A TREATISE ON THE LIMITATIONS OF POLICE POWER IN THE UNITED STATES

Da Capo Press Reprints in

AMERICAN CONSTITUTIONAL AND LEGAL HISTORY

GENERAL EDITOR: LEONARD W. LEVY
Claremont Graduate School

A TREATISE ON THE
LIMITATIONS OF
POLICE POWER
IN THE
UNITED STATES

By Christopher G. Tiedeman

DA CAPO PRESS • NEW YORK • 1971

A Da Capo Press Reprint Edition

This Da Capo Press edition of
*A Treatise on the Limitations of
Police Power in the United States*
is an unabridged republication of the
first edition published in St. Louis,
Missouri, in 1886.

Library of Congress Catalog Card Number 73-150421

SBN 306-70104-9

Published by Da Capo Press
A Division of Plenum Publishing Corporation
227 West 17th Street, New York, N.Y. 10011
Manufactured in the United States of America

A TREATISE ON THE LIMITATIONS OF POLICE POWER IN THE UNITED STATES

A TREATISE

ON THE

LIMITATIONS

OF

POLICE POWER

IN THE

UNITED STATES

CONSIDERED FROM BOTH A CIVIL AND CRIMINAL STANDPOINT.

BY

CHRISTOPHER G. TIEDEMAN, A.M., LL.B.,

Professor of Law in the University of Missouri.
Author of a treatise on *"Real Property."*

ST. LOUIS:
THE F. H. THOMAS LAW BOOK CO.,
1886.

St. Louis, Mo.:
Press of Nixon-Jones Printing Co.

THESE PAGES ARE AFFECTIONATELY INSCRIBED TO
MY WIFE,

HELEN SEYMOUR TIEDEMAN,

WHOSE SCRUPULOUS REGARD FOR THE RIGHTS OF OTHERS,
AND TENDER SYMPATHY FOR THEIR WEAKNESSES,
HAVE BEEN MY GUIDE AND INSPIRATION.

PREFACE.

In the days when popular government was unknown, and the maxim *Quod principi placuit, legis habet vigorem,* seemed to be the fundamental theory of all law, it would have been idle to speak of limitations upon the police power of government; for there were none, except those which are imposed by the finite character of all things natural. Absolutism existed in its most repulsive form. The king ruled by divine right, and obtaining his authority from above he acknowledged no natural rights in the individual. If it was his pleasure to give to his people a wide room for individual activity, the subject had no occasion for complaint. But he could not raise any effective opposition to the pleasure of the ruler, if he should see fit to impose numerous restrictions, all tending to oppress the weaker for the benefit of the stronger.

But the divine right of kings began to be questioned, and its hold on the public mind was gradually weakened, until, finally, it was repudiated altogether, and the opposite principle substituted, that all governmental power is derived from the people; and instead of the king being the vicegerent of God, and the people subjects of the king, the king and other officers of the government were the servants of the people, and the people became the real sovereign through the officials. *Vox populi, vox Dei,* became the popular answer to all complaints of the individual against

(v)

the encroachments of popular government upon his rights
and his liberty. Since the memories of the oppressions o
the privileged classes under the reign of kings and nobles
were still fresh in the minds of individuals for many years
after popular government was established in the English-
speaking world, content with the enjoyment of their own
liberties, there was no marked disposition manifested by
the majority to interfere with the like liberties of the minority. On the contrary the sphere of governmental activity was confined within the smallest limits by the
popularization of the so-called *laissez-faire* doctrine, which
denies to government the power to do more than to provide
for the public order and personal security by the prevention and punishment of crimes and trespasses. Under the
influence of this doctrine, the encroachments of government
upon the rights and liberties of the individual have for the
past century been comparatively few. But the political
pendulum is again swinging in the opposite direction, and
the doctrine of governmental inactivity in economical
matters is attacked daily with increasing vehemence. Governmental interference is proclaimed and demanded everywhere as a sufficient panacea for every social evil which
threaten the prosperity of society. Socialism, Communism,
and Anarchism are rampant throughout the civilized world.
The State is called on to protect the weak against the
shrewdness of the stronger, to determine what wages a
workman shall receive for his labor, and how many hours
daily he shall labor. Many trades and occupations are being prohibited because some are damaged incidentally by
their prosecution, and many ordinary pursuits are made
government monopolies. The demands of the Socialists

and Communists vary in degree and in detail, and the most extreme of them insist upon the assumption by government of the paternal character altogether, abolishing all private property in land, and making the State the sole possessor of the working capital of the nation.

Contemplating these extraordinary demands of the great army of discontents, and their apparent power, with the growth and development of universal suffrage, to enforce their views of civil polity upon the civilized world, the conservative classes stand in constant fear of the advent of an absolutism more tyrannical and more unreasoning than any before experienced by man, the absolutism of a democratic majority.

The principal object of the present work is to demonstrate, by a detailed discussion of the constitutional limitations upon the police power in the United States, that under the written constitutions, Federal and State, democratic absolutism is impossible in this country, as long as the popular reverence for the constitutions, in their restrictions upon governmental activity, is nourished and sustained by a prompt avoidance by the courts of any violations of their provisions, in word or in spirit. The substantial rights of the minority are shown to be free from all lawful control or interference by the majority, except so far as such control or interference may be necessary to prevent injury to others in the enjoyment of their rights. The police power of the government is shown to be confined to the detailed enforcement of the legal maxim, *sic utere tuo, ut alienum non lœdas.*

If the author succeeds in any measure in his attempt to awaken the public mind to a full appreciation of the power of constitutional limitations to protect private rights against the radical experimentations of social reformers, he will feel that he has been amply requited for his labors in the cause of social order and personal liberty.

C. G. T.

UNIVERSITY OF THE STATE OF MISSOURI, COLUMBIA, MO.,
November 1, 1886.

TABLE OF CONTENTS.

PART I.

CHAPTER I.

LIMITATIONS UPON THE POLICE POWER OF THE UNITED STATES.

SECTION 1. Police power, defined and explained.
2. The legal limitations upon police power.
3. Construction of constitutional limitations.
4. The principal constitutional limitations.
5. Table of private rights.

CHAPTER II.

POLICE REGULATION OF PERSONAL SECURITY.

SECTION 10. Security to life.
11. Capital punishment.
12. Security to limb and body.
12a. Corporal punishment.
12b. Personal chastisement in certain relations.
13. Battery in self-defense.
14. Abortion.
15. Compulsory submission to surgical and medical treatment.
16. Security to health — Legalized nuisances.
17. Security to reputation — Privileged communications.
17a. Privilege of legislators.
17b. Privilege in judicial proceedings.
17c. Criticism of officers and candidates for office.
17d. Publications through the press.
18. Security to reputation — Malicious prosecution.
18a. Advice of counsel — How far a defense.

CHAPTER III.

PERSONAL LIBERTY.

SECTION 30. Personal liberty — How guaranteed.

CHAPTER IV.

POLICE CONTROL OF CRIMINAL CLASSES.

SECTION 31. The effect of crime on the rights of the criminal.
     31*a*. Due process of law.
     31*b*. Bills of attainder.
     31*c*. *Ex post facto law.*
     32. Preliminary confinement to answer for a crime.
     33. What constitutes a lawful arrest.
     33*a*. Arrest without warrant.
     34. The trial of the accused.
     34*a*. The trial must be speedy.
     34*b*. The trial must be public.
     34*c*. Accused entitled to counsel.
     34*d*. Indictment by grand jury or by information.
     34*e*. The plea of defendant.
     34*f*. Trial by jury — Legal jeopardy.
     35. Control over criminals in the penitentiary.
     35*a*. Convict lease system.

CHAPTER V.

POLICE CONTROL OF DANGEROUS CLASSES, OTHERWISE THAN BY CRIMINAL PROSECUTION.

SECTION 42. Confinement for infectious and contagious diseases.
     43. Confinement of the insane.
     44. Control of the insane in the asylum.
     45. Punishment of the criminal insane.
     46. Confinement of habitual drunkards.
     47. Police control of vagrants.
     48. Police regulation of mendicancy.
     49. Police supervision of habitual criminals.
     50. State control of minors.

CHAPTER VI.

POLICE REGULATIONS OF THE RIGHTS OF CITIZENSHIP AND DOMICILE.

SECTION 56. Citizenship and domicile distinguished.
57. Expatriation.
58. Naturalization.
59. Prohibition of emigration.
60. Compulsory emigration.
61. Prohibition of immigration.
62. The public duties of a citizen.

CHAPTER VII.

POLICE CONTROL OF MORALITY AND RELIGION.

SECTION 68. Crime and vice distinguished — Their relation to police power.
69. Sumptuary laws.
70. Church and State — Historical synopsis.
71. Police regulation of religion — Constitutional restrictions.
72. State control of churches, and congregations.
73. Religious criticism and blasphemy distinguished.
74. Permissible limitations upon religious worship.
75. Religious discrimination in respect to admissibility of testimony.
76. Sunday laws.

CHAPTER VIII.

FREEDOM OF SPEECH AND LIBERTY OF THE PRESS.

SECTION 81. Police supervision prohibited by the constitutions.

CHAPTER IX.

POLICE REGULATIONS OF TRADES AND PROFESSIONS.

SECTION 85. General propositions.
86. Prohibition as to certain classes.
87. Police regulation of skilled trades and learned professions

SECTION 88. Regulation of practice in the learned professions.
89. Regulation of sale of certain articles of merchandise.
90. Legal tender, and the regulation of the currency.
91. Legislative restraint of importations — Protective tariffs.
92. Compulsory formation of business relations.
93. Regulation of prices.
94. Usury and interest laws.
95. Prevention of speculation.
96. Prevention of combinations in restraint of trade.
97. Boycotting.
98. Contracts against liability for negligence prohibited.
99. Wager contracts prohibited.
99a. Option contracts, when illegal.
100. General prohibition of contracts, on account of public policy.
101. Licenses.
102. Prohibition of occupations in general.
103. Prohibition of the liquor trade.
104. Police control of employments in respect to locality.
105. Monopolies, creation of.

CHAPTER X.

POLICE REGULATIONS OF REAL PROPERTY.

SECTION 115. What is meant by "private property in land?"
116. Regulation of estates — Vested rights.
117. Interests in expectancy.
118. Limitation of the right of acquisition.
119. Regulation of the right of alienation.
120. Involuntary alienation.
121. Eminent domain.
121a. Exercise of power regulated by legislature.
121b. Public purpose, what is a.
121c. What property may be taken.
121d. What constitutes a taking.
121e. Compensation, how ascertained.
122. Regulation of the use of lands — What is a nuisance?
122a. What is a nuisance, a judicial question.
122b. Unwholesome trades in tenement houses may be prohibited.
122c. Confinement of objectionable trades to certain localities.
122d. Regulation of burial grounds.
122e. Laws regulating the construction of wooden buildings.
122f. Regulation of right to hunt game.
122g. Abatement of nuisances — Destruction of buildings.
123. How far the use of land may be controlled by the requirement of license.

SECTION 124. Improvement of property at the expense, and against the will, of the owner.
125. Regulation on non-navigable streams — Fisheries.
125a. Conversion of non-navigable into navigable streams.
126. Statutory liability of lessors for the acts of lessees.
127. Search warrants.
128. Quartering soldiers in private dwellings.
129. Taxation.

CHAPTER XI.

POLICE REGULATION OF PERSONAL PROPERTY.

SECTION 135. Laws regulating the creation and acquisition of interests in personal property — Real and personal property herein distinguished.
135a. Statute of uses and rule against perpetuity, as regulations of personal property.
136. Regulation and prohibition of the sale of personal property.
136a. Laws regulating disposition of personal property by will.
137. Involuntary alienation.
138. Control of property by guardian.
139. Destruction of personal property on account of illegal use.
140. Laws regulating use of personal property.
140a. Prohibition of possession of certain property.
140b. Regulation and prohibition of the manufacture of certain property.
140c. Carrying of concealed weapons prohibited.
140d. Miscellaneous regulations of the use of personal property.
141. Laws regulating the use and keeping of domestic animals.
141a. Keeping of dogs.
141b. Laws for the prevention of cruelty to animals.
142. Regulation of contracts and other rights of action.
143. Regulation of ships and shipping.

CHAPTER XII.

POLICE REGULATION OF THE RELATION OF HUSBAND AND WIFE.

SECTION 149. Marriage, a natural *status*, subject to police regulation.
150. Constitutional limitations upon the police control of marriages.
151. Distinction between natural capacity and legal capacity.

SECTION 152. Insanity as a legal incapacity.

153. The disability of infancy in respect to marriage.

154. Consanguinity and affinity.

155. Constitutional diseases.

156. Financial condition — Poverty.

157. Differences in race — Miscegenation.

158. Polygamy prohibited — Marriage confined to monogamy.

159. Marriage indissoluble — Divorce.

160. Regulation of the marriage ceremony.

161. Wife in legal subjection to the husband — Its justification.

162. Husband's control of wife's property.

163. Legal disabilities of married women.

CHAPTER XIII.

POLICE REGULATION OF THE RELATION OF PARENT AND CHILD, AND OF GUARDIAN AND WARD.

SECTION 165. Original character of the relation of parent and child — Its political aspect.

166. No limitation to State interference.

166a. People v. Turner.

167. Compulsory education.

168. Parents' duty of maintenance.

169. Child's duty to support indigent parents.

170. Relation of guardian and ward altogether subject to State regulation.

171. Testamentary guardians.

CHAPTER XIV.

POLICE REGULATION OF THE RELATION OF MASTER AND SERVANT.

SECTION 175. Terms "master and servant" defined.

176. Relation purely voluntary.

177. Apprentices.

178. State regulation of private employments.

179. State regulation of public employments.

CHAPTER XV.

POLICE REGULATION OF CORPORATIONS

SECTION 188. The inviolability of the charters of private corporations.
189. Police control of corporations.
190. Freedom from police control, as a franchise.
191. Police regulation of corporations in general.
192. Laws regulating rates and charges of corporations.
193. Police regulation of foreign corporations.
194. Police regulation of railroads.

CHAPTER XVI.

THE LOCATION OF POLICE POWER IN THE FEDERAL SYSTEM OF GOVERNMENT.

SECTION 200. The United States government one of enumerated powers.
201. Police power generally resides in the States.
202. Regulations affecting interstate commerce.
203. Police control of navigable streams.
204. Police regulation of harbors — Pilotage laws.
205. Regulation of weights and measures.
206. Counterfeiting of coins and currencies.
207. Regulation of the sale of patented articles.
208. War and rebellion.
209. Regulation of the militia.
210. Taxation.
211. Regulation of offenses against the laws of nations.
212. The exercise of police power by municipal corporations.

TABLE OF CASES CITED.

A.

Abbott v. Lindenbower (42 Mo. 162; 46 Mo. 291), 519.

Abbott v. Siegler (9 Ind. 511), 205.

Abrams v. Foshee (3 Iowa, 274), 31.

Abt v. Burgheim (80 Ill. 92), 28.

Adams v. Beale (19 Iowa, 61), 519.

Adams v. Hatchett (27 N. H. 289), 583.

Adams v. Palmer (51 Me. 494), 358, 359, 362.

Adams v. Rivers (11 Barb. 390) 407.

Adams v. Stevens (49 Me. 362), 361.

Adams Exp. Co. v. Stettaners (61 Ill. 174), 257.

Ah Foy, Ex parte (57 Cal. 92), 272.

Ah He v. Crippen (19 Cal. 491), 443.

Ah Lew v. Choate (24 Cal. 562), 443.

Ainslee v. Martin (9 Mass. 454), 139.

Albrecht v. State (8 Tex. Ct. App. 216; 34 Am. Rep. 737), 282.

Aldrich v. Parsons (6 N. Y. 555), 366.

Aldrich v. Wright (53 N. H. 398; 16 Am. Rep. 339), 28.

Aldridge v. Railroad Company (2 Stew. & P. 199), 375.

Alexander v. Hoyt (7 Wend. 89), 82.

Alexander v. Milwaukee (16 Wis. 247), 400.

Allen v. Armstrong (16 Iowa, 508), 519.

Allen v. Colby (47 N. H. 344), 463.

Allen v. Crofoot (2 Wend. 515), 41, 42.

Allen v. Mayfield (20 Ind. 293), 339.

Allen v. Staples (6 Gray, 491), 465.

Allery v. Commonwealth (8 B. Mon. 3), 80.

Albany Street, matter of (11 Wend. 149), 358, 379, 393.

Ames v. Lake Superior, etc., R. R. Co. (21 Minn. 241), 420.

Ames v. Rathbun (55 Barb. 194), 63, 65.

Ammerman v. Crosby (26 Ind. 451) 62.

American Print Works v. Lawrence (21 N. J. 248; s. c. 23 N. J. 590), 399.

American River Water Co. v. Amsden (6 Cal. 443), 617.

Am. Union Tel. Co. v. W. U. Tel. Co. (67 Ala. 26; 42 Am. Rep. 90), 592.

Anderson v. Kerns Draining Co. (14 Ind. 199), 380, 445.

Andres v. Wells (7 Johns. 260; 5 Am. Dec. 257), 54.

Andrew v. Bible Society (4 Sandf. 156), 169.

Andrews v. Spurr (8 Allen, 416), 361.

Andrews v. State (2 Sneed, 550), 86.

Annable v. Patch (3 Pick. 360), 340.

Anthony v. Lapham (5 Pick. 175), 450.

Antisdel v. Chicago, etc., R. R. Co. (26 Wis. 145), 598.

Antoni v. Belknap (102 Mass. 200), 366.

Andrews, Ex parte (18 Cal. 678), 183.

Arimond v. Green Bay Co. (31 Wis. 316), 394, 397.

Armington v. Barnet (15 Vt. 745), 376, 392, 472.

Armstrong v. Jackson (1 Blackf. 374), 367.

Arnold v. Arnold (13 Vt. 362), 174.

Arnold v. Decatur (29 Mich. 11), 375.

Arnold v. Foot (12 Wend. 330), 451.

Arnold v. Hudson River R. R. Co. (55 N. Y. 661), 405.

Arnold v. Mundy (6 N. J. 1), 617.

Arnot v. Coal Co. (60 N. Y. 558), 250.

Arundel v. McCulloch (10 Mass. 70), 617.

Ash v. Cummings (50 N. H. 591), 385, 421.

Ash v. People (11 Mich. 347), 274, 313, 434.

Ashley v. Peterson (25 Wis. 621), 465.

Ashley v. Port Huron (35 Mich. 296), 397.

Ashton v. Dakin (4 H. & N. 867), 265.

Atchison & Neb. R. R. Co. v. Baty (6 Neb. 37; 29 Am. Rep. 356), 598.

Attorney-General v. Chicago, etc., R. R. Co. (35 Wis. 425), 584, 590.

Attorney-General v. Metropolitan R. R. Co. (125 Mass. 515; 28 Am. Rep. 248), 418.

Atwood v. Welton (7 Conn. 66), 174.

Augusta & S. R. R. Co. v. Renz (55 Ga. 126), 187.

Austin v. State (10 Mo. 591), 195, 201, 304, 305.

Austine v. State (51 Ill. 236), 91.

Ayers v. Birtch (35 Mich. 501), 28.

Aymette v. State (2 Humph. 154), 503.

Ayres v. Methodist Church (3 Sandf. 351), 171.

B.

Babcock v. Thompson (3 Pick. 446), 261.

Backus v. Lebanon (11 N. H. 9), 574.

Bacon v. Callender (6 Mass. 303), 367.

Bacon v. Towne (4 Cush. 217), 61.

Bacon v. Wayne Co. (1 Mich. 461), 90.

Badore v. Newton (54 N. H. 117), 303.

Bagg v. Detroit (5 Mich. 336), 409.

Bailey v. Fiske (34 Me. 77), 537.

Bailey v. Philadelphia, etc., R. R. Co. (4 Harr. 389), 584, 585.

Bailey v. Wright (38 Mich. 96), 465.

Baker v. Beckwith (29 Ohio St. 314), 303.

Baker v. Johnson (2 Hill, 343), 396.

Baker v. Lewis (33 Pa. St. 301), 617.

Baker v. Pope (2 Hun, 556), 303.

Baker v. State (12 Ohio St. 214), 96.

Baker, matter of (29 How. Pr. 486), 115.

Balch v. Commissioners (103 Mass. 106), 386.

Baldwin v. Bk. of Newbury (1 Wall. 234), 521.

Baldwin v. Chicago (68 Ill. 418), 310.

Baldwin v. Hale (1 Wall. 223), 521.

Baldwin v. Newark (38 N. J. 158), 517.

Baldwin v. Smith (82 Ill. 163), 429.

Ball v. Gilbert (12 Met. 399)), 261.

Baltimore v. Clunity (23 Md. 449), 583.

Baltimore v. Redecke (49 Md. 217; 33 Am. Rep. 239), 312, 435.

Baltimore, etc., R. R. Co. v. Magruder (35 Md. 79; 6 Am. Rep. 310), 392, 397.

Baltimore, etc., R. R. Co. v. Nesbit (10 How. 395), 377, 583.

Baltimore, etc., R. R. Co. v. Pittsburg, etc., R. R. Co. (17 W. Va. 812), 394, 420.

Bancroft v. Cambridge (126 Mass. 438), 445.

Bank of Augusta v. Earle (13 Pet. 519), 592.

Bk. of Columbia v. Okely (4 Wheat. 235), 583.

Bank of Old Dominion v. McVeigh (20 Gratt. 457), 574.

Bank of State v. Bank of Cape Fear (13 Ired. 75), 574.

Bankhead v. Brown (25 Iowa, 540), 376, 378, 381, 383.

Baptist Church v. Wetherell (3 Paige, 296; 24 Am. Dec. 223), 164, 166.

Barbour v. Barbour (46 Me. 9), 345.

Barclay v. Howell's Lessee (6 Pet. 498), 394.

Barfoot v. Reynolds (2 Stra. 953), 29.

Barling v. West (29 Wis. 307; 9 Am. Rep. 576), 272.

Barnard v. Backhouse (52 Wis. 593) 267, 270.

Barnard v. Bartlett (10 Cush. 501), 466.

Barnes v. Barber (6 Ill. 401), 83.

Barnes v. McCrate (32 Me. 442), 42.

Barnett v. Atlantic, etc., R. R. Co. (68 Mo. 56; 30 Am. Rep. 773), 598.

Barney v. Keokuk (94 U. S. 324), 408, 420.

Barr v. Moore (87 Pa. St. 385; 30 Am. Rep. 367), 52.

Barrett v. Hyde (7 Gray, 160), 267.

Barron v. Baltimore (7 Pet. 243), 15.

Barron v. Mason (31 Vt. 189), 61.

Barry v. Croskey (2 Johns. & H. 1), 251.

Bartemeyer v. Iowa (18 Wall. 729), 304, 305.

Bartlett v. Brown (6 R. I. 37), 63.

Bartlett v. Churchill (24 Vt. 218), 26.

Bass v. Nashville (Meigs, 421; 33 Am. Dec. 154), 583.

Bates v. McDowell (58 Miss. 815), 346.

Bauer v. Clay (8 Kan. 580), 61.

Baumgardner v. Circuit Court (4 Mo. 50), 518.

Bayer v. Cockerill (2 Kan. 292), 341.

Beach v. Hancock (27 N. H. 223), 23.

Beardsley v. Bridgman (17 Iowa, 290), 54.

Beatty v. Evans (L. R. 7 H. L. C. 102), 252.

Beckman v. Railroad Co. (3 Paige, 45; 22 Am. Dec. 679), 376, 378, 379, 388.

Beebe v. State (26 Ind. 501), 197, 308.

Beecher v. Parmelee (9 Vt. 352), 28, 29.

Beer Company v. Massachusetts (27 U. S. 25), 581.

Beers v. Haughton (9 Pet. 329), 517.

Bell v. Clapp (10 Johns. 263; 6 Am. Dec. 339), 466.

Bell v. Pearcy (5 Ired. 83), 61.

Bell v. Rice (2 J. J. Marsh. 44; 9 Am. Dec. 122), 465.

Bell v. State (2 Tex. App. 216; 28 Am. Rep. 429), 93

Bellinger v. N. Y. Cent. R. R. Co. 23 N. Y. 42), 398.

Bellport v. Tooker (21 N. Y. 267; 29 Barb. 256), 165.

Bender v. Nashua (17 N. H. 477), 401.

Benedict v. Gait (3 Barb. 459), 409.

Bennett v. Bennett (13 N. J. Eq. 114), 555.

Bennett v. Boggs (1 Bald. 74), 8.

Bennett v. Borough of Birmingham (31 Pa. St. 15), 272.

Bennett v. Brooks (9 Allen, 118), 187.

Bennett v. Child (19 Wis. 365), 364.

Bennett v. Dutton (10 N. H. 481), 257.

Bennett v. Harms (51 Wis. 25), 346.

Benson v. Mayor (24 Barb. 248, 252), 8.

Benson v. Mayor, etc., of N. Y. (10 Barb. 223), 584.

Berney v. N. Y., etc., Tel. Co. (18 Md. 341), 259.

Bertholf v. O'Reilly (74 N. Y. 509; s. c. 3 Am. Rep. 323), 7, 10, 152, 196, 303, 454, 457.

Besson v. Southard (10 N. Y. 237), 63.

Bethune v. Hayes (28 Ga. 560), 313, 434.

Bevan v. Adams (19 W. R. 76), 251.

Bickham v. Smith (62 Pa. St. 45), 257.

Bigelow v. Benedict (70 N. Y. 202), 265, 266, 267.

Bigelow v. Bigelow (120 Mass. 300), 15.

Billings v. Russell (23 Pa. St. 189), 82.

Bina's Appeal (55 Pa. St. 294), 265.

Binghamton Bridge Case (3 Wall. 51), 574.

Bird v. Holbrook (4 Bing. 628), 28.

Bird v. Perkins (33 Mich. 28), 82, 83.

Bird v. Smith (8 Watts, 434), 617.

Bird v. State (50 Ga. 585), 94.

Bissell v. N. Y. Cent. R. R. Co. (25 N. Y. 442), 258.

Black v. State (36 Ga. 447), 96.

Blackman v. Halves (72 Ind. 515), 381.

Blair v. Forehand (100 Mass. 136; 1 Am. Rep. 94), 512.

Blair v. Kilpatrick (40 Ind. 312), 198.

Blair v. Milwaukee, etc., R. R. Co. (20 Wis. 254), 580.

Blake v. Rich (34 N. H. 282), 395.

Blake v. Winona, etc., R. R. Co. (19 Minn. 418; 18 Am. Rep. 345; 94 U. S. 180), 590.

Blanchard v. Blanchard (1 Allen, 223), 339.

Blanchard, Ex parte (9 Nev. 101), 291.

Blass v. Gregor (15 La. Ann. 421), 62.

Blewet v. Wyandotte, etc., R. R. Co. (72 Mo. 583), 597.

Bliss v. Hosmer (15 Ohio, 44), 392.

Bliss v. Wyman (7 Cal. 257), 63.

Blocker v. Burness (2 Ala. 354), 174.

Bloodgood v. Mohawk, etc., R. R. Co. (18 Wend. 9), 376, 377, 379, 421.

Bloom v. Richards (2 Ohio, 387), 183.

Bloomfield, etc., R. R. Co. v. Calkins (62 N. Y. 386), 408.

Bloomington v. Wahl (46 Ill. 489), 313, 434.

Bloss v. Tobey (2 Pick. 320), 439.

Blunt v. Little (3 Mason, 102), 63, 64.

Board of Education v. McLandsborough (36 Ohio St. 227), 472.

Bodwell v. Osgood (3 Pick. 379; 15 Am. Dec. 228), 49.

Bohannan v. Commonwealth (8 Bush, 481; 8 Am. Rep. 474), 461.

Bohannan v. Hammond (42 Cal. 227), 256.

Bohl v. State (3 Tex. App. 683), 177.

Bohlman v. Green Bay, etc., R. R. Co. (40 Wis. 157), 377.

Bombaugh v. Bombaugh (11 Serg. & R. 192), 340.

Booneville v. Ormrod (26 Mo. 193), 420.

Boston v. Cummings (16 Ga. 102), 8, 77.

Boston v. Schaffer (9 Pick. 415), 272, 274.

Boston Glass Manufactory v. Binney (4 Pick. 425), 248.

Boston Mill Dam v. Newman (12 Pick. 467), 376.

Boston & Roxbury Manf. Co. v. Newman (12 Pick. 467), 385.

Boston Water Power Co. v. Boston, etc., R. R. Co. (23 Pick. 360), 392.

Bosworth v. Swansey (10 Met. 364), 187.

Boughton v. Carter (18 Johns. 405), 394, 397.

Bowen v. Matheson (14 Allen, 499), 248.

Bowen v. Preston (48 Ind. 367), 347.

Bowling Green v. Carson (10 Bush, 64), 312, 434.

Bowman v. Middleton (1 Bay, 252), 358.

Boyd v. Bryant (35 Ark. 69; 37 Am. Rep. 6), 308, 434.

Boyd v. Cross (35 Md. 194), 61.

Boyd v. State (36 Ala. 329), 583.

Boyd v. State (2 Humph. 635), 91.

Boyle v. McLaughlin (4 H. & J. 291), 256.

Boyle v. Zacharie (6 Pet. 348), 521.

Brackett v. Norcross (1 Me. 89), 367.

Bradley v. Buffalo, etc., R. R. Co. (34 N. H. 429), 597.

Bradley v. Heath (12 Pick. 163), 36, 44, 49.

Bradley v. Rice (13 Me. 200), 452.

Bradley v. McAtee (7 Bush, 667; 3 Am. Rep. 615), 581.

Bradley v. N. Y. & N. H. R. R. Co. (21 Conn. 294), 376, 381.

Bradwell v. State (55 Ill. 535; s. c. 16 Wall. 130), 201, 202.

Brady v. Bronson (45 Cal. 640), 377.

Brainard v. Head (15 La. Ann. 489), 82, 83.

Brandon v. People (42 N. Y. 265), 94.

Bratton v. Massey (15 S. C. 277), 341.

Braveboy v. Cockfield (2 McMul. 270), 61.

Breitung v. Lindauer (37 Mich. 217), 520.

Brent v. Kimball (60 Ill. 21; 14 Am. Rep. 35), 507.

Brewer Brick Co. v. Brewer (62 Me. 62; 16 Am. Rep. 395), 472.

Brewster v. Hough (10 N. H. 138), 474.

Brick Presbyterian Church v. Mayor, etc. (5 Cow. 538), 437, 583.

Briggs v. State (29 Ga. 733), 28.

Brigham v. Meade (10 Allen, 246), 267.

Briscoe v. Bank of Kentucky (11 Pet. 257), 214.

Broadbent v. Tuscaloosa, etc., Association (45 Ala. 170), 583.

Brock v. Hishen (40 Wis. 674), 421.

Brock v. Milligan (10 Ohio, 121), 174.

Bronson v. Kinzid (1 How. 311), 520.

Bronson v. Newberry (2 Dougl. (Mich.) 38), 518.

Bronson v. Oberlin (41 Ohio St. 476; 5 Am. Rep. 90), 308, 434.

Brooklyn v. Breslin (57 N. Y. 591), 272.

Brooklyn Central, etc., R. R. Co. v. Brooklyn City R. R. Co. (33 Barb. 420), 395.

Brooklyn Park Comrs. *v.* Armstrong (45 N. Y. 234; 6 Am. Rep. 70), 380, 396, 403.

Brooklyn & Newton R. R. Co. *v.* Coney Island R. R. Co. (35 Barb. 364), 395.

Brookshaw *v.* Hopkins (Loff. 235), 108.

Brosnahan, In re John (4 McCrary, 1), 196, 297.

Brother *v.* Cannon (2 Ill. 200), 82.

Brothers *v.* Church (14 R. I. 398; 51 Am. Rep. 410), 620.

Brown *v.* Carpenter (26 Vt. 638), 508.

Brown *v.* Cayuga, etc., R. R. Co. (12 N. Y. 486), 397, 400.

Brown *v.* Duplessis (14 La. Ann. 842), 402.

Brown *v.* Eastern R. Co. (11 Cush. 97), 257.

Brown *v.* Hitchcock (36 Ohio St. 667), 518.

Brown *v.* Houston (33 La. Ann. 843; 39 Am. Rep. 284), 615.

Brown *v.* Lamphear (35 Vt. 260), 361.

Brown *v.* Leeson (2 H. Bl. 43), 261.

Brown *v.* Lawrence (3 Cush. 390), 339.

Brown *v.* Maryland (12 Wheat. 419), 615.

Brown *v.* People (29 Mich. 232), 79.

Brown *v.* Phelps (103 Mass. 240), 267.

Brown *v.* Randall (36 Conn. 56), 65.

Brown *v.* Speyer (20 Gratt. 309), 265, 267.

Brown *v.* Storm (4 Vt. 37), 366.

Brua's Appeal (5 Sm. 294), 261.

Bruffet *v.* G. W. Ry. Co. (25 Ill. 353), 575.

Bruning *v.* N. N. Canal & Banking Co. (12 La. Ann. 541), 378.

Brunswick *v.* Litchfield (2 Me. 28), 536.

Bryan *v.* Lewis (Req. & Moody, 386), 265.

Buckland *v.* Adams Express Co. (97 Mass. 124), 257.

Buckingham *v.* Smith (10 Ohio, 288), 379.

Buffalo & N. Y. R. R. Co. *v.* Brainard (9 N. Y. 100), 381.

Buffalo, etc., R. R. Co. *v.* Ferris (26 Tex. 588), 421.

Buffalo *v.* Webster (10 Wend. 99), 312, 434.

Bulkley *v.* N. Y., etc., R. R. Co. (27 Conn. 497), 597, 599.

Bulkley *v.* Naumkeag, etc., Co. (24 How. 386), 256.

Bunn *v.* Rikes (4 Johns. 426), 261.

Bunton *v.* Worley (4 Bibb, 38; 7 Am. Dec. 735), 41.

Burckholter *v.* McConnellsville (20 Ohio St. 308), 273.

Burd *v.* Dausdale (2 Binn. 80), 344.

Burden *v.* Stein (27 Ala. 104), 380.

Burgess *v.* Clark (13 Ired. 109), 385.

Burke, Ex parte (59 Cal. 6; 43 Am. Rep. 231), 183.

Burlingame *v.* Burlingame (8 Cow. 141), 41.

Burlington *v.* Bumgardner (42 Iowa 673), 281.

Burlington *v.* Putnam Ins. Co. (31 Iowa, 102), 274.

Burnap *v.* Albert (Taney, 344), 65.

Burns *v.* Erben (40 N. Y. 463), 84.

Burrows *v.* Bell (7 Gray, 301), 59.

Burt *v.* Brigham (117 Mass. 307), 377.

Bush *v.* Seabury (8 Johns. 418), 312, 434.

Butchers' Union Slaughterhouse, etc., Co. *v.* Crescent City Live Stock, etc., Co. (111 U. S. 745), 582.

Butler *v.* Palmer (1 Hill, 324) 8.

Butler's Appeal (73 Pa. St. 48), 473.

Butts v. Swartwood (2 Cow. 431), 174.

Byers v. Commonwealth (42 Pa. St. 96), 125, 127.

Buzick v. Buzick (44 Iowa, 259; 24 Am. Rep. 740), 345.

C.

Cairo v. Bross (101 Ill. 475), 272, 281.

Cairo, etc., R. R. Co. v. People (92 Ill. 97; 34 Am. Rep. 112), 598.

Calder v. Bull (3 Dall. 386), 5.

Calder v. Kurby (5 Gray, 597), 583.

Caldwell v. Alton (33 Ill. 416), 313, 434.

Caldwell v. Fulton (31 Pa. St. 484), 361.

Caldwell v. N. J. Steamboat Co. (47 N. Y. 282), 256.

Calkins v. Baldwin (4 Wend. 667; 21 Am. Dec. 168), 421.

Calkins v. Chaney (92 Ill. 463), 165.

Calkins v. State (18 Ohio St. 366), 94.

Calkins v. Sumner (13 Wis. 193), 42.

Call v. Hagger (8 Mass. 430), 516.

Callahan v. Caffarati (39 Mo. 136), 61.

Callamer v. Day (2 Vt. 144), 261.

Callender v. Marsh (1 Pick. 418), 401, 406.

Callison v. Hedrick (15 Gratt. 244), 421, 422.

Camden, etc., R. R. Co. v. Baldauf (16 Pa. St. 67), 257.

Cameron v. Durkheim (55 N. Y. 425), 265.

Cameron v. Supervisors, etc. (47 Miss. 264), 377.

Campbell v. Evans (45 N. Y. 356), 507.

Campbell v. Richardson (10 Johns. 406), 261.

Campbell v. Seaman (63 N. Y. 568), 35.

Campen v. Langley (39 Mich. 451; 33 Am. Rep. 414), 507.

Canady v. George (6 Rich. Eq. 103), 541.

Canal Com'rs v. People (5 Wend. 423), 618.

Canby v. Porter (12 Ohio, 79), 344.

Cannon v. Alsbury (1 A. K. Marsh. 76), 531.

Canton v. Nist (9 Ohio St. 439), 185.

Caplis, Ex parte (58 Miss. 358), 87.

Carew v. Rutherford (106 Mass. 1, 13), 248.

Carl v. Ayers (53 N. Y. 13), 61.

Carondelet Canal, etc., Co. v. Parker (29 La. Ann. 430; 29 Am. Rep. 339), 452, 622.

Carpenter v. Bailey (53 N. H. 590), 54.

Carpenter v. Oswego, etc., R. R. Co. (24 N. Y. 655), 411.

Carpenter v. Pennsylvania (17 How. 456), 76.

Carr v. Brady (64 Ind. 28), 346.

Carr v. Georgia R. R. Co. (1 Ga. 524), 423.

Carr v. Northern Liberties (35 Pa. St. 324), 33.

Carrier v. Brannan (3 Cal. 328), 261.

Carson v. Blazer (2 Binn. 475; 4 Am. Dec. 463), 400.

Carter v. Dow (16 Wis. 298), 511, 512.

Carter v. Dow (16 Wis. 299), 277.

Carthage v. Buckner (4 Ill. App. 317), 206.

Carton v. Ill. Cent. R. R. Co. (59 Iowa, 148; 44 Am. Rep. 672), 616.

Casborns v. People (13 Johns. 329), 97.

Cash v. Whitworth (13 La. 401), 380.

Cates v. Kellogg (9 Ind. 506), 54.

Center v. Spring (2 Clarke, 393), 63.

Central Bridge Co. *v.* Lowell (4 Gray, 474), 392.

Central Bridge *v.* Lowell (15 Gray, 106), 574.

Central City Horse Railway Co. *v.* Fort Clark, etc., Ry. Co. (87 Ill. 523), 392.

Central Ohio Salt Co. *v.* Guthrie (35 Ohio, 666), 250.

Central Park Extension, matter of (16 Abb. Pr. 56), 380.

Cen ral R. R. Co. *v.* Rockafellow (17 Ill. 541), 174.

Central R. R. Co. *v.* Hetfield (29 N. J. 206), 411.

Chagrin Falls, etc., Plank Road Co. *v.* Cane (2 Ohio St. 419), 409.

Chapman *v.* Calder (14 Pa. St. 365), 50.

Chapman *v.* Dodd (10 Min. 350), 65.

Chapman *v.* Gates (54 N. Y. 132), 421.

Charity Hospital *v.* Stickney (2 La. Ann. 550), 272.

Charles River Bridge *v.* Warren Bridge (11 Pet. 420), 76, 420.

Charleston *v.* Benjamin (2 Strobh. 508), 177, 183.

Charlestown Branch R. R. Co. *v.* Middlesex (7 Met. 78), 421.

Charlton *v.* Watton (6 C. & P. 385), 58.

Chase *v.* Chaney (58 Ill. 508), 166.

Chegaray *v.* Jenkins (5 N. Y. 376), 82.

Chesapeake, etc., Canal Co. *v.* Baltimore, etc., R. R. Co. (4 Gill & J. 5), 392.

Chestnut *v.* Shane's Lessee (16 Ohio, 599), 362.

Chicago & Alton, R. R. Co. *v.* People, ex rel. Koerner (67 Ill. 11; 16 Am. Rep. 599), 590, 594.

Chicago *v.* Bartree (100 Ill. 57), 273.

Chicago *v.* Evans (24 Ill. 52), 418.

Chicago *v.* Larned (34 Ill. 279), 470.

Chicago *v.* McGinn (51 Ill. 266; 2 Am. Rep. 295), 622.

Chicago *v.* Rumpff (45 Ill. 90), 325.

Chicago, etc., R. R. Co. *v.* Barsie (55 Ill. 226), 598.

Chicago, etc., R. R. Co. *v.* Iowa (94 U. S. 155), 234, 589, 591.

Chicago, etc., R. R. Co. *v.* Joliet (79 Ill. 25), 415.

Chicago, etc., R. R. Co. *v.* Lake (71 Ill. 333), 376, 378.

Chicago, etc., R. R. Co. *v.* Sawyer (69 Ill. 285), 256.

Chicago, etc., R. R. Co. *v.* Smith (78 Ill. 96), 377.

Chicago, etc., R. R. Co. *v.* Stein (75 Ill. 41), 398.

Chicago, etc., R. R. Co. *v.* Wilson (17 Ill. 123), 396.

Chicago Packing Co. *v.* Chicago (88 Ill. 221), 581.

Chicago, Rock Island, etc., R. R. Co. *v.* Reidy (66 Ill. 43), 599.

Child *v.* Chappell (9 N. Y. 246), 404.

Child *v.* Coffin (17 Mass. 64), 585.

Childers *v.* Mayor (3 Sneed, 356), 291.

Childs *v.* Shower (18 Iowa, 261), 367.

Chilvers *v.* People (11 Mich. 43), 272, 279, 285.

Church *v.* Higham (44 Iowa, 482), 303.

Churchill *v.* Hulbert (110 Mass. 42; 14 Am. Rep. 578), 29, 30.

Cincinnati *v.* Bryson (15 Ohio, 625), 272, 282.

Cincinnati *v.* Rice (15 Ohio, 225), 185.

Cincinnati Gazette Co. *v.* Timberlake (10 Ohio St. 548), 56, 58.

Cincinnati, H. & D. R. R. Co. *v.* Cole (29 Ohio, 125), 589.

Cincinnati M. H. Assurance Co. *v.* Rosenthal (55 Ill. 85; 8 Am. Rep. 626), 592.

City Council v. Benjamin (2 Strobh. 529), 183.

City Council v. Payne (2 Nott & McCord, 475), 84.

City Council v. Peper (1 Rich. L. 364), 272.

City Council v. Rogers (2 McCord, 495), 208.

City Council v. Wentworth St. Baptist Church (4 Strobh. 310), 437, 583.

City of Erie v. Erie Canal Co. (59 Pa. St. 174), 594.

City Railroad Co. v. City Railroad Co. (2 N. J. Eq. 61), 418.

Civil Rights Cases (109 U. S. 3), 231, 614.

Clark v. Barnes (70 N. Y. 301; 32 Am. Rep. 306), 353.

Clark v. Binney (2 Pick. 112), 57.

Clark v. Clark (56 N. H. 105), 364.

Clark v. Gibson (12 N. H. 386), 261.

Clark v. Kelliher (107 Mass. 406), 30.

Clark v. Miller (54 N. Y. 528), 420.

Clark v. Rochester (24 Barb. 482), 470.

Clarke v. May (2 Gray, 410), 83.

Clarke v. State (23 Miss. 261), 77.

Clayton v. Scott (45 Vt. 386), 83.

Clay v. Smith (3 Pet. 411), 521.

Cleveland, etc., R. R. Co. v. Curran (19 Ohio St. 1), 258.

Cleveland, etc., R. R. Co. v. Speer (56 Pa. St. 325), 574.

Clinton v. Meyers (46 N. Y. 511; 7 Am. Rep. 373), 451.

Clinton v. Phillips (58 Ill. 102; 11 Am. Rep. 52), 210.

Cloon v. Gerry (13 Gray, 201), 61.

Closson v. Staples (42 Vt. 209), 62.

Coates v. Mayor, etc. (7 Cow. 585), 437, 583.

Cobb v. Prell (15 Fed. Rep. 774), 270.

Cochran v. Van Surley (20 Wend. 380), 8.

Cochrane v. Van Surlay (20 Wend. 365), 359.

Cockroft v. Smith (11 Mod. 43), 29.

Coffin v. Coffin (4 Mass. 1; 3 Am. Dec. 189), 39, 40.

Coffin v. Rich (45 Me. 507), 585.

Cohen v. Wright (22 Cal. 293), 203.

Colburn v. Richards (13 Mass. 420), 450.

Colby v. Jackson (12 N. H. 526), 108.

Cole v. Milmine (88 Ill. 349), 267.

Coleman v. Ballandi (22 Minn. 144), 520.

Coleman v. Lewis (27 Pa. St. 291), 366.

Collins v. Hayte (50 Ill. 353), 61.

Collins v. Relief Society (73 Pa. St. 94), 627.

Colman v. Anderson (10 Mass. 105), 82.

Commissioners v. Beckwith (10 Kans. 603), 377.

Commissioners Inland Fishing v. Holyoke Water Power Co. (104 Mass. 446; 6 Am. Rep. 547), 451.

Commonwealth v. Alderman (4 Mass. 477), 96.

Commonwealth v. Alger (7 Cush. 53), 358.

Commonwealth v. Bacon (13 Ky. 210; 26 Am. Rep. 189) 435.

Commonwealth v. Bakeman (105 Mass. 53), 96.

Commonwealth v. Bearse (122 Mass. 442; 42 Am. Rep. 450), 435.

Commonwealth v. Blanding (3 Pick. 304; 15 Am. Dec. 214), 57, 191.

Commonwealth v. Boden (9 Mass. 194), 96.

Commonwealth v. Bonner (97 Mass. 587), 94.

Commonwealth v. Brennan (103 Mass. 70), 583.

Commonwealth v. Brickett (8 Pick. 138), 81.

Commonwealth v. Carlisle (Brightley, 40), 246.

Commonwealth v. Casey (134 Mass. 194) 310.

Commonwealth v. Chapin (5 Pick. 199), 451, 618.

Commonwealth v. Charlestown (1 Pick. 180), 617.

Commonwealth v. Clapp (4 Mass. 163; 3 Am. Dec. 212), 51.

Commonwealth v. Cochituate Bank (3 Allen, 42), 585.

Commonwealth v. Crotty (10 Allen, 403), 465.

Commonwealth v. Costello (133 Mass. 192), 310.

Commonwealth v. Cullen (13 Pa. St. 133), 574.

Commonwealth v. Curtis (97 Mass. 574), 91.

Commonwealth v. Dana (2 Metc. 329), 463.

Commonwealth v. Deacon (8 Serg. & R. 47), 84.

Commonwealth v. Dorsey (103 Mass. 412), 79.

Commonwealth v. Eastern R. R. Co. (103 Mass. 254; 4 Am. Rep. 555), 599.

Commonwealth v. Erie, etc., R. R. Co. (27 Pa. St. 339), 411.

Commonwealth v. Erie Ry. Co. (62 Pa. St. 286; 1 Am. Rep. 399; s. c. 15 Wall. 232), 615.

Commonwealth v. Essex Co. (13 Gray, 247), 451.

Commonwealth v. Farmers' and Mechanics' Bank (21 Pick. 542), 586.

Commonwealth v. Farrer (9 Allen, 489), 292.

Commonwealth v. Fells (9 Leigh, 620), 97.

Commonwealth v. Germania L. I. Co. (11 Phila. 553), 281.

Commonwealth v. Goddard (13 Mass. 455), 96.

Commonwealth v. Haley (4 Allen, 318), 29.

Commonwealth v. Hall (97 Mass. 570), 79.

Commonwealth v. Hamilton Manfg. Co. (120 Mass. 383), 199.

Commonwealth v. Harman (4 Pa. St. 269), 91.

Commonwealth v. Has (122 Mass. 40), 177.

Commonwealth v. Hitchings (5 Gray, 482), 15.

Commonwealth v. Hopkins (2 Dana, 418), 125, 126, 129.

Commonwealth v. Hunt (4 Metc. 11), 248, 249.

Commonwealth v. Intoxicating Liquors (115 Mass. 153), 597.

Commonwealth v. Jacobus (Leg. Gaz. Rep. (Pa.) 491), 187.

Commonwealth v. Jeandell (2 Grant Cas. 506), 187.

Commonwealth v. Kingsley (133 Mass. 578), 288.

Commonwealth v. Kirkbride (3 Brewst. 586), 108.

Commonwealth v. Kneedland (20 Pick. 206), 169, 171.

Commonwealth v. L. & N. R. R. Co. (80 Ky. 291), 187.

Commonwealth v. Leftwick (5 Rand. 657), 535.

Commonwealth v. Look (108 Mass. 452), 400.

Commonwealth v. Malone (114 Mass. 295), 28.

Commonwealth v. Matthews (122 Mass. 60), 272.

Commonwealth v. Milton (12 B. Mon. 212), 592.

Commonwealth v. Mitchell (117 Mass. 431), 91.

Commonwealth v. Morgan (107 Mass. 109), 94.

Commonwealth v. Moore (25 Gratt. 951), 282.

Commonwealth v. Morris (1 Va. Cas. 175; 5 Am. Dec. 515), 51.

Commonwealth v. Nesbit (34 Pa. St. 398), 177.

Commonwealth v. Nichols (10 Met. 259), 54.

Commonwealth v. Nichols (114 Mass. 285; 19 Am. Rep. 346), 94.

Commonwealth v. Olds (5 Lit. 140), 97.

Commonwealth v. Pa. Canal Co. (66 Pa. St. 41; 5 Am. Rep. 329), 392.

Commonwealth v. Pa. Canal Co. (66 Pa. St. 41; 5 Am. Rep. 329), 450.

Commonwealth v. Parker (9 Metc. 263), 31.

Commonwealth v. Perryman (2 Leigh, 717), 535.

Commonwealth v. Richards (18 Pick. 434), 94.

Commonwealth v. Richter (1 Pa. St. 467), 400.

Commonwealth v. Scott (123 Mass. 239; 25 Am. Rep. 87), 94.

Commonwealth v. Semmes (11 Leigh, 665), 80.

Commonwealth v. Specht, (8 Pa. St. 312), 177.

Commonwealth v. Stodder (2 Cush. 562), 272, 281, 312.

Commonwealth v. Standard Oil Co. (101 Pa. St. 119), 593.

Commonwealth v. Stowell (9 Met. 572), 97.

Commonwealth v. Sturtivant (117 Mass. 122), 91.

Commonwealth v. Taylor (5 Cush. 605), 91.

Commonwealth v. Temple (14 Gray, 75), 418.

Commonwealth v. Tuck (20 Pick. 365), 96.

Commonwealth v. Waite (9 Allen, 264), 292.

Commonwealth v. Wilkinson (16 Pick. 175; 24 Am. Dec. 624), 409.

Commonwealth v. Williams (6 Gray, 1), 519.

Commonwealth v. Wilson (14 Phila. 384), 292.

Commonwealth v. Wolf (3 Serg. & R. 48), 177.

Commonwealth v. Wood (11 Gray, 85), 31.

Commonwealth v. Wyatt, (6 Rand. 694), 24.

Concord R. R. Co. v. Greely (17 N. H. 47), 379.

Conedy v. Marcy (13 Gray, 373), 361.

Coney v. Owen (6 Watts, 435), 367.

Conkey v. Hart (14 N. Y. 22), 518.

Conn, Ex parte (13 Nev. 424), 281.

Conn. River R. R. Co. v. County Comrs. (127 Mass. 50; 34 Am. Rep. 338), 421.

Connolly v. Boston (117 Mass. 64; 19 Am. Rep. 396), 187.

Connors v. People (50 N. Y. 240), 94, 95.

Conway v. Caleb (37 Ill. 82), 519.

Conwell v. Emrie (2 Ind. 35), 399.

Cook v. Gregg (46 N. Y. 439) 507.

Cook v. Hill (3 Sandf. 341), 50.

Cook v. Moffat (5 How. 295), 521.

Cook v. So. Park Comrs. (61 Ill. 115), 420.

Cooley v. Wardens (12 How. 299), 628.

Cooper v. Cooper (76 Ill. 57), 364.

Cooper v. Utterbach (37 Md. 282), 62.

Cooper v. Williams (5 Ohio, 391; 24 Am. Dec. 299), 379.

Cooper v. Williams (7 Me. 273), 375.

Coosa River St. B. Co. v. Barclay (30 Ala. 120), 518.

Corbett v. Underwood (83 Ill. 324), 265, 267.

Cordes v. Miller (39 Mich. 581; 33 Am. Rep. 330), 439.

Corfield v. Coryell (4 Wash. C. C. 380), 196.

Cornell v. Barnes (7 Hill, 35), 83.

Cornell v. State (6 Lea, 624), 24.

Corning v. McCullough (1 N. Y. 47), 518.

Corwin v. N. Y. & Erie R. R. Co., (13 N. Y. 42), 598.

Cosby v. Railroad Co. (10 Bush, 288), 411.

Coster v. N. J. R. R. Co. (22 N. J. 227), 396.

Coster v. Mayor, etc. (43 N. Y. 399), 403.

Cotes v. Davenport (9 Iowa, 227), 33.

Coulson v. Harris (43 Miss. 728).

Council Bluffs v. Kansas City, etc., R. R. Co. (45 Iowa, 338; 24 Am. Rep. 773), 617.

County Court v. Griswold (58 Mo. 175), 380.

Cousins v. State (59 Ala. 113; 20 Am. Rep. 290), 282.

Cox v. Louisville, etc., R. R. Co. (48 Ind. 178), 411.

Craft v. McConoughy (79 Ill. 346), 249.

Craig v. Kline (65 Pa. St. 399; 3 Am. Rep. 636), 620.

Craig v. Missouri (4 Pet. 35), 214.

Craig v. Railroad Co. (39 Barb. 449; 39 N. Y. 404), 418.

Cranston v. Mayor of Augusta (61 Ga. 572), 512.

Cratty v. Bangor (57 Me. 423; 2 Am. Rep. 56), 187.

Cravens v. Winter (38 Iowa, 471), 347.

Crawford v. Branch Bank (7 How. 279), 585.

Crawford v. Delaware (7 Ohio St. 459), 401, 402, 410.

Crawford v. Wick (18 Ohio, 190), 250.

Creal v. Keokuk (4 Greene, Iowa, 47), 401.

Crenshaw v. State River Co. (6 Rand. 245), 385.

Cronin v. People (82 N. Y. 318; 37 Am. Rep. 564), 312, 434.

Crossby v. Warren (1 Rich. L. 388), 429.

Croxall v. Shererd (5 Wall. 288), 339.

Cubbinson v. McCreery (7 Watts & S. 262), 174.

Cummerford v. McAvoy (15 Ill. 311), 54.

Cummings v. Maxwell (45 Me. 190), 579.

Cummings v. Missouri (4 Wall. 277), 203.

Cummings v. Perham (1 Met. 555), 510.

Cunningham v. Brown (18 Vt. 123), 42.

Cunningham v. Mitchell (67 Pa. St. 78), 82, 83.

Cunningham v. Welde (56 Iowa, 369), 346.

Cupp v. Comrs. of Seneca (19 Ohio St. 173), 422.

Curran v. Shattuck (24 Cal. 427), 423.

Currie v. White (45 N. Y. 822), 265.

Currier v. Marietta, etc., R. R. Co. (11 Ohio St. 228), 378, 397.

Curtis v. Whipple (24 Wis. 350), 385.

Cusack v. White (2 Mill, 279), 541, 542.

Cushman v. Smith (34 Me. 247), 421.

Cusic v. Douglass (3 Kans. 123), 520.

D.

Dalby v. India Life Ins. Co.(15 C. B. 365), 261.

Dale v. Lyon (10 Johns. 447 (6 Am. Dec. 346), 54.

Dame v. Dame (38 N. H. 429), 369.

Danks v. Quackenbush (1 N. Y. 129), 517.

Dartmouth College Case (4 Wheat. 519), 72.

Dartmouth College v. Woodward (4 Wheat. 418), 574.

Dash v. Van Kleek (1 Johns. 477), 76.

Davenport v. Kelly (7 Iowa, 109), 324.

Davenport v. Lynch (6 Jones L. 545), 63, 65.

Davidson v. B. & M. R. R. Co. (3 Cush. 91), 400, 401.

Davidson v. Johonnot (7 Met. 395), 359.

Davidson v. New Orleans (96 U. S. 97), 445.

Davidson v. Ramsay Co. (18 Minn. 481), 470.

Davie v. Wisher (72 Ill. 262), 63.

Davis v. Burrell (10 C. B. 821), 30.

Davis v. McNees (8 Humph. 40), 41.

Davis v. Merrill (47 N. H. 208), 109.

Davis v. O'Farrell (4 Greene, 168), 347.

Davis v. Somerville (128 Mass. 594), 187.

Davis v. State (17 Ala. 354), 94.

Davis v. State (68 Ala. 58; 44 Am. Rep. 128), 504.

Davis v. Wilson (61 Ill. 527), 53.

Day v. Cochrane (24 Miss. 261), 344.

Day v. State (7 Gill, 321), 463.

Dean v. Sullivan R. R. Co. (22 N. H. 316), 395.

Deansville Cemetery Association, matter of (66 N. Y. 569; 23 Am. Rep. 86), 378, 386.

Decatur Co. v. Humphreys (47 Ga. 565), 377.

Decorah v. Dunstan (38 Iowa, 96).

Delaplaine v. Cook (7 Wis. 44), 519.

Delaware, etc., R. R. Co. v. Starrs (69 Pa. St. 36), 257.

Del Costa v. Jones (Comp. 729), 261.

Delphi v. Evans (36 Ind. 90), 33, 377.

DeMill v. Lockwood (3 Blatchf. 56), 338.

Den v. Bolton (12 N. J. 206), 166.

Denny v. Tyler (3 Allen, 225), 109.

Denten v. English (3 Brev. 147), 541.

Deutzel v. Waldie (30 Cal. 144), 358.

Detroit v. Michigan (34 Mich. 125), 33.

Detroit v. Plankroad Co. (13 Mich. 140), 584.

Devries v. Phillips (63 N. C. 53), 94.

Dewees v. Miller (4 Harr. 347), 261.

Dial v. Holter (6 Ohio St. 229), 50.

Dickey v. Tennison (27 Mo. 373), 381, 420.

Dickson's Exr. v. Thomas (97 Pa. St. 278), 267.

Dieffendorf v. Ref. Col. Church (20 Johns. 12) 166.

Dietz v. Langfitt (63 Pa. St. 234), 62.

Dingley v. Boston (100 Mass. 544), 396, 445.

Dingman v. People (51 Ill. 277), 580.

Ditchburn v. Goldsmith (4 Campb. 152), 261.

Diver v. Diver (56 Pa. St. 106), 364.

Dobbins v. State (14 Ohio St. 493), 917.

Doe v. Deavors (11 Ga. 79), 470.
Doe v. Douglass (8 Blackf.10),8, 359.
Donnaher's Case (16 Miss. 649), 411.
Donahue v. Richards (38 Me. 376), 161.
Done v. People (5 Park. 364), 21.
Donnell v. State (48 Miss. 661), 232.
Donnelly v. Decker (58 Wis. 461; 46 Am. Rep. 637), 445.
Dorman v. State (34 Ala. 232), 8.
Dorman v. State (34 Ala. 216), 308.
Dorsey, matter of (7 Port. (Ala.) 293), 203.
Dothage v. Stuart (35 Mo. 570), 367.
Doty v. Burdick (83 Ill. 473), 29.
Dougherty v. Commonwealth (69 Pa. St. 286), 86.
Doughty v. Conover (42 N. J. L. 192), 451.
Douglass v. Pike Co. (101 U. S. 677), 515.
Douglass v. Turnpike Co. (22 Md. 219), 409.
Dowling v. Mississippi (13 Miss. 664), 79.
Downing v. Porter (8 Gray, 539), 465.
Doyle v. Ins. Co. (94 U. S. 535), 592.
Draining Co. Case (11 La. Ann. 338), 445.
Drehman v. Stifel (41 Mo. 184; 8 Wall. 595), 517.
Drehman v. Stifle (8 Wall. 595), 73.
Drenan v. People (10 Mich. 169), 84.
Dronberger v. Reed (11 Ind. 420), 422.
Dubs v. Dubs (31 Pa. St. 154), 345.
Duncan v. Burnett (11 S. C. 333; 32 Am. Rep. 476), 520.
Duncan v. Thwaites (3 B. & C. 556), 58.

Dunham v. Powers (42 Vt. 1), 42.
Dunham v. Rochester (5 Cow. 462), 272.
Dunlap v. Glidden (31 Me. 435), 42.
Dunlap v. Hunting (2 Denio, 643). 83.
Dunlap v. Snyder (17 Barb. 561), 508.
Dunman v. Strother (1 Tex. 89), 261.
Dunn v. City Council (Harp. 129), 394.
Dunn v. Sargent (101 Mass. 336), 344, 346.
Dunn v. Winters (2 Humph. 512), 50.
Durham v. Angier (20 Me. 242), 345.
Durach's Appeal (62 Pa. St. 491), 472.
Dustin v. Cowdry (23 Vt. 631), 29.

E.

Eames v. State (6 Humph. 53), 84.
Eames v. Whittaker (123 Mass. 342), 41.
Earl v. Camp (16 Wend. 562), 83.
East Kingston v. Towle (48 N. H. 57; 2 Am. Rep. 170), 513, 519.
East St. Louis v. Wehrung (46 Ill. 392), 273.
Eaton v. Boston, C. & M. R. R. Co. (51 N. H. 504), 376, 397.
Eaton v. Keegan (114 Mass. 433), 208.
Edgecombe v. Burlington (46 Vt. 118), 386.
Edgerton v. State (69 Ind. 588), 187.
Edgewood R. R. Co.'s Appeal (79 Pa. St. 277), 379.
Edings v. Seabrook (12 Rich. L. 504), 400.
Edwards v. Davis (16 Johns. 281), 564.
Edwards v. Jagers (19 Ind. 407), 575.
Edwards v. Kearzey (96 U. S. 595), 521.

Edwards v. Pope (4 Ill. 473), 358.

Elam v. Badger (23 Ill. 498), 36.

Eldridge v. Smith (34 Vt. 484), 396.

Elliott v. Brown (2 Wend. 497), 26.

Elliott v. Fair Haven, etc., R. R. Co. (32 Conn. 579), 395, 418.

Elliott v. Fitchburg R. R. Co. (10 Cush. 191), 450.

Ellis v. Jones (51 Mo. 180), 518.

Ellis v. Pac. R. R. Co. (51 Mo. 200), 377.

Embury v. Conner (3 N. Y. 511), 379, 395.

Emonert v. Hays (59 Ill. 11), 342, 357.

Emporia v. Soden (28 Kans. 588; 37 Am. Rep. 265), 398.

Emporia v. Vollmer (12 Kans. 622), 277.

English v. State (35 Tex. 472; 14 Am. Rep. 374), 503.

Erskine v. Hohnbach (14 Wall. 613), 82.

Ervine's Appeal (16 Pa. St. 256),359.

Erwin v. State (29 Ohio St. 186), 26.

Escanaba Company v. Chicago (107 U. S. 678), 619.

Eslave v. Farmer (7 Ala. 543), 342.

Estep v. Hutchman (14 Serg. & R. 435), 359.

Estes v. Redsey (8 Wend. 560), 30.

Evans v. Montgomery (4 Watts & S. 218), 76, 517, 518.

Evergreen Cemetery v. New Haven (43 Conn. 234), 386.

Everingham v. Meighan (55 Wis. 354), 267.

Ewing v. Sandford (19 Ala. 605), 62.

Exempt Firemen's Fund v. Roome (93 N. Y. 313; 45 Am. Rep. 217), 592.

F.

Fagnan v. Knox (65 N. Y. 525), 61.

Fairchilds v. Adams (11 Cush. 549), 50.

Falconer v. Campbell (2 McLean, 195), 76.

Fales v. Wadsworth (23 Me. 553), 519.

Fanning v. Gregory (16 How. 524), 621.

Fareira v. Gabell (89 Pa. St. 89), 265.

Faris v. Starke (3 B. Mon. 4), 61.

Farley v. Dowe (45 Ala. 324), 520.

Farmer v. Lewis (1 Bush (Ky.), 66), 495.

Farmers' Loan, etc., Association v. Stone (U. S. C. C. Miss., 18 Cent. L. J. 472), 591.

Farmers' & Mechanics' Bk v. Smith (6 Wheat. 131), 521.

Farnam v. Feeley (55 N. Y. 551), 61.

Farness v. Fox (1 Cush. 134), 339.

Farnsworth Co. v. Lisbon (62 Me. 451), 473.

Farnsworth v. Storrs (5 Cush. 412), 50.

Farr v. Rasco (9 Mich. 353), 54.

Farrington v. Tennessee (95 U. S. 679), 575.

Fawcett v. Charles (13 Wend. 473), 56.

Fell v. State (42 Md. 1; 20 Am. Rep. 83), 288, 583.

Fenwick v. Gill (38 Mo. 510), 367.

Ferraria v. Vasconcellos (31 Ill. 25), 165.

Ferrier, Ex parte (103 Ill. 367; 42 Am. Rep. 10), 135, 559.

Ferring v. Irwin (55 N. Y. 486), 403.

Ferris v. Bramble (5 Ohio St. 109), 381.

Fertilizing Co. v. Hyde Park (97 U. S. 25), 581.

Field v. Des Moines (39 Iowa, 575), 399.

Fillebrowne v. Grand Trunk, etc., Co. (55 Me. 462), 256, 257.

Fire Department of Milwaukee v. Helfenstein (16 Wis. 136), 592.

Fisher v. Forrester (33 Pa. St. 501), 63, 65.

Fisher v. Horricon Co. (10 Wis. 351), 385.

Fisher v. Manufacturing Co. (12 Pick. 67), 385.

Fisher v. McGirr (1 Gray, 26), 304, 463.

Fisher v. Provin (25 Mich. 347), 364.

Fisher's Case (6 Leigh, 619), 203.

Fitchburg R. R. Co. v. Grand Junction R. R. Co. (1 Allen, 552; 4 Allen, 198), 599.

Fitzgerald v. Robinson (112 Mass. 371), 37, 166.

Fletcher v. Fletcher (1 El. & El. 420), 109.

Fletcher v. Peck (6 Cranch, 81), 76.

Flickinger v. Wagner (46 Md. 581), 62.

Flint v. Pike (4 B. & C. 473), 57.

Flint v. Woodhull (25 Mich. 99), 575.

Foley v. People (1 Ill. 31), 80.

Fouville v. Casey (1 Murphy, 389), 265.

Foote v. State (59 Md. 264), 24.

Forbes v. Halsey (26 N. Y. 563), 519.

Forbes v. Johnson (11 B. Mon. 48), 41, 49.

Ford v. Chicago, etc., R. R. Co. (14 Wis. 609), 375, 411.

Foster v. Essex Bank (10 Mass. 245), 586.

Foster v. Scripps (39 Mich. 376; 33 Am. Rep. 403), 52.

Fountain v. Draper (49 Ill. 441), 303.

Fowler v. Chichester (26 Ohio St. 9), 54.

Fowler v. Halbert (4 Bibb, 54), 367.

Fowler, matter of (53 N. Y. 60), 376.

Fowles v. Bowen (30 N. Y. 20), 37.

Fox v. Ohio (5 How. 410), 15, 628.

Fox v. W. P. R. R. Co. (31 Cal. 588), 421.

Frank, Ex parte (52 Cal. 606; 28 Am. Rep. 642), 282.

Frankford, etc., R. R. Co. v. Philadelphia (58 Pa. St. 119), 579.

Frankfort, etc., R. Co. v. Philadelphia (58 Pa. St. 119), 272.

Franklin Bank v. Cooper (36 Me. 179), 585, 586.

Frasher v. State (3 Tex. App. 263), 537.

Franz v. Railroad Co. (55 Iowa, 107), 395, 403, 409, 415.

Freleigh v. State (8 Mo. 606), 291.

French v. Camp (18 Me. 433), 617.

French v. White (24 Conn. 174), 380.

Fretwell v. Troy (18 Kans. 271), 273.

Friend v. Woods (6 Gratt. 139), 256.

Frolickstein v. Mobile (40 Ala. 725), 185.

Frommer v. Richmond (31 Gratt. 646), 272.

Fry v. State (63 Ind. 552), 292.

Fuhr v. Dean (26 Mo. 116), 30.

Fuller v. Edings (11 Rich. L. 239), 400.

Furman Street, matter of (17 Wend. 649), 401.

G.

Gabel v. Houston (29 Tex. 335), 310.

Gaggans v. Turnipseed (1 S. C. 40; 7 Am Rep. 23), 515.

Gaines v. Union Transp. Co. (28 Ohio St. 418), 257.

Gallaway v. Burr (32 Mich. 332), 61.

Galveston, etc., R. R. Co. v. Gierse (51 Tex. 189), 597.

Garcia v. Territory (1 New Mex. 415) 24.

Gardner v. Newburg (2 Johns. Ch. 162; 7 Am. Dec. 526), 380, 392, 398.

Garland, Ex parte (4 Wall. 333), 72, 73, 203.

Garr v. Selden (4 N. Y. 91) 41, 42.

Garrett v. Cheshira (69 N. C. 396; 12 Am. Rep. 647), 521.

Gatlin v. Tarboro (78 N. C. 419) 282, 283.

Gaussby v. Perkins (30 Mich. 492) 303.

Gavin v. Burton (8 Ind. 69) 531.

Gee v. Patterson (63 Me. 49), 61.

Georgia Penitentiary Co. v. Nelms (65 Ga. 499; 38 Am. Rep. 793), 99.

Gerard v. People (4 Ill. 363), 96.

German Congregation v. Pressler (17 La. Ann. 127), 165.

Germania v. State (7 Md. 1), 272.

Gibbon v. Ogden (9 Wheat. 1), 605, 610.

Gibbs v. Gale (7 Md. 76), 519.

Giesy v. Cincinnati, etc., R. R. Co. (4 Ohio St. 308), 395, 396.

Gilbert v. People (1 Denio, 41), 44.

Gilbert v. Showerman (23 Mich. 448), 34.

Gillam v. Sioux City, etc., R. R. Co. (26 Minn. 268), 597.

Gillinwater v. Miss., etc., R. R. Co. (13 Ill. 1), 377.

Gilman v. Lockwood (4 Wall. 409), 521.

Gilman v. Philadelphia (3 Wall. 712), 619.

Gilmer v. Lime Point (18 Cal. 229), 376, 378.

Gilmore v. Woodcock (69 Me. 118), 261.

Glascock v. Bridges (15 La. Ann. 672) 65.

Glossom v. McFerran (79 Ky. 236) 365.

Glover v. Powell (10 N. J. Eq. 211), 397.

Goddard v. Jacksonville (15 Ill. 588), 304.

Goelett v. Gori (31 Barb. 314) 364.

Good v. Elliott (3 T. R. 993), 260.

Good v. Zercher (12 Ohio, 368), 358.

Goodell v. Jackson (20 Johns. 693, 710), 143.

Goodenough v. McGrew (44 Iowa, 670), 303.

Goodman v. Han. and St. Jo. R. R. Co. (45 Mo. 33), 366.

Goodman v. State (Meigs, 197) 93.

Gore v. Martin (66 N. C. 371), 82.

Gorgan v. State (44 Ala. 9), 96.

Gorman v. Pac. R. R. Co. (26 Mo. 441), 580, 597.

Goshern v. Kern (63 Ind. 468), 284.

Goshen v. Storlington (4 Conn. 259), 5.

Goslin v. Cannon (1 Harr. 3), 37, 41.

Gottbehuet v. Hubachek (36 Wis. 515), 52.

Gould v. Gardner (8 La. Ann. 11), 63.

Gould v. Hudson River R. R. Co. (6 N. Y. 522), 398, 400.

Gove v. Blethen (21 Minn. 80; 18 Am. Rep. 380), 52.

Gowen v. Penobscot R. R. Co. (44 Me. 140), 579, 583, 585.

Gozzler v. Georgetown (6 Wheat. 593), 401.

Grace v. Mitchell (31 Wis. 533), 83.

Grammar School v. Burt (11 Vt. 632), 574.

Grand Rapids Booming Co. v. Jarvis (30 Mich. 308), 397.

Grand Rapids, etc., R. R. Co. v. Heisel (38 Mich. 62; 31 Am. Rep. 306), 402, 415.

Grant v. Courten, (24 Barb. 232), 8.

Grant *v.* Hamilton (3 McL. 100), 261.

Graves *v.* Otis (2 Hill, 466), 401.

Gray *v.* Coffin (9 Cush. 200), 585.

Gray *v.* First Division, etc. (13 Minn. 315), 411.

Gray *v.* Harris (107 Mass. 492; 9 Am. Rep. 61), 450.

Gray *v.* Hornbeck (31 Mo. 400), 361.

Gray *v.* Kimball (42 Me. 299), 463.

Gray *v.* Pentland (2 Serg. & R. 23), 49.

Great Falls Manfg. Co. *v.* Fernald (47 N. H. 444), 385.

Great West. R. R. Co. *v.* Hawkins (17 Mich. 57; 18 Mich. 427), 257.

Green *v.* Goddard (2 Salk. 641), 28.

Green *v.* Portland (32 Me. 431), 402.

Green *v.* Reading (9 Watts, 382),401.

Green *v.* State (58 Ala. 190; 29 Am. Rep. 739), 537.

Green *v.* Swift (47 Cal. 536), 400.

Greenough *v.* Greenough (11 Pa. St. 489), 357.

Gregory *v.* Wattoma (58 Iowa, 711), 267.

Gregory *v.* Wendall (39 Mich. 337), 267, 269.

Griffin *v.* Griffin (8 B. Mon. 120), 542.

Griffin *v.* Wilcox (21 Ind. 370), 516.

Griffith *v.* Commissioners (20 Ohio, 609), 5.

Griffs *v.* Sellars (4 Dev. & Bat. 176), 61.

Grills *v.* Jonesboro (8 Baxt. 247), 310.

Grimes *v.* Coyle (6 B. Mon. 301), 37, 41.

Grinnell *v.* West. Union Tel. Co. (113 Mass. 299; 18 Am. Rep. 485), 259.

Griswold *v.* Bragg (48 Conn. 579), 367.

Groesbeck *v.* Seeley (13 Mich. 329), 519.

Grosvenor *v.* United Society (118 Mass. 78), 166.

Grove *v.* Brandenburg (7 Blackf. 234), 42.

Grover *v.* Jones (52 Mo. 68), 364.

Grumon *v.* Raymond (1 Conn 39), 83.

Guerin *v.* Moore (25 Minn. 462), 346.

Guild *v.* Rogers (8 Barb. 502), 518.

Guilford *v.* Supervisors (13 N. Y. 143), 8.

Guillotte *v.* New Orleans (12 La. Ann. 432), 237.

Gunn *v.* Barry (15 Wall. 610), 521.

Gunarrsohn *v.* Sterling (92 Ill. 669), 273.

Gunnison *v.* Twitchell (38 N. H. 68), 345.

Gut *v.* State (9 Wall. 35), 79.

Guyer *v.* Andrews (11 Ill. 494), 83.

H.

Haas *v.* Chicago & N. W. R. R. Co. (41 Wis. 44), 599.

Hadgar *v.* Supervisors (47 Cal. 222), 445.

Haight *v.* Cornell (15 Conn. 74), 50.

Haile *v.* State (38 Ark. 564; 42 Am. Rep. 3), 503.

Hale *v.* Everett (53 N. H. 9), 165.

Hale *v.* Lawrence (1 Zab. 714; 3 Zab. 590), 3.

Hale *v.* Hawkins (5 Humph. 357), 61.

Halloway *v.* Sherman (12 Iowa, 282), 518.

Ham *v.* Kendall (111 Mass. 298), 366.

Ham *v.* Salem (100 Mass. 350), 380.

Hamersly *v.* New York (56 N. Y. 533), 421.

Hamilton *v.* Eno (81 N. Y. 116), 52.

Hamilton *v.* Keith (5 Bush, 458), 575.

Hamilton v. Lomax (26 Barb. 615), 531.

Hamilton v. St. Louis Co. (15 Mo. 23), 8.

Hammett v. Philadelphia (65 Pa. St. 146; 3 Am. Rep. 615), 581.

Hammond v. Haines (25 Md. 541), 273.

Hampden v. Walsh (L. R. 12 B. D. 192), 261.

Hampton v. Wilson (4 Dev. 468), 54.

Hand v. Ballou (12 N. Y. 541), 519.

Hanton v. Small (3 Sandf. 230), 265.

Happy v. Morton (93 Ill. 398), 165.

Harbor Comrs. v. Pashley (19 S. C. 315), 625.

Hardeman v. Downer (39 Ga. 425), 520.

Harden v. Comstock (2 A. K. Marsh. 480; 12 Am. Dec. 168), 43.

Harding v. Funk (8 Kan. 315), 385.

Harding v. Goodlett (3 Yerg. 40; 24 Am. Dec. 546), 378.

Harding v. Stanford Water Co. (41 Conn. 87), 397.

Harkrader v. Moore (44 Cal. 144), 62.

Harmon v. Dreher (2 Speer's Eq. 87), 166.

Harmony v. Mitchell (1 Blatchf. 549), 495.

Harp v. Osgood (2 Hill, 216), 81.

Harper v. Richardson (22 Cal. 251), 421.

Harpham v. Whitney (77 Ill. 32), 62.

Harrigan v. Conn. River Lumber Co. (129 Mass. 580; 37 Am. Rep 387), 620.

Harris v. Huntington (2 Tyler, 129; 4 Am. Dec. 728), 49.

Harris v. Lumbridge (83 N. Y. 92), 265, 267, 268.

Hart v. People (26 Hun, 396), 291.

Hart v. State (40 Ala. 32), 79.

Hartung v. People (22 N. Y. 95, 105), 77.

Harrison v. Baltimore (1 Gill, 264), 102.

Harrison v. Harrison (43 Vt. 417), 28.

Harrison v. N. O., etc., R. R. Co. (34 La. Ann. 462; 44 Am. Rep. 438), 415.

Harvey v. Brydges (13 M. & W. 437), 30.

Harvey v. Lackawanna, etc., R. R. Co. (47 Pa. St. 428), 400.

Harvey v. Thomas (10 Watts, 63), 381.

Hastings v. Lusk (22 Wend. 410; 34 Am. Dec. 380), 43, 44.

Hatch v. Douglass (48 Conn. 116), 267.

Hatch v. Lane (105 Mass. 394), 36, 37.

Hatch v. Vt. Cent. R. R. Co. (25 Vt. 49), 398, 400.

Hatfield v. Gano (15 Iowa, 177), 31.

Hathorn v. Lyon (2 Mich. 93), 344.

Hathorn v. Stinson (12 Me. 183), 451.

Haverhill Bridge Prop. and County Comrs. (103 Mass. 120; 4 Am. Rep. 518), 421.

Hawkins v. Lumsden (10 Wis. 359), 54.

Hawthorn v. Calef (2 Wall. 10), 518, 574.

Hay v. Cohoes Company (3 Barb. 47), 385.

Hay v. Kennedy (41 Pa. St. 378), 256.

Haynes v. Burlington (38 Vt. 350), 394, 397.

Haynes v. Carter (9 La. Ann. 265), 580.

Haynes v. State (17 Ga. 465), 26.

Haynes v. Thomas (7 Ind. 38), 402.

Hays v. Risher (32 Pa. St. 169), 376.

Hayward v. Mayor of N. Y. (7 N. Y. 314), 396.

Hazen v. Essex Company (12 Cush. 475), 386.

Head v. Goodwin (37 Me. 181), 265.

Heald v. Builders' Ins. Co. (111 Mass. 38), 265.

Hector v. State (2 Mo. 166), 97.

Hedderich v. State (101 Ind. 564; 51 Am. Rep. 768), 310.

Hellams v. Abercrombie (15 S. C. 110), 187.

Hemingway v. Scales (42 Miss. 1; 2 Am. Rep. 586), 364.

Henderson's Distilled Spirits (14 Wall. 44), 284, 463.

Hendirckson v. Decon (1 N. J. Eq. 577), 166.

Hennesey v. People (21 How. Pr. 239), 439.

Henry v. Dubuque, etc., R. R. Co. (10 Iowa, 540), 423.

Henry v. Dubuque & Pac. R. R. Co. (2 Iowa, 288), 395.

Henry v. Underwood (1 Dana, 247), 375.

Henson v. Moore (104 Ill. 403), 344, 346.

Hepburn v. Griswold (8 Wall. 603), 213, 606.

Herber v. State (7 Texas, 69), 24, 77.

Herrick v. Randolph (13 Vt. 525), 472.

Hess v. Baltimore, etc., Railroad Co. (52 Md. 242; 36 Am. Rep. 371), 418.

Hess v. Johnson (3 W. Va. 645), 517.

Hewitt v. Charrier (16 Pick. 353), 204.

Heyne v. Blair (62 N. Y. 19), 61.

Hey Sing Jack v. Anderson (57 Cal. 251), 465, 498.

Heyward v. Mayor (7 N. Y. 324), 358, 359.

Hibbard v. People (4 Mich. 125), 463.

Hibblewhite v. McMorine (5 M. & W. 58), 265.

Hickman's Case (4 Harr. 580), 381.

Hilbourne v. Fogg (99 Mass. 11), 30.

Hildreth v. Lowell (11 Gray, 345), 380.

Hill v. Decatur (22 Ga. 203), 273.

Hill v. Kessler (63 N. C. 437), 520.

Hill v Miles (9 N. H. 9), 49.

Hill v. Wait (5 Vt. 124), 83.

Hills v. Miller (3 Paige, 256), 404.

Hilton v. Eckersley (6 El. & Bl. 47, 66), 246.

Hinckley v. Baxter (13 Allen, 139), 366.

Hinchman v. R. R. Co. (17 N. J. Eq. 75; 20 N. J. Eq. 360), 418.

Hinchman v. Richie (2 Law Rep. (N. S.) 180), 109.

Hinckley v. Penobscot (42 Me. 89), 187.

Hinde v. Gray (1 M. & G. 195), 249.

Hinman v. Chicago, etc., R. R. Co. (28 Iowa, 491), 598.

Hirn v. State (1 Ohio St. 15), 581.

Hirsh v. State (21 Gratt. 785), 273, 282.

Hitchcock v. Coker (6 Ad. & El. 438), 249.

Hoar v. Wood (3 Metc. 193), 44.

Hoare v. Silverlock (9 C. B. 20), 56.

Hobart v. Milwaukee, etc., R. R. Co. (27 Wis. 194; 9 Am. Rep. 461), 419.

Hobbs, Ex rel. (1 Woods, 537), 537.

Hockett v. State (Sup. Ct. Ind., Cent. L. J., July 9, 1886), 590.

Hoffman v. State (20 Md. 475), 96.

Hoffman v. Steigers (28 Iowa, 302), 364.

Holbrook v. Finney (4 Mass. 565; 3 Am. Dec. 243), 340.

Holliday v. Sterling (62 Mo. 321). 62.

Hollister v. Nowlen (19 Wend. 234), 257.

Holloway v. Commonwealth (11 Bush, 344), 26.

Holly v. Mix (3 Wend. 350), 84.

Holyoke Co. v. Lyman (15 Wall. 500), 451, 575.

Home Ins. Co. v. Augusta (50 Ga. 530), 272, 281.

Homestead Cases (22 Gratt. 266; 12 Am. Rep. 507), 521.

Hood v. Finch (8 Wis. 381), 420.

Hook v. Hackney (16 Serg. & R. 385), 52.

Hooker v. Haven, etc., Co. (16 Conn. 146; 36 Am. Dec. 477), 422.

Hooker v. Miller (37 Iowa, 613; 18 Am. Rep. 18), 28.

Hooker v. New Haven, etc., R. R. Co. (14 Conn. 186), 397, 400.

Hooker v. Vandewater (4 Denio, 340), 249, 251.

Hooper v. Bridgewater (102 Mass. 512), 380.

Hooper v. Wells (27 Cal. 11), 257.

Hoover v. State (59 Ala. 59), 537.

Hopt v. Utah (110 U. S. 574), 76.

Horn v. Atlantic, etc., R. R. Co. (35 N. H. 169), 598, 599.

Hornby v. Close (L. R. 2 Q. B. 183), 246.

Horne v. Ashford (3 Bing. 322), 249.

Horton v. Hendershot (1 Hill, 118), 83.

Hosmer v. Loveland (19 Barb. 111), 50.

Hotchkiss v. Oliphant (2 Hill, 510–513), 52.

House of Refuge v. Ryan (37 Ohio St. 197), 559.

Houston, etc., R. R. Co. v. Odum (53 Tex. 343), 411.

Howard v. Kentucky, etc., Ins. Co. (13 B. Mon. 282), 583.

Howard v. Moot (64 N. Y. 262), 519.

Howard v. Proctor (7 Gray, 128), 82.

Howard v. Thompson (21 Wend. 319), 49.

Howard v. Zeyer (18 La. Ann. 407), 367.

Huber v. Reilly (53 Pa. St. 115), 76.

Huckenstein's Appeal (70 Pa. St. 102; 10 Am. Rep. 669), 34.

Hudson v. Geary (4 R. I. 485), 177, 310.

Hulett v. Inlow (57 Ind. 412; 26 Am. Rep. 64), 364.

Hull v. Hull (48 Conn. 250), 265.

Humes v. Mo. Pac. R. R. Co. (82 Mo. 22; 52 Am. Rep. 369), 598.

Humes v. Tabor (1 R. I. 464), 465.

Hunscom v. Hunscom (15 Mass. 184), 174.

Hunt v. Bennett (19 N. Y. 173), 52.

Hunt v. Peake (5 Cow. 475), 531.

Hunter v. Burnsville Pike Co. (56 Ind. 213), 586.

Huntington v. Chessbro (57 Ind. 74), 272.

Hunting v. Johnson (66 N. C. 189), 346.

Huntley v. Rice (10 East, 22), 261.

Hunt's Lessee v. McMahon (5 Ohio, 132), 367.

Hutchins v. Com. (2 Va. Cas. 331), 535.

Hutton v. City of Camden (39 N. J. 122; 23 Am. Rep. 209), 428.

Hylton v. United States (3 Dall. 171), 469.

I.

Illinois Cent. R. R. Co. v. Arnold (47 Ill. 173), 598.

Illinois Cent. R. R. Co. v. Read (37 Ill. 484), 258.

Ilsley v. Nichols (12 Pick. 270), 465.

Imhoff v. Whitmer (21 Pa. St. 243), 497.

Imlay v. Union Branch R. R. Co. (26 Conn. 249), 395, 410, 411.

Indian Bagging Co. v. Cock & Co. (14 La. Ann. 164), 251.

Indiana Cent. R. W. Co. v. Gapen (10 Ind. 292), 598.

Indiana Cent. R. R. Co. v. Mundy (21 Ind. 48), 258.

Indianapolis, etc., R. R Co. v. Allen (31 Ind. 394), 257.

Indianapolis, etc., R. R. Co. v. Fowler (22 Ind. 316), 597.

Indianapolis, etc., R. R. Co. v. Kercheval (16 Ind. 84), 581, 597.

Indianapolis, etc., R. R. Co. v. Marshall (27 Ind. 300), 597.

Indianapolis R. R. Co. v. Smith (52 Ind. 428), 402.

Inge v. Police Jury (14 La. Ann. 117), 380.

Inglis v. Sailor's Snug Harbor (3 Pet. 99), 139.

Inhabitants of Springfield v. Conn. River R. R. Co. (4 Cush. 71), 410.

Inland Fishery Comrs. v. Holyoke Water Power Co. (104 Mass. 446), 575.

Inman Steamship Co. v. Tinker (94 U. S. 238), 625.

Intoxicating Liquor Cases (25 Kans. 751; 37 Am. Rep. 284), 324.

Iron R. R. Co. v. Ironton (19 Ohio St. 209), 375.

Iron R. R. Co. v. Lawrence Furnace Co. (29 Ohio St. 208), 590.

Israel v. Brooks (23 Ill. 575), 61.

J.

Jackson v. Burns (3 Binn. 85), 139.

Jackson v. Butler (8 Minn. 117), 516.

Jackson v. Commonwealth (19 Gratt. 656), 86, 93.

Jackson v. Edwards (7 Paige, 391; 22 Wend. 498), 345.

Jackson v. Hathaway (15 Johns. 447), 395.

Jackson v. Lyon (9 Cow. 664), 344.

Jackson v. Rutland, etc., R. R. Co. (25 Vt. 150), 395.

Jacobs v. Allard (42 Vt. 303; 1 Am. Rep. 331), 449.

Jacobs v. Cone (5 Serg. & R. 335), 86.

Jacobs, matter of (98 N. Y. 98), 196, 312, 430.

Jacobus v. St. Paul, etc., R. R. Co. (20 Minn. 125), 258.

Jacoway v. Denton (25 Ark. 641), 515.

James v. Rowland (42 Md. 462), 357.

Janes, matter of (30 How. Pr. 446), 115, 116.

Jarvis v. Hathaway (3 Johns. 180), 41.

Jeck v. Anderson (57 Cal. 251; 40 Am. Rep. 115), 498.

Jeffersonville, etc., R. R. Co. v. Nichols (30 Ind. 321), 598.

Jenkins v. Jenkins (82 N. C. 202), 346.

Jennings v. Paine (4 Wis. 358), 43, 44.

Jerome v. Ross (7 Johns. Ch. 315; 11 Am. Dec. 484), 392.

Joannes v. Bennett (5 Allen, 170), 37.

John and Cherry Street (19 Wend. 676), 358.

Johns v. State (55 Md. 350), 93.

Johns v. State (78 Ind. 332), 177, 186.

Johnson v. Atlantic, etc., R. R. Co. (35 N. H. 569), 392, 397.

Johnson v. Fletcher (54 Miss. 628; 28 Am. Rep. 388), 520.

Johnson v. Hall (6 Cal. 359), 261.

Johnson v. Hanahan (1 Strobh. 313), 30.

Johnson v. Irasburg (47 Vt. 28; 19 Am. Rep. 111), 187.

Johnson v. Lonsley (12 C. B. 468), 261.

Johnson v. People (31 Ill. 469), 187.

Johnson v. Philadelphia (60 Pa. St. 445), 272, 274, 281.

Johnson v. Russell (37 Cal. 670), 261.

Johnson v. Simonton (43 Cal. 542), 295, 297.

Johnston v. Commonwealth (10 Harris, 102), 183.

Jordan v. Woodward (40 Me. 317), 385.

Jones v. Andrews (10 Allen, 18), 188.

Jones v. Fletcher (41 Me. 254), 465.

Jones v. Galena, etc., R. R. Co. (16 Iowa, 6), 597.

Jones v. Harris (1 Strobh. 160), 174.

Jones v. Lees (1 H. & N. 189), 246.

Jones v. Marable (6 Humph. 116), 342.

Jones v. People (14 Ill. 196), 304.

Jones v. Perry (10 Yerg. 59), 358.

Jones v. State (1 Ga. 610), 79.

Jones v. Voorhees (10 Ohio, 145), 257.

Judges, Opinions of (48 Me. 591), 470.

Judson v. Bridgeport (25 Conn. 426), 377.

Juillard v. Greenman (110 U. S. 421), 213, 216, 607.

K.

Kallock v. Superior Court (56 Cal. 229), 92.

Kane v. Baltimore (15 Md. 240), 380.

Kansas Pac. Ry. Co. v Mower (16 Kan. 573), 597.

Karney v. Paisley (13 Iowa, 89), 519.

Kean v. Stetson (5 Pick. 492), 617.

Kearney v. Taylor (15 How. 494), 362.

Keenan v. State (8 Wis. 132), 84.

Keene's Appeal (64 Pa. St. 274), 361.

Keller v. Corpus Christi (50 Tex. 614; 32 Am. Rep. 513), 399.

Kellinger v. 42nd St., etc., R. R. Co. (50 N. Y. 206), 403, 418.

Kellum v. Jansorn (17 Pa. St. 467), 30.

Kellum v. State (66 Ind. 588), 583.

Kelly v. Scott (5 Gratt. 479), 531.

Kendall v. State (65 Ala. 492), 97.

Kendricks v. State (10 Humph. 497), 94.

Kennedy v. Insurance Company (11 Mo. 204), 347.

Kennett's Petition (24 N. H. 135), 400.

Kerwhacker v. Cleveland, etc., R. R. Co. (3 Ohio St. 172), 407.

Kester v. Stark (19 Ill. 328), 531.

Keyser v. School District (35 N. H. 480), 366.

Keyser v. Stansifer 6 Ohio 363), 165.

Kidder v. Parkhurst (3 Allen, 393), 41, 42.

Kimball v. Bates (50 Me. 308), 65.

Kincaid's Appeal (66 Pa. St. 423; 5 Am. Rep. 377), 437, 583.

King v. Root (4 Wend. 113; 21 Am. Dec. 102), 52.

King v. Ward (77 Ill. 603), 61, 65.

Kingsbury v. Kirwan (71 N. Y. 612), 266, 268.

Kinney v. Cent. R. R. Co. (32 N. J. 407; 34 N. J. 513), 258.

Kinney's Case (30 Gratt. 858) 537.

Kipp v. Paterson (26 N. J. 298), 281.

Kirby v. Chitwood (4 B. Mon. 95), 358, 359.

Kirby v. Shaw (90 Pa. St. 258) 472.

Kirkman v. Handy (11 Humph. 406), 34.

Kirkpatrick v. Bonsall (72 Pa. St. 155), 267.

Kirkpatrick v. Eagle Lodge (26 Kans. 384) 50.

Kirkpatrick v. Kirkpatrick (39 Pa. St. 288), 61.

Kirkland v. Hotchkiss (100 U. S. 491), 472.

Kleizer v. Symmes (40 Ind. 462), 50.

Klinck v. Colby (46 N. Y. 274 (7 Am. Rep. 360), 37, 41.

Knight v. Knight (90 Ill. 208), 29.

Kniper v. Louisville (7 Bush, 599), 272.

Knowles v. Peck (42 Conn. 386; 19 Am. Rep. 542), 37.

Knowles v. People (15 Mich. 408), 94.

Knoxville v. Bird (12 Lea, 121; 47 Am. Rep. 326), 439.

Kohlheimer v. State (39 Miss. 548), 96.

Kohn v. Koehler (21 Hun, 466) 291.

Kramer v. Cleveland, etc., R. R. Co. (5 Ohio St. 140), 372.

Krevet v. Meyer (24 Mo. 107), 30.

Kroop v. Forman (31 Mich. 144), 377.

Kuttes v. Smith (2 Wall. 491), 366.

L.

Lacey v. Davis (4 Mich. 140), 519.

Lackland v. North Mo. R. R. Co. (31 Mo. 180), 402.

La Croix v. County Comrs. (50 Conn. 321; 47 Am. Rep. 648), 583.

La Croix v. Fairfield Co. Comrs. (49 Conn. 591), 288.

Ladd v. Southern C. P. & M. Co. (53 Tex. 172), 594.

Lafayette v. Bush (19 Ind. 326), 401.

Lakeview v. Rose Hill Cemetery (70 Ill. 192; s. c. 22 Am. Rep. 71), 3, 13, 437, 438, 583.

Lakeview v. Setz (44 Ill. 81) 429, 433.

Lake Shore, etc., R. R. Co. v. Chicago, etc., R. R. Co. (97 Ill. 506), 392.

Lamb v. Lane (4 Ohio St. 167), 420.

Lambe v. St. Louis (15 Mo. 610), 33.

Lancaster Co. Bk. v. Stauffer (10 Pa. St. 398), 344, 345.

Lane v. Dorman (4 Ill. 238), 358.

Lang v. Weeks (2 Ohio (N. s.) 519), 246, 251.

Larkin v. Noonan (19 Wis. 82), 49.

Lasure v. State (10 Ohio St. 43), 79.

Laughlin v. Clawson (27 Pa. St. 330), 63.

Law, Ex parte (35 Ga. 285), 203.

Lawrence, In re (1 Redf. Sur. Rep. 310), 342.

Lawrence v. Lanning (4 Ind. 194), 61.

Lawson v. Hicks (38 Ala. 279), 44.

Lawyer v. Cipperly (7 Paige, 281), 165.

Lea v. White (4 Sneed, 111), 41.

Leachman v. Dougherty (81 Ill. 324) 83.

Learned v. Cutler (18 Pick. 9), 345.

Leavenworth v. Booth (15 Kan. 627), 279, 281.

Lebanon v. Griffin (45 N. H. 558).

Lebanon v. Olcott (1 N. H. 339), 376.

Leclaire v. Davenport (13 Iowa, 210), 313, 324, 434.

Lee v. Pembroke Iron Co. (57 Me. 481; 2 Am. Rep. 59), 450.

Lee v. State (26 Ark. 260; 7 Am. Rep. 611), 96.

Legal Tender Cases (12 Wall. 457), 213, 607.

Lemay v. Williams (32 Ark. 166), 63.

Lemmon v. Chicago, etc., R. R. Co. (32 Iowa, 151), 598.

Lessley v. Phipps (49 Miss. 790), 521.

Lenz v. Charlton (23 Wis. 478), 519.

Lester v. State (33 Ga. 339), 97.

Lester v. Thurmond (51 Ga. 118), 44.

Levy v. Brannan (39 Cal. 485) 63.

Lewellen v. Lockhardts (21 Gratt. 570), 273, 282.

Lewis v. Avery (8 Vt. 287), 83.

Lewis v. Bk. of Kentucky (12 Ohio St. 132), 586.

Lewis v. Chapman (16 N. Y. 369), 36, 37, 55.

Lewis v. Few (5 Johns. 1), 51, 54.

Lewis v. Levy (E. B. & E. 537), 56, 58.

Lewis v. Littlefield (15 Me. 233), 261.

Lewis v. Lyman (22 Pick. 437).

Lewis v. State (51 Ala. 1), 26.

Lewis v. Washington (5 Gratt. 265), 383.

Lexington, etc., R. R. Co. v. Applegate (8 Dana, 289; 33 Am. Dec. 497), 411.

Ligat v. Commonwealth (19 Pa. St. 456), 420.

Lincoln v. Alexander (52 Cal. 482; 28 Am. Rep. 639), 496.

Lincoln, etc., Bank v. Richardson (1 Greenl. 79), 585.

Lincoln v. Smith (27 Vt. 328), 304.

Lindenmuller v. People (33 Barb. 568), 178, 183.

Linsley v. Hubbard (44 Conn. 109; 26 Am. Rep. 431), 365.

Litchfield v. Cudworth (15 Pick. 28), 344.

Little Miama, etc., R. R. Co. v. Dayton (23 Ohio St. 510), 392.

Little Rock, etc., R. R. Co. v. Payne (33 Ark. 816; 34 Am. Rep. 55), 519, 598.

Liverpool Ins. Co. v. Mass. (1 Wall. 506), 592.

Livingston v. Mayor, etc. (8 Wend. 85; 22 Am. Dec. 622), 446.

Livingston v. Tanner (14 N. H. 64), 30.

Livingston's Lessee v. Moore (7 Pet. 469), 15.

Lock v. Dane (9 Mass. 360), 76.

Locke v. United States (7 Cranch, 339), 463.

Logan v. Matthews (6 Pa. St. 417), 187.

Logan v. Musick (81 Ill. 415), 265.

Logan v. Walton (12 Ind. 639), 346, 347.

Logan v. Payne (43 Iowa, 523; 22 Am. Rep. 261), 317.

Lonas v. State (3 Heisk. 287), 537.

Long v. Fuller (68 Pa. St. 170), 380, 421.

Long v. Marvin (15 Mich. 60), 344.

Long v. State (12 Ga. 233), 84.

Longmer v. Smith (1 B. & C. 1), 265.

Longville v. State (4 Tex. App. 312), 272.

Longworth v. Worthington (6 Ohio, 9), 367.

Look v. Dean (108 Mass. 116; 11 Am. Rep. 323), 108, 109.

Loomis v. Terry (17 Wend. 496), 28.

Loomis v. Spencer (1 Ohio St. 153), 82.

Lord v. Litchfield (36 Conn. 116; 4 Am. Rep. 41), 579.

Lott v. Hubbard (44 Ala. 593), 82.

Lott v. Sweet (33 Mich. 308), 108.

Loughbridge v. Harris (42 Ga. 500), 378, 385.

Louisville & N. R. R. Co. v. Burke (6 Caldw. 45), 597.

Louisville, etc., R. R. Co. v. Ballard (2 Met. (Ky.) 165), 580.

Love v. Shartzer (31 Cal. 487), 367.

Love v. Sheffelin (7 Fla. 40), 205.

Low v. Galena, etc., R. R. Co. (18 Ill. 324), 396.

Loweree v. Newark (38 N. J. 151), 421.

Lowery v. Rainwater (70 Mo. 152; 35 Am. Rep. 420), 463, 498.

Lucas v. Case (9 Bush, 562), 50, 165, 166.

Lucas v. Sawyer (17 Iowa, 517), 346.

Luminary, The (8 Wheat. 401), 463.

Lumsden v. Cross (10 Wis. 282), 519.

Lund v. New Bedford (121 Mass. 286), 377.

Lyman v. Boston, etc., R. R. Co. (4 Cush. 288), 599.

Lynch v. Brudie (63 Pa. St. 206), 267.

Lyon v. Culbertson (83 Ill. 33), 265, 267.

Lyon v. Jerome (26 Wend. 484), 376.

Lyons v. Jerome (15 Wend. 569), 392.

M.

Mabry v. Tarver (1 Humph. 94), 272.

Macomber v. Godfrey (108 Mass. 219; 11 Am. Rep. 349), 450.

Macy v. Indianapolis (17 Ind. 267), 401.

Madison, etc., R. R. Co. v. Whiteneck (8 Ind. 217), 598.

Magee v. Young (40 Miss. 164), 346.

Maguire v. Smock (42 Ind. 1), 251.

Maguire, matter of (57 Cal. 604; 40 Am. Rep. 125), 199.

Mahala v. State (10 Yerg. 532), 97.

Mahon v. N. Y. Cent. R. R. Co. (24 N. Y. 658), 411.

Malone v. Murphy (2 Kan. 250), 61.

Manderson v. Lukens (23 Pa. St. 31), 339.

Manhattan Fertilizing Co. v. Van Keuren (8 C. E. Green, 251), 428.

Mansfield v. Clark (23 Mich. 519), 375.

Marburg v. Cole (49 Md. 402; 33 Am. Rep. 266), 364.

March v. Portsmouth, etc., R. R. Co. (19 N. H. 372), 394, 397.

Marsh v. Ellsworth (50 N. Y. 309), 42, 43.

Marsh v. Russell (2 Lans. 75), 249.

Marshall v. Gunter (6 Rich. 419), 41, 44.

Marshall v. King (24 Miss. 90), 339, 342.

Marshalltown v. Blum (58 Iowa, 184; 43 Am. Rep. 116), 615.

Marten v. Van Shaik (4 Paige, 479), 54.

Martin v. Hughes (67 N. C. 293), 520.

Martin v. Hunter's Lessee (1 Wheat. 304), 605.

Marysville Turnpike Co. v. How, (14 B. Mon. 429), 575.

Mason v. Halle (12 Wheat. 370), 518.

Mason v. Mason (4 N. H. 110), 54.

Massie v. Mann (17 Iowa, 131), 205.

Mather v. Hood (8 Johns. 447), 83.

Matthew v. Fiestel (3 E. D. Smith, 90), 507.

Matthews v. Beach (5 Sandf. 259), 58.

Mattocks v. Stearns (9 Vt. 326), 344.

Maul v. Stark (25 Tex. 166), 77.

Maull v. Vaughn (45 Ala. 134), 520.

Maurer v. People (43 N. Y. 1), 86.

Maurice v. Maurice (43 N. Y. 380), 339.

Maurice v. Worden (54 Md. 233; 39 Am. Rep. 384), 41.

Maxey v. Loyal (38 Ga. 531), 518.

Maxwell v. Jonesboro (11 Heisk. 257), 310.

Maxwell v. Palmerston (21 Wend. 407), 507.

May v. Fletcher (40 Ind. 575), 346.

Mayor v. Phelps (27 Ala. 55), 272.

Mayor, etc., v. Beasley (1 Humph. 232), 283.

Mayor of New York v. 2d Ave. R. R. Co. (32 N. Y. 261), 272, 281.

Mayor of City of Hudson v. Thorne (2 Paige, 161), 324.

Mayor, etc., v. Yuille (3 Ala. 137), 272.

Mayrant v. Richardson (1 Nott & McCord, 348; 9 Am. Dec. 707), 51.

Mays v. Cincinnati (1 Ohio St. 268), 272, 281.

McAlister v. Clark (33 Conn. 91), 453.

McAndrew v. Electrical Tel. Co. (17 C. B. 3), 259.

McArthur v. Franklin (16 Ohio St. 200), 345.

McBee v. Fulton (47 Md. 403; 28 Am. Rep. 465), 56.

McDonald v. Redwing (13 Minn. 38), 399.

McDonough v. Webster (68 Me. 530), 261.

McCarty v. Blevins (13 Tenn. 195), 265.

McCarty v. Fremont (26 Cal. 196), 28.

McClain, Ex parte (61 Cal. 435; 44 Am. Rep. 554), 308.

McClary v. Lowell (44 Vt. 116; 8 Am. Rep. 366), 187.

McComb v. Akron (15 Ohio, 474; s. c. 18 Ohio, 229), 401.

McCoy v. Erie, etc., R. R. Co. (42 Md. 498), 258.

McCoy v. Grandy (3 Ohio St. 463), 369.

McCracken v. Hayward (2 How. 608), 515.

McCulloch v. Maryland (4 Wheat. 428), 470, 472.

McCurdy v. Canning (64 Pa. St. 39), 364.

McFadden v. Commonwealth (23 Pa. St. 12), 96.

McFarland v. Butler (8 Minn. 116), 516.

McGatrick v. Wason (4 Ohio St. 566), 177.

McGaughey v. Henry (15 B. Mon. 383), 342.

McGinnis v. Watson (41 Pa. St. 9), 166.

McGoon v. Scales (9 Wall. 31), 586.

McGregor v. Erie Railway (35 N. J. L. 115), 593.

McKay v. Campbell (2 Sawyer, 118), 143.

McKee v. People (32 N. Y. 239), 97.

McKeon v. Lee (51 N. Y. 300; 10 Am. Rep. 659), 34.

McKewn v. Hunter (30 N. Y. 624), 62.

McKinney v. Salem (77 Ind. 213), 583.

McLaughlin v. Cowley (127 Mass. 316), 41, 43.

McLaughlin v. State (45 Ind. 338), 79.

McLaughlin, Ex parte (41 Cal. 211; 10 Am. Rep. 272), 97.

McLean v. Cook (23 Wis. 364), 82.

McMillan v. Birch (1 Binn. 178; 2 Am. Dec. 426), 43, 50.

McMillan v. Michigan, etc., R. R. Co. (16 Mich. 79), 256.

McMillan v. McNiell (4 Wheat. 209), 521.

McPherson v. State (29 Ark. 225), 26.

McPherson v. State (22 Ga. 478), 28.

Mechanics' Bank v. De Bolt (1 Ohio St. 591), 575.

Medway v. Natick (1 Mass. 88), 537.

Medway v. Needham (16 Mass. 157) 537.

Meeker v. Wright (75 N. Y. 262), 364.

Meliget's Appeal (17 Pa. St. 449), 346.

Memphis v. Water Co. (5 Heisk. 492), 317.

Memphis & C. R. R. Co. v. Payne (37 Miss. 700), 422, 423.

Merchants' Dispatch Co. v. Smith (76 Ill. 542), 256.

Merriam v. Mitchell (13 Me. 439), 62.

Merrill v. Sherburne (1 N. H. 199; 8 Am. Dec. 52), 345.

Metcalf v. Putnam (9 Allen, 97), 361.

Metropolitan Board v. Barrie (34 N. Y. 657), 285, 304.

Metropolitan Board v. Heister (37 N. Y. 661), 312.

Metropolitan Board of Excise v. Barrie (34 N. Y. 657), 583.

Metropolitan Board of Health v. Heister (37 N. Y. 661), 434.

Metropolitan R. R. Co. v. Quincy R. R. Co. (12 Allen, 262), 418.

Michaels v. N. J. Cent. R. R. Co. (30 N. Y. 571), 257.

Mifflin v. Railroad Co. (16 Pa. St. 182), 411.

Millburn v. Cedar Rapids, etc., R. R. Co. (12 Iowa, 246), 395, 402, 403, 409.

Miller v. Miller (9 Pa. St. 74), 451.

Miller v. Miller (10 Met. 393), 342.

Miller v. Miller (16 Mass. 59), 340.

Miller v. Troosh (14 Minn. 365), 385.

Miller v. Clark (4 Bosw. 632), 205.

Milliken v. City Council (54 Tex. 388; 38 Am. Rep. 629), 351.

Mills v. Brooklyn (32 N. Y. 489), 33.

Mills v. Commonwealth (13 Pa. St. 631), 31.

Mills v. Lockwood (42 Ill. 111), 361.

Mills v. Williams (11 Ired. 558), 574.

Mills v. Williams (16 S. C. 594), 187.

Mills, matter of (1 Mich. 392), 203.

Milnor v. N. Y., etc., R. R. Co. (53 N. Y. 164), 593.

Milwaukee v. Gross (21 Wis. 241), 312, 434.

Milwaukee Industrial School v. Supervisor (40 Wis. 328; 28 Am. Rep. 702), 559.

Mississippi Soc. of Arts v. Musgrove (44 Miss. 820) 583.

Missouri Val. R. R. Co. v. Caldwell (8 Kan. 244), 257.

Mitchell v. Harmony (13 How. 115), 495.

Mitchell v. Lemon (34 Md. 176), 85.

Mitchell v. Williams (27 Ind. 62), 512.

Mitchinson v. Cross (58 Ill. 366), 61.

Mithoff v. Carrollton (12 La. Ann. 185), 380.

Mobile v. Kimball (102 U. S. 691), 624.

Mobile v. Yuille (3 Ala. (N. s.) 140), 208, 237.

Mobile & M. R. R. Co. v. Steiner (61 Ala. 559), 590.

Mobile, etc., R. R. Co. v. Moseley (52 Miss. 127), 575.

Mobile, etc., R. R. Co. v. State (51 Miss. 137), 599.

Monongahela Nav. Co. v. Coons (6 Watts & S. 101), 400.

Monroe v. Smelley (25 Tex. 586), 261.

Moore v. Allegheny City (18 Pa. St. 55), 82.

Moore v. Boyd (24 Me. 247), 29.

Moore v. City of N. Y. (8 N. Y. 110), 343, 345.

Moore v. Frost (3 N. H. 127), 345.

Moore v. Illinois (14 Ohio, 13), 628.

Moore v. Kent (37 Iowa, 20), 347.

Moore v. Monroe (64 Iowa, 367; 52 Am. Rep. 444), 162.

Moore v. Railway Co. (34 Wis. 173), 377.

Moore v. State (43 N. J. 203), 76, 517.

Moore v. State (48 Miss. 147; 12 Am. Rep. 367), 583.

Moore v. State (36 Miss. 137), 80.

Moreau v. Detachmendy (18 Mo. 522), 346.

Morehead v. State (9 Humph. 635), 91.

Morey v. Brown (42 N. H. 373), 511, 512.

Morgan v. King (18 Barb. 84; 35 N. Y. 454), 617.

Morgan v. King (35 N. Y. 454), 398.

Morgan v. Nolte (37 Ohio St. 23; 41 Am. Rep. 485), 125, 127.

Morrill v. State (38 Wis. 428; 20 Am. Rep. 12), 282.

Morris v. Wrenshall (34 Md. 494), 518.

Morris Run Coal Co. v. Barclay Coal Co. (68 Pa. 43), 250.

Morrison v. Davis, (20 Pa. St. 171), 256.

Morse v. Goold (11 N. Y. 281), 517, 520.

Mortimer v. McCallan (6 M. & W. 58), 265.

Morton, matter of (10 Mich. 208), 466.

Moseley v. State (33 Tex. 671), 97.

Moses v. Pittsburg, etc., R. R. Co. (21 Ill. 516), 395, 409, 415.

Mott v. Dawson (46 Iowa, 533), 51.

Mott v. Palmer (1 Const. 571), 366.

Mount v. Commonwealth (2 Duv. 93), 96.

Mt. Carmel v. Wabash (50 Ill. 69), 277.

Mount Washington Road Co., petition of (35 N. H. 134), 376.

Mounts v. State (14 Ohio, 295), 96.

Mouse v. Switz (19 How. 275), 252.

Mower v. Watson (11 Vt. 536; 34 Am. Dec. 704), 44.

Mowry v. Whipple (8 R. I. 360), 61, 62.

Muhlerbrinck v. Commonwealth (42 N. J. L. 364; 36 Am. Rep. 518), 272.

Mummy v. Johnston (3 A. K. Marsh. 220), 361.

Munger v. Tonawando R. R. Co. (4 N. Y. 349), 396.

Municipality v. Dubois (10 La. Ann. 56), 283.

Munn v. Illinois (94 U. S. 113), 229, 235, 236, 240, 342, 588, 590.

Munn v. State (1 Ga. 243), 503.

Murphy v. Chicago (29 Ill. 279), 401.

Murphy v. Larson (77 Ill. 172), 63.

Murray v. Commonwealth (79 Pa. St. 311), 26.

Murray v. County Com'rs (12 Met. 455), 409.

Murray v. Menefee (20 Ark. 561), 400.

Murray v. Sharp (1 Bosw. 539), 397.

Murray v. The Charming Betsey (2 Cranch, 64), 139.

Mussey v. Scott (32 Vt. 82), 29.

N.

Nashville, etc., R. R. Co. v. Hodges, (7 Lea, 663), 473.

Nathan v. State (8 How. 73), 615, 616.

Neass v. Mercer (15 Barb. 318), 519.

Nelson v. Sheboygan Nav. Co. (4 Mich. 7; 38 Am. Dec. 222), 622.

Nesbit v. Trumbo (39 Ill. 110), 391.

Neth v. Crofut (30 Conn. 580), 82.

Nevitt v. Bk. of Port Gibson (6 Smedes & M. 513), 585, 586.

New Albany, etc., R. R. Co. v. Tilton (12 Ind. 3), 598.

New Albany, etc., R. R. Co. v. Maiden (12 Ind. 10), 598.

New Albany, etc., R. R. Co. v. O'Dailey (13 Ind. 353), 395, 402, 410, 415.

New Brunswick, etc., Co. v. Tiers (24 N. J. 697), 256.

New Castle, etc., R. R. Co. v. Peru, etc., R. R. Co. (3 Ind. 464), 392.

Newcome v. Smith (1 Chandl. 71), 385.

N. J. St. Nav. Co. v. Merchants' Bk. (6 How. 344), 256.

Newman, Ex parte (9 Cal. 509), 176, 177, 179, 182, 183.

New Orleans v. Eclipse Towboat Co. (33 La. Ann. 647; 39 Am. Rep.) 279, 625.

New Orleans v. Fourchy (30 La. Ann. pt. 1, 910), 473.

New Orleans v. Guillotte (12 La. Ann. 818), 324.

New Orleans v. Kauffman (29 La. Ann. 283; 29 Am. Rep. 328), 282.

New Orleans v. People's Bank (32 La. Ann. 82), 473.

New Orleans v. Stafford (27 La. Ann. 417; 21 Am. Rep. 563), 312, 313, 434.

New Orleans, etc., R. R. Co. v. Gay (32 La. Ann. 471), 395.

N. O., etc., R. R. Co. v. Southern, etc., Tel. Co. (53 Ala. 211), 392.

N. O. Ins. Co. v. N. O., etc., R. R. Co. (20 La. Ann. 302), 257.

N. Y., etc., R. R. Co. v. Kip (46 N. Y. 546; 7 Am. Rep. 383), 379, 396.

N. Y. Cent. R. R. Co. v. Met. Gas Co. (63 N. Y. 326), 376.

Niccolls v. Ingersoll (7 Johns. 145), 81.

Nichols v. Bridgeport (23 Conn. 189), 377.

Nicholson v. N. Y., etc., R. R. Co. (22 Conn. 74), 415.

Nichols v. Somerset, etc., R. R. Co. (43 Me. 356), 421.

Nichols, matter of (8 R. I. 50), 518.

Noel v. Ewing (9 Ind. 37), 346, 549.

Nolan v. State (55 Ga. 521), 96.

Noland v. Busby (28 Ind. 154), 82.

Nolin v. Franklin (4 Yerg. 163), 506.

Noonan v. Orton (32 Wis. 106), 36.

Norfleet v. Cromwell (70 N. C. 634; 16 Am. Rep. 787), 445.

Norris v. Vt. Cent. R. R. Co. (28 Vt. 99), 397.

Norris v. Beyea (13 N. Y. 273), 344.

North v. Phillips (89 Pa. St. 250), 265, 267.

N. C., etc., R. R. Co. v. California Cent. R. R. Co. (83 N. C. 489), 392.

N. E. & S. W. R. R. Co., Ex parte (37 Ala 679), 580.

North Mo. R. R. Co. v. Gott (25 Mo. 540), 376.

North Mo. R. R. Co. v. Lackland (25 Mo. 515), 376.

Norwich Gaslight Co. v. Norwich City Gas Co. (25 Conn. 19), 317.

Noyes v. Jenkins (55 Ga. 586), 265.

Noyes v. Spalding (27 Vt. 420), 265, 267.

Nugent v. State (4 Stew. & Port. 72), 97.

O.

Oaks, matter of (8 Law Reporter, 122), 108.

O'Bannon v. Louisville, etc., R. R. Co. (8 Bush, 348), 598.

O'Brien v. Commonwealth (6 Bush, 503), 94.

O'Brien v. Kustener (27 Mich. 292), 366.

O'Connor v. Pittsburg (18 Pa. St. 187), 401, 406.

O'Donoghue v. McGovern (23 Wend. 26), 50, 55.

O'Ferrall v. Simplot (4 Iowa, 381), 346.

Ogden v. Saunders (12 Wheat. 213), 76, 515, 517, 519.

Ogden v. Stock (34 Ill. 522), 366.

O'Hara v. Lexington, etc., R. R. Co. (1 Dana, 232), 375.

O'Hara v. Stack (90 Pa. St. 477), 165.

Ohio & M. R. R. Co. v. Lackey (78 Ill. 55; 20 Am. Rep. 259), 599.

Ohio & Miss. R. R. Co. v. McClelland (25 Ill. 140), 597.

Ohio, etc., R. R. Co. v. Selby (47 Ind. 471), 258.

O'Kelly v. Williams (74 N. C. 281), 346.

Oliver v. Memphis, etc., R. R. Co. (30 Ark. 128), 515.

Olmstead v. Camp (33 Conn. 532), 376, 378, 385.

Olmstead v. Partridge (16 Gray, 383), 63.

Orange Co. Bank v. Brown (9 Wend. 85), 256.

O'Reilly v. Kankakee Val. Draining Co. (32 Ind. 169), 445.

Oregon St. Nav. Co. v. Winsor (20 Wall. 64), 251.

Ormond v. Martin (37 Ala. 598), 367.

Ormsby v. Douglass (37 N. Y. 477), 37, 55.

Orr v. Box (22 Minn. 485), 82.

Orr v. Quimby (54 N. H. 590), 421.

Osborn v. Hart (24 Wis. 89; 1 Am. Rep. 161), 381.

Osborn v. Nicholson (13 Ark. 654), 515, 516.

Osborne v. Mobile (44 Ala. 493), 592.

Osgood v. Howard (6 Greenl. 452), 366.

Oswego v. Oswego Canal Co. (6 N. Y. 257), 404.

Ould v. Richmond (23 Gratt. 464; 14 Am. Rep. 139), 282.

Our House v. State (4 Greene, Iowa, 172), 304.

Owners of Ground v. Mayor, etc., of Albany (15 Wend. 374), 380.

Oystead v. Shed (13 Mass. 520), 465.

P.

Pacific Ins. Co. v. Soule (7 Wall. 433), 469.

Pa. R. R. Co. v. Butler (57 Pa. St. 335), 258.

Packet Company v. Keokuk (95 U. S. 80), 625.

Pacquette v. Pickness (19 Wis. 219), 367.

Page v. Fazackerly (36 Barb. 392), 237.

Paine v. Woods (108 Mass. 170), 452.

Palairet's Appeal (67 Pa. St. 479), 359.

Palmer v. State (39 Ohio St. ——), 297.

Palmore v. State (29 Ark. 248), 28.

Pangburn v. Bull (1 Wend. 345), 62.

Pardy v. N. Y. &. N. H. R. R. Co. (61 N. Y. 353), 592.

Paris v. Mason (37 Texas, 447), 377.

Parker v. Bidwell (3 Conn. 84), 81.

Parker v. Metropolitan R. R. Co. (109 Mass. 507), 590, 621.

Parker v. McQueen (18 B. Mon. 16), 54.

Parker v. Milldam Co. (20 Me. 353; 37 Am. Dec. 56), 400.

Parker v. Savage (6 Lea, 406), 421.

Parver v. Com. (5 Wall. 475), 15.

Pasley v. Freeman (3 J. R. 51), 252.

Passmore v. W. U. Tel. Co. (78 Pa. St. 238,), 259.

Patten v. People (18 Mich. 314), 28.

Patterson v. Kentucky (97 U. S. 501), 207, 295, 613.

Patterson v. People (46 Barb. 625), 26.

Pattison v. Jones (8 B. & C. 578), 36.

Patton v. Patton (39 Ohio St. 590), 493.

Paul v. Detroit (32 Mich. 108), 394.

Payne v. Payne (18 Cal. 291), 359.

Payson v. Caswell (22 Me. 212), 61.

Pearce v. Savage (45 Me. 101), 339.

Peck v. Chicago, etc., R. R. Co. (94 U. S. 164), 589.

Peck v. Gurney (L. R. 6 H. L. Cas. 377), 251.

Peddicord v. Baltimore, etc., R. R. Co. (34 Md. 463), 411.

Peik v. Chicago, etc., R. R. Co. (94 U. S. 164), 234, 593.

Pekin v. Winkel (77 Ill. 56), 402.

Penniman's Case (103 U. S. 714), 518.

Pennsylvania, etc., R. R. Co. v. N. Y., etc., R. R. Co. (23 N. J. Eq. 157), 398.

Penn. R. R. Co. v. Riblet (66 Pa. St. 164; 5 Am. Rep. 360), 597, 599.

Penrose v. Erie Canal Co. (56 Pa. St. 46), 516, 518.

Pensacola, etc., R. R. Co. v. W. U. Tel. Co. (96 U. S. 1), 326.

People v. Barrett (2 Caines, 304), 96.

People v. Boston, etc., R. R. Co. (70 N. Y. 569), 597.

People v. Brighton (20 Mich. 57), 377.

People v. Canal Appraisers (13 Wend. 355), 398.

People v. Cipperly (Ct. App. N. Y. Feb. 5, 1886), 292.

People v. Colman (3 Cal. 46), 473.

People v. Commissioners (59 N. Y. 92), 581.

People v. Cook (10 Mich. 164), 96.

People v. Fisher (14 Wend. 9), 248, 250.

People v. Forbes (4 Park. 611), 122.

People v. German Church (53 N. Y. 103), 166.

People v. Goodwin (18 Johns. 187), 97.

People v. Gray (4 Park. 616), 122.

People v. Green (3 Mich. 496), 421.

People v. Hawley (3 Gibbs, 330), 304.

People v. Hennesy, 15 Wend. 147), 93.

People v. Hubbard (24 Wend. 369), 465.

People v. Ingersoll (58 N. Y. 1), 515.

People v. Jackson (3 Hill, 92), 31.

People v. Jackson, etc., Plank Road Co. (9 Mich. 282), 13, 68.

People v. Jackson, etc., Plank Road Co. (9 Mich. 285), 583, 585.

People v. Kerr (37 Barb. 357; 27 N. Y. 188), 395, 400, 403, 409.

People v. Kniskern (54 N. Y. 52), 420.

People v. Manchester (9 Wend. 351), 574.

People v. Marx (99 N. Y. 377), 196, 296.

People v. Marx (99 N. Y. 307; 52 Am. Rep. 314), 196, 296.

People v. Mayor of N. Y. (4 N. Y. 419), 446, 470.

People v. McGowan (17 Wend. 386), 96.

People v. McMahon (15 N. Y. 385), 91.

People v. Mulholland (82 N. Y. 324; 37 Am. Rep. 568), 273.

People v. Murphy (45 Cal. 137); 94.

People v. Nearing (27 N. Y. 306), 380.

People v. Olmstead (30 Mich. 431), 79.

People v. Phillips, (1 Park. 95), 122.

People v. Phillips (42 N. Y. 200), 91.

People v. Plank Road Co. (9 Mich. 285), 133.

People v. Ruggles (8 Johns. 289; 5 Am. Dec. 335), 168, 169, 171.

People v. Smith (21 N. Y. 595), 373, 375, 376.

People v. Smith (1 Cal. 9), 80.

People v. Smith (20 Johns. 63), 82.

People v. Sullivan (7 N. Y. 396), 26.

People v. Thurber (13 Ill. 557), 272, 281, 283.

People v. Thurber, (13 Ill. 554), 592.

People v. Township Board of Salem (20 Mich. 452), 388.

People v. Toynbec (20 Barb. 218), 5.

People v. Turner (55 Ill. 280; 8 Am. Rep. 645), 11, 135, 556.

People v. Tyler (7 Mich. 161), 96.

People v. Tyler (36 Cal. 522), 94.

People v. Wabash, etc., R. R. Co. (104 Ill. 476), 617.

People v. Webb (28 Cal. 467), 96.

People v. Weisenbach (60 N. Y. 385), 556.

Peoria, etc., R. R. Co. v. Duggan (109 Ill. 537; 50 Am. Rep. 619), 598.

Pequest Case (41 N. J. L. 175), 446.

Percy, Ex parte (36 N. Y. 651), 203.

Perdue v. Ellis (18 Ga. 586), 304.

Perkins v. Eaton (3 N. H. 152), 261.

Perkins v. Mitchell (31 Barb. 461), 40.

Perkins v. N. Y. Cent. R. R. Co. (24 N. Y. 197), 258.

Perry v. Phipps (10 Ired. L. 259), 508.

Perry v. Wilson (7 Mass. 395), 375.

Perry's Case (3 Gratt. 632), 76, 175.

Petillon v. Hipple (90 Ill. 420), 261.

Pettigrew v. Evansville (25 Wis. 223), 394, 397.

Phelps v. Racey (60 N. Y. 10; 19 Am. Rep. 140), 500.

Phila. Ass'n, etc., v. Wood (39 Pa. St. 73), 470.

Phila. & B. R. R. Co. v. Lehman (56 Md. 209), 187.

Philadelphia, etc., R. R. Co. v. Derby (14 How. 468), 258.

Phila., etc., R. R. Co. v. Quigley (21 How 202), 50.

Phila. & Trenton R. R. Co., cases of (6 Whart. 25; 36 Am. Dec. 202), 411.

Phila. W. B. R. R. Co. v. Bowers (4 Houst. 506), 594, 597.

Phillips v. Bonham (16 La. Ann. 387), 63.

Phillips v. Disney (16 Ohio, 639), 346.

Phillips v. Ives (1 Rawle, 36), 261.

Phillips v. Ocmulgee Mills Co. (55 Ga. 633), 265.

Phillips v. Trull (11 Johns. 477), 84.

Phillips v. Wickham (1 Paige, 590), 545.

Pickering v. Cease (79 Ill. 328), 265, 267.

Pierce v. Hubbard (10 Johns. 405), 82.

Pierce v. Kimball (9 Me. 54; 23 Am. Dec. 537), 208.

Pierce v. People (106 Ill. 11; 46 Am. Rep. 683), 592, 593.

Pingry v. Washburn (1 Aiken, 264), 585.

Piqua Bank v. Knoop (16 How. 369), 574.

Pistauque Bridge Co. v. N. H. Bridge (7 N. H. 35), 392.

Pitford v. Armstrong (Wright, Ohio, 94), 28.

Pitt v. Cox (43 Pa. St. 486), 396.

Pittock v. O'Neill (63 Pa. St. 253; 3 Am. Rep. 544), 57.

Pittsburg v. Scott (1 Pa. St. 809), 381.

Pittsburg, etc., R. R. Co. v. S. W. Penn. R. R. Co. (77 Pa. St. 173), 599.

Pittsburg, C. & St. L. R. R. Co. v. Brown (67 Ind. 45; 33 Am. Rep. 73), 597.

Pittsburg, etc., R. R. Co. v. Crown (57 Ind. 45; 33 Am. Rep. 73), 424.

Pixley v. Boynton (79 Ill. 351), 265, 267.

Planters' Bk. v. Sharp (6 How. 301), 574, 586.

Platteville v. Bell (43 Wis. 488), 310.

Pleuler v. State (11 Neb. 547), 273, 583.

Plumb v. Sawyer (21 Conn. 351), 344.

Pocopson Road (16 Pa. St. 15), 381.

Polenskie v. People (73 N. Y. 65), 292.

Poler v. N. Y. Cent. R. R. Co. (16 N. Y. 476), 598.

Pollard's Lessee v. Hagan (3 How. 212), 367.

Pomeroy v. Chicago, etc., R. R. Co. (16 Wis. 640), 411.

Poncher v. N. Y. Cent. R. R. Co. (49 N. Y. 263), 258.

Pond v. People (8 Mich. 150), 28, 461.

Pontiac v. Carter (32 Mich. 164), 401.

Pool v. Lewis (46 Ga. 162; 5 Am. Rep. 526), 451.

Pope v. Macon (23 Ark. 644), 367.

Pope v. State (22 Ark. 371), 94.

Porter v. Mariner (50 Mo. 364), 518.

Portland Bank v. Apthorp (12 Mass. 252), 472.

Potter v. Sealey (8 Cal. 217), 63.

Potter v. Titcomb (22 Me. 300).

Powell v. M. & B. Mfg. Co. (3 Mason, 369), 366.

Powell v. Mills (30 Miss. 231), 256.

Powers v. Bears (12 Wis. 213), 421.

Powers v. Dubois (17 Wend. 63), 52.

Power's Appeal (29 Mich. 504), 377, 420.

Pratt v. Brown (3 Wis. 603), 376, 379, 385.

Pratt v. Jones (25 Vt. 303), 519.

Pratt v. Tefft (14 Mich. 191), 346.

Presbyterian Society, etc., v. Auburn, etc., R. R. Co. (3 Hill, 567), 411.

Prescott v. State (19 Ohio St. 184; 2 Am. Rep. 388), 136, 559.

Preston v. Drew (33 Me. 559), 304.

Price v. State (36 Miss. 533), 96.

Price v. State (19 Ohio, 423), 96.

Price v. Talley (10 Ala. 946).

Pritchard v. Citizens' Bank (8 La. 130; 23 Am. Dec. 132), 344.

Proctor v. Andover (42 N. H. 348), 381.

Proctor v. Jennings (6 Nev. 83; 3 Am. Rep. 240), 450.

Prohibition Amendment Cases (24 Kans. 700), 288, 304.

Proprietors, etc., v. Nashua R. R. Co. (10 Cush. 388), 394, 397.

Protzman v. Indianapolis, etc., R. R. Co. (9 Ind. 467), 395, 402, 410, 415.

Prough v. Entriken (11 Pa. St. 81), 65.

Providence Bank v. Billings (4 Pet. 561), 470, 472.

Providence Savings Institute v. Skating Rink (52 Mo. 452), 518.

Pugh v. Ottenheimer (6 Ore. 231; 25 Am. Rep. 513), 344.

Pumpelly v. Green Bay, etc., Co. (13 Wall. 166), 397, 401.

Putnam *v.* Douglass Co. (6 Ore. 378; 25 Am. Rep. 527), 420.

Putnam *v.* Payne (13 Johns. 312), 509.

Q.

Quackenbush *v.* Danks (1 Denio, 128; 3 Denio, 594; 1 N. Y. 129), 520.

Quain *v.* Russell (12 Hun, 376), 303.

R.

Radcliffe's Ex'rs *v.* Mayor of Brooklyn (4 N. Y. 195; *s. c.* 7 N. Y. 195), 401, 406.

Rafferty *v.* People (69 Ill. 111; 72 Ill. 37; 18 Am. Rep. 601), 82.

Railroad *v.* Hecht (29 Ark. 661; 95 U. S. 170), 583.

Railroad *v.* Reeves (10 Wall. 176), 256.

Railroad Co. *v.* Combs (10 Bush, 382; 19 Am. Rep. 67), 411.

Railroad Co. *v.* Husan (95 U. S. 465), 624.

Railroad Co. *v.* Lockwood (17 Wall. 357), 257.

Railroad Co. *v.* Richmond (96 U. S. 521), 400.

Railroad Co. *v.* Shurmeir (7 Wall. 272), 395.

Railway Co. *v.* Philadelphia (101 U. S. 528), 473.

Railway *v.* Renwick (102 U. S. 180), 398.

Raleigh, etc., R. R. Co. *v.* Davis (2 Dev. & Bat. 451), 376.

Rand *v.* Commonwealth (9 Gratt. 738), 79.

Ratch *v.* Flanders (29 N. H. 304), 345.

Ratzky *v.* People (29 N. Y. 124), 77.

Raulston *v.* Jackson (1 Sneed, 128), 61.

Raymond *v.* Leavitt (46 Mich. 447), 249.

Reaper's Bank *v.* Willard (24 Ill. 433), 580.

Rearick *v.* Wilcox (81 Ill. 77), 52.

Rector *v.* Smith (11 Iowa, 302), 37, 41, 42.

Read *v.* Beall (42 Miss. 572), 288.

Reed *v.* Case (4 Conn. 166; 10 Am. Dec. 110), 81.

Reddall *v.* Bryan (14 Md. 444), 380.

Reeder *v.* Purdy (41 Ill. 261), 29.

Reeves *v.* Treasurer (8 Ohio St. 333), 33, 380, 381.

Reid *v.* DeLorme (2 Brev. 76), 49, 50.

Reid *v.* Kirk (12 Rich. 54), 366.

Reiser *v.* Tell Association (39 Pa. St. 137), 357.

Reitenbaugh *v.* Chester Val. R. R. Co. (21 Pa. St. 100), 377.

Reithmuller *v.* People (44 Mich. 280), 289.

Remington *v.* Congdon (2 Pick. 310), 50.

Renck *v.* McGregor (32 N. J. 70), 84.

Respublica *v.* Dennie (4 Yeates, 207; 2 Am. Dec. 402), 191.

Respublica *v.* Montgomery (1 Yeates, 419), 84.

Rex *v.* De Berenger (3 M. & S. 67), 249.

Rexford *v.* Knight (11 N. Y. 308), 396, 421.

Rex *v.* Waddington (1 East, 43), 246.

Reynolds *v.* United States (98 U. S. 145), 172, 539.

Rice *v.* Parkman (16 Mass. 326), 358, 365.

Rice *v.* Wadsworth (27 N. H. 104), 82.

Rich *v.* Chicago (59 Ill. 286), 420.

Rich *v.* Flanders (39 N. H. 304), 519.

Richards *v.* Nye (5 Ore. 382), 83.

Richardson *v.* Kelley (85 Ill. 491), 261.

Richardson v. Vt. Cent. R. R. Co. (25 Vt. 465), 400.

Richmond T. & P. R. R. Co. v. City of Richmond (26 Gratt. 83; 96 U. S. 521), 597.

Richmond Manfg. Co. v. Atlantic Delaine Co. (10 R. I. 106; 14 Am· Rep. 658), 449.

Richmond R. R. Co. v. Louisa R. R. Co. (13 How. 71), 392.

Ridge Street, In re (29 Pa. St. 391), 401.

Ring v. Wheeler (7 Cow. 725), 44.

Ritchie v. Boynton (114 Mass. 431), 208.

Rison v. Farr (24 Ark. 161), 516.

River Rendering Co. v. Behr (77 Mo. 91; 46 Am. Rep. 6), 504.

River Rendering Co. v. Behr (7 Mo. App. 345), 316.

Roach v. People (77 Ill. 25), 26.

Robbins v. Treadway (2 J. J. Marsh. 540; 19 Am. Dec. 152), 51.

Robbins v. State (8 Ohio St. 131), 31.

Roberts v. Chicago (26 Ill. 249), 33, 401.

Roberts v. Ogle (38 Ill. 459), 507.

Roberts v. Whiting (16 Mass. 186), 344.

Robertson v. Bullions (11 N. Y. 243), 165.

Robertson v. State (12 Tex. App. 541), 288.

Robinson v. Hamilton (60 Iowa, 134; 46 Am. Rep. 63), 206.

Robinson v. Richardson (13 Gray, 456), 464.

Robinson v. Swope (12 Bush, 21), 381.

Robinson, Ex parte (12 Nev. 263; 28 Am. Rep. 798), 615.

Robinson, Ex parte (12 Nev. 263), 282, 283.

Rochester Water Com'rs, In re (66 N. Y. 413), 392.

Rockford, etc., R. R. Co. v. Hillman (72 Ill. 235), 299.

Rockwell v. Hubbell's Adm'rs (2 Dougl. (Mich.) 197), 518.

Rockwell v. Nearing (35 N. Y. 302), 507.

Rodemacher v. Milwaukee, etc., R. R. Co. (41 Iowa, 297; 20 Am Rep· 592), 599.

Rogers v. Woodbury (15 Pick. 156), 366.

Rohen v. Sawen (5 Cush. 281), 84.

Rome v. Addison (34 N. H. 306), 397.

Roser, Ex parte (60 Cal. 177), 183.

Ross' Case (2 Pick. 169), 5.

Ross v. Innis (26 Ill. 259), 63.

Ross v. Irving (14 Ill. 171), 367.

Roth v. Eppy (80 Ill. 283), 303.

Roth v. House of Refuge (31 Md. 329), 559.

Rover v. Webster (3 Clarke, 502), 63, 65.

Rowe v. Addison (39 N. H. 306), 394.

Royston v. Royston (21 Ga. 161), 346.

Ruchizky v. De Haven (97 Pa. St. 202), 267.

Rudolph v. Winters (7 Neb. 125), 267.

Ruggles v. Nantucket (11 Cush. 433), 399.

Ruggles v. People (91 Ill. 256), 590.

Ruloff v. People (45 N. Y. 213), 84.

Rumsey v. Berry (65 Me. 570), 265, 267, 268.

Ruohs v. Backer (6 Heisk. 395; 19 Am. Rep. 598), 41, 44.

Russell v. Anthony (21 Kan. 450; 30 Am. Rep. 436), 52.

Russell v. Mayor of N. Y. (2 Denio, 461), 399.

Russell v. Richards (10 Me. 429), 366.

Russell v. Rumsey (35 Ill. 362), 346, 358.

Rust v. Lowe (6 Mass. 90), 394.

Ruth, In re (32 Iowa, 253), 324.

Ryckman v. Coleman (13 Abb. Pr. 398), 205.

Ryder v. Innerarity (4 Stew. & P. 14), 361.

Ryerson v. Brown (35 Mich. 333; 24 Am. Rep. 564), 378, 385.

S.

Sadler v. Langham (34 Ala. 311), 379, 381, 385.

Sager v. Portsmouth, etc., R. R. Co. (31 Me. 228), 257.

Sala v. New Orleans (2 Woods, U. S. C. C. 188), 575.

Sallee v. Smith (11 Johns. 500), 463.

Sampson v. Henry (13 Pick. 336), 29.

Sampson v. Shaw (101 Mass. 145), 250.

Sanborn v. Benedict (78 Ill. 309), 265.

Sanford v. Bennett (24 N. Y. 20), 54.

Sandford v. Nichols (13 Mass. 286; 7 Am. Dec. 151), 463, 465.

Sante v. State (2 Clarke (Iowa) 165), 304.

Santissima Trinidad, The (7 Wheat. 283), 139.

Sappington v. Watson (50 Mo. 83), 61.

Satterlee v. Matthewson (2 Pet. 380), 76.

Saunders v. Baxter (6 Heisk. 369), 56.

Saunders v. Mills (6 Bing. 213), 57.

Savannah v. Charlton (36 Ga. 460), 272, 280.

Sawyer v. Davis (136 Mass. 239; 49 Am. Rep. 27), 424.

Sawyer v. Vt., etc., R. R. Co. (105 Mass. 196), 597.

Sawyer, etc., v. Taggart (14 Bush, 730), 265, 269.

Schmidt v. Weidman (63 Pa. St. 173), 65.

School Dist. v. Boston, etc., R. R. Co. (102 Mass. 552), 257.

Schurmeier v. St. Paul, etc., R. R. Co. (10 Minn. 82), 411.

Schwuchon v. Chicago (68 Ill. 444), 288.

Scott v. Wakem (3 Fost. & Fin. 328), 108.

Scribner v. Rapp (5 Watts, 311; 30 Am. Dec. 327), 165.

Scripps v. Reilly (38 Mich. 10), 57.

Scudder v. Trenton, etc., Co. (1 N. J. Eq. 694; 23 Am. Dec. 756), 378.

Seamen's Friend Society v. Boston (116 Mass. 181), 473.

Searight v. Calbraith (4 Dall. 324), 215.

Seers v. West (1 Murphy, 291), 272.

Selman v. Wolf (27 Tex. 78), 617.

Servatius v. Pichel (34 Wis. 292), 50.

Sessions v. Crunkleton (20 Ohio St. 349), 445.

Shanks v. Dupont (3 Pet. 242), 139.

Shannon v. Frost (3 B. Mon. 253), 165.

Sharpe v. Johnson (59 Mo. 577; 76 Mo. 660), 65.

Sharpless v. Mayor (21 Pa. St. 147), 8.

Sharpless v. Mayor, etc., (21 Pa. St. 145), 472.

Shaul v. Brown (28 Iowa, 57; 4 Am. Rep. 151), 61.

Shaw v. Clark (49 Mich. 384), 267.

Shaw v. Dennis (10 Ill. 405), 82.

Shehan v. Barnett (6 B. Mon. 594), 359.

Sheldon v. Van Buskirk (2 N. Y. 473), 82.

Sheldon v. Wright (5 N. Y. 497), 83.

Sheperd v. Buff., N. Y. & Erie R. R. Co. (35 N. Y. 641), 598.

Shepherd v. People (25 N. Y. 124), 77.

Shepherd v. People (25 N. Y. 406), 77.

Shepherdson v. Milwaukee, etc., R. R. Co. (6 Wis. 605), 421.

Sheppard v. Comrs. of Ross Co. (7 Ohio, 271), 361.

Sherborne v. Coleback (2 Vent. 175), 260.

Sherman v. Brick (32 Cal. 241), 381.

Shock v. McChesney (4 Yeates, 507; 2 Am. Dec. 415), 42.

Shore v. State (6 Mo. 640), 80.

Shorter v. People (2 N. Y. 193), 26.

Shover v. State (10 Ark. 259), 183.

Shreveport v. Levy (27 La. Ann. 671), 160, 186.

Shrunk v. Schuylkill Nav. Co. (14 Serg. & R. 71), 400.

Schultz v. Cambridge (38 Ohio St. 659), 310.

Shurtleff v. Stevens (51 Vt. 501; 31 Am. Rep. 698), 50, 59.

Siebold, Ex parte (100 U. S. 385), 627.

Simmons v. State (12 Mo. 268), 272.

Simms v. Railroad Co. (12 Heisk. 621), 421.

Simond's Ex'rs v. Gratz (2 Pen. & Watts, 412), 186.

Simpson v. Ammons (1 Binn. 175), 340.

Simpson v. Savings Bank (56 N. H. 466), 517.

Sioux City v. School District (55 Iowa, 150), 473.

Sirocco v. Geary (3 Cal. 69), 399.

Skinner v. Hartford Bridge Co. (29 Conn. 523), 401.

Slaughter v. Commonwealth (13 Gratt. 767), 272, 592.

Slaughter-house Cases (16 Wall. 106), 196, 234, 322, 434.

Sloan v. Pac. R. R. Co. (61 Mo. 24; 21 Am. Rep. 397), 584, 591, 594.

Sneider v. Heidelberger (45 Ala. 126), 520.

Smith v. Atkins (18 Vt. 461), 265.

Smith v. Connelly (1 T. B. Mon. 58), 385.

Smith v. Cooper (28 Ga. 543), 257.

Smith v. Eastern R. R. Co. (35 N. H. 356), 597.

Smith v. Howard (28 Iowa, 51), 42.

Smith v. Kelly (23 Miss. 167), 342.

Smith v. Knoxville (3 Head, 245), 310.

Smith v. Maryland (18 How. 71), 15.

Smith v. Nelson (18 Vt. 511), 165.

Smith v. N. Y. Cent. R. R. Co. (24 N. Y. 222), 258.

Smith v. N. C. R. R. Co. (64 N. C. 235), 257.

Smith v. Packard (12 Wis. 370), 518.

Smith v. Smith (21 Ill. 244), 261.

Smith v. Thomas (2 Bing. N. C. 372), 37.

Smith v. Van Gilder (26 Ark. 521), 518.

Smith v. Washington (20 How. 135), 401.

Snow v. Allen (1 Stark. 409), 63, 65.

Snydecker v. Brosse (51 Ill. 357), 465.

Snyder v. Penn. R. R. Co. (55 Pa. St. 340), 411.

Sohier v. Mass. Gen. Hospital (3 Cush. 483), 358, 359, 362, 365.

Sohier v. Trinity Church (109 Mass. 1), 165.

Somar v. Canaday (53 N. Y. 298; 13 Am. Rep. 523), 345.

Somerville v. Richards (37 Miss. 299), 84.

Sommers v. Johnson (4 Vt. 278; 24 Am. Dec. 604), 518.

Sommer v. Wilt (4 Serg. & R. 20), 63.

Soule v. Winslow (66 Me. 447), 63.

South, etc., R. R. Co. v. Henlein (52 Ala. 606), 257.

So. Ca. R. R. Co. v. Steiner (44 Ga. 546), 411.

Southern Express Co. v. Caperton (44 Ala. 101), 257.

Southern Express v. Moon (39 Miss. 822), 257.

Southwestern R. R. Co. v. Telegraph Co. (46 Ga. 43), 421.

Southwick v. Southwick (49 N. Y. 510), 519.

Spaids v. Barrett (57 Ill. 289), 41, 43.

Sparhawk v. Union 'Passenger R. Co. (54 Pa. St. 401), 187.

Spealman v. Railroad Co. (71 Mo. 434), 598.

Specht v. Commonwealth (8 Pa. St. 312), 183.

Speer v. Commonwealth (23 Gratt. 935; 14 Am. Rep. 164), 615.

Spengle v. Davy (15 Gratt. 381), 61.

Spiering v. Andree (45 Wis. 330; 30 Am. Rep. 744), 51.

Spiller v. Woburn (12 Allen, 127), 161, 162.

Spinney, Ex parte (10 Nev. 323), 204.

Sprague v. Birchard (1 Wis. 457), 83.

Sprague v. Worcester (13 Gray, 493), 401.

Sprecker v. Wakeley (11 Wis. 432), 520.

Spring v. Russell (3 Watts, 294), 375.

Springer v. United States (102 U. S. 586), 466.

Spring Valley Waterworks v. Schottler (110 U. S. 347), 590, 591.

Stackpole v. Hennen (6 Mart. (N. s.) 481; 17 Am. Dec. 187), 44.

Stacy v. Vermont Cent. R. R. Co. (27 Vt. 39), 377.

Staehlin v. Destrehan (2 La. Ann. 1019), 28.

Stanford v. Worn (27 Cal. 171), 377.

Stanley v. Stanley (26 Me. 196), 585.

Stanley v. Webb (4 Sandf. 21), 56, 57, 58.

Stanton v. Allen (5 Denio, 434), 251.

Stanton v. Hart (27 Mich. 539), 62, 63.

Starr v. Camden, etc., R. R. Co. (24 N. J. 592), 411.

State v. Abbott (8 W. Va. 741), 28.

State v. Accommodation Bk. (26 La. Ann. 288), 575.

State v. Addington (77 Mo. 118), 296.

State v. Ah Chew (16 Nev. 5C; 40 Am. Rep. 488), 294.

State v. Ah Sam (15 Nev. 27; 37 Am. Rep. 454), 294.

State v. Alman (64 N. C. 364), 86, 96.

State v. Ambs (20 Mo. 214), 177.

State v. Arlin (39 N. H. 179), 77.

State v. Balt. & O. R. R. (15 W. Va. 362; 36 Am. Rep. 803), 177, 180, 186.

State v. Bank of So. Ca. (1 S. C. 63), 521.

State v. Battle (7 Ala. 259), 96.

State v. Bartlett (55 Me. 200), 94.

State v. Baughman (20 Iowa, 497), 304.

State v. Bostick (4 Harr. 563) 91.

State v. Bott (31 La. Ann. 663; 33 Am. Rep. 224), 177.

State v. Brennan's Liquors (25 Conn. 278), 304, 305, 318.

State v. Brennan's Liquors (25 Conn. 278), 463, 466.

State v. Brockman (46 Mo. 566), 91.

State v. Brown (19 Fla. 563), 273.

State v. Burgoyne (7 Lea, 173; 40 Am. Rep. 60), 304, 583.

State v. Burnham (9 N. H. 34), 37, 40, 49.

State v. Burwell (63 N. C. 661), 28.

State v. Buzzard (4 Ark. 18), 503.

State v. Callendine (8 Iowa, 288), 96.

State v. Cameron (40 Vt. 555), 94.

State v. Carney (20 Iowa, 82), 304.

State v. Cassidy (22 Minn. 312; 21 Am. Rep. 767), 272, 276.

State v. Champeau (53 Vt. 313; 36 Am. Rep. 754), 96.

State v. Chandler (2 Harr. 553), 168, 169.

State v. Christman (67 Ind. 328), 310.

State v. Cincinnati Gas Co. (18 Ohio St. 262), 395, 402.

State v. Cincinnati, etc., Gas Co. (18 Ohio St. 292), 317.

State v. Cleaves (59 Me. 298; 8 Am. Rep. 422), 94.

State v. Clottu (33 Ind. 409), 8, 561.

State v. Columbus Gaslight, etc., Co. (34 Ohio St. 216; 32 Am. Rep. 390), 590.

State v. Common Pleas (36 N. J. 72; 13 Am. Rep. 422), 304.

State v. Connor (5 Cold. 311), 96.

State v. Cook (24 M'nn. 247), 583.

State v. Cooper (22 N. J. L. 52), 31.

State v. Cornwall (27 Ind. 62), 512.

State v. Corson (59 Me. 137), 79.

State v. County Court (19 Ark. 360), 473.

State v. Curtis (5 Humph. 601), 97.

State v. Dixon (75 N. C. 275), 26.

State v. Donehey (8 Iowa, 396), 304.

State v. Drainage Co. (45 N. J. L. 91), 446.

State v. Duelle (48 Mo. 282), 82.

State v. East Orange (12 Vroom, 127), 594, 597.

State v. Endom (23 La. Ann. 663), 282, 283.

State v. Farris (45 Mo. 183), 166.

State v. Freeman (38 N. H. 426), 310.

State v. Garvey (28 La. Ann. 955; 26 Am. Rep. 123), 91.

State v. Garvey (42 Conn. 232), 96.

State v. Gazley (5 Ohio, 21), 272.

State v. Gibson (10 Ired. 214), 29.

State v. Gibson (36 Ind. 389; 10 Am. Rep. 45), 537.

State v. Goff (20 Ark. 289), 188.

State v. Graves (19 Md. 351), 422.

State v. Green (16 Iowa, 239), 96.

State v. Guild (10 N. J. 163; 18 Am. Dec. 404), 91.

State v. Gurney (37 Me. 156), 304.

State v. Hairston (63 N. C. 451), 537.

State v. Harris (10 Iowa, 441), 273.

State v. Hayne (4 Rich. L. 403), 282.

State v. Hebrew Congregation (30 La. Ann. 205; 33 Am. Rep. 217), 166.

State v. Herod (29 Iowa, 123), 272.

State v. Herod (29 Iowa, 123), 580.

State v. Hibbard (3 Ohio, 33), 272.

State v. Hoboken (33 N. J. L. 280), 272, 274, 281.

State v. Hoboken (33 N. J. 280), 444.

State v. Holmes (48 N. H. 377), 84.

State v. Hooker (17 Vt. 658), 94.

State v. Hooper (5 Ired. 201), 537.

State v. Hudson (78 Mo. 302), 273.

State v. Indianapolis (69 Ind. 375; 35 Am. Rep. 223), 473.

State v. Jackson (80 Mo. 175), 537.

State v. Jervey (4 Strobh. 304), 82.

State v. Johnson (75 N. C. 174), 28.

State v. Jumel (13 La. Ann. 399), 503.

State v. Kearney (1 Hawks, 53), 23.

State v. Kennedy (20 Iowa, 569), 26.

State v. Kennedy (67 N. C. 25), 537.

State v. Kenney (76 N. C. 251; 22 Am. Rep. 683), 537.

State v. Lathrop (10 La. Ann. 398), 281.

State v. Laverack (34 N. J. 201), 395, 409.

State v. Lawrence (57 Me. 375), 94.

State v. Learned (47 Me. 426), 79.

State v. Lee (10 R. I. 494), 67.

State v. Little (1 N. H. 257), 96.

State v. Larry (7 Barb. 95), 187.

State v. Lowborne (66 N. C. 538), 91.

State v. Ludington (33 Wis. 107), 303.

State v. Ludwig (21 Minn. 202), 310.

State v. Lutz (65 N. C. 503), 82.

State v. Madden (81 Mo. 421), 544.

State v. Manning (14 Texas, 402), 79.

State v. McGinniss (37 Ark. 362), 615.

State v. McNally (34 Me. 210), 82.

State v. Messenger (27 Minn. 119), 421.

State v. Miller (48 Me. 576), 498.

State v. Mills (34 N. J. 177), 473.

State v. Milwaukee Gas-light Co. (29 Wis. 454), 317.

State v. Mitchell (3 Blackf. 229), 503.

State v. Moffett (1 Greene (Iowa), 247), 617.

State v. Morris (77 N. C. 512), 582.

State v. Maxey (1 McMull. 501), 122.

State v. Mayor of Mobile (5 Port. 279; 30 Am. Dec. 564), 420.

State v. Mayor of Newark (35 N. J. L. 157), 574.

State v. Mugler (29 Kans. 252; 44 Am. Rep. 634), 304.

State v. Ned (7 Port. 217), 96.

State v. Nelson (26 Ind. 366), 96.

State v. New Jersey, etc., R. R. Co. (29 N. J. L. 170), 429.

State v. North (27 Mo. 464), 473, 615, 616.

State v. Norvell (2 Yerg. 24), 97.

State v. Noyes (47 Me. 198), 3.

State v. Noyes (30 N. H. 279), 304.

State v. Noyes (47 Me. 189), 392, 574, 583.

State v. Ober (52 N. H. 459; 13 Am. Rep. 88), 95.

State v. O'Flaherty (7 Nev. 153), 79.

State v. Parker (33 N. J. 213), 473.

State v. Paul (5 R. I. 185), 304.

State v. Peckham (3 R. I. 293), 304.

State v. Penny (19 S. C. 218) 627.

State v. Phalen (3 Harr. 441), 291.

State v. Plunkett (3 Harr. N. J. 5), 273.

State v. Prescott (27 Vt. 194), 304.

State v. Prince (63 N. C. 529), 91.

State v. Proudfit (3 Ohio, 33), 272.

State v. Redman (17 Iowa, 329), 97.

State v. Reid (1 Ala. 612), 503

State v. Reinhardt (63 N. C. 547), 537.

State v. Roane (2 Dev. 58), 84.

State v. Roberts (1 Dev. 259), 91.

State v. Roberts (11 Gill & J. 506), 272, 281.

State v. Rockafellow (6 N. J. 332), 80.

State v. Ross (76 N. C. 242), 537.

State v. Ryan (13 Minn. 370), 79.

State v. Scott (1 Bailey, 294), 83.

State v. Seary (20 Mo. 489), 304.

State v. Seymour (35 N. J. L. 47), 377.

State v. Sherman (20 Mo. 265), 273.

State v. Shippen (10 Minn. 223), 26.

State v. Slack (6 Ala. 676), 97.

State v. Smith (32 Me. 369), 31.

State v. Smith (11 La. Ann. 633), 503.

State v. Smythe (14 R. I. 100; 51 Am. Rep. 344), 292, 499.

State v. Snow (3 R. I. 68), 304, 466, 498.

State v. Southern, etc., R. R. Co. (24 Tex. 80), 575.

State v. Spier (1 Dev. 491), 96.

State v. Staley (14 Minn. 105), 91.

State v. Start (7 Iowa, 499), 203.

Staten v. State (30 Miss. 619), 28.

State v. Sterling (8 Mo. 797), 291.

State v. Stockton (61 Mo. 382), 28.

State v. Strauss (49 Md. 288), 310.

State v. Summons (19 Ohio, 139), 80

State v. Thomas (64 N. C. 74), 93.

State v. Tombeckbee Bk. (2 Stew. 30), 575.

State v. Vaigneur (5 Rich. 391), 91.

State v. Vance (17 Iowa, 138), 28.

State v. Walker (26 Ind. 346), 97.

State v. Washington (44 N. J. L. 605; 43 Am. Rep. 402), 289.

State v. Watkins (3 Mo. 480), 203.

State v. Weed (21 N. H. 262), 82.

State v. Welch (36 Conn. 215) 310.

State v. Wentworth (65 Me. 254; 20 Am. Rep. 688), 95.

State v. Wheeler (25 Conn. 290), 8, 304.

State v. Wheeler (44 N. J. L. 88), 449.

State v. Wilforth (74 Mo. 528; 41 Am. Rep. 330), 503.

State v. Williams (2 Rich. 418), 77, 79.

State v. Williams (11 S. C. 288), 291.

State v. Wilson (48 N. H. 398), 79.

State v. Wiseman (68 N. C. 203), 96.

State v. Woodward (89 Ind. 110; 46 Am. Rep. 160), 583.

Stearns v. Sampson (59 Me. 569; 8 Am. Rep. 442), 30.

Steele v. Gellatly (41 Ill. 39), 346.

Steele v. Spruance (22 Pa. St. 256), 367.

Stein v. Burden (24 Ala. 130), 394, 397.

Stein v. Mayor (24 Ala. 614), 8.

Stein v. Mobile (49 Ala. 362; 20 Am. Rep. 283), 515.

Sterling v. Warden (51 N. H. 239; 12 Am. Rep. 80), 30.

Stetson v. City Bank (2 Ohio St. 114), 586.

Stevens v. Middlesex Canal (12 Mass. 466), 376.

Stevens v. Paterson, etc., R. R. Co. (34 N. J. 532), 398.

Stewart v. Hartman (46 Ind. 331), 381.

Stewart v. Potts (49 Miss. 949), 282.

St. Helen's Smelting Co. v. Tipling (11 H. L. Cas. 642), 34.

Stiles v. Nokes (7 East, 493), 57.

St. Joseph, etc., R. R. Co. v. Callender (13 Kans. 496), 377.

St. Louis v. Green (70 Mo. 562; s. c. 6 Mo. App. 590), 272, 282.

St. Louis v. Manfg. Sav. Bank (49 Mo. 574), 575.

St. Louis v. Weber (14 Mo. 547), 313, 434.

St. Louis, etc., R. R. Co. v. Teters (68 Ill. 144), 377.

Stockton v. Whitmore (50 Cal. 554), 377.

Stokes v. New York (14 Wend. 87), 209.

Stokes v. People (53 N. Y. 164), 79.

Stone v. Mayor, etc., of N. Y. (25 Wend. 157), 399.

Stone v. Mississippi (101 U. S. 814), 581, 582.

Stone v. Stevens (12 Conn. 219), 61.

Stone v. Stone (32 Conn. 142), 564.

Stoneman v. Commonwealth (25 Gratt. 887), 28.

Storey v. Wallace (60 Ill. 51), 57.

Story v. Elliott (8 Cow. 27), 183.

Story v. Firman (25 N. Y. 214), 518.

Story v. N. Y. Elevated R. R. Co. (90 N. Y. 122), 403, 407.

Story v. Salomon (71 N. Y. 420), 266, 267, 268.

Stoughton v. Taylor (2 Paine, 655), 139.

Stover v. People (56 N. Y. 315), 94.

Stover v. State (10 Ark. 259), 178.

St. Paul v. Smith (27 Minn. 164; 38 Am. Rep. 296), 272.

St. Paul v. Traeger (25 Minn. 248; 33 Am. Rep. 462), 272, 281.

Stratton v. Collins (43 N. J. 563), 472.

Strauss v. Meyer (48 Ill. 385), 41.

Street v. Wood (15 Barb. 105), 49, 50.

Street Railway v. Cummingsville (14 Ohio St. 523), 395, 402, 410.

Stringfellow v. State (26 Miss. 155), 93.

Strong v. Clem (12 Ind. 37), 347.

Strong v. State (1 Blackf. 193), 77.

Struthers v. Railroad Co. (87 Pa. St. 282), 411.

Sturdevant v. Norris (30 Iowa, 65), 346.

Sturgeon v. St. Louis, etc., R. R. Co. (60 Mo. 569), 257.

Sturgis v. Crowninshield (4 Wheat. 122), 518, 521.

Sturgis v. Ewing (18 Ill. 176), 342, 357.

Sullivan v. Oneida (61 Ill. 242), 79, 466.

Sutton v. Asken (66 N. C. 172; 8 Am. Rep. 500), 346.

Summons v. State (5 Ohio St. 325), 94.

Sunderlin v. Bradstreet (46 N. Y. 188; 7 Am. Rep. 322), 37.

Supervisors of Doddridge Co. v. Stout (9 W. Va. 703), 377.

Swain v. Mizner (8 Gray, 182), 465.

Swan v. Williams (2 Mich. 427), 376.

Sweeney v. Baker (13 W. Va. 159; 31 Am. Rep. 757), 51, 52.

Sweet v. Wabash (41 Ind. 7), 282.

Swindler v. Hilliard (2 Rich. 286), 256.

T.

Taggert v. Western, etc., R. R. Co. (24 Md. 563), 579, 580.

Talbot v. Hudson (16 Gray, 417), 421.

Talbot v. Janson, (3 Dall. 133), 139.

Tapley v. Smith (18 Me. 12), 366.

Tarlton v. Baker (18 Vt. 9), 261.

Tarner v. State (67 Ind. 595), 187.

Tatem v. Wright et al. (23 N. J. L. 429), 592.

Taylor v. Church (8 N. Y. 452), 37, 52.

Taylor v. Marcy (25 Ill. 518), 421.

Taylor v. Miles (5 Kans. 498; 7 Am. Rep. 558), 519.

Taylor v. Plymouth (8 Met. 462), 399.

Taylor v. Porter (4 Hill, 140), 381.

Taylor v. Porter (4 Hill, 145), 5, 358.

Taylor v. Sample (51 Ind. 423), 347.

Taylor v. State (35 Tex. 97), 96.

Temple v. Sumner (51 Miss. 13), 272.

Teneyck v. Canal Co. (18 N. J. 200; 37 Am. Dec. 233), 379.

Tennessee v. Sneed (96 U. S. 69), 517.

Tenney v. Lanz (16 Wis. 566), 277.

Tenney v. Lenz (16 Wis. 566), 512, 513.

Tenney, Ex parte (2 Duv. (Ky.) 351), 203.

Territory v. Dakota (2 Dak. 155), 453.

Terry v. Fellows (21 La. Ann. 375), 42, 56, 59.

Terry v. Olcott (4 Conn. 442), 291.

Theilan v. Porter (14 Lea, 622; 52 Am. Rep. 173), 441.

Thien v. Voegtlander (3 Wis. 461), 385.

Thomas v. Crosswell (7 Johns. 264; 5 Am. Dec. 269), 52.

Thomas v. Leland (24 Wend. 65), 472.

Thomas v. Tiles (3 Ohio, 74), 246, 251.

Thompson v. Commonwealth (20 Gratt. 724), 91.

Thompson v. Commonwealth (81 Pa. St. 314), 516.

Thompson v. Spraigue (69 Ga. 409; 47 Am. Rep. 760), 627.

Thorn v. Blanchard (5 Johns. 508), 49.

Thorne v. Travelers' Ins. Co. (80 Pa. St. 15; 8 Am. Rep. 626), 592.

Thornton v. Marginal Freight Railway (123 Mass. 32), 575.

Thorpe v. Rutland, etc., R. R. (27 Vt. 140), 2, 4, 578, 581, 597.

Thrall v. Hill (110 Mass. 328), 265.

Thunder Bay, etc., Co., v. Speechly (31 Mich. 332), 398.

Tidewater Co. v. Coster (3 C. E. Green, 518), 446.

Tifft v. Griffin (5 Ga. 185), 519.

Tillson v. Robbins (68 Me. 295; 28 Am. Rep. 50), 52.

Tinicum Fishing Co. v. Carter (61 Pa. St. 21), 400.

Tinicum Fishing Co. v. Carter (90 Pa. St. 85; 35 Am. Rep. 632), 622.

Todd v. Jackson (26 N. J. L. 525), 30.

Toledo, etc., R. R. Co. v. Fowler (22 Ind. 316), 597.

Toledo, etc., R. R. Co. v. Jacksonville (67 Ill. 37), 581, 594, 597.

Tomlin v. Dubuque, etc., R. R. Co. (32 Iowa, 106; 7 Am. Rep. 176), 398.

Tonawanda R. R. Co. v. Munger (5 Denio, 255), 407.

Torrey v. Field (10 Vt. 353), 56.

Towanda Bridge, In re (91 Pa. St. 216), 392.

Tower v. Tower (18 Pick. 262), 510.

Town Council v. Harbers (6 Rich L. 96), 273.

Town of Guilford v. Supervisors (13 N. Y. 143), 8.

Trammell v. Bradley (37 Ark. 356), 308.

Transportation Co. v. Chicago (99 U. S. 635), 401.

Travis v. Smith (1 Pa. St. 234), 61.

Treat v. Lord (42 Me. 552), 617.

Tredway v. Railroad Co. (43 Iowa, 527), 598.

Tremont v. Clarke (33 Me. 482), 82.

Trenton Ins. Co. v. Johnson (4 Zabr. 576), 261.

Tribble v. Frame (1 J. J. Marsh. 599), 30.

True v. Int. Tel. Co. (60 Me. 9), 259.

Trustees v. Keeting (4 Denio, 341), 273.

Trustees Brooks Academy v. George, 14 W. Va. 411; 35 Am. Rep. 760), 494.

Trustees E. F. Fund v. Roome (93 N. Y. 313), 281.

Trustees of Griswold College v. State (46 Iowa, 275; 26 Am. Rep. 138), 473.

Trustees of M. E. Church v. Ellis (38 Ind. 3), 473.

Trustees of Watertown v. Cowen (4 Paige, 510), 404.

Trustees, etc., v. Indiana (14 How. 268), 574.

Tuckahoe Canal Co. v. R. R. Co. (11 Leigh, 42; 36 Am. Dec. 374), 392.

Turner v. Franklin (29 Mo. 285), 82.

Turner v. Maryland (107 U. S. 38), 208, 615.

Turner v. State (4 Ala. 21), 77.

Turner v. Walker (3 G. & J. 380), 63.

Turney v. Wilson (7 Yerg. 540), 256.

Tuthill v. Scott (44 Vt. 525; 5 Am. Rep. 301), 450.

Tweedy v. State (5 Iowa, 433), 26.

Twitchell v. Com. (7 Wall. 321) 15.

Twitchell v. Shaw (10 Cush. 46), 83.

Tyler v. Beacher (44 Vt. 648), 378, 381, 385.

Tyler v. W. U. Tel. Co. (60 Ill. 421; 14 Am. Rep. 38), 259.

U.

Underwood v. People (32 Mich. 1), 111.

Underwood v. Robinson (106 Mass. 296), 82.

Union Nat. Bk. of Chicago v. Carr (15 Fed. Rep. 438), 268.

Union Pac. Ry. v. U. S. (99 U. S. 700), 589.

United States v. Bainbridge (1 Mason, 71), 555.

United States v. DeWitt (9 Wall. 541), 613

United States v. Gillies (1 Pet. C. C. 159), 139.

United States v. Hamilton (3 Dall. 17), 80.

United States v. Harris (1 Sumn. 21), 375.

United States v. Marigold (9 How. 560), 628.

United States v. Perez 9 Wheat. 579), 96.

United States v. Reed (56 Mo. 565), 377.

Universalist Society v. Providence (6 R. I. 235), 474.

University of No. Ca. v. N. C. R. R. Co. (76 N. C. 103; 22 Am. Rep. 671), 494.

Updegraph v. Commonwealth (11 S. & R. 394), 169, 171.

Usher v. Severance (21 Me. 9; 37 Am. Dec. 33) 58.

V.

Van Arnsdale v. Laverty (69 Pa. St. 103), 49.

Van Baalen v. People (40 Mich. 458), 274.

Van Baumback v. Bade (9 Wis. 559), 515.

Van Buren v. Downing (41 Wis. 122), 615.

Vanderbelt v. Adams (7 Cow. 349), 439.

Vanderveer v. Mattocks (3 Ind. 479), 84.

Vanderzee v. McGregory (12 Wend. 545), 49.

Van Deusen v. Newcomer (40 Mich. 90), 104, 107, 109.

Vandine, Petitioner (9 Pick. 187; 7 Am. Dec. 351), 316.

Van Duzer v. Van Duzer (6 Paige, 366), 344.

Varden v. Mount (78 Ky. 86; 39 Am. Rep. 356), 507.

Varner v. Martin (21 W. Va. 548), 379, 381, 383.

Van Rensselaer v. Snyder (9 Barb. 302; 13 N. Y. 299), 518.

Varrick v. Smith, 5 Paige, 137), 5, 358, 375, 397.

Vansee v. Lee (1 Hill (S.C.), 197; 26 Am. Dec. 168), 41.

Veazie v. Mayo (45 Me. 560; 49 Me. 156), 599.

Veazie Bank v. Fenno (8 Wall. 533), 469.

Venard v. Cross (8 Kan. 248) 385.

Vincennes v. Richards (23 Ind. 381), 401.

Vidal v. Girard's Exrs. (2 How. 127), 167.

Virginia, etc., R. R. Co. v. Sayers (26 Gratt. 328), 257.

Vise v. Hamilton Co. (19 Ill. 18), 90.

Vogelsang v. State (9 Ind. 112), 183.

W.

Wabash, St. L. & P. R. R. Co. v. People (105 Ill. 231), 617.

Wadleigh v. Gilman (12 Me. 403), 439.

Wadsworth v. Sharpsteen (8 N. Y. 388), 497.

Wager v. Troy Union R. R. Co. (25 N. Y. 526), 410, 418.

Waite v. Merrill (4 Me. 102; 16 Am. Dec. 238), 165.

Wakeman v. Dalley (44 Barb. 498), 252.

Wolcott v. Heath (78 Ill. 433), 265.

Walden v. Dudley (49 Mo. 419), 82.

Wales v. Stetson (2 Mass. 143), 574.

Walker v. Deaver (5 Mo. App. 139), 346.

Walker v. Springfield (94 Ill. 364), 281.

Wall v. State (51 Ind. 453), 28.

Wall v. Trumbull (16 Mich. 228), 83.

Walling v. Michigan (116 U. S. 446), 615.

Walpole v. Saunders (16 E. C. L. R. 276), 260.

Walter v. People (32 N. Y. 147), 79.

Walter v. Sample (25 Pa. St. 275), 63.

Walther v. Warner (25 Mo. 277), 421.

Walton v. Commonwealth (16 B. Mon. 15), 79.

Walton v. Fill (1 Dev. & B. 507), 30.

Wamesit Power Co. v. Allen (120 Mass. 352), 377.

Ward v. Farwell (97 Ill. 693), 586.

Ward v. Greenville (1 Baxt. 228; 35 Am. Rep. 700), 310.

Ward v. State (31 Md. 279; s. c. 12 Wall. 418), 615.

Ware v. Miller (9 S. C. 13), 518.

Ware v. Owens (42 Ala. 212), 346.

Warner v. Paine (2 Sandf. 195), 43.

Warner v. Shed (10 Johns. 138), 82.

Warren v. Commonwealth (37 Pa. St. 45), 79.

Warren v. Mayor, etc., of Charlestown (2 Gray, 98), 304.

Warren v. St. Paul, etc., R. R. Co. (18 Minn. 384), 376.

Wartman v. Philadelphia (33 Pa. St. 202), 312, 313, 315, 434.

Warwick v. Cooper (5 Sneed, 659), 531.

Washburn v. Gilman (64 Me. 163; 18 Am. Rep. 246), 449.

Washington Bridge Co. v. State (18 Conn. 53), 584.

Waterman v. Johnson (13 Pick. 261), 452.

Waterworks v. Schotler (110 U. S. 347), 234.

Waterworks Co. v. Burkhardt (41 Ind. 364), 375, 378, 396.

Watkins v. Walker Co. (18 Texas, 585), 392.

Watson v. Avery (2 Bush, 332), 165.

Watson v. Jones (13 Wall. 679), 165, 166.

Watson v. Mercer (8 Pet. 88), 76, 362.

Watson v. N. Y. Cent. R. R. Co. (47 N. Y. 157), 518.

Watson v. Watson (9 Conn. 140), 82, 83.

Watson v. Watson (13 Conn. 88), 344.

Watson, In re (15 Fed. Rep. 511), 615.

Wayne Co. v. Waller, (90 Pa. St. 99; 35 Am. Rep. 636), 90.

Weaver v. Fegely (29 Pa. St. 27), 627.

Weaver v. Gregg (6 Ohio St. 547), 346.

Webb v. Den (17 How. 576), 519.

Webb v. Dunn (18 Fla. 721), 626.

Webbe v. Commonwealth (33 Gratt. 898), 282.

Webber v. Gay (24 Wend. 485), 82, 83.

Webster v. Potter (105 Mass. 416), 366.

Weeks v. Milwaukee (10 Wis. 242), 473.

Weil v. Ricord (9 C. E. Green, 169), 428.

Weise v. Smith (3 Ore. 445; 8 Am. Rep. 621), 617.

Weister v. Hade (52 Pa. St. 474), 472.

Welch v. Boston, etc., R. R. Co. 41 Conn. 333), 257.

Welch v. Hotchkiss (39 Conn. 140), 274.

Welch v. Hotchkiss (39 Conn. 144), 439, 441.

Welch v. Stowell (2 Dougl. Mich. 332), 441.

Weller v. Snover (42 N. J. L. 341), 451, 498.

Wells v. N. Y. Cent. R. R. Co. (24 N. Y. 181), 258.

Wells v. Somerset, etc., R. R. Co. (47 Me. 345), 392.

Welsh v. Chicago, B. & Q. R. R. Co. (53 Iowa, 632), 598.

West v. Sansom (44 Ga. 295), 516.

West v. Stewart (7 Pa. St. 122), 366.

West Jersey R. R. Co. v. Cape May, etc., Co. (34 N. J. Eq. 164), 411.

West River Bridge v. Dix (6 How. 507), 392.

W. U. Tel. Co. v. Carew (15 Mich. 525), 259.

W. U. Tel. Co. v. Graham (1 Cal. 230), 259.

W. U. Tel. Co. v. Mayor (28 Ohio St. 521), 472.

W. U. Tel. Co. v. Tyler (74 Ill. 168), 259.

Westervelt v. Gregg (12 N. Y. 202), 344.

Weston v. Foster (7 Met. 297), 395.

W. Va. Transportation Co. v. Volcanic Oil, etc., Co. (5 W. Va. 382), 377, 378.

Wheeler v. Friend (22 Tex. 683), 261.

Wheeler v. Nesbit (24 How. (U. S.) 545), 61.

Wheeler v. Shields (3 Ill. 348), 54.

Wheeler, etc., Transportation Co. v. City of Wheeling (9 W. Va. 170; 27 Am. Rep. 552), 625.

Wheeling Bridge Case (13 How. 518; 18 How. 421), 618.

Wheelock v. Young (4 Wend. 647), 392.

Whitcomb v. Gilman (35 Vt. 497), 188.

White v. Carroll (42 N. Y. 166; 1 Am. Rep. 503), 42.

White v. Carroll (42 N. Y. 161), 205.

White v. Charleston (1 Hill (S. C.) 571), 399.

White's Creek Turnpike Co. v. Davidson Co. (3 Tenn. Ch. 396), 584.

White v. Hart (13 Wall. 646), 515.

White v. Flynn (23 Ind. 46), 519.

White v. Graves (107 Mass. 325; 9 Am. Rep. 38), 345.

White v. Moses (21 Cal. 44), 359.

White v. Nashville, etc., R. R. Co. (7 Heisk. 588), 421.

White v. Nichols (3 How. 266), 36, 37.

White v. Tucker (16 Ohio St. 468), 62.

White v. Yazoo (27 Miss. 357), 33.

Whitehead v. Latham (83 N. C. 232), 518.

Whitehead v. Root (2 Metc. (Ky.) 584), 265.

Whitman v. Devere (33 Wis. 70), 303.

Whiteman's Ex'rs v. Wilmington, etc., R. R. Co. (2 Harr. 514), 376.

White River Turnpike Co. v. Vt. Cent. R. R. Co. (21 Vt. 590), 392.

White River Turnpike v. Central R. R. Co. (21 Vt. 590), 376.

Whitney v. Allen (62 Ill. 472), 49.

Whitney v. Bartholomew (21 Conn. 213), 34.

Whitney v. Peckham (15 Mass. 242), 61.

Whitney v. Richardson (31 Vt. 300), 367.

Whittaker v. Perry (38 Vt. 107), 29.

Whittingham v. Bowen (22 Vt. 317), 381.

Wicker v. Hotchkiss (62 Ill. 107), 63.

Wiggins v. Chicago (68 Ill. 372).

Wiggins Ferry Co. v. East St. Louis (107 U. S. 365), 621, 625.

Wilcox v. Hemming (58 Wis. 144; 46 Am. Rep. 625), 507.

Wild v. Deig (43 Ind. 45; 13 Am. Rep. 399), 381.

Wilder v. Me. Cent. R. R. Co. (65 Me. 332), 597.

Wiley v. Owens (39 Ind. 429), 273.

Wilkerson v. Rust (57 Ind. 172), 303.

Wilkinson v. Arnold (13 Ind. 45), 63.

Wilkinson v. Leland (2 Pet. 657), 5, 358, 359, 362.

Willard v. Stone (17 Cow. 22), 521.

Williams v. Carr (80 N. C. 294), 267, 269.

Williams v. Commonwealth (2 Gratt. 568), 96.

Williams v. Courtney (77 Mo. 587).

Williams v. Haines (27 Iowa, 251), 518.

Williams v. Mayor of Detroit (2 Mich. 560), 445.

Williams v. Nat. Bridge Plankroad Co. (21 Mo. 580), 409.

Williams v. N. Y. Central R. R. Co. (16 N. Y. 97), 411.

Williams v. School District (33 Vt. 271), 380.

Williams v. Taylor (6 Bing. 183), 61.

Williams v. Tiedemann (6 Mo. App. 269), 267, 268.

Williams v. Van Meter (8 Mo. 339), 63.

Williams v. Williams (4 Thomp. & C. 251), 108.

Williams' (Isaac) Case (2 Cranch, 82), 139.

Williamson v. Field (2 Sandf. Ch. 533), 339.

Williamson v. Willis (15 Gray, 427), 82.

Wilmarth v. Burt (7 Met. 257), 83.

Wilson v. Blackbird Creek Marsh Co. (2 Pet. 245), 376.

Wilson v. Brown (58 Ala. 62; 29 Am. Rep. 727), 520.

Wilson v. Iowa (2 Ohio St. 319), 31.

Wilson v. John's Island Church (2 Rich. Eq. 192), 166.

Wilson v. McNamee (102 U. S. 572), 627.

Wilson v. Mayor of N. Y. (1 Denio, 595), 401.

Wilson v. N. Y. (1 Denio, 595), 33.

Wilson v. Noonan (35 Wis. 321), 52.

Wilson v. Ohio, etc., R. R. Co. (64 Ill. 542), 76.

Wilson v. Supervisors of Sutter (47 Cal. 91), 473.

Wilson v. Wilson (37 Mo. 1).

Winchell v. State (7 Cow. 525), 86.

Winchester v. Nutter (52 N. H. 507), 261.

Winnebiddle v. Porterfield (9 Pa. St. 137), 61.

Wingate v. Sluder (6 Jones (N. C.), 552), 472.

Winnsboro v. Smart (11 Rich. L. 551), 311, 434.

Winona, etc., R. R. Co. v. Waldron 11 Minn. 575), 597.

Wisconsin River Improvement Co. v. Manson (43 Wis. 255; 28 Am. Rep. 542), 622.

Witham v. Gowen (14 Me. 362), 61.

Witham v. Osburn (4 Ore. 318; 18 Am. Rep. 287), 381.

Withers v. Buckley (20 How. 84), 619.

Withers v. State (36 Ala. 252), 203.

Withington v. Corey (2 N. H. 115), 367.

Woart v. Winnick (3 N. H. 473), 76, 77.

Wood v. Kelley (30 Me. 47), 452.

Wood v. Weir (5 B. Mon. 544), 63.

Woodbury v. Grimes (1 Col. 100), 518.

Woodman v. Howell (45 Ill. 367), 28.

Wood Mowing Machine Co. v. Caldwell (54 Ind. 270; 23 Am. Rep. 641), 592.

Woodruff v. Fisher (17 Barb. 224), 445, 446.

Woodruff v. Neal (28 Conn. 165), 407.

Woolever v. Stewart (36 Ohio St. 146; 38 Am. Rep. 566), 450.

Woolf v. Chalker (31 Conn. 121), 508.

Wolfe v. Covington, etc., R. R. Co. (15 B. Mon. 404), 411.

Worcester v. N. & W. R. R. Co. (109 Mass. 103), 575.

World v. State (50 Md. 54), 125, 130.

Worthington v. Scribner (108 Mass. 487; 12 Am. Rep. 736), 41.

Wright v. Carter (27 N. J. 76), 409.

Wright v. Cradlebaugh (3 Nev. 341), 519.

Wright v. Dunham (13 Mich. 414), 519.

Wright v. State (5 Ind. 290), 96.

Wyatt v. Buell (47 Cal. 624), 41.

Wyick v. Aspinwall (17 N. Y. 190), 50.

Wyman v. Fiske (3 Allen, 238), 266.

Wyman v. Mayor of N. Y. (11 Wend. 487), 404.

Wynehamer v. People (13 N. Y. 390), 8.

Wynehamer v. People (3 Kern. (N. Y.) 435), 304.

Wynne v. Wright (1 Dev. & B. L. 19), 272.

Y.

Yale, Ex parte (24 Cal. 241), 203.

Yarborough, Ex parte (110 U. S. 651), 614.

Yates v. Milwaukee (12 Wis. 673), 209.

Yates v. Milwaukee (10 Wall. 497), 398, 430.

Yates v. Mullen (24 Ind. 278), 366.

York v. Pease (2 Gray, 282), 50.

York Co. v. Central R. R. Co. (3 Wall. 107), 257.

Young v. Beardsley (11 Paige, 93), 519.

Young v. Harrison (6 Ga. 130), 574.

Young v. McKenzie (3 Ga. 31), 381.

Young v. Thomas (17 Fla. 169), 272, 282.

Young v. West. Un. Tel. Co. (65 N. Y. 163), 259.

Youngblood v. Sexton (32 Mich. 406; 20 Am. Rep. 654), 273, 276, 282, 283, 286.

Z.

Zabriskie v. Hackensack, etc., R. R. Co. (17 N. J. Eq. 178), 574.

Zell v. Reame (31 Pa. St. 304), 30.

Zimmerman v. Union Canal Co. (1 Watts & S. 846), 400.

Zumhoff v. State (4 Greene, Iowa, 526), 304.

CONSTITUTIONAL LIMITATIONS

UPON THE

POLICE POWER IN THE UNITED STATES

PART I.

CHAPTER I.

LIMITATIONS UPON THE POLICE POWER IN THE UNITED
STATES.

SECTION 1. Police power, defined and explained.
    2. The legal limitations upon police power.
    3. Construction of constitutional limitations.
    4. The principal constitutional limitations.
    5. Table of private rights.

§ 1. **Police power—Defined and explained.**—The private
rights of the individual, apart from a few statutory rights,
which when compared with the whole body of private rights
are insignificant in number, do not rest upon the mandate
of municipal law as a source. They belong to man in a
state of nature; they are natural rights, rights recognized
and existing in the law of reason. But the individual, in a
state of nature, finds in the enjoyment of his own rights
that he transgresses the rights of others. Nature wars upon
nature, when subjected to no spiritual or moral restraint.
The object of government is to impose that degree of
restraint upon human actions, which is necessary to the
uniform and reasonable conservation and enjoyment of
private rights. Government and municipal law protect
and develop, rather than create, private rights. The

conservation of private rights is attained by the imposition of a wholesome restraint upon their exercise,
such a restraint as will prevent the infliction of injury
upon others in the enjoyment of them; it involves a provision of means for enforcing the legal maxim, which enunciates
the fundamental rule of both the human and the natural law,
sic utere tuo, ut alienum non lœdas. The power of the government to impose this restraint is called POLICE POWER.
By this "general police power of the State, persons and
property are subjected to all kinds of restraints and burdens, in order to secure the general comfort, health and
prosperity of the State; of the perfect right in the legislature to do which no question ever was or upon acknowledged general principles ever can be made, so far as natural
persons are concerned."[1] Blackstone defines the police
power to be "the due regulation and domestic order of the
kingdom, whereby the inhabitants of a State, like members
of a well-governed family, are bound to conform their general behavior to the rules of propriety, good neighborhood
and good manners, and to be decent, industrious and inof-
fensive in their respective stations."[2] Judge Cooley says:[3]
"The police of a State, in a comprehensive sense, embraces
its whole system of internal regulation, by which the State
seeks not only to preserve the public order and to prevent
offenses against the State, but also to establish for the intercourse of citizens with citizens those rules of good manners and good neighborhood which are calculated to prevent
a conflict of rights, and to insure to each the uninterrupted
enjoyment of his own so far as it is reasonably consistent
with a like enjoyment of rights by others."[4] The conti-

[1] Redfield, C. J., in Thorpe *v.* Rutland, etc., R. R., 27 Vt. 140.
[2] 4 Bl. Com. 162.
[3] Cooley, Const. Lim. 572.
[4] The following other definitions present the same ideas in different
language, but they are added, *ex abundante cautela*, with the hope that
they may assist in reaching a clear conception of the scope of the police
power. "The police power of a State is co-extensive with self-protec-

§ 1

nental jurists include, under the term *Police Power*, not only those restraints upon private rights which are imposed for the general welfare of all, but also all the governmental institutions, which are established with public funds for the better promotion of the public good, and the alleviation of private want and suffering. Thus they would include the power of the government to expend the public moneys in the construction and repair of roads, the establishment of hospitals and asylums and colleges, in short, the power to supplement the results of individual activity with what individual activity can not accomplish. " The governmental

tion, and is not inaptly termed ' the law of overruling necessity.' It is that inherent and plenary power in the State, which enables it to prohibit all things hurtful to the comfort and welfare of society." Lakeview *v.* Rose Hill Cemetery, 70 Ill. 192. "With the legislature the maxim of law ' *salus populi suprema lex*,' should not be disregarded. It is the great principle on which the statutes for the security of the people are based. It is the foundation of criminal law, in all governments of civilized countries, and of other laws conducive to the safety and consequent happiness of the people. This power has always been exercised, and its existence cannot be denied. How far the provisions of the legislature can extend, is always submitted to its discretion, *provided its acts do not go beyond the great principle of securing the public safety*, and its duty to provide for the public safety, within well defined limits and with discretion, is imperative. * * * All laws for the protection of lives, limbs, health and quiet of the person, and for the security of all property within the State, fall within this general power of government." State *v.* Noyes, 47 Me. 189. "There is, in short, no end to these illustrations, when we look critically into the police of large cities. One in any degree familiar with this subject would never question a right depending upon invincible necessity, in order to the maintenance of any show of administrative authority among the class of persons with which the city police have to do. To such men any doubt of the right to subject persons and property to such regulations as public security and health may require, regardless of mere private convenience, looks like mere badinage. They can scarcely regard the objector as altogether serious. And, generally, these doubts in regard to the extent of governmental authority come from those who have had small experience." Hale *v.* Lawrence, 1 Zab. 714; 3 Zab. 590. While it is true that a small experience in such matters is calculated to increase one's doubts in respect to the exercise of the power, a large and practical experience is likely to make one recklessly disregardful of private rights and constitutional limitations.

§ 1

provision for the public security and welfare in its daily necessities, that provision which establishes the needful and necessary, and therefore appears as a bidding and forbidding power of the State, is the scope and character of the police."[1] But in the present connection, as may be gathered from the American definitions heretofore given, the term must be confined to the imposition of restraints and burdens upon persons and property. The power of the government to embark in enterprises of public charity and benefit can only be limited by the restrictions upon the power of taxation, and to that extent alone can these subjects in American law be said to fall within the police power of the State.

It is to be observed, therefore, that the police power of the government, as understood in the constitutional law of the United States, is simply the power of the government to establish provisions for the enforcement of the common as well as civil-law maxim, *sic utere tuo, ut alienum non lœdas.* " This police power of the State extends to the protection of the lives, limbs, health, comfort and quiet of all persons, and the protection of all property within the State. According to the maxim, *sic utere tuo, ut alienum non lœdas*, it being of universal application, it must of course be within the range of legislative action to define the mode and manner in which every one may so use his own as not to injure others."[2] Any law which goes beyond that principle, which undertakes to abolish rights, the exercise of which does not involve an infringement of the rights of others, or to limit the exercise of rights beyond what is necessary to provide for the public welfare and the general security, cannot be included in the police power of the government. It is a governmental usurpation, and violates the principles

---

[1] Bluntschli, Mod. Stat., vol. II., p. 276. See *v.* Mohl's comprehensive discussion of the scope of Police Power in the introductory chapter to his Polizeiwissenschaft.

[2] Thorpe *v.* Rutland, etc., R. R., 27 Vt. 150.

§ 1

of abstract justice, as they have been developed under our republican institutions.

§ 2. **The legal limitations upon police power.** — This is the subject of the present work, viz.: The legal limitations upon the police power of American governments, national and State. Where can these limitations be found, and in what do they consist? The legislature is clearly the department of the government which can and does exercise the police power, and consequently in the limitations upon the legislative power, are to be found the limitations of the police power. Whether there be other limitations or not, the most important and the most clearly defined are to be found in the national and State constitutions. Whenever an act of the legislature contravenes a constitutional provision, it is void, and it is the duty of the courts so to declare it, and refuse to enforce it. But is it in the power of the judiciary to declare an act of the legislature void, because it violates some abstract rule of justice, when there is no constitutional prohibition? Several eminent judges have more or less strongly insisted upon the doctrine that the authority of the legislature is not absolute in those cases in which the constitution fails to impose a restriction; that in no case can a law be valid, which violates the fundamental principles of free government, and infringes upon the original rights of men, and some of these judges claim for the judiciary, the power to annul such an enactment, and to forbid its enforcement.[1] Judge Chase expresses himself as follows : " I cannot subscribe to the omnipotence of a State legislature, or that it is absolute and without control, although its authority should not be expressly re-

[1] Judge Chase in Calder *v.* Bull, 3 Dall. 386; Judge Story in Wilkinson *v.* Leland, 2 Pet 657; Judge Bronson in Taylor *v.* Porter, 4 Hill, 145; Judge Strong in People *v.* Toynbec, 20 Barb. 218; Judge Hosmer in Goshen *v.* Storlington, 4 Conn. 259; Chancellor Walworth in Varick *v.* Smith, 5 Paige, 137; Judge Spaulding in Griffith *v.* Commissioners, 20 Ohio, 609; Ch. J. Parker, in Ross' Case, 2 Pick. 169.

strained by the constitution or fundamental law of the State. The people of the United States erected their constitutions or forms of government, to establish justice, to promote the general welfare, to secure the blessings of liberty, and to protect their persons and property from violence. The purposes for which we enter into society, will determine the nature and terms of the social compact; and as they are the foundation of the legislative power, they will decide what are the proper objects of it. The nature and ends of of legislative power will limit the exercise of it. This fundamental principle flows from the very nature of our free republican governments, that no man should be compelled to do what the laws do not require, nor to refrain from acts which the laws permit. There are acts which the Federal or State legislature cannot do, without exceeding their authority. There are certain vital principles in our free republican governments, which will determine and overrule an apparent and flagrant abuse of legislative power; as to authorize manifest injustice by positive law, or to take away that security for personal liberty or private property for the protection whereof the government was established. An act of the legislature (for I cannot call it a law), contrary to the great first principles of the social compact, cannot be considered a rightful exercise of legislative authority. The obligation of a law in governments, established on express compact and on republican principles, must be determined by the nature of the power on which it is founded. * * * The legislature may enjoin, permit, forbid and punish; they may declare new crimes, and establish rules of conduct for all its citizens in future cases; they may command what is right, and prohibit what is wrong, but they cannot change innocence into guilt, or punish innocence as a crime; or violate the right of an antecedent lawful private contract, or the right of private property. To maintain that our Federal or State legislature possesses such powers, if they had not been expressly

§ 2

restrained, would in my opinion be a political heresy, altogether inadmissible in our free republican governments." But notwithstanding the opinions of these eminently respectable judges, the current of authority, as well as substantial constitutional reasoning, is decidedly opposed to the doctrine. It may now be considered as an established principle of American law that the courts, in the performance of their duty to confine the legislative department within the constitutional limits of its power, cannot nullify and avoid a law, simply because it conflicts with the judicial notions of natural right or morality, or abstract justice." [1]

[1] "The question whether the act under consideration is a valid exercise of legislative power is to be determined solely by reference to constitutional restraints and prohibitions. The legislative power has no other limitation. If an act should stand when brought to the test of the constitution, the question of its validity is at an end, and neither the executive nor judicial department of the government can refuse to recognize or enforce it. The theory, that laws may be declared void when deemed to be opposed to natural justice and equity, although they do not violate any constitutional provision, has some support in the *dicta* of learned judges, but has not been approved, so far as we know, by any authoritative adjudication, and is repudiated by numerous authorities. Indeed, under the broad and liberal interpretation now given to constitutional guaranties, there can be no violation of fundamental rights, which will not fall within the express or implied prohibition and restraints of the constitution and it is unnecessary to seek for principles outside of the constitution, under which legislation may be condemned." Bertholf *v.* O'Reilly, 74 N. Y. 509. "Defendant insists that we should pronounce the law now in question to be void, on the ground that it is opposed to natural right and the fundamental principles of civil liberty. We are by no means prepared to accede to the doctrine involved in this claim, that under a written constitution like ours, in which the three great departments of government, the executive, legislative and judicial, are confided to distinct bodies of magistracy, the powers of each of which are expressly confined to its own proper department, and in which the powers of each are unlimited, in its appropriate sphere, except so far as they are abridged by the constitution itself, it is competent for the judicial department to deprive the legislature of powers which they are not restricted from exercising by that instrument. It would seem to be sufficient to prevent us from thus interposing, that the power exercised by the legislature is properly legislative in its character, which is unquestionably the case with respect to the law

§ 2

While it is true that the courts have no authority to override the legislative judgment on the question of expediency or abstract justice in the enactment of a law, and if a case, arising under the statute, should come up before them for adjudication, they are obliged by their official oaths to enforce the statute notwithstanding it offends the commonest principles of justice, it is nevertheless true that a law which does not conform to the fundamental principles of free government and natural justice and morality, will prove ineffectual and will become a dead letter. No law can be enforced, particularly in a country governed directly by the popular will, which does not receive the moral and active support of a large majority of the people ; and a law, which violates reason and offends against the prevalent conceptions of right and justice, will be deprived of the power necessary to secure its enforcement. The passage of such statutes, however beneficent may be the immediate object of them, will not only fail of attaining the particular end in view, but it tends on the one hand to create in those who are likely to violate them a contempt for the whole body of restrictive laws, and on the other hand, to inspire in those, from whom the necessary moral support is to be expected, a fear and distrust, sometimes hate, of legal restraint which is very destructive of their practical value. And such is particularly the case with police regulations. When confined within their proper limits, viz. : to compel every one to so use his own and so conduct himself as not to injure his neighbor or infringe upon his rights,

---

we have been considering, and that the consideration contains no restrictions upon its exercise in regard to the subject of it.'' State *v.* Wheeler, 25 Conn. 290. See, also, Butler *v.* Palmer, 1 Hill, 324; Cochran *v.* Van Surley, 20 Wend. 380; Grant *v.* Courten, 24 Barb. 232; Benson *v.* Mayor, 24 Barb. 248, 252; Wynehamer *v.* People, 13 N. Y. 390; Town of Guilford *v.* Supervisors, 13 N. Y. 143; Sharpless *v.* Mayor, 21 Pa. St. 147; Bennett *v.* Boggs, 1 Bald. 74; Doe *v.* Douglass, 8 Blackf. 10; State *v.* Clottu, 33 Ind. 409; Stein *v.* Mayor, 24 Ala. 614; Dorman *v.* State, 34 Ala. 232; Boston *v.* Cummings, 16 Ga. 102; Hamilton *v.* St. Louis Co., 15 Mo. 23.

§ 2

police regulations should, and usually would, receive in a reasonably healthy community the enthusiastic support of the entire population. There have been, however, so many unjustifiable limitations imposed upon private rights and personal liberty, sumptuary laws, and laws for the correction of personal vice, laws which have in view the moral and religious elevation of the individual against his will, and sometimes in opposition to the dictates of his conscience, (all of which objects, however beneficent they may be, do not come within the sphere of the governmental activity), that the modern world looks with distrust upon any exercise of police power; and however justifiable, reasonable and necessary to the general welfare may be a particular police regulation, it often meets with a determined opposition, and oftener with a death-dealing apathy on the part of those who are usually law-abiding citizens and active supporters of the law. Goethe makes Mephistopheles give the cause of this opposition in the following expressive language:—

"Ich weisz mich trefflich mit der Polizei
Doch mit dem Blutbann schlecht mich abzufinden,"

which, roughly translated, means "I can get along very well with the police, but badly with the hereditary monopoly." (Blutbann.) [1]

But these are considerations, which can alone be addressed to the legislative department of the government. If an unwise law has been enacted, which does not infringe upon any constitutional limitation, the only remedy is an appeal to the people directly, or through their representatives, to repeal the law. The courts have no authority to interpose.

[1] Reference is here made to those numerous monopolies, created in various industries for the benefit of certain powerful families and made hereditary, which proved beneficial to their possessors, while they were correspondingly oppressive to the poorer classes. This was one of the crying evils of the old French civilization which led up to the Revolution.

§ 2

§ 3. Construction of constitutional limitations.— But although these fundamental principles of natural right and justice cannot, in themselves, furnish any legal restrictions upon the governmental exercise of police power, in the absence of express or implied constitutional limitations, yet they play an important part in determining the exact scope and extent of the constitutional limitations. Wherever by reasonable construction the constitutional limitation can be made to avoid an unrighteous exercise of police power, that construction will be upheld, notwithstanding the strict letter of the constitution does not prohibit the exercise of such a power. The unwritten law of this country is in the main against the exercise of police power, and the restrictions and burdens, imposed upon persons and private property by police regulations, are jealously watched and scrutinized. "The main guaranty of private rights against unjust legislation is found in that memorable clause in the bill of rights, that no man shall be deprived of life, liberty or property, without due process of law. This guaranty is not construed in any narrow or technical sense. The right to life may be invaded without its destruction. One may be deprived of his liberty in a constitutional sense without putting his person in confinement. Property may be taken without manual interference therewith, or its physical destruction. The right to life includes the right of the individual to his body in its completeness and without its dismemberment, the right to liberty, the right to exercise his faculties and to follow a lawful avocation for the support of life, the right of property, the right to acquire property and enjoy it in any way consistent with the equal rights of others and the just exactions and demands of the State." [1] In searching for constitutional restrictions upon police power, not only may resort be had to those plain, exact and explicit provisions

[1] Bertholf v. O'Reilly, 74 N. Y. 509.

of the constitution, but those general clauses, which have acquired the name of " glittering generalities," may also be appealed to as containing the germ of constitutional limitation, at least in those cases in which there is a clearly unjustifiable violation of private right. Thus, almost all of the State constitutions have, incorporated in their bills of rights, the clause of the American Declaration of Independence that all men " are endowed by their Creator with certain inalienable rights; that among these are life, liberty and the pursuit of happiness." If, for example, a law should be enacted, which prohibited the prosecution of some employment which did not involve the infliction of injury upon others, or which restricts the liberty of the citizen unnecessarily, and in such a manner that it did not violate any specific provision of the constitution, it may be held invalid, because in the one case it interfered with the inalienable right of property, and in the other case it infringed upon the natural right to life and liberty. " There is living power enough in those abstractions of the State constitutions, which have heretofore been regarded as mere ' glittering generalities,' to enable the courts to enforce them against the enactments of the Legislature, and thus declare that all men are not only created free and equal, but remain so, and may enjoy life and pursue happiness in their own way, provided they do not interfere with the freedom of other men in the pursuit of the same objects." [1] This is a novel doctrine, and one which perhaps is as liable

---

[1] Judge Redfield's annotation to People v. Turner, 55 Ill. 280; 10 Am. Law Reg. (N. s.) 372. At a very early day, before the adoption of the present constitution of the United States, it was judicially decided in Massachusetts that slavery was abolished in that State by a provision of the State constitution, which declared that " all men are born free and equal, and have certain natural, essential and inalienable rights," etc. This clause was held to be inconsistent with the *status* of slavery, and therefore impliedly emancipated every slave in Massachusetts. See Draper, Civil War in America, vol. I., p. 317; Bancroft, Hist. of U. S. vol. x., p. 365; Cooley Principles of Const., p. 213.

§ 3

to give rise to dangerous encroachments by the judiciary upon the sphere and powers of the legislature, as the doctrine that a law is invalid which violates abstract principles of justice. If it be recognized as an established rule of constitutional law, it must certainly be confined in its application to clear cases of natural injustice. Wherever there is any doubt as to the legitimate character of legislation, it should be solved in favor of the power of the Legislature to make the enactment. In all cases the courts should proceed with caution in the enforcement of this most elastic constitutional provision.

While we find a tendency in one direction to stretch the constitutional restrictions over a great many cases of legislation, which would not fall within the strict letter of the constitution, in order that due force and effect may be given to the fundamental principles of free government; on the other hand, where the letter of the constitution would prohibit police regulations, which by all the principles of constitutional government have been recognized as beneficent and permissible restrictions upon the individual liberty of action, such regulations will be upheld by the courts, on the ground that the framers of the constitution could not possibly have intended to deprive the government of so salutary a power, and hence the spirit of the constitution permits such legislation, although a strict construction of the letter may prohibit. But in such a case the regulation must fall within the enforcement of the legal maxim, *sic utere tuo, ut alienum non lædas.* " Powers which can only be justified on this specific ground (that they are police regulations) and which would otherwise be clearly prohibited by the constitution, can be such only as are so clearly necessary to the safety, comfort and well-being of society, or so imperatively required by the public necessity, as to lead to the rational and satisfactory conclusion that the framers of the constitution could not, as men of ordinary prudence and foresight, have intended to prohibit their exercise in the particular case,

§ 3

notwithstanding the language of the prohibition would otherwise include it." [1]   And in all such cases it is the duty of the courts to determine whether the regulation is a reasonable exercise of a power, which is generally prohibited by the constitution.   " It is the province of the law-making power to determine when the exigency exists for calling into exercise the police power of the State, but what are the subjects of its exercise is clearly a judicial question." [2]

§ 4. **The principal constitutional limitations.** — The principal constitutional limitations, which are designed to protect private rights against the arbitrary exercise of governmental power, and which therefore operate to limit and restrain the exercise of police power, are the following : —

1. No bill of attainder or *ex post facto* law shall be passed by the United States,[3] or by the States.[4]

2. No State shall pass any law impairing the obligation of a contract.[5]

3. Neither slavery nor involuntary servitude, except as a punishment for crime whereof the party shall have been duly convicted, shall exist within the United States, or any place subject to their jurisdiction.[6]

4. The right of the people to be secure in their persons, houses, papers, and effects, against unreasonable searches and seizures, shall not be violated; and no warrants shall issue but upon probable cause, supported by oath or affirmation, and particularly describing the place to be searched, and the person or thing to be seized.[7]

---

[1] Christiancy, J., in People *v.* Jackson and Mich. Plank Road Co., 9 Mich. 285.

[2] Lake View *v.* Rose Hill Cemetery, 70 Ill. 192.

[3] U. S. Const., art. I., § 9.

[4] U. S. Const., art. I., § 10.

[5] U. S. Const., art. I., § 10.

[6] U. S. Const. Amend., Art. VIII.

[7] U. S. Const. Amend., art. IV.

5. No soldier shall, in time of peace, be quartered in any house without the consent of the owner; nor in time of war, but in a manner to be prescribed by law.[1]

6. The right of the people to keep and bear arms shall not be infringed.[2]

7. Congress shall make no law respecting an establishment of religion or prohibiting the free exercise thereof; or abridging the freedom of speech, or of the press, or the right of the people, peaceably to assemble, and to petition the government for a redress of grievances.[3]

8. No person shall be held to answer for a capital, or otherwise infamous crime, unless on a presentment or indictment of a grand jury, except in cases arising in the land or naval forces, or in the militia, when in actual service in time of war or public danger; nor shall any person be subject for the same offense to be twice put in jeopardy of life or limb; nor shall be compelled in any criminal case to be a witness against himself, nor be deprived of life, liberty, or property, without due process of law; nor shall private property be taken for public use without just compensation.[4]

9. In all criminal prosecutions, the accused shall enjoy the right to a speedy and public trial, by an impartial jury of the State and district wherein the crime shall have been previously ascertained by law, and to be informed of the nature and cause of the accusation; to be confronted with the witnesses against him; to have compulsory process for obtaining witnesses in his favor, and to have the assistance of counsel for his defense.[5]

---

[1] U. S. Const. Amend., art. III.
[2] U. S. Const. Amend., art. II.
[3] U. S. Const. Amend., art. I.
[4] U. S. Const. Amend., art. V.
[5] U. S. Const. Amend., art. V.

§ 4

10. Excessive bail shall not be required, nor excessive fines imposed, nor cruel and unusual punishment inflicted.[1]

11. The privilege of the writ of *habeas corpus* shall not be suspended, unless when in cases of rebellion or invasion the public safety may require it.[2]

12. No State shall make or enforce any law which shall abridge the privilges or immunities of citizens of the United States, nor shall any State deprive any person of life, liberty or property, without due process of law ; nor deny to any person within its jurisdiction the equal protection of the laws.[3]

13. The right of the citizens of the United States to vote shall not be denied or abridged by the United States, or by any State, on account of race, color, or previous condition of servitude.[4]

Here are given only the provisions of the Federal constitution, but they either control the action of the States, as well as of the United States, or similar provisions have been incorporated into the bills of rights of the different State constitutions, so that the foregoing may be considered to be the chief limitations in the United States upon legislative interference with natural rights. Where the States are not expressly named in connection with any clause of the United States constitution, the provision is construed by the best authorities to apply solely to the United States.[5] But all of these limitations have been repeated in the State bill of rights, with some little but unimportant change of phraseology, together with other more minute limitations.

---

[1] U. S. Const. Amend., art. VIII.
[2] U. S. Const., art. I., § 9.
[3] U. S. Const., Amend. art. XIV.
[4] U. S. Const. Amend., art. XV.
[5] Barron *v.* Baltimore, 7 Pet. 243 ; Livingston's Lessee *v.* Moore, *Ib.* 469 ; Fox *v.* Ohio, 5 How. 410 ; Smith *v.* Maryland, 18 How. 71 ; Parvear *v.* Com., 5 Wall. 475 ; Twitchell *v.* Com., 7 Wall. 321 ; Com. *v.* Hitchings, 5 Gray, 482 ; Bigelow *v.* Bigelow, 120 Mass. 300, etc.

§ 4

§ 5. **Table of private rights.** — Police power, being the imposition of restrictions and burdens npou the natural and other private rights of individuals, it becomes necessary to tabulate and classify these rights, and in presenting for discussion the field and scope for the exercise of police power, the subject-matter will be subdivided according to the rights upon which the restrictions and burdens are imposed. The following is

THE TABLE OF PRIVATE RIGHTS.

(*a.*) Personal rights.
      1. Personal security — Life.
                    — Limb.
                    — Health.
                    — Reputation.
      2. Personal liberty.
      3. Private property — Real.
                    — Personal.

(*b.*) Relative Rights
      arising between 1. Husband and wife.
                     2. Parent and child.
                     3. Guardian and ward.
                     4. Master and servant.

(*c.*) Statutory Rights
      embracing all those rights which rest upon legislative grant.

§ 5

CHAPTER II.

POLICE REGULATION OF PERSONAL SECURITY.

SECTION 10. Security to life.
    11. Capital punishment.
    12. Security to limb and body.
    12a. Corporal punishment.
    12b. Personal chastisement in certain relations.
    13. Battery in self-defense.
    14. Abortion.
    15. Compulsory submission to surgical and medical treatment.
    16. Security to health — Legalized nuisances.
    17. Security to reputation — Privileged communications.
    17a. Privilege of legislators.
    17b. Privilege in judicial proceedings.
    17c. Criticism of officers and candidates for office.
    17d. Publications through the press.
    18. Security to reputation — Malicious prosecution.
    18a. Advice of counsel — How far a defense.

§ 10. **Security to Life.**—The legal guaranty of the protection of life is the highest possession of man. It constitutes the condition precedent to the enjoyment of all other rights. A man's life includes all that is certain and real in human experience, and since its extinction means the deprivation of all temporal rights, the loss of his own personality, so far as this world is concerned, the cause or motive for its destruction must be very urgent, and of the highest consideration, in order to constitute a sufficient justification. If there be any valid ground of justification in the taking of human life, it can only rest upon its necessity as a means of protection to the community against the perpetration of dangerous and terrible crimes by the person whose life is to be forfeited. When a person commits a crime, that is, trespasses upon the rights of his fellow-men, he subjects his own rights to the possibility of forfeiture, including even the forfeiture of life itself ; and the only consideration, independently of constitutional limitations, being, whether the given forfeiture, by exerting a deterrent influence, will furnish the necessary protection against future infringements of the same rights.   That is, of course, only a question of expedience addressed to the wise discretion of legislators, and does not concern the courts.   Except as a punishment for crime, no man's life can be destroyed, not even with his consent.   Suicide, itself, is held to be a crime, and one who assists another in the commission of suicide is himself guilty of a crime.[1]   This rule of the common law is in apparent contradiction with the maxim of the common law, which in every other case finds ready acquiescence, viz. : an injury (*i. e.* a legal wrong) is never committed against one who voluntarily accepts it, *volenti non fit injuria*.   If a crime be in every case a trespass upon the rights of others[2] suicide is not a crime, and it would not be a crime to assist one " to shuffle off this mortal coil."   But the dread of the uncertainties of the life beyond the grave so generally " makes us rather bear those ills we have, than fly to others that we know not of," that we instinctively consider suicide to be the act of a deranged mind ; and on the hypothesis that no sane man ever commits suicide the state may very properly interfere to prevent self-destruction, and to punish those who have given aid to the unfortunate man in his attack upon himself, or who have with his consent, or by his direction, killed a human being.   But if we hold suicide to be in any case the act of a sane man, I cannot see on what legal grounds he can be prevented from taking his own life.   It would be absurd to speak of a man being under a legal obligation to society to live as long as possible.   The immorality of the act does not make it a crime,[3] and since it is

[1] 4 Bl. Com. 188, 189.
[2] See *post*, § 68.
[3] See *post*, § 68.

§ 10

not a trespass upon the rights of any one, it is not an act that the State can prohibit. But even if suicide be declared a crime, the act has carried the criminal beyond the jurisdiction of the criminal courts, and consequently no punishment could be inflicted on him. The common law in providing that the body of a suicide should be buried at the cross-roads with a stake driven through it, and that his property shall be forfeited to the crown, violated the fundamental principle of constitutional law that no man can be condemned and punished for an offense, except after a fair trial by a court of competent jurisdiction, in which the accused is given an opportunity to be heard in his own defense. It is somewhat different where one man kills another at the latter's request. If it be held that the man who makes the request is sane, the killing is no more a crime than if it was done by the unfortunate man himself. But in consideration of the difficulty in proving the request, and the frequent opportunities for felonious murders the allowance of such deeds would afford, the State can very properly prohibit the killing of one man by another at the latter's request. These considerations would justify this exercise of police power, and in only one case is it supposed that any fair reason may be given for allowing it, and that is, where one is suffering from an incurable and painful disease. If the painful sufferer, with no prospect of a recovery or even temporary relief from physical agony, instead of praying to God for a deliverance, should determine to secure his own release, and to request the aid of a physician in the act, the justification of the act on legal grounds may not be so difficult. But even in such a case public, if not religious, considerations would justify a prohibition of the homicide.

§ 11. **Capital punishment.** — That capital punishment may be imposed for the commission of crimes against the life of another, and crimes against those rights of personal secur-

ity, which are in the estimation of the generality of mankind
as dear as life itself, for example, arson and rape, seems to admit of no doubt, not even in the realms of reason and natural
justice.   Certainly there is no constitutional prohibition
against its infliction for these offenses.   These are *mala in
se*, violations of the natural rights of man, and there is in
the breast of every human being a natural fear of punishment, proportionate to each and every violation of human
rights.   In the absence of a regularly established society,
in a state of nature, the power to inflict this punishment for
natural crimes is vested in every individual, since every one
is interested in providing the necessary protection for life.
" Whereof," Mr. Blackstone says, " the first murderer,
Cain, was so sensible, that we find him expressing his apprehensions, that *whoever* should find him would slay him." [1]
In organized society, a supreme power being established,
which is able and is expressly designed to provide for the
public security, the government succeeds to this natural right
of the individual.   " In a state of society this right is transferred from individuals to the sovereign power, whereby
men are prevented from being judges in their own causes,
which is one of the evils that civil government was intended to
remedy."[2]   These cases of capital punishment are readily justified, but it would seem to be a matter of very grave doubt,
certainly on rational grounds, whether the legislature had
the power to provide capital punishment for the commission
of a crime which is only a *malum prohibitum*, an act which
by the law of nature is not a violation of human rights.
But whatever may be the final settlement of this question,
by the common-law capital punishment was inflicted for
numerous crimes of very different characters and grades of
heinousness.   Says Blackstone: " It is a melancholy truth,
that among the variety of actions which men are daily liable

[1] 4 Bl. Com. 8.
[2] 4 Bl. Com. 8.

§ 11

to commit, no less than a hundred and sixty have been declared by act of Parliament to be felonies without benefit of
clergy ; or in other words, to be worthy of instant death." [1]
Sir Matthew Hale justifies this practice of inflicting capital
punishment for crimes of human institution in the following language : " When offenses grow enormous, frequent
and dangerous to a kingdom or state, destructive or highly
pernicious to civil societies, and to the great insecurity and
danger of the kingdom or its inhabitants, severe punishment
and even death itself is necessary to be annexed to laws in
many cases by the prudence of law-givers." [2]

It may now be considered as a settled doctrine that, in
the absence of an express constitutional prohibition, the infliction of capital punishment rests entirely in the discretion
of the legislature. The only constitutional limitation
which can bear upon the subject under discussion, is that
found in both the national and State constitutions, which
prohibits the imposition of " cruel and unusual punishments." [3] Capital punishment in itself is not " cruel,"
but the mode of its infliction may be " cruel and unusual,"
and hence contravene this constitutional provision. Thus,
for example, would be those cruel punishments of colonial
times and of the common law, such as burning at the stake,
breaking on the wheel, putting to the rack, and the like.
In the present temper of public opinion, these would undoubtedly be considered " cruel and unusual punishments,"
and therefore, forbidden by the constitution. [4] But would
the infliction of capital punishment for offenses, not involving the violation of the right to life and personal security,
be such a " cruel and unusual " punishment, as that it
would be held to be forbidden by this constitutional provision. It would seem to me that the imposition of the

---

[1] 4 Bl. Com. 18.
[2] 4 Bl. Com. 9.
[3] U. S. Const. Amend., art. 8.
[4] Done v. People, 5 Park. 364.

§ 11

death penalty for the violation of the revenue laws, *i.e.*, smuggling, or the illicit manufacture of liquors, or even for larceny or embezzlement, would properly be considered as prohibited by this provision as being " cruel and unusual." But if such a construction prevailed, it would be difficult to determine the limitations to the legislative discretion.

There has been so little litigation over this provision of our constitutions, that it is not an easy matter to say what is meant by the clause. Judge Cooley says : " Probably any punishment declared by statute for any offense, which was punished in the same way at common law, could not be regarded as cruel and unusual in the constitutional sense. And probably any new statutory offense may be punished to the extent and in the mode permitted by the common law for offenses of a similar nature." [1]   Capital punishment can be inflicted, in organized society, only under the warrant of a court of justice, having the requisite jurisdiction, and it must be done by the legal officer, whose duty it is to execute the decrees of the court.   The sentence of the court must be followed implicitly.   The sheriff is not authorized to change the mode of death, without becoming guilty of the crime of felonious homicide.[2]

SECTION. 12. Security to limb and body — General statement.
    12*a*. Corporal punishment.
    12*b*. Personal chastisement in certain relations.

§ 12. **Security to limb and body — General statement.** — This right is as valuable, and as jealously guarded against violation, as the primary right to life.   Not only does it involve protection against actual bodily injuries, but it also includes an immunity from the unsuccessful attempts to inflict bodily injuries, a protection against assaults, as well as batteries.   This protection against

[1] Cooley Const. Lim. 403, 404.
[2] 4 Bl. Com. 402–404.

§ 12

the hostile threats of bodily injury is as essential to one's happiness as immunity from actual battery.[1] But however high an estimate may be placed generally upon this right of personal security of limb and body, there are cases in which the needs of society require a sacrifice of the right; usually, however, where the wrongful acts of the person, whose personal security is invaded, have subjected him to the possibility of forfeiture of any right, as a penalty for wrong-doing.

§ 12*a*. **Corporal punishment.**— The whipping-post constituted at one time a very common instrument of punishment, and in the colonial days of this country it ornamented the public square of almost every town. At present corporal punishment is believed to be employed only in Delaware and Maryland.[2] It was much resorted to in England as a punishment for certain classes of infamous crimes. "The general rule of the common law was that the punishment of all infamous crimes should be disgraceful; as the pillory for every species of *crimen falsi*, as forgery, perjury and other offenses of the same kind. Whipping was more peculiarly appropriated to petit larceny and to crimes which betray a meanness of disposition, and a deep taint of moral depravity."[3] It does seem as if there are crimes so infamous in character, and betoken such a hopeless state of moral iniquity, that they can only be controlled and arrested by the degrading punishment of a public whipping. It is now being very generally suggested as the only appropriate punishment for those cowardly creatures, who lay their hands in violence upon their defenseless wives. But public opin-

---

[1] "Without such security society loses most of its value. Peace and order and domestic happiness, inexpressibly more precious than mere forms of government, cannot be enjoyed without the sense of perfect security." Gilchrist, J., in Beach *v.* Hancock, 27 N. H. 223.

[2] In Maryland it has been revived as a punishment for wife beating.

[3] Taylor, Ch. J., in State *v.* Kearney, 1 Hawks, 53.

§ 12*a*

ion is still strongly opposed to its infliction in any case.
The punishment is so degrading that its infliction leaves the
criminal very little chance for reformation, unless he betakes
himself to a land, whither the disgrace will not follow him,
or be generally known.[1]

In respect to the constitutional right to impose the
penalty of corporal punishment for crime, Judge Cooley
says: " We may well doubt the right to establish
the whipping post and the pillory in the States in
which they were never recognized as instruments of
punishment, or in States whose constitutions, revised
since public opinion had banished them, have forbidden
cruel and unusual punishment. In such States the public
sentiment must be regarded as having condemned them as
' cruel;' and any punishment, which if ever employed at all
has become altogether obsolete, must certainly be looked
upon as ' unusual.' " [2] The fact, that this mode of punishment has become obsolete, has made it impossible to secure
any large number of adjudications on the constitutionality
of a statute, which authorized or directed the infliction of
corporal punishment. But so far as the courts have passed
upon the question, they have decided in favor of its constitutionality, and held that whipping was not a " cruel and
unusual " punishment.[3] It has also been recognized as a
legitimate power in keepers of prisons and wardens of
penitentiaries to administer corporal punishment to refrac-
tory prisoners.[4] But whatever may be the correct view in

[1] "Among all nations of civilized man, from the earliest ages, the infliction of stripes has been considered more degrading than death itself."
Herber v. State, 7 Texas, 69.

[2] Cooley Const. Lim. *330.

[3] Commonwealth v. Wyatt, 6 Rand. 694; Foote v. State, 59 Md. 264
(for wife-beating); Garcia v. Territory, 1 New Mex. 415. In the last
case, the corporal punishment was inflicted for horse stealing.

[4] Cornell v. State, 6 Lea, 624. This power is exercised generally
throughout the country; it is hard to say, to what extent with the direct
sanction of law.

§ 12a

respect to the constitutionality of laws imposing corporal punishment, this mode of punishment has now become very generally obsolete, and no court would presume to employ it upon the authority of the English common law. A statute would be necessary to revive it.[2]

§ 12*b*. **Personal chastisement in certain relations.**— As a natural right, in consequence of the duty imposed upon the husband, parent, guardian and master, it was conceded by the common law that they could inflict corporal punishment, respectively, upon the wife, child pupil, ward and apprentice. But as the domestic relations, and the relative rights and duties growing out of them will, receive a more detailed treatment in a subsequent chapter, the reader is referred to that chapter.[2]

§ 13. **Battery in self-defense.** — One of the primary restrictions upon individual liberty, growing out of the organization of society and the institution of government, is that which limits or takes away the right to undertake the remedy of one's own wrongs, and provides a remedy in the institution of courts and the appointment of ministerial officers, who hear the complaints of parties, and condemn and punish all infractions of rights. But the natural right of protecting one's own rights can only be taken away justly where the law supplies in its place, and through the ordinary judicial channels, a reasonably effective remedy. In most cases, where the remedy should be preventive, in order that it may be effectual, the law is clearly powerless to afford the necessary protection, and hence it recognizes in private persons the right to resist by the use of force all attacks upon their natural rights. The degree of force,

---

[1] 1 Bishop Crim. Law. § 722. Under the national government, both the whipping post and the pillory were abolished by act of Congress in 1839. 5 U. S. Stat. at Large, ch. 36, § 5.

[2] See *post*, §§ 160, 165, 172.

§ 13

which one is justified in using in defense of one's rights, is determined by the necessities of the case. He is authorized to use that amount of force which is necessary to repel the assailant.[1] And in defending his rights, as a general rule, he may use whatever force is necessary for their protection, although it extends to the taking of life. But before using force in repelling an assault upon one's person, certainly where the necessary force would involve the taking of life, the law requires the person, who is assailed, to retreat before his assailant, and thus avoid a serious altercation as long as possible. When escape is impossible, then alone is homicide justifiable. Says Blackstone: " For which reason the law requires that the person, who kills another in his own defense, should have retreated as far as he conveniently or safely can, to avoid the violence of the assault, before he turns upon his assailant; and that not fictitiously, or in order to watch his opportunity, but from a real tenderness of shedding his brother's blood." [2] In the excitement which usually attends such occurrences, it would be requiring too much of the party assailed to adjust to a nicety the exact amount of force which would be sufficient to furnish him and his rights with the necessary protection, and hence he is required to exercise that degree of care which may be expected from a reasonably prudent man under similar circumstances.[3]

Blackstone also justifies, in cases of extreme necessity, the taking of the life of another, for the preservation of one's own life, where there is no direct attack upon the

---

[1] Bartlett v. Churchhill, 24 Vt. 218; Elliott v. Brown, 2 Wend. 497; Murray v. Commonwealth, 79 Pa. St. 311; Lewis v. State, 51 Ala. 1; McPherson v. State, 29 Ark. 225; Holloway v. Commonwealth, 11 Bush, 344; Erwin v. State, 29 Ohio St. 186; Roach v. People, 77 Ill. 25; State v. Kennedy, 20 Iowa, 569; State v. Shippen, 10 Minn. 223.

[2] 4 Bl. Com. 217. See People v. Sullivan, 7 N. Y. 396; State v. Dixon, 75 N. C. 275; Haynes v. State, 17 Ga. 465; Tweedy v. State, 5 Iowa, 433.

[3] Shorter v. People, 2 N. Y. 193; Patterson v. People, 46 Barb. 625.

§ 13

personal security, but the circumstances, surrounding the persons, require the death of one of them. He says: "There is one species of homicide *se defendendo* where the party slain is equally innocent as he who occasions his death: and yet this homicide is also excusable from the great universal principle of self-preservation, which prompts every man to save his own life preferable to that of another, where one of them must inevitably perish. As, among others, in that case mentioned by Lord Bacon,[1] where two persons being shipwrecked, and getting on the same plank, but finding it not able to save them both, one of them thrusts the other from it, whereby he is drowned. He who thus preserves his own life at the expense of another man's is excusable through unavoidable necessity, and the principle of self-defense; since both remaining on the same weak plank is a mutual, though innocent, attempt upon, and an endangering of each other's life."[2]   But, of late, the doctrine has been repudiated by the English Courts in a case, which has created widespread interest. A shipwreck had occurred, and some four or five persons occupied one of the life-boats. They were without provisions, and after enduring the pangs of hunger until they were almost bereft of reason, one person, a young boy, was selected by the others to die for their benefit. The boy was killed, and the others subsisted on his flesh and blood, until they were overtaken by a vessel, and carried to England. Their terrible experience was published in the papers, and the ship having been an English vessel, they were arrested on the charge of murder, and convicted, notwithstanding the strong effort of counsel to secure from the court a recognition of the principle advocated by Blackstone. A contrary doctrine is laid down by the Court, that no one has a right to take the life of another to save his own, except when it is endangered by the attacks of the other person. Even in cases of the extremest

---

[1] Elem. c. 5.
[2] 4 Bl. 186.

§ 13

necessity the higher law must be obeyed, that man shall not save his life at the expense of another, who is not responsible for the threatening danger.

Homicide is not only justifiable when committed in defense of one's life, but it is likewise excusable, when it is necessary to the protection of a woman's chastity. She may employ whatever force is necessary to afford her protection against the assault, even to the taking of life.[1] So may one use any degree of force that may be necessary to protect any member of his family, a wife, child, etc.[2] So may a battery be justified which is committed in defense of one's property, both real and personal, providing, always, that the force used is not excessive.[3] And where one is assaulted in one's dwelling, he is not required to retreat, but he may take the trespasser's life, if such extreme force is necessary to prevent an entrance.[4] But, although one may resist to any extent the forcible taking away of any property from himself, yet homicide in resisting a simple trespass to property, where there is no violence offered to the person, is never justifiable, except in the case of one's dwelling.[5]

In all these cases, the assault and battery are justified,

[1] Staten v. State, 30 Miss. 619; Briggs v. State, 29 Ga. 733.

[2] Commonwealth v. Malone, 114 Mass. 295; Stoneman v. Commonwealth, 25 Gratt. 887; State v. Johnson, 75 N. C. 174; Staten v. State, 30 Miss. 619; Patten v. People, 18 Mich. 314.

[3] Green v. Goddard, 2 Salk. 641; Beecher v. Parmele, 9 Vt. 352; Harrison v. Harrison, 43 Vt. 417; Ayers v. Birtch, 35 Mich. 501; Woodman v. Howell, 45 Ill. 367; Abt v. Burgheim, 80 Ill. 92; Staehlin v. Destrehan, 2 La. Ann. 1019; McCarty v. Fremont, 23 Cal. 196.

[4] State v. Burwell, 63 N. C. 661; McPherson v. State, 22 Ga. 478; State v. Abbott, 8 W. Va. 741; Pitford v. Armstrong, Wright (Ohio), 94; Wall v. State, 51 Ind. 453; Pond v. People, 8 Mich. 150; State v. Stockton, 61 Mo. 382; Palmore v. State, 29 Ark. 248.

[5] State v. Vance, 17 Iowa 138. See Loomis v. Terry, 17 Wend. 496. See, also, Bird v. Holbrook, 4 Bing. 628; Aldrich v. Wright, 53 N. H. 398 (16 Am. Rep. 339); Hooker v. Miller, 37 Iowa, 613 (18 Am. Rep. 18), where it is held that the use of spring guns and other like instruments, which cause the death of trespassers upon the land, is not permissible.

§ 13

only where they are employed in protecting rights against threatened injury. One cannot use force in recovering property or rights which have been taken or denied,[1] or in punishing those who have violated his rights. It is no part of one's legal rights to *avenge* the wrongs of himself and of his family.[2]

At common law it was the right of one, who was unlawfully disseised, to recover his lands by force of arms, using whatever force was necessary to that end. But in the reign of Richard II., a statute was passed which prohibited entries upon land, in support of one's title, " with strong hand or a multitude of people, but only in a peaceable and easy manner." [3] Similar statutes have been passed in most of the States of this country, and the effect of the statute has been the subject of more or less extensive litigation. The question has been mooted from an early period, whether the purpose of the statute was to take away the common-law civil right to recover one's lawful possession by force of arms, or simply to provide a punishment for the breach of the public peace thereby occasioned. Although there are decisions, which maintain that the statute has this double effect, and that such a forcible entry would lay the lawful owner open to civil actions for trespass and for assault and battery,[4] yet the weight of authority, both in this country and England, is certainly in favor of confining the operation of the statute to a criminal prosecution for the prohibited entry. The decisions cited below maintain that the plea of *liberum*

[1] Commonwealth v. Haley, 4 Allen, 318; Sampson v. Henry, 13 Pick. 336; Churchill v. Hulbert, 110 Mass. 42 (14 Am. Rep. 578).

[2] Cockroft v. Smith, 11 Mod. 43; Barfoot v. Reynolds, 2 Stra. 953; State v. Gibson, 10 Ired. 214.

[3] Tiedeman on Real Property, § 228.

[4] Reeder v. Pardy, 41 Ill. 261; Doty v. Burdick, 83 Ill. 473; Knight v. Knight, 90 Ill. 208; Dustin v. Cowdry, 23 Vt. 631; Whittaker v. Perry, 38 Vt. 107 (but see *contra* Beecher v. Parmelee, 9 Vt. 352; Mussey v. Scott, 32 Vt. 82). See Moore v. Boyd, 24 Me. 247.

§ 13

tenementum is a good plea to every action of trespass *quare clausum fregit*, and even if the tenant is forcibly expelled and suffers personal injuries therefrom, no civil action for any purpose will lie, unless the force used was greater than what was necessary to effect his expulsion.[1]

§ 14. **Abortion.** — In the act of abortion, there is a two-fold violation of rights. In the first place, it involves a violation of personal security to the limbs and body of the woman. The fœtus is part of the body of the woman and an unnatural expulsion of it inflicts injury upon the mother. But since the maxim of the law is, *volenti non fit injuria,* there is at common law no crime of assault and battery against the woman, where she procures or assents to the abortion. But abortion involves also the destruction of the life-germ of the fœtus, which is considered, even by the common law, to be a living human being for certain purposes. Mr. Blackstone says : " Even an infant *in ventre sa mère*, or in the mother's womb, is, for many purposes, which will be specified in the course of these commentaries, treated in law as if actually born." [2] But the fœtus was not supposed to have such an actual separate existence as to make abortion a crime against the unborn child, until it had reached that stage of its growth when it is said to " quicken." Consequently at common law, where an abortion is commit-

---

[1] Harvey *v.* Brydges, 13 M. & W. 437; Davis *v.* Burrell, 10 C. B. 821; Hilbourne *v.* Fogg, 99 Mass. 11; Churchill *v.* Hulbert, 110 Mass. 42 (15 Am. Rep. 578); Clark *v.* Kelliher, 107 Mass. 406; Stearns *v.* Sampson, 59 Me. 569 (8 Am. Rep. 442); Sterling *v.* Warden, 51 N. H. 239 (12 Am. Rep. 80); Livingston *v.* Tanner, 14 N. H. 64; Estes *v.* Redsey, 8 Wend. 560; Kellum v. Jansorn, 17 Pa. St. 467; Zell *v.* Reame, 31 Pa. St. 304; Todd *v.* Jackson, 26 N. J. L. 525; Walton *v.* Fill, 1 Dev. & B. 507; Johnson *v.* Hanahan, 1 Strobh. 313; Tribble *v.* Frame, 1 J. J. Marsh. 599; Krevet *v.* Meyer, 24 Mo. 107; Fuhr *v.* Dean, 26 Mo. 116. But where force is used after a peaceable entry to eject a tenant, it is lawful and will not sustain a prosecution for assault and battery. Stearns *v.* Sampson, 59 Me. 569 (8 Am Rep. 442).

[2] 1 Bl. Com.·154.

§ 14

ted upon a woman, with her consent, before the child had quickened, it is no crime unless the death of the mother ensues.[1] The crime of abortion is now regulated by statute in the different States, and is generally made a crime, under all circumstances, to procure the miscarriage of a pregnant woman, whether she consents to the act, or the child has not quickened, and even where she herself, unaided, attempts the abortion.

§ 15. **Compulsory submission to surgical and medical treatment.** — Although it has never been brought before the courts for adjudication, it is nevertheless a most interesting question of police power, whether a person who is suffering from disease can be forced to submit to a surgical operation or medical treatment. We can readily understand the right of a parent or guardian to compel a child to submit to necessary medical treatment, and likewise the right of the guardian or keeper of an insane person to treat him in a similar manner. So also can we justify the exercise of force in administering remedies to one who is in the delirium of fever. But can a sane, rational man or woman of mature age be forced to submit to medical treatment, though death is likely to follow from the consequent neglect? If the disease is infectious or contagious, we recognize without question the right of the State to remove the afflicted person to a place of confinement, where he will not be likely to communicate the disease to others;[2] and we recognize the right of the State to keep him confined, as long as the danger to the public continues. Inasmuch as the confinement of such a person imposes a burden upon the community, all means for lessening that burden may be

---

[1] Commonwealth *v.* Parker, 9 Metc. 263; State *v.* Cooper, 22 N. J. L. 52; see Abrams *v.* Foshee, 3 Iowa, 274; Hatfield *v.* Gano, 15 Iowa, 177; People *v.* Jackson, 3 Hill, 92; Wilson *v.* Iowa, 2 Ohio St. 319; Robbins *v.* State, 8 Ohio St. 131; State *v.* Smith, 32 Me. 369; Commonwealth *v.* Wood, 11 Gray, 85; Mills *v.* Commonwealth, 13 Pa. St. 631.

[2] See *post*, § 42.

employed as a legitimate exercise of police power ; and
if a surgical operation or medical treatment be necessary
to effect a cure, the patient cannot lawfully resist the treatment.   Not only is this true, but it seems that medical and
surgical treatment can be prescribed, against the consent
of the individual, as a preventive of contagious and infectious diseases.   Thus in England, and probably in some of
the United States, vaccination has been made compulsory.[1]
When one remembers the terrible scourges suffered from
small-pox in the past, and thinks of the moderation and
control of them effected by a general vaccination of the
the people, no one would hesitate to answer all philosophical objections to compulsory vaccination by an appeal to the
legal maxim, *salus populi suprema lex.*   In the same manner, where medical attendance and surgical operations
are necessary to procure the successful delivery of a child,
the consent of the woman is not necessary.   The saving
of her life and the life of the child is a sufficient justification for this invasion of the right of personal security.   But where the neglect of medical treatment will not
cause any injury to others, it is very questionable if any
case can be suggested in which the employment of force,
in compelling a subjection to medical treatment of one who
refused to submit, could be justified, unless it be upon
the very uncertain and indefinite ground that the State
suffers a loss in the ailment of each inhabitant, which
may be guarded against or cured by the proper medical
treatment.

§ 16. **Security to health — Legalized nuisance.** — The
security against all causes of injury to health and bodily
comfort is also highly essential to human happiness, and
those acts of individuals which produce injury to health,

---

[1] In Montreal, Canada, during the winter of 1885-86, the enforcement
of such a law was resisted by a large part of the population, and serious
riots ensued.

§ 16

or seriously interfere with bodily comfort, are called nuisances and are, as a general rule, prohibited. But it is not every annoyance to health and comfort, which constitutes a nuisance.[1] Where the annoyance proceeds from some natural cause, and is not the consequence of an act of some individual, it is no nuisance, if the public or private owner should fail to remove the cause of annoyance.[2] Thus, it is not actionable, if the owner of swamp lands fails to drain his lands, and in consequence the neighbors are made sick by the injurious exhalations.[3] Nor is it any ground for an action against a municipal corporation, that it has failed to provide proper remedies for the prevention of nuisances and other annoyances to health and bodily comfort.[4] And although, as a general proposition, no one has a right to do any act which will cause injury to the health or disturb seriously the bodily comfort or mental quietude of another, yet this right of security to health and comfort cannot be left absolute in a state of organized society. It must give way to the reasonable demands of trade, commerce, and the other vital interests of society. While the state cannot take away absolutely the private rights of individuals by the legalization of nuisances,[5] yet in most cases of nuisances, affecting the personal health and comfort, there is involved the consideration of what constitutes a reasonable use of one's property, and that is a question of fact, the answer to which varies according to the circumstances of each case. One is expected to submit

[1] See *post*, § 122, for a more thorough discussion of nuisances.

[2] See *post*, § 124, in respect to the power of the state to compel the owner of land to remove natural causes of annoyance.

[3] Reeves *v.* Treasurer, 8 Ohio St. 333.

[4] Roberts *v.* Chicago, 26 Ill. 249. See Wilson *v.* New York, 1 Denio, 595; Mills *v.* Brooklyn, 32 N. Y. 489; Carr *v.* Northern Liberties, 35 Pa. St. 824; Detroit *v.* Michigan, 34 Mich. 125; Delphi *v.* Evans, 36 Ind. 90; Cotes *v.* Davenport, 9 Iowa, 227; Lamber *v.* St. Louis, 15 Mo. 610; White *v.* Yazoo, 27 Miss. 357.

[5] See Cooley on Torts, 616.

§ 16

to a reasonable amount of discomfort for the convenience
or benefit of his neighbor. If a discomfort were wantonly
caused from malice or wickedness, a slight degree of inconvenience might be sufficient to render it actionable ; but if
it were to result from pursuing a useful employment in a
way which but for the discomfort to others would be reasonable and lawful, it is perceived that the position of both
parties must be regarded, and that what would have been
found wholly unreasonable before may appear to be clearly
justified by the circumstances.[1] Instead of being a question of personal health and comfort on the one hand, and
a profitable use of property on the other hand, the question
is, on whom in equity should the loss fall, where two adjoining or contiguous land proprietors find their interests clashing in the attempted use of the land by one for a purpose
or trade, which causes personal discomfort to the other,
who is residing upon his land.   The injury to the personal
comfort and health is not in such a case an absolute one.
For, as was said by the court in one of the leading cases,[2]
" the people who live in such a city, i.e., where the principal industry consists of manufactures, or within its sphere
of influence, do so of choice, and they voluntarily subject
themselves to its peculiarities and its discomforts for the
greater benefits they think they derive from their residence or
business there."   If a noisome or unhealthy trade is plied in
a part of a city, which is given up principally to residences, it
might be considered a nuisance, while the same trade might,
in a less populous neighborhood, or in one which is devoted to trade and manufacturing, be considered altogether
permissible.[3]

[1] Cooley on Torts, 596.

[2] Huckenstein's Appeal, 70 Pa. St. 102 (10 Am. Rep. 669).

[3] St. Helen's Smelting Co. v. Tipling, 11 H. L. Cas. 642; Whitney v.
Bartholomew, 21 Conn. 213; McKeon v. Lee, 51 N. Y. 300 (10 Am. Rep.
659); Huckenstein's Appeal, 70 Pa. St. 102 (10 Am. Rep. 669); Gilbert v.
Showerman, 23 Mich. 448; Kirkman v. Handy, 11 Humph. 406; Cooley

§ 16

SECTION 17. Security to reputation — Privileged communications.

17a. Privilege of legislators.

17b. Privilege in judicial procedings.

17c. Criticism of officers and candidates for office.

17d. Publication through the press.

§ 17. Security to reputation — Privileged communications.

— A man's reputation, the opinion entertained of him by his neighbors, is another valuable possession, and the security to which is most jealously, but, it must be confessed in most cases, ineffectually guarded against infractions. The breath of suspicion, engendered by a slanderous lie, will tarnish a fair name, long after the injurious statement has been proved to be an unfounded falsehood. But the aim of all legislation on the subject is to provide the proper protection against slander and libel, and failure in ordinary cases is caused by the poverty of the means of penal judicature, and does not arise from any public indifference. But dear to man as is the security to reputation, there are cases in which it must yield to the higher demands of public necessity and general welfare. Malice is generally inferred from a false and injurious statement or publication, and the slanderer and libeler are punished accordingly. But there are special cases, in which for reasons of public policy, or on account of the rebuttal of the presumption of malice by the co-existence of a duty to speak or an active interest in the subject, the speaker or writer is held to be "privileged," that is, relieved from liability for the damage which has been inflicted by his false

on Torts, 596–605; 1 Dillon's Municipal Corp., § 374, note. "If one lives in a city he must expect to suffer the dirt, smoke, noisome odors, noise and confusion incident to city life. As Lord Justice James beautifully said in Salvin v. North Brancepeth Coal Co., L. M. 9 Ch. Ap. 705, 'if some picturesque haven opens its arms to invite the commerce of the world, it is not for this court to forbid the embrace, although the fruit of it should be the sights and sounds and smells of a common seaport and shipbuilding town, which would drive the Dryads and their masters from their ancient solitude.'" Earl, J., in Campbell v. Seaman, 63 N. Y. 568.

§ 17

charges.   These privileged communications are divided
into two classes; first, those which are made in a public or
official capacity, and which for reasons of public policy are
not permitted to be the subject of a judicial action ; and secondly, all those cases in which the circumstances rebut the
presumption of malice.   In these cases of the second class,
the privilege is only partial.   As already stated, the circumstances are held to rebut the presumption of malice, and
throws upon the plaintiff the burden of proving affirmatively that the defendant was actuated by malice in making
the false statement which has injured the plaintiff's reputation.   In these cases, the proof of express malice revives
the liability of the alleged slanderer.[1]   As Mr. Cooley says,
" they are generally cases in which a party has a duty to
discharge, which requires that he should be allowed to
speak freely and fully that which he believes ; or where he
is himself directly interested in the subject-matter of the
communication, and makes it with a view to the protection
or advancement of his own interest, or where he is communicating confidentially with a person interested in the communication, and by way of advice." [2]   The cases of a private
nature are very numerous, and for a full and exhaustive
discussion of them, reference must be made to some work
on slander and libel.   Under this rule of exemption are
included answers to inquiries after the character of one, who
had been employed by the person addressed, and who is
soliciting employment from one who makes the inquiry,[3]

---

[1] " It properly signifies this and nothing more; that the excepted instances shall so far change the ordinary rule with respect to slanderous
or libelous matter as to remove the regular and usual presumption of
malice, and to make it incumbent on the party complaining to show
malice."   Daniel, J., in White v. Nichols, 3 How. 266, 287.   See Lewis v.
Chapman, 16 N. Y. 369.

[2] Cooley Const. Lim. 425.

[3] Pattison v. Jones, 8 B. & C. 578; Bradley v. Heath, 12 Pick. 163;
Hatch v. Lane, 105 Mass. 394; Elam v. Badger, 23 Ill. 498; Noonan v.
Orton, 32 Wis. 106.   So also is a subsequent communication, to one who

§ 17

the answer of all inquiries between tradesmen concerning the financial credit and commercial reputation of persons who desire to enter into business dealings with the inquirers.[1] While the private reports of mercantile agencies are privileged,[2] the published reports of such agencies, which are distributed among the customers, are held not to constitute one of the privileged classes.[3]

All *bona fide* communications are privileged, where there is a confidential relation of any kind, existing between the parties in respect to the subject-matter of the inquiry. "All that is necessary to entitle such communications to be regarded as privileged is, that the relation of the parties should be such as to afford reasonable ground for supposing an innocent motive for giving the information, and to deprive the act of an appearance of officious intermeddling with the affairs of another."[4]

The first class of privileged communications, enumerated above, is absolutely privileged, and there is no right of action, even though the false statement is proved to be prompted by malice. They are few in number, and the privilege rests upon public policy, and usually have reference to the administration of some branch of the government. They will be discussed in a regular order.

§ 17a. **Privilege of legislators.**—In order that the

had employed a clerk upon the former's recommendation, of the facts which have induced a change of opinion. Fowles *v.* Bowen, 30 N. Y. 20.

[1] Smith *v.* Thomas, 2 Bing. N. C. 372; White *v.* Nichols, 3 How. 266; Cooley on Torts, 216.

[2] Lewis *v.* Chapman, 16 N. Y. 369; Ormsby *v.* Douglass, 37 N. Y. 477.

[3] Taylor *v.* Church, 8 N. Y. 452; Sunderlin v. Bradstreet, 46 N. Y. 188 (7 Am. Rep. 322). See note 2, p. 55.

[4] Lewis *v.* Chapman, 16 N. Y. 369. See Todd *v.* Hawkins, 8 C. & P. 88; Cockagne *v.* Hodgkisson, 5 C & P. 543; Klinck *v.* Colby, 46 N. Y. 274 (7 Am. Rep. 360); Joannes *v.* Bennett, 5 Allen, 170; Hatch *v.* Lane, 105 Mass. 394; Fitzgerald *v.* Robinson, 112 Mass. 371; State *v.* Burnham, 9 N. H. 34; Knowles *v.* Peck, 42 Conn. 386 (19 Am. Rep. 542); Goslin *v.* Cannon, 1 Harr. 3; Grimes *v.* Coyle, 6 B. Mon. 301; Rector *v.* Smith, 11 Iowa, 302.

§ 17a

legislator may, in the performance of his official duties, feel himself free from all restraining influences, and able to act without fear or favor of any one whatsoever, it is usually provided by a constitutional clause, that he shall not be subjected elsewhere to any legal liability for any statement he may have made in speech or debate.[1]   Inasmuch as this absolute privilege is established in behalf of the legislator, not for his own benefit, but with a view to promote the public good, and inasmuch as the houses of Congress, and of the State legislatures, have the power to punish their members for disorderly behavior and unparliamentary language, a most liberal construction is given to this constitutional provision.   " These privileges (the privilege of legislators from arrest and from liability for false statements in speech or debate) are thus secured, not with the intention of protecting the members against prosecutions for their own benefit, but to support the rights of the people, by enabling their representatives to execute the functions of their office without fear of prosecutions civil or criminal. I therefore think that the article ought not to be construed strictly, but liberally, that the full design of it may be answered.   I will not confine it to delivering an opinion, uttering a speech, or haranguing in debate, but will extend it to the giving of a vote, to the making of a written report, and to every other act resulting from the nature and in the execution of the office ; and I would define the article as securing to every member exemption from prosecution for everything said or done by him, as a representative, in the exercise of the functions of that office, without inquiring

---

[1] The provision in the United States constitution is, " And for any speech or debate in either house they (the members of Congress) shall not be questioned in any other place." U. S Const. art. I., § 6.   It is believed that similar provisions are to be found in every State constitution having reference to members of State legislatures, except those of North Carolina, South Carolina, Mississippi, Texas, California and Nevada.   Cooley Const. Lim. *446, note 1.

§ 17a

whether the exercise was regular and according to the rules
of the house, or irregular and against their rules. I do not
confine the member to his place in the house, and I am satisfied that there are cases in which he is entitled to this privilege when not within the walls of the representatives'
chamber. He cannot be exercising the functions of his
office as the member of a body, unless the body be in existence. The house must be in session to enable him to
claim this privilege, and it is in session, notwithstanding
occasional adjournments for short intervals for the convenience of its members. If a member, therefore, be out of
the chamber, sitting in committee, executing the commission of the house, it appears to me that such a member is
within the reason of the article, and ought to be considered
within the privilege. The body of which he is a member is
in session, and he, as a member of that body, is in fact discharging the duties of his office. He ought, therefore, to
be protected from civil or criminal prosecutions for everything said or done by him in the exercise of his functions,
as a representative, in debating or assenting to or drafting a
report. Neither can I deny the member his privilege when
executing the duties of his office, in convention of both
houses, although the convention should be holden in the
senate chamber.''[1] But even to so absolute a privilege as
this, there is a limitation. Because a man holds the position
of a legislator, the public interests do not require that he
be given unlimited license to slander whom he pleases, and
to screen himself from a just retribution under his legislative privilege. It is only when he is acting in his official
capacity, that he can claim this protection. If, therefore,
the slanderous statement has no relevancy to any public busi-

---

[1] Coffin *v.* Coffin, 4 Mass. 1, 27 (3 Am. Dec. 189). The constitutional
provision, which was in force when this case arose, was as follows:
"The freedom of deliberation, speech and debate in either house, cannot be the foundation of any accusation or prosecution, action or complaint, in any other court or place whatever."

§ 17*a*

ness or duty, is not even remotely pertinent to public questions then under discussion, the legislator in his utterance of them subjects himself to civil and criminal liability.[1] A similar exemption from responsibility for official utterances is guaranteed to the President of the United States and to the governors of the several States.[2]

§ 17b. **Privilege in judicial proceedings.**—The object of all judicial proceedings is the furtherance of justice by preventing or punishing wrongs and providing protection to rights. Although the law does not support, and is not designed to foster, a litigious spirit, yet whenever one, from all the facts within his knowledge, is justified in believing that he has suffered a wrong ; in other words, if the facts within his knowledge make out a *prima facie* cause of action, he has a right to call to his aid the whole power of the law in the protection and enforcement of his rights, and it is to the public interest that a sufficient remedy be provided, and a resort to the courts be encouraged, in order to diminish the temptation, which is always present, to redress one's own wrongs. Now, if one, in stating his cause of action to the court, will subject himself to liability for every mistake of fact that he might innocently make, appeals to the courts in such cases would thus be discouraged. It is therefore consonant with the soundest public policy, to protect from civil liability all false accusations contained in the affidavits, pleadings, and other papers, which are preliminary to the institution of a suit. But the courts are not to be made the vehicles for slanderous villification, and hence the false accusations are privileged only when made in good faith, with the intention to prosecute, and under circumstances, which induced the affirmant, as a reasonably prudent man, to believe them to be true. The

---

[1] Coffin v. Coffin, 4 Mass. 1 (3 Am. Dec. 189); State v. Burnham, 9 N. H. 34; Perkins v. Mitchell, 31 Barb. 461.
[2] Cooley on Torts, 214.

§ 17b

good faith rebuts the presumption of malice, and the affiant is protected under his privilege, as long as the statement is pertinent to the cause of action, and where he is not actuated by malice in making it. If the statement is not pertinent, or if express malice be proved, the liability attaches.[1] All allegations in pleadings, if pertinent, are said to be absolutely privileged,[2] except where the libelous words in the pleadings refer to third person, and not to the defendant. Then they are only privileged, when they are pertinent and are pronounced in good faith.[3] Not only are false statements privileged, when made in preliminary proceedings, but a false statement has also been held to be privileged, where it has been made to one, after the commission of a crime, with a view to aid him in discovering the offender and bringing him to justice.[4] And so, likewise, is a paper privileged, which is signed by several persons, who thereby agree to prosecute others, whose names are given in the paper, and who are therein charged with the commission of a crime.[5]

In the same manner is the report of the grand jury privileged, notwithstanding, in making it, they have exceeded their jurisdiction.[6]

[1] Kine v. Sewell, 3 Mees. & W. 297; Kidder v. Parkhurst, 3 Allen, 393; Worthington v. Scribner, 108 Mass. 487 (12 Am. Rep. 736); Eames v. Whittaker, 123 Mass. 342; Jarvis v. Hathaway, 3 Johns. 180; Allen v. Crofoot, 2 Wend. 515; Burlingame v. Burlingame, 8 Cow. 141; Garr v. Selden, 4 N. Y. 91; Maurice v. Worden, 54 Md. 233 (39 Am. Rep. 384); Vaussee v. Lee, 1 Hill (S. C.), 197 (26 Am. Dec. 168); Marshall v. Gunter, 6 Rich. 419; Lea v. Sneed, 4 Sneed, 111; Grimes v. Coyle, 6 B. Mon. 301; Bunton v. Worley, 4 Bibb, 38 (7 Am. Dec. 735); Strauss v. Meyer, 48 Ill. 385; Spaids v. Barrett, 57, Ill. 289; Wyatt v. Buell, 47 Cal. 624.

[2] Strauss v. Meyer, 48 Ill. 385; Lea v. White, 4 Sneed, 111; Forbes v. Johnson, 11 B. Mon. 48.

[3] McLaughlin v. Cowley, 127 Mass. 316; Davis v. McNees, 8 Humph. 40; Ruohs v. Packer, 6 Heisk. 395 (19 Am. Rep. 598); Wyatt v. Buell, 47 Cal. 624.

[4] Goslin v. Cannon, 1 Harr. 3.

[5] Klinck v. Colby, 46 N. Y. 427 (7 Am. Rep. 360).

[6] Rector v. Smith, 11 Iowa, 302.

§ 17b

When the case is called up in court for trial, the chief aim of the proceeding is the ascertainment of the truth, and all the protections thrown around the *dramatis personæ* in a judicial proceeding are designed to bring out the truth, and to insure the doing of justice. We therefore find as a familiar rule of law, that no action will lie against a witness for any injurious and false statement he might make on the witness-stand. If he is guilty of perjury, he subjects himself to a criminal liability, but in no case does he incur any civil liability.[1] But he is only privileged when the statement is pertinent to the cause and voluntarily offered. He is not the judge of what is pertinent, and is protected if his statement is prompted by a question of counsel, which is not forbidden by the court.[2]

The statements of the judge are privileged for similar reasons,[3] and in the same manner are jurors privileged in statements which they make during their deliberations upon the case.[4]

The most important case of privilege, in connection with judicial proceedings, is that of counsel in the conduct of the cause. In order that the privilege may prove beneficial to the party whom the counsel represents, it must afford him the widest liberty of speech, and complete immunity from liability for any injurious false statement. It is, therefore, held very generally, that the privilege of counsel is as broad as that of the legislator, and that he sustains no civil liabil-

---

[1] Dunlap *v.* Glidden, 31 Me. 435; Barnes *v.* McCrate, 32 Me. 442; Cunningham *v.* Brown, 18 Vt. 123; Allen *v.* Crofoot, 2 Wend. 515 (20 Am. Dec. 647); Garr *v.* Selden, 4 N. Y. 91; Marsh *v.* Ellsworth, 50 N. Y. 309; Grove *v.* Brandenburg 7 Blackf. 234; Shock *v.* McChesney, 4 Yeates, 507 (2 Am. Dec. 415); Terry *v.* Fellows, 21 La. Ann. 375; Smith *v.* Howard, 28 Iowa, 51.

[2] See Barnes *v.* McCrate, 32 Me. 442; Kidder *v.* Parkhurst, 3 Allen, 393; White *v.* Carroll, 42 N. Y. 166 (1 Am. Rep. 503); Calkins *v.* Sumner, 13 Wis. 193.

[4] Dunham *v* Powers, 42 Vt. 1; Rector *v.* Smith, 11 Iowa, 302.

[3] Cooley on Torts, 214; Townshend on Slander and Libel, § 227.

§ 17b

ity for false, injurious statements, however malicious an intent may have actuated their utterance, provided they are pertinent to the cause on trial.[1] Nowhere is the privilege of counsel more clearly elucidated than in the following extract from an opinion of Chief Justice Shaw: "We take the rule to be well settled by the authorities, that words spoken in the course of judicial proceedings, though they are such as impute crime to another, and, therefore, if spoken elsewhere, would import malice and be actionable in themselves, are not actionable, if they are applicable and pertinent to the subject of inquiry. The question, therefore, in such cases is, not whether the words spoken are true, but whether they were spoken in the course of judicial proceedings, and whether they are relevant or pertinent to the cause or subject of inquiry. And in determining what is pertinent, much latitude must be allowed to the judgment and discretion of those who are entrusted with the conduct of a cause in court, and a much larger allowance made for the ardent and excited feelings with which a party or counsel, who naturally and almost necessarily identifies himself with his client, may become animated, by constantly regarding one side only of an interesting and animated controversy, in which the dearest rights of such a party may become involved. And if these feelings sometimes manifest themselves in strong invectives, or exaggerated expressions, beyond what the occasion would strictly justify, it is to be recollected that this is said to a judge who hears both sides, in whose mind the exaggerated statement may be at once controlled and met by evidence and argument of a contrary tendency from the other party, and who, from the impartiality of his position, will naturally give to an exaggerated

---

[1] Hastings v. Lusk, 22 Wend. 410 (34 Am. Dec. 380); Warner v. Paine, 2 Sandf. 195; Marsh v. Ellsworth, 50 N. Y. 309; McMillan v. Birch, 1 Binney, 178 (2 Am. Dec. 426); McLaughlin v. Cowley, 127 Mass. 316; Harden v. Comstock, 2 A. K. Marsh. 480 (12 Am. Dec. 168); Spaids v. Barnett, 57 Ill. 289; Jennings v. Paine, 4 Wis. 358.

§ 17b

assertion, not warranted by the occasion, no more weight than it deserves. Still, this privilege must be restrained by some limit, and we consider that limit to be this: that a party or counsel shall not avail himself of his situation to gratify private malice by uttering slanderous expressions, either against a party, witness or third person, which have no relation to the cause or subject-matter of the inquiry. Subject to this restriction, it is, on the whole, for the public interest, and best calculated to subserve the purposes of justice, to allow counsel full freedom of speech in conducting the causes and advocating and sustaining the rights of their constituents ; and this freedom of discussion ought not to be impaired by numerous and refined distinctions." [1]

While the importance of an almost unrestricted liberty of speech to a counsel is recognized and conceded, and likewise the difficulty in restraining abuses of the privilege, still the commonness of the abuse would well make the student of police power pause to consider, if there be no remedy which, while correcting the evil, will not tend to hamper the counsel in the presentation of his client's case. Personal invective against one's opponent, the " browbeating " of hostile witnesses, are the ready and accustomed weapons of poor lawyers, while really able lawyers only resort to them when their cause is weak. If the invective was confined to the subject-matter furnished and supported by the testimony before the court, and consisted of exaggerated and abusive presentations of proven facts, while even this would seem reprehensible to us, there are no possible means of preventing it. But it is not within the privilege of counsel to gratify private malice by uttering slanderous

---

[1] Hoar v. Wood, 3 Metc. 193. See Bradley v. Heath, 12 Pick. 163; Mower v. Watson, 11 Vt. 536 (34 Am. Dec. 704); Gilbert v. People, 1 Denio, 41; Ring v. Wheeler, 7 Cow. 725; Hastings v. Lusk, 22 Wend. 410 (34 Am. Dec. 380); Stackpole v. Hennen, 6 Mart. (N. s.) 481 (17 Am. Dec. 187); Marshall v. Gunter, 6 Rich. 419; Lester v. Thurmond, 51 Ga. 118; Ruohs v. Backer, 6 Heisk. 395 (19 Am. Rep. 598); Lawson v. Hicks, 38 Ala. 279; Jennings v. Paine, 4 Wis. 358.

§ 17b

·expressions, either against a party, a witness or a third person, which have no relation to the subject-matter of the inquiry. Counsel should be confined to what is relevant to the cause, whatever may be his motive for going outside of the record. The courts are too lax in this regard. No legislation is needed ; they have the power in their reach to reduce this evil, for it is an evil, to a minimum. The most salutary remedy would be raising the standard of qualification for admission to the bar. The number of poor lawyers, now legion, would be greatly reduced, and consequently the abuse of this privilege lessened.

§ 17c. **Criticism of officers and candidates for office.** — When a man occupies an official position, or is a candidate for office, the people whom he serves, or desires to serve, are interested in his official conduct, or in his fitness and capacity for the office to which he aspires. It would seem, therefore, that, following out the analogy drawn from cases of private communications, affecting the reputation of persons, in whom the parties giving and receiving the communications are interested, any candid, honest, canvass of the official's or candidate's character and capacity would be privileged, and the party making the communication will not be held liable, civilly or criminally, if it proves to be false. But here, as in the case of private communications, one or the other of the parties, who were concerned in the utterance of the slander or publication of the libel, must have been interested in the subject-matter of the communication. In the case of officials and candidates for office, in order to be privileged, the criticism must be made by parties who are interested personally in the conduct and character of the official or candidate. The subject-matter of the communication must, therefore, relate to his official conduct, if the party complained of be an officer, and, if he be a candidate for office, the communication should be confined to a statement of objections to his capacity and fitness for office.

§ 17c

Not that in either case the man's private conduct cannot be discussed under a similar privilege, although such a distinction is advocated in an English case.[1] In this case, Baron Alderson says : "It seems there is a distinction, although I must say I really can hardly tell what the limits of it are, between the comments on a man's public conduct and upon his private conduct. I can understand that you have a right to comment on the public acts of a minister, upon the public acts of a general, upon the public judgments of a judge, upon the public skill of an actor; I can understand that; but I do not know where the limit can be drawn distinctly between where the comment is to cease, as being applied solely to a man's public conduct, and where it is to begin as applicable to his private character; because, although it is quite competent for a person to speak of a judgment of a judge as being an extremely erroneous and foolish one,— and no doubt comments of that sort have great tendency to make persons careful of what they say,— and although it is perfectly competent for persons to say of an actor that he is a remarkably bad actor, and ought not to be permitted to perform such and such parts, because he performs them so ill, yet you ought not to be allowed to say of an actor that he has disgraced himself in private life, nor to say of a judge or of a minister that he has committed a felony, or anything of that description, which is in no way connected with his public conduct or public judgment; and, therefore, there must be some limits, although I do not distinctly see where those limits are to be drawn." Judge Cooley, in criticising this opinion,[2] says : "The radical defect in this rule, as it seems to us, consists in its assumption that the private character of a public officer is something aside from, and not entering into or influencing his public conduct; that a thoroughly dishonest man may be a just minister, and that a judge, who is corrupt and debauched in private

---

[1] Gathercole v. Miall, 15 Mees. & W. 319.
[2] Cooley Const. Lim. 440.

§ 17c

life may be pure and upright in his judgments ; in other words, that an evil tree is as likely as any other to bring forth good fruits. . Any such assumption is false to human nature, and contradictory to general experience ; and whatever the law may say, the general public will still assume that a corrupt life will influence public conduct, and that a man who deals dishonestly with his fellows as individuals will not hesitate to defraud them in their aggregate and corporate capacity, if the opportunity shall be given him.''

Where the private character would indicate the possession of evil tendencies, which can manifest themselves in, and influence, his official conduct to the detriment of the public, it would seem but natural that the same privilege should be extended to such a communication concerning a candidate for office, as if the same evil tendency had been manifested by some previous public or official conduct. In both cases, the conduct is brought forward as evidence of the same fact, his unfitness for the office to which he aspires. But a candidate for office may possess defects of character, which cannot in any way affect the public welfare by influencing or controlling his official conduct, and inasmuch as the privilege is granted, if at all, for the sole purpose of promoting a free discussion of the fitness of the candidate for office, such an object can be attained without opening the floodgates of calumny upon a man, and depriving him of the ordinary protection of the law, because he has presented himself as a candidate for the suffrages of the people. Thus while vulgarity of habits or speech, unchastity, and the like, may be considered great social and moral evils, they can hardly be considered to affect a candidate's fitness for any ordinary office. Integrity, fidelity to trusts, are not incompatible with even libertinism, which is attested by the acts and lives of some of the public men of every country.[1] Whereas dishonesty, in whatever form it may manifest

[1] But the retirement from public life during the present year, of a prominent English statesman on account of his conviction of the act of

§ 17c

itself, blind bigotry, and the like, do enter largely into the composition of one's official capacity, and consequently the discussion of any acts which tend to establish these characteristics would come within the privilege, although these acts may be of a private nature.   But, although it may be justifiable in charging a candidate with vulgarity or unchastity, and the like, if they are true, there is no reason why they should be privileged, because they do not enter into the determination of the candidate's fitness for office, and only raises a question of preference.

Where the party is holding an office instead of being a candidate for office, the only public interest to be subserved in the establishment of a privilege is the faithful performance of his official duty, and where the office is one, the incumbent of which can only be removed for malfeasance in office, only those communications should be held to be privileged, which criticise his public conduct.   If, however, the office is appointive, and the incumbent is removable at the pleasure of the appointive power, the privilege should be as extensive as that which should relate to candidates, as already explained.

The foregoing statement presents what it is conceived should be the law.   An investigation of the authorities, however, reveals a different condition of the law.   The cases which fall under the subject of this section are naturally, as well as by the variance in the authorities, divided into two classes: *First*, where the office is one of appointment, and the criticism is contained in a petition or address to the appointing or removing power ; and, *secondly*, where the office is elective, and the criticisms appear in publications of the press, or are made in speeches at public meetings, and are intended to influence the votes of the electors at large, who will be called upon to pronounce for

adultery, would indicate that public sentiment is changing in this regard, and at no distant day will require that the private character of public men shall be as pure as their public character.

§ 17c

or against the candidate.   In the cases of the first class, it has been very generally held that the communications are privileged as long as they are *bona fide* statements, and the burden of establishing malice in their utterance is thrown upon the plaintiff.   The Supreme Court of New York characterizes a contrary ruling in the court below, as " a decision which violates the most sacred and unquestionable rights of free citizens; rights essential to the very existence of a free government, rights necessarily connected with the relation of constituent and representative, the right of petitioning for a redress of grievances, and the right of remonstrating to the competent authority against the abuse of official functions." [1]   Not only are these petitions privileged when they are presented, but also when they are being circulated for the purpose of procuring signatures. [2]

This privilege is not confined to communications, in the form of petitions, which relate to the incompetency, and call for the removal, of public officials.   It is applied also to similar cases arising in the management and government of other and private bodies, whether incorporated or unincorporated.   Thus all communications to church tribunals in reference to the moral character of its members, both lay and clerical, are protected by this privilege so as not

---

[1] Thorn *v.* Blanchard, 5 Johns. 508.   In Howard *v.* Thompson, 21 Wend. 319, it was held in order that plaintiff may sustain his action in such a case, he must not only prove actual malice, but also show the want of probable cause, the action being considered by the court of the nature of an action for malicious prosecution.   See, generally, in support of the privilege, Bodwell *v* Osgood, 3 Pick. 379 (15 Am. Dec. 228); Bradley *v.* Heath, 12 Pick. 163; Hill *v.* Miles, 9 N. H. 9; State *v.* Burnham, 9 N. H. 34 (31 Am. Dec. 217); Howard *v.* Thompson, 12 Wend. 545; Gray *v.* Pentland, 2 Serg. & R. 23; Van Arnsdale *v.* Laverty, 69 Pa. St. 103; Harris *v.* Huntington, 2 Tyler, 129 (4 Am. Dec. 728); Reid *v.* DeLorme, 2 Brev. 76; Forbes *v.* Johnson, 11 B. Mon. 48; Whitney *v.* Allen, 62 Ill. 472; Larkin *v.* Noonan, 19 Wis. 82.

[2] Vanderzee *v.* McGregory, 12 Wend. 545; Street v. Wood, 15 Barb, 105.

§ 17c

to be actionable, if they were not prompted by malice.[1]
The same privilege protects a communication to the lodge
of some secular organization, preferring charges against a
member.[2] In all these cases the privilege only extends to
the communication or petitions, which are presented to the
body or person, in whom the power of appointment and
removal is vested, and if a petition is prepared, but never
presented to the proper authority, any other publication of
it would not be privileged.[3]

There is apparently no rational difference, so far as the
justification of the privilege is concerned, between those
cases, in which there is a remonstrance or petition to the
body or person having the power of appointment and removal, and the cases of appeal or remonstrance to the general public, pronouncing the candidate for an elective office
unfit for the same, either through incompetency or dishonesty, and one would naturally expect such a privilege.
The electors, and the public generally, are interested in
knowing the character and qualifications of those who apply for their suffrages ; and the public welfare, in that
regard, is best promoted by a full and free discussion of
all those facts and circumstances in the previous life of the
candidate, which are calculated to throw light upon his

---

[1] Kershaw v. Bailey, 1 Exch 743; Farnsworth v. Storrs, 5 Cush. 412;
Remington v. Congdon, 2 Pick. 310; York v Pease, 2 Gray, 282; Fairchild
v. Adams, 11 Cush. 549; Shurtleff v. Stevens, 51 Vt. 501 (31 Am. Rep.
698) ; Haight v. Cornell, 15 Conn. 74; O'Donaghue v. McGovern, 23 Wend.
26; Wyick v. Aspinwall, 17 N. Y. 190; Chapman v. Calder, 14 Pa. St. 365;
McMillan v. Birch, 1 Binn. 178 (2 Am. Dec. 426;) Reid v. DeLorne, 2
Brev. 76; Dunn v. Winters, 2 Humph. 512; Lucas v. Case, 9 Bush, 562;
Dial v. Holter, 6 Ohio St. 228; Kleizer v. Symmes, 40 Ind. 562; Servatius v. Pichel, 34 Wis. 292.

[2] Streety v. Wood, 15 Barb. 105; Kirkpatrick v. Eagle Lodge, 26 Kan.
384. A report by officers of a corporation to a meeting of its stockholders
falls under the same rule. Philadelphia, etc. R. R. Co. v. Quigley, 21
How. 202.

[3] Fairman v. Ives, 5 B. &. Ald. 642; Woodward v. Lander, 6 L. & P.
548; State v. Burnham, 9 N. H. 34; Hosmer v. Loveland, 19 Barb. 111;
Cook v. Hill, 3 Sandf. 341.

§ 17c

fitness for the office for which he applies. Where the statements respect only the mental qualification of the candidate, it has been held that they are privileged. "Talents and qualifications for office are mere matters of opinion, of which the electors are the only competent judges." [1] But where the communication impugns the character of the candidate, it appears that the privilege does not cover the case, and the affirmant makes the statement at his peril, being required by the law to ascertain for himself the truth or falsity of it. And the same rule applies to the deliberations of public meetings, as well as to the statements of an individual. In the leading case on this subject [2] the court say: "That electors should have a right to assemble, and freely and openly to examine the fitness and qualifications of candidates for public offices, and communicate their opinions to others, is a position to which I most cordially accede. But there is a wide difference between this privilege and a right irresponsibly to charge a candidate with direct, specific, and unfounded crimes. It would, in my judgment, be a monstrous doctrine to establish that, when a man becomes a candidate for an elective office, he thereby gives to others a right to accuse him of any imaginable crime with impunity. Candidates have rights as well as electors; and those rights and privileges must be so guarded and protected as to harmonize one with the other. If one hundred or one thousand men, when assembled together, may undertake to charge a man with specific crimes, I see no reason why it should be less criminal than if each one should do it individually at different times and places. All that is required in the one case or

---

[1] Mayrant v. Richardson, 1 Nott & McCord, 348 (9 Am. Dec. 707); Commonwealth v. Clapp, 4 Mass. 163 (3 Am. Dec. 212); Commonwealth v. Morris, 1 Va. Cas. 175 (5 Am. Dec. 515); Sweeney v. Baker, 13 W. Va. 158 (31 Am. Rep. 757); Mott v. Dawson, 46 Iowa, 533. But see Robbins v. Treadway, 2 J. J. Marsh 540 (19 Am. Dec. 152); Spiering v. Andree, 45 Wis. 330 (30 Am. Rep. 744).

[2] Lewis v. Few, 5 Johns. 1, 35.

§ 17c

the other is, not to transcend the bounds of truth. If a man has committed a crime, any one has a right to charge him with it, and is not responsible for the accusation; and can any one wish for more latitude than this? Can it be claimed as a privilege to accuse *ad libitum* a candidate with the most base and detestable crimes? There is nothing upon the record showing the least foundation or pretence for the charges. The accusation, then, being false, the *prima facie* presumption of law is, that the publication was malicious, and the circumstance of the defendant being associated with others does not *per se* rebut this presumption.'' This position of the New York court has not only been sustained by later cases in the same State, but it has been followed generally by the other American courts, and it may be considered as the settled doctrine in this country.[1]

§ 17*d*.   **Publications through the press.** — It has been often urged in favor of the press, that a general and almost unrestricted privilege should be granted the proprietors of newspapers for all statements that might be received and printed in their paper in good faith, which subsequently prove to be false and injurious to some individual, provided it pertain to a matter in which the public may justly be supposed to be interested. This view has of late met with a strong support in Judge Cooley. In criticising an opinion of the New York court to the contrary,[2] he says:

---

[1] See King *v.* Root, 4 Wend. 113 (21 Am. Dec. 102); Powers *v.* Dubois, 17 Wend. 63; Hunt *v.* Bennett, 19 N. Y. 173; Hamilton *v.* Eno, 81 N.Y. 116; Thomas *v.* Crosswell, 7 Johns. 264 (5 Am. Dec. 269); Tillson *v.* Robbins, 68 Me. 295 (28 Am. Rep. 50); Hook *v.* Hackney, 16 Serg. & R. 385; Sweeney *v.* Baker, 13 W. Va., 158 (31 Am. Rep. 757); Foster *v.* Scripps, 39 Mich. 376 (33 Am. Rep. 403); Wilson *v.* Noonan, 35 Wis. 321; Gottbehuet *v.* Hubachek, 36 Wis. 515; Gove *v.* Blethen, 21 Min. 80 (18 Am. Rep 380); Rearick *v.* Wilcox, 81 Ill. 77; Russell *v.* Anthony, 21 Kan. 450 (30 Am. Rep. 436). See Barr *v.* Moore, 87 Pa. St. 385 (30 Am. Rep. 367.)

[2] Hotchkiss *v.* Oliphant, 2 Hill, 510–513, per Nelson, Ch. J.

§ 17*d*

"If this strong condemnatory language were confined to the cases in which private character is dragged before the public for detraction and abuse to pander to a depraved appetite for scandal, its propriety and justice and the force of its reasons would be at once conceded. But a very large proportion of what the newspapers spread before the public relates to matters of public concern, in which, nevertheless, individuals figure, and must, therefore, be mentioned in any account or discussion. To a great extent also, the information comes from abroad; the publisher can have no knowledge concerning it, and no inquiries which he could make would be likely to give him more definite information, unless he delays the publication, until it ceases to be of value to his readers. Whatever view the law may take, the public sentiment does not brand the publisher of news as libeler, conspirator or villain, because the telegraphic dispatches transmitted to him from all parts of the world, without any knowledge on his part concerning the facts, are published in his paper, in reliance upon the prudence, care and honesty of those who have charge of the lines of communication, and whose interest it is to be vigilant and truthful. The public demand and expect accounts of every important meeting, of every important trial, and of all the events which have a bearing upon trade and business, or upon political affairs. It is impossible that these shall be given in all cases without matters being mentioned derogatory to individuals; and if the question were a new one in the law, it might be worthy of inquiry whether some line of distinction could not be drawn which would protect the publisher when giving in good faith such items of news as would be proper, if true, to spread before the public, and which he gives in the regular course of his employment, in pursuance of a public demand, and without any negligence, as they come to him from the usual and legitimate sources, which he has reason to rely upon; at the same time leaving him liable when he makes his columns

§ 17d

the vehicle of private gossip, detraction and malice."[1] We believe that the law should "protect the publisher when giving in good faith such items of news as would be proper, if true, to spread before the public." But the difficulty is experienced in determining what is proper to be published in an ordinary newspaper. It seems to us that, whenever an event occurs in which the public generally is justified in demanding information, the published accounts will be covered by the ordinary privilege, which is granted to the injurious and false statements of private individuals, when they are made to those who have a legitimate interest in the subject-matter.[2] But there is no reason why any special protection should be thrown around the publisher of news. Any such special protection, which cannot in reason be extended to "the village gossiper" would in the main only serve to protect newspaper publishers in the publication of what is strictly private scandal. Except in one large class of cases, in which we think both the press and the individual are entitled to the protection asked for, viz. : in criticisms upon public officials and candidates for office, the general demand of Judge Cooley may be granted, indeed is now granted by the law which denies "that conductors of the public press are entitled to peculiar indulgences and have special rights and privileges."[3] But the

---

[1] Cooley Const. Lim. *454.

[2] See Commonwealth v. Nichols, 10 Met. 259; Mason v. Mason, 4 N. H. 110; Carpenter v. Bailey, 53 N. H. 590; Lewis v. Few, 5 Johns. 1; Andres v. Wells, 7 Johns. 260 (5 Am. Dec. 257); Dale v. Lyon, 10 Johns. 447 (6 Am. Dec. 346); Marten v. Van Shaik, 4 Paige, 479; Sandford v. Bennett, 24 N. Y. 20; Hampton v. Wilson, 4 Dev. 468; Parker v. McQueen, 8 B. Mon. 16; Fowler v. Chichester, 26 Ohio St. 9; Cates v. Kellogg, 9 Ind. 506; Farr v. Rasco, 9 Mich. 353; Wheeler v. Shields, 3 Ill. 348; Cummerford v. McAvoy, 15 Ill. 311; Hawkins v. Lumsden, 10 Wis. 359; Beardsley v. Bridgman, 17 Iowa, 290.

[3] "The law recognizes no such peculiar rights, privileges or claims to indulgence. They have no rights but such as are common to all. They have just the same rights that the rest of the community have and no more. They have the right to publish the truth, but no right to publish

§ 17d

demands of the press extend beyond the limits set down by Judge Cooley. The privilege they ask for is intended to furnish protection for all those thrilling accounts of crime and infamous scandal, the publication of which appears to be required by a depraved public taste, but which the thoughtful citizen would rather suppress than give special protection to the publisher. The only two cases in which a change in the existing law of privilege would perhaps be just and advisable, are, *first*, the public criticism of public officials and political candidates, and, *secondly*, the reports of failures or financial embarrassments of commercial personages. In the second case, the privilege is granted to individuals, and even to those well-known mercantile agencies, when they make private reports to their subscribers of the financial standing of some merchant; [1] but the privilege does not appear to extend to the publication of such items in the newspapers. [2]

---

falsehood to the injury of others with impunity." King *v.* Root, 4 Wend. 113 (21 Am. Dec. 102).

[1] Lewis *v.* Chapman, 16 N. Y. 369; Ormsby *v.* Douglass, 37 N. Y. 477.

[2] Thus, the reports of a mercantile agency, published and distributed among its subscribers, have been held not to be privileged. Taylor *v.* Church, 8 N. Y. 452; Sunderlin *v.* Bradstreet, 46 N. Y. 188 (7 Am. Rep. 322). "It may be assumed that if any one, having an interest in knowing the credit and standing of the plaintiffs, or whom the defendants supposed and believed to have had such interest, had made the inquiry of the defendants, and the statement in the alleged libel had been made in answer to the inquiry in good faith; and upon information upon which the defendants relied, it would have been privileged. This was the case of Ormsby *v.* Douglass, 37 N. Y. 477. The business of the defendant in that case was of a similar character to that of the present defendants; and the statement complained of was made orally, to one interested in the information, upon personal application at the office of the defendant who refused to make a written statement. There was no other publication, and it was held that the occasion justified the defendant in giving such information as he possessed to the applicant.

"In the case at bar, it is not pretended that but few, if any, of the persons to whom the 10,000 copies of the libelous publication were transmitted, had any interest in the character or pecuniary responsibility of the plaintiffs; and to those who had no such interest there was no just

§ 17*d*

The principal inquiry that concerns us in the present connection is, to what extent privileged communications remain
so, when they are published through the public press.   The
privilege does not extend beyond the necessity which justifies its existence.   Thus, for example, the law provides for
the legal counsellor and advocate a complete immunity from
responsibility for anything he says in the conduct of a
cause.   The privilege rests upon the necessity for absolute
freedom of speech, in order to insure the attainment of justice between the parties.   A publication of his speech will
not aid in the furtherance of justice, and hence it is not
privileged.   But the law favors the greatest amount of
publicity in legal proceedings, it being one of the political
tenets prevailing in this country, that such publicity is a
strong guaranty of personal liberty, and furthers materially
the ends of justice.   Hence we find that fair, impartial
accounts of legal proceedings, which are not *ex parte* in
character, are protected and are recognized as justifiable
publications.[1]   The publication is privileged only when it
is made with good motives and for justifiable ends.[2]   Ob-
servations or comments upon the proceedings do not come

occasion or propriety in communicating the information.   The defendants, in making the communication, assumed the legal responsibility
which rests upon all who, without cause, publish defamatory matter of
others, that is, of proving the truth of the publication, or responding in
damages to the injured party.   The communication of the libel, to those
not interested in the information, was officious and unauthorized, and,
therefore, not protected, although made in the belief of its truth, if it
were in point of fact false."   Judge Allen in Sunderlin *v.* Bradstreet,
supra.

[1] Lewis *v.* Levy, E. B. & E. 537; Hoare *v.* Silverlock, 9 C. B. 20;
Torrey *v.* Field, 10 Vt. 353; Stanley *v.* Webb, 4 Sandf. 21; Fawcett *v.*
Charles, 13 Wend. 473; McBee *v.* Fulton, 47 Md. 403 (28 Am. Rep. 465);
Cincinnati Gazette Co. *v.* Timberlake, 10 Ohio St. 548.   The privilege is
also extended to the publication of investigations ordered by Congress.
Terry *v.* Fellows, 21 La. Ann. 375.

[2] Saunders *v.* Baxter, 6 Heisk. 369.

§ 17*d*

within the privilege.[1] Nor, it seems, do the defamatory speeches come within the privilege thus accorded to the publication of legal proceedings.[2] But *ex parte* proceedings, and all preliminary examinations, though judicial in character, do not come within the privilege, and are not protected when published in the newspaper. In one case, the court say: "It is our boast that we are governed by that just and salutary rule upon which security of life and character often depends, that every man is presumed innocent of crimes charged upon him, until he is proved guilty. But the circulation of charges founded on *ex parte* testimony, of statements made, often under excitement, by persons smarting under real or fancied wrongs, may prejudice the public mind, and cause the judgment of conviction to be passed long before the day of trial has arrived. When that day of trial comes, the rule has been reversed, and the presumption of guilt has been substituted for the presumption of innocence. The chances of a fair and impartial trial are diminished. Suppose the charge to be utterly groundless. If every preliminary *ex parte* complaint, which may be made before a police magistrate, may with entire impunity be published and scattered broadcast over the land, then the character of the innocent, who may be the victim of a conspiracy, or of charges proved afterwards to have arisen entirely from misapprehension, may be cloven down without any malice on the part of the publisher. The refutation of slander, in such cases, generally follows its propagation at distant intervals, and brings often but an imperfect balm to wounds which have become festered, and perhaps incurable. It is not to be denied that occasionally

---

[1] Stiles *v.* Nokes, 7 East, 493; Clark *v.* Binney, 2 Pick. 112; Commonwealth *v.* Blanding, 3 Pick. 304 (15 Am. Dec. 214); Pittock *v.* O'Neill, 63 Pa. St. 253 (3 Am. Rep. 544); Scripps *v.* Reilly, 38 Mich. 10; Storey *v.* Wallace, 60 Ill. 51.

[2] Saunders *v.* Mills, 6 Bing. 213; Flint *v.* Pike, 4 B. & C. 473. See Stanley *v.* Webb, 4 Sandf. 21.

§ 17*d*

the publication of such proceedings is productive of good, and promotes the ends of justice. But in such cases, the publisher must find his justification, not in privilege, but in the truth of the charges." [1]

But the English courts have lately shown an inclination to depart from this doctrine, particularly in relation to the publication of police reports. In a late case, [2] Lord Camp-bell indorses and acts upon the following quotation from an opinion of Lord Denman, expressed before a committee of the House of Lords in 1843: " I have no doubt that (police reports) are extremely useful for the detection of guilt by making facts notorious, and for bringing those facts more correctly to the knowledge of all parties in unraveling the truth. The public, I think, are perfectly aware that those proceedings are *ex parte*, and they become more and more aware of it in proportion to their growing intelligence; they know that such proceedings are only in the course of trial, and they do not form their opinions until the trial is had. Perfect publicity in judicial proceedings is of the highest importance in other points of view, but in its effect upon character, I think it desirable. The statement made in open court will probably find its way to the ears of all in whose good opinion the party assailed feels an interest, probably in an exaggerated form, and the imputation may often rest upon the wrong person; both these evils are prevented by correct reports." The publication of police reports, or of any other preliminary proceedings of a judicial nature, will bring the news to the ears of countless numbers of strangers, who, not knowing the party accused, will not likely be prejudiced in his favor, and certainly would not have heard or have taken any interest in the rumor of the man's guilt,

---

[1] Stanley *v.* Webb, 4 Sandf. 21. See Usher *v.* Severance, 21 Me. 9 (37 Am. Dec. 33); Matthews *v.* Beach, 5 Sandf. 259; Cincinnati Gazette Co. *v.* Timberlake, 10 Ohio St. 548; Duncan *v.* Thwaites, 3 B. & C. 556; Charlton *v.* Watton, 6 C. & P. 385.

[2] Lewis *v.* Levy, E. B. & E. 537.

§ 17*d*

but for the publication. The readers of these reports, who are inclined to receive them in the judicial frame of mind, suggested by Lord Denman, are not numerous, and very few will dismiss from their minds all suspicions against the innocence of the accused when there has been a failure to convict him of the charge. Even when there has been a trial of the defendant, and the jury has brought in a verdict of acquittal, the publication of the proceedings is calculated to do harm to the reputation of the defendant. But the public welfare demands the freest publicity in ordinary legal proceedings, and the interest of the individual must here give way. On the other hand, there is no great need for the publication of the preliminary examinations. In only a few cases can the publication prove of any benefit to the public. The public demand being small, the sacrifice of private interest is not justified.

Not only is the publication of the proceedings of a court of law privileged ; but the privilege extends to the publication in professional and religious journals of proceedings had before some judicial body or council, connected with the professional or religious organization, which the publishing paper represents.[1] And so likewise would be privileged the publication of legislative proceedings, and the proceedings of congressional and legislative investigating committees.[2]

Section 18. Security to reputation — Malicious prosecution.
    18a. Advice of counsel, how far a defense.

§ 18 **Security to reputation — Malicious prosecution**— Although a prosecution on the charge of some crime may result in a verdict of acquittal, even where the trial would furnish to a judicial mind a complete vindication, by remov-

[1] Burrows, *v.* Bell, 7 Gray, 301 ; Shurtleff *v.* Stevens, 51 Vt. 501 (31 Am. Rep. 698).
[2] Terry *v.* Fellows, 21 La. Ann. 375.

§ 18

ing all doubts of the innocence of the accused, it will nevertheless leave its mark upon the reputation. Even a groundless accusation will soil one's reputation. But it is to the interest of the public, as well as it is the right of the individual, that resort should be made to the courts. for redress of what one conceives to be a wrong. While a litigious spirit is to be deprecated, since in the institution of legal order the right to self-defense is taken away, except as an immediate preventive of attacks upon person and property, it is not only expedient but just, that when a man believing that he has a just claim against the defendant, or that this person has committed some act which subjects him to a criminal prosecution, sets the machinery of the law in motion, he should not be held responsible for any damage that might be done to the person prosecuted, in the event of his acquittal. The good faith of the prosecutor should shield him from liability. Any other rule would operate to discourage to a dangerous degree the prosecution of law-breakers, and hence it has been recognized as a wise limitation upon the right of security to reputation. But the interests of the public do not require an absolute license in the institution of groundless prosecutions. The protection of privilege is thrown around only those who in good faith commence the prosecution for the purpose of securing a vindication of the law, which they believe to have been violated. Hence we find that the privilege is limited, and, as it is succinctly stated by the authorities, in order that an action for malicious prosecution, in which the prosecutor may be made to suffer in damages, may be sustained, three things must concur: there must be an acquittal of the alleged criminal, the suit must have been instituted without probable cause, and prompted by malice.

A final acquittal is necessary, because a conviction would be conclusive of his guilt. And even where he is convicted in the court below, and a new trial is ordered by the superior court for error, the conviction is held to be conclus-

§ 18

ive proof of the existence of probable cause.[1] But an acquittal, on the other hand, does not prove the want of probable cause, does not even raise the *prima facie* presumption of a want of probable cause. Probable cause, as defined by the Supreme Court of the United States, is " the existence of such facts and circumstances as would excite belief in a reasonable mind, acting on the facts within the knowledge of the prosecutor, that the person charged was guilty of the crime, for which he was prosecuted."[2]

The want of probable cause cannot be inferred ; it must be proven affirmatively and independently of the presence of actual malice. The plainest proof of actual malice will not support an action for malicious prosecution, if there be probable cause. With probable cause, the right to institute the prosecution is absolute, and the element of malice does not affect it.[3] But when it has been shown that the defendant in the prosecution has been acquitted and that the suit had been instituted without probable cause, the malice need not be directly and affirmatively proved. It may be inferred from the want of probable cause. The want of probable cause raises the *prima facie* presumption of malice, and

---

[1] Witham *v.* Gowen, 14 Me. 362; Payson *v.* Caswell, 22 Me. 212; Whitney *v.* Peckham, 15 Mass. 242; Bacon *v.* Towne, 4 Cush. 217; Kirpatrick *v.* Kirkpatrick, 39 Pa. St. 288; Griffs *v.* Sellars, 4 Dev. & Bat. 176.

[2] Wheeler *v.* Nesbit, 24 How. (U. S.) 545. See Gee *v.* Patterson, 63 Me. 49; Barron *v.* Mason, 31 Vt. 189; Mowry *v.* Whipple, 8 R. I. 360; Stone *v.* Stevens, 12 Conn. 219; Carl *v.* Ayres, 53 N. Y. 13; Farnam *v.* Feeley, 55 N. Y. 551; Fagnan *v.* Knox, 65 N. Y. 525; Winebiddle *v.* Porterfield, 9 Pa. St. 137; Boyd *v.* Cross, 35 Md. 194; Spengle *v.* Davy, 15 Gratt. 381; Braveboy *v.* Cockfield, 2 McMul. 270; Raulston *v.* Jackson, 1 Sneed, 128; Faris *v.* Starke, 3 B. Mon. 4; Collins *v.* Hayte, 50 Ill. 353; Gallaway *v.* Burr, 32 Mich. 332; Lawrence *v.* Lanning, 4 Ind. 194; Shaul *v.* Brown, 28 Iowa, 57 (4 Am. Rep. 151) ; Bauer *v.* Clay, 8 Kan. 580.

[3] Williams *v.* Taylor, 6 Bing. 183; Cloon *v* Gerry, 13 Gray 201 ; Heyne *v.* Blair, 62 N. Y. 19; Travis *v.* Smith, 1 Pa. St. 234; Bell *v.* Pearcy, 5 Ired. 83; Hall *v.* Hawkins, 5 Humph. 357; Israel *v.* Brooks, 23 Ill. 575; King *v.* Ward, 77 Ill. 603; Mitchinson *v.* Cross, 58 Ill. 366; Callahan *v.* Caffarati, 39 Mo. 136; Sappington v. Watson, 50 Mo. 83; Malone *v.* Murphy, 2 Kan. 250.

§ 18

throws upon the prosecutor the burden of proving that he was not actuated by malice in the commencment of the prosecution.[1] But this presumption may be rebutted by the presentation of facts, which indicate that the prosecutor was actuated solely by the laudable motives of bringing to justice one whom he considers a criminal. The want of probable cause is not inconsistent with perfect good faith. The prosecutor may have been honestly mistaken in the strength of his case. But when a man is about to institute a proceeding which will do irreparable damage to a neighbor's reputation, however it may terminate, it is but natural that he should be required to exercise all reasonable care in ascertaining the legal guilt of the accused. As it was expressed in one case:[2] "Every man of common information is presumed to know that it is not safe in matters of importance to trust to the legal opinion of any but recognized lawyers; and no matter is of more legal importance than private reputation and liberty. When a person resorts to the best means in his power for information, it will be such a proof of honesty as will disprove malice and operate as a defense proportionate to his diligence." In order, therefore, that the prosecutor may, where a want of probable cause has been established against him, claim to have acted in good faith and thus screen himself from liability, he must show that he consulted competent legal counsel, and that the prosecution was instituted in reliance upon the opinion of counsel that he had a good cause of action.

[1] Merriam v. Mitchell, 13 Me. 439; Mowry v. Whipple, 8 R. I. 360; Closson v. Staples; 42 Vt. 209; Pangburn v. Bull, 1 Wend. 345; McKewn v. Hunter, 30 N. Y. 624; Dietz v. Langfitt, 63 Pa. St. 234; Cooper v. Utterbach, 37 Md. 282; Flickinger v. Wagner, 46 Md. 581; Ewing v. Sanford, 19 Ala. 605; Blass v. Gregor, 15 La. Ann. 421; White v. Tucker, 16 Ohio St. 468; Ammerman v. Crosby, 26 Ind. 451; Harpham v. Whitney, 77 Ill. 32; Holliday v. Sterling, 62 Mo. 321; Harkrader v. Moore, 44 Cal. 144.
[2] Campbell, J. in Stanton v. Hart, 27 Mich. 539.

§ 18

§ 18a. **Advice of counsel, how far a defense.**— It is remarkable with what uncertainty the books speak of the manner, in which the advice of counsel constitutes a defense to the action for malicious prosecution. Some of the cases hold that it is proof of probable cause ;[1] some maintain that it disproves malice, in most cases imposing no limitation upon its scope,[2] while others, and it is believed the majority of cases, refer to it as establishing both the absence of malice and the presence of a probable cause.[3] If the position of these courts is correct, which hold that the advice of counsel establishes the existence of probable cause, then the advice of counsel will constitute an absolute bar to all actions for malicious prosecution, whenever there has been a

[1] See Olmstead v. Partridge, 16 Gray, 383; Besson v. Southard, 10 N. Y. 237; Laughlin v. Clawson, 27 Pa. St. 330; Fisher v. Forrester, 33 Pa. St. 501; Ross v. Innis, 26 Ill. 259; Potter v. Sealey, 8 Cal. 217; Levy v. Brannan, 39 Cal. 485. Mr. Cooley, in his work on Torts, p. 183, says: "A prudent man is, therefore, expected to take such advice (of counsel), and when he does so, and places all the facts before his counsel, and acts upon his opinion, proof of the fact *makes out a case of probable cause,* provided the disclosure appears to have been full and fair, and not to have withheld any of the material facts."

[2] Snow v. Allen, 1 Stark. 409; Sommer v. Wilt, 4 Serg. & R. 20; Davenport v. Lynch, 6 Jones L. 545; Stanton v. Hart, 27 Mich. 539; Murphy v. Larson, 77 Ill. 172; Williams v. Van Meter, 8 Mo. 339; Center v. Spring, 2 Clarke, 393; Rover v. Webster, 3 Clarke, 502.

[3] See Soule v. Winslow, 66 Me. 447; Bartlett v. Brown, 6 R. I. 37; Ames v. Rathbun, 55 Barb. 194; Walter v. Sample, 25 Pa. St. 275; Turner v. Walker, 3 G. & J. 380; Gould v. Gardner, 8 La. Ann. 11; Phillips v. Bonham, 16 La. Ann. 387; Lemay v. Williams, 32 Ark. 166; Wood v. Weir, 5 B. Mon. 544; Wicker v. Hotchkiss, 62 Ill. 107; Davie v. Wisher, 72 Ill. 262; Wilkinson v. Arnold, 13 Ind. 45; Bliss v. Wyman, 7 Cal. 257. In the case of Blunt v. Little, 3 Mason, 102, Mr. Justice Story said: "It is certainly going a great way to admit the evidence of any counsel that he advised a suit upon a deliberate examination of the facts, for the purpose of *repelling the imputation of malice and establishing probable cause.* My opinion, however, is that such evidence is admissible." So, also, in Walter v. Sample, 25 Pa. St. 275, we find the law stated thus: "Professors of the law are the proper advisers of men in doubtful circumstances, and their advice, when fairly obtained, exempts the party who acts upon it from the imputation of *proceeding maliciously* and without *probable cause.*

§ 18a

full and fair disclosure of all the facts within the knowledge of the prosecutor; and the proof of actual malice as the cause of the prosecution will not render him liable, not even where the procurement of professional opínion was to furnish a cloak for his malice, or as a matter of precaution, to learn whether it was safe to commence proceedings. But probable cause does not rest upon the sincerity of the prosecutor's belief, nor upon its reasonableness, as shown by facts which are calculated to influence his judgment peculiarly, and not the judgment of others. It must be established by facts, which are likely to induce *any* reasonable man to believe that the accused is guilty. If probable cause depends upon the honest reasonable belief of the prosecutor in the guilt of the accused, it is certainly based upon reasonable grounds, if his legal adviser tells him that he has a good cause of action. But his belief does not enter into the determination of the question of probable cause. Although his honest belief in the guilt of the accused is necessary to shield him from a judgment for malicious prosecution, it is not because such belief is necessary to establish probable cause, but because its absence proves that the prosecution was instituted for the gratification of his malice. The opinion of counsel can not supplant the judgment of the court as to what is probable cause, and such would be the effect of the rule, that the advice of counsel establishes probable cause. As Mr. Justice Story said: "What constitutes a probable cause of action is, when the facts are given, matter of law upon which the court is to decide; and it can not be proper to introduce certificates of counsel to establish what the law is."[1]

The better opinion, therefore, is that the advice of counsel only furnishes evidence of his good motives, in rebuttal to the inference of malice from the want of probable cause. It does not constitute a conclusive presumption of good

[1] Blunt *v.* Little, 3 Mason, 102.
§ 18*a*

faith on the part of the prosecutor. If, therefore, there are facts, which establish the existence of malice, and show that the procurement of professional opinion was to cloak his malice, or as a matter of precaution to learn whether it was safe to commence proceedings, the defense will not prevail, and the prosecutor will, notwithstanding, be held liable.[1]

[1] Burnap v. Albert, Taney, 344; Ames v. Rathbun, 55 Barb. 194; Kimball v. Bates, 50 Me. 308; Brown v. Randall, 36 Conn. 56; Prough v. Entriken, 11 Pa. St. 81; Fisher v. Forrester, 33 Pa. St. 501; Schmidt v. Weidman, 63 Pa. St. 173; Davenport v. Lynch, 6 Jones L. 545; Glascock v. Bridges, 15 La. Ann. 672; King v. Ward, 77 Ill. 603; Rover v. Webster, 3 Clarke, 502; Chapman v. Dodd, 10 Minn. 350. In Snow v. Allen, 1 Stark. 409, one of the earliest cases in which the advice of counsel was set up as a defense, Lord Ellenborough inquired: "How can it be contended here that the defendant acted maliciously? He acted ignorantly. * * * He was acting under what he thought was good advice, it was unfortunate that his attorney was mislead by Higgin's Case (Cro. Jac. 320); but unless you can show that the defendant was actuated by some purposed malice, the plaintiff can not recover." In Sharpe v. Johnstone (59 Mo. 577; s. c. 76 Mo. 660), Judge Hough said (76 Mo.) 674: "Although defendants may have communicated to counsel learned in the law, all the facts and circumstances bearing upon the guilt or innocence of the plaintiff, which they knew or by any reasonable diligence could have ascertained, yet, if, notwithstanding the advice of counsel, they believed that the prosecution would fail, and they were actuated in commencing said prosecution, not simply by angry passions or hostile feelings, but by a desire to injure and wrong the plaintiff, then most certainly they could not be said to have consulted counsel in good faith, and the jury would have been warranted in finding that the prosecution was malicious." See the annotation of the author to Sharpe v. Johnstone, in 21 Am. Law. Reg. (N. S.) 582.

§ 18a

CHAPTER III.

PERSONAL LIBERTY.

§ 30. Personal liberty — How guaranteed. — It is altogether needless in this connection to indulge in a panegyric upon the blessings of guaranteed personal liberty. The love of liberty, of freedom from irksome and unlawful restraints, is implanted in every human breast. In the American Declaration of Independence, and in the bills of rights of almost every State constitution, we find that personal liberty is expressly guaranteed to all men equally. But notwithstanding the existence of these fundamental and constitutional guaranties of personal liberty, the astounding anomaly of the slavery of an entire race in more than one-third of the States of the American Union, during three-fourths of a century of national existence, gave the lie to their own constitutional declarations, that " *all* men are endowed by their Creator, with certain alienable rights, among which are the right to life, liberty, and the pursuit of happiness." But, happily, this contradiction is now a thing of the past, and in accordance with the provisions of the thirteenth amendment to the constitution of the United States, it is now the fundamental and practically unchangeable law of the land, that " neither slavery nor involuntary servitude, except as a punishment for crime whereof the party shall have been duly convicted, shall exist within the United States, or any place subject to their jurisdiction.[1]

But to a practical understanding of the effect of these constitutional guaranties, a clear idea of what personal liberty consists is necessary. It is not to be confounded with a license to do what one pleases. Liberty, according

---

[1] U. S. Const. Amend., art. XIII.

§ 30 (66)

to Montesquieu, consists " only in the power of doing what
we ought to will, and in not being constrained to do what
we ought not to will." No man has a right to make such
a use of his liberty as to commit an injury to the rights of
others. His liberty is controlled by the oft quoted maxim,
sic utere tuo, ut alienum non lædas. Indeed liberty is that
amount of personal freedom, which is consistent with a
strict obedience to this rule. " Liberty," in the words of
Mr. Webster, " is the creature of law, essentially different
from that authorized licentiousness that trespasses on right.
It is a legal and refined idea, the offspring of high civilization, which the savage never understood, and never can
understand. Liberty exists in proportion to wholesome
restraint; the more restraint on others to keep off from us,
the more liberty we have. It is an error to suppose that
liberty consists in a paucity of laws. If one wants few
laws, let him go to Turkey. The Turk enjoys that blessing.
The working of our complex system, full of checks on legislative, executive and judicial power, is favorable to liberty
and justice. Those checks and restraints are so many
safeguards set around individual rights and interests.
That man is free who is protected from injury." [1] While
liberty does not consist in a paucity of laws, still it is only
consistent with a limitation of the restrictive laws to those
which exercise a wholesome restraint. " That man is free
who is protected from injury," and his protection involves
necessarily the restraint of other individuals from the commission of the injury. In the proper balancing of the contending interests of individuals, personal liberty is secured
and developed ; any further restraint is unwholesome and
subversive of liberty. As Herbert Spencer has expressed
it, " every man may claim the fullest liberty to exercise
his faculties compatible with the possession of like liberty
by every other man." [2]

[1] Webster's Works, vol. II., p. 393.
[2] Social Statics, p. 94.

§ 30

The constitutional guaranties are generally unqualified, and a strict construction of them would prohibit all limitations upon liberty, if any other meaning but the limited one here presented were given to the word. But these guaranties are to be liberally construed, so that the object of them may be fully attained. They do not prohibit the exercise of police power in restraint of licentious trespass upon the rights of others, but the restrictive measures must be kept within these limits. " Powers, which can be justified only on this specific ground (that they are police regulations), and which would otherwise be clearly prohibited by the constitution, can be such only as are so clearly necessary to the safety, comfort and well-being of society, or so imperatively required by the public necessity, as to lead to the rational and satisfactory conclusion that the framers of the constitution could not, as men of ordinary prudence and foresight have intended, to prohibit their exercise in the particular case, notwithstanding the language of the prohibition would otherwise include it." [1]

The restrictions upon personal liberty, permissible under these constitutional limitations, are either of a public or private nature. In consequence of the mental and physical disabilities of certain classes, in the law of domestic relations, their liberty is more or less subjected to restraint, the motive being their own benefit. These restraints are of a private nature, imposed under the law by private persons who stand in domestic relation to those whose liberty is restrained. This subject will be discussed in a subsequent connection. [2] In this connection we are only concerned with those restraints which are of a public nature, i.e., those which are imposed by government. They may be subdivided under the following headings: 1. The police

---

[1] Christiancy, J., in People v. Jackson & Mich. Plank Road Co., 9 Mich. 285.

[2] See *post*, ch. 12, 13, 14, and §§ 149-178.

§ 30

control of the criminal classes. 2. The police control of dangerous classes, other than by criminal prosecutions. 3. The regulation of domicile and citizenship. 4. Police control of morality and religion. 5. Police regulation of the freedom of speech and of the press. 6. Police regulation of trades and professions.

§ 30

CHAPTER IV.

POLICE CONTROL OF CRIMINAL CLASSES.

SECTION 31. The effect of crime on the rights of the criminal.
 31a. Due process of law.
 31b. Bills of attainder.
 31c. *Ex post facto law.*
 32. Preliminary confinement to answer for a crime.
 33. What constitutes a lawful arrest.
 33a. Arrest without warrant.
 34. The trial of the accused.
 34a. The trial must be speedy.
 34b. The trial must be public.
 34c. Accused entitled to counsel.
 34d. Indictment by grand jury or by information.
 34e. The plea of defendant.
 34f. Trial by jury — Legal jeopardy.
 35. Control over criminals in the penitentiary.
 35a. Convict lease system.

§ **31. The effect of crime on the rights of the criminal.** — The commission of crime, in the discretion of the government, subjects all rights of the criminal to the possibility of forfeiture. Life, liberty, political rights, statutory rights, relative rights, all or any of them may be forfeited by the State, in punishment of a crime. When a man commits a crime he forfeits to a greater or less extent his right of immunity from harm. The forfeiture for crime is usually confined to life, liberty and property, and political rights, although all rights in the wisdom of the legislature may be subjected to forfeiture, and the forfeiture of liberty is the most common.

§ **31a. Due process of law.** — But the forfeiture of rights is limited and controlled by constitutional restrictions, and it

§ 31a   (70)

may be stated as a general proposition, that such a forfeiture, as a punishment for crime, can only be effected after a judicial examination and a conviction of the crime charged. In the Magna Charta, in the charter of Henry III., in the Petition of Right, in the Bill of Rights, in England, and in this country in all the constitutions, both State and national, it is substantially provided that no man shall be deprived of his life, liberty, or property, unless by the judgment of his peers or the law of the land. In some State constitutions, the clause "without due process of law" is employed in the place of " the judgment of his peers or the law of the land;" but the practical effect is the same in all cases, whatever may be the exact phraseology of this constitutional provision.[1] Perhaps the scope of the limitation cannot be better explained than by the words of Mr. Webster: " By the law of the land is most clearly intended the general law; a law which hears before it condemns; which proceeds upon inquiry, and renders judgment only after trial. The meaning is that every citizen shall hold his life, liberty, property and immunities under the protection of the general rules which govern society. Everything which may pass under the form of an enactment is not therefore to be considered the law of the land. If this were so, acts of attainder, bills of pains and penalties, acts of confiscation, acts reversing judgments, and acts directly transferring one man's estate to another, legislative judgments, decrees and forfeitures in all possible forms, would be the law of the land. Such a strange construction would render constitutional provisions of the highest importance completely inoperative and void. It would tend directly to establish the union of all powers in the legislature. There would be no general permanent law for courts to administer or men to live under. The administration of justice would be an empty form, an idle ceremony. Judges would sit to exe-

---

[1] Cooley Const. Lim. *352, *353.

§ 31a

cute legislative judgments and decrees, not to declare the law or administer the justice of the country." [1]

§ 31*b*. **Bills of attainder.** — A further limitation is imposed by the constitution of the United States, which prohibits the enactment of *bills of attainder* by Congress and by the legislatures of the several States.[2] A bill of attainder is a legislative conviction for crime, operating against a particular individual, or some one or more classes of individuals. According to the ancient English meaning of the term, it included only those legislative enactments, which pronounced the judgment of death. But a broader signification is given to the word in this constitutional limitation, and it includes all attempts on the part of Congress to inflict punishment and penalties upon individuals for alleged crimes of every description. The term *bill of attainder* is now used to include all bills of pains and penalties. " I think it will be found that the following comprise those essential elements of bills of attainder, in addition to the one already mentioned (which was that certain persons were declared attainted and their inheritable blood corrupted), which distinguish them from other legislation, and which made them so obnoxious to the statesmen who organized our government: 1. They were convictions and sentences pronounced by the legislative department of the government, instead of the judicial. 2. The sentence pronounced and the punishment inflicted were determined by no previous law or fixed rule. The investigation into the guilt of the accused, if any such were made, was not necessarily or generally conducted in his presence or that of his counsel, and no recognized rule of evidence governed the inquiry." [3]

---

[1] Dartmouth College Case, 4 Wheat. 519; Webster's Works, vol. V., p. 487. For a full and exhaustive discussion and treatment of this constitutional limitation, see Cooley Const. Lim. *351-*413.

[2] U. S. Const., art. I., §§ 9, 10.

[3] Miller, J., in Ex parte Garland, 4 Wall. 333.

§ 31*b*

Since the formation of the Union, there has happily been but one occasion when there was any inducement to the enactment of such legislative judgments and convictions, and that was at the close of the late civil war. Congress provided by statute that in order that one may enter upon the performance of the duties of any office of trust or profit under the government of the United States, excepting the President of the United States, he shall theretofore take and subscribe an oath that he had not aided or given countenance to the rebellion against the United States. A second act was passed, prescribing a similar oath to be taken by candidates for admission to practice in any of the courts of the United States. The Supreme Court held that the latter statute was void, because it offended this constitutional provision, prohibiting the enactment of bills of attainder.[1] Inasmuch as the right to hold a public office is a privilege and not a right, the former act of Congress, which provided the so called " iron-clad " oath of office, would not be unconstitutional, unless the qualifications of the candidates for office, to which the statute applied, are stipulated in the constitution. Congress, or a legislature, has no power to change the qualifications for office, where they have already been determined by the constitution.[2] It is, probably, for this reason that the office of President was excluded from the operation of this statute. In article I., section 1, of the constitution of the United States, the oath of office is prescribed which the President is required to take before entering upon the duties of his office.

Similar legislation was enacted in some of the States. In Missouri, the constitution of '65 contained a clause, which required a similar oath to be taken by all voters, officers of State, county, town, or city, to be elected or already elected ; attorneys at law, in order to practice law ; clergymen, in order to teach, and preach or solemnize mar-

[1] Ex parte Garland, 4 Wall. 333; Drehman v. Stifle, 8 Wall. 595.
[2] See Cooley Const. Lim. *64, note.

§ 31b

riages; professors and teachers of educational institutions, etc. Although the State court, as it was then constituted, did not hesitate to pronounce these provisions valid, the Supreme Court of the United States has declared them void as being in violation of the national constitution, which prohibits the enactment of bills of attainder by the States.[1]

§ 31c. **Ex post facto laws.**— Another constitutional provision, intended to furnish to individual liberty ample protection against the exercise of arbitrary power, prohibits the enactment of *ex post facto* laws by Congress as well as by the State legislatures.[2] The literal meaning of the prohibition is that no law can be passed which will apply to and change the legal character of an act already done. But at a very early day in the history of the Constitution, the clause was given a more technical and narrow construction, which has ever since limited the application of the provision. In the leading case,[3] Judge Chase explains the meaning of the term *ex post facto* in the following language: " The prohibition in the letter is not to pass any law concerning or after the fact ; but the plain and obvious meaning

---

[1] Cummings *v.* Missouri, 4 Wall. 277; *s. c.* State *v.* Cummings, 36 Mo. 263. The constitutional provision was likewise upheld in the following cases: State *v.* Garesche, 36 Mo. 256, in its application to an attorney; State *v.* Bernoudy, 36 Mo. 279, in the case of the recorder of St. Louis. In State *v.* Adams, 44 Mo. 570, after the Cummings Case had been decided by the Supreme Court of the United States against the State, and after also a change in the *personnel* of the State court, a legislative act, which declared the Board of Curators of St. Charles College deprived of their office, for failure to take the oath of loyalty, was held to be void as being a bill of attainder. A statute of this kind was likewise passed by the legislature of West Virginia, and although sustained at first by the Supreme Court of the State (Beirne *v.* Brown, 4 W. Va. 72; Pierce *v.* Karskadon, 4 W. Va. 234), it was subsequently held by the Supreme Court of the State, and of the United States, that the act was unconstitutional. Kyle *v.* Jenkins, 6 W. Va. 371; Lynch *v.* Hoffman, 7 W. Va. 553; Pearce *v.* Karskadon, 16 Wall. 234.

[2] U. S. Const., art. I., §§ 9 and 10.

[3] Calder *v.* Bull, 3 Dall. 386, 390.

§ 31c

and intention of the prohibition is this: that the legislatures
of the several States shall not pass laws after a fact done by
a subject or citizen, which shall have relation to such fact,
and punish him for having done it. The prohibition, considered in this light, is an additional bulwark in favor of the
personal security of the subject, to protect his person from
punishment by legislative acts having a retrospective operation. I do not think it was inserted to secure the citizen in
his private rights of either property or contracts. The prohibitions not to make anything but gold and silver a tender
in payment of debts, and not to pass any law impairing the
obligation of contracts, were inserted to secure private
rights; but the restriction not to pass any *ex post facto* law
was to secure the person of the subject from injury or punishment, in consequence of such law. If the prohibition
against making *ex post facto* laws was intended to secure
personal rights from being affected or injured by such laws,
and the prohibition is sufficiently extensive for that object,
the other restraints I have enumerated were unnecessary,
and therefore improper, for both of them are retrospective.

" I will state what laws I consider *ex post facto* laws,
within the words and the intent of the prohibition. 1st.
Every law that makes an action, done before the passing of
the law, and which was innocent when done, criminal, and
punishes such action. 2d. Every law that aggravates a
crime, or makes it greater than it was when committed.
3d. Every law that changes the punishment, and inflicts a
greater punishment than the law annexed to the crime when
committed. 4th. Every law that alters the legal rules of
evidence, and receives less or different testimony than the
law required at the time of the commission of the offense,
in order to convict the offender. All these and similar
laws are manifestly unjust and oppressive. In my opinion,
the true distinction is between *ex post facto* laws and retrospective laws. Every *ex post facto* law must necessarily be
retrospective, but every retrospective law is not an *ex post*

§ 31c

facto law ; the former only are prohibited. Every law that takes away or impairs rights vested, agreeably to existing laws, is retrospective, and is generally unjust, and may be oppressive ; and there ·is a good general rule, that a law should have no retrospect ; but there are cases in which laws may justly, and for the benefit of the community, and also of individuals, relate to a time antecedent to their commencement; as statutes of oblivion or of pardon. They are certainly retrospective, and literally both concerning and after the facts committed. But I do not consider any law *ex post facto*, within the prohibition that mollifies the rigor of the criminal law; but only those that create or aggravate the crime, or increase the punishment, or change the rules of evidence for the purpose of conviction. Every law that is to have an operation before the making thereof, as to commence at an antecedent time, or to save time from the statute of limitations, or to excuse acts which were unlawful, and before committed, and the like, is retrospective. But such laws may be proper or necessary, as the case may be. There is a great and apparent difference between making an unlawful act lawful, and the making an innocent action criminal, and punishing it as a crime. The expressions *ex post facto* are technical ; they had been in use long before the revolution, and had acquired an appropriate meaning by legislators, lawyers, and authors." [1] It is not difficult to understand the scope of the constitutional pro-

---

[1] See Fletcher *v.* Peck, 6 Cranch, 87; Ogden *v.* Saunders, 12 Wheat. 213; Satterlee *v.* Matthewson, 2 Pet. 380; Watson *v.* Mercer, 8 Pet. 88; Charles River Bridge *v.* Warren Bridge, 11 Pet. 420; Carpenter *v.* Pennsylvania, 17 How. 456; Hopt *v.* Utah, 110 U. S. 574; Lock *v.* Dane, 9 Mass. 360; Woart *v.* Winnick, 3 N. H. 473; Dash *v.* Van Kleek, 7 Johns. 477; Moore *v.* State, 43 N. J. 203; Perry's Case, 3 Gratt. 632; Evans *v.* Montgomery, 4 Watts & S. 218; Huber *v.* Reilly, 53 Pa. St. 115. But a retrospective law will be *ex post facto*, notwithstanding it does not provide for a criminal prosecution. The exaction of any penalty for the doing of an act, which before the law was altogether lawful, makes the law *ex post facto*. Falconer *v.* Campbell, 2 McLean, 195; Wilson *v.* Ohio, etc., R. R. Co., 64 Ill. 542.

§ 31c

tection against *ex post facto* laws, except as to those cases, in which it is held that when a less punishment is inflicted, the law is not *ex post facto*. The difficulty in these cases is a practical one, arising from an uncertainty concerning the relative grievousness and weight of different kinds of punishment. That a law is constitutional, which mitigates the punishment of crimes already committed, cannot be doubted.[1] But all punishments are degrading, and in no case of an actual change of punishment, as for example, from imprisonment to whipping, or *vice versa*, can the court with certainty say that the change works a mitigation of the punishment. But while the courts of many of the States have undertaken to decide this question of fact,[2] the New York Court of Appeals has held that " a law changing the punishment for offenses committed before its passage is *ex post facto* and void, under the constitution, unless the change consists in the remission of some separable part of the punishment before prescribed, or is referable to prison discipline or penal administration, as its primary object." [3]

---

[1] Woart *v.* Winnick, 3 N. H. 179; State *v.* Arlin, 39 N. H. 179; Hartung *v.* People, 22 N. Y. 95, 105; Shepherd *v.* People, 25 N. Y. 124; State *v.* Wiliams, 2 Rich. 418; Boston *v.* Cummings, 16 Ga. 102; Strong *v.* State, 1 Blackf. 193; Clarke *v.* State, 23 Miss. 261; Maul *v.* State, 25 Tex. 166; Turner *v.* State, 40 Ala. 21.

[2] See State *v.* Arlin, 39 N. H. 179; State *v.* Williams, 2 Rich. 418; Strong *v.* State, 1 Blackf. 193; Herber *v.* State, 7 Tex. 69.

[3] Davies, J., in Ratzky *v.* People, 29 N. Y. 124. See Shepherd *v.* People, 25 N. Y. 406. " In my opinion," says Denio, J., in Hartung *v.* People, 22 N. Y. 95, 105, " it would be perfectly competent for the legislature, by a general law, to remit any separable portion of the prescribed punishment. For instance, if the punishment were fine and imprisonment, a law which should dispense with either the fine or the imprisonment might, I think, be lawfully applied to existing offenses; and so, in my opinion, the term of imprisonment might be reduced, or the number of stripes diminished, in cases punishable in that manner. Anything which, if applied to an individual sentence, would fairly fall within the idea of a remission of a part of the sentence, would not be liable to objection. And any change which should be referable to prison discipline or penal administration, as its primary object, might also be made to take effect upon past as well as future offenses; as changes in the manner or

§ 31c

Except in regard to the material changes in the rules of evidence which tend to make conviction easier, laws for the regulation of criminal procedure are always subject to repeal or amendment, and the new law will govern all prosecutions that are begun or are in progress after its enactment, it matters not when the offenses were committed. Such a law is not deemed an *ex post facto* law when applied

kind of employment of convicts sentenced to hard labor, the system of supervision, the means of restraint, or the like. Changes of this sort might operate to increase or mitigate the severity of the punishment of the convict, but would not raise any question under the constitutional provision we are considering. The change wrought by the act of 1860, in the punishment of the existing offenses of murder, does not fall within either of these exceptions. If it is to be construed to vest in the governor a discretion to determine whether the convict should be executed or remain a perpetual prisoner at hard labor, this would only be equivalent to what he might do under the authority to commute a sentence. But he can, under the constitution, only do this once for all. If he refuses the pardon, the convict is executed according to the sentence. If he grants it, his jurisdiction of the case ends. The act in question places the convict at the mercy of the governor in office at the expiration of one year from the time of the conviction, and of all of his successors during the lifetime of the convict. He may be ordered to execution at any time, upon any notice, or without notice. Under one of the repealed sections of the Revised Statutes, it was required that a period should intervene between the sentence and the execution of not less than four, nor more than eight weeks. If we stop here, the change effected by the statute is between an execution within a limited time, to be prescribed by the court, or a pardon or commutation during that period, on the one hand, and the placing the convict at the mercy of the executive magistrate for the time, and his successors, to be executed at his pleasure at any time after one year, on the other. The sword is indefinitely suspended over his head, ready to fall at any time. It is not enough to say, if ever that can be said, that most persons would probably prefer such a fate to the former capital sentence. It is enough to bring the law within the condemnation of the constitution, that it changes the punishment after the commission of the offense, by substituting for the prescribed penalty a different one. We have no means of saying whether one or the other would be the most severe in a given case. That would depend upon the disposition and temperament of the convict. The legislature can not thus experiment upon the criminal law. The law, moreover, prescribes one year's imprisonment, at hard labor in the State prison, in addition to the punishment of death. In every case of the execution of a capital sen-

§ 31c

to the prosecution of offenses commited before the change in the law.[1]

§ 32. **Preliminary confinement to answer for a crime.**— It is the benign principle of every system of jurisprudence that one is presumed to be innocent of all criminal accusations, until he is proven to be guilty, and that presumption is so strong that the burden is thrown upon the prosecution of proving the guilt beyond the shadow of a doubt, in order to secure a conviction. But, notwithstanding this general presumption of innocence, the successful prosecution and punishment of crimes require that the necessary precautions be taken to secure the presence of the accused during the trial and afterwards, in case of conviction, and the fear of a default in attendance becomes greater in proportion as the likelihood of conviction increases. In order, therefore, that the laws may be enforced, and the guilty be brought to trial and punishment, it is necessary that every one, against whom a charge of crime has been laid, should submit to arrest by the proper officer, whose duty it is to bring the accused before the court or officer by whom the order for arrest has been issued.

tence, it must be preceded by the year's imprisonment at hard labor. * * * It is enough, in my opinion, that it changes it (the punishment) in any manner, except, by dispensing with divisible portions of it; but upon the other definition announced by Judge Chase, where it is implied that the change must be from a less to a greater punishment, this act can not be sustained."

[1] Gut v. State, 9 Wall. 35; State v. Learned, 47 Me. 426; State v. Corson, 59 Me. 137; Commonwealth v. Hall, 97 Mass. 570; Commonwealth v. Dorsey, 103 Mass. 412; State v. Wilson, 48 N. H. 398; Walter v. People, 32 N. Y. 147; Stokes v. People, 53 N. Y. 164; Warren v. Commonwealth, 37 Pa. St. 45; Rand v. Commonwealth, 9 Gratt. 738; State v. Williams, 2 Rich. 418; Jones v. State, 1 Ga. 610; Hart v. State, 40 Ala. 32; State v. Manning, 14 Tex. 402; Dowling v. Mississippi, 13 Miss. 664; Walton v. Commonwealth, 16 B. Mon. 15; Lasure v. State, 10 Ohio St. 43; McLaughlin v. State, 45 Ind. 338; Brown v. People, 29 Mich. 232; People v. Olmstead, 30 Mich. 431; Sullivan v. Oneida, 61 Ill. 242; State v. Ryan, 13 Minn. 370; State v. O'Flaherty, 7 Nev. 153.

Since the preliminary confinement is ordered only to insure the attendance of the accused at the trial, the confinement can only be continued as long as there .s any reasonable danger of his default. Where, therefore, the punishment upon conviction will not exceed a fine or imprisonment of short duration, it became customary at an early day to release him upon giving a bond for his appearance, signed by sureties, in the sum which he will have to pay upon conviction, or in such a sum as would probably be sufficient to outweigh the impulse to flee from the threatened imprisonment. This was called *giving bail.* At common law, bail could not be demanded as a matter of right, except in cases of misdemeanor, and felonies were not bailable as a rule. But the severity of the common law in this regard has been greatly moderated, until at the present day, as a general rule, all offenses are bailable as a matter of course, except in cases of homicide and other capital cases. In all capital cases, it is usually provided that bail should be refused, where the evidence of guilt is strong or the presumption great, and in all such cases it is left to the discretion of the judge to whom application is made, whether bail should be granted or refused.[1] When a person is bailed, he is released from the custody of the State authorities, but he is not remanded completely to his liberty. The one who has furnished the security, and is therefore responsible for his default, has in theory the custody of the accused in the place of the State, and he has in fact so much of a control over the accused, that he may re-arrest the latter, whenever he wishes to terminate his responsibility, and deliver the principal to the officers of the law. But the imprisonment by the bail can only be temporary and for the purpose of

[1] United States *v.* Hamilton, 3 Dall. 17; State *v.* Rockafellow, 6 N. J. 332; Com. *v.* Semmes, 11 Leigh, 665; State *v* Summons, 19 Ohio, 139; Allery *v.* Com., 8 B. Mon. 3; Moore *v.* State, 36 Miss. 137; Foley *v.* People, 1 Ill. 31; Shore *v.* State, 6 Mo. 640; People *v.* Smith, 1 Cal. 9.

§ 32

returning him to the custody of the law, and must be done with as little violence as possible.   This can be done at any time before the forfeiture of the bond for non-appearance has been judicially declared ; it may be done by the bail or by his duly constituted agent, and the arrest can be made wherever the accused can be found, even though it is without the State.[1]

The constitutions of most of the States, as well as the constitution of the United States, provide that excessive bail shall not be required.   What constitutes excessive bail, must from the necessities of the case be left with the discretion of the judge or magistrate, to whom application for release on bail is made.   Any misjudgment in such a case, or a willful requirement of excessive bail, could not be remedied, except by application to some other court or judge possessing jurisdiction over the case.   That bail may be called reasonable, which will be sufficient to secure the attendance of the accused at the trial by outweighing or overcoming the inducement to avoid punishment by a default ; and the court or judge, in determining the amount of the bail, must take into consideration all the circumstances which will increase or diminish the probability of a default, the nature of the offense, and of the punishment, the strength or weakness of the evidence, the wealth or impecuniosity of the accused, etc.

Section 33. What constitutes a lawful arrest.
    33a. Arrests without a warrant.

§ 33. **What constitutes a lawful arrest.** — As a general proposition, no one can make a lawful arrest for a crime, except an officer who has a warrant issued by a court or magistrate having the competent authority.   If the process

[1] See Commonwealth *v.* Brickett, 8 Pick. 138; Parker *v.* Bidwell, 3 Conn. 84; Reed *v.* Case, 4 Conn. 166 (10 Am. Dec. 110); Niccolls *v.* Ingersoll, 7 Johns. 145; Harp *v.* Osgood, 2 Hill, 216.

§ 33

is fair on its face, that is, nothing appears upon its face to lead the officer to an inquiry into the jurisdiction of the court, then the officer who makes the arrest has acted lawfully, notwithstanding the court or magistrate which issued the process had no jurisdiction over the case.[1]

A distinction is made by the cases between courts of general and of inferior jurisdiction, in respect to what process is fair on its face. If the process issued from a court of general jurisdiction, the officer is allowed to indulge in the presumption that the case came within the jurisdiction of the court, and need make no inquiry into the details of the case, nor need the warrant contain recitals to show that the court had jurisdiction. But if the process issued from a magistrate or court of inferior and limited jurisdiction, the warrant must contain sufficient recitals to satisfy the officer that the case was within the jurisdiction of the court, in order to be fair on its face. This distinction is very generally recognized and applied.[2]

---

[1] Cooley on Torts, 172, 173, 460. See State v. McNally, 34 Me. 210; State v. Weed, 21 N. H. 262; Underwood v. Robinson, 106 Mass. 296; Neth v. Crofut, 30 Conn. 580; Warner v. Shed, 10 Johns. 138; Brainard v. Head, 15 La. Ann. 489. See, also, generally, as to what process is fair on its face, Erskine v. Hohnbach, 14 Wall. 613; Watson v. Watson, 9 Conn. 140; Tremont v. Clarke, 33 Me. 482; Colman v. Anderson, 10 Mass. 105; Howard v. Proctor, 7 Gray, 128; Williamston v. Willis, 15 Gray, 427; Rice v. Wadsworth, 27 N. H. 104; Sheldon v. Van Buskirk, 2 N. Y. 473; Alexander v. Hoyt, 7 Wend. 89; Webber v. Gay, 24 Wend. 485; Chegaray v. Jenkins, 5 N Y. 376; Moore v. Alleghany City, 18 Pa. St. 55; Billings v. Russell, 23 Pa. St. 189; Cunningham v. Mitchell, 67 Pa. St. 78; State v. Jervey, 4 Strob. 304; State v. Lutz, 65 N. C. 503; Gore v. Martin, 66 N. C. 371; Bird v. Perkins, 33 Mich. 28; Loomis v. Spencer, 1 Ohio St. 153; Noland v. Busby, 28 Ind. 154; Lott v. Hubbard, 44 Ala. 593; Brother v. Cannon, 2 Ill. 200; Shaw v. Dennis, 10 Ill. 405; McLean v. Cook, 23 Wis. 364; Orr v. Box, 22 Minn. 485; Turner v. Franklin, 29 Mo. 285; State v. Duelle, 48 Mo. 282; Walden v. Dudley, 49 Mo. 419. The officer can not receive the warrant signed in blank by the judge or magistrate, and fill up the blanks himself. Such a warrant would be void. Pierce v. Hubbard, 10 Johns. 405; People v. Smith, 20 Johns. 63; Rafferty v. People, 69 Ill. 111; s. c. 72 Ill. 37 (18 Am. Rep. 601).

[2] Cooley on Torts, pp. 173, 464.

§ 33

The officer is bound to know whether under the law the warrant is defective, and not fair on its face, and he is liable as a trespasser, if it does not appear on its face to be a lawful warrant. His ignorance is no excuse.[1] It has been held in several of the States [2] that where an officer has knowledge of the illegality of the warrant, although it is fair on its face, he can not with safety act under it, the protection of process fair on its face being granted to those who ignorantly rely upon its apparent validity. But the better opinion is that the officer is not required in any case to pass judgment upon the validity of a warrant that is fair on its face, and his knowledge of extra-judicial facts will not deprive him of the right to rely upon its apparent validity.[3]

§ 33a. **Arrests without a warrant.**— Although it is the general rule of law that there can be no arrest without a warrant of the nature just described, yet there are cases in which the requirement of a warrant would so obstruct the effectual enforcement of the laws, that the ends of justice would be defeated. For public reasons, therefore, in a few

[1] Grumon v. Raymond, 1 Conn. 39; Lewis v. Avery, 8 Vt. 287; Clayton v. Scott, 45 Vt. 386. But where the matter of jurisdiction is a question of fact and not a question of law, upon which the court issuing the warrant has pronounced judgment, the officer is protected by the warrant, and is not responsible for any error of the court. Clarke v. May, 2 Gray, 410; Mather v. Hood, 8 Johns. 447; Sheldon v. Wright, 5 N. Y. 497; State v. Scott, 1 Bailey, 294; Wall v. Trumbull, 16 Mich. 228.

[2] Barnes v. Barber, 6 Ill. 401; Guyer v. Andrews, 11 Ill. 494; Leachman v. Dougherty, 81 Ill. 324; Sprague v. Birchard, 1 Wis. 457, 464; Grace Mitchell, 31 Wis. 533, 539.

[3] Wilmarth v. Burt, 7 Met. 257; Twitchell v. Shaw, 10 Cush. 46; Grumon v. Raymond, 1 Conn. 40; Watson v. Watson, 9 Conn. 140, 146; Webber v. Gay, 24 Wend. 485; Cunningham v. Mitchell, 67 Pa. St. 78; Wall v. Trumbull, 16 Mich. 228; Bird v. Perkins, 33 Mich. 28; Brainard v. Head, 15 La. Ann. 489; Richards v. Nye, 5 Ore. 382. But he may, if he chooses, refuse to serve such a warrant, and waive the protection which he may claim from its being fair on its face. Horton v. Hendershot, 1 Hill, 118; Cornell v. Barnes, 7 Hill, 35; Dunlap v. Hunting, 2 Denio, 643; Earl v. Camp, 16 Wend. 562. See Davis v. Wilson, 61 Ill. 527; Hill v. Wait, 5 Vt. 124.

§ 33a

cases, the personal security of the citizen is subjected to the further liability of being arrested by a police officer or private individual without a warrant. But the right thus to arrest without a warrant must be confined to the cases of strict public necessity. The cases are few in number, and may be stated as follows: —

1. When a felony is being committed, an arrest may be made without warrant to prevent any further violation of the law.[1]

2. When the felony has been committed, and the officer or private individual is justified, by the facts within his knowledge, in believing that the person arrested has committed the crime.[2]

3. All breaches of the peace, in assaults and batteries, affrays, riots, etc., for the purpose of restoring order imdiately.[3]

4. The arrest of all disorderly and other persons who may be violating the ordinary police regulations for the preservation of public order and health, such as vagrants,

[1] Ruloff v. People, 45 N. Y. 213; Keenan v. State, 8 Wis. 132. But see Somerville v. Richards, 37 Mich. 299.

[2] But the belief must be a reasonable one. If the facts within his knowledge do not warrant his belief in the guilt of the innocent person whom he has arrested, he will be liable in an action for false imprisonment. State v. Holmes, 48 N. H. 377; Holly v. Mix, 3 Wend. 350; Reuck v. McGregor, 32 N. J. 70; Commonwealth v. Deacon, 8 Serg. & R. 47; State v. Roane, 2 Dev. 58; Long v. State, 12 Ga. 233; Eames v. State, 6 Humph. 53. Less particularity, in respect to the reasonableness of the suspicions against an individual, is required of an officer who makes an arrest without warrant, than of a private person. The suspicions must be altogether groundless, in order to make the officer liable for the wrongful arrest. See Marsh v. Loader, 14 C. B. (N. S.) 535; Lawrence v. Hedger, 3 Taunt. 14; Rohan v. Sawin, 5 Cush. 281; Holley v. Mix, 3 Wend. 350; Burns v. Erben, 40 N. Y. 463; Drennan v. People, 10 Mich. 169.

[3] Philips v. Trull, 11 Johns. 477; Respublica v. Montgomery; 1 Yeates, 419; City Council v. Payne 2 Nott & McCord, 475; Vandeveer v. Mattocks, 3 Ind. 479.

§ 33a

gamblers, beggars, who are found violating the laws in the public thoroughfares.[1]

SECTION 34. The trial of the accused.
 34a. Trial must be speedy.
 35b. Trial must be public.
 34c. Accused entitled to counsel.
 34d. Indictment by grand jury or by information.
 34e. The plea of defendant.
 34f. Trial by jury — Legal jeopardy.

§ 34. **The trial of the accused.** — "No man shall be deprived of his life, liberty, or property except by the judgment of his peers or the law of the land." One who has committed a crime can be punished by man, not because he has violated the law of God, or the law of nature (if the two systems of law can be considered distinguishable), but because he has broken the law of man. In order that a man may be lawfully deprived of his life or liberty, he must be convicted of a breach of the human laws, and the conviction must be secured according to the provisions of these laws. If, according to the existing rules of the substantial and remedial law, one charged with a crime is not guilty or can not be convicted of it, he stands free before the law notwithstanding he has violated the God-given rights of others; and to take away his life or his liberty would be as much an infringement of his constitutional rights, as would a like deprivation be of a man who leads a strictly moral life, and scrupulously respects the natural rights of his fellow-men. A man's life, liberty, or property can not be taken away, except by due process of law. It is not proposed to explain all the rules of law governing the conduct and management of criminal prosecutions, since the

---

[1] See Mitchell v. Lemon, 34 Md. 176, in which it was held that one may be arrested without a warrant, who was found violating the rules laid down by the city board of health for the preservation of the public health.

§ 34

object of the present outline of the subject is simply to make a statement of the leading constitutional protections to personal liberty. The trial must be conducted in complete accordance with the rules of practice and the law of evidence, in order that a conviction may lawfully support an imprisonment for crime. But these rules of practice and pleading may be changed by the legislature to any extent, provided the constitutional limitations to be presently mentioned are not violated.

As already explained, a temporary confinement of one accused of crime is permissible, in fact necessary, for the purpose of insuring the presence of the alleged criminal at the trial; for in cases of felony no one can be tried and convicted in his absence, even though his absence is voluntary.[1] But this confinement is only temporary, and can justifiably continue only for as long a time as is reasonably required by the prosecuting attorney to prepare the case of the State for trial.

34*a*. **The trial must be speedy.**— It is, therefore, one of the constitutional limitations for the protection of personal liberty, that the trial be speedy. A man accused of a crime is entitled to a speedy trial, not merely because he is under a personal restraint, but also because his reputation is under a cloud, as long as the criminal accusation remains undisposed of. As a general proposition, the accused is entitled to a trial at the next term of the court after the commission of the crime, or after the accused has been apprehended ; and if it should prove to be necessary for any cause, except the

---

[1] Winchell v. State, 7 Cow. 525; Maurer v. People, 43 N. Y. 1; Jacobs v. Cone, 5 Serg. & R. 335; State v. Alman, 64 N. C. 364; Andrews v. State, 2 Sneed, 550; Jackson v. Commonwealth, 19 Gratt. 656. In capital cases, the record must show affirmatively that the accused was present throughout the trial, and particularly when the verdict is brought in and sentence pronounced. Dougherty v. Commonwealth, 69 Pa. St. 286. But it seems that the accused need not always be personally present at the trial for misdemeanors. Cooley Const. Lim. 390.

§ 34*a*

fault of the accused, to adjourn the court without bringing the prisoner to trial, in ordinary cases he would then be entitled to bail, although originally he was not. This is, however, largely a matter of discretion for the court.[1] When the prisoner is ready for trial, the solicitor for the State is not entitled to delay, unless he satisfies the court that he has exercised due diligence, yet for some cause, the shortness of time, or the absence of material witnesses, etc., he is not prepared to proceed to trial.[2] The continuance of cases must necessarily be largely left to the discretion and good faith of the prosecuting attorney, although it is the duty of the court to be watchful in behalf of the prisoners, who may through the carelessness or malice of the attorney for the State be kept in prison, indefinitely, awaiting a trial. The discretionary character of the duties of prosecuting attorneys furnishes them with powerful means of oppression, if they choose to employ them, and they are too often careless and indifferent to the suffering they cause to the accused, and too frequently ignore his legal right to a speedy trial.[3]

§ 34b. **Trials must be public.**— The next constitutional requirement is that the trial must be public. The object of this provision is to prevent the establishment of secret tribunals of justice, which can be made effective instruments for the oppression of the people. But there is a difficulty in determining what amount of publicity in criminal trials would satisfy this requirement of the constitution. It would not do to say that every person has a constitutional right to attend every criminal trial, whether he had an interest in the

[1] See Ex parte Caplis, 58 Miss. 358.
[2] Cooley Const. Lim. 311, 312.
[3] While I am writing, an account of a most flagrant case of official disrespect of private rights of this character has come to my ears. In my neighborhood, a man has been allowed to linger in jail on the charge of burglary, for many days, awaiting his preliminary examination, because the prosecuting attorney was in attendance upon political picnics.

§ 34b

prosecution or not, for that would necessitate the construction for judicial purposes of a much larger building than is really needed for the ordinary conduct of the courts. Then, too, since this constitutional requirement was established for the protection of the accused, it would not be violating any rights of his, if the courts should be closed, in the trial of causes in which great moral turpitude is displayed, to those who are drawn thither by no real interest in the prosecution or the accused, or for the performance of a public duty, but merely for the gratification of a prurient curiosity. The admission of such persons may justly be considered injurious to the public morals, and not at all required as a protection against the oppression of star chambers. But, while it is undoubtedly true that this constitutional requirement could be satisfied, notwithstanding the public generally is excluded from attendance upon trials, where on account of the nature of the case public morals would likely be corrupted by an unnecessary exposure of human depravity, still it must be conceded that the present public sentiment in America is opposed to any exclusion of the public from attendance upon the sessions of the criminal courts, and an attempt of that kind, even if the court possessed the power under the constitution and laws, and that seems questionable, would raise a most dangerous storm of public indignation against the offending judge. It is only through the action of the legislature that it would be possible to impose effectively the limitations proposed. In framing these limitations, numerous difficulties would present themselves; and it would finally be ascertained that but two methods were feasible, viz.: either to leave it to the discretion of the court who shall be admitted to witness the trial, or to exclude the public altogether, and admit only the officers of the court, including members of the bar and jurors, the parties to the suit, witnesses, and others who are personally interested in the accused or the subject of the suit, and those whose

§ 346

presence is requested by the parties to the cause. Such is believed to be the law prevailing in Germany.[1] Such a provision would seem to make the trial sufficiently public in order to protect the individual against unjust and tyrannical prosecutions, and likewise furnish the community with abundant means for enforcing a proper administration of the courts.

In the same connection, it would be well, in carrying out the same object, to exclude the reporters of the ordinary newspapers. While, as a matter of course, the preservation and publication of criminal trials and statistics are necessary to the public good, it is not only unnecessary as a protection of personal liberty, that they should appear in the ordinary public print, but it is highly injurious to the public morals, as well as revolting to the sensibilities of any one possessing a fair degree of refinement. The most enterprising of the American journals of the larger cities present daily to their reading public a full history of the criminal doings of the previous day, and the length of the reports increases with the nastiness of the details. The amount of moral filth, that is published in the form of reports of judicial proceedings, renders the daily paper unfit to be brought into a household of youths and maidens. There is greater danger of the corruption of the public morals through the publication of the proceedings of our criminal courts, than through the permission of attendance upon the sessions of the court. Only a few will or can avail themselves of that privilege, whereas thousands get to learn through the press of the disgusting details of crime.

§ 34c. **Accused entitled to counsel.** — The State, in all criminal prosecutions, is represented by a solicitor, learned

---

[1] The writer remembers how on one occasion, while he was a student of the law at the University of Goettingen, he was bidden to leave the criminal court, because the case about to be tried was one involving deep moral turpitude.

§ 34c

in the law, and unless the accused was likewise represented by legal counsel, he would usually be at the mercy of the court and of the prosecuting attorney. The prosecution might very easily be converted into a persecution. It was one of the most horrible features of the early common law of England, that persons accused of felonies were denied the right of counsel, the very cases in which the aid of counsel was most needed; and it was not until the present century that in England the right of counsel was guaranteed to all persons charged with crime.[1] But in America the constitutional guaranty of the right of counsel in all cases, both criminal and civil, is universal, and this has been the practice back to an early day. Not only is it provided that prisoners are entitled to counsel of their own appointment, but it is now within the power of any judge of a criminal court, and in most States it is held to be his imperative duty, to appoint counsel to defend those who are too poor to employ counsel; and no attorney can refuse to act in that capacity, although he may be excused by the court on the presentation of sufficient reasons.[2]

On the continent of Europe, the prisoner is allowed the aid of counsel during the trial, but until the prosecuting attorney is through with his inquisitorial investigation of the prisoner, and has, by alternately threatening, coaxing,

---

[1] In 1836, by Stat. 6 and 7 Will. IV., ch. 114. Before this date, English jurists indulged in the pleasing fiction that the judge will be counsel for the prisoner. "It has been truly said that, in criminal cases, judges were counsel for the prisoners. So, undoubtedly, they were, as far as they could be, to prevent undue prejudice, to guard against improper influence being excited against prisoners; but it was impossible for them to go further than this, for they could not suggest the course of defense prisoners ought to pursue; for judges only saw the deposition so short a time before the accused appeared at the bar of their country, that it was quite impossible for them to act fully in that capacity." Baron Garrow in a charge to a grand jury, quoted in Cooley Const. Lim. *332, n. 2.

[2] Wayne Co. v. Waller, 90 Pa. St. 99 (35 Am. Rep. 636); Bacon v. Wayne Co., 1 Mich. 461; Vise v. Hamilton Co., 19 Ill. 18.

§ 34c

and entrapping the accused into damaging admissions, procured all the attainable evidence for the State, he is denied the privilege of counsel. The counsel gains access to his client when the prosecuting attorney is satisfied that he can get nothing more out of the poor prisoner, who, finding himself perhaps for the first time in the clutches of the law, and unable to act or to speak rationally of the charge against him, will make his innocence appear to be a crime. Not so with the English and American law. From the very apprehension of the prisoner, he is entitled to the aid of counsel, and while his admissions, freely and voluntarily made, are proper evidence to establish the charge against him, it is made the duty of all the officers of the law, with whom he may come into contact, to inform him that he need not under any circumstances say anything that might criminate him. Confessions of the accused, procured by promises or threats, are not legal testimony, and cannot be introduced in support of the case for the State.[1]

§ 34d. **Indictment by grand jury or by information.**— The prevailing criminal procedure, throughout the United States, with perhaps a few exceptions, provides in cases of felony for accusations to be made by an indictment by a grand jury.[2] But these are matters of criminal procedure

[1] Commonwealth v. Taylor, 5 Cush. 605; Commonwealth v. Curtis, 97 Mass. 574; Commonwealth v. Sturtivant, 117 Mass. 122; Commonwealth v. Mitchell, 117 Mass. 431; People v. Phillips, 42 N. Y. 200; People v. McMahon, 15 N. Y. 385; State v. Guild, 10 N. J. 163 (18 Am. Dec. 404); Commonwealth v. Harman, 4 Pa. St. 269; State v. Bostick, 4 Harr. 563; Thompson v. Commonwealth, 20 Gratt. 724; State v. Roberts, 1 Dev. 259; State v. Lowhorne, 66 N. C. 538; State v. Vaigneur, 5 Rich. 391; Frain v. State, 40 Ga. 529; State v. Garvey, 28 La. Ann. 955 (26 Am. Rep. 123); Boyd v. State, 2 Humph. 635; Morehead v. State, 9 Humph. 635; Austine v. State, 51 Ill. 236; State v. Brockman, 46 Mo. 566; State v. Staley, 14 Minn. 105.

[2] In some of the States all accusations are now made by information filed by the prosecuting attorney, and probably in all of the States prosecutions for minor misdemeanors are begun by information.

that are subject to constant change by the legislature, and it cannot be doubted that no constitutional limitation would be violated, if the grand jury system were abolished.[1]

§ 34e. **The plea of defendant.** — According to the early common law, it was thought that before the trial could proceed, the defendant had to plead to the indictment. In treason, petit felony, and misdemeanors, a refusal to plead or standing mute, was equivalent to a plea of guilty and the sentence was pronounced as if the prisoner had been regularly convicted. But in all other cases, it was necessary to have a plea entered, before judgment could be pronounced; and unless the defendant could be compelled to plead, the prosecution would fail. It was the custom in such cases to resort to tortures of the most horrible kind in order to compel the defendant to plead ; and where the refusal was shown to be through obstinacy or a design to frustrate the ends of justice, and not because of some physical or mental infirmity (and these matters were determined by a jury summoned for that purpose), the court would pronounce the terrible sentence of "*peine forte et dure.*"[2] But at the present day the necessity of a voluntary plea to the indictment does not seem to be considered so pressing, as to require the application of this horrible penalty. Respect for the common law requirement is manifested only by the court ordering the plea of *not guilty* to be

---

[1] Kallock *v.* Superior Court, 56 Cal. 229. But the United States Constitution requires indictment by grand jury in those cases in which it was required at common law. See United States Const., Amend., art., V.

[2] Which was as follows: "That the prisoner be remanded to the prison from whence he came; and put into a low dark chamber; and there be laid on his back, on the bare floor, naked, unless where decency forbids; that there be placed upon his body, as great a weight of iron as he could bear, and more; that he have no sustenance, save only, on the first day, three morsels of the worst bread; and, on the second day, three draughts of standing water, that should be nearest to the prison door; and in this situation such should be alternately his daily diet till he died, or (as anciently the judgment ran) till he answered." 4 Bl. Com. 423.

§ 34e

entered, whenever the prisoner failed or refused to plead, and the trial then proceeds to the end as if he had voluntarily pleaded.

If, upon arraignment, the prisoner should plead guilty, it would appear, from a superficial consideration of the matter, that no further proof need be required. But, strange as it may seem, there have been cases in which the accused has pleaded guilty, and it has afterwards been discovered that no crime had been committed. A tender regard for the liberty of the individual would suggest the requirement of extraneous evidence to prove the commission of a crime, and the plea of guilty be admitted only to connect the prisoner with the crime. This would be sufficient precaution in ordinary criminal cases, but in capital cases it would be wise to authorize a refusal of all pleas of guilty; for a mistake in such cases would be irremediable.[1]

If the plea is *not guilty*, it becomes necessary for the State to show by competent, legal evidence, that the defendant has committed the crime wherewith he is charged. Except in a few cases, where the subject-matter of the testimony forms a part of a public record, or consists of the dying declaration of the murdered man in a case of homicide, which are made exceptions to the rule by the necessities of criminal jurisprudence, the evidence is presented to the court by the testimony of witnesses. It is the invariable rule of the criminal law, which is believed to be guaranteed by the constitutional limitations, that the testimony must be given in open court by the witnesses orally, so that the defendant will have an opportunity to cross-examine them.[2]

---

[1] In Stringfellow *v.* State, 26 Miss. 155, a confession of murder was held not sufficient to warrant conviction, unless supported by other evidence showing the death of the man supposed to have been murdered. See, also, People *v.* Hennesy, 15 Wend. 147.

[2] Jackson *v.* Commonwealth, 19 Gratt. 656; Johns *v.* State, 55 Md. 350; State *v.* Thomas, 64 N. C. 74; Bell *v.* State, 2 Tex. App. 216 (28 Am. Rep. 429); Goodman *v.* State, Meigs, 197. But if there has been a preliminary examination before a coroner or magistrate, or a previous trial, when the

§ 34e

One of the most important constitutional requirements in this connection, and that which most distinguishes the common-law system of criminal procedure from that of the European Continent, is that the accused can never be compelled to criminate himself by his evidence. Nor can he be compelled to testify to any degree whatever. On the continent of Europe he is compelled to answer every question that is propounded to him by the presiding judge. In England and America he may now testify in his own behalf, but the privilege of remaining silent is so strictly guarded, that it is very generally held to be error for the State to comment on, and to drawn adverses inferences from, his failure to take advantage of the opportunity to testify in his own behalf. The Anglo-Saxon spirit of fair play requires the State to convict the accused without the aid of extorted confessions, and will not allow such criticisms on his silence.[1] But if he goes upon the witness-stand, while he still has the privilege of deciding how far and as to what facts he shall testify, and may refuse to answer questions which may tend to criminate him, the State attorney may comment on the incompleteness of the evidence and his refusal to answer proper questions. Having put himself upon the stand,

defendant had an opportunity to cross-examine the witness, it will be allowable to make use of the minutes of the previous examination in all cases where the witness is since deceased, has become insane, or is sick, or is kept away by the defendant. Commonwealth v. Richards, 18 Pick. 434; State v. Hooker, 17 Vt. 658; Brown v. Commonwealth, 73 Pa. St. 321; Summons v. State, 5 Ohio St. 325; O'Brien v. Commonwealth, 6 Bush, 503; Pope v. State, 22 Ark. 371; Davis v. State, 17 Ala. 354; Kendricks v. State, 10 Humph. 479; People v. Murphy, 45 Cal. 137.

[1] See Commonwealth v. Bonner, 97 Mass. 587; Commonwealth v. Morgan, 107 Mass. 109; Commonwealth v. Nichols, 114 Mass. 285 (19 Am. Rep. 346); Commonwealth v. Scott, 123 Mass. 239 (25 Am. Rep. 87); State v. Cameron, 40 Vt. 555; Brandon v. People, 42 N. Y. 265; Connors v. People, 50 N. Y. 240; Stover v. People, 56 N. Y. 315; Devries v. Phillips, 63 N. C. 53; Bird v. State, 50 Ga. 585; Calkins v. State, 18 Ohio St. 366; Knowles v. People, 15 Mich. 408; People v. Tyler, 36 Cal. 522; See, contra, State v. Bartlett, 55 Me. 200; State v. Lawrence, 57 Me. 375; State v. Cleaves, 59 Me. 298 (8 Am. Rep. 422).

§ 34e

very little weight can be given to his testimony, if he does not tell the whole truth, as well as nothing but the truth.[1]

It is hardly necessary to state that a full opportunity must be given to the accused to defend himself against the charge of the State.   Without such an opportunity, the proceeding would be only *ex parte*.

§ 34*f*. **Trial by jury — Legal jeopardy.** — All prosecutions are tried at common law by a jury, and in some of our State constitutions the right of trial by jury is expressly guaranteed.   Where the right is guaranteed without restriction, it means a common-law trial by jury; and where at common law certain offenses were triable by the court without the aid of a jury, the jury is not now required.[2] Whether in the absence of an express guaranty of the trial by jury, it could be abolished by the legislature, is difficult to determine.   If one can keep his judgment unbiased by the prevailing sentiment, which makes of the jury " the palladium of liberty," " the nation's cheap defender," etc., it would seem that he must conclude that the jury is not needed to make the trial " due process of law ; " and where the constitutional clause reads in the alternative, as it did in the *Magna Charta*, " by the judgment of his peers or the law of the land," the presumption becomes irresistible that when the trial by jury is not expressly guaranteed the power of the legislature to abolish the jury system is free from constitutional restraint.   But in the present temper of public opinion concerning the sacredness of the right of trial by jury, it would not be surprising if the courts should pronounce an express guaranty to be unnecessary.

The last constitutional requirement concerning criminal

---

[1] State *v*. Ober, 52 N. H. 459 (13 Am. Rep. 88); State *v*. Wentworth, 65 Me. 234 (20 Am. Rep. 688); Connors *v*. People, 50 N. Y. 240.

[2] What are the common-law characteristics of a jury trial, are so fully set forth and explained in books of criminal procedure, that any statement of them in this connection is unnecessary.

§ 34*f*

trials to be considered is that which declares that no person shall " be subject for the same offense to be twice put in jeopardy of life or limb." A person is said to have been in legal jeopardy when he is brought before a court of competent jurisdiction for trial, on a charge that is properly laid before the court, in the form of an indictment or an information, and a jury has been impaneled and sworn to try him. When this is done, the defendant is entitled to have the case proceed to a verdict, and if the prosecution should be dropped by the entry of a *nolle prosequi* against the defendant's will, it is of the same effect as if the case had ended in acquittal of the defendant. There cannot be any second prosecution for the same offense.[1] But if the prosecution should fail on account of some defect in the indictment, or for want of jurisdiction,[2] or if for unavoidable reasons, the court has to adjourn and the jury be discharged without a verdict,[3] as when the death of a judge or of a juror

---

[1] Commonwealth *v.* Tuck, 20 Pick. 365; People *v.* Barrett, 2 Caines, 304; State *v.* Alman, 64 N. C. 364; Nolan *v.* State, 55 Ga. 521; Grogan *v.* State, 44 Ala. 9; State *v.* Connor, 5 Cold. 311; Mounts *v.* State, 14 Ohio, 295; Baker *v.* State, 12 Ohio St. 214; State *v.* Callendine, 8 Iowa, 288. But see State *v.* Champeau, 53 Vt. 313 (36 Am. Rep. 754), in which a *nolle prosequi* at this stage is held not to constitute a bar to a second prosecution. See, generally, as to what constitutes a legal jeopardy, State *v.* Garvey, 42 Conn. 232; People *v.* McGowan, 17 Wend. 386; Commonwealth *v.* Alderman, 4 Mass. 477; State *v.* Little, 1 N. H. 257; Williams *v.* Commonwealth, 2 Gratt. 568; Hoffman *v.* State, 20 Md. 475; State *v.* Spier, 1 Dev. 491; McFadden *v.* Commonwealth, 23 Pa. St. 12; State *v.* Ned, 7 Port. 217; Lee *v.* State, 26 Ark. 260 (7 Am. Rep. 611); O'Brian *v.* Commonwealth, 9 Bush, 333 (15 Am. Rep. 715); Price *v.* State, 19 Ohio, 423; Wright *v.* State, 5 Ind. 292; State *v.* Nelson, 26 Ind. 366; People *v.* Cook, 10 Mich. 164; State *v.* Green, 16 Iowa, 239; People *v.* Webb, 28 Cal. 467.

[2] Commonwealth *v.* Bakeman, 105 Mass. 53; Black *v.* State, 36 Ga. 447; Kohlheimer *v.* State, 39 Miss. 548; Mount *v.* Commonwealth, 2 Duv. 93; Gerard *v.* People, 4 Ill. 363; Commonwealth *v.* Goddard, 13 Mass. 455; People *v.* Tyler, 7 Mich. 161.

[3] See United States *v.* Perez, 9 Wheat. 579; Commonwealth *v.* Boden, 9 Mass. 194; Hoffman *v.* State, 20 Md. 425; State *v.* Wiseman, 68 N. C. 203; State *v.* Battle, 7 Ala. 259; Taylor *v.* State, 35 Tex. 97; Wright *v.* State, 5 Ind. 290; Price *v.* State, 36 Miss. 533. The result is the same if

§ 34*f*

occurs,[1] or the jury is unable, after a reasonable effort, to agree upon a verdict, and a mistrial has to be ordered.[2] A second prosecution may also be instituted when a verdict is set aside, or the judgment reversed, on the ground of error.[3]

SECTION 35.— Imprisonment for crime — Hard labor — Control of convict in prison.
    35a.— Convict lease system.

§ 35. **Imprisonment for crime — Hard labor— Control of convicts in prison.**—The most common mode of punishment for crime at the present day is confinement in some jail or penitentiary. The liberty of the convict is thus taken away for a specified period, the length of which is graded according to the gravity of the offense committed. What shall be the proper amount of imprisonment to be imposed as a reasonable punishment for a particular crime is a matter of legislative discretion, limited only by the vague and uncertain constitutional limitation, which prohibits the infliction of " cruel and unusual punishments." [4] Within the walls of the prison the convict must conduct himself in an orderly manner, and conform his actions to the ordinary prison regulations. If he should violate any of these regulations, he may be subjected to an appropriate

---

the adjournment without a verdict is ordered with the express or implied consent of the defendant. Commonwealth v. Stowell, 9 Met. 572; State v. Slack, 6 Ala. 676.

  [1] Nugent v. State, 4 Stew. & Port. 72; Commonwealth v. Fells, 9 Leigh, 620; Mahala v. State, 10 Yerg. 532; State v. Curtis, 5 Humph. 601; Hector v. State, 2 Mo. 166.

  [2] People v. Goodwin, 18 Johns. 187; State v. Prince, 63 N. C. 529; Lester v. State, 33 Ga. 329; Moseley v. State, 33 Tex. 671; State v. Walker, 26 Ind. 346; Commonwealth v. Olds, 5 Lit. 140; Dobbins v. State, 14 Ohio St. 493; Ex parte McLaughlin, 41 Cal. 211; 10 Am. Rep. 272.

  [3] See State v. Lee, 10 R. I. 494; Casborus v. People, 13 Johns. 329; McKee v. People, 32 N. Y. 239; State v. Norvell, 2 Yerg. 24; Kendall v. State, 65 Ala. 492; State v. Redman, 17 Iowa, 329.

  [4] As to the meaning of this limitation, see, ante, §§ 11, 12.

§ 35

punishment, and for serious cases of insubordination, corporal punishment is very often inflicted, even in those
States in which the whipping-post has been abolished.[1]

For minor offenses, it is usual to confine the criminal in
the county jail, and the punishment consists only of a deprivation of one's liberty.   But for more serious and graver
offenses, the statutes provide for the incarceration of the
convict in the penitentiary, where he is required to perform
hard labor for the benefit of the State.   The product of
his labor is taken by the State in payment of the cost of
his maintenance.   It cannot be doubted that the State has
a constitutional right to require its convicts to work during
their confinement, and there has never been any question
raised against the constitutionality of such regulations.
The penitentiary system is now a well recognized feature
of European and American penology.

§ 35a.   **Convict lease system.** — An interesting question
has lately arisen in this country, in respect to the State
control of convicts.   In many of the Southern States, instead of confining the convict at hard labor within the walls of
the penitentiary, in order to get rid of the burden of maintaining and controlling them within the penitentiary, provision was made for leasing the convicts to certain contractors
to be worked in different parts of the date, usually in the construction of railroads.   The entire control of the convict was
transferred to the lessee, who gave bond that he would take
care and guard them, and promised to pay a penalty to the
State for the escape of each convict.   The frequency of the
reports of heartless cruelty on the part of lessees towards
the convicts, prompted by avarice and greed, and rendered
possible by the most limited supervision of the State, has
aroused public sentiment in opposition to the convict lease
system in some of these States, and we may confidently

[1] See *ante*, § 12a.
       § 35a

expect a general abolition of the system at no very distant day. But it is still profitable to consider the constitutionality of the law, upon which the convict lease system is established. In Georgia, the constitutionality of the law was questioned, but sustained. In pronouncing the statute constitutional, the court said: " In the exercise of its sovereign rights for the purpose of preserving the peace of society, and protecting the rights of both person and property, the penitentiary system of punishment was established. It is a part of that police system necessary, as our lawmakers thought, to preserve order, peace and the security of society. The several terms of these convicts fixed by the judgments of the courts under the authority of the law, simply subject their persons to confinement, and to such labor as the authority may lawfully designate. The sentence of the courts under a violated law confers upon the State this power, no more; the power to restrain their liberty of locomotion, and to compel labor not only for the purposes of health, but also to meet partially or fully the expenses of their confinement. The confinement necessarily involved expenses of feeding, clothing, medical attention, guards, etc., and this has been in its past history a grievous burden upon the taxpayers of the State. Surely it was competent for the sovereign to relieve itself of this burden by making an arrangement with any person to take charge of these convicts and confine them securely to labor in conformity with the judgments against them for a time not exceeding their terms of sentence. It was a transfer by the State to the lessee of the control and labor of these persons in consideration that they would feed, clothe, render medical aid and safely keep them during a limited period." [1] It cannot be doubted that, as a general proposition, in the absence of express constitutional limitations as to the place of imprisonment and labor, the convict could

---

[1] Georgia Penitentiary Co. v. Nelms, 65 Ga. 499 (38 Am. Rep. 793).

§ 35a

be confined and compelled to labor in any place within the
State, and in fact he may be compelled to lead a migratory
life, going from place to place, performing the labor required of him by the law of the land. And the only case
in which such a disposition of the convict may be questioned, would be where this law was made to apply to one,
who had been convicted under a different law, the terms of
which allowed or required the sentence to provide for confinement at hard labor within the walls of the penitentiary.
A convict under such a sentence could not, in the enforcement of a subsequent statute, be taken out of the penitentiary and be compelled to work in other parts of the State.
The application of the new law to such a case would give it
a retrospective operation, and make it an *ex post facto* law.
But ordinary constitutional limitations would not be violated
in the application of such a law to those who may be convicted subsequently. The convict lease system is not open
to constitutional objection, because it provides for the convict to be carried from place to place, performing labor
wherever he is required. The objectionable feature of the
system is the transfer to private persons, as a vested right,
of the control over the person and actions of the convict.
It is true that all the rights of the individual are subject to
forfeiture as a punishment for crime, and the State government, as the representative of society, is empowered to
declare the forfeiture under certain constitutional limitations. The State may subject the personal liberty of the
convict to restraint, but it cannot delegate this power of
control over the convict, any more than it can delegate to
private individuals the exercise of any of its police powers.
The maxim, *delegatus non delegare potest* finds an appropriate application in this connection. Certainly, when we
consider the great likelihood of cruel treatment brought
about by the greed and avarice of the lessees of the convicts, personal interest outweighing all considerations of
humanity, it would not require any stretch of the meaning

§ 35a

of words to declare the convict lease system a " cruel and unusual punishment." The State may employ its convicts in repairing its roads, in draining swamp lands, and carrying on other public works ; the State may even lease the convicts to labor, the lessee assuming the expense of maintaining and guarding them, provided the State through its officials has the actual custody of them ; but the State cannot surrender them to the custody of private individuals. Such a system resembles slavery too much to be tolerated in a free State.

§ 35a

CHAPTER V.

POLICE CONTROL OF DANGEROUS CLASSES, OTHERWISE THAN BY CRIMINAL PROSECUTION.

SECTION 42. Confinement for infectious and contagious diseases.
 43. Confinement of the insane.
 44. Control of the insane in the asylum.
 45. Punishment of the criminal insane.
 46. Confinement of habitual drunkards.
 47. Police control of vagrants.
 48. Police regulation of mendicancy.
 49. Police supervision of habitual criminals.
 50. State control of minors.

§ 42. Confinement for infectious and contagious diseases. — The right of the State, through its proper officer, to place in confinement, and to subject to regular medical treatment, those who are suffering from some contagious or infectious disease, on account of the danger to which the public would be exposed if they were permitted to go at large, is so free from doubt that it has been rarely questioned.[1] The danger to the public health is a sufficient ground for the exercise of police power in restraint of the liberty of such persons. This right is not only recognized in cases where the patient would otherwise suffer from neglect, but also where he would have the proper attention at the hands of his relatives. While humanitarian impulses would prompt such interference for the benefit of the homeless, the power to confine and to subject by force to medical treatment those who are afflicted with a conta-

---

[1] Harrison v. Baltimore, 1 Gill, 264. In this case it was held that it was competent for the health officer to send to the hospital persons, on board of an infected vessel, who have the infectious disease, and all others on board who may be liable to the disease, if it be necessary, in his opinion, to prevent the spread of the disease.

§ 42   (102)

gious or infectious disease, rests upon the danger to the public, and it can be exercised, even to the extent of transporting to a common hospital or *lazaretto* those who are properly cared for by friends and relatives, if the public safety should require it.

But while it may be a legitimate exercise of governmental power to establish hospitals for the care and medical treatment of the poor, whatever may be the character of the disease from which they are suffering, unless their disease is infectious, their attendance at the hospital must be free and voluntary. It would be an unlawful exercise of police power, if government officials should attempt to confine one in a hospital for medical treatment, whose disease did not render him dangerous to the public health. As a matter of course, the movements of a person can be controlled, who is in the delirium of fever, or is temporarily irrational from any other cause; but such restraint is permissible only because his delirium disables him from acting rationally in his own behalf. But if one, in the full possession of his mental faculties, should refuse to accept medical treatment for a disease that is not infectious or contagious, while possibly, in a clear case of beneficial interference in an emergency, no exemplary or substantial damages could be recovered, it would nevertheless be an unlawful violation of the rights of personal liberty to compel him to submit to treatment. The remote or contingent danger to society from the inheritance of the disease by his children would be no ground for interference. The danger must be immediate.

§ 43. **The confinement of the insane.** — This is one of the most important phases of the exercise of police power, and there is the utmost need of an accurate and exact limitation of the power of confinement. In the great majority of the cases of confinement for insanity, it is done at the request and upon the application of some loving friend or relative; the parent secures the confinement of his insane child, the husband that of his demented wife, and *vice versa;* and no doubt in comparatively few cases is there the slightest ground for the suspicion of oppression in the procurement of the confinement. But cases of the confinement of absolutely sane people, through the promptings of greed and avarice, or through hate and ignorance, do occur, even now, when public opinion is thoroughly aroused on the subject, and they occurred quite frequently in England, when private insane asylums were common. Although these cases of unjust confinement are probably infrequent, perhaps rare, still the idea of the forcible confinement in an insane asylum of a sane person is so horrible, and the natural fear is so great that the number of such cases is underestimated, because of the difficulty experienced in procuring accurate statistical knowledge (that fear being heightened by the well known differences of opinion, among medical experts on insanity, whenever a case comes up in our courts for the adjudication upon the sanity or insanity of some one), one is inclined, without hesitation, to demand the rigorous observance of the legal limitations of power over the insane, and it becomes a matter of great moment, what constitutional limitations there are, which bear upon this question.[1]

In what relation does the insane person stand to the State? It must be that of guardian and ward. The State may authorize parents and relatives to confine and care for the insane person, but primarily the duty and right of confinement is in the State. " This relation is that of a ward, who is a stranger to his guardian, of a guardian who has no acquaintance with his ward." [2] In the consideration of the rights and duties incident to this relation, it will be neces-

[1] For a careful, able, and elaborate discussion of the rights of the insane, and of the power of the State over them, see Judge Cooley's opinion in the case of Van Deusen *v.* Newcomer, 40 Mich. 90.

[2] Preface to Harrison's Legislation on Insanity.

§ 43

sary, first, to consider the circumstances under which the confinement would be justifiable, and the grounds upon which forcible confinement can be sustained, and then determine what proceedings, preliminary to confinement, are required by the law to make the confinement lawful.

The duty of the State, in respect to its insane population, is not confined to a provision of the means of confinement, sufficient to protect the public against any violent manifestations of the disease. The duty of the State extends further, and includes the provision of all the means known to science for the successful treatment of the diseased mind. This aspect of the duty of the State is so clearly and unequivocally recognized by the authorities and public opinion in some of the States, that the statutes impose upon the State asylums the duty of receiving all *voluntary* patients for medical treatment, upon the payment of the proper reasonable fees, and retaining them as long as such patients desire to remain. In this respect the insane asylum bears the same relation to the public as the hospital does. As long as coercion is not employed, there would seem to be no limit to the power of the State to provide for the medical treatment of lunatics, except the legislative discretion and the fiscal resources of the State. But when the lunatic is subjected to involuntary restraint, then there are constitutional limitations to the State's power of control.

If the lunatic is dangerous to the community, and his confinement is necessary as a means of protecting the public from his violence, one does not need to go farther for a reason sufficient to justify forcible restraint. The confinement of a violent lunatic is as defensible as the punishment of a criminal. The reason for both police regulations is the same, viz. : to insure the safety of the public.

But all lunatics are not dangerous. It is sometimes maintained by theorists that insanity is always dangerous to the public, even though it may be presently of a mild and apparently harmless character, because of the insane pro-

§ 43

pensity for doing mischief, and the reasonable possibility of a change in the character of the disease. But the same might be said of every rational man in respect to the possibility of his committing a crime. Some one has said, all men are potential murderers. The confinement of one who is liable to outbursts of passion would be as justifiable as the confinement of a harmless idiot, whose *dementia* has never assumed a violent form, and is not likely to change in the future, simply for the reason that there is a bare possibility of his becoming dangerous.

But the State, in respect to the care of the insane, owes a duty to these unfortunate people, as well as to the public. The demented are as much under a natural disability as minors of tender age, and the State should see that the proper care is taken of them. The position has been already assumed and justified that the State may make provision for the reception and cure of voluntary patients, suffering from any of the forms of *dementia*, and for the same reason that the proper authority may forcibly restrain one who is in the delirium of fever and subject him to medical treatment, the State has undoubtedly the right to provide for the involuntary confinement of the harmlessly insane, in order that the proper medical treatment may be given, and a cure effected. The benefit to the unfortunate is a sufficient justification for the involuntary confinement. He is not a rational being, and cannot judge for himself what his needs are. Judge Cooley says: "An insane person, without any adjudication,[1] may also lawfully be restrained of his liberty, for his own benefit, either because it is necessary to protect him against a tendency to suicide or to stray away from those who would care for him, or because a proper medical treatment requires it."[2] If the possible cure of the patient be the only ground upon which a harm-

---

[1] As to the necessity of adjudication in any case of confinement of the insane, see *post*.

[2] Cooley on Torts, 179.

§ 43

less lunatic could be confined, as soon as it has become clear that his is a hopeless case, for which there is no cure, he becomes entitled to his liberty. As already stated, the mere possibility of his becoming dangerous, through a change in the character of the disease, will not justify his further detention. But the confinement of a hopeless case of harmless lunacy may be continued, where the lunacy is so grave that the afflicted person is unable to support himself or to take ordinary care of himself, and where if discharged he will become a burden upon the public. That manifestly could only happen where the lunatic was a pauper. If he is possessed of means, and his friends and relatives are willing to take care of him, the forcible confinement cannot be justified. These points are so clearly sustained by reason that authorities in support of them would not be necessary, if they could be found.[1] The difficulties, in respect to the question of confinement of the insane, arise only when we reach the discussion of the preliminary proceedings, which the law requires to justify the forcible restraint of an insane person.

It is a constitutional provision of all the States, as well as of the United States, that " no man shall be deprived of his life, liberty, and property, except by due process of law." There must be a judicial examination of the case, with a due observance of all the constitutional requirements in respect to trials; and the restraint of one's liberty, in order to be lawful, must be in pursuance of a judgment of a court of competent jurisdiction, after one has had an opportunity to be heard in his own defense. This is the general rule. The imprisonment of a criminal, except as preliminary to the trial, can only be justified when it rests upon the judgment of the court. Since this constitutional provision is general and sweeping in its language, there can be no doubt of its application to the case of confinement

---

[1] The opinion of Judge Cooley in Van Deusen *v.* Newcomer, 40 Mich. 90, supports them in the main.

§ 43

of the insane, and we would, from a consideration of this constitutional guaranty, be forced to conclude that, except in the case of temporary confinement of the dangerously insane, no confinement of that class of people would be permissible, except when it is done in pursuance of a judgment of a court, after a full examination of the facts and after an opportunity has been given to the person charged with insanity to be heard in his own defense. Indeed, there is no escape from this conclusion. But the adjudications and State legislation do not seem to support this position altogether.

It is universally conceded that every man for his own protection may restrain the violence of a lunatic, and any one may, at least temporarily, place any lunatic under personal restraint, whose going at large is dangerous to others.[1] But this restraint has been held by some authorities to be justifiable without adjudication, only while the danger continues imminent, or as preliminary to the institution of judicial proceedings by which a judgment for permanent confinement may be obtained.[2] It is believed that no court would justify a permanent confinement of an insane person at the instance of a stranger without adjudication; and in almost all of the States the statutes provide for an adjudication of the question of insanity in respect to any supposed lunatic found going at large and without a home, and forbid the confinement of such person, except after judgment by the court.[3] It may be assumed, therefore, that in those States the permanent confinement of an alleged insane person can not be justified by proof of his insanity, not even of his dangerous propensities, where the confine-

[1] Colby v. Jackson, 12 N. H, 526; Brookshaw v. Hopkins, Loff. 235; Williams v. Williams, 4 Thomp. & C. 251; Scott v. Wakem, 3 Fost. & Fin. 328; Lott v. Sweet, 33 Mich. 308.

[2] Colby v. Jackson, 12 N. H. 526; Matter of Oaks, 8 Law Reporter, 122; Com. v. Kirkbride, 3 Brewst. 586.

[3] Harrison's Legislation on Insanity; Look v. Dean, 108 Mass. 116 (11 Am. Rep. 323).

§ 43

ment was at the instance of a stranger or an officer of the law, unless it be in pursuance of a judgment of a court of competent jurisdiction.

But where the confinement is on the request of relatives, whose natural love and affection would ordinarily be ample protection against injustice and wrong, there is a tendency to relax the constitutional protection, and hold that relatives may procure the lawful confinement of the insane, without a judicial hearing, provided there is actual insanity. The cases generally hold that extra-judicial confinement at the instance of relatives is lawful, where the lunntic is harmless, as well as in the case of dangerous lunacy, and it would appear that this is the prevailing opinion.[1] If the objections to a judicial hearing were sustainable at all, it would seem that, in these cases of confinement on the request of relatives, there would be the least need of this constitutional protection, particularly as the person confined can always, by his own application, or through the application of any one who may be interested in him, have his case brought before a court for a judicial hearing, in answer to a writ of *habeas corpus*. And it may be that he needs no further protection. But there is still some room for the unlawful exercise of this power of control, prompted by cupidity or hate. This danger may be extremely limited, and the cases of intentional confinement of sane persons may be rare; still the fact that they have occurred, the difficulty in procuring a hearing before the court after confinement, as well as the explicit declaration of the constitution that no man's liberty can be restrained, except by due process of law, urge us to oppose the prevailing opinion, and to require a judicial hearing to justify any case of confinement, except where an imme-

[1] See Hinchman *v.* Richie, 2 Law Reporter (N. S.), 180; Van Duesen *v.* Newcomer, 40 Mich. 90; Fletcher *v.* Fletcher, 1 El. & El. 420; Denny *v.* Tyler, 3 Allen, 225; Davis *v.* Merrill, 47 N. H. 208; Cooley on Torts, 179; Look *v.* Dean, 108 Mass. 116 (11 Am. Rep. 323).

§ 43

diately threatening danger renders a temporary restraint of the insane person necessary, as a protection to the public or to himself.

§ 44. **Control of the insane in the asylum.** — Another important question is, how far the keepers of an insane person may inflict punishment for the purpose of control. When one is confined in an asylum, on account of insanity, the very mental helplessness would prompt a humanitarian method of treatment, as the best mode of effecting a cure, and the keepers should be severely punished for every act of cruelty, of whatever nature it may be. But still every one will recognize the necessity at times for the infliction of punishment, not only for the proper maintenance of order and good government in the asylum, but also for the good of the inmates. Because one is insane, it does not necessarily follow that he is not influenced in his actions by the hope of reward and the fear of punishment, and, when the infliction of punishment is necessary, it is justifiable. But there is so great an opportunity for cruel treatment, without any means of redress or prevention, that the most stringent rules for the government and inspection of asylums should be established and enforced. But within these limitations any mode of reasonable punishment, even corporal punishment, is probably justifiable on the plea of necessity.

§ 45. **Punishment of the criminal insane.** — It is probably the rule of law in every civilized country, that no insane man can be guilty of a crime, and hence can not be punished for what would otherwise be a crime. The ground for this exception to criminal responsibility is, that there must be a criminal intent, in order that the act may constitute a crime, and that an insane person can not do an intentional wrong. Insanity, when it is proven to have existed at the time when the offense was committed, con-

§ 45

stitutes a good defense, and the defendant is entitled to an acquittal. If the person is still insane, he can be confined in an asylum, until his mental health is restored, when he will be entitled to his release, like any other insane person. In some of the States, a verdict of acquittal on the ground of insanity, in a criminal prosecution, raises a *prima facie* presumption of insanity at the time of acquittal, which will authorize his commitment to an asylum, without further judicial investigation. Other State statutes provide for his detention, until it can be ascertained by a special examination whether the insanity still continues. But as soon as it is made plain that his reason is restored, he is entitled to his liberty. If his confinement was intentionally continued after his restoration to reason, it would practically be a punishment for the offense or wrong. Mr. Cooley says : " It is not possible constitutionally to provide that one shall be imprisoned as an insane person, who can show that he is not insane at all." [1] This is very true, but I will attempt to show that there is no constitutional objection to the confinement of the criminal insane, after restoration to sanity, as a punishment for the offense which was committed under the influence of insanity. The chief objection to be met in the argument in favor of the punishment of insane persons for the crime or wrong which they have committed, lies in the commonly accepted doctrine, that a criminal intent, which an insane person is not capable of harboring, constitutes the essential element of a crime. Without the intent to do wrong there can be no crime. But that is merely an assumption, which rests upon a fallacy in respect to the grounds upon which the State punishes for crime, and which, as soon as it is recognized as a controlling principle, is practically abrogated by dividing criminal intent into *actual* and *presumed*. It is found on applying the rule to the ordinary experiences of life,

[1] Underwood *v.* People, 32 Mich. 1; Cooley on Torts, 178, n. 2.

§ 45

that it does not fulfill all the demands of society; for a strict adherence to the principle would exclude from the list of crimes very many offenses, which the general welfare requires to be punished. A man, carried away by a sudden heat of passion, slays another. The provocation enabled the animal passions in him to fetter and blind the reason, and without any exercise of will, if by will we mean a rational determination, these passions, differing only in degree and duration from the irresistible impulse of insanity, urged him on to the commission of an act, which no one so bitterly regrets as he does himself, after his mental equilibrium has been restored. Where is the criminal intent in most cases of manslaughter? We are told that the law will presume an intent from the unlawful act.

A man becomes intoxicated with drink, and thus bereft of his reason he commits a crime. Momentarily he is as much a *non compos mentis* as the premanently insane. But he is nevertheless punished for his wrongful act ; and we are told, in response to our inquiry after the criminal intent, that the law will again presume it from the act ; for by intoxication he has voluntarily deprived himself of his reasoning faculties, and can not be permitted to prove his drunkenness, in order to claim exemption from criminal responsibility. A man handles a fire-arm or some other dangerous machine or implement with such gross negligence that the lives of all around are endangered, and one or more are killed. The law, at least in some of the States, makes the homicide a crime, and punishes it as one grade of manslaughter, and very rightly. But where is the criminal intent? By the very description of the act, all criminal intent is necesarily excluded. It is negligence, which is punished as a crime.

Now these cases of *presumed* intent are recognized as exceptions to the rule, which requires an actual intent to do wrong in order to constitute a crime, because it is felt that something in the way of punishment must be inflicted to prevent the too frequent occurrence of such wrongs, even

§ 45

though there is involved in the commission of them no willful or intentional infraction of right.

The idea, that the intent was a necessary element of a crime, was derived from the conception of a wrong in the realms of ethics and religion, and is but an outcome of the doctrine of free will. When a man has the power to distinguish and choose between right and wrong, and intentionally does a wrong thing, he is then guilty of immorality, and if the act is forbidden by law, of a crime; and punishment ought to follow as a just retribution for the wrongful act. But if a man can not, from any uncontrollable cause, distinguish between right and wrong, or if the act is an accident, and he does harm to his neighbor, not having rationally determined to do a thing which he knew to be wrong, he is not guilty of a moral wrong, nor of a crime. If the human punishment of crimes rested upon the same grounds, and proceeded upon the same principles, on which, as we are told, the God of the Universe metes out a just retribution for the infractions of His laws, then clearly there can be no punishment of wrongful acts, as crimes, where there is no moral responsibility. But the punishment of crimes does not rest upon the same grounds and principles. The human infliction of punishment is an exercise of police power, and there is no better settled rule than that the police power of a State must be confined to those remedies and regulations which the safety, or at least the welfare, of the public demands. We punish crimes, not because the criminals deserve punishment, but in order to prevent the further commission of the crime by the same persons and by others, by creating the fear of punishment, as the consequence of the wrongful act. A man, laboring under an insane propensity to kill his fellow-man, is as dangerous, indeed he is more dangerous, than the man who for gain, or under the influence of his aroused passions, is likely to kill another. The insane person is more dangerous, because the same influences are not at work on him, as would have weight with a rational, but evil disposed person. And this circumstance would no doubt require special and peculiar regulation for the punishment of the insane, in order that it may serve as a protection to the public, and a restraint upon the harmful actions of the lunatic. If, therefore, the protection to the public be the real object of the legal punishment of crimes, it would be as lawful to punish an insane person for his wrongful acts as one in the full possession of his mental faculties. The lunatic can be influenced by the hope of reward and the fear of punishment, and he can be prevented in large measure from doing wrong by subjecting him to the fear of punishment. This is the principle upon which the lunatics are controlled in the asylums. It would be no more unconstitutional to punish a lunatic outside of the asylum.

It is not likely that this view of the relation of the insane to the criminal law will be adopted at an early day, if at all; for the moral aspect of punishment has too strong a hold upon the public.[1] But if its adoption were possible, it would reduce to a large extent the number of crimes which are alleged to have been committed under the influence of an insanity, which has never been manifested before the wrongful occurrence, and has, immediately thereafter, entirely disappeared.

§ 46. **Confinement of habitual drunkards.**— It is the policy of some States, notably New York, to establish asylums for the inebriate, where habitual drunkards are received and subjected to a course of medical treatment, which is calculated to effect a cure of the disease of drinking, as

[1] So strong an influence has this theory over the public mind that in a late number of the *North American Review*, a writer attempts to prove the "certainty of endless punishment" for the violation of God's laws, by showing *inter alia* that even human laws are retributive and not corrective, that a criminal is punished for the vindication of a broken law, and not that crime may be prevented. See vol. 140, p. 154.

§ 46

it is claimed to be. A large part of human suffering is the almost direct result of drunkenness, and it is certainly to the interest of society to reduce this evil as much as possible. The establishment and maintenance of inebriate asylums can, therefore, be lawfully undertaken by the State. The only difficult constitutional question, arising in this connection, refers to the extent to which the State may employ force in subjecting the drunkard to the correcting influences of the asylum. Voluntary patients can, of course, be received and be retained, as long as they consent to remain. But they can not be compelled to remain any longer than they desire, even though they have, upon entering the the asylum, signed an agreement to remain for a specified time, and the time has not expired.[1] The statutes might authorize the involuntary commitment of inebriates, who are so lost to self-control that the influence of intoxicating liquor amounts to a species of insanity, called dipsomania.[2] But if the habit of drunkenness is not so great as to deprive the individual of his rational faculties, the State has no right to commit him to the asylum for the purpose of effecting a reform, no more than the State is authorized to forcibly subject to medical and surgical treatment one who is suffering from some innocuous disease. If the individual is rational, the only case in which forcible restraint would be justifiable, would be where the habit of drunkenness, combined with ungovernable fiery passions, makes the individual a source of imminent danger. Every community has at least one such character, a passionate drunkard, who terrorizes over wife and children, subjects them to cruel treatment, and is a frequent cause of street brawls, constantly breaking the peace and threatening the quiet and safety of law-abiding citizens. The right of the State to commit such a person to the inebriate asylum, even where

---

[1] Matter of Baker, 29 How. Pr. 486.
[2] Matter of Janes, 30 How. Pr. 446.

§ 46

there has been no overt violation of the law, can not be questioned.   A man may be said to have a natural right to drink intoxicating liquor as much as he pleases, provided that in doing so he does not do or threaten positive harm to others.   Where, from a combination of facts or circumstances, his drunkenness does directly produce injury to others,— whether they be near relatives, wife and children, or the community at large, — the State can interfere for the protection of such as are in danger of harm, and forcibly commit the drunkard to the inebriate asylum.   It may be said that any form of drunkenness produces harm to others, in that it is calculated to reduce the individual to pauperism, and throw upon the public the burden of supporting him and his family.   But that is not a proximate consequence of the act, and no more makes the act of drunkenness a wrong against the public or the family, than would be habits of improvidence and extravagance.   For a poor man intoxication is an extravagant habit.   The State can only interfere, when the injury to others is a proximate and direct result of the act of drunkenness, as, for example, where the drunkard was of a passionate nature and was in the habit of beating those about him, while in this drunken frenzy.   This is a direct and proximate consequence, and the liability to this injury would be sufficient ground for the interference of the State.   But in all of these cases of forcible restraint of inebriates, the restraint is unlawful, except temporarily to avert a threatening injury to others, unless it rests upon the judgment of a court, rendered after a full hearing of the cause.   The commitment on *ex parte* affidavits would be in violation of the general constitutional provision, that no man can be deprived of his liberty, except by due process of law.[1]

§ 47. **Police control of vagrants.** — The vagrant has been

---

[1] Matter of Janes, 30 How. Pr. 446.

§ 47

very appropriately described as the chrysalis of every species of criminal. A wanderer through the land, without home ties, idle, and without apparent means of support, what but criminality is to be expected from such a person? If vagrancy could be successfully combated, if every one was engaged in some lawful calling, the infractions of the law would be reduced to a surprisingly small number; and it is not to be wondered at that an effort is so generally made to suppress vagrancy. The remedy is purely statutory, as it was not an offense against the common law. The statutes are usually very explicit as to what constitute vagrancy, and a summary proceeding for conviction, before a magistrate and without a jury, is usually provided, and the ordinary punishment is imprisonment in the county jail.

The provision of the State statutes on the subject bear a very close resemblance, and usually set forth the same acts as falling within the definition of vagrancy. Webster defines a vagrant or vagabond to be " one who wanders from town to town, or place to place, having no certain dwelling, or not abiding in it, and usually without the means of livelihood." In the old English statutes, they are described as being " such as wake on the night, and sleep on the day, and haunt customable taverns and ale-houses, and routs about; and no man wot from whence they come, nor whither they go." The English, and some of the American statutes have stated very minutely what offenses are to be included under vagrancy. But, apart from those acts which would fall precisely under Mr. Webster's definition, the acts enumerated in the statutes in themselves constitute distinct offenses against public peace, morality, and decency, and should not be classified with vagrancy, properly so-called. Thus, for example, an indecent exposure of one's person on the highway, a boisterous and disorderly parade of one's self by a common prostitute, pretending to tell fortunes and practicing other deceptions upon the public,

§ 47

and other like acts, are distinct offenses against the public, and the only apparent object of incorporating them into the vagrant act is to secure convictions of these offenses by the summary proceeding created by the act.[1] Mr. Webster's definition will therefore include all acts that can legitimately come within the meaning of the word *vagrancy*.

What is the tortious element in the act of vagrancy? Is it the act of listlessly wandering about the country, in America called "tramping?" Or is it idleness without visible means of support? Or is it both combined? Of course, the language of the particular statute, under which the proceeding for conviction is instituted, will determine the precise offense in that special case, but the offense is usually defined as above. If one does anything which directly produces an injury to the community, it is to be supposed that he can be prevented by appropriate legislation. While an idler running about the country is injurious to the State indirectly, in that such a person is not a producer, still it would not be claimed that he was thus inflicting so direct an injury upon the community as to subject him to the possibility of punishment. A man has a legal right to live a life of absolute idleness, if he chooses, provided he does not, in so living, violate some clear and well defined duty to the State. To produce something is not one of those duties, nor is it to have a fixed permanent home. But it is a duty of the individual so to conduct himself that he will be able to take care of himself, and prevent his becoming a public burden. If, therefore, he has sufficient means of support, a man may spend his whole life in idleness and wandering from place to place. The gist of the offense, therefore, is the doing of these things, when one has no visible means of support, thus threatening to become a public burden. The statutes generally make use of the words, "without visible means of support." What is

---

[1] See 2 Broom & Hadley's Com. 467, 468.

§ 47

meant by "visible means?" Is it a man's duty to the public to make his means of support visible, or else subject himself to summary punishment? Is it not rather the duty of the State to show affirmatively that this "tramp" is without means of support, and not simply prove that his means of support are not apparent? Such would be a fair deduction by analogy from the requirements of the law in respect to other offenses. But the very difficulty, in proving affirmatively that a man has no means of support, is, no doubt, an all-sufficient reason for this departure from the general rule in respect to the burden of proof, and for confining the duty of the State to the proof that the person charged with vagrancy is without *visible* means of support, and throwing upon the individual the burden of proving his ability to provide for his wants.

An equally difficult question is, what amount and kind of evidence will be sufficient to establish a *prima facie* case of invisibility of the means of support? If a man is found supporting himself in his journeyings by means of begging, no doubt that would be deemed sufficient evidence of not having proper means of support. But suppose it cannot be proven that he begs. Will the tattered and otherwise dilapidated condition of his attire be considered evidence of a want of means? The man may be a miser, possessed of abundant means, which he hoards to his own injury. Has he not a right to be miserly, and to wear old clothes as long as he conforms to the requirement of decency, and may he not, thus clad, indulge in a desire to wander from place to place? Most certainly. He is harming no one, provided he pays for all that he gets, and it would be a plain violation of his right of liberty, if he were arrested on a charge of vagrancy, because he did not choose to expend his means in the purchase of fine linen. Or will the lack of money be evidence that he has no visible means of support? In the first place how can that be ascertained? Has the State a right to search a man's pockets in order to confirm a sus-

§ 47

picion that he has no means of support? And even if such a search was lawful, or the fact that the defendant was without money was established in some other way, the lack of money would be no absolute proof of a want of means.

Again, a man may have plenty of money in his pocket, and yet have no lawful means of support. And if he is strongly suspected of being a criminal, he is very likely to be arrested as a vagrant. Indeed, the vagrant act is specially intended to reach this class of idlers, as a means of controlling them and ridding the country of their injurious presence. But there is no crime charged against them. They are usually arrested on mere suspicion of being, either concerned in a crime recently committed, or then engaged in the commission of some crime. That suspicion may rest upon former conviction for crime, or upon the presumptions of association, or the police officer may rely upon his ability to trace the lines of criminality upon the face of the supposed offender. But in every case, where there is no overt criminal act, an arrest for vagrancy is based upon the suspicion of the officer, and it is too often unsupported by any reasonably satisfactory evidence. It is true that very few cases of unjust arrests, *i.e.*, of innocent persons, for vagrancy occur in the criminal practice; but with this mode of proceeding it is quite possible that such may occur. Moreover, the whole method of proceeding is in direct contradiction of the constitutional provisions that a man shall be convicted before punishment, after proof of the commission of a crime, by direct testimony, sufficient to rebut the presumption of innocence, which the law accords to every one charged with a violation of its provisions. In trials for vagrancy, the entire process is changed, and men are convicted on not much more than suspicion, unless they remove it, to employ the language of the English statute, by " giving a good account of themselves. " It reminds one of the police regulation of Germany, which provides that upon the arrival of a person at an inn or boarding-

§ 47

house, the landlord is required to report the arrival to the police, with an account of one's age, religion, nationality, former residence, proposed length of stay, and place of destination. Every one is thus required to "give a good account of" himself, and the regulation is not confined in its operations to suspicious characters. Whatever may be the theoretical and technical objections, to which the vagrancy laws are exposed, and although the arrest by mistake of one who did not properly come under the definition of a vagrant would possibly subject the officer of the law to liability for false imprisonment, the arrest is usually made of one who may, for a number of the statutory reasons, be charged with vagrancy, and no contest arises out of the arrest. But if the defendant should refuse to give testimony in defense, and ask for an acquittal on the ground that the State had failed to establish a *prima facie* case against him, unless the statute provided that a want of lawful means of support is sufficiently proved by facts which otherwise would create a bare suspicion of impecuniosity, the defendant would be entitled to a discharge. Punishment for vagrancy is constitutional, provided the offense is proven, and conviction secured in a constitutional manner. And since the summary conviction deprives one of the common-law right of trial by jury, the prosecutions should and must be kept strictly within the limitation of the statute.

The constitutionality of the vagrancy laws has been sustained by the courts, although in none of the cases does it appear that the court considered the view of the question here presented. The discussion cannot be more fitly closed than by the following quotation from an opinion of Judge Sutherland, of the New York judiciary: "These statutes declaring a certain class or description of persons vagrants, and authorizing their conviction and punishment as such, as well as certain statutes declaring a certain class or description of persons to be disorderly persons, and authorizing their arrest as such, are in fact rather in the nature of

§ 47

public regulations to prevent crime and public charges and burdens, than of the nature of ordinary criminal laws, prohibiting and punishing an act or acts as a crime or crimes. If the condition of a person brings him within the description of either of the statutes declaring what persons shall be esteemed vagrants, he may be convicted and imprisoned, whether such a condition is his misfortune or his fault. His individual liberty must yield to the public necessity or the public good; but nothing but public necessity or the public good can justify these statutes, and the summary conviction without a jury, in derogation of the common law, authorized by them. They are constitutional, but should be construed strictly and executed carefully in favor of the liberty of the citizen. Their description of persons who shall be deemed vagrants is necessarily vague and uncertain, giving to the magistrate in their execution an almost unchecked opportunity for arbitrary oppression or careless cruelty. The main object or purpose of the statutes should be kept constantly in view, and the magistrate should be careful to see, before convicting, that the person charged with being a vagrant is shown, either by his or her confession, or by competent testimony, to come exactly within the description of one of the statutes." [1]

§ 48. **Police regulation of mendicancy.** — Somewhat akin to the evil of vagrancy, and growing out of it, is common and public mendicancy. The instincts of humanity urge us to relieve our fellow-creatures from actual suffering, even though we fully recognize in the majority of such cases that the want is the natural consequence of vices, or the punishment which nature imposes for the violation of her laws. It would be unwise for State regulation to prohibit obedience to this natural instinct to proffer assistance

[1] People v. Forbes, 4 Park. 611. See, also, in affirmance of the constitutionality of vagrant laws, People v. Phillips, 1 Park. 95; People v. Gray, 4 Park. 616; State v. Maxey, 1 McMull. 501.

§ 48

to suffering humanity.[1] Indeed, it would seem to be the absolute right of the possessors of property to bestow it as alms upon others, and no rightful law can be enacted to prohibit such a transfer of property. It certainly could not be enforced. But while we recognize the ennobling influence of the practice of philanthrophy, as well as the immediate benefit enjoyed by the recipient of charity, it must be conceded that unscientific philanthropy, more especially when it takes the form of indiscriminate almsgiving, is highly injurious to the welfare of the community. Beggars increase in number in proportion to the means provided for their relief. Simply providing for their immediate wants will not reduce the number. On the contrary their number is on the increase. State regulation of charity is therefore necessary, and is certainly constitutional. A sound philanthropy would call for the support of those who cannot from mental or physical deficiencies provide themselves with the means of subsistence, and include even those who in their old age are exposed to want in consequence of the lavish gratification of their vices and passions. But all charity institutions should be so conducted that every one, coming in contact with them, would be stimulated to work. Poor-houses should not be made too inviting in their appointments. After providing properly for the really helpless, it would then be fit and proper for the State to prohibit all begging upon the streets and in public resorts. Those who are legitimate subjects of charity should be required to apply to the public authorities. All others should be sent to the jail or work-house, and compelled to work for their daily bread. It is conceded that the State cannot prohibit the practice of private philanthropy, but it can prohibit public and professional begging, and, under the vagrant laws, punish those who practice it.

[1] The religious aspect of the question is not considered here.

§ 48

§ 49. Police supervision of habitual criminals. — A very large part of the duties of the police in all civilized countries is the supervision and control of the criminal classes, even when there are no specific charges of crime lodged against them. A suspicious character appears in some city, and is discovered by the police detectives. He bears upon his countenance the indelible stamp of criminal propensity, and he is arrested. There is no charge of crime against him. He may never have committed a crime, but he is arrested on the charge of vagrancy, and since by the ordinary vagrant acts the burden is thrown upon the defendant to disprove the accusation, it is not difficult in most cases to fasten on him the offense of vagrancy, particularly as such characters will usually prefer to plead guilty, in order to avoid, if possible, a too critical examination into their mode of life. But to punish him for vagrancy is not the object of his arrest. The police authorities had, with an accuracy of judgment only to be acquired by a long experience with the criminal classes, determined that he was a dangerous character; and the magistrate, in order to rid the town of his presence, threatens to send him to jail for vagrancy if he does not leave the place within twenty-four hours. In most cases, the person thus summarily dealt with has been already convicted of some crime, is known as a confirmed criminal, and his photograph has a place in the " rogues' gallery." Now, so far as this person has been guilty of a violation of the vagrant laws, he is no doubt subject to arrest and can and should be punished for vagrancy, in conformity with the provisions of the statute. But so far as the police, above and beyond the enforcement of the vagrant law, undertake to supervise and control the actions of the criminal classes, except when a specific crime has been committed and the offender is to be arrested therefor, their action is illegal, and a resistance to the control thus exercised must lead to a release and acquittal of the offender. This is certainly true where the control and

§ 49

supervision of the habitual criminals are not expressly authorized by statute.   But in some of our States, in connection with the punishment of vagrancy, provision is made for the punishment of any " common street beggar, common prostitute, habitual disturber of the peace, known pickpockets, gambler, burglar, thief, watch-stuffer, ball-game player, a person who practices any trick, game, or device with intent to swindle, a person who abuses his family, and any suspicious person who cannot give a reasonable account of himself." [1]   Laws of this character have been enacted, and the constitutionality of them sustained in Ohio, Maryland, Pennsylvania and Kentucky.[2]   The only serious constitutional objection to these laws for the punishment of habitual criminals is that they provide a punishment for the existence of a *status* or condition, instead of for a crime or wrong against society or an individual.   If an individual has become an habitual criminal, *i.e.*, that he has committed, and is still committing, a number of offenses against the law, for each and every offense he may be punished, and the punishment may very properly be made to increase with every repetition of the offense.   But this person can hardly be charged with the *crime* of being a common or habitual law-breaker.   After meting out to him the punishment that is due to his numerous breaches of the law, he has paid the penalty for his infractions of the law, and stands before it a free man.

There can be no doubt that constant wrong-doing warps the mind, and more or less permanently changes the character, producing a common or habitual criminal.   But to say that the being an habitual criminal is a punishable offense, is to say that human punishment is endless, for it is an attempt to punish a condition of mind and character, which

[1] Rev. Stat. Ohio, § 2108.

[2] Morgan *v.* Nolte, 37 Ohio St. 23 (41 Am. Rep. 485); Byers *v.* Commonwealth, 42 Pa. St. 96; World *v.* State, 50 Md. 54; Commonwealth *v.* Hopkins, 2 Dana, 418.

§ 49

only years of patient and arduous struggle can obliterate or
change. The practical effect of such laws, when vigorously
enforced, is to make of such a person an outlaw, without
home or country, driven from post to post, for his habitual
criminality is an offense against such laws of every community into which he may go, it matters not where the
offenses were committed which made him an habitual criminal.[1] Even the habitual criminal has a right to a home, a
resting-place. If the hardened character of the criminal
makes his reform an impossibility, and renders him so dangerous to the community that he cannot be allowed to live
as other men do, he may be permanently confined for life
as a punishment of the third, fifth, or other successive commission of the offense ; he may be placed under police surveillance, as is the custom in Europe, and he may be compelled, by the enforcement of the vagrant laws, to engage
in some lawful occupation. But it is impossible to punish
him, as for a distinct offense, for being what is the necessary
consequence of those criminal acts, which have been already
expiated by the infliction of the legal punishment.

But the laws have been generally sustained, wherever
their constitutionality has been brought into question. In
criticising the objection just made, the Supreme Court of
Ohio say : " The only limitations to the creation of offenses
by the legislative power are the guaranties contained in the
bill of rights, neither of which is infringed by the statute in
question. It is a mistake to suppose that offenses must be
confined to specific acts of commission or omission. A general course of conduct or mode of life, which is prejudicial
to the public welfare, may likewise be prohibited and punished as an offense. Such is the character of the offense in
question. * * * At common law a common scold was
indictable ; so also a common barrator ; and, by various
English statutes, summary proceedings were authorized

[1] Commonwealth v. Hopkins, 2 Dana, 418.
§ 49

against idlers, vagabonds, rogues, and other classes of disorderly persons.[1] In the several States in this country similar offenses are created. In some of the States it is made an offense to be a common drunkard, a common gambler, a common thief, each State defining the offenses according to its own views of public policy. * * * In such cases the offense does not consist of particular acts, but in the mode of life, the habits and practices of the accused in respect to the character or traits which it is the object of the statute creating the offense to suppress." [2] A practical difficulty in enforcing snch laws would arise in determining what kind of evidence, and how much, it was necessary to convict one of being a common or habitual criminal. Conceding the constitutionality of the law which makes habitual criminality a distinct punishable offense, the position assumed by the Kentucky court, in respect to the quality and character of the evidence needed to procure a conviction under the law, cannot be questioned. The court say : " It is the general course of conduct in pursuing the business or practice of unlawful gaming, which constitutes a *common gambler*. As a man's character is no doubt formed by, and results from, his habits and practices; and we may infer, by proving his character, what his habits and practices have been. But we do not know any principle of law, which sanctions the introduction of evidence to establish the character of the accused, with a view to convict him of offending against the law upon such evidence alone. If the statute had made it penal to possess the character of a common gambler, the rejected testimony would have been proper. But we apprehend that the question whether a man is, or is not, a com-

---

[1] See Stephen's Dig. of Crim. Law, art. 193.

[2] Morgan *v.* Nolte, 37 Ohio St. 23 (41 Am. Rep. 485). And it is also held to be constitutional to provide for the punishment of such offenses by a summary conviction without jury trial. Byers *v.* Commonwealth, 42 Pa. St. 89.

§ 49

mon gambler, depends upon matters of fact — his practices, and not his reputation or character; and, therefore, the facts must be proved, as in other cases.

" The attorney for the Commonwealth offered to prove by a witness, that the accused ' had played at cards for money,' since February, 1833, and before the finding of the indictment. The court rejected the evidence, and we think erroneously. How many acts there were, of playing and betting, or the particular circumstances attending each, cannot be told, inasmuch as the witness was not allowed to make his statement. Every act, however, of playing and betting at cards, which the testimony might establish, would have laid some foundation on which the venire could have rested, in coming to the conclusion, whether the general conduct and practices of the accused did, or did not, constitute him a *common gambler*. One, or a few acts of betting and playing cards might be deemed insufficient, under certain circumstances, to establish the offense. For instance, if the acccused, during the intervals between the times he played and bet, was attending to some lawful business, his farm, his store, or his shop, it might thereby be shown that his playing and betting were for pastime and amusement merely. Under such circumstances the evidence might fail to show the accused was a common gambler. Thus, while many acts of gaming may be palliated, so as to show that the general conduct and practices of an individual are not such as to constitute him a *common gambler;* on the other hand, a single act may be attended with such circumstances as to justify conviction. For example, if an individual plays and bets, and should at the time display all the apparatus of an open, undisguised, common gambler, it would be competent for the jury, although he was an entire stranger, to determine that he fell within the provisions of the statute. The precise nature of the acts which the testimony would have disclosed, had it been heard, is unknown; but we perceive enough to

§ 49

convince us that it was relevant and ought to have been heard.

"The attorney for the Commonwealth offered to prove by a witness, that the accused had, within the period aforesaid, set up and kept faro banks and other gaming tables, at which money was bet, and won and lost, at places without the county of Fayette, where the indictment was found; and the court excluded the testimony. In this the court clearly erred. It makes no difference where the gaming takes place. If a person has gamed until he is a common gambler, without the county of Fayette, he may go to that county for the purpose of continuing his practices. In such a case it was the object of the statute to arrest him as soon as possible by conviction, and requiring the bond provided for in the sixth section of the act of 1833. The testimony should have been admitted." [1]

[1] Commonwealth *v.* Hopkins, 2 Dana, 418. In the following opinion is discussed the amount and character of the evidence required to convict one of being a common thief: "The act of the assembly under which appellant was indicted, provides that 'any evidence of facts or reputation, proving that such a person is habitually and by practice a thief, shall be sufficient for his conviction, if satisfactorily establishing the fact.' In order to justify a conviction of a party of the offense created by the act, there must be proof of either facts or reputation, sufficient to satisfy the jury that the party accused is by *practice* and *habit* a thief. The offense is but a misdemeanor, and it must, therefore, be prosecuted within one year from the time of its commission. It is necessary, in order to justify conviction, that the proof should establish the fact that the accused was 'a common thief' within one year before the prosecution was begun, and therefore, evidence of 'acts of larceny,' committed more than a year before the indictment was found, would not be admissible. Though the conviction of the accused of the larceny of a watch was within a year before this prosecution was begun, it was contended that, standing alone, it was not sufficient to prove that the accused was by *habit* and *practice* a thief, and that it was not admissible, unless connected with an offer to follow it up with other proof to the same point, and that, as no such offer was made, the criminal court erred in admitting it. It did not matter that the record of the conviction of the accused, of larceny in 1877, did not prove the whole issue. The court had no right to require the State's attorney to disclose in advance what other proof he intended to offer. While the record of conviction was not of itself legally sufficient

§ 49

Another phase of police supervision is that of photograph-
ing alleged criminals, and sending copies of the photograph
to all detective bureaus.   If this be directed by the law as
punishment for a crime of which the criminal stands convicted, or if the man is in fact a criminal, and the photograph is obtained without force or compulsion, there can be
no constitutional or legal objection to the act; for no right
has been violated.   But the practice is not confined to the
convicted criminals.   It is very often employed against
persons who are only under suspicion.   In such a case, if
the suspicion is not well founded, and the suspected person
is in fact innocent, such use of his protograph would be a
libel, for which every one could be held responsible who
was concerned in its publication.   And it would be an
actionable trespass against the right of personal security,
whether one is a criminal or not, to be compelled involuntarily to sit for a photograph to be used for such purposes,
unless it was imposed by the statutes as a punishment for
the crime of which he has been convicted.

These are the only modes of police supervision of habitual criminals which the American law permits.   But on the
continent of Europe, it seems that the court may, even in
cases of acquittal of the specific charge, under certain
limitations which vary with each statute, subject an evil
character after his discharge to the supervision and control
of the police.   Such persons are either confined within

to convict, it was a link in the chain of evidence admissible *per se*, when
offered, as tending to prove the issue.   Its legal effect was a question for
the jury to determine, they being under our constitution the judges of
the law and the facts in criminal cases.   So also with respect to the
objection to the evidence of the reputation of the accused, as given by the
police officer.   Reputation is but a single fact, and the whole may be given
in evidence, commencing at a period more than a year before the indictment was found.   The reputation which the accused bore at a time more
than a year before the indictment, was admissible, though it would not
of itself justify a conviction, and unless followed up with proof that such
reputation continued, and was borne by the accused within a year before
the indictment was found."   World *v.* State, 50 Md. 4.

§ 49

certain districts, or are prohibited from residing in certain localities. They are sometimes compelled to report to certain police officers at stated times, and other like provisions for their control are made. This police supervision lasts during life, or for some stated period which varies with the gravity of the offense and the number of offenses which the person under supervision has committed. Similar regulations have been established in England, by " The Habitual Criminal Act."[1]

As a punishment for crime, there can be no doubt of the power of the legislature to institute such police regulations, unless the length of time, during which the convicted criminal is kept under surveillance, would expose the regulation to the constitutional objection of being a cruel and unusual punishment. But to enforce such a regulation in any other manner, or under any other character, than as a punishment for a specific crime, would clearly be a violation of the right of personal liberty, not permitted by the constitution.

Police supervision of prostitutes, so universal a custom in the European cities, is sometimes considered in the same light, but is essentially different. Prostitution is an offense against the law, and these city ordinances render lawful the practice by authorizing its prosecution under certain limitations and restrictions, among which are police supervision and inspection. But the subjection to this control is voluntary on the part of the prostitute, in order to render practices lawful which are otherwise unlawful. It is rather in the character of a license, under certain restraints, to commit an offense against public morality.

§ 50. **State control of minors.** — It is not proposed to discuss in this connection the power of the State to interfere with the parent's enjoyment of his natural right to the

[1] 32 and 33 Vict., ch. 99. See Polizeiaufsicht in Von Holtzendorff's Rechtslexikon, vol. 2, pp. 322, 323.

§ 50

care and education of his minor child.   The regulation of
this relative right will be explained in a subsequent section.[1]
Here we shall make reference only to the power of the
State to take into its care and custody the young children
who have been robbed by death of parental care, and but
for State interference would be likely to suffer want, or at
least to grow up in the streets, without civilizing influences,
and in most cases to swell the vicious and criminal classes.
There can be no doubt that, in the capacity of a *parens
patriæ*, the State can, and should, make provision for the
care and education of these wards of society, not only for
the protection of society, but also for the benefit of the children themselves.   The State owes this duty to all classes,
who from some excessive disability are unable to take care
of themselves.   It is clear, as has already been stated, and
explained in several connections, the State has no right to
force a benefit upon a full grown man, of rational mind,
against his will.   But the minor child is not any more capable of determining what is best for himself than a lunatic
is.   Being, therefore, devoid of the average mental powers
of an adult, he is presumed to be incapable of taking care of
himself, and the State has the right, in the absence of some
one upon whom the law of nature imposes this duty, to take
the child in custody, and provide for its nurture and education.   This subjection to State control continues during
minority.

Now, there are two ways in which the State can interfere
in the care and management of a child without parental care.
It can either appoint some private person as guardian, into
whose custody the child is placed, or it may direct him to
be sent to an orphan asylum or reformatory school,
especially established for the education and rearing of
children who cannot be otherwise cared for.   The right of
the State to interfere in either way, has never been disputed,

_____
[1] See *post*, §§ 165, 166a.

§ 50

but a serious and important question has arisen as to the necessary formalities of the proceedings, instituted to bring such children under the control of the State. As already explained, the constitution provides, in the most general terms, that no man shall be deprived of his liberty, except by due process of law. Of course, minors are as entitled to the benefit of this constitutional protection as any adult, within, what must necessarily be supposed to have been, the intended operation of this provision. In the nature of things, we cannot suppose the authors of this provision to have intended that, before parents could exercise control over their minor children, and restrain them of their liberty, they would be compelled to apply to a court for a decretal order authorizing the restraint. The law of nature requires the subjection of minors to parental control, and we therefore conclude that " the framers of the constitution could not, as men of ordinary prudence and foresight, have intended to prohibit [such control] in the particular case, notwithstanding the language of the prohibition would otherwise include it." [1] The subjection of minors to control being a natural and ordinary condition, when it is clearly established that the State, as *parens patriæ*, succeeds to the parent's rights and duties, in respect to the care of the child, due process of law would be no more necessary to support the assumption of control by the State than it is necessary to justify the parental control. The child is not deprived of a natural right, and hence he is not deprived of his liberty in any legal sense of the term. In a late case the Supreme Court of Illinois has, in an opinion exhibiting considerable warmth of feeling, declared that an adjudication is necessary before the child can be deprived of its natural liberty.[2]

[1] Christiancy, J., in People *v.* Plank Road Co., 9 Mich. 285.

[2] " In cases of writs of *habeas corpus* to bring up infants, there are other rights besides the rights of the father. If improperly or illegally restrained, it is our duty, *ex debito justitiæ* to liberate. The welfare and

§ 50

This is really only a *dictum* of the court, so far as it affirms the right of a child to a trial, before the State can place him under restraint, for in this case the boy was taken from the custody of his father, and the real question at issue was whether the State had a right to interfere with the father's control of the boy.   This aspect of the

rights of the child are also to be considered. The disability of minors does not make slaves or criminals of them. They are entitled to legal rights, and are under legal liabilities. An implied contract for necessaries is binding on them. The only act which they are under a legal incapacity to perform, is the appointment of an attorney. All their other acts are merely voidable or confirmable. They are liable for torts and punishable for crime. Every child over ten years of age may be found guilty of crime. For robbery, burglary, or arson, any minor may be sent to the penitentiary. Minors are bound to pay taxes for support of the government, and constitute a part of the militia, and are compelled to endure the hardship and privation of a soldier's life, in defense of the constitution and the laws; and yet it is assumed that to them liberty is a mere chimera. It is something of which they may have dreamed, but have never enjoyed the fruition.

" Can we hold children responsible for crime, liable for torts, impose onerous burdens upon them, and yet deprive them of the enjoyment of liberty without charge or conviction of crime? The bill of rights declares that ' all men are, by nature, free and independent, and have certain inherent and inalienable rights — among these are life, liberty, and the pursuit of happiness.' This language is not restrictive; it is broad and comprehensive, and declares a grand truth; that ' all men,' all people, everywhere, have the inherent and inalienable right to liberty. Shall we say to the children of the State, you shall not enjoy this right — a right independent of all human laws and regulations? It is declared in the constitution; is higher than the constitution and law, and should be held forever sacred.

"Even criminals can not be convicted and imprisoned without due process of law — without regular trial, according to the course of the common law. Why should minors be imprisoned for misfortune? Destitution of proper parental care, ignorance, idleness and vice, are misfortunes, not crimes. In all criminal prosecutions against minors for grave and heinous offenses, they have the right to demand the nature and cause of the accusation, and a speedy public trial by an impartial jury. All this must precede the final commitment to prison. Why should children, only guilty of misfortune, be deprived of liberty without ' due process of law? '

§ 50

question will be presented subsequently.[1] The following calm, dispassionate language of the Supreme Court of Ohio commends itself to the consideration of the reader. It was a case of committal to reformatory school on an *ex parte* examination by the grand jury, of a boy under sixteen, who had been charged with crime, under statutes which authorize and direct the proceeding:—

"The proceeding is purely statutory; and the commitment, in cases like the present, is not designed as a punishment for crime, but to place minors of the description, and for the causes specified in the statute, under the guardianship of the public authorities named, for proper care and discipline, until they are reformed, or arrive at the age of majority. The institution to which they are committed is a school, not a prison, nor is the character of this detention affected by the fact that it is also a place where juvenile convicts may be sent, who would otherwise be condemned to confinement in the common jail or penitentiary. * * * Owing to the *ex parte* character of the proceeding, it is possible that the commitment of a person might be made on a false and groundless charge. In such a case neither the infant nor any person who would, in the absence of such commitment, be entitled to his custody and services, will be without remedy. If the remedy pro-

---

[1] "It cannot be said that in this case there is no imprisonment. This boy is deprived of a father's care; bereft of home influences; has no freedom of action; is committed for an uncertain time; is branded as a prisoner; made subject to the will of others, and thus feels that he is a slave. Nothing could more contribute to paralyze the youthful energies, crush all noble aspirations, and unfit him for the duties of manhood. Other means of a milder character; other influences of a more kindly nature; other laws less in restraint of liberty would better accomplish the reformation of the depraved, and infringe less upon inalienable rights." People *v.* Turner, 55 Ill. 280. But see, *contra*, Ex parte Ferrier, 103 Ill. 367 (42 Am. Rep. 10).

[1] See *post*, § 166*a*.

§ 50

vided in the twentieth section should not be adequate or available, the existence of a sufficient cause for the detention might, we apprehend, be inquired into by a proceeding in *habeas corpus*." [1]

[1] Prescott *v.* State, 19 Ohio St. 184 (2 Am. Rep. 388).

§ 50

CHAPTER VI.

POLICE REGULATIONS OF THE RIGHTS OF CITIZENSHIP AND
DOMICILE.

SECTION 56. Citizenship and domicile distinguished.
    57. Expatriation.
    58. Naturalization.
    59. Prohibition of emigration.
    60. Compulsory emigration.
    61. Prohibition of immigration.
    62. The public duties of a citizen.

§ 56. Citizenship and domicile distinguished. — The distinction between citizenship and domicile has been so often explained in elementary treatises that only a passing reference will be needed here, in order to refresh the memory of the reader. Mr. Cooley defines a citizen to be " a member of the civil state entitled to all its privileges." [1] Mr. Blackstone's definition of allegiance, which is the obligation of the citizen, is " the tie which binds the subject to the sovereign, in return for that protection which the sovereign affords the subject." [2] Citizenship, therefore, is that political *status* which supports mutual rights and obligations. The State, of which an individual is a citizen, may require of him various duties of a political character ; while he is entitled to the protection of the government against all foreign attacks, and is likewise invested with political rights according to the character of the government of the State, the chief of which is the right of suffrage.

Domicile is the place where one permanently resides. One's permanent residence may be, and usually is, in the country of which he is a citizen, but it need not be, and

---

[1] Cooley on Const. Law, 77.
[2] 1 Bl. Com. *441.

very often is not.   One can be domiciled in a foreign land.
While a domicile in a foreign State subjects the individual
and his personal property to the regulation and control of
the law of the domicile, *i.e.*, creates a local or temporary
allegiance on the part of the individual to the State in
which he is resident, and although he can claim the protection of the laws during his residence in that State, he does
not assume political obligations or acquire political rights,
and can not claim the protection of the government, after
he has taken his departure from the country.   Only a citizen can claim protection outside of the country.

There is no permanent tie binding the resident alien to
the State, and there is no permanent obligation on the part
of either.   The individual is at liberty to abandon his domicile, whenever he so determines, without let or hindrance
on the part of the State, in which he has been resident.
This is certainly true of a domicile in a foreign country.

§ 57.   **Expatriation.** — But it has been persistently maintained by the European powers, until within the last twenty
years, that the citizen cannot throw off his allegiance, and by
naturalization become the citizen of another country.   The
older authorities have asserted the indissolubility of the allegiance of the natural-born subject to his sovereign or State.
Mr. Blackstone says, " it is a principle of universal law that
the natural-born subject of one prince cannot by any act of
his own, no, not by swearing allegiance to another, put off or
discharge his natural allegiance to the former ; for this natural allegiance was intrinsic and primitive, and antecedent
to the other ; and cannot be divested without the concur-
rent act of the prince to whom it was due." [1]   Although all
the States of Europe have provided for the naturalization
of aliens, they have uniformly denied to their own subjects
the right of expatriation.   But when emigration to this
country became general, this right was raised to an interna-

[1] 1 Bl. Com. *446.

§ 57

tional question of great importance, and in conformity with their own interests and their general principles of civil liberty, the United States have strongly insisted upon the natural and absolute right of expatriation. This question has been before the courts of this country,[1] and at an early day the Supreme Court of the United States showed an inclination to take the European view of this right.[2] But the question has been finally settled in favor of the right of expatriation, so far at least as the government of the United States is concerned, by an act of Congress in the following terms : —

" Whereas, the right of expatriation is a natural and inherent right of all people, indispensable to the enjoyment of the rights of life, liberty and the pursuit of happiness ; and whereas, in the recognition of this principle, this government has freely received emigrants from all nations, and invested them with the rights of citizenship ; and whereas it is claimed, that such American citizens, with their descendants, are subjects of foreign States, owing allegiance to the governments thereof ; and whereas it is necessary to the maintenance of public peace that this claim of foreign allegiance should be promptly and finally disavowed: therefore, be it enacted by the Senate and House of Representatives of the United States of America, in Congress assembled, that any declaration, instruction, opinion, order or decision of any officer of this government, which denies,

---

[1] See Inglis *v.* Sailor's Snug Harbor, 3 Pet. 99; Shanks *v.* Dupont, 3 Pet. 242; Stoughton *v.* Taylor, 2 Paine, 655; Jackson *v.* Burns, 3 Binn. 85.

[2] " In the first place, she was born under the allegiance of the British crown, and no act of the government of Great Britain has absolved her from that allegiance. Her becoming a citizen of South Carolina did not, *ipso facto*, work any dissolution of her original allegiance, at least so far as the rights and claims of the British crown were concerned." Shanks *v.* Dupont, 3 Pet. 242. See Talbot *v.* Janson, 3 Dall. 133; Isaac William's case, 2 Cranch, 82, note; Murray *v.* The Charming Betsey, 2 Cranch, 64; The Santissima Trinidad, 7 Wheat. 283; United States *v* Gillies, 1 Pet. C. C. 159; Ainslee *v.* Martin, 9 Mass. 454.

§ 57

restricts, impairs or questions the right of expatriation is
hereby declared inconsistent with the fundamental principles of this government.'' [1]

The United States government has actively sought the
establishment of treaties with other countries, in which the
absolute right of expatriation is unqualifiedly recognized;
and such great success has attended these efforts, that
expatriation may now be asserted to be a recognized international right, which no government can deny.[2]

§ 58. **Naturalization.** — In order that one may expatri-
ate himself, he must, by naturalization, become the citizen of
another State. International law does not recognize the
right to become a cosmopolitan. But because expatriation
is recognized as a right indispensable to the enjoyment of
the rights of life, liberty, and the pursuit of happiness, and
which cannot be abridged or denied to any one, it does not
follow that one has a natural and absolute right to become
the citizen of any State which he should select. A State
has as absolute a right to determine whom it shall make
citizens by naturalization, as the individuals have to determine of what State they will be citizens. Citizenship by
birth within the country does not depend upon the will of
society. By a sort of inheritance the natural-born citizen
acquires his right of citizenship. But when a foreigner
applies for naturalization, his acquisition of a new citizenship depends upon the agreement of the two contracting
parties.

The State, therefore, has the unqualified right to deny
citizenship to any alien who may apply therefor, and the
grounds of the objection cannot be questioned. The alien
has no political rights in the State, and he cannot attack
the motive of the State in rejecting him.

[1] Act of July 27, 1868, 15 Stat. at Large, 223, 224.
[2] The United States have entered into such treaties with almost all the
countries of Europe.

§ 58

§ 59. **Prohibition of emigration.** — Political economy teaches us that national disaster may ensue from an excessive depopulation of the country. When the population of a country is so small that its resources can not be developed, it is an evil which emigration in any large degree would render imminent; and the temptation would, under such circumstances, be great to prohibit and restrain the emigration to other lands, while the impulse would increase in proportion to the growth of the evil of depopulation. Has the State the right to prohibit emigration, and prevent it by the institution of the necessary police surveillance? It cannot be questioned that the State may deny the right of emigration to one who owes some immediate service to the State, as for example in the case of war when one has been drafted for the army, or where one under the laws of the country is bound to perform some immediate military service.[1] But it would seem, with this exception, that the natural and unrestricted right of emigration would be recognized as a necessary consequence of the recognition of the right of expatriation. If expatriation is indispensable to the enjoyment of the rights of life, liberty and the pursuit of happiness, the right of emigration must be more essential; for expatriation necessarily involves emigration, although emigration may take place without expatriation. But this right of prohibition was once generally claimed and exercised and Russia still exercises the right.[2]

§ 60. **Compulsory emigration.** — General want and suffering may be occasioned by over-population. Indeed, according to the Malthusian theory, excessive population is the great and chief cause of poverty. From the standpoint of public welfare, it would seem well for the State to determine how many and who, should remain domiciled in

---

[1] The compulsory military service for four of the best years of a man's life has been the chief moving cause of emigration of the Germans.

[2] Phillemore International Law, 348, 349.

§ 60

the country, in order that the population may be regulated
and kept within the limits of possible well-being, and transport the excess of the population to foreign uninhabited
lands, or to other parts of the same country, which are
more sparsely settled. But from the standpoint of the individual and of his rights, this power of control assumes a
different aspect. If government is established for the benefit of the individual, and society is but a congregation of
individuals for their mutual benefit; once the individual is
recognized as a part of the body politic, he has as much
right to retain his residence in that country as his neighbor;
and there is no legal power in the State to compel him to
migrate, in order that those who remain may have more
breathing space. Let those emigrate who feel the need of
more room.

Another cause of evil, which prompt the employment of
the remedy of compulsory emigration, would be an ineradicable antagonism serious enough to cause or to threaten social disorder and turmoil. Can the government make a forced
colonization of one or the other of the antagonistic races?
This is a more stubborn evil than that which arises from excessive population; for want, especially when the government
offers material assistance, will drive a large enough number
out of the country to keep down the evil. The only modern
case of forcible emigration, known to history, is that of the
Acadians. Nova Scotia was originally a French colony,
and when it was conquered by the British, a large non-
combatant population of French remained, but refused to
take the oath of allegiance. The French in the neighboring
colonies kept up communication with these French inhabitants of Nova Scotia and, upon the promise to recapture the
province, incited them to a passive resistance of the British
authority. The presence of such a large hostile population
certainly tended to make the British hold upon Nova Scotia
very insecure, and the English finally compelled these French
people to migrate. While the circumstances tend to miti-

§ 60

gate the gravity of this outrage upon the rights of the individual, the act has been universally condemned.[1] The State
has no right to compel its citizens to emigrate for any cause,
except as a punishment for crime. It may persuade and
offer assistance, but it can not employ force in effecting
emigration, whatever may be the character of the evil, which
threatens society, and which prompts a compulsory emigration of a part of its population.

But it does not follow from this position, that the State
has not the right to compel the emigration of residents of
the country, who are not citizens. The obligation of the
State to resident aliens is only temporary, consists chiefly
in a guaranty of the protection of its laws, as long as the
residence continues, and does not deprive the State of the
power to terminate the residence by their forcible removal.
They can be expelled, whenever their continued residence
for any reason becomes obnoxious or harmful to the citizen or to the State.

Although the aborigines of a country may not, under the
constitutional law of the State, be considered citizens,[2] they

---

[1] While the above was being written, the world was startled by the
expulsion from France of the Orleans and Bonaparte princes, who are in
the line of inheritance of the lost crown. These princes were not charged
with any offense against the existing government of France, or against
France. They were monarchists, and, it is true, they refused to abjure
their claims to the throne of France. But, beyond the formation of
marital alliances with the reigning families of Europe, they were not
charged with any actions hostile or menacing to the present government.
The ineradicable antagonism between monarchy and republicanism may
possibly furnish justification for these expulsions; but one who has thoroughly assimilated the doctrine of personal liberty can hardly escape the
conclusion that they were at least questionable exercises of police power.

[2] This is the rule of law in this country in respect to the legal status
of the Indian. As long as he continues his connection with his tribe,
and consequently occupies towards the United States a more or less foreign relation, it would be unwise as well as illogical to invest him with
the rights of citizenship. Goodell *v.* Jackson, 20 Johns. 693, 710; McKay
v. Campbell, 2 Sawyer, 118. But it is claimed, with much show of reason
for it, that as soon as he abandons the tribal relation, and subjects him-

§ 60

are likewise not alien residents and cannot be expelled from the country or forcibly removed from place to place, except in violation of individual liberty.   But the treatment offered by the United States government to the Indians would indicate that they have reached a different conclusion.   The forcible removal of the Indians from place to place, in violation of the treaties previously made with them, although there is a pretence that the treaties have become forfeited on account of their wrongful acts, differs in character but little from the expulsion of the Acadians, for whose sufferings the world felt a tender sympathy.

§ 61. **Prohibition of immigration.** — Since the State owes no legal duty to a foreigner, and the foreigner has no legal right to a residence in a country of which he is not a citizen, a government may restrain and even absolutely prohibit immigration, if that should be the policy of the State.   The policy of each State will vary with its needs.   In this country, the need of immigration has been so great that we offer the greatest possible inducements to immigrants to settle in our midst.   So general and unrestricted has immigration been in the past, that a large class of our people have denied the right to refuse ingress to any foreigner, unless he is a criminal.   As a sentiment, in conformity with the universal brotherhood of man, this position may be justified ; but, as a living legal principle, it cannot be sustained.   The government of a country must protect its own people at all hazards.   Races are too dissimilar to bring into harmonious relations with each other under one government, and the presence in the same country of antagonistic races always engenders social and economical disturbances.   If they are already citizens of the same country, as, for example, the negroes and the whites of the Southern States,

self to the jurisdiction of our government, he becomes as much a citizen of the United States as any other native.   See Story on Constitution, § 1933.

§ 61

there is no help for the evil but a gradual solution of the problem by self-adaptation to each other, or a voluntary exodus of the weaker race. But when an altogether dissimilar race seeks admission to the country, not being citizens, the State may properly refuse them the privilege of immigration. And this is the course adopted by the American government towards the Chinese who threaten to invade and take complete possession of the Pacific coast. After making due allowance for the exaggerations of the evil, there can be no doubt that the racial problem, involved in the Chinese immigration, was sufficiently serious to justify its prohibition. The economical problem, arising from a radical difference in the manners and mode of life of the Chinese, not to consider the charges of their moral depravity, threatened to disturb the industrial and social conditions of those States, to the great injury of the native population. It was even feared that the white population, not being able to subsist on the diet of the Chinese, and consequently being unable to work for as low wages, would be forced to leave the country, and as they moved eastward, the Chinese would take their place, until finally the whole country would swarm with the almond-eyed Asiatic. Self-preservation is the first law of nature, with States and societies, as with individuals. It can not be doubted that the act of Congress, which prohibited all future Chinese immigration, was within the constitutional powers of the United States.

The United States government have also instituted police regulations for the purpose of preventing pauper immigration, and when an immigrant is without visible means of support, the steamship company which transported him is required to take him back. The purpose of these regulations itself suggests the reasons that might be advanced in justification of them, and, therefore, no statement of them is necessary.

§ 61

§ 62. **The public duties of a citizen.** — In return for the protection guaranteed to the citizen, he is required to do whatever is reasonable and necessary in support of the government and the promotion of the public welfare. It will not be necessary to enter into details, for these duties vary with a change in public exigencies. The object of taxation is treated more particularly in a subsequent section.[1] The ordinary public duties of an American citizen, are to assist the peace officers in preserving the public order and serving legal processes, and to obey all commands of the officers to aid in the suppression of all riots, insurrections and other breaches of the peace; to serve as jurors in the courts of justice, to perform military service, in time of peace as well as in war. It is common for the States to require its male citizens to enroll themselves in the State militia, and receive instruction and to practice in military tactics, and in time of war there can be no doubt of the power of the government to compel a citizen to take up arms in defense of the country against the attacks of an enemy, in the same manner as it may require the citizen to aid in suppressing internal disorders.[2] At an earlier day, it was also a common custom to require of the citizens of a town or city the duty of assisting in the quenching of accidental fires and the prevention of conflagrations, and in some of the States

---

[1] See *post*, § 129 *et seq.*

[2] But defensive warfare must in this connection be distinguished from offensive warfare. The duty of the citizen to repel an attack upon his country is clear, but it is certainly not considered in the United States a duty of the citizen to aid the government in the prosecution of an offensive war, instituted for the purpose of aggrandizement. But the question involves the practical difficulty of determining which party in a particular war is on the defensive, and which is the attacking party. It is not necessary for the territory of one's country to be invaded, in order that the war may be offensive. Substantial and valuable international rights may be trespassed without a blow being struck or a foot of land invaded, and usually both parties claim to be on the defensive. But the difficulty in answering this question of fact does not affect the accuracy of the theoretic distinction, although it does take away its practical value.

§ 62

(notably South Carolina) every male citizen, between certain ages, was at one time required to be an active member of a militia or fire company.[1]

It was also at one time the common duty of a citizen to perform, or supply at his expense, labor upon the public roads, in order to keep them in repairs. But this specific duty is each day becoming more uncommon, and the repairs are being made by employees of the State or municipal community, whose wages are paid out of the common fund. Indeed, the general tendency at the present day is to relieve the citizen of the duty of performing these public duties by the employment of individuals who are specially charged with them, and perform them as a matter of business. Even in regard to the matter of military service in time of war, this tendency is noticeable. Whenever a draft is made by the government for more men, and one whose name is found in the list desires to avoid the personal performance of this public duty, he is permitted to procure a substitute. The duty of acting as juror is about the only public duty, whose performance is still required to be personal, and even that is somewhat in danger of substitutive performance. The flimsy and unreasonable excuses, too often given and received for discharge from jury duty, are fast paving the way to the appointment of professional jurymen.

---

[1] But it is now found to be more profitable, in combating the danger of fire in municipal life, to employ men who are specially charged with the performance of this duty. Voluntary, or unprofessional, fire departments are now to be found, in the United States, only in the villages and small towns.

§ 62

CHAPTER VII.

POLICE CONTROL OF MORALITY AND RELIGION.

SECTION 68. Crime and vice distinguished—their relation to Police power.
69. Sumptuary laws.
70. Church and State — Historical synopsis.
71. Police regulation of religion — Constitutional restrictions.
72. State control of churches, and congregations.
73. Religious criticism and blasphemy distinguished.
74. Permissible limitations upon religious worship.
75. Religious discrimination in respect to admissibility of testimony.
76. Sunday laws.

§ 68. **Crime and vice distinguished — Their relation to police power.**— In legal technics, crime is any act which involves the violation of a public law, and which by theory of law constitutes an offense against the State. Crimes are punished by means of prosecution by State officers. When an act violates some private right, and it is either so infrequent, or so easily controlled by private or individual prosecutions, that the safety of society does not require it to be declared a crime, and the subject of a criminal prosecution, it is then denominated a *trespass*, or tort. The same act may be both a tort and a crime, and with the exception of those crimes which involve the violation of strictly public rights, such as treason, malfeasances in office, and the like, all crimes are likewise torts. The same act works an injury to the State or to the individual whose right is invaded, and according as we contemplate the injury to the State or to the individual, the act is a crime or a tort. The injury to the State consists in the disturbance of the public peace and order. The injury to the individual consists in the trespass upon some right.

§ 68 (148)

But from either standpoint the act must be considered as an infringement of a right. The act must constitute an *injuria, i. e*, the violation of a right.

The distinction thus given between a crime and a tort is purely technical, and proceeds from the habit of the common-law jurist to account for differences in legal rules and regulations by fictitious distinctions, which were in fact untrue. There is no essential difference between a crime and a tort, except in the remedy. No act can be properly called either a crime or a tort, unless it be a violation of some right, and with the exception of those crimes which consist in the violation of some public right, such as treason, crimes are nothing more than violations of private rights, which are made the subject of public prosecution, because individual prosecution is deemed an ineffectual remedy. The idea of an injury to the State, as the foundation for the criminal prosecution is a pure fiction, indulged in by the jurists in order to conform to the iron cast maxim, that no one but the party injured can maintain an action against the wrong-doer. A crime, then, is a trespass upon some right, public or private, and the trespass is sought to be redressed or prosecuted whether the remedy be a criminal prosecution or a private suit.

A vice, on the other hand, consists in an inordinate, and hence immoral, gratification of one's passions and desires. The primary damage is to one's self. When we contemplate the nature of a vice, we are not conscious of a trespass upon the rights of others. If the vice gives rise to any secondary or consequential damage to others we are only able to ascertain the effect after a more or less serious deliberation. An intimate acquaintance with sociology reveals the universal interdependence of individuals in the social state ; *no man liveth unto himself*, and no man can be addicted to vices, even of the most trivial character, without doing damage to the material interests of society, and affecting each individual of the community to a greater or less degree.

§ 68

But the evils to society, flowing from vices, are indirect and remote and do not involve trespasses upon rights. The indolent and idle are actual burdens upon society, if they are without means of support, and in any event society suffers from them because they do not, as producers, contribute their share to the world's wealth. We may very well conceive of idleness becoming so common as to endanger the public welfare. But these people are not guilty of the *crime* of indolence; we can only charge them with the *vice* of idleness.

Now, in determining the scope of police power, we concluded that it was confined to the imposition of burdens and restrictions upon the rights of individuals, in order to prevent injury to others; that it consisted in the application of measures for the enforcement of the legal maxim, *sic utere tuo, ut alienum non lædas*. The object of police power is the prevention of crime, the protection of rights against the assaults of others. The police power of the government cannot be brought into operation for the purpose of exacting obedience to the rules of morality, and banishing vice and sin from the world. The moral laws can exact obedience only *in foro conscientiæ*. The municipal law has only to do with trespasses. It cannot be called into play in order to save one from the evil consequences of his own vices, for the violation of a right by the action of another must exist or be threatened, in order to justify the interference of law. It is true that vice always carries in its train more or less damage to others, but it is an indirect and remote consequence; it is more incidental than consequential. At least it is so remote that very many other causes co-operate to produce the result, and it is difficult, if not impossible, to ascertain which is the controlling and real cause.[1]

---

[1] Thus the intemperance of a man may result in the suffering of his wife from want, because of his consequent inability to earn the requisite means of support. But she may have been equally responsible for her own suffering on account of her recklessness in marrying him, or she may

§ 68

Because of this uncertainty, and practical inability to determine responsibility, it has long been established as the invariable rule of measuring the damages to be recovered in an action for the violation of a right, that only the proximate and direct consequences are to be considered. *In jure non remota causa, sed proxima spectatur.* If this is a necessary limitation upon the recovery of damages where a clearly established legal right is trespassed upon, there surely is greater reason for its application to a case where there is no invasion of a right, in a case of *damnum absque injuria.* It is apparently conceded by all, that vice cannot be punished unless damage to others can be shown as accruing or threatening. It cannot be made a legal wrong for one to become intoxicated in the privacy of his room, when the limitation upon his means did not make drunkenness an extravagance. If he has no one dependent upon him, and does not offend the sensibility of the public, by displaying his intoxication in the public highways, he has committed no wrong, *i.e.*, he has violated no right, and hence he cannot be punished. When, therefore, the damage to others, imputed as the cause to an act in itself constituting no trespass, is made the foundation of a public regulation or prohibition of that act, it must be clearly shown that the act is the real and predominant cause of the damage. The intervention of so many co-operating causes in all cases of remote damage makes this a practical impossibility. Certainly the act itself cannot be made unlawful, because in certain cases a remote damage is suffered by others on account of it.

It may be urged that this rule for the measurement of damages may be changed, and the damages imputed to the remote cause, without violating any constitutional limitation,

be extravagant and wasteful; or she may by her own conduct have driven him into intemperance, and many other facts may be introduced to render it very doubtful to which of these moral delinquencies her suffering might be traced as the real moving cause.

§ 68

and such has been the ruling of the New York Court of Appeals.[1]

If this rule rested purely upon the will of the governing power, if it was itself a police regulation, instituted for the purpose of preventing excessive and costly legislation, its abrogation would be possible. But it has its foundation in fact. It is deduced from the accumulated experience of ages that the proximate cause is always the predominant in effecting the result, it is a law of nature, immutable and unvarying.[2] The abrogation of this rule violates the constitutional limitation " no man shall be deprived of his life, liberty or property, except by due process of law," when in pursuance thereof one is imprisoned or fined for a damage which he did not in fact produce. The inalienable right to " liberty

---

[1] Bertholf v. O'Rielly, 74 N. Y. 309, 509 (30 Am. Rep. 323). In this case it was held that the legislature has power to create a cause of action for damages, in favor of one who was injured in person or property by the act of an intoxicated person, against the owner of real property, whose only connection with the injury is that he leased premises, where liquor causing the intoxication was sold or given away, with the knowledge that the intoxicating liquors were to be sold thereon. "The act of 1873 is not invalid because it creates a right of action and imposes a liability not known to the common law. There is no such limit to legislative power. The legislature may alter or repeal the common law. It may create new offenses, enlarge the scope of civil remedies, and fasten the responsibility for injuries upon persons against whom the common law gives no remedy. We do not mean that the legislature may impose upon one man liability for an injury suffered by another, with which he has no connection. But it may change the rule of the common law, which looks only to the proxi_ mate cause of the mischief, in attaching legal responsibility, and allow a recovery to be had against those whose acts contributed, though re motely, to produce it. This is what the legislature had done in the act of 1873. That there is or may be a relation in the nature of cause and effect, between the act of selling or giving away intoxicating liquors, and the injuries for which a remedy is given, is apparent, and upon this relation the legislature has proceeded in enacting the law in question. It is an extension by the legislature, of the principles expressed in the maxim sic utere tuo, ut alienum non lœdas to cases to which it has not before been applied, and the propriety of such an application is a legislative and not a judicial question.

[2] See post, § 129.

§ 68

and the pursuit of happiness " is violated, when he is prohibited from doing what does not involve a trespass upon others.

In order, therefore, that vices may be subjected to legal control and regulation, it will be necessary to show that it constitutes a trespass upon some one's rights, or proximately causes damage to others, and that is held to be a practical impossibility. Under the established rules of constitutional construction, it is quite probable that proximate damage without trespass upon rights may be made actionable, and the vice which causes it to be prohibited, without infringing the constitution ; but the further practical difficulty is to be met and avoided that a trespass upon one's rights, or the threatening danger of such a trespass, is necessary to procure from the people that amount of enthusiastic support, without which a law becomes a dead letter. It is the universal experience that laws can not be enforced which impose penalties upon acts which do not constitute infringements upon the rights of others. But this is not a constitutional objection, and does not affect the binding power of the law, if a sufficient moral force can be brought together to secure its enforcement. This is a question of expediency, which can only be addressed to the discretion of the legislature.

§ 69. **Sumptuary laws.** — Of the same general character as laws for the correction of vices, are the sumptuary laws of a past civilization. Extravagance in expenditures, the control of which was the professed design of these laws, was proclaimed to be a great evil, threatening the very foundations of the State ; but it is worthy of notice that in those countries and in the age in which they were more common, despotism was rank, and the common people were subjected to the control of these sumptuary laws, in order that by reducing their consumption they may increase the sum of enjoyment of the privileged classes. The diminution of their

§ 69

means of luxuriant living was really the danger against which
the sumptuary laws were directed. In proportion to the
growth of popular yearning for personal liberty, these laws
have become more and more unbearable, until now it is the
universal American sentiment, that these laws, at least in
their grosser forms, and hence on principle, are violations
of the inalienable right to "liberty and the pursuit of happiness," and involve a deprivation of liberty and property — through a limitation upon the means and ways of
enjoyment — without due process of law. Judge Cooley,
says: "The ideas which suggested such laws are now ex-
ploded utterly, and no one would seriously attempt to justify them in the present age. The right of every man to do
what he will with his own, not interfering with the recip-
rocal right of others, is accepted among the fundamentals
of our law."[1] It is true that a public and general extravagance in the ways of living would lead to national decay.
Nations have often fallen into decay from the corruption
caused by the individual indulgence of luxurious tastes.
But this damage to others is very remote, if it can be
properly called consequential, and in any event of its becoming a widespread evil, the nation would be so honey-
combed with corruption that the means of redemption, or
regeneration, except from without, would not be at hand.
The enforcement of the laws could not be secured. The
inability to secure a reasonable enforcement of a law is
always a strong indication of its unconstitutionality in a
free State.

Public sentiment in the United States is too strong in its
opposition to all laws which exert an irksome restraint upon
individual liberty, in order that sumptuary laws in their
grosser forms may be at all possible. But as far as the
liquor prohibition laws have for their object the prevention
of the consumption of intoxicating liquors, they are sumpt-

---

[1] Cooley Const. Lim. *385.

§ 69

ary laws, and are constitutionally objectionable on that ground, if the measures are not confined to the prohibition of the sale of liquors. This is the usual limitation upon the scope of the prohibition laws. But it is said that in the States of Wisconsin and Nevada laws have been enacted by the Legislature, prohibiting the act of "treating" to intoxicating drinks, making it a misdemeanor, and punishable by fine or imprisonment. There is probably very little doubt that a large proportion of the intemperance among the youth of this country may be traced to this peculiarly American custom or habit of "treating." But inasmuch as the persons, who are directly injured — and this is the only consequential injury which can be made the subject of legislation — are all willing participants, except in the very extreme cases of beastly intoxication, when one or more of the parties "treated" cannot be considered as rational beings — *volenti non fit injuria* — these regulations are open to the constitutional objection of a deprivation or restraint of liberty, in a case in which no right has been invaded. The manifest inability to secure, even in the slightest degree, an enforcement of these curious experiments in legislation has been their most effective antidote. But while, as a general proposition, we may freely use what ever food or clothing taste or caprice may suggest, without the exercise of any governmental restraint, there are some exceptions to the rule, which will probably be admitted without question. Certainly no one would seriously doubt the constitutionality of the laws, to be found on the statute book of every State, which provide for the punishment of an indecent exposure of the person in the public thoroughfares. Every one can be required to appear in public in decent attire. It is not definitely settled what is meant by indecent attire, but probably the courts would experience no difficulty in reaching the conclusion that any attire is indecent, which left exposed parts of the human body which according to the common custom of the country are invari-

§ 69

ably covered. It is questionable that the courts can go
farther in the requirement of decent attire, as, for example,
to prohibit appearance in the streets in what are usually
worn as undergarments, provided that the body is properly
covered to prevent exposure.

Another phase of police power, in this connection, is the
prohibition of the appearance in public of men in women's
garb, and *vice versa*. The use of such dress could serve no
useful purpose, and tends to public immorality and the perpetration of frauds. Its prohibition is, therefore, probably constitutional. But it does not follow that a law, which
prohibited the use by men of a specific article of women's
dress, or to women the use of particular piece of men's
clothing, would be constitutional. The prohibition must be
confined to those cases, in which immorality or the practice
of deception is facilitated, viz., where one sex appears
altogether in the usual attire of the other sex.

§ 70. **Church and State — Historical synopsis.** —
Religious liberty, in all its completeness, is a plant of
American growth. In no other country, and in no preceding age, was there anything more than religious toleration, and even toleration was not a common experience.
Everywhere, the State was made the instrument for the
propagation of the doctrines of some one religious sect, and
all others were either directly prohibited, or so greatly discriminated against in the bestowal of State patronage, as to
amount, in effect, to an actual prohibition. On the other
hand, the State would secure the support of the church in
the enforcement of its mandates. Before the American
era, the gradual development of the human soul, under the
workings of the forces of civilization, had long since done
away with physical torture. Heretics were not burned at
the stake, or put to the rack, but the same cruel intolerance
exacted the creation of social and political distinctions,
which were equally effective in oppressing those who dif-

fered in their religious faith with the majority. Protestant England and Germany oppressed the Catholics, and Catholic France and Italy oppressed the Protestants, while the infidel received mercy and toleration at the hands of neither. Most of the immigrants to the American colonies were refugees from religious oppression, driven to the wilds of America, in order to worship the God of the Universe according to the dictates of their conscience. The Puritans of New England, the Quakers of Pennsylvania, the English Catholics of Maryland, and the Huguenots of the Carolinas, sought on this continent that religious liberty which was not to be found in Europe. I should not say " religious liberty," for that is not what they sought. They desired only to be freed from the restraint of an intolerant and opposing majority. They desired only to settle in a country where the adherents of their peculiar creed could control the affairs of State. Notwithstanding their sad experience in the old world, when they settled in America, they became as intolerant of dissenters from the faith of the majority, as their enemies had been towards them. Church and State were not yet separate. Each colony was dominated by some sect, and the others fared badly. The performance of religious duties was enforced by the institution of statutory penalties. The clergyman, particularly of New England, was not only the shepherd of the soul, but he was likewise, in some sense, a magistrate. " The heedless one who absented himself from the preaching on a Sabbath was hunted up by the tithing man, was admonished severely, and, if he still persisted in his evil ways, was fined, exposed in the stocks or imprisoned in the cage. To sit patiently on the rough board seats, while the preacher turned the hour-glass for the third time, and with his voice husky from shouting, and the sweat pouring in streams down his face, went on for an hour more, was a delectable privilege. In such a community the authority of the reverend man was almost supreme. To speak disrespectfully concerning him, to jeer

§ 70

at his sermons, or to laugh at his odd ways, was sure to bring down on the offender a heavy fine." [1]   The religious liberty of the colonial period meant nothing more than freedom from religious restraint for the majority, while the minority suffered as much persecution as the immigrants had themselves suffered in Europe, a striking illustration of the accuracy of the doctrine that there are no worse oppressors than the oppressed when they have in turn become the ruling class.   It is no exaggerated view to take of the probabilities, that the grand establishment of religious liberty of to-day would not have been attained, at least in the present age, if the rapid increase in the number of religious sects, each one of which was predominant in one or more of the colonies, had not militated against the successful union of the colonies into one common country.   " In some of the States, Episcopalians constituted the predominant sect ; in others, Presbyterians ; in others, Congregationalists ; in others, Quakers, and in others, again, there was a close numerical rivalry among contending sects. It was impossible that there should not arise perpetual strife and perpetual jealousy on the subject of ecclesiastical ascendancy, if the national government were left free to create a religious establishment.   The only security was in extirpating the power." [2]   Congress was therefore denied by the first amendment to the Constitution of the United States the power to make any law respecting an establishment of religion or prohibiting the free exercise thereof. " Thus, the whole power over the subject of religion is left exclusively to the State governments, to be acted upon according to their own sense of justice and the State constitutions ; and the Catholic and Protestant, the Calvinist and the Armenian, the Jew and the infidel, may sit down at

---

[1] McMaster's Hist. of People of U. S., vol. I., p. 31.
[2] Story on the Constitution, § 1879.

§ 70

the common table of the national councils, without any inquisition into their faith or mode of worship."[1]

Proceeding from this limitation upon the power of the national government to regulate religion, there was ultimately incorporated into the constitutions of almost all of the States a prohibition of all State interference in matters of religion, thus laying the foundation for that development of a complete and universal religious liberty, a liberty enjoyed alike by all, whatever may be their faith or creed. Thus and then, for the first time in the history of the world, was there a complete divorce of church and State. But even with the enactment of the constitutional provisions, religious liberty was not assured to all. Legal discriminations, on account of religious opinions, exist in some of the States to the present day, and public opinion in most American communities is still in a high degree intolerant.[2] The complete abrogation of all State interference in matters of religion is of slow growth, and can only be attained with the growth of public opinion.

§ 71. **Police regulation of religion — Constitutional restrictions.** — If there were no provisions in the American constitutions specially applicable to the matter of police regulation of religion, the considerations which would deny to the State the control and prevention of vice would also constitute insuperable objections to State interference in matters of religion. But the rivalry and contention of the religious sects not only demanded constitutional prohibition of the interference of the national government, but gave rise to the incorporation of like prohibitions in the various State constitutions. The exact phraseology varies with each constitution, but the practical effect is believed in the main to be the same in all of them. These provisions not only prohibit all church establishments, but also guarantee

[1] Story on Constitution, § 1879.
[2] See *post*, § 75.

§ 71

to each individual the right to worship God in his own way, and to give free expression to his religious views. The prohibition of a religious establishment not only prevents the establishment of a distinctively State church, but likewise prohibits all preferential treatment of the sects in the bestowal of State patronage or aid. A law is unconstitutional which gives to one or more religious sects a privilege that is not enjoyed equally by all.[1] " Whatever establishes a distinction against one class or sect is, to the extent to which the distinction operates unfavorably, a persecution ; and if based on religious grounds, a religious persecution. The extent of the discrimination is not material to the principle, it is enough that it creates an inequality of right or privilege." [2]

But while religious establishments and unequal privileges are prohibited, and the State in its dealings with the individual is to know no orthodoxy or heterodoxy, no Christianity or infidelity, no Judaism or Mohammedanism, the law cannot but recognize the fact that Christianity is in the main the religion of this country. While equality, in respect to the bestowal of privileges, is to be strictly observed, the recognition of the prevailing religion, in order to foster and encourage the habit of worship as a State policy, is permissible, provided there is no unnecessary discrimination in favor of any particular sect. It is said that only *unnecessary* discrimination is prohibited. By that is meant that, in the encouragement of religious worship, there is in some cases an unavoidable recognition of the overwhelming prevalence of the Christian religion in this country. The masses of this country, if they profess any religious creed at all, are Christians. Thus, for example, it has been long the custom to appoint chaplains to the army and navy of the United States, and the sessions of Congress and of the State legisla-

---

1 Shreveport *v.* Levy, 27 La. Ann. 671.
2 Cooley Const. Lim. *469.

§ 71

tures are usually opened with religious exercises. These chaplains are naturally Christian clergymen. If they were the teachers of any other religion, their public ministrations would fail in the object of their appointment, viz. : the encouragement of religious worship, because such exercises would offend the religious sensibilities and arouse the opposition of the masses, instead of exciting in them a greater desire for spiritual enlightenment. But these regulations can go no further than the institution and maintenance of devotional exercises. If attendance upon these exercises is made compulsory upon the army and navy, and upon the members of the legislative bodies, there would be a clear violation of the religious liberty of the person who was compelled to attend against his will. The Jew and the infidel cannot be forced to attend them.[1]

This question has of late years been much discussed in its bearings upon the conduct of religious exercises in the public schools of this country. It has been held that the school authorities may compel the pupils to read the Bible in the schools, even against the objection and protest of the parents.[2] But it would appear that this view is erroneous. It is true that the regulation does not constitute such a gross violation of the religious liberty of the child, as it would, if attendance upon the school was compulsory. It is true that the Hebrew or infidel need not attend the public schools, if he objects to the religious exercises conducted there. But such a regulation would amount to the bestowal of unequal privileges, which is as much prohibited by our constitutional law as direct religious proscription. In accordance with the permissible recognition of Christianity as the prevailing religion of this country, it may be permitted of the school authorities to provide for devotional exercises according to the Christian faith, but neither teacher nor pupil can lawfully

---

[1] Cooley Const. Lim. *471.

[2] See Donahue v. Richards, 38 Me. 376; Spiller v. Woburn, 12 Allen, 127.

11   § 71

be compelled to attend.[1]   All education must be built upon
the corner-stone of morality, in order that any good may
come out of it to the individual or to society ; and an educational course, which did not incorporate the teaching of
moral principles, would at least be profitless, if not abso-

---

[1] Speller *v.* Woburn, 12 Allen, 127.   In Iowa by statute it was provided
that the Bible shall not be excluded from the public schools but that no
pupil shall be required to read it contrary to the wishes of his parent or
guardian.   In declaring the statute to be constitutional, the court says:
" The plaintiff's position is that by the use of the school-house as a place for
reading the Bible, repeating the Lord's prayer and singing religious songs,
it is made a place of worship ; and so his children are compelled to attend
a place of worship, and he, as a taxpayer, is compelled to pay taxes for
building and repairing a place of worship.   We can conceive that exercises like those described might be adopted with other views than those
of worship, and possibly they are in the case at bar; but it is hardly to
be presumed that this is wholly so.   For the purposes of the opinion it
may be conceded that the teachers do not intend wholly to exclude the
idea of worship.   It would follow that the school-house is, in some sense,
for the time being, made a place of worship.   But it seems to us that if
we should hold that it is made a place of worship within the meaning of
of the constitution, we should put a very strained construction upon it.
" The object of the provision, we think, is not to prevent the casual use of
a public building as a place for offering prayer, or doing other acts of religious worship, but to prevent the enactment of a law, whereby any person
can be compelled to pay taxes for building or repairing any place, designed
to be used distinctively as a place of worship.   The object, we think, was
to prevent an improper burden.   It is, perhaps, not to be denied that the
principle, carried out to its extreme logical results, might be sufficient to
sustain the appellant's position, yet we cannot think that the people of
Iowa, in adopting the constitution, had such an extreme view in mind.
The burden of taxation by reason of the casual use of a public building
for worship, or even such stated use as that shown in the case at bar, is
not appreciably greater.   We do not think indeed that the plaintiff's real
objection grows out of the matter of real taxation.   We infer from his
argument that his real objection is that the religious exercises are made a
part of the educational system into which his children must be drawn, or
made to appear singular, and perhaps be subjected to some inconvenience.   But so long as the plaintiff's children are not required to be in
attendance at the exercises, we cannot regard the objection as one of
great weight.   Besides, if we regard it as of greater weight than we do,
we should have to say that we do not find anything in the constitution or
law upon which the plaintiff can properly ground his application for relief."   Moore *v.* Monroe, 64 Iowa, 367 (52 Am. Rep. 444).

§ 71

lutely dangerous. The development of the mind without the elevation of the soul, only sharpens the individual's wits and makes him more dangerous to the commonwealth. The teaching of morality is therefore not in any sense objectionable ; on the contrary, it should be made the chief aim of the public school system. But religion should be carefully distinguished from morality. The Jew, the Christian, the Chinese, the Mohammedans, the infidels and atheists, all may alike be taught the common principles of morality, without violating their religious liberty. The law exacts an obedience to the more vital and fundamental principles of morality, and the State can as well provide for moral instruction in its public schools. It is its duty to do so. But moral instruction does not necessitate the use of the Bible, or any other recognition of Christianity, and such recognition is unconstitutional, when forced upon an unwilling pupil.

§ 72. **State control of churches and congregations.** — In the English law of corporations, one of the classifications is into *ecclesiastical* and *lay*. The religious incorporations were called ecclesiastical, and because of the legal recognition and establishment of church and religion, they are possessed of peculiar characteristics, which called for this special classification. But in this country there is no need for it. In conformity with the general encouragement of religious worship, voluntary religious societies are at their request incorporated under the general laws, in order that they may hold and transmit property, and do other necessary acts as a corporate body, which without incorporation would be the joint acts of the individual members, with the general liability of partners. All religious societies are alike entitled to incorporation, and whatever privileges are granted to one society or sect, must be granted to all, in order not to offend the constitutional prohibition.

Upon the incorporation of a religious society, two differ-

§ 72

ent bodies, co-existing and composed of the same members, are to be recognized. The religious organization, together with all the spiritual affairs of the society, has received no legal recognition and has, in fact, no legal *status*, except as it might affect the temporal affairs and civil rights of the members of the corporation, wherewith it is so intimately bound up that it is difficult at times to trace the line of demarcation. There has been no incorporation of the spiritual organization. Its members have only become incorporators of the religious corporation. While the corporation and the spiritual organization are usually composed of the same members, it is not at all impossible for what appears, to clericals and laymen alike, as a remarkable anomaly to happen, viz. : that some of the members of the corporation are not members of the spiritual corporation, and some members of the latter do not belong to the temporal society. Of course, this is only possible when the organic law of the corporation does not require membership in the spiritual organization, as a condition of membership in the legal incorporation. The law cannot undertake to regulate the religious affairs of the society, or overrule the decisions and actions of the properly constituted authorities of the church in respect to such religious affairs. The creed, articles of faith, church discipline, and ecclesiastical relations generally, are beyond State regulation or supervision. " Over the church, as such, the legal or temporal tribunals of the State do not profess to have any jurisdiction whatever, except so far as is necessary to protect the civil rights of others, and to preserve the public peace. All questions relating to the faith and practice of the church and its members belong to the church judicatories to which they have voluntarily subjected themselves." [1] But whenever the civil and property

---

[1] Walworth, Chancellor, in Baptist Church *v.* Wetherell, 3 Paige, 296 (24 Am. Dec. 223). " In this country the full and free right to entertain any religious belief, to practice any religious principle, and to teach any religious doctrine which does not violate the laws of morality and prop-

§ 72

rights of the individual are invaded, the State is justified and expected to exercise the same control and supervision as it would in the case of any other incorporation.[1] The legal corporations may be established simply upon the basis of a community of property, without introducing any religious qualification as a member,[2] and in that case there is no opportunity whatsoever for State interference in the religious affairs of the organization. But this is not usually the case. Membership in the corporation assumes ordinarily a more or less religious aspect, and depends upon the performance of certain religious conditions. The civil rights of such a member may, therefore, be materially affected by the decisions of the ecclesiastical authorities, and

erty, and which does not infringe personal rights, is conceded to all. The law knows no heresy, and is committed to the support of no dogma, the establishment of no sect. The right to organize voluntary religious associations, to assist in the expression and dissemination of any religious doctrine, and to create tribunals for the decision of controverted questions of faith within the association, and for the ecclesiastical government of all the individual members, congregations, and officers within the general associations, is unquestioned. All who unite themselves to such a body do so with an implied consent to this government, and are bound to submit to it. But it would be a vain consent and would lead to the total subversion of such religious bodies, if any one aggrieved by one of their decisions could appeal to the secular courts and have them reversed. It is the essence of these religious unions, and of their right to establish tribunals for the decision of questions arising among themselves, that those decisions should be binding in all cases of ecclesiastical cognizance, subject only to such appeals as the organism itself provides for." Watson v. Jones. 13 Wall. 679. See, also, Sohier v. Trinity Church, 109 Mass. 1; Lawyer v. Cipperly, 7 Paige, 281; Robertson v. Bullions, 11 N. Y. 243; Bellport v. Tooker, 21 N. Y. 267 (29 Barb. 256); O'Hara v. Stack, 90 Pa. St. 477; Keyser v. Stansifer, 6 Ohio, 363; Shannon v. Frost, 3 B. Mon. 253; Lucas v. Case, 9 Bush, 297; Ferraria v. Vascóncellos, 31 Ill. 25; Calkins v. Chaney, 92 Ill. 463; German Congregation v. Pressler, 17 La. Ann. 127.

[1] Watson v. Jones, 13 Wall. 679; Smith v. Nelson, 18 Vt. 511; Hale v. Everett, 53 N. H. 9; Ferraria v. Vasconcellos, 31 Ill. 25; Watson v. Avery, 2 Bush, 332; Happy v. Morton, 93 Ill. 398.

[2] Waite v. Merrill, 4 Me. 102 (16 Am. Dec. 238); Scribner v. Rapp, 5 Watts. 311 (30 Am. Dec. 327).

§ 72

to that extent and for the protection of such civil rights are these decisions on religious matters subject to review.   The religious status cannot be determined in any event by a civil court, except as it bears upon and interferes with the temporal or civil rights of the individual.   And even then the courts are not permitted to review and determine the essential accuracy of the decision.   The court must confine its investigation to ascertaining, whether the proper religious authorities had had cognizance of the case, and had complied with their organic law in the procedure and how far the decision affects the civil rights under the by-laws and charter of the corporation.[1]

§ 73. Religious criticism and blasphemy distinguish-

[1] "When a civil right depends upon an ecclesiastical matter, it is the civil court and not the ecclesiastical which is to decide. But the civil tribunal tries the civil right and no more, taking the ecclesiastical decisions out of which the civil right arises as it finds them." Harmon v. Dreher, 2 Speer's Eq. 87.

"The entire separation of church and State is not the least of the evidences of the wisdom and forethought of those who made our nation's constitution. It was more than a happy thought, it was an inspiration. But although the State has renounced authority to control the internal management of any church, and refuses to prescribe any form of church government, it is nevertheless true that the law recognizes the existence of churches, and protects and assures their right to exist, and to possess and enjoy their powers and privileges. Of course, wherever rights of property are invaded, the law must interpose equally in those instances where the dispute is as to church property as in those where it is not, and it also takes note of, but does not itself enforce, the discipline of the church, and the maintenance of church order and internal regulation." State v. Hebrew Congregation, 30 La. Ann. 205 (33 Am. Rep. 217). See, also, Watson v. Jones, 13 Wall. 679; Grosvenor v. United Society, 118 Mass. 78; Dieffendorf v. Ref. Col. Church, 20 Johns. 12; Baptist Church v. Wetherell, 3 Paige, 301 (24 Am. Dec. 223); People v. German Church, 53 N. Y. 103; Hendirckson v. Decon, 1 N. Y. Eq. 577; Den v. Bolton, 12 N. J. 206; McGinnis v. Watson, 41 Pa. St. 9; Wilson v. Johns Island Church, 2 Rich Eq. 192; Lucas v. Case, 9 Bush, 297; Chase v. Chaney, 58 Ill. 508; State v. Farris, 45 Mo. 183. See Fitzgerald v. Robinson, 112 Mass. 371, in which it was held that an excommunication would not be permitted to affect property and other civil rights.

§ 73

ed.—The recognition of Christianity by the State is not, and need not be, confined to the provision for Christian devotional exercises in the various governmental departments and State institutions, as has been explained and claimed in a preceding section.[1] The fostering and encouragement of a worshipful attitude of mind, the development and gratification of the religious instinct, should be of great concern to the State. While morality is distinguishable from religion, the most important principles of morality receive their highest sanction and their greatest efficacy, as a civilizing force, in becoming the requirements of religion. A high morality is inconsistent with a state of chronic irreligiousness. Anything, therefore, that is calculated to diminish the people's religious inclinations is detrimental to the public welfare, and may therefore be prohibited. Public contumely and ridicule of a prevalent religion not only offend against the sensibilities of the believers, but likewise threaten the public peace and order by diminishing the power of moral precepts. Inasmuch, therefore, as Christianity is essentially the religion of this country, any defamation of its founder or of its institutions, as well as all malicious irreverence towards Deity, must and can be prohibited. These acts or offenses are generally comprehended under the name of *blasphemy*.

Mr. Justice Story, in the Girard will case, said that, " although Christianity be a part of the common law of the State, yet it is only so in the qualified sense, that *its divine origin and truth are admitted*, and therefore it is not to be maliciously and openly reviled and blasphemed, against, *to the annoyance of believers or the injury of the public.*"[2] The " divine origin and truth" of the Christian religion are not admitted by the common law of this country. The only thing that the law can admit, in respect to

[1] See *ante*, § 71.
[2] Vidal *v.* Girard's Exrs., 2 How. 127.

§ 73

Christianity, is its potent influence in carrying on the development of civilization, and more especially in compelling the recognition and observance of moral obligations. If the laws against blasphemy rested upon the admission by the law of the "divine origin and truth" of the Christian religion, they would fall under the constitutional prohibitions, which withdraw religion proper from all legal control. Blasphemy is punishable, because, as already stated, it works an annoyance to the believer and an injury to the public. While religion proper is by the constitutional limitations taken out of the field of legislation, they were "never meant to withdraw religion in general, and with it the best sanctions of moral and social obligation from all consideration and notice of the law. * * * To construe it as breaking down the common-law barriers against licentious, wanton and impious attacks upon Christianity itself, would be an erroneous construction of its (their) meaning." [1] But it is only as a moral power that any religion can receive legal recognition. "The common law adapted itself to the religion of the country just so far as was necessary for the peace and safety of civil institutions ; but it took cognizance of offenses against God only when, by their inevitable effects they became offenses against man and his temporal security." [2] The essential element of blasphemy is malicious impiety. "In general, blasphemy may be described as consisting in speaking evil of the Deity with an impious purpose to derogate from the divine majesty, and to alienate the minds of others from the love of and reverence of God. It is purposely using words concerning God, calculated and designed to impair and destroy the reverence, respect and confidence due to Him, as the intelligent Creator, Governor and Judge of the world. It embraces the idea of detraction, when used towards the Supreme Being; as

[1] People v. Ruggles 8, Johns. 289 (5 Am. Dec. 335).
[2] State v. Chandler, 2 Harr. 553.

§ 73

' calumny ' usually carries the same idea when applied to an individual. It is a willful and malicious attempt to lessen men's reverence of God by denying His existence, or His attributes as an intelligent Creator, Governor and Judge of men, and to prevent their having confidence in Him as such."[1]

The laws against blasphemy, at least in respect to the more special details, have reference solely to Christianity. If their authority rested on the religious character of the offense, the equality of all religion before the law would require that these laws should embrace blasphemy, against whatever religion it may be directed. And while that would be, under our constitutional provisions, both permissible and commendable, since the laws are designed to prevent widespread irreligiousness and disturbance of the public order, there would be no illegal discrimination, if the provisions of the law should in the main be confined to blasphemy against the Christian religion. " Nor are we bound, by any expressions in the constitution, as some have strongly supposed, either not to punish at all, or to punish indiscriminately, the like attacks upon the religion of Mahomet or the Grand Lama; and for this plain reason, that the case assumes that we are a Christian people, and the morality of the country is deeply ingrafted in Christianity."[2]

In order that an utterance or writing may be considered a legal blasphemy, it must be accompanied by malice and a willful purpose to offend the sensibilities of Christians. The malice or evil purpose is the gravamen of the wrong. The very same words, at least the same thoughts, may under other circumstances, and with a different purpose, be lawful, and the free expression of them may be

---

[1] Shaw, ch. J., in Commonwealth v. Kneeland, 20 Pick. 206. See also, People v. Ruggles, 8 Johns. 289 (5 Am. Dec. 335); Updegraph v. Com., 11 S. & R. 394; State v. Chandler, 2 Harr. 553; Andrew v. Bible Society, 4 Sandf. 156.

[2] Kent Ch. J. in People v. Ruggles, 8 Johns 289 (5 Am. Dec. 225).

§ 73

guaranteed by the constitutional provisions in respect to religious liberty. Religious liberty is impossible without freedom of expression and profession of one's faith and doctrines. Religious liberty implies the utmost freedom in the promulgation of the creed one professes, and exhortation to non-believers to embrace that faith. The serious and honest discussion of the doctrinal points of the Christian or any other religion is protected from infringement by our constitutional limitations. But no one can claim, under these provisions of the constitution, the right of indulgence in " offensive levity, or scurrilous and opprobrious language," which serves no good purpose, and, when done in public, is likely to bring about more or less disturbance of the public order. Such actions and such language, whether written or spoken, constitute a nuisance, which comes within the jurisdiction of law. It is legal blasphemy. The statute against blasphemy " does not prohibit the fullest inquiry and the freest discussion, for all honest and fair purposes, one of which is, the discovery of truth. It admits the freest inquiry, when the real purpose is the discovery of truth, to whatever result such inquiries may lead. It does not prevent the simple and sincere avowal of a disbelief in the existence and attributes of a supreme intelligent being, upon suitable and proper occasions. And many such occasions may exist; as where a man is called a witness, in a court of justice and questioned upon his belief, he is not only permitted, but bound, by every consideration of moral honesty to avow his unbelief, if it exists. He may do it inadvertently in the heat of debate, or he may avow it confidentially to a friend, in the hope of gaining new light on the subject, even perhaps whilst he regrets his unbelief; or he may announce his doubts publicly, with the honest purpose of eliciting a more general and thorough inquiry, by public discussion, the true and honest purpose being the discovery and diffusion of

§ 73

truth.   None of these constitute the willful blasphemy prohibited by this statute." [1]

§ 74. **Permissible limitations upon religious worship.** — While the constitution of the United States prohibits all interference with the free exercise of religion according to the dictates of the conscience, and guarantees before the law a substantial equality to all systems of religion, by the influence of natural social forces, Christianity has become a part of the common law of this country to the extent of those of its moral precepts, which have a bearing upon social order, and the breach of which is pronounced by common opinion to be injurious to the welfare of society.   Immorality and crime, according to public sentiment as it has been given public expression in the laws of the country, cannot be sanctioned and permitted to those, who through their mental aberrations have adhered to and professed a religion, which authorizes and perhaps commands the commission of what is pronounced a crime.   An act is still a crime, notwithstanding the actor's religious belief in its justifiableness.   So far, therefore, as religious worship involves the commission of a crime, or constitutes a civil trespass against the rights of others, it can and will be prohibited.   As Judge Cooley happily expresses it: " Opinion must be free ; religious error the government

---

[1] Com. v. Kneeland, 20 Pick. 206, 220, see Updegraph v. Com., 11 S. & R. 394; People v. Ruggles, 8 Johns. 289 (5 Am. Dec. 335).   In speaking of charitable uses, Judge Duer, in Ayres v. Methodist Church, 3 Sandf. 351, said: " If the Presbyterian and the Baptist, the Methodist and the Protestant Episcopalian, must each be allowed to devote the entire income of his real and personal estate, forever, to the support of missions, or the spreading of the Bible, so must the Roman Catholic his to the endowment of a monastery or the founding of a perpetual mass for the safety of his soul; the Jew his to the translation and publication of the Mishua, or the Talmud; and the Mohametan (if in that *colluries gentium* to which this city [New York], like ancient Rome, seems to be doomed, such shall be among us), the Mohametan his to the assistance or relief of the annual pilgrims to Mecca."

§ 74

should not concern itself with; but when the minority of
any people feel impelled to indulge in practices or to observe ceremonies that the general community look upon as
immoral excess or license, and therefore destructive of public morals, they have no claim to protection in so doing.
The State can not be bound to sanction immorality or
crime, even though there be persons in a community with
minds so perverted or depraved or ill-informed as to believe
it to be countenanced or commanded of heaven. And the
standard of immorality or crime must be the general sense
of the people embodied in the law. There can be no
other." [1] Thus it has been held by the Supreme Court of
the United States that the religious liberty of the Mormons
of Utah is not infringed by the act of Congress providing
penalties for the practice of polygamy, which is sanctioned
or commanded by their religious creed. [2] In many of the
State constitutions, — notably, California, Colorado, Connecticut, Florida, Georgia, Illinois, Maryland, Minnesota,
Mississippi, Missouri, Nevada, New York, South Carolina,
there are provisions to the effect that the constitutional
guaranty of religious liberty is not to justify or sanction
immoral or licentious acts, the practice of which threatens
the peace or moral order of society.

Of late years the question of police regulation of religious
worship has assumed a rather important as well as curious
phase, in consequence of the formation of religious unions,
variously called Salvation Army, Band of Holiness, etc.,
which parade in the public streets, conduct religious exercises in the market place, or other prominent thoroughfares, and do other things of a like character, with the
desire to attract the attention of those classes of society
which are beyond the reach of the ordinary Christian and
moral influences. As long as these unions are quiet and

---

[1] Cooley on Torts, 34.
[2] Reynolds v. United States, 98 U. S. 145.

§ 74

peaceable in their actions, neither creating any public disturbance nor obstructing the thoroughfare, and are not by their utterances so rudely offensive to the public sentiment, as tinged and colored by the prevailing influence of Christianity as to endanger the public peace, there will probably be no question raised against the continuance of their public parades and exhibitions. But suppose an Israelite, a Chinaman, a Mohammedan, the infidel or the atheist, should undertake in the public streets to preach upon the peculiar doctrines of their respective religions, and in their efforts to win disciples should enter upon a free and searching criticism of the distinctive doctrines of the Christian religion, will they be permitted to proceed with their efforts at proselytism, and outrage the prevailing sentiment by utterances, which however honest are held by the majority of the community to be little less than blasphemous? If the public peace is endangered by these public meetings, they can be lawfully prohibited, whether the doctrines taught be Christian or Hebrew, infidel or Mohammedan. All religions are equal before the law, and the Christian has no more right to disturb the public peace by preaching the gospel of Christ in the streets of the Jewish or other unchristian quarter of a city, than has the Jew or infidel a right to threaten the public peace by the promulgation of his religious doctrines in a Christian community. But would it be permissible to prohibit by law discourses which are designed to assail and supplant the Christian religion with some other creed? The quiet and peace of mind of a Christian believer is greatly disturbed, and his inalienable right to " the pursuit of happiness " invaded, by hearing upon the public streets and highways animadversions and free criticisms of the Christian doctrines and institutions, in whose divine origin and truth he has implicit faith. And being a trespass it would seem permissible to prohibit all such discussions. But the Jew's or infidel's right to " the pursuit of happiness " is as much invaded by the Christian

§ 74

exhorter's animadversions upon their religious tenets, and is entitled to equal protection. We therefore conclude, *first*, that public religious discussions are not nuisances at common law, that is, independently of statute, unless they incite the populace to breaches of the peace, or obstruct the thoroughfare, and in that case the breach of the peace or obstruction of locomotion constitutes the offense against the law rather than the discourse. However, on the ground that all religious discussions on the public streets are more or less calculated to disturb the mental rest and quiet of those whose religious opinions are assailed, we hold that these public meetings can be prohibited altogether. But a law which prohibited those only, which are conducted by the opponents of the Christian religion, would be unconstitutional on account of the discrimination against other religions and in favor of the Christian religion. All religious discourses in the street and other public places should be prohibited or none at all.

§ 75. **Religious discrimination in respect to admissibility of testimony.**— According to the English common law, no one was a competent witness, who did not believe in the existence of God, and of a state of rewards and punishments hereafter. This rule has been recognized and enforced to its fullest extent in the earlier cases,[1] and it was almost universally required by the courts of this country, that the witness, in order to be competent, should believe in a superintending Providence, who can and would punish perjury.[2] The reason for the rule was declared to be, that without such belief an oath could not be made binding upon

---

[1] See Atwood *v.* Welton, 7 Conn. 66.

[2] See Arnold *v.* Arnold, 13 Vt. 362; Hunscom *v* Hunscom, 15 Mass. 184; Butts *v.* Swartwood, 2 Cow. 431; Cubbison *v.* McCreery, 7 Watts & S. 262; Jones *v.* Harris, 1 Strobh. 160; Blocker *v.* Burness, 2 Ala. 354; Brock *v.* Milligan, 10 Ohio, 121; Central R. R. Co. *v.* Rockafellow, 17 Ill. 541.

§ 75

the conscience, and such a person's testimony was therefore unworthy of belief. The growth of public opinion towards the complete recognition of religious liberty is exerting its influence upon this rule, and in many of the State constitutions there are provisions which abolish this and every other religious qualification of witnesses.[1] Mr. Cooley says, "wherever the common law remains unchanged, it must, we suppose, be held no violation of religious liberty to recognize and enforce its distinctions." But it would appear to us that the enforcement of such a law would violate the constitutional guaranty of religious liberty, and hence the enactment of this constitutional provision was an implied repeal of the common-law requirement.[2]

§ 76. **Sunday laws.** — The most common form of legal interference in matters of religion is that, which requires the observance of Sunday as a holy day. In these days, the legal requirements do not usually extend beyond the compulsory cessation of labor, the maintenance of quiet upon the streets, and the closing of all places of amusements; but the public spirit which calls for a compulsory observance of these regulations is the same which in the colonial days of New England imposed a fine for an unexcused absence from divine worship. Although other reasons have been assigned for the State regulation of the observance of Sunday, in order to escape the constitutional objections that can be raised against it, if it takes the form of a religious institution,[3] those who are most active in securing the enforcement of the Sunday laws do so, because of the religious character of the day, and not for any economical

---

[1] Such a provision is to be found in Arkansas, California, Florida, Indiana, Iowa, Kansas, Michigan, Minnesota, Missouri, Nebraska, Nevada, New York, Ohio, Oregon, Wisconsin.

[2] See Perry's Case, 3 Gratt. 632.

[3] See *post*.

§ 76

reason.   While it is not true that the institution of a special day of rest for all men is " a *purely* religious idea," [1] it is because of the strong influence of the religious idea that there are active supporters of such laws.   Whatever economical reasons may be urged in favor of the Sunday laws, requiring the observance of the day as a day of general rest from labor, their influence upon the people would be powerless to secure an enforcement of these laws.   The effectiveness of the laws is measured by the influence of the Christian idea of Sunday as a religious institution.   " Derived from the Sabbatical institutions of the ancient Hebrew, it has been adopted into all the creeds of succeeding religious sects throughout the civilized world; and whether it be the Friday of the Mohamedan, the Saturday of the Israelite, or the Sunday of the Christian, it is alike fixed in the affections of its followers, beyond the power of eradication, and in most of the States of our confederacy, the aid of the law to enforce its observance has been given under the pretense of a civil, municipal or police regulation." [2]

But Sunday, as a religious institution, can receive no legal recognition.   It is manifest that the religious liberty of the Jew or the infidel would be violated by a compulsory observance of Sunday as a religious institution.   While such a regulation, if it did not extend to a prohibition of the Jew's religious observance of the seventh day, or to a compulsory attendance upon Christian worship, may not amount to a direct infringement of his religious liberty, he may still reasonably claim that it operates indirectly as a discrimination against his religion, by requiring him to respect Sunday as a day of rest, while his conscience requires of him a like observance of Saturday. [3]   But the legal establishment of Sunday as a religious institution, would violate the Christian's religious liberty, as much as that of the Jew.   The compul-

---

1 Terry, Ch. J., in Ex parte Newman, 9 Cal. 509.
2 Opinion of Terry, Ch. J., 9 Cal., p. 509.
3 Cooley's Const. Lim. *476.

§ 76

sory observance of a religious institution against conscience is no more a violation of the constitutional limitations than a like compulsion in conformity with one's religious convictions. " The fact that the Christian voluntarily keeps holy the first day of the week does not authorize the legislature to make that observance compulsory. The legislature cannot compel a citizen to do that which the constitution leaves him free to do, or omit, at his election." [1] We therefore conclude that Sunday laws, so far as they require a religious observance of the day, are unconstitutional, and cannot be enforced. If these laws can be sustained at all, they must be supported by some other unobjectionable reasons.[2] But there have been decisions in favor of the compulsory observance of Sunday as a religious institution.[3]

---

[1] Burnett, J., in Ex parte Newman, 9 Cal. 510.

[2] "Under the constitution of this State, the legislature cannot pass any act, the legitimate effect of which is forcibly to establish any merely religious truth, or enforce any merely religious observances. The Legislature has no power over such a subject. When therefore a citizen is sought to be compelled by the legislature to do any affirmative religious act, or to refrain from doing anything, because it violates simply a religious principle or observance, the act is unconstitutional." Burnett, J., in Ex parte Newman, 9 Cal. 510. See, also, Com. v. Has, 122 Mass. 40; Com. v. Specht, 8 Pa. St. 312; Com. v. Wolf, 3 Serg. & R. 48; Com. v. Nesbit, 34 Pa. St. 398; Hudson, v. Geary, 4 R. I. 485; State v. Balt. & O. R. R., 15 W. Va. 362 (36 Am. Rep. 803); Charleston v. Benjamin, 2 Strobh. 508; McGatrick v. Wason, 4 Ohio St. 566; Johns v. State, 78 Ind. 332; Bohl v. State, 3 Tex. App. 683; State v. Bott, 31 La. Ann. 663 (33 Am. Rep. 224).

[3] Scott, J., in State v. Ambs, 20 Mo. 214, 216, uses this language: "Those who question the constitutionality of our Sunday laws seem to imagine that the constitution is to be regarded as an instrument formed for a State composed of strangers collected from all quarters of the globe, each with a religion of his own, bound by no previous social ties, nor sympathizing in any common reminiscences of the past; that, unlike ordinary laws, it is not to be construed in reference to the State and condition of those for whom it was intended, but that the words in which it is comprehended are alone to be regarded without respect to the history of the people for whom it was made. It is apprehended, that such is not the mode by which our organic law is to be interpreted. We must regard the people for whom it was ordained, It appears to have been made by Christian men. The constitution on its face shows that the Christian religion

12   § 76

Notwithstanding the strictly religious aspect the observance of a general day of rest has always assumed among all people, and under all systems of religion ; although the observance of such a day has always been taught to be a divine injunction ; it is claimed, with much show of reason, that this custom, even as a religious institution, was originally established as a sanitary regulation, designed to procure for the individual that periodical rest from labor so necessary to the recuperation of the exhausted energies : and the religious character was given to it, in order to secure its more universal observance. In the primitive ages of all nations, theology, medicine and law were administered by the same body of men, and it was but natural that they should apply to a much needed sanitary regulation, the spiritual influence of theology and its obligation of law. Under this view of the matter, the observance of a day of rest was, in the order of history, primarily a sanitary regulation, and secondarily a religious institution. Under our constitutional limitations, it is only in its primary character that an observance of the law can be exacted.

All sanitary regulations operate directly upon the individual, and from the medical standpoint, their primary object is the benefit to the individual. It is so likewise with the observance of a day of rest. It is the individual which is primarily benefited by the cessation from labor, and the community or society is only remotely and indirectly bene-

was the religion of its framers. * * * They, then, who engrafted on our constitution the principles of religious freedom contained therein, did not regard the compulsory observance of Sunday, as a day of rest, a violation of those principles. They deemed a statute compelling the observance of Sunday necessary to secure a full enjoyment of the rights of conscience. How could those who conscientiously believe that Sunday is hallowed time, to be devoted to the worship of God, enjoy themselves in its observance amidst all the turmoil and bustle of worldly pursuits, amidst scenes by which the day was desecrated, which they conscientiously believe was holy ?'' See also, Stover v. State, 10 Ark. 259, 263; Lindenmuller v. People, 33 Barb. 568.

§ 76

fited by the increased vitality of his offspring and possibly relief from the public burden of an early decrepitude, the result of overwork. The failure to observe this law of nature, calling for rest from labor on every seventh day, — for this has been demonstrated by the experience of ages to be a law of nature, — is, like every other inordinate gratification of one's desires, a vice, and not the subject of law. The possible evil, flowing from this " vice," will not justify the State authorities in entering the house and premises of a citizen, and there compel him to lay down his tool or his pen, and refrain from labor, on the ground that his unremittent toil will possibly do damage to society through his children. How can it be proved *a priori* that that man needs the rest that the law requires him to take? He may be fully able to continue his labor, at least during a portion of the Sunday, without doing any damage to anybody.[1] Furthermore, it may be shown that he has for special reasons, or because his religion requires it, abstained from labor for the required time on some other day. And having done so, from the individual standpoint, he has substantially complied with the requirements of the law.[2] Then must the conclusion be.

---

[1] "Again it may be well considered that the amount of rest which would be required by one half of society may be widely disproportionate to that required by the other. It is a matter of which each individual must be permitted to judge for himself, according to his own instincts and necessities. As well might the legislature fix the days and hours for work, and enforce their observance by an unbending rule which shall be visited alike upon the weak and strong; whenever such attempts are made, the law-making power leaves its legitimate sphere, and makes an incursion into the realms of physiology, and its enactments like the sumptuary laws of the ancients, which prescribe the mode and texture of people's clothing, or similar laws which might prescribe and limit our food and drink, must be regarded as an invasion, without reason or necessity, of the natural rights of the citizens, which are guaranteed by the fundamental law." Terry, Ch. J., Ex parte Newman, 9 Cal. 508.

[2] "It appears to us that if the benefit of the individual is alone to be considered, the argument against the law which he may make, who has already observed the seventh day of the week, is *unanswerable*." Cooley's Const. Lim. *476, *477.

§ 76

reached, that there are no satisfactory grounds upon which Sunday laws can be sustained, and the constitutional objections avoided?

It matters not what is the moving cause, or what amount of gratification is had out of the act, the commission of a trespass upon another's rights, or the reasonable fear of such a trespass, always constitutes sufficient ground for the exercise of police power. The prevention of a trespass is the invariable purpose of a police regulation. It is the right of every one to enjoy quietly, and without disturbance, his religious liberty, and his right is invaded as much by noise and bustle on his day of rest, varying only in degree, as by a prohibition of religious worship according to one's convictions. Noisy trades and amusements, and other like disturbances of the otherwise impressive quiet of a Sunday, may therefore be prohibited on that day, in complete conformity with the limitations of police power.[1] But the prosecution of noiseless occupations, and the indulgence in quiet, orderly amusements, since they involve no violation of private right, cannot be prohibited by law without infringing upon the religious liberty of those who are thus prevented, and such regulations would therefore be unconstitutional. It is barely possible, but doubtful, that a law could be sustained under the principles here advanced, which required that the front doors of stores and places of amusement should be kept closed on Sunday, but not otherwise interfering with the noiseless occupations and diversions. The total prohibition of such employments and labor on Sunday, except possibly for a reason to be suggested and explained later, could only be justified by the

---

[1] " While I am thus resting on the Sabbath in obedience to law, it is right and reasonable that my rest should not be disturbed by others. Such a disturbance by others of my rest, is in its nature a nuisance, which the law ought to punish, and Sabbath-breaking has been frequently classed with nuisances and punished as such." State v. B. & O. R. R., 15 W. Va. 362 (36 Am. Rep. 803, 814.)

§ 76

religious character of the day, and we have already seen that that aspect of Sunday cannot be taken into account, in framing the Sunday laws.

But there is, perhaps, a constitutional reason why the prohibition of labor on Sunday should be extended to other than noisy trades and employments. The reason calls for the avoidance of an indirectly threatened trespass, rather than the prohibition of a direct invasion of right. In the ideal state of nature, when free agency and independence of the behests of others may be considered factual, the prosecution of a noiseless trade or other occupation could not in any sense be considered as, either constituting a trespass, or threatening one. Each man, being left free to do as he pleased, would then have the equal liberty of joining in the religious observance of the day or continuing his labor, subject to the single condition, that he must not in doing so disturb the religious worship of others. But we are not living in a state of nature. Whatever the metaphysicians or theologians may tell us about free will, in the complex society of the present age, the individual is a free agent to but a limited degree. He is in the main but the creature of circumstances. Like the shuttle, he may turn to the right or to the left, but the web of human events is woven, unaffected by this freedom of action. Those who most need the cessation from labor, are unable to take the necessary rest, if the demands of trade should require their uninterrupted attention to business. And if the law did not interfere, the feverish, intense desire to acquire wealth, so thoroughly a characteristic of the American nation, inciting a relentless rivalry and competition, would ultimately prevent, not only the wage-earners, but likewise the capitalists and employers themselves, from yielding to the warnings of nature, and obeying the instinct of self-preservation by resting periodically from labor, even if the mad pursuit of wealth should not warp their judgment and destroy this instinct. Remove the prohibition of law, and this whole-

§ 76

some sanitary regulation would cease to be observed. No
one, if he would, could do so. The prohibition of labor
for these reasons may be contradictory of the constitutional
affirmation of the equality of all men ; and the prohibitory
law may be practically unenforcible ; but it would be difficult to establish any positive constitutional objection to
it.[1] It has been urged that this law, when founded upon
this reason, of protection to the individual, may be sustained, if it was confined in its operations to slaves,
minors, apprentices and others who are required to obey
the commands, of others, and designed to protect them
from the cruelty of incessant toil.[2] But the slave or
apprentice is no more bound to obey the behests of others,
and to work at their command, than the free laborer, clerk,
and even the employer himself, under the irresistible force
of competition, in the struggle for existence and the accumulation of wealth. "It is no answer to the requirements of
the statute that mankind will seek cessation from labor by the
natural influences of self-preservation. The position assumes
that all men are independent, and at liberty to work whenever they choose. Whether this be true or not in theory, it is
false in fact ; it is contradicted by every day's experience.
The relation of superior and subordinate, master and servant,
principal and clerk, always have and always will exist.

---

[1] See *post* § 178.

[2] "The question arising under this act is quite distinguishable from
the case where the legislature of a State, in which slavery is tolerated,
passes an act for the protection of the slave against the inhumanity of the
master in not allowing sufficient rest. In this State, every man is a free
agent, competent, and able to protect himself, and no one is bound by law
to labor for a particular person. Free agents must be left free as to
themselves. Had the act under consideration been confined to infants, or to
persons bound by law to obey others, then the question presented would
have been very different. But if we cannot trust free agents to regulate
their own labor, its time and quantity, it is difficult to trust them to
make their own contracts. If the legislature could prescribe the ' days ' of
rest for them, then it would seem that the same power could prescribe
hours to work, rest and eat." Burnett, J., in Ex parte Newman, 9 Cal. 510.

§ 76

Labor is in a great degree dependent on capital, and unless the exercise of power which capital affords is restrained, those who are obliged to labor will not possess the freedom for rest which they would otherwise exercise. Necessities for food and raiment are imperious, and exactions of avarice are not easily satisfied. It is idle to talk of a man's freedom to rest, when his wife and children are looking to his daily labor for their daily support. The law steps in to restrain the power of capital. Its object is not to protect those who can rest at their pleasure, but to afford rest to those who need it, and who, from the conditions of society, could not otherwise obtain it. * * * The authority for the enactment, I find in the great object of all governments, which is protection. Labor is necessarily imposed by the condition of our race, and to protect labor is the highest office of our laws." [1] For various reasons, laws have been generally sustained, which compel the closing of the stores of business.[2] If the reasoning here pre-

---

[1] Dissenting opinion of Judge Field in Ex parte Newman, 9 Cal. 502, 518. The opinion of Judge Field although rejected by the majority of the court in Ex parte Newman, was after a change in the *personnel* of the court adopted as the rule in California in Ex parte Andrews, 18 Cal. 678, and was affirmed in many other later cases, the last being Ex parte Burke, 59 Cal. 6 (43 Am. Rep. 231); Ex parte Roser, 60 Cal. 177.

[2] Vogelsang v. State, 9 Ind. 112; Shover v. State, 10 Ark. 259; Warne v. Smith, 8 Conn. 14; Lindenmuller v. People, 33 Barb. 549; Story v. Elliott, 8 Cow. 27; Johnston v. Com., 10 Harris, 102; Bloom v. Richards, 2 Ohio, 387; City Council v. Benjamin, 2 Strobh. 529; Specht v. Com., 8 Pa. St. 312. In the last case, the court expresses itself thus: " It intermeddles not with the natural and indefeasible right of all men to worship Almighty God according to the dictates of their own consciences; it compels none to attend, erect or support any place of worship, or to maintain any ministry against his consent; it pretends not to control or to interfere with the rights of conscience, and it establishes no preference for any religious establishment or mode of worship. It treats no religious doctrine as paramount in the State; it enforces no unwilling attendance upon the celebration of divine worship. It says not to the Jew or Sabbatarian, 'You shall desecrate the day, you esteem as holy, and keep sacred to religion that *we* deem to be so! It enters upon no discussion of the rival claims of the first or seventh days of the week, nor pretends

§ 76

sented be correct, and the premises into which it has been formulated be impregnable, the following conclusion is inevitable, viz. : that no Sunday law is constitutional which does more than prohibit those acts, which are noisy and are therefore calculated to disturb the quiet and rest of Sunday worshipers, or which in their commission demand or are likely to demand, the services of others, who cannot refuse to serve, on account of the common interdependence of mankind.   The doing of any act, which is noiseless and does not require the service of others, can not be prohibited. It is not maintained that this limitation upon the power of the State to regulate the observance of Sunday, is recognized and indorsed by the decisions of our courts.   On the contrary, there are police regulations in the different States, which are sustained in violation of this rule of limitation. The laws which prohibit quiet and orderly amusements cannot be sustained under the rule, and so also those laws, which make void the commercial paper and deeds which are executed on Sunday.   Other instances of existing legislation, contradictory of this rule of limitation, may be cited, but it is not necessary.   But although not generally supported by the authorities, it is believed to be the correct rule.   The same reasons, which are here advanced, would likewise support and justify legislation, designed to protect the Jew in his religious observance of Saturday, and the Mohamedan in his enjoyment of Friday.   But if the rule

to bind upon the conscience of any man any conclusion upon a subject which each must decide for himself. It intrudes not into the domestic circle to dictate when, where, or to what God its inmates shall address their orisons; nor does it presume to enter the synagogue of the Israelite, or the church of the seventh-day Christian, to command or even persuade their attendance in the temples of those who especially approach the altar on Sunday. It does not in the slightest degree infringe upon the Sabbath of any sect, or curtail their freedom of worship. It detracts not one hour from any period of time they may feel bound to devote to this object, nor does it add a moment beyond what they may choose to employ. Its sole mission is to inculcate a temporary weekly cessation from labor, but it adds not to this requirement any religious obligation."

§ 76

were carried to the extreme, of giving equal protection to the enjoyment of the religious days of every sect, the business prosperity of the country would be seriously impaired. Although the Jew and the Mohamedan have the same right to the quiet and undisturbed enjoyment of his holy day, the public welfare, which likewise is the main spring to the Sunday laws, requires that his enjoyment of his religion should sustain the burden and annoyance occasioned by the general prosecution of trades and occupations on their holy days. [In Charleston, S. C., it is said that an ordinance requires all vehicles on Saturday to pass the Jewish synagogues in a slow walk, in order to reduce disturbance of the worship to a minimum.] The selection of Sunday, as the day of rest to be observed by all, is not justified by its religious character, although its religious character, in the eyes of the masses of this country, suggests the reason of its selection in preference to some other day. The interference of the State is, after all, for the purpose of promoting the public welfare, for the purpose of securing to society the benefits arising from a general periodical cessation from labor ; and that object can be best attained by setting apart as a legal day of rest, that day which is looked upon as a holy day by the vast majority of our people. In some of our States, there are statutory exceptions in favor of those who conscientiously observe some other day of the week as a holy day, and abstain from labor on that day, and in Ohio, it has been held that a statute which did not contain such an exception, was for that reason unconstitutional.[1] But in other States, it is held that the Sunday law in its application to the orthodox Jew, was not in violation of the article in the State constitution, which declares that no person shall " upon any pretense whatever be hurt, molested, or restrained in his religious sentiments or persuasions." [2] The restraint upon the right to engage in lawful employment and

---

[1] Cincinnati v. Rice, 15 Ohio, 225; Canton v. Nist, 9 Ohio St. 439.
[2] Frolickstein v. Mobile, 40 Ala. 725.

§ 76

to do otherwise lawful acts, is reasonable, because necessary to the successful maintenance of a general day of rest.[1]

While it is claimed that the State can not go beyond the limitations that have been presented, in enacting laws for the observance of Sunday as a day of rest, it rests with the discretion of the legislature how far the enactment should extend within these limitations, and the scope of the legislation has varied with the public policy in each State. We have already noticed exemptions from the operation of the Sunday laws in favor of the Jew. In some of the States only a person's ordinary calling is intended to be sup-

[1] "The legislature obviously regarded it as promotive of the mental, moral and physical well-being of men, that they should rest from their labors at stated intervals; and in this all experience shows they were right. If then, rest is to be enjoined as a matter of public policy at stated intervals, it is obvious that public convenience would be much promoted by the community generally resting on the same day, for otherwise, each individual would be much annoyed and hindered in finding that those, with whom he had business to transact, were resting on the day on which he was working. The legislature, holding these views in selecting the particular day of rest, doubtless selected Sunday, because it was deemed a proper day of rest by a majority of our people who thought it a religious duty to rest on that day; and in selecting this day for these reasons, the legislature acted wisely. The law requires that the day be observed as a day of rest, not because it is a religious duty, but because such observance promotes the physical, mental and moral well-being of the community; and Sunday is selected as the day of rest, because if any other day had been named, it would have imposed unnecessarily onerous obligations on the community, inasmuch as many of them would have rested on Sunday as a religious duty, and the requirement of another day to be observed as a day of rest, would have resulted in two days being observed instead of one, and thus time would have been uselessly wasted. This I conceive is the main object of our law; but it is not its only object." State v. Balt. & O. R. R. Co., 15 W. Va. 362 (36 Am. Rep. 803, 814); an exemption of this kind was declared unconstitutional in Louisiana, because it discriminated between religious sects. Shreveport v. Levy, 26 La. Ann. 67. But it was held valid in Indiana. Johns v. State, 78 Ind. 332. In Simonds' Exrs. v. Gratz, 2 Pen. & Watts, 412, it was held that it was no ground for a continuance that a Jew had conscientious scruples against attendance at the trial of his cause on Saturday.

§ 76

pressed;[1] and there is an universal exception in favor of
works of charity and necessity. But what constitutes
charity and necessity is not viewed in the same light in
every State. It is a common rule that traveling on Sunday, except in cases of charity or necessity, is unlawful,
and any one injured while so doing cannot recover damages.[2] But whether a certain act is looked upon as a necessity, will depend largely upon the condition of public
sentiment, its mere fitness and propriety being the only
standard of right and wrong.[3] We must therefore expect to find contradictory conclusions upon this question of
necessity. In Pennsylvania it is not considered a work of
necessity for a barber to shave his customers on Sunday,[4]
while it is deemed a necessity in Texas.[5] In some States
the running of railroad trains and the operation of street
railroads are held to be necessary.[6] In other States both
have been held to be violations of the Sunday laws.[7] The
transportation of cattle received on Sunday,[8] feeding stock
and gathering the necessary feed,[9] the gathering of grain
which may be injured if left in the field until Monday,[10]
the expenditure of the labor necessary to prevent waste of

[1] Mills v. Williams, 16 S. C. 594, 597, approving Hellams v. Abercrombie, 15 S. C. 110, 113; Bennett v. Brooks, 9 Allen, 118.

[2] Hinckley v. Penobscot, 42 Me. 89; Cratty v. Bangor, 57 Me. 423 (2
Am. Rep. 56); Johnson v. Irasburg, 47 Vt. 28 (19 Am. Rep. 111); Bos-
worth v. Swansey, 10 Met. 364; Connolly v. Boston, 117 Mass. 64 (19
Am. Rep. 396); Davis v. Somerville, 128 Mass. 594.

[3] See Davis v. Somerville, 128 Mass. 594; McClary v. Lowell, 44 Vt.
116 (8 Am. Rep. 366); Logan v. Matthews, 6 Pa. St. 417; Johnson v.
People, 31 Ill. 469.

[4] Com. v. Jacobus, 1 Leg. Gaz. Rep. (Pa.) 491.

[5] State. v. Lorry, 7 Barb. 95.

[6] Com. v. Louisville & Nashville R. R. Co., 80 Ky. 291; Augusta &
S. R. R. Co. v. Renz, 55 Ga. 126.

[7] Sparhawk v. Union Passenger R. Co., 54 Pa. St. 401; Com. v. Jeandell, 2 Grant Cas. 506.

[8] Phil. & B. R. R. Co. v. Lehman, 56 Md. 209.

[9] Edgerton v. State, 69 Ind. 588.

[10] Turner v. State, 67 Ind. 595.

§ 76

sap in making maple sugar,[1] have been held to be lawful
because they were works of necessity.   In other States
similar acts were held to be unlawful, on the ground of not
being deemed necessary.[2]

1 Whitcomb v. Gilman, 35 Vt. 497.
2 State v. Goff, 20 Ark., 289; Jones v. Andrews, 10 Allen, 18.

§ 76

CHAPTER VIII.

FREEDOM OF SPEECH AND LIBERTY OF THE PRESSES

§ 81. **Police supervision prohibited by the constitutions.** — A popular goverument, and hence freedom from tyranny, is only possible when the people enjoy the freedom of speech, and the liberty of the press. If the individual is not free to publish by word of mouth or writing, or through the press, the complaints of encroachments of the government or of individuals upon his rights and liberties, he is deprived of his liberty, and he is not a freeman. Even if there were no special constitutional restrictions upon the governmental control of these rights, the State regulation would be unconstitutional, which denied the right of the individual to publish what he pleases, or prohibited the publication of newspapers or other periodicals or books, on the general ground that they would involve the deprivation of liberty and the right to pursue happiness. But the liberty of speech and of the press is not to be confounded with a licentiousness and a reckless disregard of the rights of others. No one can claim the right to slander or libel another, and the constitutions do not permit or sanction such wrongful acts. Liberty of speech and of the press, therefore, means the right to speak or publish what one pleases, the utterance of which does not work an injury to any one, by being false. The common law provided for the due punishment of such trespasses upon the right to reputation, and ordinarily these remedies, which prevail generally, afford sufficient protection to the individual and the public. But sometimes, and oftener in these later days, when the press has acquired extraordinary

(189)

power, these remedies prove ineffectual.   The tendency of
the press, at least of this country, is to publish sensational,
and oftener false, accounts of individual wrongs and immor-
alities, to such an extent that newspapers too often fall
properly within the definition of obscene literature.   If
possible, the publication of such matter should be suppressed, or at least published in such a way, as to do little
or no harm to the morals of the community.

Then again, we have newspapers, in whose columns we
find arguments and appeals to passion, designed to incite
the individual who may be influenced thereby to the commission of crimes, appeals to " dynamiters," socialists and
nihilists, and all other classes of discontents, who believe
the world has been fashioned after a wrong principle, and
needs to be remodeled.   Of course, those who do these
reprehensible things may be punished for each overt act.
But the only effective remedy would be the establishment
of a censorship over the press, by which such publication
may be prevented, instead of being punished after the evil
has been done.   Under the general constitutional provisions, this supervision of the press would be permissible,
and would not infringe the liberty of the individual.   It
would be only such a restraint upon the liberty of the
speech and of the press, as would promote public welfare,
and would be sanctioned as an exercise of the police power
of the government.   But such a control of the press would
be very liable to abuse, and through it the absolute suppression of the press would be rendered possible, if the
government should fall into the hands of designing men,
and at all events it would be an effective engine of oppression.

Profiting by their experience in the colonial days, when
the English government exercised a control over the press,
sometimes to the extent of prohibiting the publication of
the paper, and always to the extent of suppressing all pro-
tests and arguments against England's oppressive acts; our

§ 81

forefathers provided by constitutional provisions, both in the Federal and in the State constitutions, that the liberty of speech and of the press shall not be abridged by any law. The provision varies in phraseology in the different constitutions, but the limitation upon the power of government is the same in all cases. While this constitutional provision prohibits all control or supervision of the press in the way of a license or censorship, the slanderer or libeler may still be punished. He suffers the penalty inflicted by the law for the abuse of his privilege. The opinion of Chief Justice Parker of Massachusetts, has been frequently quoted, and generally recognized as presenting the correct construction of this constitutional provision. In Commonwealth *v.* Blanding,[1] he says: " Nor does our constitution or declaration of rights abrogate the common law in this respect, as some have insisted. The sixteenth article declares that ' liberty of the press is essential to the security of freedom in a State ; it ought not, therefore, to be restrained in this Commonwealth. The liberty of the press, not its licentiousness: this is the construction which a just regard to the other parts of that instrument, and to the wisdom of those who founded it, requires. In the eleventh article, it is declared that ' every subject of the Commonwealth ought to find a certain remedy, by having recourse to the laws, for injuries or wrongs which he may receive in his person, property, or character ; ' and thus the general declaration in the sixteenth article is qualified. Besides, it is well understood and received as a commentary on this provision for the liberty of the press, that it was intended to prevent all such *previous restraints* upon publications as had been practiced by other governments, and in early times here to stifle the efforts of patriots towards enlightening their fellow-subjects upon their rights and the duties of rulers. The

---

[1] 3 Pick. 304, 313. See, also, Story on Constitution, § 1889; 2 Kent, 17; Wharton's State Trials, 323; Respublica *v.* Dennie, 4 Yeates, 207 (2 Am. Dec. 402).

§ 81

liberty of the press was to be unrestrained, but he who used it was to be responsible in case of its abuse; like the right to keep fire-arms, which does not protect him who uses them for annoyance or destruction."

But while all *previous restraints* are forbidden by this provision of the constitution, the permissible restraints upon the freedom of speech and of the press are not confined to responsibility for private injury. All obscene or blasphemous publications may be prohibited, as tending to do harm to the public morals. So, likewise, may the publication of all defamatory statements, whether true or false, concerning private individuals, in whom the public have no concern, be prohibited, as was the case at common law, and is now in some of the States, on the ground that such publications do no good, and excite breaches of the peace. In neither case is there any private injury inflicted, but the harm to the public welfare is the justification of the prohibition.

" The constitutional liberty of speech and of the press, as we understand it, implies a right to freely utter and publish whatever the citizen may please, and to be protected against any responsibility for so doing, except so far as such publications, from their blasphemy, obscenity, or scandalous character, may be a public offense, or as, by their falsehood and malice, they may injuriously affect the standing, reputation, or pecuniary interests of individuals." [1]

So, also, is it not to be inferred from the prohibition of a censorship of the press, that the press, can without liability for its wrongful use, make use of the constitutional privilege for the purpose of inciting the people to the commission of crime against the public. The newspapers of anarchists and nihilists cannot be subjected to a censorship, or be absolutely suppressed; but if the proprietors should in their

[1] Cooley Const. Lim. 521 (*422).

§ 81

columns publish inflammatory appeals to the passion of discontents, and urge them to the commission of crimes against the public or against the individual, they may very properly be punished, and without doubt the right to the continued publication may be forfeited as a punishment for the crime.

§ 81

CHAPTER IX.

POLICE REGULATIONS OF TRADES AND PROFESSIONS.

SECTION 85. General propositions.
  86. Prohibition as to certain classes.
  87. Police regulation of skilled trades and learned professions.
  88. Regulation of practice in the learned professions.
  89. Regulation of sale of certain articles of merchandise.
  90. Legal tender, and the regulation of the currency.
  91. Legislative restraint of importations — Protective tariffs.
  92. Compulsory formation of business relations.
  93. Regulation of prices.
  94. Usury and interest laws.
  95. Prevention of speculation.
  96. Prevention of combinations in restraint of trade.
  97. Boycotting.
  98. Contracts against liability for negligence prohibited.
  99. Wager contracts prohibited.
  99a. Option contracts, when illegal.
  100. General prohibition of contracts, on account of public policy.
  101. Licenses.
  102. Prohibition of occupations in general.
  103. Prohibition of the liquor trade.
  104. Police control of employments in respect to locality.
  105. Monopolies, creation of.

§ 85. **General propositions.** — It will probably not be disputed that every one has a right to pursue in a lawful manner, any lawful calling which he may select. The State can neither compel him to pursue any particular calling, nor prohibit him from engaging in any lawful business, provided he does so in a lawful manner. It is equally recognized as beyond dispute, that the State, in the exercise of its police power, is, as a general proposition, authorized to subject all occupations to a reasonable regulation, where such regulation is required for the protection of public interests, or for the public welfare. It is also conceded

§ 85   (194)

that there is a limit to the exercise of this power, and that it is not an unlimited arbitrary power, which would enable the legislature to prohibit a business, the prosecution of which inflicts no damage upon others. But the difficulty is experienced, when an attempt is made to lay down a general rule, by which the validity of a particular regulation may be tested. There can be no objection raised to such a regulation, unless it contravenes some constitutional provision. "The State legislatures have the power, unless there be something in their own constitution to prohibit it, of entirely abolishing or placing under restrictions any trade or profession, which they may think expedient." [1] It is a matter of great doubt, whether in any of the State constitutions there is any special limitation upon the power of the legislature to regulate and enjoin the prosecution of trades and occupations, and if there is any limitation it must be inferred from the general clauses, such as " every man has an inalienable right to life, liberty, and the pursuit of happiness," or " no man shall be deprived of his life, liberty and property, except by due process of law." No man's liberty is safe, if the legislature can deny him the right to engage in a harmless calling ; there is certainly an interference with his right to the pursuit of happiness in such a case; and such a prohibition would be a deprivation of his liberty " without due process of law." Judge Cooley says in this connection : " What the legislature ordains and the constitution does not prohibit must be lawful. But if the constitution does no more than to provide that no person shall be deprived of life, liberty, or property, except by due process of law, it makes an important provision on this subject, because it is an important part of civil liberty to have the right to follow all lawful employments." [2] If these general

---

[1] Austin v. State, 10 Mo. 591.

[2] Cooley on Torts, p. 277. "No proposition is now more firmly settled than that it is one of the fundamental rights and privileges of every American citizen to adopt and follow such lawful industrial pursuits, not

constitutional provisions contain the only limitations upon
the legislative power to regulate employments, in order to
determine what are the specific limitations which these provisions impose, it will be necessary to refer to the limitations upon the police power in general.

It has already been determined that, in the exercise of the
police power, personal liberty can be subjected to only such
restraint as may be necessary to prevent damage to others or
to the public.[1] Police power, generally, is limited in its

injurious to the community, as he may see fit. Slaughterhouse Cases,
16 Wall. 106; Corfield v. Coryell, 4 Wash. C. C. 380; Matter of Jacobs,
98 N. Y. 98. The term 'liberty,' as protected by the constitution, is not
cramped into a mere freedom from physical restraint of the person of the
citizen, as by incarceration, but is deemed to embrace the right of man to
be free in the enjoyment of the faculties with which he has been endowed
by the Creator, subject only to such restraints as are necessary for the
common welfare. In the language of Andrews, J., in Bertholf v.
O'Rielly (74 N. Y. 515), the right to liberty embraces the right of man
' to exercise his faculties and to follow the lawful avocations for the support of life,' and as expressed by Earl, J., in In re Jacobs (98 N. Y. 98),
' one may be deprived of his liberty, and his constitutional right thereto
violated, without the actual restraint of his person. Liberty in its broad
sense, as understood in this country, means the right not only of freedom
from servitude, imprisonment or restraint, but the right to use his
faculties in all lawful ways, to live and work where he will, to earn his
livelihood in any lawful calling, and to pursue any lawful trade or avocation.' " People v. Marx, 99 N. Y. 377, 386. "The evidence in favor of
the petitioner is abundant and of the highest kind that the article he sells,
forbidden by the Missouri statute, is wholesome. It is not so much
urged that anything in the constitution of Missouri forbids or limits its
power in this respect by express language, as that the exercise of such a
power in regard to a property shown to be entirely innocent, incapable
of any injurious results or damage to the public health and safety, is an unwarranted invasion of public and private rights, an assumption of power
without authority in the nature of our institutions, and an interference
with the natural rights of the citizen and the public, which does not come
within the province of legislation. The proposition has great force, and
in the absence of any presentation of the motives and circumstances,
which governed the legislature in enacting the law, we should have
difficulty in saying it is unsound." Justice Miller, In re John Brosnahan,
Jr., 4 McCrary, 1.

[1] See *ante*, § 30.

§ 85

exercise to the enforcement of the maxim, *sic utere tuo ut alienum non lœdas.*[1]

Whenever, therefore, the prosecution of a particular calling threatens damage to the public or to other individuals, it is a legitimate subject for police regulation to the extent of preventing the evil. It is always within the discretion of the legislature to institute such regulations when the proper case arises, and to determine upon the character of the regulations. But it is a strictly judicial question, whether the trade or calling is of such a nature, as to require or justify police regulation. The legislature cannot declare a certain employment to be injurious to the public good, and prohibit it, when, as a matter of fact, it is a harmless occupation. " The position, however, is taken on the part of the State, that it is competent for the legislature, whenever it shall deem proper, to declare the existence of any property and pursuit deemed injurious to the public, *nuisances*, and to destroy and prohibit them as such ; and that such an action of the legislature is not subject to be reviewed by the courts. We deny this position. We deny that the legislature can enlarge its power over property or pursuits by declaring them nuisances, or by enacting a definition of a nuisance that will cover them. Whatever it has a right by the constitution to prohibit or to confiscate, it may thus deal with, without first declaring the matter to be a nuisance ; and whatever it has not a right by the constitution to prohibit and confiscate, it cannot thus deal with, even though it first declare it a nuisance." [2] It is also a judicial question whether the police regulation extends beyond the threatened evil, and prohibits that which involves no threatening danger to the public. If it is unconstitutional to impose police regulations upon an innocent calling, it must be likewise unconstitutional to place an occupation under police restraint beyond what is necessary to dissipate the threatening evil.

[1] See *ante*, § 1.
[2] Beebe *v.* State, 26 Ind. 501.

§ 85

The legislature has the choice of means to prevent evil to the public, but the means chosen must not go beyond the prevention of the evil, and prohibit what does not cause the evil. To illustrate, the keeping of a public gambling house is in itself a public evil, and the legislature may place it under whatever police control it may see fit, even to the extent of prohibiting the keeping of them. But the profession of medicine is a proper and necessary calling, and if pursued only by men, possessed of skill, instead of threatening public evil, is of the highest value to a community. The only evil, involved in the prosecution of that calling, is that which arises from the admission of incompetent men into the profession. The police regulation of the practice of medicine must, therefore, be confined to the evil, and any prohibition or other restrictive regulation which went beyond the exclusion of ignorant or dishonest men, would be unconstitutional. The police regulation of trades and professions, must, therefore, be limited to such restrictions and limitations as may be necessary to prevent damage to the public or to third persons. Keeping these general rules in mind, we will now consider the various methods of police interference with employments.

§ 86. **Prohibition as to certain classes.** — A calling may be generally harmless, when prosecuted by some classes of persons, and very harmful when engaged in by others. Thus, for example, it can readily be seen that the keeping of billiard saloons, of bar-rooms, and other public resorts by women, will prove highly injurious to the public morals, while there is no such peculiar danger arising from the keeping of such places by men. A law which prohibited women from engaging in these occupations would be for that reason justifiable under the constitutional limitations.[1]

[1] See Blair v. Kilpatrick, 40 Ind. 312, in which it was held that the granting of liquor licenses to men only, did not violate the constitutional provisions against the granting of special privileges. But under the con-

§ 86

Regulations have also been sustained, which were designed to prevent men of bad repute from engaging in employments, which from their nature are likely to become public nuisances, if conducted without safeguards. Thus it has been common, for this reason, to require hackmen, and keepers of places of public resort, to take out a license, and to give security for their good behavior or testimonials of good character. It has also been held that " the State may forbid certain classes of persons being employed in occupations which their age, sex, or health renders unsuitable for them, as women and young children are sometimes forbidden to be employed in mines and certain kinds of manufacture." [1] In so far as the employment of a certain class in a particular occupation may threaten or inflict damage upon the public or third persons, there can be no doubt as to the constitutionality of any statute which prohibits their prosecution of that trade. But it is questionable, except in the case of minors, whether the prohibition can rest upon the claim that the employment will prove hurtful to them. Minors are under the guardianship of the State, and their actions can be controlled so that they may not injure themselves. But when they have arrived at majority they pass out of the state of tutelage, and stand before the law free from all restraint, except that which may be necessary to prevent the infliction by them of injury upon others. It may be, and probably is, permissible for the State to prohibit pregnant women

stitution of California, which provides that no person shall be disqualified by sex from pursuing any lawful vocation, it was held that a similar regulation, excluding females from employment in certain kinds of drinking saloons, was unconstitutional. Matter of Maguire, 57 Cal. 604 (40 Am. Rep. 125).

[1] Cooley Const. Law, p. 231. In Com. *v.* Hamilton Manfg. Co., 120 Mass. 383, it was held that a statute prohibiting the employment of all persons under eighteen, and of all women in laboring in any manufacturing establishment more than 60 hours per week (Mass. Stat. 1874), violates no contract implied in the granting of a charter to any manufacturing company, nor any right reserved under the constitution to any citizen, and may be maintained as a health or police regulation.

§ 86

from engaging in certain employments, which would be likely to prove injurious to the unborn child, but there can be no more justification for the prohibition of the prosecution of certain callings by women, because the employment will prove hurtful to themselves, than it would be for the State to prohibit men from working in the manufacture of white lead, because they are apt to contract lead poisoning, or to prohibit occupation in certain parts of iron smelting works, because the lives of the men so engaged are materially shortened.

§ 87. **Police regulation of skilled trades and learned professions.** — Where the successful prosecution of a calling requires a certain amount of technical knowledge and professional skill, and the lack of them in the practitioner will result in material damage to the one who employs him, it is a legitimate exercise of police power to prohibit any one from engaging in the calling who has not previously been examined by the lawfully constituted authority and received a certificate in testimony of his qualification to practice the profession. The right of the State to exercise this control over skilled trades and the learned professions, with a single exception in respect to teachers and expounders of religion, has never been seriously questioned. Thus we find in every State statutes which provide for the examination of those who wish to engage in the practice of the law, of medicine and surgery, of pharmacy, and sometimes we find statutes which require all engineers to be examined before they are permitted to take charge of an engine. So, also, in England, it was once made necessary for one to serve an apprenticeship before he was permitted to pursue any one of the skilled trades. That is not now the law in the United States, but there would be no constitutional objection to such a statute, if it were enacted. Judge Cooley says: "No one has any right to practice law or medicine except under the regulations the State may prescribe. * * *

§ 87

The privilege may be given to one sex and denied to the other, and other discriminations equally arbitrary may doubtless be established."[1] A distinguished judge of Missouri says there can be no doubt "that the legislature of Missouri can declare the practice of law or medicine an unlawful calling, if they thought fit to do so."[2] If the rules heretofore laid down for the determination of the limitation of the police control of employments be sustainable, the position of these distinguished judges is untenable. The professions of law and medicine are profitable employments, to the public as well as to the practitioners ; and the only elements of danger arising from the practice of them lies in the admission of incompetent persons into them. (Any prohibition which extends further than to prevent the admission of incompetent men will be unconstitutional. It has been held that women can be denied the right to engage in the practice of law.[3] In the State court the principal ground for a denial of the plaintiff's right to engage in the practice of law was maintained to be that, "as a married woman (she) would be bound neither by her express contracts, nor by those implied contracts, which it is the policy of the law to create between attorney and client." In the Supreme Court of the United States, although the opinion of the court, delivered by Justice Miller, was rested upon the fact that the practice of law in Illinois was not one of the privileges and immunities of *citizens of the United States* as such, and therefore did not come within the jurisdiction of the court, in a separate opinion by Judge Bradley, in which Judges Field and Swayne concur, it is claimed that the statutes of a State may prohibit a woman from practicing law, because on account of the supposed difference in her mental capacity she cannot acquire that degree of skill which the

---

[1] Cooley on Torts, pp. 289, 290.
[2] Napton, J., in Austin *v.* State, 10 Mo. 591.
[3] Bradwell *v.* State, 55 Ill. 535; *s. c.* 16 Wall. 130.

§ 87

successful practice of the law requires.[1] Of course, a married woman, under her strict common-law disabilities, cannot make binding contracts, and it would be impossible for her to be sued on any express or implied obligation which she may have incurred in the practice. This no doubt would furnish a justification for a statute which prohibited married women from engaging in the practice of law, provided the disabilities thus imposed by the law are themselves constitutional.[2] But in respect to the inability of woman to attain the standard of professional skill required by the law to insure clients against the ignorant blunderings of attorneys, one is forced to the conclusion that this, like very many other venerable distinctions between the sexes, is the result of sexual prejudice.

Judge Cooley's position, in respect to the unlimited power of the State to regulate the practice of law and medicine, is that the practice of these professions is a privilege, and cannot be demanded as a matter of right. I can see no ground upon which this claim may be supported, so far as it refers to medicine. The physician and surgeon derives no peculiar benefit from the State, and there can be no substantial difference between his right to pursue his calling and that of a teacher to ply his vocation, or of the mer-

[1] "In the nature of things it is not every citizen of every age, sex, and condition that is qualified for every calling and position. It is the prerogative of the legislator to prescribe regulations founded upon nature, reason and experience for the due admission of qualified persons to professions and callings demanding special skill and confidence. This fairly belongs to the police power of the State; and in my opinion, in view of the peculiar characteristics, destiny and mission of woman, it is within the province of the legislature to ordain what offices, positions, and callings shall be filled and discharged by men, and shall receive the benefit of those energies and responsibilities, and that decision and firmness which are presumed to predominate in the sterner sex. For these reasons I think that the laws of Illinois now complained of are not obnoxious to the charge of abridging any of the privileges and immunities of citizens of the United States." Opinion of Justice Bradley, concurred in by JJ. Swayne and Field, in Bradwell v. Illinois, 16 Wall. 142.

[2] As to which see *post*, § 162.

§ 87

-chant to engage in business. They are not enjoying any peculiar privilege. Nor can I see any reason for looking upon the practice of law, outside of the courts, as a privilege. I cannot see why it is a peculiar privilege, derivable from the State, for an attorney to draw up a deed, or to make a will for a client. But inasmuch as courts are creatures of the law, and independently of the State, there can be no courts and no advocates, the right to appear for another in a court of justice may be considered a privilege which may be denied or granted at the pleasure of the State authorities. In England, at an early day, one accused of crime was not allowed to have counsel, and the right to appear by counsel in any case, rests upon rule of law. Yet even with this concession, it may still be claimed that such a privilege should be granted equally and to all, to avoid the constitutional objection to the granting of unequal or special privileges and immunities.[1]

In respect to the regulation of the practice of medicine, the constitutionality of laws has likewise been questioned.[2]

---

[1] The constitutionality of the regulations of the right to practice law has often been questioned. Thus a statute has been held to be unconstitutional which required attorneys to take an oath that they have not engaged in dueling, as a condition precedent to practicing law. Matter of Dorsey, 7 Port. (Ala.) 293. It had also been held to be unconstitutional for a statute to prohibit one from engaging in the practice of law who had served in the Confederate Army in the war of the rebellion, or to require them to take an oath that they have never taken up arms against the United States. Ex parte Tenney, 2 Duv. (Ky.) 351; Ex parte Law, 35 Ga. 285; Ex parte Garland, 4 Wall. 333; Cummings v. Missouri, 4 Wall. 277 But it is constitutional to require attorneys to take the oath of allegiance to the United States government. Cohen v. Wright, 22 Cal. 293; Ex parte Yale, 24 Cal. 241. And in order that he may be disbarred, precise and specific charges of malpractice or unprofessional behavior must be brought against him, and he must have an opportunity to be heard in his own defense. State v. Watkins, 3 Mo. 480; Matter of Mills, 1 Mich. 392; State v. Start, 7 Iowa, 499; Fisher's Case, 6 Leigh, 619; Withers v. State, 36 Ala. 252; Ex parte Percy, 36 N. Y. 651.

[2] By a Massachusetts law it was provided that no one can be permitted to recover by legal process the fees he has earned in the practice of medicine and surgery, unless he has been licensed by the Massachusetts Med-

In respect to the clerical profession, the constitutional guaranties against encroachments on religious liberty and freedom of worship would be violated, if an attempt were made by the State to determine who shall minister to the spiritual wants of the people. Every individual, and every body of people, have a constitutional right to select their own clergymen and expounders of religion, and it can never, under our present constitutions, which ordain a complete separation of church and State, become a matter of State regulation as it is in some of the states of Europe.[1]

§ 88. **Regulation of practice in the learned professions.**—Not only does the State undertake to prescribe the terms and conditions for the admission of members to the learned professions, so as to exclude dishonest and incompetent men, but in some instances laws have been enacted to regulate the practice of the professions. Thus at common law attorneys were prohibited from making contracts with their clients to receive a certain portion of what is recovered in a suit, as compensation for their services. This was called *champerty*. It is still the law everywhere, in the absence of a repealing statute ; but public opinion, in respect to the character of the offense, has so far changed that the law has become a dead letter, and reputable attorneys are daily accepting fees, contingent upon the success of the suit, and proportionate to the amount recovered in the judgment. It is also a common rule of the court that attorneys will not be allowed to become bail or surety for their clients in a pending suit.[1]

ical Society or was graduated as a doctor of medicine in Harvard University: the statute was held to be constitutional. Hewitt *v.* Charier, 16 Pick. 353. So, also, an act of Nevada, providing that graduation from a medical college was necessary to receive a license to practice medicine except in the case of those who have practiced for ten years in that State, was held to be not unconstitutional, because it does not make a similar exception in favor of those who had practiced for the same length of time elsewhere. Ex parte Spinney, 10 Nev. 323.

[1] Cooley on Torts, p. 290; Cooley Const. Law, pp. 231, 232.

§ 88

In the practice of medicine, an attempt has often been made by the old school of medicine, the school of allopathy, to bring homeopathy into legal disrepute, and to deny to practitioners of that school equal privileges before the law; but the police power of the State can never be exercised in favor of or against any system of medicine.   The police power can be brought to bear upon quacks, and disreputable practitioners, to whichever school they may belong, but when reputable and intelligent members of the profession differ in theories of practice, the State has no power to determine which of them, if either, is wrong.[2]

In the practice of medicine, however, there are legal regulations which the members of the profession are obliged to observe.   It is well known that when a death occurs, the physician who has been in attendance upon the deceased is obliged by the law to furnish a certificate, setting forth the cause of death ; this certificate being required, before there can be a burial, without a coroner's inquest.   It is also required sometimes of physicians to report to the health officer all cases of infectious or contagious diseases, which they have in charge.   Such regulations are readily justifiable; the first, because the physician's certificate assists in preventing the burial of those who have met with a wrongful or violent death ; and the second, because information concerning the location of cases of infectious and contagious diseases will enable the health officers to employ safeguards to prevent an epidemic.   But it is not quite so clear that the State has the right to require physicians and midwives to report to some officer, within a certain time, all births and deaths which may come under their supervision, subject to a penalty for failing to perform the duty thus re-

[1] Love *v.* Sheffelin, 7 Fla. 40; Massie *v.* Mann, 17 Iowa, 131; Miles *v.* Clarke, 4 Bosw. 632; Ryckman *v.* Coleman, 13 Abb. Pr. 398.   But see Abbott *v.* Zeigler, 9 Ind. 511.

[2] See White *v.* Carroll, 42 N. Y. 161.

§ 88

quired of them. This regulation is now becoming quite common, and the object of it is to facilitate the collection of statistics. In a case before the Supreme Court of Iowa, such a law was sustained as constitutional, and probably the practical utility of the law, and the absence of any excessive burden in requiring this duty of the physician, will in all cases furnish sufficient justification for the enactment of the law.[1]

In support of legislation for the prevention of intoxication, it has been held not unreasonable for an ordinance to make it unlawful for a physician to prescribe liquor for a well man.[2] As an attempt to evade a law, it is clearly permissible to prohibit it, and if any question can arise in that connection, it would have reference to the validity of the law whose enforcement is designed to be attained by the ordinance. If it was permissible for the State or town to prohibit the sale of liquor except for medicinal purposes, it was proper enough for the town or State to prohibit an evasion of the law by means of false prescriptions.

Although the clerical profession cannot be subjected to police supervision, so far as to determine the character of its *personnel*, or of the doctrines to be taught, yet, clergymen in the performance of duties, which are collateral to their main duties, and which have a civil phase as well as a religious phase, may be subjected to the regulations of of the State. Thus it is becoming more and more common

---

[1] " The statute requires the collection of statistics pertaining to the population of the State, and the health of the people, which may impart information useful in the enactment of laws, and valuable to science and the medical profession, to whom the people look for remedies for disease and for means tending to preserve health. The objects of the statute are within the authority of the State and may be attained in the exercise of its police power. Similar objects are contemplated by statutes requiring a census to be periodically taken, the constitutionality of which we have never heard questioned." Robinson *v.* Hamilton, 60 Iowa, 134 (46 Am. Rep. 63).

[2] Carthage *v.* Buckner, 4 Ill. App. 317.

§ 88

for State laws to prohibit the solemnization of marriages unless the parties have previously received a marriage license from some civil officer, and requiring the clergyman to return the license, with a certificate from himself, announcing the day of the marriage. Marriage is a civil *status*, as well as a religious institution, and the two are so intimately blended that its regulation by the State in its former character controls its regulation by the church.

§ 89. **Regulation of sale of certain articles of merchandise.** — The regulations, which would fall under this heading, are very numerous, and most of them are free from all doubt in respect to their validity under our constitutional limitations. They are instituted either for the purpose of preventing injury to the public, or thwarting all attempts of the vendor to defraud the vendee.

A regulation, whatever may be its character, which is instituted for the purpose of preventing injury to the public, and which does tend to furnish the desired protection, is clearly constitutional. A good example of this class of regulations, would be the Kentucky statute, which is also found in other States, providing for the inspection of kerosene and other oils, with a view to prohibit the sale of such as ignite below a certain degree of heat. Such a law is a plain and reasonable exercise of the police power of the State.[1] So would be any law, providing for the inspection of fresh meat, and other provisions, in order that the public welfare may be protected from the danger, arising from the consumption of unwholesome food.

But where there is no danger of injury to the public, it is difficult to determine how far the State may by its police regulations attempt to protect private individuals against each other's frauds. A fraud is, of course, a trespass upon another's private rights, and can always be punished, when

---

[1] Patterson *v.* Kentucky, 97 U. S. 501.

§ 89

committed. It is therefore but rational to suppose that the State may institute any reasonable preventive remedy, when the frequency of the frauds, or the difficulty experienced in circumventing them, is so great that no other means will prove efficacious. Where, therefore, police regulations are established, which give to private parties increased facilities for detecting and preventing fraud, as a general proposition, these laws are free from all constitutional objections. Laws, which provide for the inspection and grading of flour, the inspection of tobacco,[1] the inspection and regulation of weights and measures,[2] the regulation of weight of bread,[3] requiring all lumber to be surveyed, by a public surveyor,[4] providing for the weighing of coal and other articles of heavy bulk on the public scales,[5] are constitutional exercises of police power, so far as they permit one party to compel the other to comply with the regulation, in the absence of their agreement to the contrary. For example, it is permissible for a statutory regulation to provide for standard weights and measures, and to compel their use, when the parties have not agreed upon the use of others. But it cannot be reasonable to prohibit the use of any other mode of measurement.[6] It is an excessive exercise of police power, when the law compels one to make use of the means provided for his own protection against fraud. The same distinction would apply to regulations, requiring the inspection and weighing of articles of merchandise by the inspector and weigher, and charging a certain fee for the same, even when the parties have agreed in good faith to waive the compliance with the regulation. There is only one ground, upon which this fea-

---

[1] Turner v. Maryland, 107 U. S. 38 (22 Am. Law Reg. N. S. 198, note.)
[2] Ritchie v. Boynton, 114 Mass. 431; Eaton v. Keegan, 114 Mass. 433; Durgin v. Dyer, 68 Me. 143; Woods v. Armstrong, 34 Ala. 150.
[3] Mobile v. Tuille, 3 Ala. (N. S.) 140.
[4] Pierce v. Kimball, 9 Me. 54 (23 Am. Dec. 537).
[5] City Council v. Rogers, 2 McCord, 495.
[6] See Eaton v. Keegan, 114 Mass. 433.

§ 89

ture of such laws may be justified; and that is, to insure
the State against the expense of maintaining a public inspection, and the provision will fall under the head of exceptional burdens or special taxation, which in some of the
States is prohibited. But the authorities do not support
this view of such regulations. The regulation is in most
cases made absolute, and the observance of it is obligatory
upon all. Thus it has been held that a city ordinance may
require hay or coal to be weighed by city weighers.[1] Of
the same character, is the New York law, which provides
that the sale of oleomargarine, or other product resembling
butter, shall be prohibited, unless the box or other recepta-
cle, in which it is kept, shall have the true name of the article
plainly stamped upon it. The object of the law is the prevention of fraud, and is a reasonable police regulation. Of
a similar character is the law, which provides that druggists
must, in the sale of all poisons, have upon the label of each
package the word " Poison " printed in clear type, the
name of the poison and a statement of the ordinary anti-
dotes. The regulation is a reasonable and justifiable one,
and works no peculiar hardship upon the pharmacist. But
the regulation of the sale of poison assumes an interesting
and peculiar form, when it is extended, as it is in some of
the States, to a requirement, that the druggist must keep a
register of the poisons sold, and the names of purchasers.
Probably a double purpose is intended in the enforcement
of this regulation, viz. : the prevention of suicide by checking the purchase of poison for such a purpose, and the
prevention of homicide by poison, by facilitating the conviction in furnishing evidence of the purchase of poison. It
is probable that the law is easily sustainable on either ground.
While the common-law rule making suicide a crime and
providing a certain punishment, may be open to serious

---

[1] Stokes v. New York, 14 Wend. 87; Yates v. Milwaukee, 12 Wis.
673.

constitutional objections,[1] it is reasonable to suppose a man, who commits suicide, to be sufficiently insane to justify State interference, in order to prevent his infliction of bodily injury upon himself.[2]

§ 90. **Legal tender and regulation of currency.** — Although Sociologists, like Herbert Spencer, may doubt the necessity, and condemn the practice, of the regulation of currency by the government; and although the private coining of money may be permitted without any detriment to the public interests, arising from the general debasement of the coin: no constitutional question can arise in respect to the exclusive exercise by government of the power to coin money in the United States; for the United States constitution gives to the national government this exclusive right.[3] But apart from any special constitutional provision, and on general principles of constitutional law, this phase of police power may be justified on the plea of public necessity. The most devoted disciple of the *laissez faire* doctrine will admit that so delicate a matter as the determination of the standard value of the current coin can only be obtained by governmental regulation. In the colonial days, and in the days of the confederation, one of the greatest evils, and the in most serious obstacle to commercial intercourse between the States, was the almost endless variety of coin that passed current in different places, and the difficulty was increased by the employment of the same names to denote, in different places, coins of different values. If the States and colonies could not, without the interference of the general government, procure for them-

---

[1] See *ante*, § 10.

[2] On the other hand it has been held to be unconstitutional to require druggists to furnish the names of parties to whom he sells liquor. Clinton *v.* Phillips, 58 Ill. 102 (11 Am. Rep. 52).

[3] See U. S. Const., art. I., § 8, in which it is provided that Congress shall have power "to coin money, regulate the value thereof, and of foreign coin."

§ 90

selves coin of uniform value, it would be still more difficult for the commercial world to attain the same end. The only safe course is to vest in the Supreme Power — in this country, in the United States government — the exclusive control of the coin.

The necessity for a public coinage may not be so great as the State regulation of the value of the coins, but the danger of a general debasement of the coin, and the great possibilities of committing fraud upon persons who generally would not have the means at hand for detecting the fraud, would be a sufficient justification of the denial to private individuals of the right to coin money.

As already stated, in respect to the exclusive power of the United States, to coin money and to regulate the value thereof, no doubt can arise. But grave difficulties are met with, in determining the limitations upon the power of the government to declare what shall be a legal tender in the payment of debts. In fact, the governmental power to coin money is mainly incidental to the regulation of the matter of legal tender. Of course, the power to facilitate exchange by the creation of an ample currency does not necessarily involve the creation of legal tender. For example, national bank notes are currency, but they are not legal tender. But the need of a determination by law, what shall constitute a legal tender for the payment of debts, led inevitably to the demand for the creation of a sufficient quantity of the things, called money, which are required by law to be tendered in payment of debts. I do not mean to say that the demand for a legal tender preceded, in point, of historical sequence, the need of a currency. But from the standpoint of police power, the necessity of a legal tender requires a regulation of the currency of the government, instead of the latter bearing the relation of cause to the former.

Now, what can government declare to be a legal tender? There can be no doubt that the government has the power

§ 90

to declare its own coin to be legal tender. And it may, no doubt, provide that certain foreign coin shall be legal tender at their real value, as estimated by Congress ; nor can it be doubted that the several States have no right to declare anything else but gold and silver to be a legal tender.[1] But it is not an easy matter to determine the limitations of the power of the United States government, in the matter of legal tender. The question has assumed a practical form by the enactment of laws by Congress, in 1862, 1863, and 1878, declaring the treasury notes of the United States to be legal tender in payment of all debts, public and private. The acts of 1862 and 1863 were passed when the country was rent in twain by a gigantic civil war, which threatened the existence of the Union ; and they were prompted by the desire to force the notes into circulation, and procure funds and materials for the prosecution of the war. In reporting the first act to the Senate, the chairman of the committee on finance (Sumner) said : " It is put on the ground of absolute, overwhelming necessity; that the government has now arrived at that point when it must have funds, and those funds are not to be obtained from ordinary sources, or from any of the expedients to which we have heretofore had recourse, and therefore, this new, anomalous and remarkable provision must be resorted to in order to enable the government to pay off the debt that it now owes, and afford circulation which will be available for other purposes." [2] In other words, in order to furnish the government with the means, which the exigencies of war demanded, Congress made use of a power which is possessed by the government for promoting the welfare of the commercial world, by providing a uniform mode of settlement of debts. The establishment of a legal tender has for its object the bestowal of benefits upon the private interests of

[1] See art. I., § 10.
[2] Cong. Globe, 1861–2, Part I., 764.

§ 90

individuals, and was not intended to be a source of revenue. It cannot be doubted that this is the real object of a legal tender. The question then arises, can Congress employ this power for the purpose of increasing the revenue.

The question has been before the United States Supreme Court several times. In the first case,[1] the acts of 1862–63, were declared to be unconstitutional in so far as they make the treasury notes of the United States legal tender in payment of existing debts. In the Legal Tender Cases,[2] the opinion of the court in Hepburn v. Griswold, was overruled, and the acts of 1862 and 1863, in making the treasury notes legal tender, were declared to be constitutional, whether they applied to existing or subsequent debts, the burden of the opinion being that Congress had the right, as a war measure, to give to these notes the character of legal tender. In 1878, Congress passed an act, providing for the re-issue of the treasury notes, and declared them to be legal tender in payment of all public and private debts. In a case, arising under the act of 1878, the Supreme Court has finally affirmed the opinion set forth in 12 Wallace, and held further, that, the power of the government to make the treasury notes legal tender, when the public exigencies required, being admitted, it becomes a question of legislative discretion, when the public welfare demands the exercise of the power.[3] This decision will probably constitute the final adjudication of this question; and while it must be considered as settled, at least for the present, that the United States has the power to make its treasury notes legal tender, it is but proper that, in a work on police power, the rule of the court should be criticised and tested by the application of the ordinary rules of constitutional law. The decision is so important, that full extracts from the opinion

[1] Hepburn v. Griswold, 8 Wall. 603.
[2] 12 Wall. 457.
[3] Juillard v. Greenman, 110 U. S. 421.

§ 90

of the court, and the dissenting opinion of Justice Field, have been inserted in the note below.[1]

[1] " By the Constitution of the United States, the several States are prohibited from coining money, emitting bills of credit, or making anything but gold and silver coin a tender in payment of debts. But no intention can be inferred from this to deny to Congress either of these powers. Most of the powers granted to Congress are described in the eighth section of the first article; the limitations intended to be set to its powers, so as to exclude certain things which might be taken to be included in the ninth section; the tenth section is addressed to the States only. This section prohibits the States from doing some things which the United States are expressly prohibited from doing, as well as from doing some things the United States are expressly authorized to do, and from doing some things neither expressly granted nor expressly denied to the United States. Congress and the States equally are expressly prohibited from passing any bill of attainder, or *ex post facto* law, or granting any title of nobility. The States are forbidden, while the President and Senate are expressly authorized, to make treaties. The States are forbidden, but Congress is expressly authorized, to coin money. The States are prohibited from emitting bills of credit; but Congress, which is neither expressly authorized nor expressly forbidden to do so, has, as we have already seen, been held to have the power of emitting bills of credit, and of making every provision for their circulation as currency, short of giving them the quality of legal tender for private debts — even by those who have denied its authority to give them this quality.

"It appears to us to follow, as a logical and necessary consequence, that Congress has the power to issue the obligations of the United States in such form, and to impress upon them such qualities as currency for the purchase of merchandise, and the payment of debts, as accords with the usage of sovereign governments. The power, as incident to the power of borrowing money and issuing bills or notes of the government for money borrowed, of impressing upon those bills or notes the quality of being a legal tender for the payment of private debts, was a power universally understood to belong to sovereignty, in Europe and America, at the time of the framing and adoption of the constitution of the United States. The governments of Europe, acting through the monarch or the legislature, according to the distribution of powers under their respective constitutions, had and have as sovereign a power of issuing paper money as of stamping coin. * * * The power of issuing bills of credit, and making them, at the discretion of the legislature, a tender in payment of private debts, had long been exercised in this country by the several colonies and States; and during the Revolutionary war the States upon the recommendation of the congress of the confederation, had made the bills issued by Congress a legal tender. See Craig v. Missouri, 4 Pet. 35, 453; Briscoe v. Bank of Kentucky, 11 Pet. 257, 313, 334, 336; Legal

§ 90

A perusal of the decisions in these leading cases will disclose the fact that the members of the courts, and the attorneys in the causes, have not referred to, the same constitutional provision for the authority to make the treasury

Tender Cases, 12 Wall. 557, 558, 622. The exercise of this power not being prohibited to Congress by the constitution, it is included in the power expressly granted to borrow money on the credit of the United States.

"This position is fortified by the fact that Congress is vested with the exclusive exercise of the analogous power of coining money, and regulating the value of domestic and foreign coin, and also, with the paramount power of regulating foreign and inter-state commerce. Under the power to borrow money on the credit of the United States, and to issue circulating notes for the money borrowed, its power to define the quality and force of those notes as currency is as broad as the like power over a metallic currency under the power to coin money, and to regulate the value thereof. Under the two powers, taken together, Congress is authorized to establish a national currency, either in coin or in paper, and to make that currency lawful money for all purposes, as regards the national government or private individuals.

"The power of making the notes of the United States a legal tender in payment of private debts, being included in the power to borrow money and to provide a national currency, is not defeated or restricted by the fact that its exercise may affect the value of private contracts. If, upon a just and fair interpretation of the whole constitution, a particular power or authority appears to be vested in Congress, it is no constitutional objection to its existence, or to its exercise, that the property or the contracts of individuals may be incidentally affected." * * * "So, under the power to coin money and to regulate its value, Congress may (as it did with regard to gold by the act of June 28, 1834, ch. 95, and with regard to silver, by act of Feb. 28, 1878, ch. 20) issue coins of the same denominations as those already current by law, but of less intrinsic value than those, by reason of containing a less weight of the precious metals, and thereby enable debtors to discharge their debts by the payment of coins of less than the real value. A contract to pay a certain sum in money, without any stipulation as to the kind of money in which it shall be paid, may always be satisfied by payment of that sum in any currency which is lawful money at the place and time at which payment is to be made. 1 Hale P. C. 192, 194; Bac. Abr., Tender, B. 2; Pothier, Contract of Sale, No. 416; Pardessus, Droit Commercial, No. 204, 205; Searight, v Calbraith, 4 Dall. 324. As observed by Mr. Justice Strong, in delivering the opinion of the court in the *Legal Tender Cases*, ' every contract for the payment of money, simply, is necessarily subject to the constitutional power of the government over the currency, whatever that power may

§ 90

notes legal tender.   Some have claimed it to be a power,
implied from the power to levy and carry on war, others
refer it to the power to borrow money, etc.   If the
power to make the treasury notes legal tender cannot be

be, and the obligation of the parties is, therefore, assumed with reference
to that power.'

"Congress, as the legislature of a sovereign nation, being expressly
empowered by the Constitution 'to lay and collect taxes, to pay the debts
and provide for the common defense and general welfare of the United
States,' and 'to borrow money on the credit of the United States,' and
'to coin money and regulate the value thereof and of foreign coin; ' and
being clearly authorized, as incidental to the exercise of those great
powers, to emit bills of credit, to charter national banks, and to provide
a national currency for the whole people, in the form of coin, treasury
notes and national bank bills; and the power to make the notes of the
government a legal tender in payment of private debts being one of the
powers belonging to sovereignty in other civilized nations, and not expressly withheld from Congress by the constitution; we are irresistibly
impelled to the conclusion that the impressing upon the treasury notes of
the United States the quality of being a legal tender in payment
of private debts is an appropriate means, conducive and plainly
adapted to the execution of the undoubted powers of Congress, consistent with the letter and spirit of the constitution, and, therefore,
within the meaning of that instrument, 'necessary and proper for carrying into execution the powers vested by this constitution in the government of the United States.'

"Such being our conclusion in matter of law, the question whether at
any particular time, in war or in peace, the exigency is such, by reason of
unusual and pressing demands on the resources of the government, or of
the inadequacy of the supply of gold and silver coin to furnish the currency needed for the uses of the government and of the people, that it is,
as matter of fact, wise and expedient to resort to this measure is a political question, to be determined by Congress when the question of exigency arises, and not a judicial question, to be afterwards passed upon
by the courts." Opinion of court by J. Gray, in Juillard v. Greenman,
110 U. S. 421.

"It must be evident, however, upon reflection, that if there were any
power in the government of the United States to impart the quality of
legal tender to its promissory notes, it was for Congress to determine
when the necessity for its exercise existed; that war merely increased the
urgency for money; it did not add to the powers of the government nor
change their nature; that if the power exists it might be equally exercised when a loan was made to meet ordinary expenses in time of peace,
as when vast sums were needed to support an army or navy in time of

§ 90

shown to be prohibited by the United States constitution, then there would be very little difficulty in determining the power of the government in the premises.   The power to

war.   The wants of the government could never be the measure of its powers.   But in the excitement and apprehensions of the war these considerations were unheeded; the measure was passed as one of overruling necessity in a perilous crisis of the country.   Now, it is no longer advocated as one of necessity, but as one that may be adopted at any time. Never before was it contended by any jurist or commentator on the constitution that the government, in full receipt of ample income, with a treasury overflowing, with more money on hand than it knows what to do with, could issue paper money as a legal tender.   What was in 1862 called 'the medicine of the constitution' [by Sumner], has now become its daily bread.   So it always happens that whenever a wrong principle of conduct, political or personal, is adopted on the plea of necessity, it will afterwards be followed on a plea of convenience.

"The advocates of the measure have not been consistent in the designation of the power upon which they have supported its validity, some placing it on the power to borrow money, some on the coining power; and some have claimed it as an incident to the general powers of the government.   In the present case it is placed by the court upon the power to borrow money, and the alleged sovereignty of the United States over the currency.   It is assumed that this power, when exercised by the government, is something different from what it is when exercised by corporations or individuals, and that the government has, by the legal tender provision, the power to enforce loans of money because the sovereign governments of European countries have claimed and exercised such power.

*   *   *   "As to the terms *to borrow money*, where, I would ask, does the court find any authority for giving to them a different interpretation in the constitution from what they receive, when used in other instruments, as in the charters of municipal bodies or of private corporations, or in the contracts of individuals?   They are not ambiguous; they have a well-settled meaning in other instruments.   If the courts may change that in the constitution, so it may the meaning of all other clauses; and the powers which the government may exercise will be found declared, not by plain words in the organic law, but by words of a new significance resting in the minds of the judges.   Until some authority beyond the alleged claim and practice of the sovereign governments of Europe be produced, I must believe that the terms have the same meaning in all instruments wherever they are used; that they mean a power only to contract for a loan of money, upon considerations to be agreed upon between the parties.   The conditions of the loan, or whether any particular security shall be given to the lenders, are matters of arrange-

§ 90

make and regulate legal tender being denied by the United
States constitution to the States, the power must be exercised, if at all, by the United States government; and the

ment between the parties, they do not concern any one else. They do
not imply that the borrower can give to his promise to refund the money,
any security to the lender outside of the property or rights which he possesses. The transaction is completed when the lender parts with his
money, and the borrower gives his promise to pay at the time and in the
manner and with the securities agreed upon. Whatever stipulations may
be made to add to the value of the promises or to secure its fulfilment,
must necssarily be limited to the property rights and privileges which
the borrower possesses. Whether he can add to his promises any element which will induce others to receive them beyond the security which
he gives for their payment, depends upon his promise to control such
element. If he has a right to put a limitation upon the use of other
persons' property, or to enforce an exaction of some benefit from them,
he may give such privilege to the lender; but if he has no right thus to
interfere with the property or possessions of others, of course he can give
none. It will hardly be pretended that the government of the United
States has any power to enter into any engagement that, as security for its
notes, the lender shall have special privileges with respect to the visible
property of others, shall be able to occupy a portion of their lands or their
houses, and thus interfere with the possession and use of their property.
If the government cannot do that, how can it step in and say, as a condition of loaning money, that the lender shall have a right to interfere with
contracts between private parties? A large proportion of the property
of the world exists in contracts and the government has no more right
to deprive one of their value by legislation operating directly upon them
than it has a right to deprive one of the value of any visible and taxable
property.

"No one, I think, will pretend that individuals or corporations
possess the power to impart to their evidences of indebtedness any
quality by which the holder will be able to affect the contracts of other
parties, strangers to the loan; nor would any one pretend that congress
possesses the power to impart any one quality to the notes of the United
States, except from the clause authorizing it to make laws necessary and
proper to the execution of its powers. That clause, however, does not
enlarge the expressly designated powers; it merely states what Congress
could have done without its insertion in the constitution. Without it
Congress could have adopted any appropriate means to borrow; but that
can only be appropriate for that purpose which has some relation of
fitness to the end, which has respect to the terms essential to the contract, or to the securities which the borrower may furnish for the repay-
ment of the loan. The quality of legal tender does not touch the terms of

§ 90

United States government can exercise it, if the power is not prohibited by the constitution altogether, even though it is not expressly or impliedly delegated to the general govern-

the contract; that is complete without it; nor does it stand as a security for the loan, for a security is a thing pledged, over which the borrower has some control, or in which he holds some interest.

" The argument presented by the advocates of legal tender is, in substance this: The object of borrowing is to raise funds, the addition of the quality of legal tender to the notes of the government will induce parties to take them, and funds will thereby be more readily loaned. But the same thing may be said of the addition of any other quality which would give to the holder of the notes some advantage over the property of others, as for instance, that the notes should serve as a pass on the public conveyances of the country, or as a ticket to places of amusement, or should exempt his property from State and municipal taxation or entitle him to the free use of the telegraph lines, or to a percentage from the revenues of private corporations. The same consequence, a ready acceptance of the notes, would follow; and yet no one would pretend that the addition of privileges of this kind with respect to the property of others, over which the borrower has no control, would be in any sense an appropriate measure to the execution of the power to borrow.

" * * * The power vested in Congress to coin money does not in my judgment fortify the position of the court as its opinion affirms. So far from deducing from that power any authority to impress the notes of the government with the quality of legal tender, its existence seems to me inconsistent with a power to make anything but coin a legal tender. The meaning of the terms ' to coin money ' is not at all doubtful. It is to mould metallic substance into forms convenient for circulation and to stamp them with the impress of government authority indicating their value with reference to the unit of value established by law. Coins are pieces of metal of definite weight and value, stamped such by the authority of the government.

" * * * The clause to coin money must be read in connection with the prohibition upon the States to make anything but gold and silver coin a tender in payment of debts. The two taken together clearly show that the coins to be fabricated under the authority of the general government, and as such to be a legal tender for debts, are to be composed principally, if not entirely, of the metals of gold and silver. Coins of such metals are necessarily a legal tender to the amount of their respective values without any legislative enactment, and the statutes of the United States providing that they shall be such tender is only declaratory of their effect when offered in payment. When the constitution says, therefore, that Congress shall have the power to coin money, interpreting that clause with the prohibition upon the States, it says it shall have

§ 90

ment, at least if the position elsewhere taken [1] in respect to the powers of the United States be correct.

But it is my opinion that, while the constitution of the United States does not prohibit Congress from making any other coins, than gold and silver, legal tender, it does prohibit it from giving the character of legal tender to the United States treasury notes, or to anything else, which does not have and pass for, its intrinsic value. When gold or silver, or any other article of value is coined and is made a legal tender for the payment of all debts, at its true value, it is a very reasonable exercise of police power; for no one is deprived of his property against his will and without due process of law. It is merely a determination by law what coin is genuine, and which, therefore, was bargained for, by the parties to the contract. And when the value of the metal is inclined to be slightly variable from time to time, as in the case of silver, relative to gold, the establishment of a uniform value, when justly made, is likewise no unreasonable regulation. But if a money of a given denomination should

the 'power to make coins of the precious metals a legal tender, for that alone which is money can be a legal tender. If this be the true import of the language, nothing else can be made a legal tender. We all know that the value of the notes of the government in the market, and in the commercial world generally, depends upon their convertibility on demand into coin; and as confidence in such convertibility increases or diminishes, so does the exchangeable value of the notes vary. So far from becoming themselves standard of value by reason of the legislative declaration to that effect, their own value is measured by the facility with which they can be exchanged into that which alone is regarded as money by the commercial world. They are promises of money, but they are not money in the sense of the constitution. * * * Now, to coin money is, as I have said, to make coins out of metallic substances, and the only money the value of which Congress can regulate is coined money, either of our mints or of foreign countries. It should seem, therefore, that to borrow money is to obtain a loan of coined money, that is, money composed of precious metals, representing value in the purchase of property and payment of debts.' " Dissenting opinion of J. Field in Juillard v. Greenman, *supra*.

[1] See *post*, § 200.

§ 90

be coined, of less value than existing coins of the same denomination, and the people were required to take them at
their nominal value, it would be a fraud upon the people,
and I can see no reason why such a law should not be declared unconstitutional.   Congress has full power to change
the value of coins from time to time, but no law is constitutional which compels the creditor of existing debts to receive these coins of less value, when the parties contemplated
payment in the older coins of a higher value, but of the
same denomination.   If Congress should coin a dollar in
gold or silver, whose intrinsic value was only eighty-five
cents in existing coin, no law can compel its acceptance as
equivalent to a dollar, worth one hundred cents.   The enforcement of such a law would deprive creditors of fifteen
per cent of their loans, without due process of laws, and
hence in violation of the constitution of the United States.
Mr. Justice Gray says in Juillard v. Greenman,[1] that such
a law would not infringe any constitutional limitation, but
it seems to me to be a plain violation of the constitutional
provision, that " no man shall be deprived of his life, liberty
or property, without due process of law."

   " Undoubtedly Congress has power to alter the value of
coins issued, either by increasing or diminishing the alloy
they contain; so it may alter at its pleasure their denominations; it may hereafter call a dollar an eagle, and it may
call an eagle a dollar.   But if it be intended to assert that
Congress may make the coins changed the equivalent of
those having a greater value in their previous condition,
and compel parties contracting for the latter to receive
coins with diminished value, I must be permitted to deny
any such authority.   Any such declaration on its part
would be not only inoperative in fact but a shameful disregard of its constitutional duty.   As I said on a former
occasion : ' The power to coin money as declared by this

[1] 110 U. S. 449.

§ 90

court is a great trust devolved upon Congress, carrying
with it the duty of creating and maintaining a uniform
standard of value throughout the Union, and it would be a
manifest abuse of the trust to give to the coins issued by its
authority any other than their real value. By debas-
ing the coins, when once the standard is fixed, is meant
giving to the coins by their form and impress a certificate
of their having a relation to that standard different from
that which, in truth, they possess; in other words, giving
to the coins a false certificate of their value." [1] But even
in such a case, where a contract stipulates for the payment
of lawful money, and the law should subsequently alter the
value of the coin, so that the lawful money in use, when the
contract is to be performed, is of less intrinsic value; and by
construction of law the contract is supposed to refer to
what is lawful money at the time of performance; there still
may not be any absolutely arbitrary deprivation of private
property. But when the government undertakes to make
its own notes legal tender, a thing which has no intrinsic
value, whose value as currency depends upon the public
credit of the government, and rises and falls with it; instead
of its being the reasonable exercise of a police regulation,
the object of which is to facilitate exchange, and provide a
satisfactory legal settlement of private obligations by providing a uniform currency of recognized value, it is an arbitrary taking of private property, compelling private
individuals to become creditors of the government against
their will.

Making the treasury notes legal tender is not induced by
any desire to provide an easy method of making legal settlements of obligations, the only legitimate object of
establishing a legal tender of any kind, but for the purpose
of increasing the revenue of the government. The Su-

---

[1] Dissenting opinion of Justice Field in Juillard *v.* Greenman, 110 U.
U. 465.

§ 90

preme Court, in the opinion of Justice Gray, freely acknowledge this to be the purpose, and justify the exercise of the
power, by claiming it to be implied from the power to
borrow money. This clearly is unjustifiable under any
known rules of constitutional construction. The acts of
1862, and 1863, were justified as war measures, on the plea
of necessity. It may be that the government of a country
in a state of war, when its very existence is threatened, may
compel its citizens to become creditors of the government.
It may issue its treasury notes, and compel the creditors of
the government of all classes to receive its notes in payment of its debts. It may, possibly, appropriate to its own
use the materials necessary for the prosecution of the war,
paying for them at their market value in its treasury
notes. It may compel the citizens to serve in its land and
naval forces, and be paid for their services in treasury notes.
But it is difficult to see how it facilitates the borrowing of
money by the government to make the treasury notes legal
tender in the payment of debts between private parties. It
has been claimed that the character of legal tender increases the purchasing power of the treasury notes. If
this were so, it would be a faint justification of the law as a
war measure. But it is not true. The purchasing power
of a government treasury note, or of any other paper currency, depends upon the popular confidence in its ready
convertibility into specie. There is no difference in the
purchasing power of treasury notes and national bank notes,
although one is made legal tender, and the other is not.
Both are received as the equivalent of a gold or silver dollar, because of the confidence in the convertibility of both
of them into coin; whereas, during the civil war, when
many brave and true men were fearful of the result and the
popular confidence in the durability of the United States
government was greatly shaken; although the notes were
made legal tender, they sunk steadily in value, until at one
time, one dollar in gold was the equivalent of two and a

§ 90

half dollars in treasury notes. The treasury notes of the Confederate States fared worse, because their credit was impaired to a greater degree. Therefore, we must conclude, that even as a war measure it was unconstitutional to make the treasury notes legal tender in payment of private debts, because it did not in any sense assist them in borrowing money or procuring money's equivalent, for the prosecution of the war.

It is probable that the latest decision of the Supreme Court on this subject will be treated by the present generation as final. But inasmuch as decisions of courts, even of last resort, do not make law, but are merely evidence, albeit the highest and usually most reliable kind of evidence, of what the law is, it is the duty and within the province of jurists to combat error in decisions as in any other source of law, even when there is very little hope of a general adoption of their views.

§ 91. **Legislative restraint of importations — Protective tariffs.** — The reader, who has carefully followed the line of argument adopted, and the tests applied, in each case of the exercise of police power, will scarcely need any special elaboration of the grounds upon which it is held to be a violation of civil liberty for the government to do any act which is intended to and does restrain importations. Whatever may be thought of the justice of an import tax, in the abstract, the United States constitution expressly grants to the United States government the power to lay such a tax upon all importations. A tariff for revenue, therefore, comes within the legitimate exercise of police power. It is one mode of taxation. But no claim can be successfully made to an express or implied power to establish a tariff whose object is to restrain importations for the protection of competing home industries. The only provision on the subject is article 1, section 8, where it is provided that Congress shall have power " to lay and col-

§ 91

lect taxes, duties, imposts, and excises to pay the debts
and provide for the common defense and general welfare of
the United States." Here is found only an authority to
establish a tariff for revenue. In the days when the constitutionality of tariff laws used to be discussed, it appears
to have been conceded by the abler statesmen, that there
was no authority in the constitution for creating a tariff for
protection, and the claim was usually made that they may
establish " a tariff for revenue with incidental protection."
This is clearly an inconsistency. A tariff for revenue,
when carried to its logical extreme, would involve the institution of a policy, which would encourage importations,
and discourage home manufactures, for the greater the imposts the larger will be the revenue. On the other hand,
the principle of protection, when pushed to its extremity,
would restrain importations, and, if possible, the tariff
would be so constructed that there would be no imports,
and hence no revenue. While a tariff for revenue so constructed as to operate as an intentional restraint upon home
industries would not be just or wise, all tariffs should be
constructed with the single object in view of raising revenue,
and so far as there is any attempt to afford the so-called incidental protection, Congress exceeds the express power
to lay imposts.

But, in accordance with the rule of constitutional construction advocated and explained in a subsequent section,[1]
since the States are denied the power to lay imposts or
duties upon imports, " without the consent of Congress,"
" except what may be absolutely necessary for executing its
inspection laws,"[2] we claim that Congress may, without
express grant of such a power, lay imposts for the purposes of protection, if the constitution does not prohibit it.
But we also claim that a tariff for protection is prohibited by

---

[1] See *post*, § 200.
[2] U. S. Cons., art. I., § 10.

§ 91

the constitution, not in express terms, but by the general clause which provides that no one shall " be deprived of life, liberty or property, without due process of law." [1] It would be as constitutional for a State to prohibit one class of citizens from trading with another, as it is for the United States to prohibit, totally or partially, the dealing of citizens with foreign countries. It is a part of the civil liberty of a citizen of a constitutional State to be permitted to have business relations with whom he pleases. Even though a protective tariff does not compel the consumer to pay more for the home products than he would have to pay for the foreign articles in the absence of a protective tariff, and the home products were of the same value and intrinsic merit, protection is unconstitutional, because it interferes with the civil liberty of the citizen, when he is not threatening any evil to the public. But protective tariffs are usually needed, either because it is impossible to manufacture the home products as cheaply, or because they are of an inferior character. Hence, the consumer is made to pay more for his goods, and the tariff furthermore deprives him of his property, without due process of law. Without express constitutional authority, nothing but free trade is permissible under a constitutional government and in a free State.

§ 92. **Compulsory formation of business relations.** — It is a part of civil liberty to have business relations with whom one pleases. Judge Cooley says: " It is a part of every man's civil rights that he be left at liberty to refuse business relations with any person whomsoever, whether the refusal rests upon reason, or is the result of whim, caprice, prejudice or malice." [2] Business relations must be voluntary in order to be consistent with civil liberty. An attempt of the State to compel one man to enter into bus-

[1] U. S. Const. Amend., art. 5.
[2] Cooley on Torts, p. 278.

§ 92

iness relations with another, can only be justified by some
public reason or necessity. In an ordinary private business
relation, the State cannot constitutionally interfere, whatever reason may be assigned for one's refusal to have
dealings with another. It is no concern of the State or of
the individual, what those reasons are. It is his constitutional right to refuse to have business relations with a
particular individual, with or without reason. But there
are cases in which it has long been held to be within the
scope of legislative authority to interfere with, and compel,
the formation of business relations. The common law of
England, and of this country, has for centuries justified
this power of control over common carriers and innkeepers.
No man is compelled to become a common carrier or innkeeper ; but if he holds himself out to the world as such, he
is obliged to enter into business relations with all, under
impartial and reasonable regulations. The common carrier
must carry for all, within his regular line of business, and
the innkeeper must provide accommodation for all who
come to him, as long as he has room for them. These two
cases have for so long a time been recognized as exceptions
to the general rule, in respect to the voluntary character
of business relations, that the reasons for them are rarely,
if ever, demanded, and certainly not questioned. But a
determination of the constitutional reasons for these exceptions, if there are any, will help to discover the limitations
of legislative power in respect to other kinds of business.
It is stated usually, that the business of a common carrier
is a *quasi* public business, meaning that the public have
some rights in it, as, for example, the right to a compulsory formation of business relations, which they do not
possess in respect to a purely private business. But that
is rather a statement of what is, rather than a reason for
its existence. A similar statement is usually made in regard to the peculiar liability of innkeepers, and ordinarily
deemed sufficient. But if this regulation of the business

§ 92

of a common carrier, and of an innkeeper, is justifiable under our constitutional limitations, there must be some good public reason for the regulation, and not merely a matter of public convenience. Where the common carrier enjoys, in the prosecution of his business, unusual privileges or franchises, as in the case of railroads, ferries, street car companies and the like,[1] one need not go further for a reason to justify such a police regulation. Since the State grants the common carrier a privilege, not equally enjoyed by others, for the promotion of the public convenience, it might very well arrange for the impartial carriage of all, under reasonable regulations. And inasmuch as the common carriers, who do not have any special privileges, like hackmen, draymen, and drivers of express and furniture wagons, make a special use of a general privilege, in plying their trade, it may not be unreasonable for the State to compel them to carry all who may offer themselves or their goods. But no such reasons can be assigned for a similar regulation of innkeepers. They enjoy no privileges of any kind. Every man has a natural right to keep an inn, provided he so conducts it as not to violate the rights of others, or to constitute a public nuisance. If the business was of such a nature, that for the protection of the public from injury it is necessary to make a monopoly and grant it to one or more, as a special privilege,[2] then it would be the duty of the State to provide for the impartial entertainment of all who present themselves, and comply with the reasonable regulations of the inn. But the inn is no more likely to be productive of public injury than is the boarding house, from which the inn is distinguished. The keeper of a boarding house is not obliged to receive as a guest any one who comes. The threatening danger to the public, arising from the improper conduct of the inn, is, therefore, not the reason

---

[1] See *post,* §§ 189–194.
[2] See *post,* § 105

§ 92

for the rule of law, which obliges the innkeeper to receive as his guest, any traveler of decent behavior, who may apply. The object of the rule is to make it convenient for travelers to find lodging upon arriving in a strange place. It is a worthy object, but no man can be compelled to lodge another, simply because he is a traveler, and a stranger. No sufficient reason can be assigned ; unless the reason, given by Chief Justice Waite in a later case,[1] may be accepted as a proper one. He says: " Looking to the common law, from whence came the right which the constitution protects, we find that when private property is affected with a public interest, it ceases to be *juris privati* only. This was said by Lord Chief Justice Hale more than two hundred years ago, in his treatise De Portibus Maris, 1 Harg. Law Tracts, 78, and has been accepted without objection as an essential element in the law of property ever since. Property does become clothed with a public interest, when used in a manner to make it of public consequence, and affect the community at large. When, therefore, one devotes his property to a use in which the public has an interest, he, in effect, grants to the public an interest in that use, and must submit to be controlled by the public for the common good, to the extent of the interest he has thus created. He may withdraw his grant by discontinuing the use, but, so long as he maintains the use, he must submit to the control." [2] In this case, the business in question was the storage of grain in bulk in the Chicago elevators. As applied to the particular case, the rule thus laid down by Chief Justice Waite would give to the legislature the right to regulate any business, which should become a public necessity. The public utility of the business clothes it with a public interest, and authorizes police regulation to prevent imposition or oppression where the business be-

[1] Munn *v.* Illinois, 94 U. S. 113.
[2] pp. 125, 126.

§ 92

comes a *virtual* monopoly.[1] It is unquestionable that the State can, and indeed it is its duty to, subject to police control a monopoly, created by law; but in this case it is laid down for the first time that where the circumstances, surrounding a particular business, or its character, make it a "virtual monopoly," the State can regulate the conduct of the business, so that all having concern in it, will be treated impartially and fairly. I say this rule has been laid down for the first time, although the chief justice refers to it as a long established rule, and refers to Lord Hale as his authority. A careful study of Hale's writings will disclose the fact that to no case does he refer in which the business does not under the law constitute a privilege, more or less of a legal monopoly. There is nothing in his writings to justify the application of his rule or his reason-

[1] "In this connection it must also be borne in mind that, although in 1874, there were in Chicago fourteen warehouses adapted to this particular business, and owned by about thirty persons, nine business firms controlled them, and that the prices charged and received for storage were such as have been from year to year agreed upon and established by the different elevators or warehouses in the city of Chicago, and which rates have been annually published in one or more newspapers printed in said city, in the month of January in each year, as the established rates for the year then next ensuing such publication. Thus it is apparent that all the elevating facilities through which these vast productions of seven or eight great States of the West must pass on the way to four or five of the States on the seashore may be a 'virtual' monopoly.

"Under such circumstances it is difficult to see why, if the common carrier, or the miller, or the ferryman, or the innkeeper, or the wharfman, or the baker, or the cartman or the hackney coachman, pursues a public employment and exercises 'a sort of public office,' these plaintiffs in error do not. They stand, to use again the language of their counsel, in the very 'gateway of commerce,' and take toll from all who pass. Their business most certainly 'tends to a common charge, and is become a thing of public interest and use.' * * * Certainly, if any business can be clothed 'with a public interest, and cease to be *juris privati* only,' this has been." Opinion of Waite, Ch. J., *supra*. See *post*, § 93, for extracts from the dissenting opinion of Justice Field.

§ 92

ing to a business, which is a virtual monopoly, but is not made so by law.[1]

But even this is not a satisfactory reason for compelling all innkeepers to receive all guests applying to them at the present day. Perhaps at an early day, when the number of travelers was limited, and was not large enough to support more than one inn in most places, innkeeping may have been a virtual monopoly. But that town is very small, in this country, which cannot boast of at least two inns, and the actual rivalry and competition to secure guests will dispel all notions of a virtual monopoly. No reason but public convenience can be suggested for the existence of this law in respect to innkeepers, and it is by no means a satisfactory one. The public convenience can never justify the interference of the State with one's private business.

Of late a disposition to bring within this category the theaters and other places of public amusements has been displayed by legislatures, both State and national, in order to prevent discrimination by the managers and proprietors of such places against the negro, " on account of his race, color, or previous condition of servitude." The United States statute, which has lately been declared to be unconstitutional, because the law encroaches upon the domain of the State legislatures,[2] and which corresponds in all essential particulars to the State statutes on the same subject, provided " that all persons within the jurisdiction of the United States shall be entitled to the full and equal enjoyment of the accommodations, advantages, facilities and privileges of inns, public conveyances on land and water, theaters and other places of public amusement, subject only to the conditions and limitations established by law, and applicable alike to citizens of every race and color, regardless of any

---

[1] See *post*, § 93, for lengthy quotations from Lord Hale.
[2] See Civil Rights Cases, 109 U. S. 3.

§ 92

previous condition of servitude." So far as these statutes refer to the enjoyment of the privileges of inns and public conveyances, they merely affirm the common law, and grant no new right. But in respect to theaters and other places of public amusement, the regulation is certainly novel. The only legal reason for the regulation is public convenience, unless the circumstances are such that the business becomes a virtual monopoly. And to justify the regulation on these grounds is, certainly, going very far toward removing all limitation upon the power of the State to regulate the private business of an individual. In the Supreme Court case,[1] in which Chief Justice Waite justifies the police control of " a virtual monopoly," on the ground that the use of the elevator is a public necessity to all merchants, who are engaged in the shipment of grain through Chicago to all points of the country. So, also, may the entertainment at an inn be considered a public necessity to all travelers. But attendance upon theatrical and other public amusements can in no sense be considered a necessity, nor is the business a franchise or legal monopoly. Such legislation should, therefore, be condemned as unconstitutional. But it has been sustained in Mississippi against all objections,[2] and Judge Cooley justifies it in the following language : " Theaters and other places of public amusement exist wholly under the authority and protection of State laws; their managers are commonly licensed by the State, and in conferring the license it is no doubt competent for the State to impose the condition that the proprietors shall admit and accommodate all persons impartially. Therefore, State regulations corresponding to those established by Congress must be clearly within the competency of the legislature, and might be established as suitable regulations of police." [3]

---

[1] Munn v. Illinois, *supra*.

[2] Donnell v. State, 48 Miss. 661.

[3] Cooley on Torts, p. 285. See *post*, § 101, concerning licenses as police regulations.

§ 92

§ 93. **Regulation of Prices and charges.** — A most interesting question, somewhat like, and resting upon the same grounds as the one discussed in the preceding section, is the right of the government to regulate prices and charges for things and services. The exercise of this power was quite common in past ages ; and there appeared to be no well defined limitations upon the power, if any at all were recognized. But under a constitutional and popular government, there must necessarily be some limitation. It is a part of the natural and civil liberty to form business relations, free from the dictation of the State, that a like freedom should be secured and enjoyed in determining the conditions and terms of the contract which constitutes the basis of the business relation or transaction. It is, therefore, the general rule, that a man is free to ask for his wares or his services whatever price he is able to get and others are willing to pay ; and no one can compel him to take less, although the price may be so exorbitant as to become extortionate. No one has a natural right to the enjoyment of another's property or services upon the payment of a reasonable compensation ; for we have already recognized the right of one man to refuse to have dealings with another on any terms, whatever may be the motive for his refusal. But there are exceptions to the rule which can be justified on constitutional grounds. This general freedom from the State regulation of prices and charges can only be claimed as a natural right so far as the business is itself of a private character, and is not connected with, or rendered more valuable by, the enjoyment of some special privilege or franchise. Whenever the business is itself a privilege or franchise, not enjoyed by all alike, or the business is materially benefited by the gift by the State of some special privileges to be enjoyed in connection with it, the business ceases to be strictly private, and becomes a *quasi* public business, and to that extent may be subjected to police regulation. A special privilege or franchise is granted to individuals because of some supposed benefit to the public, and in order that the benefit may be assured to the public, the State may justly institute regulations to that end. The regulation of prices in such cases, will therefore, be legitimate and constitutional.[1]

But the regulation of prices will not be justified in any case where the law merely declares the prosecution of the business to be a privilege or franchise. If it be without legislation a natural right, no law can make it a privilege by requiring a license. The deprivation of the natural right to carry on the business must be justifiable by some public reason or necessity. Otherwise the general or partial prohibition is unconstitutional, and furnishes no justification for the regulation of prices and charges, incident to the business.[2]

But some of the courts are inclined to extend the exercise of this power of control to other cases, which do not come within the classes mentioned, viz.: those in which no special privilege or franchise is enjoyed, and in which there is no legal monopoly, but in which the circumstances conspire to create in favor of a few persons a virtual monopoly out of

---

[1] Chicago, etc., R. R. Co. v. Iowa, 94 U. S. 155; Peik v. Chicago, etc., R. R. Co., 94 U. S. 164; Slaughterhouse Cases, 16 Wall. 36; Waterworks v. Schotler, 110 U. S. 347. Judge Cooley classifies the cases as follows: —

"1. Where the business is one, the following of which is not a matter of right, but is permitted by the State as a matter of privilege or franchise. Under this head may be classed the business of setting up lotteries, of giving shows, and of keeping billiard-tables for hire; of selling intoxicating drinks, and of keeping a ferry or toll bridge.

"2. When the State on public grounds renders to the business special assistance by taxation, or under the eminent domain, as is done in the case of railroads.

"3. When, for the accommodation of the business special privileges are given in the public streets, or exceptional use allowed of public property or public easements, as in the case of hackmen, draymen, etc. Commonwealth v. Gage, 114 Mass. 328.

"4. When exclusive privileges are granted in consideration of some special return to the public and in order to secure something to the public not otherwise attainable." Cooley's Principles Constitution, p. 234.

[2] See post, § 102.

§ 93

a business of supreme necessity to the public. The leading case is that of Munn *v.* Illinois, already mentioned in the preceding section.[1] It has so important a bearing upon the question under discussion, that we will quote again Chief Justice Waite's statement of the rule laid down in that case. He says : " Looking, then, to the common law, from whence came the right which the constitution protects, we find that when private property is ' affected with a public interest, it ceases to be *juris privati* only.' This was said by Lord Chief Justice Hale, more than two hundred years ago, in his treatise *De Portibus Maris*,[2] and has been accepted without objection as an essential element in the law of property ever since. Property does become clothed with a public interest when used in a manner to make it of public consequence, and affect the community at large. When, therefore, one devotes his property to a use in which the public has an interest, he, in effect, grants to the public an interest in that use, and must submit to be controlled by the common good, to the extent of the interest he has thus created. He may withdraw his grant by discontinuing the use ; but, so long as he maintains the use, he must submit to the control." [3] Although the application of these principles to the case in question only constitutes a precedent for justifying the regulation of prices in those cases, where the business is a virtual monopoly and of great necessity to the public,[4] yet the language is broad enough to justify almost any case of regulation of prices. Under this rule,

[1] Munn *v.* People, 69 Ill. 80; *s. c.,* 94 U. S. 113.
[2] 1 Harg. Law Tracts, 78.
[3] Munn *v.* Illinois, 94 U. S. 125, 126.
[4] In the case in question, the use of the Chicago elevator was necessary to all dealers in grain in that city, and was controlled by nine firms, who annually established rates of charges for the regulation of the business. Says Chief Justice Waite: "Thus it is apparent that all the elevating facilities through which these vast productions ' of seven or eight great States of the West ' must pass on the way ' to four or five of the States on the seashore ' may be a virtual monopoly." p. 131.

§ 93

the attainment of the object of all individual activity, viz. :
to make oneself or one's services indispensable to the public, furnishes in every case the justification of State interference. Only the more or less unsuccessful will be
permitted to enjoy his liberty without governmental molest-
ation. We feel with Mr. Justice Field, who dissents
from the opinion of the court, that "if this be sound law, if
there be no protection, either in the principles upon which
our republican government is founded, or in the prohibitions of the constitution against such an invasion of private
rights, all property and all business in the State are held
at the mercy of a majority of its legislature." [1] For the
same reasons, we find the Supreme Court of Alabama justifying an act of the legislature which authorized the town
council of Mobile to license bakers, and regulate the weight
and price of bread. In declaring the act to be constitutional, the court said: " There is no motive, however, for this
interference on the part of the legislature with the lawful ac-

[1] "The public has no greater interest in the use of buildings for the
storage of grain than it has in the use of buildings for the residences of
families, nor, indeed anything like so great an interest; and, according
to the doctrine announced, the legislature may fix the rent of all tene-
ments used for residences, without reference to the cost of their erection.
If the owner does not like the rates prescribed, he may cease renting his
houses. He has granted to the public, says the court, an interest in the
use of the buildings, and 'he may withdraw his grant by discontinuing
the use; but, so long as he maintains the use, he must submit to the control.' The public is interested in the manufacture of cotton, woolen and
silken fabrics, in the construction of machinery, in the printing and publication of books and periodicals, and in the making of utensils of every
variety, useful and ornamental; indeed, there is hardly an enterprise or
business engaging the attention and labor of any considerable portion of
the community, in which the public has not an interest in the sense
in which that term is used by the court in its opinion; and the doctrine which allows the legislature to interfere with and regulate the
charges which the owners of property thus employed shall make for
its use, that is, the rates at which all these different kinds of business
shall be carried on, has never before been asserted, so far as I am aware,
by any judicial tribunal in the United States." Dissenting opinion of
Justice Field in Munn v. Illinois, 94 U. S. 136.

§ 93

tions of individuals or the mode in which private property shall be enjoyed, unless such calling affects public interests, or private property is employed in a manner which directly affects the body of the people."

" Upon this principle, in this State, tavern keepers are licensed and required to enter into bond, with surety, that they will provide suitable goods and lodgings for their guests, and stabling and provender for their horses. The county court is required, at least, once a year, to settle the rates of innkeepers, and upon the same principle is founded the control which the legislature has always exercised in the establishment and regulation of mills, fences, bridges, turnpike roads and other kindred subjects." [1]

Chief Justice Waite relies upon Lord Hale as an authority for his recognition of the rule as of common-law origin. But there is nothing in Lord Hale's writings to support the broad application which the Chief Justice makes of his language. In every case to which Lord Hale applies this doctrine, there is a grant of a special privilege or franchise, and the enjoyment of it is regulated by law so that the public may derive from it the benefit which constituted the consideration of the grant. Thus, in respect to ferries, he says, the king "has a right of franchise or privilege, that no man may set up a common ferry for all passengers, without a prescription time out of mind, or a charter from the king." And he proceeds to make the claim that " every ferry ought to be under a public regulation, viz. : that it give attendance at due times, keep a boat in due order, and take but reasonable toll." So, also, in respect to wharves and wharfingers, the same writer says : —

" A man, for his own private advantage may, in a port or town, set up a wharf or crane, and may take what rates he and his customers can agree for cranage, wharfage,

<hr>

[1] Mayor v. Yuille, 3 Ala. 137 (36 Am. Dec. 441). See Page v. Fazackerly, 36 Barb. 392; Guillotte v. New Orleans, 12 La. Ann. 432.

§ 93

housellage, pesage ; for he doth no more than is lawful for
any man to do, viz., make the most of his own.   *   *   *
If the king or subject have a public wharf, *unto which all
persons that come to that port must come* and unlade *or* lade
their goods, as for the purpose, because they are the only
wharves licensed by the king,   *   *   *   or because there is
no other wharf in that port, as it may fall out where a port
is newly erected ; in that case there cannot be taken arbitrary
and excessive duties for cranage, wharfage, pesage, etc.,
neither can they be enhanced to an immoderate rate ; but the
duties must be reasonable and moderate, though settled by
the king's license or charter.   For now the wharf and crane
and other conveniences are affected with a public interest,
and they cease to be *juris privati* only ; as if a man set out
a street in new building on his own land, it is now no longer
a bare private interest, but is affected by a public interest."[1]
At common law, the right of property in a wharf or pier
was a franchise.   Lord Hale, therefore, cannot be cited in
support of the doctrine that the State may regulate the
prices charged in a business which from the circumstances
becomes a virtual monopoly.   And even if he did justify
such regulations, his opinions can hardly be set up in opposition to the rational prohibition of the American constitution.   By all the known rules of constitutional construction
the conclusion must be reached that the regulation of prices
in such a case is unconstitutional ; and while the common
law is still authority for the propriety and justification of
laws, which antedate the American constitutions, it cannot
be cited to defeat the plain meaning of the constitution in
respect to laws subsequently enacted.

§ 94. **Usury and interest laws.** — It has long been the
custom in England and in this country to regulate the rate
of interest.

[1] De Portibus Maris, 1 Harg. Law Tracts, 78.

The regulation of interest may be of two kinds. So far as the legislature undertakes to determine what rate of interest can be recovered on contracts for the payment of money, in the absence of the express stipulation of the parties, it is a reasonable police regulation, the object of which is to aid the parties in effecting settlements, when they have not previously agreed upon any rate of interest. If the parties are not satisfied with the statutory rate, they can agree upon any other rate. But it is different when the legislature undertakes to prescribe what rate of interest the parties to a contract may agree upon. The rate of interest, like the price of merchandise, is determined ordinarily by the relation of supply and demand. Free trade in money is as much a right as free trade in merchandise. If the owner of the property in general has a natural right to ask whatever price he can get for his goods, the owner of money may exact whatever rate of interest the borrower may be willing to give. For interest is nothing more than the price asked for the use of money. No public reason can be urged for imposing this restriction upon the money lender, and the utter futility of such laws, in attempting to control the rate of interest, is, or should be, a convincing proof of their unreasonableness. It has been suggested that originally these laws were based upon the fact that the lending of money was a special privilege. "The practice of regulating by legislation the interest receivable for the use of money, when considered with reference to its origin, is only the assertion of a right of the government to control the extent to which a privilege granted by it may be exercised and enjoyed. By the ancient common law it was unlawful to take any money for the use of money; all who did so were called usurers, a term of great reproach, and were exposed to the censure of the church, and if, after the death of a person, it was discovered that he had been a usurer while living, his chattels were forfeited to the king, and his land escheated to the

§ 94

lord of the fee. No action could be maintained on any promise to pay for the use of money, because of the unlawfulness of the contract. Whilst the common law thus condemned all usury, Parliament interfered, and made it lawful to take a limited amount of interest. It was not upon the theory that the legislature could arbitrarily fix the compensation which one could receive for the use of property, which, by the general law, was the subject of hire for compensation, that Parliament acted, but in order to confer a privilege which the common law denied. The reasons which led to this legislation originally have long since ceased to exist; and if the legislation is still persisted in, it is because a long acquiescence in the exercise of a power, especially when it was rightfully assumed in the first instance, is generally received as sufficient evidence of its continued lawfulness." [1]

But, of course, this reason furnishes no justification for the present existence of such laws. In the light of modern public opinion, the lending of money on interest is in no sense a privilege, and no law can make it so. The biblical injunction against the taking of interest, and the fact that the original money lenders of Europe were Jews; in other words, respect for the teachings of the Bible on the subject, and hate for the despised Jew, probably combined to bring the usury laws into being. In the Middle Ages, the Jew had no rights at all. Every recognition of his natural rights was a privilege. Suffice it to say, that on no satisfactory grounds can usury laws be justified. But their enactment has so long been recognized as a constitutional exercise of legislative authority, and the fact that they become dead letters as soon as enacted, render it very unlikely that the courts will pronounce them unconstitutional, however questionable legal writers and authorities may consider them. Mr. Cooley says that the usury laws are " difficult to defend

---

[1] Field, J., in Munn v. Illinois, 94 U. S. 136; 10 Bac. Abr. 264.

§ 94

on principle; but the power to regulate the rate of interest has been employed from the earliest days, and has been too long acquiesced in to be questioned now."[1] I differ with the learned judge in his opinion that long acquiescence in such laws precludes an inquiry into their constitutionality; but will readily accede that the easy evasion of them makes it unimportant whether they are questioned or not, except that it may be considered as highly injurious to enact any law which is not or cannot be enforced, in that the successful defiance or evasion of a particular law tends to lessen one's reverence for law in general.

§ 95. **Prevention of Speculation.** — Free trade is an undoubted constitutional right. Every man has the constitutional right, not only to determine with whom he will have business dealings, and to whom he shall offer his goods or his services, but he also has the right, in most cases, whether he shall offer them to any one at all. He may refuse, without giving any reasons, to sell his goods or to tender his services. He cannot ordinarily be compelled to do either. The only exceptions that suggest themselves, are cases in which the right of eminent domain is exercised,[2] and those in which the State in the emergency of war makes forced sales of the property of private individuals for war purposes,[3] and all cases of compulsory performance of duties to the State. In all other cases a man cannot lawfully be compelled to part with his property, or to render services against his will. Circumstances may conduce to make a particular business a virtual monopoly in the hands of one man or one partnership. But I apprehend that he cannot for that reason be subjected to police regulation. Because one man has the capital wherewith to buy up all the corn or wheat in our great Western markets, and to cause in con-

---

[1] Cooley's Principles of Const. Law, p. 235.
[2] See *post*, § 121.
[3] See *post*, § 137.

sequence a rise in the values of these commodities, does not justify State interference with his liberty of action, any more than would the police regulation of the whole capitalist class be permissible. And yet this one man occupies an economical position, differing only in degree from the capitalists as a class. The same qualities and characteristics which enabled him to become a capitalist, will urge him to make the most of the wealth he has accumulated or inherited, and he will so manipulate it as to increase its returns if possible. Each successful increase in the returns from capital, increase the price of the commodity, in the manufacturing or preparation or handling of which the capital has been invested. It is only in extraordinarily abnormal cases that any one man can acquire this power over his fellow-men, unless he is the recipient of a privilege from the government, or is guilty of dishonest practices. The remedy for the first case, in a constitutional government is to withhold dangerous privileges, or if the grant of them is conducive to the public welfare, to subject their enjoyment to police regulation, so that the public may derive the benefit expected and receive no injury. In the second class of cases, a rigid prosecution of dishonest practices will be an efficient remedy.

The common law did not recognize this view of a right to be free from police regulation, in the matter of trade. While the general right to buy and sell without let or hindrance was recognized, certain sales were held to be illegal, and punished as misdemeanors, which are exceedingly common at the present day, and, if not legal, are acknowledged by the commercial world as legitimate transactions. These were sales, known at common law by the names, *forestalling*, *regrating*, and *engrossing*. Says Blackstone: "The offense of *forestalling* the market is an offense against public trade. This, which (as well as the two following) is also an offense at common law, was described by statute 5 and 6 Edw. 6, ch. 14, to be the buying or contracting for any merchandise or victual coming in the way to market; or

§ 95

dissuading persons from bringing their goods or provisions there; any of which practices make the market dearer to the fair trade. *Regrating* was described by the same statute to be the buying of corn or other dead victual, in any market, and selling it again in the same market, or within four miles of the place. For this also enhances the price of provisions, as every successive seller must have a successive profit. *Engrossing* was also described to be the getting into one's possession, or buying up, large quantities of corn or other dead victuals, with intent to sell them again. This must, of course, be injurious to the public, by putting it in the power of one or two rich men to raise the price of provisions at their own discretion. And so the total engrossing of any other commodity with an intent to sell it at an unreasonable price is an offense indictable and finable at the common law." [1] In Russell on Crimes,[2] these offenses are stated as follows: " Every practice or device by art, conspiracy, words, or news, to enhance the price of victuals or other merchandise, has been held to be unlawful; as being prejudicial to trade and commerce, and injurious to the public in general. Practices of this kind come under the notion of forestalling, which anciently comprehended, in its significance, regrating and engrossing and all other offenses of the like nature. Spreading false rumors, buying things in the market before the accustomed hour, or buying and selling again the same thing in the same market, are offenses of this kind. Also if a person within the realm buy merchandise in gross, and sell the same in gross, it has been considered to be an offense of this nature, on the ground that the price must be thereby enhanced, as each person through whose hands it passed would endeavor to make his profit of it." As stated by Blackstone, these acts are no longer recognized by the American criminal law as

[1] 4 Bl. Com. 154.
[2] 1 Russ. Crimes (Grea. Ed.), 168.

§ 95

offenses against the public, or as being in any way illegal. The purchase of merchandise, or any other commodity, that may be the subject of sale, expecting a rise in the price, in other words, speculation, is legal, whether the buyer intends to sell again, in gross, or in retail. A man has a constitutional right to buy anything in any quantity, providing he use only fair means, and set his own price on it, or refuse to sell at all. Where one man, acting independently, does this, he can be only considered guilty of a wrong to the public, when he secures the possession of these things by the practice of fraud, or endeavors by false reports to enhance the price of a commodity which he offers for sale. These are distinct acts of fraud or deception, and it is proper for the law to declare them illegal. Further the law cannot go. Mr Bishop, in discussing these common-law offenses, denies that *regrating*, as distinguishable from *forestalling* and *engrossing*, can be considered a criminal offense in this country,[1] but he recognizes the other two offenses, in a modified form. In respect to forestalling, he says: "In reason, the essence of the common law, on the subject of forestalling, considered distinct from engrossing and regrating, seems to be, that, whenever a man, *by false news, or by any kind of deception*, gets into his hands a considerable amount of any one article of merchandise, and holds it for an undue profit, thereby creating a perturbation in what pertains to the public interests, he is guilty of the offense of forestalling." [2] As stated by Mr. Bishop, the common law in making a criminal offense of forestalling is no more open to constitutional objection than the punishment or prohibition of any other act of fraud or deception. But Mr. Bishop's position, in regard to *engrossing*, is not as free from criticism. He says: "Whenever a man, for the purpose of putting things, as it were, out of joint, and obtaining an un-

[1] 1 Bishop Crim. Law, § 970.
[2] 1 Bishop Crim. Law, § 968.

§ 95

due profit, purchases large quantities of an article of merchandise, to hold it, not for a fair rise, but to compel buyers to pay a price greatly above, as he knows, what can be regularly sustained in the market, he may, on principle, be deemed, with us, to be guilty of the common-law offense of engrossing." [1] It is, without doubt, an immoral act, to ask an unconscionably high price for a commodity, taking advantage of the pressing wants of the people; and it may, under a high code of morals, be held to be an extortion, for one to purchase and hold merchandise for the purpose of gaining from its sale more than a fair profit; but it cannot be claimed that there is a trespass upon the rights of others in doing so, or that the rights of others are thereby threatened with injury. One is simply exercising his ordinary rights in demanding whatever price he pleases for his property. But apart from this objection, the great difficulty, if not impossibility, in ascertaining what is an extortionate price, and the practical inability, to enforce it, would predetermine such a law to become a dead letter.

§ 96. **Prevention of combinations in restraint of trade.** — While the manipulation of capital by single individuals cannot threaten the public welfare by the general oppression of the masses ; when two or more people combine their energies and their capital, the acquisition of this extraordinary power becomes easier and more common. In fact, it may be stated that, practically, combination is absolutely necessary in all cases to its acquisition. But combinations are beneficial, as well as injurious, according to the motives and aims with which they were formed. It is, therefore, impossible to prohibit all combinations. The prohibition must rest upon the objectionable character of the object of the combination. One of these objectionable objects is the restraint of trade. At common law, and it is

[1] Bishop Crim. Law, § 969.

§ 96

still the law in most, if not all, of the States, [in some there are statutory regulations on the subject], all combinations in restraint of trade were unlawful, and no contracts, founded upon the combination, would be enforced by the courts.[1]

The cases are numerous and apply to almost all kinds of combinations, the object of which is the extortion of the public. As expressed by one judge, " a combination is criminal, whenever the act to be done has a necessary tendency to prejudice the public; or to oppress individuals, by unjustly subjecting them to the power of the confederates, and giving effect to the purpose of the latter, whether of extortion or of mischief.[2] Even where this effect is more or less remote, the combination will be void. Thus the English court has refused to enforce an agreement, entered into by several employers in the same line of business, to suspend or carry on the business, in obedience to the direction of the majority.[3] So also, are all combinations among employees void, whose object is the restraint or control of a particular trade. The obligations of the individual member to obey the orders of the league or combination, to refuse to offer his services to one, against whom the combination is directed, cannot be enforced in the courts.[4]

Labor organizations are very common in this country, and a consideration of their rights and powers inside of the law is therefore necessary. It can hardly be denied that so far as these organizations have charitable objects in view, the care of their sick and indigent members, the dissemination of useful literature among them and their enlightenment on

---

[1] 1 Hawk Pleas C., ch. 80, § 1; 1 Bl. Com. 150; Rex v. Waddington, 1 East, 43; 1 Smith's Lead. Cas. 367, 381; Lang v. Weeks, 2 Ohio (N. S.) 519; Thomas v. Tiles, 3 Ohio, 74; Barry v. Croskey, 2 Johns. & H. 1; Jones v. Lees, 1 H. & N. 189, Gulich v. Ward, 5 Halst. 87; Benjamin on Sales, 799.

[2] Com. v. Carlisle, Brightley, 40.

[3] Hilton v. Eckersley, 6 El. & Bl, 47, 66.

[4] Hornby v. Close, L. R. 2 Q. B. 183.

§ 96

matters connected with their trade, they are lawful. For such purposes the formation of associations can never be prohibited in any free State. Their prohibition would be a violation of constitutional liberty. But so far as these combinations have for their object the control of trade, and of the price of labor, they constitute combinations in restraint of trade, and all contracts founded upon them are void. A successful combination of labor will raise the price of labor and hence the cost of the commodity above its normal value in the same manner as the combination of capitalists will increase the cost of the commodity by increasing the return to capital. Free trade is only possible by a prohibition of both classes of combinations which, if successful, are equally dangerous to the public safety and comfort.

But at common law the combinations of employees for their mutual protection against the demands of their employers are not punishable criminally, nor actionable civilly, unless they commit some distinct offense against the public or against an individual. While an agreement among workmen to labor for not less than a given sum, or to refuse to work for a particular employer, or to work with employees, who do not belong to the union or organization, and the like, will not be enforced by the courts against one who refuses to fulfill his obligations, since it is against public policy; there is no common-law wrong done to the public or to the individuals who may be affected by the combination, as long as they do not by threats or acts of trespass against the rights of persons and property, attempt an interference with the freedom of others to employ and be employed by whom they please. Says Chapman, Ch. J. : "Every man has a right to determine what branch of business he will pursue, and to make his own contracts with whom he pleases, and on the best terms he can. He may change from one occupation to another, and pursue as many different occupations as he pleases, and competition in business is lawful. He may refuse to deal with any man

§ 96

or class of men; and it is no crime for any number of persons, without an unlawful object in view, to associate themselves together and agree that they will not work for or deal with certain men or classes of men, or work under a certain price or without certain conditions. * * * Freedom is the policy of this country."[1]   Mr. Bishop states that in England and in this country, combinations among workmen to raise the price of wages are indictable at common law.[2]   In England, statutes have been passed making such combinations a criminal offense, but it is not a crime, independently of statute, for workmen to combine to enhance the price of labor.[3]   But there can be no question concerning the power of the State to make such combinations criminal misdemeanors, if the public safety should require it.   The power to declare an act unlawful being admitted, the choice of remedies for its prevention is wholly within the discretion of the legislative power.[4]

§ 96a.   A combination to " corner " the market. — One of the commonest cases of combinations in restraint of trade, is where two or more dealers in a staple commodity undertake to " corner the market."   Dos Passos defines " a corner " in the following language: " A scheme or combination of one or more ' bulls ' who are ' long ' of certain stocks or securities, to compel the ' bears,' or persons ' short ' of the stock to pay a certain price for the same. Or it may be a combination to force a fictitious and unnatural rise in the market, for the purpose of obtaining the

---

1 Carew v. Rutherford, 106 Mass. 1, 13, citing Conn. v. Hunt, 4 Met. 111; Boston Glass Manufactory v. Binney, 4 Pick. 425; Bowen v. Matheson, 14 Allen, 499.

2 2 Bishop Crim. Law, §§ 224, 225, citing Rex v. Mawbey, 6 T. R. 619; Com. v. Hunt, 4 Met. 11; People v. Fisher, 14 Wend. 9.

3 Com. v. Hunt, 4 Met. 111.   See post, § 97 on Boycotting.

4 See People v. Fisher, 14 Wend. 9, in which it is held that the New York statute, concerning conspiracy, makes it a misdemeanor for workmen to combine to raise their wages.

§ 96a

advantage of dealers, purchasers, and all persons whose necessities or contracts compel them to use or obtain the thing ' cornered.' " [1] In New York, Illinois, Georgia, and Nebraska, there are statutes prohibiting " cornering," and providing remedies for the breach of the statute, but it is safe to assert that the act is unlawful at common law, and independent of statute. A combination to raise funds, or create fictitious prices by the spread of false rumors, is clearly criminal conspiracy, for it injures every one who would have to make purchases of the commodity and were compelled to pay a higher price in consequence of the false rumors.[2] So, also, will a combination be void, which is formed for the purpose of enhancing the price of a commodity by the making of fictitious sales. There is as much fraud in these cases as where the combination attained their ends by setting false rumors in motion. In both cases there is a fraud against the public.[3] These cases are plain, because in both classes of cases there is a distinct act of deception or fraud. But the illegality of combinations is pushed to the extreme limit, when it is held that a combination to enhance the price of a commodity is always unlawful, even where there is no deception or fraud, and when the combination do nothing more than hold the goods which they control for higher prices. But that is the common-law rule. Such combinations are quite common in later days, and public opinion is very tolerant of them, rarely, if ever, condemning the practice as immoral, but there can be no question concerning their illegality. In Raymond v. Leavitt,[4] plaintiff loaned defendant $10,000 for purpose of

[1] Dos Passos on Stock Brokers, p. 454.

[2] Rex v. De Berenger, 3 M. & S. 67. See, also, Hitchcock v. Coker, 6 Ad. & El. 438; Hinde v. Gray, 1 M. & G. 195; Horne v. Ashford, 3 Bing. 322; Com. v. Hunt, 4 Met. 111.

[3] Marsh v. Russell, 2 Lans. 75; Stanton v. Allen, 5 Denio, 434; 2 Kent Com. 699; Bissbane v. Adams, 3 Comst. 129; Hooker v. Vandewater, 4 Denio, 349. See Craft v. McConoughy, 79 Ill. 346.

[4] 46 Mich. 447.

§ 96a

controlling wheat market at Detroit for parties called the May *deal.* The scheme was " to force a fictitious rise in values." The court held that the money advanced for the purpose of making a " corner " in wheat, could not be recovered by any legal measures and this, too, independently of statute. " There is no doubt that modern ideas of trade have practically abrogated some common-law doctrines which are supposed to unduly hamper commerce." * * * " But we do not feel called upon to regard so much of the common law to be obsolete as treats these combinations as unlawful, whether they should now be held punishable as crimes or not. The statute of New York, which is universally conceded to be a limitation of the common-law offenses is referred to in Arnot *v.* Coal Co.,[1] as rendering such conspiracies unlawful, and this had been previously held in People *v.* Fisher,[2] where the subject is discussed at length. There may be some difficulty in determining such conduct to be in violation of public policy, where it has not before been covered by statutes as precedents. But in the case before us the conduct of the parties comes within the undisputed censure of the laws of the land, and we cannot sustain the transaction, *without doing so on the ground that such dealings are so manifestly sanctioned by usage and public approval, that it would be absurd to suppose the legislature, if attention were called to them, would not legalize them.* We do not think public opinion has become so thoroughly demoralized ; and until the law is changed, we shall decline enforcing such contracts. If parties see fit to invest money in such ventures, they must get it back by other than legal measures." [3]

---

[1] 60 N. Y. 558.

[2] 14 Wend. 9.

[3] See Sampson *v.* Shaw, 101. Mass. 145; Crawford *v.* Wick, 18 Ohio, 190; Morris Run Coal Co. *v.* Barclay Coal Co., 68 Pa. 173; Central Ohio Salt Co. *v.* Guthrie, 35 Ohio, 666. "Whenever a particular staple is essential to the health and comfort of a community, a combination to absorb it, for the purpose of extortion, is invalid." 1 Hawk. P C., ch. 80, § 1; 1 Bl. Com. 150; Rex *v.* Waddington, 1 East, 43; Indian Bagging

§ 96*a*

Of the same character would be an agreement between
all the transportation companies of a particular territory,
which was made for the purpose of preventing competition,
and controlling the rates of charges for transportation.
Such agreements are void.[1] The only ground upon which
the prohibition of combinations in such cases may be justified is that such combinations tend to give to the members of them an undue and dangerous power over the needs
and necessities of the people ; and for that reason it is a
legitimate exercise of police power to prohibit such combinations.   Such a law does not interfere with the equal freedom of all to do what they will with their own.   Every
one is left free to do or act as he pleases, but he is not allowed to deny to others an equal freedom, not even with
their consent.   Public policy, the public safety, requires the
prohibition.

Since the common law made it an indictable offense for
one man to " corner " the market, there can be no question
that the combination of two or more to buy up any article
of merchandise, and force the payment of exorbitant
prices, is a criminal conspiracy, and may be punishable
without further legislation, if public opinion did not look
so leniently upon such transactions.[2]

Co. v. Cock & Co., 14 La Ann. 164; 1 Smith's Lead. Cas. 307, 381; Lang
v. Weeks, 2 Ohio (N. s.), 519; Thomas v. Tiles, 3 Ohio, 74; Barry v.
Croskey, 2 Johns. & H. 1.

[1] Maguire v. Smock, 42 Ind. 1; Staunton v. Allen, 5 Denio, 434; Hooker
v. Vandewater, 4 Denio, 349; Oregon St. Nav. Co. v. Winsor, 20 Wall. 64.

[2] " By the law of New York, no conspiracies are punishable criminally,
except those there stated, and among others the conspiracy of two or
more persons ' to commit any act injurious to the public health, to public
morals, or trade or commerce, or for the perversion or obstruction of justice, or due administration of the laws ' shall constitute a misdemeanor.
Under this broad and comprehensive language, which is practically the rule
in all the States, either by adoption of the common law or express statute,
it will not be difficult to punish infamous conspiracies or combinations,
whether their object be to affect the necessaries of life, or securities,
or other property in which the public have an interest." Dos Passos on
Stock Brokers 462, 463; Peck v. Gurney, L. R. 6 H. L. C. 377; Pasley

§ 96a

§ 97. **Boycotting.** — In the last few years, and particularly in the current year, the industrial world has been greatly agitated by the employment by trade unions in their contest with the employers of a system of warfare, known as boycotting. The origin of the term is involved in some uncertainty, but the name is believed to have arisen during the Irish land troubles a few years ago, in consequence of the manifesto of the Irish land league, that the payment of rents will be refused, if they were not reduced to what was claimed by the league to be a reasonable amount. During the disturbances which followed this attempt to carry the manifesto into effect, the peasants came into conflict with a landlord named Boycott. He had been known to be specially severe in making terms with his tenants, and when he refused to accede to the demands of the league and evicted his tenants for refusing to pay rent, almost the entire population of that community combined to force him to terms. The bakers, butchers and other tradesmen refused to have dealings with him. He could buy nothing wherewith to feed his family. All his domestic servants left him, and he could get none to take their place. He and his family were left alone in the midst of a populous community. Existence under such circumstances became unbearable, and he was forced to yield. The success of the combination was hailed with delight by the Irish peasantry and their sympathizers, and the method or plan adopted to attain the end desired became known as " the boycott." The boycott, unaffected by complications arising from distinct trespasses upon the rights of others, may be defined as being a combination to force one to terms by

v. Freeman, 3 J. R. 51; Bevan v. Adams, 19 W. R. 76; Beatty v. Evans, L. R. 7 H. L. C. 102; Pontifex v. Bignold's, 3 Scott, N. R. 390; Moore v. Burke, 4 F. & F. 258; Cross v. Lockett, 6 Abb. Pr. 247; Wakeman v. Dalley, 44 Barb. 498; Cazeaux v. Mali, 25 Barb. 578; Mouse v. Switz, 19 How. 275; In re Chandler, 13 Am. Law Reg. (N. S.) 260; s. c. Biss. C. C. 53; *sub. nom.* Ex parte Young.

§ 97

abstaining from having business and social relations with him. And in order to make the combination more effective in its operations against one person, the members of the union usually threaten to "boycott" all others who may dare to have relations of any kind with the objectionable person. So far as the managers of a boycott are able to keep themselves and their followers from interfering with the rights of person or of property of those who are boycotted, their action is not illegal at common law, and is not illegal in any American State in which the common law has not been changed by statute. For while all contracts or agreements to obey the orders of a trade union in its contests with employers are void, and cannot be enforced in a court of law, the combinations of labor do not constitute a civil or criminal wrong, as long as the members of the combination do not employ force, or otherwise interfere with the legal rights of their opponents.[1] As has already been stated,[2] it is the constitutional right of every American citizen to refuse to have business and social relations with any one who may displease him, and his motives for abstaining from associating with the objectionable person can not be inquired into. So also is it no criminal or civil wrong at common law to conspire or combine to do an act which is lawful for the single individual to do.[3] As long, therefore, as boycotters simply refrain from having dealings with the objectionable person, and induce others to do the same by applying the boycott to them, they commit no crime and are liable for no civil wrong. But the boycott, pure and simple, is very rarely efficacious in bringing the employer or capitalist to terms; and the boycotters, after trying for a while to keep within the law respecting the rights of their powerful opponent, soon are forced either to surrender to the enemy, or to do

[1] See *ante*, § 96.
[2] See *ante*, §§ 95, 96.
[3] See *ante*, § 96.

§ 97

violence to his personal and property rights. It happened thus in the great railroad strikes of the present year and in all other prominent cases of boycott. A legitimate engine of industrial warfare was turned into an illegal trespass upon private right. And so it will always be in the absence of police regulation. The sharp competition of modern trade; the rapid increase in the productivity of labor-saving machines; in fact, all the characteristics of modern industry tend to sharpen the struggle for existence on the part of the weaker; and the latter has presented to him the alternative of barely eking out an existence on a mere pittance, or wresting by unlawful means a more comfortable living from those, who by a superior physical or intellectual strength, or by chicanery, have been able to gather together an undue share of the world's wealth, and public disorder and general insecurity ensues. So far as we are able to fathom the mysteries of social life, the whole social fabric is in danger when the personal and property rights of the individual are not afforded ample protection against unlawful attacks. Public disorder, which is the ordinary accompaniment of the boycott, is also highly injurious to the commonwealth. In accordance, therefore, with the maxim *salus populi suprema lex*, the boycott may be properly prohibited by law. But, in the absence of a statute, boycotts, when not accompanied by overt attacks upon personal or property rights, like all other strikes on the part of labor organizations, are legal and cannot be suppressed by law.

In consequence of the punishment of boycotters in New York and in the United States courts, it has become the popular impression that the boycott is, according to the common law, a criminal offense. But this is a mistake. On the statute books of New York, and of the United States, there are statutes defining the crime of conspiracy, the

§ 97

language of which is sufficiently broad to cover boycotting, and to make it a criminal offense.[1]

§ 98. **Contracts against liability for negligence prohibited.** — The liability for negligence is imposed by the law, and does not arise out of the contract of the parties. The duty, in the performance of which the negligence occurred, may arise out of, and rest upon, contract; but the exercise of care in the performance of a duty, whether the duty is legal or contractual, is an obligation often of general application. Ordinarily, the performance of a legal duty, or the liability for an improper performance, may be waived by agreement of the persons who may be affected by it. The law does not ordinarily compel persons to avail themselves of the protection it affords them. But where the duty is of so general a nature, as that the proper performance of it, even where the private individual is most affected by it, becomes a matter of public policy, the right may very properly be denied to the private individual to relieve by contract from the liability for improper performance. A private person, probably, cannot be forced to sue on the tort, but the law may declare void any contract, by which he relieves the person, on whom the duty rests, from liability. This is the rule at common law in respect to liability for negligence. No man can by contract relieve himself from liability for negligence in the performance of any duty

---

[1] See *ante*, § 96. In 2 Rev. Stat. N. Y. 691, § 8, it is declared to be a punishable conspiracy to combine "to commit any act injurious to the public health, to public morals, or to trade or commerce, or for the perversion or obstruction of justice, or the due administration of the laws." So, also, is it declared by the United States Revised Statutes (§ 5407, p. 1052) to be a criminal conspiracy, "if two or more persons in any State or Territory conspire for the purpose of impeding, hindering, obstructing, or defeating, in any manner, the due course of justice in any State or Territory, with intent to deny to any citizen the equal protection of the laws, or to injure him or his property for lawfully enforcing or attempting to enforce, the right of any person, or class of persons, to the equal protection of the laws." See also, §§ 1977 1991, 2004–2010, 5506–5510.

§ 98

to the public generally, or to a particular individual, whether the duty arises out of a contract or is imposed by the law, but particularly so where the law imposes the duty. This restriction upon the contracts of individuals has particular application to contracts with common carriers and telegraph companies. In respect to the common carrier, the common law imposed the obligation to guarantee the safe delivery of the goods intrusted to his care for transportation, and he is liable for the failure to deliver them at the place of destination in every case, except where they are proven to have been destroyed by the intervention of some unavoidable natural agency, or by the act of the public enemy. The exercise of the highest degree of care constitutes no defense. Public policy requires the imposition of this extraordinary obligation.[1] But the imposition of this extraordinary obligation is not deemed to be so far required by public policy,

[1] Coggs v. Bernard, 2 Ld. Raym. 909; Railroad v. Reeves, 10 Wall. 176; Bulkley v. Naumkeag, etc., Co., 24 How. 386; Fillebrown v. Grand Trunk, etc., Co., 55 Me. 462; Caldwell v. N. J. Steamboat Co., 47 N. Y. 282; Orange Co. Bk. v. Brown, 9 Wend. 85; Hayes v. Kennedy, 41 Pa. St. 378; Morrison v. Davis, 20 Pa. St. 171; Boyle v. McLaughlin, 4 H. & J. 291; New Brunswick, etc., Co. v. Tiers, 24 N. J. 697; Friend v. Woods, 6 Gratt. 139; Swindler v. Hilliard, 2 Rich. 286; Turney v. Wilson, 7 Yerg. 540; Powell v. Mills, 30 Miss. 231; Chicago, etc., R. R. Co. v. Sawyer, 69 Ill. 285; Merchants' Dispatch Co. v. Smith, 76 Ill. 542; McMillan v. Michigan, etc., R. R. Co., 16 Mich. 79; Bohannan v. Hammond, 42 Cal. 227. The exceptions to this general liability as an insurer are usually stated to be "the act of God, or of the public enemy." The "act of God" means any natural cause, which could not be avoided by human foresight. "What is precisely meant by the expression 'act of God' as used in the case of common carriers, has undergone discussion, but it is agreed that the notion of exception is those losses and injuries occasioned exclusively by natural causes, such as could not be prevented by human care, skill, and foresight. All the cases agree in requiring the entire exclusion of human agency from the cause of the injury or loss. If the loss or injury happen in any way through the agency of man, it can not be considered the act of God; nor even if the act or negligence of man contributes to bring or leave the goods of the carrier under the operation of natural causes that work to their injury, is he excused. In short, to excuse the carrier, the act of God, or vis divina, must be the sole and immediate cause of the injury. If there be any co-operation of man, or any admixture of human means,

§ 98

as that parties may not be permitted by contract to release the carrier from it. Common carriers may limit their common-law liability to acts of negligence by contract with the consignor. But the contract must be freely and voluntarily made. The carrier cannot refuse to take goods for carriage under the common-law liability, if the consignor should refuse his assent to a limitation.[1] But public policy would not permit the enforcement of a contract, which not only released the carrier of his common-law liability as an insurer, but likewise from the consequences of his negligence. It is the almost invariable rule of law in the United States, that common carriers are forbidden to relieve themselves by contract from liability for injuries caused by the negligence of the carrier or his servants. This is the rule of law, whether the carrier be a natural person or a corporation.[2] In New York and New Jersey, it has been held not

---

the injury is not, in a legal sense, the act of God." Wright, J., in Michaels v. N. J. Cent. R. R. Co., 30 N. Y. 571.

[1] New Jersey Steam Nav. Co. v. Merchant's Bank, 6 How. 344; Railroad Co. v. Manufacturing Co., 16 Wall. 318; Fillebrowne v. Grand Trunk R. Co., 55 Me 462; Brown v. Eastern R. Co., 11 Cush. 97; Buckland v. Adams Express Co., 97 Mass. 124; Hollister v. Nowlen, 19 Wend. 234; Bennett v. Dutton, 10 N. H. 481; McCoy v. Erie, etc., R. R. Co., 42 Md. 498; Smith v. N. C. R. R., 64 N. C. 235; Southern Express Co. v. Caperton, 44 Ala. 101; Jones v. Voorhees, 10 Ohio, 145; McMillan v. Michigan, etc., R. R., 16 Mich. 79.

[2] New Jersey, etc., Co. v. Merchants' Bk., 6 How. 344; York Co. v. Central R. R. Co., 3 Wall. 107; Sager v. Portsmouth, etc., R. R. Co., 31 Me. 228; School Dist. v. Boston, etc., R. R. Co., 102 Mass. 552; Camden, etc., R. R. v. Baldauf, 16 Pa. St. 67; Bickham v. Smith, 62 Pa. St. 45; Delaware, etc., R. R. v. Starrs, 69 Pa. St. 36; Welch v. Boston, etc., R. R., 41 Conn. 333; Virginia, etc., R. R. v. Sayers, 26 Gratt. 328; Smith v. N. C. R. R., 64 N. C. 235; Swindler v. Hilliard, 2 Rich. 286; Berry v. Cooper, 28 Ga. 543; Indianapolis, etc., R. R. v. Allen, 31 Ind. 394; Southern Express v. Moon, 39 Miss. 822; Gaines v. Union Transp. Co., 28 Ohio St. 418; Great West. R. R. v. Hawkins, 17 Mich. 57; s. c. 18 Mich. 427; Adams Exp. Co. v. Stettaners, 61 Ill. 174; Sturgeon v. St. Louis, etc., R. R., 65 Mo. 569; South, etc., R. R. v. Henlein, 52 Ala. 606; Mo. Val. R. R. v. Caldwell, 8 Kan. 244; N. O. Ins. Co. v. N. O., etc., R. R., 20 La. Ann. 302; Hooper v. Wells, 27 Cal. 11.

§ 98

to be against public policy for common carriers to make
contracts, whereby to release themselves from liability
for the negligence of their servants, although it is forbidden them to divest themselves of responsibility for
their own negligence; and in the case of railroad corporations this principle has been carried so far as to enable a
release from liability for the negligence of every agent of
the corporation, except the board of directors.[1] The prohi-
tion of contracts in release of liability for negligence is the
same, whether it refers to the carriage of goods or of passengers.   In the latter cases, such contracts· are against
public policy, and, therefore, void, even where the passenger is traveling on a free pass, whether the pass is
given in conjunction with the transportation of freight for
hire, as in the case of " drover's passes," [2] but also where
it is given as a matter of courtesy.[3] The cases generally
maintain that the common carrier is held to the same degree
of care, whether the carriage is gratuitous or for a consideration, but it would seem but natural to require of the
common carrier, in cases of free passes, only that degree
of care, which is required of all bailees, where the bailment
is exclusively for the benefit of the bailor, viz. : slight care,
and it has been so held in Illinois.[4]

The same restriction against contractual releases from

---

[1] Wells *v.* N. Y. Cent. R. R., 24 N. Y. 181; Perkins *v.* N. Y. Cent. R. R.,
24 N. Y. 197; Smith *v.* N. Y. Cent. R. R., 24 N. Y. 222; Bissell v. N. Y.
Cent. R. R., 25 N. Y. 442; Poucher *v.* N. Y. Cent. R. R., 49 N. Y. 263;
Kinney *v.* Cent. R. R., 32 N. J. 407; *s. c.* 34 N. J. 513.

[2] Railroad Co. *v.* Lockwood, 17 Wall. 357; Cleveland, etc., R. R. *v.*
Curran, 19 Ohio St. 1; Ohio, etc., R. R. *v.* Selby, 47 Ind. 471.

[3] Philadelphia, etc., R. R. *v.* Derby, 14 How. 468; Pa. R. R. Co. *v.*
Butler, 57 Pa. St. 335; Ind. Cent. R. R. *v.* Mundy, 21 Ind. 48; Jacobus *v.*
St. Paul. etc., R. R., 20 Minn. 125.

[4] " While we hold this argument did not exempt the railroad company
from the gross negligence of its employees, we are free to say that it does
exempt it from all other species or degrees of negligence not denominated gross, or which might have the character of recklessness." Ill.
Cent. R. R. *v.* Read, 37 Ill. 484.

§ 98

liability for negligence has been applied to telegraph companies, but with a notable exception. The general rule, that one can not by contract relieve himself from responsibility for negligence, applies. But in consequence of the great liability to the commission of errors in the transmission of messages ; arising from the limited control over the electrical current, and the great exposure to accidents to the wires, and to the electrical apparatus at both ends ; it has very generally been held to be a reasonable and permissible stipulation, that the telegraph company will not be responsible for errors in transmission of messages, whether they arise from the intervention of natural causes or the negligence of the operators, unless the message is repeated. Such a contract would be equivalent to an agreement to send the message for a less sum, upon condition of being relieved from liability for errors or delays.[1]

SECTION 99. Wagering contracts prohibited.
   99a. Option contracts, when illegal.

§ 99. **Wagering contracts prohibited.** — At all times in the history of the English and American law, gambling of every variety has been the subject of police regulation.

[1] McAndrew v. Electrical Tel. Co., I7 C. B. 3; Grinnell v. West. Union Tel. Co., 113 Mass. 299 (18 Am. Rep. 485); True v. Int. Tel. Co., 60 Me. 9; Young v. West. Union Tel. Co., 65 N. Y. 163; Passmore v. W. U. Tel. Co., 78 Pa. St. 238; Berney v. N. Y., etc., Tel. Co., 18 Md. 341; W. U. Tel. Co. v. Carew, 15 Mich. 525. In Illinois, it is not permitted to telegraph companies to stipulate that they will not be responsible for errors arising solely from the negligence of the operators. They can stipulate against liability for errors, only where they occur through some natural cause beyond the company's control. Tyler v. West. Union Tel. Co., 60 Ill. 421 (14 Am. Rep. 38); West. Union Tel. Co. v. Tyler, 74 Ill. 168. See Wann v. West. Union Tel. Co., 37 Mo. 472; Sweatland v. Ill., etc., Tel. Co., 27 Iowa, 432; Candee v. West. Union Tel. Co., 34 Wis. 471; West. Union Tel. Co. v. Graham, 1 Col. 230. In the last case it was held that the condition against liability, where the message is not repeated, is no defense in an action for failure to deliver.

§ 99

The lower and more common forms of gambling, when conducted as a business, are now uniformly prohibited and the prosecution of them made a penal offense. Ordinarily, however, wagers or bets are only so far prohibited or regulated that the courts refuse to perform the contracts. Independently of statute, no wager of any kind constitutes a penal offense. It requires statutory legislation to make betting a misdemeanor. Indeed, such legislation would be open to serious constitutional objections. Gambling or betting of any kind is a vice and not a trespass, and inasmuch as the parties are willing victims of the evil effects, there is nothing which calls for public regulation.[1] But when they pursue gambling as a business, and set up a gambling house, like all others who make a trade of vice, they may be prohibited and subjected to severe penalties.[2] And so, also, if they apply to the courts for aid in enforcing the contracts made in the indulgence of this vice, the courts can properly refuse to assist them.

A wager or bet, according to Mr. Bouvier, is " a contract by which two parties or more agree that a certain sum of money or other things, shall be paid or delivered to one of them on the happening, or not happening, of an uncertain event." Employing the word in this sense, it is pretty well settled that all wager contracts were not void at common law. The distinction between the legal and the illegal wagers seems to rest upon the good or evil character of the event or act, which constitutes the subject-matter of the wager. If the wager was about a harmless and legal act or event, the wager was itself legal, and the wager contract could be enforced.[3] But if the wager has reference to the

[1] See, *ante*, § 68.

[2] See, *post*, § 102.

[3] Thus it was lawful at common law to bet that A. has purchased a wagon of B. (Good *v*. Elliott, 3 T. R. 693); or to bet on a cricket-match. Walpole *v*. Saunders, 16 E. C. L. R. 276. See, also, generally, in support of the position taken above, Sherborne *v*. Colebach, 2 Vent. 175; Hussey

§ 99

happening or doing of some act which is illegal or against good morals, the wager is void and will not be enforced.[1] In no part of the civilized world are contracts for the insurance of life or property against accidental destruction held to be invalid.

The English doctrine is clearly sustained, as a part of the common law, by the decision of some of the American courts.[2] But, except in the matter of insurance contracts, all wager contracts are declared to be invalid in Maine, Massachusetts, New Hampshire, Vermont, and Pennsylvania, whatever may be the character of the event or act, which constitutes the foundation for the wager.[3] In many of the States the common law is changed by statutes which prohibit all wager contracts, and forbid their enforcement by the courts. Thus, by the New York Revised Statutes,[4] " all wagers, bets, or stakes, made to depend upon any race,

---

v. Crickell, 3 Campb. 168; Grant v. Hamilton, 3 M. L. 100; Cousins v. Mantes, 3 Taunt. 515; Johnson v. Lonsley, 12 C. B. 468; Dalby v. India Life Ins. Co., 15 C. B. 365; Hampden v. Walsh, L. R. 12 B. D. 192.

[1] Thus, wagers are void, which rest upon the result of an illegal game (Brown v. Leeson, 2 H. Bl. 43); which involve the abstinence from marriage (Huntley v. Rice, 10 East. 22); which refer to the expected birth of an illegitimate child (Ditchburn v. Goldsmith, 4 Campb. 152); or to the commission of adultery. Del Costa v. Jones, Comp. 729. See, also, to the same effect, Shirley v. Sankey, 2 Bos. & P. 130; Etham v. Kingsman, 1 B. & Al. 684.

[2] Bunn v. Rikes, 4 Johns. 426; Campbell v. Richardson, 10 Johns. 406; Dewees v. Miller, 5 Harr. 347; Trenton Ins. Co. v. Johnson, 4 Zabr. 576; Dunman v. Strother, 1 Tex. 89; Wheeler v. Friend, 22 Tex. 683; Monroe v. Smelley, 25 Tex. 586; Grant v. Hamilton, 3 McLean (U. S. C. C.), 100; Smith v. Smith, 21 Ill. 244; Richardson v. Kelley, 85 Ill. 491; Petillon v. Hipple, 90 Ill. 420; Carrier v. Brannan, 3 Cal. 328; Johnson v. Hall, 6 Cal. 359; Johnson v. Russell, 37 Cal. 670.

See Lewis v. Littlefield, 15 Me. 233; McDonough v. Webster, 68 Me. 530; Gilmore v. Woodcock, 69 Me. 118; Babcock v. Thompson, 3 Pick. 446; Ball v. Gilbert, 12 Met. 399; Sampson v. Shaw, 101 Mass. 150; Perkins v. Eaton, 3 N. H. 152; Clark v. Gibson, 12 N. H. 386; Winchester v Nutter, 52 N. H. 507; Collamer v. Day, 2 Vt. 144; Tarlton v. Baker, 18 Vt. 9; Phillips v. Ives, 1 Rawle, 36; Brua's Appeal, 5 Sm. 294.

[4] 1 Rev. Stats. N. Y. 661, § 8.

§ 99

or upon any gaming by lot or chance, casualty, or unknown or contingent event whatever, shall be unlawful.   All contracts for, or on account of, any money or property or thing in action so wagered, bet or staked shall be void.''[1] It is to be observed, that in all of these judicial and legislative determinations of the illegality of wagering contracts, although they differ in respect to the legality of particular wagers, they all rest upon the proposition that the prohibited wagers tend to develop and increase the spirit of gambling and at the same time serve no useful purpose. For these reasons all contracts, based upon such wagers, are declared to be illegal.   Inasmuch as insurance contracts serve a useful purpose, they are not prohibited; and it is not likely that a law, prohibiting them, would be sustained. It is, therefore, the evil effect of betting, coupled with its practical uselessness, that justifies its prohibition ; for all unobjectionable contracts have, as an incident of property, an inalienable right to some effective remedy in the courts of the country.[2]

§ 99*a*. **Option contracts, when illegal.** — The common forms of gambling are not difficult to define or distinguish from harmless or unobjectionable transactions.   The enforcement of the law against gambling in such cases is not trammeled with confusion as to what constitutes the *gravamen* of the offense.   It is the staking of money on the issue of games of chance, or on the happening or not happening of a contingent event or act, in those cases in which the wager does not promote a public or private good.   For many years, in all parts of the commercial world, a species of commercial gambling has been devised and developed, and which is still increasing in proportions.   Large bodies of men in our commercial centers congregate daily in the ex-

[1] Similar legislation is to be found in New Hampshire, Virginia, West Virginia, Wisconsin, Missouri, Illinois, Ohio and Iowa, and other States.
[2] See, *post*, § 142.

§ 99*a*

changes for the purpose of betting on the rise and fall in the price of stocks, cotton, and produce. The business is disguised under the name of speculation, but it is in nothing different from the wager on the result of some game of cards. The card player bets that he will win the game. The merchant, dealing in "futures," bets that the price of a commodity will, at a future day, be a certain sum, more or less than the ruling market price. In neither case does the result add anything to the world's wealth; there is only an exchange of the ownership of property without any benefit to the former owner. In the liquidation of both bets A. passes over to B. a certain proportion of his property. Under the guise of speculation, it is given an air of respectability which makes the indulgence in it all the more dangerous to the public welfare. The disreputable character of the common forms of gambling, made so by public condemnation, is the chief protection against the evil. But men of respectability are engaged in option dealing; and the apparent respectability of the business develops, to a most alarming extent, the gambling spirit in all classes of society. Instead of striving to produce something that will increase the world's wealth, while they accumulate their own, these men are bending every energy, and taxing their ingenuity, to take away what his neighbor has already produced. Apart from this injury to the public material and moral welfare, the commercial gambling, when developed to its present enormous proportions, unsettles the natural values of commodities, and the fate of the producer is made to depend upon the relative strength of the "bulls" and "bears." Conceding the truth of these charges, and the evil effect of this species of gambling which has never been seriously questioned, it would be a legitimate exercise of police power to prohibit these commercial transactions. The difficulty lies not in the justification of this prohibitory legislation, but in discovering the wrongful element in the transactions, and in

§ 99a

distinguishing them from legitimate trading. The so-called
" option contracts " are in form contracts for the sale or
purchase of commercial commodities for future delivery, at
a certain price, with the option to one or both of the parties in settlement of the contract to pay the difference
between the contract price, and the price ruling on the day
of delivery, the difference to be paid to the seller, if the
market price is lower than the contract price, and to the
purchaser, if the market price is higher. Such a contract
has three striking elements : first, it is a contract for future
delivery; secondly, the delivery is conditional upon the will
of one or both of the parties ; and thirdly, the payment of
differences in prices, in the event that the right of refusal
is exercised by one of the parties. If the common-law
offense of *regrating* were still recognized in the criminal
law, all contracts for future delivery may be open to serious
question.[1] But that rule of the common law is repudiated,
and it may now be considered as definitely settled that a
contract for future delivery of goods is not for that reason
invalid. If they infringe the law, it must be for some other
reason than that the contract stipulates for future delivery.
This is not only true, when the vendor has the goods in his
possession at the time of sale, but also when he expects to
buy them for future delivery. Lord Tenterden claimed
that in the latter case the contract was a wager on the price
of the commodity, and for that reason should not be enforced.[2] But the position here taken has since been

[1] See *ante,* § 95.

[2] " I have always thought, and shall continue to think until I am told
by the House of Lords that I am wrong, that if a man sells goods to
be delivered on a future day, and neither has the goods at the time, nor
has entered into any prior contract to buy them, nor has any reasonable
expectation of receiving by assignment, but means to go into the market
and to buy the goods which he has contracted to deliver, he cannot maintain an action on such contract. Such a contract amounts, on the part of
the vendor, to a wager on the price of the commodity, and is attended

§ 99*a*

repudiated by the English courts, on the ground that it is not a wager, and if a wager, not one which tends to injure the public.[1] The late English opinion is generally followed in the United States, and it may be stated, as the general American rule, that *bona fide* contracts for the future delivery of goods are not invalid, because at the time of sale the vendor has not in his actual or potential possession the goods which he has agreed to sell.[2]

It is also held to be an unobjectionable feature in such contracts, that the vendee has no expectation of receiving the goods purchased into his actual possession, but intends to resell them before the delivery of the possession to him.[3]

with the most mischievous consequences." Lord Tenterden in Bryan *v.* Lewis, Req. & Moody, 386. See, also, Longmer *v.* Smith, 1 B. & C. 1.

[1] " I have always entertained considerable doubt and suspicion as to the correctness of Lord Tenterden's doctrine in Bryan *v.* Lewis. It excited a good deal of surprise in my mind at the time, and when examined, I think it is untenable. I cannot see what principle of law is at all affected by a man's being allowed to contract for the sale of goods, of which he has not possession at the time of the bargain, and has no reasonable expectation of receiving. Such a contract does not amount to a wager, inasmuch as both the contracting parties are not in the vendor's possession; and even if it were a wager, it is not illegal, because it has no necessary tendency to injure third parties." Baron Parke in Hibblewhite *v.* McMorine, 5 M. & W. 58. See Mortimer *v.* McCallan, 6 M. & W. 58; Wells *v.* Porter, 3 Scott, 141.

[2] Head *v.* Goodwin, 37 Me. 181; Rumsey *v.* Berry, 65 Me. 570; Lewis *v.* Lyman, 22 Pick. 437; Thrall *v.* Hill, 110 Mass. 328; Heald *v.* Builders' Ins. Co., 111 Mass. 38; Smith *v.* Atkins, 18 Vt. 461; Noyes *v.* Spaulding, 27 Vt. 420; Hull *v.* Hull, 48 Conn. 250; Hauton *v.* Small, 3 Sandf. 230; Currie *v.* White, 45 N. Y. 822; Bigelow *v.* Benedict, 70 N. Y. 202; Bina's Appeal, 55 Pa. St. 294; Brown *v.* Speyer, 20 Gratt. 309; Phillips *v.* Ocmulgee Mills, 55 Ga. 633; Noyes *v.* Jenkins, 55 Ga. 586; Fonville *v.* Casey, 1 Murphy, 389; Whitehead *v.* Root, 2 Metc. (Ky.) 584; McCarty *v.* Blevins, 13 Tenn. 195; Wilson *v.* Wilson, 37 Mo. 1; Logan *v.* Musick, 81 Ill. 415; Pixley *v.* Boynton, 79 Ill. 351; Pickering *v.* Cease, 79 Ill. 328; Lyon *v.* Culbertson, 83 Ill. 33; Corbett *v.* Underwood, 83 Ill. 324; Sanborn *v.* Benedict, 78 Ill. 309; Wolcott *v.* Heath, 78 Ill. 433.

[3] Ashton *v.* Dakin, 4 H. & N. 867; Sawyer, Wallace & Co. *v.* Laggart, 14 Bush, 730; Cameron *v.* Durkheim, 55 N. Y. 425. But see *contra*, Brua's Appeal, 55 Pa. St. 294; Fareira *v.* Gabell, 89 Pa. St. 89; North *v.* Phillips 89 Pa. St. 250.

§ 99*a*

To quote the words of the Kentucky court, "sales for future delivery have long been regarded and held to be indispensable in modern commerce, and as long as they continue to be held valid, one who buys for future delivery has as much right to sell as any other person, and there cannot, in the very nature of things, be any valid reason why one who buys for future delivery may not resolve, before making the purchase, that he will resell before the day of delivery, and especially when, by the rules of trade and the terms of his contract, the person to whom he sells will be bound to receive the goods from the original seller, and pay the contract price." [1]

Nor is a contract necessarily hurtful to the public welfare, which provides on payment of a valuable consideration that one at a future day shall have the right to buy certain property or sell other property, according as one or the other happens to be advantageous to him. One may have a lawful and beneficial end in view in acquiring such a right of refusal.[2] "Mercantile contracts of this character are not infrequent, and they are consistent with a *bona fide* intention on the part of both parties to perform them. The vendor of goods may expect to produce or acquire them in time for a future delivery, and, while wishing to make a market for them, is unwilling to enter into an absolute obligation to deliver, and therefore bargains for an option which, while it relieves him from liability, assures him of a sale, in case he is able to deliver; and the purchaser may, in the same way, guard himself against loss beyond the consideration paid for the option, in case of his inability to take the goods, there is no inherent vice in such a contract." [3] And

[1] Sawyer et al. *v.* Taggart, 14 Bush, 730.

[2] Story *v.* Salomon, 71 N. Y. 420; Kingsbury *v.* Kirwan, 71 N. Y. 612; Harris *v.* Lumbridge, 83 N. Y. 92; Bigelow *v.* Benedict, 70 N. Y. 202.

[3] Bigelow *v.* Benedict, 70 N. Y. 202. In this case, A., for a valuable consideration, agreed to purchase gold coin of B. at a named price, the coin to be delivered at any time within six months that B. might choose.

§ 99*a*

the consideration for this option may very properly be the difference between the ruling market price and the price specified in the contract. For that would be the damage to the other party resulting from the sale of the option or refusal.[1]

If each of the preceding propositions is correct, then the illegality of option contracts must rest upon the intention of the parties not to deliver the goods bargained for, but merely to pay the difference between the market price and contract price. The cases are unanimous in the opinion that a contract, for the payment of difference in prices, arising out of the rise and fall in the market price above or below the contract price, is a wager on the future price of the commodity, and is therefore invalid.[2] If the contracts were in form, as well as in fact, agreements to pay the difference in prices, they could be easily avoided, and thrown out of court. But the contracts never assume the form of wagers on the price of the commodity. They are always in form undistinguishable from those option contracts, in

---

This case, as a legitimate transaction, is more easily understood than where the option is to buy certain goods or to sell others, but the latter can exist under lawful circumstances and have a lawful end in view. See Story v. Salomon, 71 N. Y. 420.

[1] Story v. Salomon, 71 N. Y. 420; Harris v. Lumbridge, 83 N. Y. 92, and the cases cited in the next note.

[2] Rumsey v. Berry, 65 Me. 574; Wyman v. Fiske, 3 Allen, 238; Brigham v. Meade, 10 Allen, 246; Barratt v. Hyde, 7 Gray, 160; Brown v. Phelps, 103 Mass. 303; Hatch v. Douglass, 48 Conn. 116; Noyes v. Spaulding, 27 Vt. 240; Story v. Salomon, 71 N. Y. 420; Bigelow v. Benedict, 70 N. Y. 202; Harris v. Lumbridge, 83, 82, N. Y. 92; North v. Phillips, 89 Pa. St. 250; Ruchizky v. De Haven, 97 Pa. St. 202; Dickson's Ex'or v. Thomas, 97 Pa. St. 278; Kirkpatrick v. Bonsall, 72 Pa. St. 155; Brown v. Speyer, 20 Gratt. 296; Williams v. Carr, 80 N. C. 294; Williams v. Tiedemann, 6 Mo. App. 269; Lyon v. Culbertson, 83 Ill. 33; Cole v. Milmine, 88 Ill. 349; Corbitt v. Underwood, 83 Ill. 324; Pickering v. Cease, 79 Ill. 338; Pixley v. Boynton, 79 Ill. 351; Barnard v. Backhouse, 52 Wis. 593; Sawyer v. Taggert, 14 Bush, 727; Gregory v. Wendall, 39 Mich. 337; Shaw v. Clark, 49 Mich. 384; Gregory v. Wattoma, 58 Iowa, 711; Everingham v. Meighan, 55 Wis. 354; Rudolph v. Winters 7 Neb. 125.

§ 99a

which the parties in good faith have bargained for the refusal of the goods, and which are valid contracts.   The following is a good illustration of the ambiguity of the form
of the contract.   " For value received, the bearer (S.)
may call on the undersigned for one hundred (100) shares
of the capital stock of the Western Union Telegraph Company, at seventy-seven and one-half (77½) per cent, at
any time in thirty (30) days from date. Or the bearer may,
at his option, deliver the same to the undersigned at
seventy-seven and one-half (77½) per cent., any time
within the period named, one day's notice required." [1]
There is no evidence on the face of this contract of the
determination of the parties to settle on the differences in
price ; and while such a contract may be used as a cover for
commercial gambling, it is not necessarily a wager on the
future price of the commodity.

It is the ordinary rule of law that where a writing is
susceptible of two constructions, one of which is legal, and
the other illegal, that construction will prevail, which is in
conformity with the law.[2]   Applying this rule to the construction of option contracts,it has very generally been
held that these contracts are valid and enforcible, unless it
be proven affirmatively that the parties did not intend to
make a delivery of the goods bargained for, but to settle
on the differences.[3]   And if it be shown that only one of
the parties entertained this illegal intention, while the other
acted in good faith, the contract will be void as to the

---

[1] Story v. Salomon, 71 N. Y. 420.

[2] " It is a general rule, that wheresoever the words of a deed, or of
the parties without deed, may have a double intendment, and the one
standeth with law and right, and the other is wrongful and against law,
the intendment that standeth with the law shall be taken."   Coke on
Lyttleton, 42, 183.

[3] Story v. Salomon, 71 N. Y. 420; Kingsbury v. Kirwan, 71 N. Y. 612;
Harris v. Lumbridge, 83 N. Y. 92; Williams v. Tiedemann, 6 Mo. App.
274; Union Nat. Bank of Chicago v. Carr, 15 Fed. Rep. 438; and cases
cited in preceding note.

§ 99a

first, but will be enforcible in behalf of the second.[1]   In
delivering the opinion of the New York Court of Appeals[2]
Earl, J. said: "On the face of the contract the plaintiff provided for the contingency that on that day he
might desire to purchase the stock, or he might desire to
sell it, and in either case there would have to be a delivery
of the stock, or payment in damages in lieu thereof.   We
should not infer an illegal intent unless obliged to.   Such a
transaction, unless intended as a mere cover for a bet or
wager on the future price of the stock, is legitimate and
condemned by no statute, and that it was so intended was
not proved.   If it had been shown that neither party intended to deliver or accept the shares, but merely to pay
differences according to the rise or fall of the market, the
contract would have been illegal."   This rule of construction is adopted by most of the courts, in determining the
legality of these questionable contracts, but a different rule
has been laid down by the Supreme Court of Wisconsin.
The contract, which constituted the subject of the suit, was
in form a legitimate transaction, and there was no proof
that it was used as a cover for commercial gambling.   The
court declared it to be the duty of the plaintiff to show
that he had made a *bona fide* contract for the delivery of
the commodities bought and sold, instead of throwing
upon the defendant the burden of proving that the contract
was made for the payment of differences in price, and did
not contemplate any delivery of the grain.   The court
claimed that it would " not do to attach too much weight or
importance to the mere form of the contract, for it is quite
certain that parties will be as astute in concealing their intention, as the real nature of the transaction, if it be illegal."
It may be safely assumed, that the parties will make such
contracts valid in form ; but courts must not be deceived

[1] Rumsey *v.* Berry, 65 Me. 570; Williams *v.* Carr, 80 N. C. 94; Sawyer
et al. *v.* Taggert, 14 Bush, 727; Gregory *v.* Wendall, 39 Mich. 337.
[2] Story *v.* Salomon, *supra*.

§ 99a

by what appears on the face of the agreement. It is often
necessary to go behind, or outside of, the words of the
contract — to look into the facts and circumstances which
attended the making of it — in order to ascertain whether
it was intended as a *bona fide* purchase and sale of the
property, or was only colorable. And to justify a court
in upholding such an agreement, it is not too much to require a party claiming rights under it, to make it satisfactorily and affirmatively appear that the contract was made
with an actual view to the delivery and receipt of grain,
not as an evasion of the statute against gaming, or as a
cover for a gambling transaction."[1] The power of the
legislature to change this rule of construction, and to throw
the burden of proof of the legality of the contract upon the
party asserting it, cannot be questioned. But it is not
within the power of the court to change it, as was done by
the Wisconsin court. For the effective prevention of this
commercial gambling, this change is most needful, and with
one other regulation, which will be suggested here, the
prohibition can be made as effective as any prohibition of
an act, which operates as a trespass only indirectly through
its injurious effects. The other needful regulation would
be the prohibition of all contracts of sale for future delivery, where the vendor has neither the actual, constructive,
nor potential possession of the goods sold. A man has an
absolute right, in his personal or representative capacity,
to sell for future delivery any goods which he may have in
his actual or constructive possession, or which he may
have the present capacity of acquiring at some future day.
One has the right to sell commodities which he has purchased from another for future delivery, or to sell a growing or other future crop, or the flour that his mill will
grind during a stated period. But one can serve no useful

---

[1] Barnard *v.* Backhous, 52 Wis. 593. See, to the same effect, Cobb.
v. Prell, 15 Fed. Rep. 774.

§ 99*a*

end by selling goods for future delivery, goods which he does not own, and which he does not expect to possess. Such future contracts may therefore be prohibited. With the aid of this legislation, and by casting the burden of proof upon him who asserts the legality of these questionable or doubtful contracts, gambling in futures may be subjected to a more effective restraint.

§ 100. **General prohibition of contracts on the ground of public policy.** — In the preceding sections, we have given many cases of contracts, which are declared to be invalid, because their enforcement is contrary to public policy, for more or less satisfactory reasons. It only remains to be stated generally, that whenever a contract is made, having for its subject-matter the commission of some offense against the law, the violation of some rule of morality, or the commission of some injury to the public health, the contract can not be enforced; and the courts will leave the parties to the contract and their property in the same position in which they are found. No right of action can be maintained, which has the invalid contract for a legal basis. It is neither possible nor advisable in this connection to refer to special cases; the principle is the same in all cases, and the whole subject will be found discussed in all of the numerous treatises upon the law of contracts.[1]

§ 101. **Licenses.** — It is the common custom in all of the towns and cities of the United States to require the payment of a certain sum of money as a license, for the privilege of prosecuting one's profession or calling. The license is required indiscriminately of all kinds of occupations, whatever may be their character, whether harmful or innocent, whether the license is required as a protection to

[1] See, also, Benjamin on Sales, and Greeenhood on Public Policy.

§ 101

the public or not. The one general object of such ordinances, as a whole, whatever other reasons may be assigned
for the requirement of a license in any particular occupation, can only be the provision of a reliable source of
revenue. It is one of " the ways and means " of defraying
the current expenses. While the courts are not uniform in
the presentation of the grounds upon which the general
requirement of a license for all kinds of employments may
be justified ; on one ground or another the right to impose
the license has been very generally recognized.[1] Whatever

[1] Boston v. Schaffer, 9 Pick. 415; Com. v. Stodder, 2 Cush. 562; Mayor
of New York v. 2nd Ave. R. R. Co., 32 N. Y. 261; Brooklyn v. Breslin, 57
N. Y. 591; State v. Hoboken, 33 N. J. L. 280; Muhlenbrinck v. Com., 42 N.
J. L. 364 (36 Am. Rep. 518); Johnson v. Philadelphia, 60 Pa. St. 445;
Bennett v. Borough of Birmingham, 31 Pa. St. 15; State v. Roberts, 11
Gill & J. 506; The Germania v. State, 7 Md. 1; Slaughter v. Com., 13
Gratt. 767; Wynne v. Wright, 1 Dev. & B. (N. C.) L. 19; Home Ins. Co.
v. Augusta, 50 Ga. 530; Savannah v. Charton, 36 Ga. 460; Mayor v.
Phelps, 27 Ala. 55; Mays v. Cincinnati, 1 Ohio St. 268; Cincinnati v.
Bryson, 15 Ohio, 625; Chilvers v. People, 11 Mich. 43; State v. Herod,
29 Iowa, 123; People v. Thurber, 13 Ill. 557; Cairo v. Bross, 101 Ill. 475;
Kniper v. Louisville, 7 Bush, 599. The licensing of hucksters has been
held to be unreasonable in Dunham v. Rochester, 5 Cow. 462; Muhlen-
brinck v. Commissioners, 42 N. J. L. 364 (36 Am. Rep. 518); Frommer v.
Richmond, 31 Gratt. 646; Barling v. West, 29 Wis. 307 (9 Am. Rep. 576);
St. Paul v. Traeger, 25 Minn. 248 (33 Am. Rep. 462); Mays v. Cincinnati,
1 Ohio St. 268. License tax upon attorneys and physicians, held to be
reasonable. Simmons v. State, 12 Mo. 268; State v. Hibbard, 3 Ohio, 33;
State v. Proudfit, 3 Ohio, 33; State v. Gazley, 5 Ohio, 21; Savannah v.
Charton, 36 Ga. 460; Young v. Thomas, 17 Fla. 169; Longville v. State,
4 Tex. App. 312. Licensing of bakers, reasonable. Mayor, etc., v.
Yuille, 3 Ala. 137. License tax on places of public amusement, reasonable. Charity Hospital v. Stickney, 2 La. Ann. 550; Seers et al. v. West,
1 Murphy, 291; Germania v. State, 7 Md. 1; Mabry v. Tarver, 1 Humph.
94. Reasonable to require license of hacks and draymen. Brooklyn v.
Breslin, 57 N. Y. 591; Frankfort, etc., R. Co. v. Philadelphia, 58 Pa. St.
119; City Council v. Pepper, 1 Rich. L. 364; St. Louis v. Green, 70 Mo.
562; Cincinnati v. Bryson, 15 Ohio, 625; Commonwealth v. Matthews,
122 Mass. 60; St. Paul v. Smith, 27 Minn. 164 (38 Am. Rep. 296). Reasonable to prohibit peddling without license. Huntington v. Cheesbro,
57 Ind. 74; Ex parte Ah Foy, 57 Cal. 92; Temple v. Sumner, 51 Miss. 13.
Reasonable to prohibit sale of milk without license. People v. Mulhol-

§ 101

refinements of reasoning may be indulged in, there are but two substantial phases to the imposition of a license tax on professions and occupations. It is either a license, strictly so-called, imposed in the exercise of the ordinary police power of the State, or it is a tax, laid in the exercise of the power of taxation. In many cases it becomes exceedingly important to determine under which power the particular license is imposed.

In preceding sections, it has been explained how the right to pursue the ordinary callings of life exists independently of government, and the pursuit of them can only be so far restrained and regulated, as such restraint and regulation may be required to prevent the doing of damage to the public or to third persons. Where the calling is not dangerous to the public, either directly or incidentally, it cannot be subjected to any police regulation whatever which does not fall within the power of taxation. But those occupations which require police regulation, because of their peculiar character, in order that harm might not come to the public, can be subjected to whatever police regulation may be necessary to avert the threatened danger. Among other measures that would be justifiable in such cases, would be a more or less rigid police supervision of those who may be permitted to pursue the calling. Hence, it would be

land, 19 Hun, 548; *s. c.* 82 N. Y. 324 (37 Am. Rep. 568); Chicago *v.* Bartree, 100 Ill. 57. Imposing heavy license on auctioneers reasonable. Wiggins *v.* Chicago, 68 Ill. 372; Decorah *v.* Dunstan, 38 Iowa, 96; Fretwell *v.* Troy, 18 Kan. 271. Licensing of liquor trade. State *v.* Cassidy, 22 Minn. 312 (21 Am. Rep. 767); Bancroft *v.* Dumas, 21 Vt. 456; State *v.* Brown, 19 Fla. 563; Lewellen *v.* Lockhardts, 21 Gratt. 570; Hirsh *v.* State, 21 Gratt. 785; Wiley *v.* Owens, 39 Ind. 429; Pleuler *v.* State, 11 Neb. 547; State *v.* Harris, 10 Iowa, 441; Hammond *v.* Haines, 25 Md. 541; Trustees *v.* Keeting, 4 Denio, 341; Town Council *v.* Harbers, 6 Rich. L. 96; State *v.* Plunkett, 3 Harr. (N. J.) 5; Burckholter *v.* McConnellsville, 20 Ohio St. 308; State *v.* Sherman, 20 Mo. 265; State ex rel. Troll *v.* Hudson, 78 Mo. 302; Gunnarssohn *v.* Sterling, 92 Ill. 669; East St. Louis *v.* Wehrung, 46 Ill. 392; Hill *v.* Decatur, 22 Ga. 203; Youngblood *v.* Sexton, 32 Mich. 406 (20 Am. Rep. 654).

lawful and constitutional for the State or town to require all those, who follow such a vocation, to take out a license. On this principle, attorneys, physicians, druggists, engineers and other skilled workmen may be required to procure a license, which would certify to their fitness to pursue their respective callings, in which professional skill is most necessary, and in which the ignorance of the practitioner is likely to be productive of great harm to the public, and to individuals coming into business relations with them. So also, the licensing of dramshops, green groceries, hackmen and the like, is justifiable, in order that these callings may be effectually brought within the police supervision, which is necessary to prevent the occupation becoming harmful to the public. The dramshop is likely to gather together the more or less disreputable and dangerous classes of society; the green grocers are likely, if not honest, to sell to their customers meat that is stale and unhealthy; and the hackmen are inclined, if not watched by the public authorities, to practice frauds upon the public against which they cannot very well protect themselves without police aid. In the regulation of all such occupations, it is constitutional to require those, who apply for a license, to pay a reasonable sum to defray the expense of issuing the license and maintaining the police supervision. What is a reasonable sum must be determined by the facts of each case; but where it is a plain case of police regulation, the courts are not inclined to be too exact in determining the expense of procuring the license, as long as the sum demanded is not altogether unreasonable.[1] The evils growing out of some occupations may be such that their suppression can only be attained to any appreciable degree by the imposition of a restraint upon the pursuit of such callings or kinds of busi-

---

[1] Boston v. Schaffer, 9 Pick. 415; Welch v. Hotchkiss, 39 Conn. 140; Johnson v. Philadelphia, 60 Pa. St. 445; State v. Hoboken, 41 N. J. L. 71; Ash v. People, 11 Mich. 347; Van Baalen v. People, 40 Mich. 458; Burlington v. Putnam Ins. Co., 31 Iowa, 102.

§ 101

ness. For example, the keeping of saloons produces public evil in proportion to the number of low groggeries, which are allowed to be opened, and in any event the evil is lessened by reducing the number of saloons of all grades of respectability. One of the most effective modes of restraining and limiting the number of saloons in any particular town or city, is to require a heavy license of the keepers of them. Such a license may, probably, be justified on the ground that, since the prosecution of the business entails more or less injury upon society, it is but just that those who make profit out of the traffic should bear the burden of liquidating the damage done to the public in the form of increased pauperism and crime. In Minnesota, an act provided for the payment of a license by all keepers of saloons and dramshops, which would be devoted to the establishment of a fund for the foundation and maintenance of an asylum for inebriates. In declaring the act to be constitutional, the court advanced the following reasons in support of it: "It is very apparent from its provisions, that the law in effect is one further regulating traffic in intoxicating drinks. Such is manifestly one of its objects, and its principal features and provisions accord with this idea. It requires of those desiring to prosecute business the procuring of a special license as a condition precedent to the exercise and enjoyment of such a right. It regards the traffic as one tending to produce intemperance, and as likely, by reason thereof, to entail upon the State the expense and burden of providing for the class of persons rendered incapable of self-support, the evil influence of whose presence and example upon society is necessarily injurious to the public welfare and prosperity, and, therefore, calls for such legislative interposition as will operate as a restraint upon the business, and protect the community from the mischief, evils and pecuniary burthens following from its prosecution. To this end the special license is required, and the business restricted to such persons as are willing to indemnify the

§ 101

State, in part, against its probable results and consequences, by contributing towards a fund that shall be devoted ex-exclusively to that purpose in the manner indicated in the act. That these provisions unmistakably partake of the nature of police regulations, are strictly of that character, there can be no doubt, nor can it be denied that their expediency or necessity is solely a legislative, and not a judicial, question.

" Regarding the law as a precautionary measure, intended to operate as a wholesome restraint upon a traffic, and as a protection to society against its consequent evils, the exacted fee is not unreasonable in amount, and the purpose to which it is devoted is strictly pertinent and appropriate. It could not be questioned but that a reasonable sum imposed in the way of an indemnity to the State against the expense of maintaining the police force to supervise the conduct of those engaged in the business and to guard against disorders and infractions of law occasioned by its prosecution, would be a legitimate exercise of police power, and not open to the objection that it was a tax for the purpose of revenue, and therefore unconstitutional. Reclaiming the inebriate, restoring him to society, prepared again to discharge the duties of citizenship, equally promotes the public welfare and tends to the accomplishment of like beneficial results, and it is difficult to see wherein the imposition of a reasonable license fee would be any less a proper exercise of the power in one case than in the other." [1]

But that disposition of the license fees is not necessary as a justification of the law which exacts them. The money, collected by way of a license as a police regulation, may go into the State treasury for general revenue purposes, and need not be devoted specially to the relief of burdens which the prosecution of the trade or occupation imposed on the State, provided that the character of the occupation is such that

---

[1] State v. Cassidy, 22 Minn. 312 (21 Am. Rep. 765).

§ 101

restrictions upon its pursuit, looking to its partial suppression, would be constitutional, whatever their character may be. Since the primary object of such a law would be to operate as a restriction upon the trade, and not to raise a revenue, the incidental increase in the revenue would constitute no valid objection to the law.[1]

The amount demanded for the license, in such a case, would be determinable by the legislature. It would be a legislative, and not a judicial question. But it is a judicial question, whether the particular occupation or trade can, under the constitutional limitations, be restrained. One, desiring to practice law or medicine, can be required to obtain a license from some court or other State authority, to which he is entitled after passing a satisfactory examination into his qualifications for the profession; and he can be required to pay a small fee to cover the expense incurred in issuing the license; but he could not be right-

---

[1] Youngblood v. Sexton, 32 Mich. 406 (20 Am. Rep. 554); Carter v. Dow, 16 Wis. 299; Tenny v. Lanz, 16 Wis. 566. "In granting licenses, the items which may be taken into consideration as elements fixing the costs of the same, would seem to be about as follows: *First*, the value of the labor and material in merely allowing and issuing the license; *second*, the value of the benefit of the license to the person obtaining the same; *third*, the value of the convenience and cost to the public in protecting such business, and in permitting it to be carried on in the community; *fourth*, and in some cases an additional amount imposed as a restraint upon the number of persons who might otherwise engage in the business. None of these items contemplates, except incidentally, the raising of revenue for general purposes. In many cases, the license, which, if issued for proper purposes would be valid, would not be valid if issued merely for the purpose of obtaining or increasing the general revenue fund.'' Leavenworth v. Booth, 15 Kan. 627. "It is no doubt true that the city was empowered to resort to other means of restraint (than requiring heavy licenses of saloon keepers), such as requiring such houses to be orderly, and in other respects to conform to such ordinances as might be adopted to properly restrain the business; but the fact that they had other powers conferred for this purpose in nowise prevented the city from exercising the power to restrain the general free sale of liquors by requiring that a license should be obtained before it could be sold." Mt. Carmel v. Wabash, 50 Ill. 69; Emporia v. Volmer, 12 Kan. 622.

§ 101

fully compelled to pay a large amount, exacted of him with
a view to reduce the number of the practitioners of these
professions, although they may be overcrowded.   A green
grocer may be required to take out a license, in order that
the proper police supervision may be maintained over his
business to prevent the sale of unwholesome meat ; and he
may be required to pay a reasonable sum to defray the expenses of this necessary police inspection; but the number
of green grocers can not be restrained by requiring a large
sum in payment for his license.   In order to justify a restrictive license, the business must itself be of such a nature,
that its prosecution will do damage to the public, whatever
may be the character and qualifications of those who engage
in it.   Such would be the keeping of a saloon or dramshop.[1]
Once having been judicially ascertained that the trade or
occupation may be restrained, it is a matter of legislative
discretion what kind of restraints can be imposed.   The
prosecution of the trade then becomes a privilege, for which
as large a price can be demanded by the State as it may see
fit.

In respect to the great majority of employments and
occupations, the principles, explained above, have no application whatever.   They not only do not threaten any
evil to the public, but their prosecution to the fullest measure of success is a public blessing.   Instead of placing trades·
in general under restraints and police regulations, in which
a license would be required, the utmost freedom can best
attain the greatest good to the public.   When, therefore,
we see municipal corporations requiring licenses for the
prosecution of all kinds of occupations and employments ;
if their action can be justified at all, it must rest upon some
other grounds than as a police regulation.   It can only be
justified as a tax upon the profession or calling.   Having the natural, inalienable right to pursue a harmless

---

[1] See *post*, § 13.

§ 101

calling, he can not be required to take out a license before he can lawfully pursue it. For what is a license? "The object of a license," says Mr. Justice Manning,[1] "is to confer a right that does not exist without a license, and consequently a power to license involves in the exercise of it, a power to prohibit under pain or penalty without a license. Otherwise a license would be an idle ceremony, giving no right, conferring no privilege, and exempting from no pain or penalty. If the right existed previous to the law requiring the license, it would not exist afterwards without a license. The fact that a license is required to do an act, is of itself a prohibition of such act without a license."[2]

"A proper license tax is not a tax at all within the meaning of the constitution, or even within the ordinary signification of the word 'tax.' * * * The imposition of a license tax is in the nature of the sale of a benefit, or privilege, to the party who would not otherwise be entitled to the same. The imposition of an ordinary tax is in the nature of the requisition of a contribution from that which the party taxed already rightfully possesses."[3]

The following case, from the Supreme Court of Minnesota, covers the ground so effectually, in presenting the distinction between a "license" and a "tax" upon occupations, that an extensive quotation is given from the opinion of the court. The city council of St. Paul had by ordinance required a license fee of twenty-five dollars from every huckster of vegetables, who plied his trade in the streets of the city. In determining whether this was a license or a tax, the court said: —

"It is apparent that provisions of this section are founded upon the assumption that the common council, under the charter, possesses the power to license the pursuit of the particular calling or business mentioned, in and along

[1] Chilvers v. People, 11 Mich. 43.
[2] Chilvers v. People, 11 Mich. 49.
[3] Leavenworth v. Booth, 15 Kan. 627.

§ 101

the streets of the city, and to prescribe, as an incident thereto, when it may be followed, what sum shall be paid for the privilege, and also to prohibit the business entirely without a license, as an efficient means for the protection and enjoyment of the power itself. The ordinance is in entire harmony with this view and no other. It was not passed as suggested by counsel, by virtue of any power of supervision and control over streets, because powers of that character are conferred for the sole purpose of putting and preserving the public streets in a fit and serviceable condition, as such, by keeping them in repair and free from all obstructions and uses tending in any way to the hinderance or interruption of public travel, and to that end alone can they be exercised. The ordinance in question has no such object in view. On the contrary, it expressly authorizes the use of the public streets for the purposes of the licensed traffic during that portion of each day, when ordinarily the travel is the greatest, and when such traffic would be most likely to interfere with the free and uninterrupted passage of vehicles and footmen, and it contains no provision in any way restricting, or calculated to regulate, the manner in which the licensed business shall be conducted as to occasion the least public inconvenience. It cannot be claimed that it was enacted in the exercise of any police power for sanitary purposes, or for the preservation of good order, peace or quiet of the city, because neither upon its face, nor upon any evidence before us, does it appear that any provision is made for the inspection of any articles sold or offered for sale under the license, or preventing the sale of any decayed or unwholesome vegetables, nor is there any restraint or regulation whatever, imposed upon the conduct of the business during the time it is permitted to be prosecuted. The annual sum exacted for the license is manifestly much in excess of what is necessary or reasonable to cover expenses incident to its issue. The business itself is of a useful character, neither hurtful nor pernicious, but benefi-

§ 101

cial to society, and recognized as rightful and legitimate, both at common law and by the general laws of the State. No regulations being prescribed in reference to its prosecution under the license, there could be little, if any, occasion for the exercise of any police authority, in supervising the business or enforcing the ordinance, and no cause for any considerable expense on that account. In view of these facts, it is quite obvious that the amount of the license fee was fixed with reference to revenue purposes, which it was the main object of the ordinance to promote, by means of a tax imposed upon the particular employment or pursuit, through the exercise of its power over the subject of granting license." [1]

It is, therefore, conclusive, that the general requirement of a license for the pursuit of any business that is not dangerous to the public, can only be justified as an exercise of the power of taxation, or the requirement of a compensation for the enjoyment of a privilege or franchise. In respect to the latter ground, no substantial objection can be well laid to the requirement of a license. When the State grants a franchise, it may demand, as a consideration for its grant, some special compensation, and afterwards tax it as property *ad valorem*. Thus insurance companies established by charter from one State have no natural right to carry on business in any other State, and permission to do so is a privilege for which the payment of a substantial sum as license may be required.[2]

[1] St. Paul *v.* Traeger, 25 Minn. 248. See, also, Mayor *v.* 2nd Ave. R. R. Co., 32 N. Y. 261; Kip *v.* Paterson, 26 N. J. 298; State *v.* Hoboken, 41 N. J. 71; Commonwealth *v.* Stodder, 2 Cush. 562; Johnson *v.* Philadelphia, 60 Pa. St. 445; Muhlenbrinck *v.* Commissioners, 42 N. J. 364 (36 Am. Rep. 518); State *v.* Roberts, 11 Gill & J. 506; Home Ins. Co. *v.* Augusta, 50 Ga. 530; Burlington *v.* Bumgardner, 42 Iowa, 673; Cairo *v.* Bross, 101 Ill. 475; Mayor *v.* Cincinnati, 1 Ohio St. 268.

[2] People *v.* Thurber, 13 Ill. 554; Commonwealth *v.* Germania, L. I. Co., 11 Phila. 553; Walker *v.* Springfield, 94 Ill. 364; State *v.* Lathrop, 10 La. Ann. 398; Ex parte Conn, 13 Nev. 424; Trustees E. F. Fund *v.* Roome, 93 N. Y. 313; Leavenworth *v.* Booth, 15 Kan. 627.

§ 101

The right of the State to tax professions and occupations, unless there is some special constitutional prohibition of it, seems to be very generally conceded. Judge Cooley says: "Taxes may assume the form of duties, imposts and excises, and those collected by the national government are very largely of this character. They may also assume the form of license fees, for permission to carry on particular occupations."[1] The State and the town authorities may impose a separate tax upon the same occupation,[2] and the fact that the property used in trade is taxed *ad valorem*, does not constitute any objection to the imposition of a license tax upon the business.[3]

The most common objection raised to the enforcement of a license tax, is that it offends the constitutional provision, which requires uniformity of taxation, since the determination of the sum that shall be required of each trade or occupation must necessarily, in some degree, be arbitrary, and the amount demanded more or less irregular. But the courts have very generally held that the constitutional requirement as to uniformity of taxation had no reference to taxation of occupations. "We are unable to perceive how the ordinance in question violates art. 127, which requires taxation to be equal and uniform. Its words are;

[1] Cooley Const. Lim. 613; Ould *v.* Richmond, 23 Gratt. 464 (14 Am. Rep. 139); Commonwealth *v.* Moore, 25 Gratt. 951; Gatlin *v.* Tarborso, 78 N. C. 419; State *v.* Hayne, 4 Rich. L. 403; Young *v.* Thomas, 17 Fla. 169 (35 Am. Rep. 328); Stewart *v.* Potts, 49 Miss. 949; State *v.* Endom, 23 La. Ann. 663; New Orleans *v.* Kaufman, 29 La. 283 (29 Am. Rep. 328); Albrecht *v.* State, 8 Tex. Ct. App. 216 (34 Am. Rep. 737); Cousins *v.* State, 59 Ala. 113 (20 Am. Rep. 290); Sweet *v.* Wabash, 41 Ind. 7; Youngblood *v.* Sexton, 32 Mich. 406 (20 Am. Rep. 654); Morrill *v.* State, 38 Wis. 428 (20 Am. Rep. 12); Ex parte Frank, 52 Cal. 606 (28 Am. Rep. 642); Ex parte Robinson, 12 Nev. 263. In Cincinnati *v.* Bryson, 15 Ohio, 625, Judge Read, in a dissenting opinion, denies that the legislature of Ohio has the power to tax occupations.

[2] Webbe *v.* Commonwealth, 33 Gratt. 898.

[3] St. Louis *v.* Green, 6 Mo. App. 590; Lewellen *v.* Lockharts, 21 Gratt. 570; Hirsh *v.* State, 21 Gratt. 785.

§ 101

' *all* keepers or owners of stables where horses and carriages are kept for hire, etc.' The argument seems to be that the business of defendant's livery stable will not bear such a tax. To this it may be again replied — this does not profess to be a tax upon capital or profits, which are property ; but on the person pursuing a certain occupation. To levy such a tax differently upon one and another in proportion to the success of each in such a pursuit would produce the very inequality of which the defendants complain. As the ordinance stands, all are taxed alike."[1]

A more serious question is the character of the remedies that may be employed for the collection of the license tax. Where the tax is laid upon property, the usual remedy is a suit at law and a sale of goods necessary to liquidate the taxes due, or, in the case of real property, a sale of the property against which the taxes are assessed. And a sale of the goods under execution, issued on a judgment for the license tax, would be an altogether unobjectionable remedy. When the tax is lawfully laid against the individual, it becomes a debt which, like any other kind of indebtedness, can be reduced to judgment, and satisfaction obtained by a sale under execution of the judgment debtor's goods. But the usual remedy is to make the payment of the license tax a condition precedent to the lawful prosecution of the business, whether the license is executed in the enforcement of a police regulation, or as means of raising revenue. As a police regulation the denial of the right to engage in the business before taking out a license is but reasonable. The license operates as a prohibition, and there would clearly

[1] Municipality *v.* Dubois, 10 La. Ann. 56. See, also, to the same effect, Youngblood *v.* Sexton, 32 Mich. 406 (20 Ann. Rep. 654) ; Gatlin *v.* Tarboro; 78 N. C. 119; Mayor, etc., *v.* Beasley, 1 Humph. 232; Ex parte Robinson, 12 Nev. 263; State *v.* Endom, 23 La. Ann. 663; People *v.* Thurber, 13 Ill. 554.

§ 101

be no constitutional objection to a law, which even made it penal to prosecute the business without a license.[1]

But the case assumes a different phase, when the occupation is merely taxed, and not licensed in the strict sense of the word. Can the State prohibit the prosecution of a trade or business until the tax is paid? Ordinarily it is conceded that this remedy may be adopted for the effectual collection of the tax. Judge Cooley says : [2] " What method shall be devised for the collection of a tax, the legislature must determine, subject only to such rules, limitations, and restraints as the constitution may have imposed. Very summary methods are sanctioned by practice and precedent." In a note on the same page, he gives among the methods of collection resorted to, the following : " Making payment a condition precedent to the exercise of some legal right, such as the institution of a suit, or voting at elections, or to the carrying on of business; requiring stamps on papers, documents, manufactured articles," etc., and the United States government has employed in the internal revenue service a large force of detectives whose duty it is to discover and bring to punishment all those who are engaged in the manufacturing of distilled spirits. The right of the United States government to make the sale and manufacture of intoxicating liquors and tobacco illegal, unless a revenue license has been previously obtained, and the tax paid, has never been successfully contested, although the prosecutions for the violation of the law have been frequent.[3] But the right of the States, in taxing the professions, to make the payment of the tax a condition precedent to the lawful pursuit of the business or profession, has been questioned, and likewise denied.[4]

---

[1] Goshen v. Kern, 63 Ind. 468. In this case the occupation was that of auctioneers.

[2] Const. Lim. 645,

[3] See Henderson's Distilled Spirits, 14 Wall 44.

[4] " What is a license? It is defined to be a right given by some compe-

§ 101

" The popular understanding of the word license undoubtedly is, a permission to do something which without license would not be allowable. This we are to suppose was the sense in which it was made use of in the constitution. But this is also the legal meaning. ' The object of a license,' says Mr. Justice Manning, ' is to confer a right that does not exist without a license.' [1] Within this definition, a mere tax upon a traffic cannot be a license of the traffic, unless the tax confers some right to carry on the traffic, which otherwise would not have existed. We do not understand that such is the case here. The very act which imposed this tax repealed the previous law, which forbade the traffic and declared it illegal. The trade then became lawful, whether taxed or not; and this law, in imposing the tax, did not declare the trade illegal in case the tax was not paid. So far as we can perceive, a failure to pay the tax no more renders the trade illegal than would a like failure of a farmer to pay a tax on his farm render its cultivation illegal. The State has imposed a tax in such a case, and made such provision as has been deemed needful to insure its payment; but it has not seen fit to make the failure to pay a forfeiture of the right to pursue the calling. If the tax is paid, the traffic is lawful; but if not paid, the traffic is

tent authority to do an act which, without such authority, would be illegal. The position of a city then is that, notwithstanding Dr. Charlton has a license from the State to practice medicine anywhere in the State, yet if he exercise the privilege thereby granted in the city of Savannah without a license from the city, it will be illegal. In other words if he acts under a license from the State, he becomes a criminal. The effect of which is to elevate the ordinance of a city above the laws of the State. * * * Under the name of license Dr. Charlton cannot be prohibited from availing himself, in the city, of a privilege conferred on him by the State. He is not here contesting the authority of the city to tax him for practicing his profession; what he contends for is, that the city shall not make that illegal which by the law of the State is legal. We see no good reason why the city may not tax the practice of any profession within the corporate limits." Savannah v. Charlton, 36 Ga. 460.

[1] Chilvers v. People, 11 Mich. 43.

§ 101

equally lawful. There is consequently nothing in the case that appears to be in the nature of license." [1]

While practice and precedent justify this summary method of collecting the tax upon occupations, it cannot be successfully denied that it is in contravention of natural right. Every one has a natural right to pursue any innocent calling, without permission from the government; and while the right of the government to tax an occupation may be conceded, the imposition of the tax creates only a debt between the individual and the State; and the same remedies may be pursued, as are permissible in the collection of ordinary debts. In cases of insolvency of the individual, the indebtedness to the State for a license tax may be given priority of payment; a very summary proceeding may be devised for reducing the license tax to judgment, and securing payment by a levy upon the goods of the individual; all these ordinary and special remedies, and others of a like character, might well be provided, but to make it illegal to pursue a trade or engage in an occupation, until the tax is paid, is clearly in violation of those fundamental principles of civil liberty, which are recognized and guaranteed by all constitutional governments. The State may make the payment of taxes generally, or of poll tax in particular, a condition precedent to the exercise of the right of suffrage, for that is generally conceded by all constitutional authorities to be a privilege, and not a natural right. But the pursuit of an employment or business is a natural right, which exists independently of State authority, and can only be abridged by the exercise of the police power of the State, in the imposition of those restrictions and burdens which are necessary to prevent, in the prosecution of the trade or business, the infliction of injury upon others. The collection of a tax does not come within the exercise of police power as a prohibitory measure.

---

[1] Cooley, J., in Youngblood v. Sexton, 32 Mich. 406.

§ 101.

Another important question, in connection with licenses, is the nature of the right or privilege acquired by a license, strictly so called. A license tax, as a tax, confers no right of any kind; it simply lays a burden upon an occupation, and creates the duty to pay the tax. But when the license fee is exacted in the exercise of the police power of the State, does its payment give to the owner of the license an irrevocable right to pursue the trade or occupation, subject to no further restrictions by the State? The question has assumed a practical form in determining the effect of the passage of a law, prohibiting the sale of intoxicating liquor, upon the licenses to sell, that have been previously granted, and the time for which they were given has not expired. Can the State, after granting a license to sell intoxicating liquors for one year, during that year revoke the license by prohibiting the sale altogether? The answer must depend upon the nature of the right acquired by the license. It has been repeatedly held that a subsequent prohibition law revokes all outstanding licenses, whatever damage might result to those who, relying upon the license, as giving the right to sell during the year, have incurred obligations and expenses, for which they cannot secure any proper reimbursement except in the continued enjoyment of the license. But, however great a hardship the revocation of the license may happen to be in particular cases, since the license is an authority to do what is otherwise prohibited, and the issue of the license is one mode of exercise of the police power; if the occupation or trade can be prohibited under the constitutional limitations, because of the injury done to the public in its prosecution, the license must be held to have been given and accepted, subject always to the constant exercise of the police power in the interest of the public, the right to the exercise of which can never be bartered away by any legislative enactment. The Court of Appeals of New York gave utterance to the following language, in explaining the right to revoke licenses:

§ 101

" These licenses to sell liquors are not contracts between the State and the person licensed, giving the latter vested rights, protected on general principles and by the constitution of the United States against subsequent legislation, nor are they property in any legal or constitutional sense. They have neither the qualities of a contract nor of property, but are merely temporary permits to do what otherwise would be an offense against a general law.   They form a portion of the internal police system of the State ; are issued in the exercise of its police powers, and are subject to the direction of the State government, which may modify, revoke or continue them as it may deem fit.   If the legislature of 1857 had declared that licenses under it should be irrevocable (which it does not, but by its very terms they are revocable), the legislatures of subsequent years would not have been bound by the declaration.   The necessary powers of the legislature over all subjects of internal police, being a part of the general grant of legislative power given by the constitution, cannot be sold, given away, or relinquished.   Irrevocable grants of property and franchises may be made, if they do not impair the supreme authority to make laws for the right government of the State ; but no one legislature can curtail the power of its successors to make such laws as they may deem proper in matters of police." [1]

[1] Metropolitan Board v. Barrie, 34 N. Y. 657.   " Nor can it be doubted that the legislature has the power to prohibit the sale of spirituous or fermented liquors in any part of the State, notwithstanding a party to be affected by the law may have procured a license, under the general license laws of the State, which has not yet expired.   Such a license is in no sense a contract made by the State with the party holding the license. It is a mere permit, subject to be modified or annulled at the pleasure of the legislature, who have the power to change or repeal the law under which the license was granted."   Fell v. State, 42 Md. 71 (20 Am. Rep. 83); Commonwealth v. Kingsley, 133 Mass. 578; La Croix v. Fairfield Co. Comrs., 49 Conn. 591; Reed v. Beall, 42 Miss. 572; Coulson v. Harris, 43 Miss. 728; Robertson v. State, 12 Tex. App. 541; Schwuchon v. Chicago, 68 Ill. 444; Prohibition Amendment Cases, 24 Kan. 700.

§ 101

By the same course of reasoning is it justified by subsequent laws to subject the licensed occupation to further restrictions.   Thus it was held that the grant of a license does not prevent the State from prohibiting by a later law the sale of liquor on certain speci fied days,[1] or from prohibiting licensed saloons being open after a certain hour in the night.[2]

§ 102. **Prohibition of occupations in general.**[3] -- If the police regulation of trades and occupations cannot be instituted and enforced, except so far as a trade or occupation is harmful or threatens to be harmful i n any way to the public, however slight the restraint may be, so much the more necessary must it be to confine the exercise of the police power to the prevention of the injuries with which the public is threatened by the prosecution of a calling, when the law undertakes to deny altogether the right to pursue the calling or profession.   In proportion to the severity or extent of the police control must the strict observance of the constitutional limitations upon police power be required. There is no easier or more tempting opportunity for the practice of tyranny than in the police control of occupations.   Good and bad motives often combine to accomplish this kind of tyranny.   The zeal of the reformer, as well as cupidity and self-interest, must alike be guarded against. Both are apt to prompt the employment of means, to attain the end desired, which the constitution prohibits.

It has been so often explained and stated, that the police power must, when exerted in any direction, be confined to the imposition of those restrictions and burdens which are necessary to promote the general welfare, in other words to prevent the infliction of a public injury, that it seems

---

Reichmuller *v.* People, 44 Mich. 280.

[2] State *v.* Washington, 44 N. J. L. 605 (43 Am. Rep. 402).

[3] See *post,* § 136, for a discussion of the prohibition of the sale of personal property.

to be an unpardonable reiteration to make any further reference to it. But the principle thus enunciated is the key to every problem arising out of the exercise of police power. Applied to the question of prohibition of trades and occupations, it declares unwarranted by the constitution any law which prohibits altogether an occupation, the prosecution of which does not necessarily, and because of its unenviable character, work an injury to the public. It is not sufficient that the public sustains harm from a certain trade or employment, as it is conducted by some who are engaged in it. Nor is it sufficient that all remedies for the prevention of the evil prove defective, which fall short of total prohibition. Because many men engaged in the calling persist in so conducting the business that the public suffer, and their actions cannot otherwise be effectually controlled, is no justification of a law which prohibits an honest man from conducting the business in such a manner as not to inflict injury upon the public. In order to prohibit the prosecution of a trade altogether, the injury to the public, which furnishes the justification for such a law, must proceed from the inherent character of the business. Where it is possible to conduct the business without harm to the public, all sorts of police regulations may be instituted, which may tend to suppress the evil. Licenses may be required, the most rigid system of police inspection may be established, and heavy penalties may be imposed for the infractions of the law; but if the business is not inherently harmful, the prosecution of it cannot rightfully be prohibited to one who will conduct the business in a proper and circumspect manner. Such an one would " be deprived of his liberty " without due process of law.

With this understanding of the constitutional limitations upon the police control of employments, it is not difficult to test the constitutionality of the various laws enacted in different States, which prohibit the prosecution of certain trades and professions.

§ 102

It has been maintained in a previous section,[1] that police power does not extend to the punishment of vice. No law can make vice a crime, unless it becomes by its consequence a trespass upon the rights of the public. But while this may be true, no man can claim the right to make a trade of vice. A business that panders to vice may and should be strenuously prohibited, if possible. Fornication is a most grievous and common vice. Under this view of the limitations of police power, it could not be made a punishable offense, although it would be commendable as well as permissible to prohibit the keeping of houses of ill-fame.[2] Gambling of every kind is an evil, a vice, which cannot consistently be punished, except indirectly by a refusal of the courts to enforce gambling contracts; [3] but the State may prohibit and punish the keeping of gambling houses, and lotteries, and the sale of lottery tickets.[4] And it is the same in respect to every vice. Vice, as vice, is not subject to police regulation, but a business may always be prohibited, whose object is to furnish means for the indulgence of a vicious propensity or desire.

Fraud is a trespass upon the rights of others, and may, therefore, always be punished. When, therefore, a business consists necessarily in the perpetration of a fraud, the business may be prohibited, although fraud furnishes no justification for the prohibition of a business, which is not necessarily fraudulent, but which only affords abundant facilities for the commission. Thus it has been held within the constitutional limitations of the power of a State legis-

---

[1] See *ante*, § 68.

[2] State *v.* Williams, 11 S. C. 288; Childers *v.* Mayor, 3 Sneed, 356.

[3] See *ante*, § 99.

[4] Freleigh *v.* State, 8 Mo. 606; State *v.* Sterling, *Ib.* 797; Terry *v.* Olcott, 4 Conn. 442; Ex parte Blanchard, 9 Nev. 101; Kohn *v.* Koehler, 21 Hun, 466; Hart *v.* People, 26 Hun, 396. See State *v.* Phalen, 3 Harr. 441, in which it is held that an act, prohibiting lotteries, cannot act retrospectively, so as to affect a lottery which is carried on under special grant of the legislature

§ 102

lature to prohibit the sale of adulterated milk, even though the adulteration is made with harmless materials, such as pure water.[1] It may be said that a perfectly *bona fide* sale may be made of adulterated milk, but the position is hardly sustainable. Adulteration is essentially fraudulent, and serves no good purpose, and the sale of the adulterated article of food may be rightfully prohibited, although it produces no unwholesome effect. Sugars are now very commonly adulterated by the use of a harmless substance called glucose. There can be no doubt of the power of the State to make the sale and manufacture of adulterated sugar a misdemeanor, but the great difficulty, that is experienced in detecting and suppressing this mode of adulteration, would not justify the absolute prohibition of the sale and manufacture of sugars.

Of late years statutes have been enacted in several States, notably Indiana and Pennsylvania, which prohibit the sale of railroad tickets, except by the authorized agents of the railroads and the *bona fide* purchaser of an unused ticket or portion of a ticket, the object of the statutes being to put an end to the business of the so-called ticket " scalpers " or brokers, and the Pennsylvania statute makes it compulsory upon the railroad company to redeem an unused ticket or portion of a ticket. It has been held in both States that the law was constitutional.[2] In both cases the law was justified as a measure for the prevention of fraud upon the railroads and upon purchasers. The preamble to the Pennsylvania statute was as follows : " Whereas numerous frauds have been practiced upon unsuspecting travelers by means of the sale by unauthorized persons of rail-

---

[1] Legislature has the power in an act forbidding the sale of impure or adulterated milk, to fix a standard by which it shall be judged. People *v.* Cipperly, Ct. App. N. Y., Feb. 5, 1886; State *v.* Smythe, 14 R. I. 100 (51 Am. Rep. 344); Commonwealth *v.* Waite, 9 Allen, 264; Commonwealth *v.* Farren, 9 Allen, 489; Polenskie *v.* People, 73 N. Y. 65.

[2] Fry *v.* State of Indiana, 63 Ind. 552 (18 Am. Law Reg. (N. S.) 425); Commonwealth *v.* Wilson, 14 Phila. (Pa.) 384.

§ 102

way and other tickets, and also upon railroads and other corporations by the fraudulent use of tickets, in violation of the contract of their purchase," etc. It is not contended that the business of ticket brokerage is in itself of a fraudulent character. The business can be honestly conducted by honest man. It is only claimed that in its prosecution the business presents manifold opportunities for the commission of fraud. As has already been stated, the police regulation of an employment may extend to any length that may be necessary for the prevention and suppression of fraud in its pursuit ; but an honest man cannot be denied the privilege of conducting tne business in an honest and lawful manner because dishonest men are in the habit of practicing gross and successful frauds upon those with whom they have dealings. If that were a justifiable ground for abolishing any business, many important, perhaps some of the most beneficial, employments and professions could be properly prohibited. There is no profession or employment, that furnishes more abundant opportunities for the practice of frauds upon defenseless victims than does the profession of the law, and that profession has its ample proportion of knaves among its votaries, although the proportion is very much smaller than is popularly supposed. But it would be idle to assert that, because of the frequency of fraudulent practices among lawyers, the State could abolish the profession and forbid the practice of the law. There is no difference in principle between the two cases. The business of ticket brokerage does afford many opportunities for fraud and deceit, and it may on that account be placed under strict police surveillance. But the business serves a useful end, when honestly conducted, and the constitutional liberty of the ticket broker is violated, when he is prohibited altogether from carrying on his business.

A still stronger ground for the total prohibition of a trade or business is when the thing offered for sale is in some

§ 102

way injurious or unwholesome. It is not enough that the thing may become harmful, when put to a wrong use. It must be in itself harmful, and incapable of a harmless use. Poisonous drugs are valuable, when properly used, but they may work serious injuries, by being improperly used, even to the extent of destroying life. But it would hardly be claimed that, on that account, their sale could be prohibited altogether. Safeguards of every kind can be thrown around the sale of them, so that damage will not be sustained from an improper use of them, but that is the limit of the police control of the trade. Thus, for example, opium is a very harmful drug, when improperly used, and it is all the more dangerous because the power of resistance diminishes rapidly in proportion to the growth of the habit of taking it as a stimulant, and a miserable, degraded death is the usual end. An opium eater or smoker, not only brings down ruin upon himself, but inflicts misery upon all who stand in more or less intimate relation with him. The habit is a most dangerous vice. But on the other hand, opium is a very useful, and indispensable drug. Many a poor sufferer has had his descent to the grave made easy and painless by the judicious use of this drug. Shall the sale of opium be prohibited altogether simply because some men are apt to misuse it to their own injury? The law can prohibit the keeping of houses where those who are addicted to the opium habit are entertained with the opium pipe; the law may subject the sale of opium to such regulations as may be calculated to diminish the temptation to acquire this evil habit, but the sale of the drug for proper purposes cannot be prohibited.[1] It is possible that the sale of opium or other poisonous drugs may be prohibited to all except those who, like physicians and druggists, furnish in their professional char-

[1] State v. Ah Sam, 15 Nev. 27 (37 Am. Rep. 454; State v. Ah Chew, 16 Nev. 50 (40 Am. Rep. 488).

§ 102

acter a safe guaranty, that no improper use shall be made of
them, and to others upon the prescription of a physician.
But that is questionable.   The sale of it can, of course, be
prohibited to minors and to all who may be suffering from
some form of dementia, and to confirmed opium eaters.
But it would seem to be taking away the free will of those
who are under the law confessedly capable of taking care of
themselves, if the law were to prohibit the sale of opium to
adults in general.   But where a thing may be put to a
wrongful and injurious use, and yet may serve in some
other way a useful purpose, the law may prohibit the sale
of such things, in any case where the vendor represents
them as fit for a use that is injurious, or merely knows that
the purchaser expects to apply them to the injurious purpose.   Thus the sale of diseased or spoiled meats or other
food, as food, intending or expecting that the purchaser
is to make use of them as food, may be prohibited.   So,
also, the sale of milk which comes from cows fed in whole
or in part upon still slops, may be prohibited, if it is true
that such milk is unwholesome as human food.[1]   In the
same manner a law was held to be constitutional, which prohibited the sale of illuminating oil which ignited below a
certain heat.[2]   But it would be unconstitutional to prohibit
altogether the sale of either of these things, if they could
be employed in some other harmless and useful way.   For
example, the oil which was prohibited for illuminating purposes, may be very valuable and more or less harmless
when used for lubricating purposes.

These principles have lately been presented for consideration and review in connection with laws prohibiting the
manufacture and sale of a substance, called oleomargarine,
which resembles butter, and is intended to be used instead,
and to supply the place in trade, of the dairy product.   It
is manufactured out of certain fatty deposits of the cow,

[1] Johnson v. Simonton, 43 Cal. 542.
[2] Patterson v. Kentucky, 97 U. S. 501.

§ 102

which contain the same chemical properties as butter, varying only in degree. In New York and Missouri, and perhaps in other States, laws have been enacted, prohibiting absolutely the sale and manufacture of the oleomargarine. Although there has been some attempt made to show that this butter substitute is unwholesome as food, it seems now to be established by the most thorough chemical analyses, that there is no unwholesome ingredient in unadulterated oleomargarine. If it were shown to be unwholesome as food, its sale for the purpose of human consumption could without doubt be prohibited. But the only valid objection to its sale is the close resemblance to genuine butter, and the consequent opportunity for the perpetration of fraud. And this was the sole ground upon which the constitutionality of the law was sustained by the Supreme Court of Missouri.[1]

But it is plain from the foregoing principles, that a total prohibition of the sale of a thing cannot be justified on any such grounds. The sale must be necessarily fraudulent, in order to admit of its absolute prohibition. The law, therefore, which prohibits the sale of oleomargarine, granting that it is a wholesome article of food, is unconstitutional, and so it is decided by the New York Court of Appeals, in considering the validity of the New York statute.[2] In the United States Circuit Court, the constitutionality of the Mis-

---

[1] "The central idea of the statute before us seems very manifest; it was, in our opinion, the prevention of facilities for selling or manufacturing a spurious article of butter, resembling the genuine article so closely in its external appearance, as to render it easy to deceive purchasers into buying that which they would not buy but for the deception. The history of legislation on this subject, as well as the phraseology of the act itself, very strongly tend to confirm this view. If this was the purpose of the enactment now under discussion, we discover nothing in its provisions which enables us, in the light of the authorities, to say that the legislature, when passing the act, exceeded the power confided to that department of the government; and, unless we can say this, we cannot hold the act as being anything less than valid." State v. Addington, 77 Mo. 118.

[2] People v. Marx, 99 N. Y. 307 (52 Am. Rep. 314).

§ 102

souri statute was disputed in a petition by the party to the cause, who prayed for the intervention of the United States courts to prevent the enforcement of the law. The petition was denied, on the ground that the United States court has no jurisdiction, but in delivering the opinion of the court, Justice Miller expressed the opinion that the law was in violation of the constitution of Missouri.[1] The practice of deception in the sale of the oleomargarine may be made punishable as a misdemeanor, and the law may require, as in Ohio, the oleomargarine to be put up for sale in packages on which shall be distinctly and durably painted, stamped, or marked, the name of each article used or entering into the composition of such substance.[2] A law has lately been proposed in New York, by which every one dealing in oleomargarine, is required to put up a sign to that effect, and in the manufacture of the substance it is required to be so colored that it may be readily distinguished from pure butter. There can be no doubt as to the constitutionality of such laws, for their only effect is the prevention of fraud. They do not interfere with the honest sale of a wholesome article of food.

It has been maintained in one case,[3] that the judgment of a town board of aldermen that a certain article of food is unwholesome, and that therefore the sale of it can be prohibited, is not open to inquiry in the ordinary courts. There can be no doubt that the scientific correctness of the judgment of the legislative body in such a case is a judicial question, and therefore subject to review by the courts, for in no other way can the legislatures be kept within the limitations of the constitution. If it is only necessary for the legislature to pronounce a calling injurious to the public, in order to justify its prohibition, there is no limit to the police power of the government. Constitutional restrictions

---

[1] In re John Brosnahan, Jr., 4 McCrary, 1.
[2] Palmer *v.* State, 39 Ohio St. — ; 3 Ohio Law J. 708.
[3] Johnson *v.* Simonton, 43 Cal. 242.

§ 102

would exert no greater influence than disorganized public opinion ; and absolutism, monarchical, aristocratic or democratic, according to the circumstances, would be the corner stone of such a government, at least in theory. The recognition of the rights of the minority would be only a matter of special grace and favor.

An important question, in this phase of police power, which will soon demand an explicit answer, is how far and in what manner the government may regulate and prohibit the manufacture and sale of dynamite and other compounds of nitro-glycerine. The deadly character of the composition; the ready opportunity which its portability and easy manufacture afford for its application to base and criminal uses; the ability of a few miscreants with a few pounds of it to endanger and perhaps destroy the lives of many people, demolish public and other buildings, and bring about a state of anarchy in general, all of which can be done with very little danger of detection; these considerations, if any, would most certainly justify the prohibition of the manufacture and sale of so dangerous an article. And yet a law would be unconstitutional which prohibited absolutely the manufacture and sale of dynamite and nitro-glycerine. For these powerful agencies are of great value and service in many legitimate trades and occupations. The business may be placed under the strictest police supervision ; heavy penalties may be imposed upon those who knowingly sell these articles to persons to be used for criminal purposes; a heavy bond of indemnity may be required of each dealer, and only men of reputable character, under license, may be permitted to carry on the business: these regulations are all reasonable and constitutional, for they do not extend beyond the prevention of the evil which threatens the public. A total prohibition of the trade in dynamite would not only prevent the evil, but also prohibit the lawful use of a most valuable agency, and would therefore be unconstitutional.

§ 102

§ 103. **Prohibition of the liquor trade.** — This phase of police supervision is not only the most common, but the moral and economical conditions, which induce its exercise, are so great and pressing, and the popular excitement attending all agitations against intemperance, like all popular agitations, is usually so little under the control of reason, that it is hard to obtain, from those who are attempting to form and mould public opinion. any approach to a dispassionate consideration of the constitutional limitations upon the police power of the State, in their application to the regulation and prohibition of the liquor trade. Drunkenness is distressingly common, notwithstanding the great increase in the number of those who practice and preach total abstinence from the use of intoxicating liquors; and the multitude of cases of misery and want, caused directly by this common vice, cry aloud for some measure whereby the evil of drunkenness may be banished from the earth. It is no wonder when the zealous reformer contemplates the careworn face of the drunkard's wife, and the rags of his children, that he appeals to the law-making power to enact any and all laws which seem to promise the banishment of drunkenness; forgetting, as it is very natural for him to do, since zealots are rarely possessed of a philosophical and judicial mind, that to make a living law, it must be demanded, and its enactment compelled by an irresistible public opinion : and where the law in question does not have for its object the prevention or punishment of a trespass upon rights, it is impossible to obtain for it the enthusiastic and practically unanimous support, which is necessary to secure a proper enforcement of it. Furthermore, if in any community public opinion is so aroused into activity as to be able to secure the enforcement of a law, having for its object the prevention of a vice, the moral force of such a public opinion will be amply sufficient to suppress it. The temperance agitator does not usually dwell on these scientific objections to temperance laws, or if he does, he either gives to them a flat and unreasoning denial, which makes all further argument impossible, or he justifies the enactment of an otherwise useless law by the claim that the enactment would arouse public attention to the evils of drunkenness, and by making persistent, though unsuccessful, attempts to enforce the law, public opinion will be educated up to the point of giving the proper support to the law. Educate public opinion up to the point of giving proper support to the law! If there is one principle that the history of law and legislation teaches with unerring precision, it is, not only the utter futility as a corrective measure of a law, whose enactment is not the necessary and unavoidable resultant of the social forces, then at play in organized society, but also the great injury inflicted upon law in general by the enactment of laws before their time. Nothing so weakens the reverence for law, and diminishes its effectiveness as a restraint upon wrong and crime, as the passage of stillborn laws, laws which are dead letters before they have been promulgated to the people. And why are laws for the prevention or punishment of vice ineffectual? Because such a law cannot enlist in its cause the strong motive power of self-interest. I do not mean that it cannot be demonstrated that each individual in the community will be benefited by the effective control of drunkenness. But I do mean that the people at large cannot be made to feel, sufficiently acutely, the necessity of enforcing these laws, in order to make them effective remedies for the suppression of the evil. A man sees a pick-pocket steal his neighbor's handkerchief, while on his way through the public streets. He will instantly, involuntarily, give the alarm, and probably would render what aid was necessary or possible, in securing the arrest of this offender against the laws of the country. The same man, a few steps further, sees another violating the law against the sale of intoxicating liquor; and although he may be an active member of some temperance organization, he will be sure to pass on his way,

§ 103

and say and do nothing to bring this offender to justice. Why this difference of action in the two cases? In the first case, the act was a trespass upon the right of property of another, and self-interest, through fear of a like trespass upon his own rights of property, prompted the man who saw the crime to aid in the arrest of the criminal. In the latter case, no man's rights were trampled upon; the unlawful act inflicted no direct damage upon the man who witnessed the violation of the law, and consequently self-interest did not impel him to activity in support of the law.

But these considerations constitute only philosophical objections to such laws, and can only be addressed to the legislative body, as reasons why they should not be passed. They do not enter into a consideration of the constitutionality of the laws after they have been enacted. If the constitution does not prohibit the enactment of these laws, the only obstacle in the way of their passage is the unwillingness of the legislators. The question to be answered is, therefore, are the laws for the regulation and prohibition of the liquor trade constitutional? The preceding sections of the present chapter contain an enunciation of all the principles of constitutional law, which are necessary to the solution of the present problem. But a recapitulation is necessary, before applying them to the particular case in question. It has been demonstrated, and satisfactorily explained in its application to a sufficient number of parallel and similar cases, in order to lay it down as an invariable rule, that no trade can be subjected to police regulation of any kind, unless its prosecution involves some harm or injury to the public or to third persons, and in any case the regulation cannot extend beyond the evil which is to be restrained. It has also been maintained and, I think satisfactorily established, that no trade can be prohibited altogether, unless the evil is inherent in the character of the trade, so that the trade, however conducted, and whatever may be the character of the person engaged in it, must necessarily produce

§ 103

injury upon the public or upon individual third persons. It has likewise been shown that, while vice, as vice, can never be the subject of criminal law, yet a trade, which has for its object or necessary consequence, the provision of means for the gratification of a vice, may be prohibited, and its prosecution made a criminal offense. These principles, if sustainable at all, must have a universal application. They admit of no exceptional cases. If the reader has given his assent to the truth of them, in their application to other cases of police regulation of employments, his inability to adhere to them, in their application to the police regulation of the liquor trade, indicates either a lack of courage to maintain his convictions in the face of popular clamor, or an obscurity of his judgment through his sympathetic emotions, which are aroused in considering the gigantic evil to be combated.

It has never been claimed that any one could be punished for drunkenness, unless he thrusts the fact upon the attention of the public, so that it offends the sensibilities of the community, and in consequence becomes a public offense. If a man displays his drunkenness on the public thoroughfares to the annoyance and inconvenience of the public, he can be punished therefor. But if he chooses to degrade himself by intoxication in the privacy of his own home or apartments, he commits no offense against the public, and is consequently not subject to police regulation. But the man who proposed to make a profit out of his proneness to drunkenness, would be guilty of a public wrong, and could be punished for it. It is perfectly reasonable for the law to prohibit the sale of liquor to minors, lunatics, persons under the influence of liquor and confirmed drunkards, and impose a penalty upon the dealer who knowingly does so In very many of the States there are statutes in which it is provided, that whoever is injured by the wrongful acts of a drunken person may maintain an action for damages against the dealer in liquor who sold or gave the liquor

§ 103

which caused intoxication in whole or in part, where the
intoxicated person was neither a confirmed drunkard, nor
a minor, nor a lunatic, nor under the influence of liquor,
when he purchased the liquor. This legislation has been
frequently sustained by the courts in its broadest application, and it is believed, has in no case been declared unconstitutional, although often contested.[1] So far as these
statutes prohibit the sale of liquor to persons who, from
their known weakness of character, may be expected to
make an improper use of it to their own harm and the
injury of others, and subject the dealer, who sells liquor to
these classes of persons, to an action for the damages that
third persons may have sustained from their drunken antics,
it cannot be doubted that the statutes are constitutional.
These persons, who are laboring under some mental or other
infirmity which renders them unable to take care of themselves, can very properly be placed under the guardianship
of the State, if not in all cases for their own benefit, at
least for the protection of the public ; and where a dealer
in intoxicating liquors sells to such an one, in violation of
the statute, he does a wrongful thing, an act prohibited by
a constitutional law, and he may therefore be held responsible for every damage flowing from his wrongful act, which
might reasonably have been anticipated. But when the
statutes go farther and make the dealer responsible for
every wrongful act committed by any and every person
while in a state of intoxication, whose intoxication was
caused by the liquor which the dealer had sold, whether
the dealer knew of his aptitude to intoxication or not, they
can only be justified on the principle that the prosecution

---

[1] Roth v. Eppy, 80 Ill. 283; Wilkerson v. Rust, 57 Ind. 172; Fountain
v. Draper, 49 Ill. 441; Church v. Higham, 44 Iowa, 482; Goodenough v.
McGrew, 44 Iowa, 670; Gaussby v. Perkins, 30 Mich. 492; Badore v.
Newton, 54 N. H. 117; Baker v. Pope, 2 Hun, 556; Quain v. Russell, 12
Hun, 376; Berthoff v. O'Reilley, 74 N. Y. 515; Baker v. Beckwith, 29
Ohio St. 314; State v. Ludington, 33 Wis. 107; Whitman v. Devere, 33
Wis. 70.

§ 103

of the liquor trade is unlawful in itself, and the constitutionality of such laws must depend upon the constitutionality of laws for the prohibition of the liquor trade in general. For no one can be held responsible for damage, flowing consequentially from an act of his, unless that act is unlawful in itself, or he has done it in an unlawful manner. If the sale of liquor is a lawful occupation he can not be held for a damage that is not the result of his failure to conduct the business in a lawful manner, and he cannot be said to have conducted a lawful business in an unlawful manner, when he sells liquor to one who may not reasonably be expected to become intoxicated.

Is then the absolute prohibition of the liquor trade a constitutional exercise of legislative authority under the ordinary constitutional limitations? It may be stated that the decisions of the courts, in different parts of the country, have very generally sustained laws for the prohibition of the sale of intoxicating liquors, in any manner, form or bulk whatever, and on the ground that the trade works an injury to society, and may, therefore, be prohibited.[1]

---

[1] Metropolitan Board Excise v. Barrie, 34 N. Y. 657; Wynehame v. People, 3 Kern, 435; Warren v. Mayor, etc., Charleston, 2 Gray, 98; Fisher v. McGirr, 1 Gray, 26; Jones v. People, 14 Ill. 196; Goddard v. Jacksonville, 15 Ill. 588; People v. Hawley, 3 Gibbs, 330; Preston v. Drew, 33 Me. 559; State v. Noyes, 30 N. H. 279; State v. Snow, 3 R. I. 68; State v. Peckham, Ib. 293; State v. Paul, 5 R. I. 185; State v. Wheeler, 25 Conn. 290; Lincoln v. Smith, 27 Vt. 328; Sante v. State, 2 Clarke (Iowa), 165; Prohibitory Am. Cases, 25 Kan. 751 (37 Am. Rep. 284); Bartemeyer v. Iowa, 18 Wall. 729; State v. Mugler, 29 Kan. 252 (44 Am. Rep. 634); Perdue v. Ellis, 18 Ga. 586; Austin v. State, 10 Mo. 591; State v. Searcy, 20 Mo. 489; Our House v. State, 4 Greene (Iowa), 172; Zumhoff v. State, Ib. 526; State v. Donehey, 8 Iowa, 396; State v. Carney, 20 Iowa, 82; State v. Baughman, Ib. 497; State v. Gurney, 37 Me. 156; State v. Burgoyne, 7 Lea, 173 (40 Am. Rep. 60); State v. Prescott, 27 Vt. 194; Lincoln v. Smith, 27 Vt. 328; State v. Brennan's Liquors, 25 Conn. 278; State v. Common Pleas, 36 N. J. 72 (13 Am. Rep. 422). "The measures best calculated to prevent those evils and preserve a healthy tone of morals in the community, are subjects proper for the consideration of the legislature. Courts of justice have nothing to do with them, other than to discharge

§ 103

The citations and quotations may be continued without
end, but the invariable argument is that the liquor trade
has, following in its train, certain evils, which would not
exist, if the trade were prohibited altogether; consequently, the trade may rightfully be prohibited. If the
necessary consequence of the sale of liquor was the intoxication of the purchaser, because the liquor could not be
used without this or other injury to the person using it and
to others, then the trade may be prohibited in accordance
with the principles, which have been established in preceding sections of this chapter, in application to other employments. In such a case, the trade would   be   essentially

their legitimate duties in carrying into execution such laws as the legislature may establish, unless, indeed, they find that the legislature in making a particular law, has disregarded the restraints imposed upon it by
the constitution of this State, or the United States." State v. Brennan,
25 Conn. 278. "There is, however, no occasion to pursue this topic.
The law in question, is, in our opinion, obnoxious to no objection, which
could be derived from the establishment of the doctrine advanced by the
defendant. It is not different in its character, although it may be more
stringent in some of its provisions from those numerous laws, which
have been passed in almost all civilized communities and in ours from the
earliest settlement of our State, regulating the traffic in spirituous
liquors, and which are based on the power possessed by every sovereign
State, to provide by law, as it shall deem fit for the health, morals, peace
and general welfare of the State, and which, whatever may have been
thought of their expediency, have been invariably sustained as being
within the competency of the legislature to enact." State v. Wheeler,
Ib. "The weight of authority is overwhelming that no such immunity
has heretofore existed, as would prevent State legislatures from regulating and even prohibiting the traffic in intoxicating drinks with a solitary exception. That exception is the case of a law operating so rigidly
upon property in existence at the time of its passage, absolutely prohibiting its sale, as to amount to depriving the owner of his property."
Justice Miller in Bartemeyer v. Iowa, 18 Wall. 129. "There certainly are
provisions in all our State constitutions, which will not permit legislative bodies wantonly to interfere with or destroy many of the natural or
constitutional rights of the citizens. Of this class are those provisions
which secure the freedom of the press and of speech, and the freedom of
debate. But we are not aware that there is any provision in our consti-
which would prevent the legislature from prohibiting dram selling
entirely." Napton, J., in Austin v. State, 10 Mo. 591.

§ 103

injurious to the public. But it does not necessarily follow that the sale of the liquor will cause the intoxication of the purchaser. The number of those who are likely to become intoxicated by the liquor they purchase is very small, in comparison with the thousands who buy and use it in moderation, without ever approaching the state of intoxication. We cannot say, therefore, that the sale of liquor necessarily causes intoxication. On the contrary, the facts establish the truth of the statement that cases, in which the sale of liquor is followed by intoxication, constitute the exception to the general rule. The liquor dealer may, and probably in the majority of cases does, become responsible for the intoxication that follows a sale in these exceptional cases by knowingly selling liquor to one who is intoxicated at the time, or is likely to become intoxicated, and he can undoubtedly be punished for such a wrong against society; but the main and proximate cause of these cases of intoxication is the weakness of the purchaser, against which no law probably can furnish for him any effective protection.

But it is often urged as a justification of prohibition that even a moderate use of intoxicating liquor is injurious to the health. A great many people, including the present writer, believe this to be true, and very probably it is. But the majority of people of the present generation think differently. Thousands maintain that it is a harmless indulgence, and as many more declare it to be positively beneficial. We, who are opposed to the use of intoxicating liquors, except for medicinal purposes, are convinced that these people are wrong; but they are entitled to their own opinions, as well as we, and it would be just as much an act of tyranny to compel them to abandon their ideas and practices, in conformity with our own views of what is good for them, as it would be to pass a law prohibiting the eating of hot bread because the majority of the people believe it to be injurious to the health. It is true that a man may be prohibited from doing that which will work an injury to

§ 103

his offspring by the inheritance of diseases caused by the prohibited practice. While it is probably true that intoxicating liquor, like any other stimulant, will produce a more or less lasting effect upon the constitution of the person addicted to its use, it is by no means a demonstrated fact that its use is the cause of any constitutional disease. Whatever injury can be attributed to the moderate use of liquor, so far at least as our present knowledge extends, is functional and not constitutional. If these reasons be well founded, then the liquor trade is not necessarily injurious, in a legal sense, to the public; and where injury does result, it is either caused by the shortcomings of the purchaser, without any participation in the wrong by the seller, as where he does not know, and cannot be supposed to know, that intoxication will very likely follow the sale; or the responsibility may be laid at the door of the seller, when he knowingly sells to one who is likely to make an improper use of it. The seller may in the latter case be punished, and his right to pursue the trade thereafter may be taken away altogether, as a penalty for his violation of the law in this regard. But the liquor trade can not, for these reasons, be prohibited altogether, if it be true that no trade can be prohibited entirely, unless its prosecution is essentially and necessarily injurious to the public. Even the prohibition of saloons, that is, where intoxicating liquor is sold and served, to be drunk on the premises, cannot be justified on these grounds.[1]

[1] As stated already, the prohibition of the sale of intoxicating liquor has seldom been declared to be unconstitutional, but in the following opinion from the Supreme Court of Indiana, which has, however, been subsequently overruled, or at least departed from, a law which prohibited the manufacture of spirituous liquor was declared to be unconstitutional: —

" The court knows, as matter of general knowledge, and is capable of judicially asserting the fact, that the use of beer, etc., as a beverage, is not necessarily hurtful, any more than the use of lemonade or ice cream. It is the abuse, and not the use, of all these beverages that is hurtful. But the legislature enacted the law in question upon the assumption that the

§ 103

It is quite common for the legislature to pass laws prohibiting the sale of intoxicating liquors in the neighborhood
of schools, colleges, and lunatic asylums, and these laws
have uniformly been sustained as constitutional, unless in
some of the States they have come under the constitutional
prohibition for being special laws, the right to enact which
is taken away from the legislature by some of the constitutions.[1]   Surely, if in any case prohibition laws can be sustained on principle, their enactment would find ample justification in the removal of temptation to drink from those
who, on account of their infancy or mental deficiencies, are
not as able to maintain an effective resistance without this
protection.   But if the principles heretofore developed be
at all reliable, as a guide in search of the constitutional
limitations upon the police control of trades and employments, these special prohibitory laws are subject to the

manufacture and sale of beer, etc., were necessarily destructive to the
community; and in acting upon that assumption, in our own judgment,
it has invaded unwarrantably the right to private property and its use as
a beverage and article of traffic.

"What harm, we ask, does the mere manufacture or sale or temperate
use of beer do to any one?   And the manufacturer or seller does not necessarily know what use is to be made by the purchaser of the article.   It may
be a proper one.   And if an improper one, it is not the fault of the manufacturer or seller, but it is thus appropriated by the voluntary act of another person, and by his own wrong.   And will the general principle be
asserted that to prevent the abuse of useful things, the government shall
assume the dispensation of them to all the citizens — put all under guardianship?   Fire-arms and gunpowder are not manufactured and sold to
shoot innocent persons with, but are often so misapplied.   Axes are not
made and sold to break heads with, but are often used for that purpose. * * *   Yet who, for all this, has ever contended that the manufacture and sale of these articles should be prohibited as being nuisances,
or be monopolized by government?   We repeat, the manufacture and
sale of liquors are not necessarily hurtful, and this court has the right to
judicially inquire into and act upon the validity of the law in question."
Beabe v. State, 6 Ind. 501.

[1] Dorman v. State, 34 Ala. 216; Boyd v. Bryant, 35 Ark. 69 (37 Am.
Rep. 6; Trammell v. Bradley, 37 Ark. 356; Ex parte McClain, 61 Cal. 436
(44 Am. Rep. 554); Bronson v. Oberlin, 41 Ohio St. 476 (52 Am. Rep. 90).

§ 103

same constitutional objection, that the trade which they prohibit is not essentially and necessarily harmful to society,
even under the peculiar circumstances which furnish a
special reason for the enactment of the law.

It has been stated that the reasons usually assigned for
the enactment of prohibitory laws, viz.: the prevention of
drunkenness, will not satisfy the constitutional requirements even in the prohibition of drinking saloons, although
most of the drunkenness from which the State suffers is
caused by the existence of taverns or saloons, where liquor
is sold to be drunk on the premises.   For it would be manifestly untrue to assert that every frequenter of a saloon
became intoxicated, and during intoxication did more or
less damage to the public, or to third persons : consequently the sale of liquor in a saloon does not necessarily
bring about the intoxication of the buyer or of his friends.
But there is another, and an all-sufficient, reason for the
prohibition of drinking saloons, if the legislature should
deem it expedient to prohibit them.   It is that they constitute the places of meeting for all the more or less disreputable and dangerous classes of the community, and breaches
of the peace of a more or less serious character almost invariably occur in bar-rooms.   It is true that there are many
comparatively quiet saloons, where men of good social
standing resort, and which are to be distinguished from the
low groggeries where the vicious and the criminal classes
congregate, but the keeping of a drinking saloon cannot be
conducted so that public disorders cannot possibly occur,
and some of the most distressing breaches of the peace,
resulting in the death of one or more, have occurred in this
better class of saloons.   The suppression and control of
the public disorders caused by the keeping of saloons constitute a heavy burden upon the tax payer, and the cause
of them may be removed by a prohibitory law, or restrained
and restricted in number by the imposition of a high license,
according as it may seem best to the law-making power.

§ 103

As a matter of course, if the absolute prohibition of drinking saloons is constitutional, it would be lawful to subject them to more or less strict police regulations, where the regulations have for their reasonable object the prevention of some special evil which the prosecution of the trade threatens to the public. Thus it has been held reasonable to compel the closing of saloons on Sunday,[1] not only because the pursuit of the business would be a violation of the ordinary Sunday laws,[2] but also because there is increased danger on that day of breaches of the peace in bar-rooms, on account of the idleness of those persons who are most likely to frequent such places. It has also been held to be reasonable, for similar reasons, to prohibit the sale of liquors on primary and other election days;[3] on court, show and fair days;[4] compelling the saloons to be closed at a certain hour in the night,[5] and in one case it was maintained to be lawful for the legislature to authorize the Board of Police Commissioners to order all saloons to be closed, "temporarily," whenever in their judgment the public peace required it.[6] It has also been declared to be reasonable to prohibit the erection of screens and shutters before places in which liquors are sold.[7]

This, therefore, is the conclusion reached after a careful

[1] Hudson v. Geary, 4 R. I. 485; Gabel v. Houston, 29 Tex. 335; State v. Ludwig, 21 Minn. 202.

[2] As to which see *ante*, § 76.

[3] State v. Christman, 67 Ind. 328.

[4] Grills v. Jonesboro, 8 Baxt. 247.

[5] State v. Welch, 36 Conn. 215; State v. Freeman, 38 N. H. 426; Smith v. Knoxville, 3 Head, 245; Maxwell v. Jonesboro, 11 Heisk. 257; Baldwin v. Chicago, 68 Ill. 418; Platteville v. Bell, 43 Wis. 488. In Ward v. Greenville, 1 Baxt. 228.(35 Am. Rep. 700), it was held to be unreasonable to compel saloons to be closed between 6 p. m. and 6. a. m. But a statute prohibiting sale of liquors between 11 p. m. and 5 a. m. was held to be constitutional. Hedderich v. State, 101 Ind. 564 (51 Am. Rep. 768.)

[6] State v. Strauss, 49 Md. 288.

[7] Commonwealth v. Costello, 133 Mass. 192; Commonwealth v. Casey, 134 Mass. 194; Shultz v. Cambridge, 38 Ohio St. 659.

§ 103

consideration of all the constitutional reasons for and against the prohibition of the liquor trade : the prohibition of the manufacture and sale of spirituous and intoxicating liquors is unconstitutional, unless it is confined to the prohibition of drinking saloons, and the prohibition of the sale of liquor to minors, lunatics, confirmed drunkards, and persons in a state of intoxication. As has already been explained, there is an almost unbroken array of judicial opinions against this position, and there is not any reasonable likelihood that there will be any immediate revulsion in the opinions of the courts. But it is the duty of a constitutional jurist to press his views of constitutional law upon the attention of the legal world, even though they place him in opposition to the current of authority.

§ 104.   **Police control of employments in respect to locality.**[1]— Another more or less common mode of police regulation of employments is the determination of the localities, in which the trade will be allowed. Very many trades are beneficial to society in general, and it would be unconstitutional to prohibit them altogether, and yet they may be subjected to whatever reasonable regulations may be needed to avert or prevent some special danger, which is threatened by the prosecution of them. Very many instances of such regulations have been given in preceding sections of this chapter. A trade may be highly dangerous or offensive to the people, when prosecuted in one locality, while the danger or offensiveness may be dissipated altogether or considerably abated, if it is carried on in a different community. Machine shops and the cotton trade may be cited as a good example of trades, which are more dangerous in one locality than in some other ; while a soap factory or a tannery may be referred to as illustrating cases, in which offensiveness would constitute a serious objection

---

[1] See *post* § 122c in respect to the confinement of objectionable trades to certain localities.

§ 104

to their prosecution in the residential portion of a city. It would not constitute any unreasonable interference with the right to pursue without restraint any lawful trade or employment, if the legislative authority should require the prosecution of such trades and occupations within a certain area of a populous city, and prohibit them outside of such area. This power has been often exercised, and but rarely questioned. It has been held reasonable to prohibit the keeping of slaughter-houses in certain parts of the city,[1] and to exclude hacks from certain streets.[2] But the prohibition as to locality must be reasonable, in order that it may not offend the constitutional limitations. If the area, in which the prosecution of a useful trade is prohibited, is so extensive that it amounts to a practical prohibition of the trade, the regulation will be unconstitutional. Thus it has been held to be unreasonable to prohibit the establishment of a steam engine in the city.[3] A law has also been declared to be unconstitutional, which prohibited the manufacture of cigars in tenement houses, on the ground that the public health or comfort was endangered by the prosecution of the trade in such places.[4] Not only has the legislature exercised the power of confining the prosecution of certain trades to certain localities, but it has very often, particularly in respect to the vending of fresh meat and vegetables, prohibited the plying of the trade in any other place than the market, established and regulated by government. This regulation is very common in all parts of this country, and has frequently been the source of litigation; but it has generally been held to be reasonable.[5] In the

---

[1] Cronin v. People, 82 N. Y. 318 (37 Am. Rep. 564); Metropolitan Board of Health v. Heister, 37 N. Y. 661; Milwaukee v Gross, 21 Wis. 241.)

[2] Commonwealth v. Stodder, Cush. 561.

[3] Baltimore v. Redecke, 49 Md. 217 (33 Am. Rep. 239).

[4] Matter of Jacobs, 98 N. Y. 98.

[5] Buffalo v. Webster, 10 Wend. 99; Bush v. Seabury 8 Johns. 418; Winnsboro v. Smart, 11 Rich. L. 551; Bowling Green v. Carson, 10 Bush, 64; New Orleans v. Stafford, 27 La. Ann. 417 (21 Am. Rep. 563); Wart-

§ 104

case of New Orleans *v.* Stafford,[1] the Supreme Court of Louisiana presents forcibly the reasons which justify this police regulation:

" Has the legislature the power to make the regulation which it made by this act of the twenty-sixth of February, 1874, declaring that private markets shall not be established, continued or kept open within twelve squares of a public market? This question, we think, must be answered in the affirmative. And the power arises from the nature of things, and what is termed a police power. It springs from the great principle,. *salus populi suprema est lex.* There is in the defendant's case no room for any well grounded complaint of the violation of a vested private right, for the privilege, if he really possessed it, of keeping a private market, was acquired subordinately to the right existing in the sovereign to exercise the police power to regulate the peace and good order of the city, and to provide for and maintain its cleanliness and salubrity. By way of illustrating this necessarily existing power to regulate the number, location and management of markets, take the city of New Orleans, in a warm climate, located in a low district of country, surrounded by marshes and swamps, which in the hot season under favorable conditions envelopes its large population in a malarious atmosphere. Under such circumstances the danger of epidemics becomes imminent. It behooves the city authorities at such periods to be on the alert to obviate local causes of disease within the limits of the city. Among such causes the decay of animal and vegetable matter is a prominent one. The markets therefore must on that account be strictly attended to and such measures adopted in regard to them as in the judg-

man *v.* Philadelphia, 33 Pa. St. 202; St. Louis *v.* Weber, 14 Mo. 547; Ash *v.* People, 11 Mich. 347; LeClaire *v.* Davenport, 13 Iowa 210. But see *contra* Bethune *v.* Hayes, 28 Ga. 560; Caldwell *v.* Alton, 34 Ill. 416; Bloomington *v.* Wahl, 46 Ill. 489.

[1] 27 La. Ann. 417 (51 Am. Rep 563.)

ment of the proper authorities, the public health may require." * * * " We presume it will not be denied that under circumstances of peril and emergency the law-maker would have the right to abolish or suspend an occupation imperiling the public safety. This power is inherent in him. He may exercise it prospectively for prevention as well as *pro rata*, for immediate effect. It is within his discretion when to exercise this power and persons under license to pursue such occupations as may in the public need and interest be affected by the exercise of the police power, embark in those occupations subject to the disadvantages which may result from a legal exercise of that power." [1]

[1] " The necessity of a public market, where the producers and consumers of fresh provisions can be brought together at stated times for the purchase and sale of those commodities is very apparent. There is nothing which more imperatively requires the constant supervision of some authority which can regulate and control it. Such authority in this country is seldom if ever vested in individuals. It can never be so well placed, as where it is put into the hands of the corporate officers who represent the people immediately interested. A municipal corporation, comprising a town of any considerable magnitude, without a public market subject to the regulation of its own local authorities, would be an anomaly which at present has no existence among us. The State might undoubtedly withhold from a town or city the right to regulate its markets, but to do so would be an act of tyranny, and a gross violation of the principle universally conceded to be just, that every community, whether large or small, should be permitted to control, in their own way, all those things which concern nobody but themselves. The daily supply of food to the people of a city is emphatically their own affair. It is true that the persons who bring provisions to the market have also a sort of interest in it, but not such an interest as entitles them to a voice in its regulation. The laws of a market (I am now using the word in its larger sense) are always made by the persons who reside at the place, and that whether they be buyers or sellers. It is, therefore, the common law of Pennsylvania, that every municipal corporation which has power to make by-laws and establish ordinances to promote the general welfare and preserve the peace of a town or city, may fix the time or places of holding public markets for the sale of food, and make such other regulations concerning them as may conduce to the public interest. We take this to be the true rule, because it is necessary and proper, in harmony with the sentiments of the people, universally practiced by the towns,

§ 104

The same principles would govern in their application to cases of a similar character. It cannot be doubted, for example, that the State may directly, or through a municipal corporation, establish a public slaughter-house, where butchers must bring their cattle to be slaughtered, and prohibit the slaughtering of cattle elsewhere. Compelling persons to pursue such callings in public places, established and regulated by the State, is looked upon as reasonable. But when the State, instead of establishing a public market or slaughter-house, and placing it under the management and control of State officials, grants to a private individual or corporation the exclusive privilege of maintaining a public market or slaughter-house, serious objections are raised to the constitutionality of the legislative act, and the franchise is often claimed to be void because it creates a monopoly.

§ 105. **Monopolies.** — As a general proposition, it may be conceded that the creation of a monopoly out of an ordinary calling is unconstitutional. But it will not do to say that all monopolies are void. Every man has, under reasonable regulations, a right to pursue any one of the ordinary callings of life, as long as its pursuit does not involve evil or danger to society. And a law which granted to one man, or a few individuals, the exclusive privilege of prosecuting the trade, would be in violation of the constitutional rights of those who are prohibited from pursuing the same calling. This is clear. On the other hand, when the State bestows upon one or more the privileges of pursuing a calling, or trade, the prosecution of which is not a common natural right, a monopoly is created, but no right of the individual is violated, for with the abolition of the monopoly thus created would disappear all right to carry on the trade. The trade never existed before as a lawful calling. Such

and universally submitted to by the residents of the country." Wartman *v.* Philadelphia, 33 Pa. St. 202.

§ 105

monopolies are valid, and free from all constitutional objections.[1] The grant of exclusive franchises is a matter of
relatively common occurrence, and is rarely questioned.

As long as the question is confined to the case of exceptional franchises, as for example, railroads, bridges, ferries,
and the like, there seems to be no doubt of the power of the
State to grant an exclusive franchise. But when the same
principle is applied to the more common and numerous
franchises, as for example, a more or less extraordinary use
of the streets of a city, the cases do not always support the
distinctions that have been made. On the one hand it has
been held to be reasonable to grant to one or more the exclusive right to remove the carcasses of animals and other
offal of a city.[2] But, on the other hand, it has been held in
some States, although a different conclusion is reached in
other States, that the exclusive grant to a company of the
right to furnish the city with gas, was unlawful and void, as
being a monopoly: " As, then, no consideration whatever, either of a public or private character, was reserved
for the grant; and as the business of manufacturing
and selling gas is an ordinary business, like the manufacturing of leather, or any other article of trade in
respect to which the government has no exclusive prerogative, we think that so far as the restriction of other
persons than the plaintiffs from using the streets for the
purpose of distributing gas by means of pipes, can fairly
be viewed as intended to operate as a restriction upon
its free manufacture and sale, it comes directly within the
definition and description of a monopoly; and although we
have no direct constitutional provision against a monopoly,
yet the whole theory of a free government is opposed to
such grants, and it does not require even the aid which may
be derived from the Bill of Rights, the first section of which

---

[1] Cooley on Torts, pp. 277, 278.

[2] Vandine, Petitioner, 9 Pick. 187 (7 Am. Dec. 351); River Rendering
Co. v. Behr, 7 Mo. App. 345.

§ 105

declares ' that no man or set of men are entitled to exclusive public emoluments ' to render them void." [1]

Certainly it is a franchise to make excavations for the laying of pipes for the distribution of the gas, very different from " the manufacture of leather ;" and being a franchise, the enjoyment of it may be made an exclusive privilege. In Tennessee it has been held that even if monopolies in general are prohibited, it is nevertheless competent to grant the exclusive right to a company to supply a city with water for a term of years.[2] In Iowa, in a case involving much doubt, it was declared to be unreasonable to grant to one person the exclusive right to run omnibuses in the city.[3] It is often stated, that the copyright and the patent of an invention are monopolies, which are permissible by law. But it seems to me that they are monopolies only so far as they make the right of manufacture exclusive. If the common-law theory in respect to these subjects be correct, that there is no natural right to the exclusive manufacture of one's own inventions and intellectual productions, then the grant of the exclusive right to manufacture is a monopoly, and cannot be better sustained than a monopoly of the manufacture of sugar or any other product. But the products of mental labor, when they take the shape of a book or an invented machine, ought to be as secure to the producer, as the products of manual labor, and it is the possible unconscious recognition of the justice of these claims, which brings about popular justification of these so-called monopolies.

Notwithstanding the contradictions of the authorities, it is not difficult to determine on principle, as enunciated above, that the grant of privileges may be made a monopoly, but

---

[1] Norwich Gas-light Co. v. Norwich City Gas Co., 25 Conn. 19; State v. Cincinnati, etc., Gas Co., 18 Ohio St. 292. But, see *contra*, State, v. Milwaukee Gas-light Co., 29 Wis. 454.

[2] Memphis v. Water Co., 5 Heisk. 492.

[3] Logan v. Payne, 43 Iowa 524 (22 Am. Rep. 261).

§ 105

that a monopoly cannot be made of the ordinary lawful occupations. But the difficulty becomes almost inexplicable,
when the exclusive privilege is granted of carrying on a business, which is prohibited to others, because the unlimited
pursuit of it works an injury to society. There is no doubt
that a trade or occupation, which is inherently and necessarily injurious to society, may be prohibited altogether;
and it does not seem to be questioned that the prosecution
of such a business may be assumed by the government and
managed by it as a monopoly.[1] If it is lawful for the State
to prohibit a particular business altogether, or to make a
government monopoly of it, the pursuit of such a business
would, if permitted to any one, be a privilege or franchise,
and like any other franchise may be made exclusive. This
is but a logical consequence of the admission, that the State
has the power to prohibit the trade altogether. Such an admission is fatal to a resistance of the power to make it a
monopoly. Not only is this true in respect to the prosecution of the prohibited trade, but the same principle applies
to those cases; where the law provides that a particular trade
shall be conducted in certain buildings or localities. We
have seen that it is reasonable to prohibit the prosecution
of certain trades except within a certain area, or in certain
public buildings, owned and managed by the State or town.
But the same objection is raised, if the State or town, instead
of constructing and maintaining these public buildings, authorizes a private individual or corporation to erect and
conduct them under police regulations. The monopoly,
thus created, is not any more objectionable on principle, because it does not interfere to any greater degree, or in any
different way, with the liberties of others who are prohibited,
than the erection and maintenance of such buildings by the
government. If the State has the constitutional power to

---

[1] For example, in the regulation of the liquor trade, it was held to be
constitutional to prohibit the sale of liquor, except by the agents of the
town. State v. Brennan's Liquors, 25 Conn. 278.

§ 105

prohibit the prosecution of such a trade in all other buildings, the prohibition is equally irksome, whether the buildings are owned by the public or by private individuals; and the grant of the right to prosecute an otherwise prohibited trade in the buildings of a private individual or corporation would create a privilege, and may therefore be made a monopoly. If there is any valid objection to this regulation, it will be found to apply equally to all like cases, whether the buildings in which the trade is required to be conducted belongs to the State or private persons; and the regulation is unconstitutional, because the prosecution of the business anywhere will not produce an injury to the public.

This doctrine has been established and applied to the case of slaughter-houses. The legislature of Louisiana provided for the erection by a certain private corporation of slaughter-houses on the Mississippi, near New Orleans, to which all butchers within a certain area were required to bring their cattle for slaughtering. The law compelled the corporation to provide convenient accommodation for all butchers, who applied, upon the payment of a reasonable compensation, and the slaughtering of animals elsewhere was absolutely interdicted. Suits were brought to resist the enforcement of the law, on the ground that it interfered with the constitutional rights of those interdicted and created a monopoly, not allowed by the constitution. The cases finally reached the Supreme Court of the United States, and the law was declared, by a divided court, to be constitutional. In delivering the opinion of the court Justice Miller said: " It cannot be denied that the statute under consideration is aptly framed to remove from the more densely populated part of the city the noxious slaughter-houses, and large and offensive collections of animals necessarily incident to the slaughtering business of a large city, and to locate them where the convenience, health and comfort of the people require they shall be located. And it must be conceded that the means adopted by the act for

§ 105

this purpose are appropriate, are stringent, and effectual. But it is said that, in creating a corporation for this purpose and conferring upon it exclusive privileges — which it is said constitute a monopoly — the legislature has exceeded its power. If this statute had imposed on the city of New Orleans precisely the same duties, accompanied by the same privileges, which it has on the corporation which it created, it is believed that no question would have been raised as to its constitutionality. In that case the effect on the butchers' pursuit of their occupation and on the public would have been the same as it is now. Why cannot the legislature confer the same powers on another corporation, created for a lawful and useful public object, that it can on the municipal corporation already existing? That wherever a legislature has the right to accomplish a certain result, and that result is best attained by means of a corporation, it has the right to create such a corporation, and to endow it with the power necessary to effect the desired and lawful purpose, seems hardly to admit of debate. The proposition is ably discussed and affirmed in the case of McCulloch v. State of Maryland in relation to the power of Congress to organize the bank of the United States to aid in the fiscal operations of the government.   *   *   *

" Unless, therefore, it can be maintained that the exclusive privileges granted by this charter for the corporation, is beyond the power of the legislature of Louisiana, there can be no just exception to the validity of the statute. And in this respect we are not able to see that these privileges are especially odious or objectionable. The duty imposed as a consideration for the privilege is well defined, and its enforcement well guarded. The prices or charges to be made by the company are limited by the statute, and we are not advised that they are on the whole exorbitant or unjust."

" The proposition is, therefore, reduced to these terms : Can any exclusive privilege be granted to any of its

§ 105

•citizens, or to a corporation, by the legislature of the State? * * *

"But it is to be observed, that all such references are to monopolies established by the monarch in derogation of the rights of the subjects, or arise out of transactions in which the people were unrepresented and their interests uncared for. The great *Case of Monopolies*, reported by Coke, and so fully stated in the brief, was undoubtedly a contest of the Commons against the monarch. The decision is based upon the ground that it was against common law and the argument was aimed at the unlawful assumption of power by the crown; for whoever doubted the authority of Parliament to change or modify the common law? The discussion in the House of Commons cited from Macaulay clearly establishes that the contest was between the crown and the people represented in Parliament.

"But we think it may be safely affirmed that the Parliament of Great Britain, representing the people in their legislative functions, and the legislative bodies of this country, have from time immemorial to the present day, continued to grant to persons and corporations privileges — privileges denied to other citizens — privileges which come within any just definition of the word monopoly, as much as those now under consideration; and that the power to do this has never been questioned or denied. Nor can it be truthfully denied that some of the most useful and beneficial enterprises set on foot for the general good, have been made successful by means of these exclusive rights, and could only have been conducted to success in that way.

"It may, therefore, be considered as established, that the authority of the legislature of Louisiana to pass the present statute is ample, unless some restraint in the exercise of that power be found in the constitution of that State, or in the amendments to the constitution of the United States."

"The statute under consideration defines these localities, and forbids slaughtering in any other. It does not, as has

21 § 105

been asserted, prevent the butcher from doing his own slaughtering. On the contrary, the Slaughter-House Company is required, under a heavy penalty, to permit any person who wishes to do so, to slaughter in their houses ; and they are bound to make ample provision for the convenience of all the slaughtering for the entire city. The butcher then is still permitted to slaughter, to prepare and to sell his own meats ; but he is required to slaughter at a specified place and to pay a reasonable compensation for the use of the accommodations furnished him at that place. The wisdom of the monopoly granted by the Legislature may be open to question, but it is difficult to see a justification for the assertion that the butchers are deprived of the right to labor in their occupation, or the people of their daily service in preparing food, or how this statute, with the duties and guards imposed upon the company, can be said to destroy the business of the butcher, or seriously interfere with its pursuit." [1]

[1] Opinion of J. Miller in Slaughter-House Cases, 16 Wall. 36. C. J. Chase and JJ. Field, Swayne and Bradley, dissent. In delivering his dissenting opinion, Justice Field said: " By the act of Louisiana, within the three parishes named, a territory exceeding one thousand one hundred square miles, and embracing over two hundred thousand persons, every man who pursues the business of preparing animal food for market must take his animals to the buildings of the favored company and must perform his work in them, and for the use of the buildings must pay a prescribed tribute to the company, and leave with it a valuable portion of each animal slaughtered. Every man in these parishes who has a horse or other animal for sale, must carry him to the yards and stables of the company, and for their use pay a like tribute. He is not allowed to do his work in his own buildings or take his animals to his own stables, or keep them in his own yards, even though they should be erected in the same district as the buildings, stables and yards of the company, and that district embraces over eleven hundred square miles. The prohibitions imposed by this act upon butchers and dealers in cattle in these parishes, and the special privileges conferred upon the favorite corporation, are similar in principle and as odious in character as the restrictions imposed in the last century upon the peasantry in some parts of France, where, as says a French writer, the peasant was prohibited to ' hunt on his own lands, to fish in his own waters, to grind at his own mill, to

§ 105

This is not the only case in which the right of the government to create such a monopoly has been sustained. In Iowa, a law was sustained, which granted to private individ-

cook at his own oven, to dry his clothes on his own machines, to whet his instruments at his own grindstone, to make his own wine, his oil and his cider at his own press, * * * or to sell his commodities at the public markets. The exclusive right of all these privileges was vested in the lords of the vicinage. The history of the most execrable tyranny of ancient times,' says the same writer, ' offers nothing like this. This category of oppressions cannot be applied to a free man, or to the peasant, except in violation of his rights.'

"But if the exclusive privileges conferred upon the Louisiana corporation be sustained, it is not perceived why exclusive privileges for the construction and keeping of ovens, machines, grindstones, wine presses, and for all the numerous trades and pursuits for the prosecution of which buildings are required, may not be equally bestowed upon other corporations or private individuals and for periods of indefinite duration. * * * This equality of right, with exemption from all disparaging and partial enactments, in the lawful pursuits of life, throughout the whole country, is the distinguishing privilege of citizens of the United States. To them, everywhere, all pursuits, all professions, all avocations are open without other restrictions than such as are imposed equally upon all others of the same age, sex, and condition. The State may prescribe such regulations for every pursuit and calling of life as will promote the public health, secure the good order and advance the general prosperity of society, but when once prescribed, the pursuits or calling must be free to be followed by every citizen who is within the conditions designated, and will conform to the regulations. This is the fundamental idea upon which our institutions rest, and unless adhered to in the legislation of the country our government will be a republic only in name. * * *

"The keeping of a slaughter-house is part of, and incidental to, the trade of a butcher — one of the ordinary occupations of human life. To compel a butcher, or rather all the butchers of a large city and an extensive district, to slaughter their cattle in another person's slaughter-house and pay him a toll therefor, is such a restriction upon the trade, as materially to interfere with its prosecution. It is onerous, unreasonable, arbitrary and unjust. It has none of the qualities of a police regulation. If it were really a police regulation, it would undoubtedly be within the power of the legislature. That portion of the act which requires all slaughter-houses to be located below the city, and to be subjected to inspection, etc., is clearly a police regulation. That portion which allows no one but the favored company to build, own, or have slaughter-houses is not a police regulation, and has not the faintest semblance of one."

§ 105

uals the exclusive right to erect and maintain a public market in which all vendors of fresh meat and vegetables were required to ply their trade.[1] And in Louisiana it was held that, not only may the municipality of New Orleans grant to private persons the exclusive privilege of erecting and maintaining a public market, in partnership with the city, but that the city council cannot legislate in respect to the regulation of the markets, without consulting the partners, where the regulation is likely to affect the financial interest of the partnership.[2] So, also, it has been held in Kansas, that a law is not unconstitutional which restricts the sale of liquors to druggists and for special purposes.[3] On the other hand, in an early case in New York, it was declared to be unconstitutional to prohibit persons in general the manufacture of pressed hay in the thickly settled parts of a city, on account of the danger of fire, and grant to one or more the exclusive privilege of engaging in that business within the prohibited district. The court says: —

"If the manufacture of pressed hay within the compact parts of the city is dangerous in causing or promoting fires, the common council have the power expressly given by their charter to prevent the carrying on of such manufacture ; but as all by-laws must be reasonable, the common council can not make a by-law which shall permit one person to carry on the dangerous business and prohibit another who has an equal right from pursuing the same business."[4]

In a case parallel with the slaughter-house cases of Louisiana, the city of Chicago passed an ordinance designating certain buildings for slaughtering all animals intended for sale or consumption in the city, the owners of the buildings

---

[1] Le Claire v. Davenport, 13 Iowa, 210, overruling Davenport v. Kelly, 7 Iowa, 109, 110. See the dissenting opinion in the latter case.

[2] New Orleans v. Guillotte, 12 La. Ann. 818.

[3] Intoxicating Liquor Cases, 25 Kan. 751 (37 Am. Rep. 284). See In re Ruth, 32 Iowa, 253.

[4] Mayor City of Hudson v. Thorne, 7 Paige, 261.

§ 105

being granted for a specified period the exclusive privilege of having all such animals slaughtered in their establishment, and exacting a certain fee from the owners of animals so slaughtered. In passing upon the constitutionality of this law, the Supreme Court of Illinois pronounced the following opinion : " The charter authorizes the city authorities to license or regulate such establishments. When that body has made the necessary regulations, required for the health or comfort of the inhabitants, all persons inclined to pursue such an occupation should have an opportunity of conforming to such regulations; otherwise the ordinance would be unreasonable and tend to oppression. Or if they should regard it for the interest of the city that such establishments should be licensed, the ordinance should be so framed that all persons desiring it might obtain licenses by conforming to the prescribed terms and regulations for the government of such business. We regard it neither as a regulation nor a license of a business to confine it to one building or to give it to one individual. Such an action is oppressive, and creates a monopoly that never could have been contemplated by the general assembly. It impairs the rights of all other persons, and cuts them off from a share in not only a legal, but a necessary, business. Whether we consider this as an ordinance or a contract, it is equally unauthorized, as being opposed to the rules governing the adoption of municipal by-laws. The principle of the equality of rights is violated by this contract. If the common council may require all of the animals for the consumption of the city to be slaughtered in a single building, or on a particular lot, and the owner be paid a specific sum for the privilege, what would prevent the making a similar contract with some other person that all of the vegetables or fruits, the flour, the groceries, the dry goods, or other commodities should be sold on his lot and he receive a compensation for the privilege? We can see no difference in principle." [1]

[1] City of Chicago v. Rumpff, 45 Ill. 90.

§ 105

This presentation of the subject readily indicates an almost hopeless contradiction of authorities; but it seems to be without doubt, that the doctrine laid down by the Supreme Court of the United States in the Slaughter-house Cases will ultimately come to be recognized as the correct one.

But there is always this limitation to be recognized upon the power to make a monopoly of any trade, to be conducted by itself or by some private individual or corporation to whom it is granted as a privilege, viz. : that the general prosecution of the trade or occupation, by every one who chooses to engage in it, produces injurious results which can only be avoided by making a monopoly of the trade.   In all parts of the civilized world, the transportation of the mails has become a government monopoly; and the railroads and the telegraph in Europe are for the most part in the hands of the government.   In our own country it has been declared by the Supreme Court of the United States, that it would be a legitimate assumption of power for the United States to make a government monopoly of the management of railroads and the telegraph, and appropriate to its use the existing lines of railroad and telegraph.[1]

Whether it is impossible for the railroads and telegraph and post-office to be conducted by private individuals or corporations, is a question about which there is a divided opinion.   In respect to the post-office, the assumption of its management by government is so universal at the present day that the objections to this monopoly are hardly worthy of a serious consideration, for it is firmly rooted in public opinion that this is a legitimate exercise of governmental authority.   The same reasons which would justify the post-office monopoly, would be sufficient to establish a claim in favor of a railroad or telegraph monopoly. They are all common means of intercourse and intercom-

---

[1] Ch. J. Waite in Pensacola, etc., R. R. Co. v. West. Union Tel. Co., 96 U. S. 1.

§ 105

munication among people of the same and of different countries, and might very properly be compared with the governmental control of the public highways on land and on water. And whatever serious doubts may be entertained by the philosopher and student concerning the legal propriety of such government monopolies; in these days of labor agitation and gigantic railroad and telegraph combinations, when a collision between the capitalist and the workingman stops the wheels of commerce, and brings all commercial intercourse to an end as long as the disagreement continues, public opinion will be very willing to indorse any reasonable proposition to place the management of railroads and telegraphs in the hands of the national government.

But the application of this principle to practical politics is very likely to result in an abuse of it, and the student of European politics meets with all sorts of monopolies, almost as varied and numerous as they were in France under the ancient *régime*, the only difference being that the general government, and not the privileged classes, own the monopolies. Thus, for example, in most of the European States, the preparation and manufacture of tobacco and cigars has been made a government monopoly. The real object of the monopoly is to increase the revenue of the country, but on no principle of constitutional law could such a monopoly be justified. There may in the future be attempts in this country to create monoplies out of trades and occupations, the prosecution of which by private individuals and corporations would not necessarily inflict injury upon the public. But a resort to the courts will furnish an ample remedy, if public opinion has not grown accustomed to a disregard of constitutional limitations and the rights of individuals.

§ 105

CHAPTER X.

POLICE REGULATIONS OF REAL PROPERTY.

Section 115. What is meant by "private property in land?"
116. Regulation of estates — Vested rights.
117. Interests of expectancy.
118. Limitation of the right of acquisition.
119. Regulation of the right of alienation.
120. Involuntary alienation.
121. Eminent domain.
121*a*. Exercise of power regulated by legislature.
121*b*. Public purpose, what is a.
121*c*. What property may be taken.
121*d*. What constitutes a taking.
121*e*. Compensation, how ascertained.
122. Regulation of the use of lands — What is a nuisance?
122*a*. What is a nuisance, a judicial question.
122*b*. Unwholesome trades in tenement houses may be prohibited.
122*c*. Confinement of objectionable trades to certain localities.
122*d*. Regulation of burial grounds.
122*e*. Laws regulating the construction of wooden buildings.
122*f*. Regulation of right to hunt game.
122*g*. Abatement of nuisances — Destruction of buildings.
123. How far the use of land may be controlled by the requirement of license.
124. Improvement of property at the expense, and against the will, of the owner.
125. Regulation of non-navigable streams — Fisheries.
125*a*. Conversion of non-navigable into navigable streams.
126. Statutory liability of lessors for the acts of lessees.
127. Search warrants.
128. Quartering soldiers in private dwellings.
129. Taxation.

§ 115. **What is meant by "private property in land?"** — An accurate answer to this question is exceedingly important, because attacks have repeatedly been made upon the existing land tenure of England and the United States by political economists, as being the chief cause of human woes; and promises are made of the advent of an era of universal prosperity, only a little short of millenium, if private property in land be only abolished. The latest writer upon this subject, Mr. Henry George, has created no little stir by his vigorous attacks upon private property in land, and has succeeded, in no small degree, in unsettling preconceived notions of the right to own land. Our interest in this connection, as a jurist and a student of police economics, lies chiefly in Mr. George's conceptions of the existing law of real property, and the meaning he and other political economists attach to the phrase "private property in land." If we have not mistaken the writer's main idea, it is no less and no more than what is set forth by Mr. Herbert Spencer in his Social Statics,[1] with a greater display of rhetoric, however, and an elaborate scheme for the confiscation of the so-called "private property in land." Both writers present their views under the impression that the existing law recognizes an absolute right of private property in land, and they both propose that this private property be abolished, and land become the common property of all, of the State or society.

Mr. Spencer's entire argument is based upon his first principle of sociology: "Every man has freedom to do all that he wills provided he infringes not the equal freedom of any other man," and in applying this principle — which we most heartily indorse as the ruling principle of police power in the United States,[2] and the necessary fundamental principle in every system of sociology in a free State — to the right of property in land, he maintains that no one "may use the earth in such a way as to prevent the rest from similarly using it ; seeing that to do this is to assume greater freedom than the rest, and consequently to break the law." Both writers maintain that land is the free gift of nature, and must ever remain the inalienable property of society. But Mr. Spencer, readily perceiving the practical

[1] pp. 130-144.
[2] See *ante*, secs. 1, 2.

§ 115

objections that might be raised to his scheme of a common
property in lands, if left unqualified, proceeds to deny that
we must, as a result of a common property in lands, " return to the times of uninclosed wilds, and subsist on roots,
berries and game." In further explanation of this scheme
he says: " Such a doctrine is consistent with the highest
state of civilization ; may be carried out without involving a
community of goods; and need cause no very serious revolution in existing arrangements. The change required
would simply be a change of landlords. Separate owner-
ships would merge into the joint stock ownership of the
public. Instead of being in the possession of individuals,
the country would be held by the great corporate body —
society. Instead of leasing his acres from an isolated proprietor, the farmer would lease them from the nation. Instead
of paying his rent to the agent of Sir John or his Grace, he
would pay it to an agent or deputy agent of the community.
Stewards would be public officials, instead of private ones;
and tenancy the only land tenure." [1] Tersely stated, Mr.
Spencer's idea is that all men must become tenants of the
State or of society, and must pay rent to the State for the
exclusive use of the land. Mr. George's proposition is essentially the same. He says: " I do not propose either to
purchase or to confiscate private property in land. The first
would be unjust ; the second needless. Let the individuals
who now hold it still retain, if they want to, possession of
what they are pleased to call *their* land. Let them continue to
call it *their* land. Let them buy and sell, and bequeath and
devise it. We may safely leave them the shell, if we take
the kernel. *It is not necessary to confiscate land; it is only
necessary to confiscate rent.*" [2] And in order that the State
need not " bother with the letting of lands," secure the benefits arising out of the position of landlord without being

---

[1] Social Statics, p. 141.
[2] Progress and Poverty, p. 364.

§ 115

subjected to its annoyances, he proposes to " appropriate rent by taxation."

Both writers recognize the absolute right of private property in the improvements which the possessor may put upon the land, and neither would claim the right of confiscation of them, directly or indirectly, except that Mr. George recognizes the right to confiscate those " improvements which in time become indistinguishable from the land itself." [1] But as a general proposition, they both recognized this right to the improvements, which are of course products of man's labor.

Mr. Spencer claims that this proposed tenantry is 'in strict conformity with his first principles. He says : " A state of things so ordered would be in perfect harmony with the moral law. Under it all men would be equally landlords ; all men would be alike free to become tenants. A., B., C., and the rest, might compete for a vacant farm as now, and one of them might take that farm, without in any way violating the principles of pure equity. All would be equally free to bid ; all would be equally free to refrain. And when the farm had been let to A., B., or C., all parties would have done that which they willed — the one in choosing to pay a given sum to his fellowmen for the use of certain lands — the other in refusing to pay that sum. Clearly, therefore, on such a system, the earth might be inclosed, occupied, and cultivated, in entire subordination to the law of equal freedom." In effect, Mr. George's position is identical. They both assert the natural right of one man to the exclusive possession of a tract or plot of land, for the period of his tenancy, provided he pays the proper rent or equivalent to society. Who is to determine what rent would be a fair equivalent for the right or privilege thus secured? Clearly, the legal representative of society

[1] Progress and Poverty, p. 308.

§ 115

in its organized condition, in other words, the government of the State.

If tenancy be for one year, of course the rent will in proportion be smaller than what would be payable in a tenancy for ten, twenty, one hundred, and one thousand years; and there would possibly be a different amount of rent exacted for a tenancy for the life of the tenant. Of course, legal limitations could be imposed upon the duration of the tenancy,[1] but would this be wise? May not cases arise, in which it would be no inducement for a tenant to make improvements, unless he was given a long lease? The desire for a permanent "local habitation" is very strong in the human breast, and Blackstone tells us that under the feudal system it was considered "that the smallest interest, which was worthy of a freeman, was one which must endure during his life."[2] Apart from any express legal restrictions, which of course may be imposed under this theory of property in lands, if the consideration or rent is adequate, there would be no more injustice to the rest of the human race to give one man the exclusive possession of a piece of land during his life, than it would be if his tenancy was only for one year. Having paid to society a fair equivalent for the use of the land, is society at all concerned in the manner of his using the land, provided he injures no one else? Would it be an act of natural injustice to society, if he for some satisfactory consideration lets some one else utilize the land, instead of doing so himself? The right of subletting is therefore a natural incident of a tenancy, unless expressly taken away.

One step farther: suppose society finds out that in a given case it can procure, through individual activity, a long felt want, but the individuals in question will not undertake the project unless they have in certain lands a more per-

[1] See *post*, § 116.
[2] 2 Bla. Com. 237.

§ 115

manent right of possession than what a tenancy for life gives them.   Suppose society conclude that they must have this want supplied, and in order to gratify this desire they give to these parties and to their heirs and assigns the exclusive possession of certain land, as long as they pay a certain rent, the amount of which is to be determined by society from time to time, and provided further, that the land may be at any time reclaimed by society, if the public exigencies shall require it, upon the payment to these parties or their heirs and assigns of a compensation for the loss of improvements, which have become inseparable from the land, and for future profits in the continued possession? Would such a contract be in violation of Mr. Spencer's first principle?   Would not the State be still the ultimate owner of the land, and the so-called proprietor only vested with the right of possession and enjoyment, in other words, a qualified property?   Would he not be essentially a tenant of the State, and his interest in the land a tenancy?

That is all "the private property in land" which the American and English laws recognize.   The present writer has stated elsewhere [1] this limitation upon the right of property in land in the following language : —

"It may be stated as a general rule, though controverted by eminent authority, that in any system of jurisprudence, there cannot be an absolute ownership in lands.   The right of property or interest in them must always be qualified, that interest being known in the English and American law as an *estate*.   A man can have only an estate in the land, the absolute right of property being vested in the State. An estate has, in respect to the real property, the three elements, the right of possession, right of enjoyment, and right of disposition, subject to the right of the State to defeat it, and appropriate it to the public use, or for the public good.   In what cases, and under what circumstances,

[1] Tiedeman on Real Property, § 19.

§ 115

the State can exercise this power of appropriation, and to what extent the rights of possession, enjoyment and disposition, may be limited by the imposition of restrictions, depends upon the policy of each system of jurisprudence. In some States the restrictions are numerous, while in others they are few, the right of property being almost absolute in the individual. But nowhere can the private right of property be said to be absolute. The absolute right of property being in the State, the right of ownership, which an individual may acquire, must, therefore, in theory at least, be held to be derived from the State, and the State has the right and power to stipulate the conditions and terms upon which the land may be held by individuals. These conditions and terms, and the rights and obligations arising therefrom, constitute what is known as *tenure* or *land tenure*."[1]

Is not then this statement of the law correct? Is there an acre of land in this country, that is not held subject to taxation and to the right of eminent domain? Taxation of real estate is essentially the same as rent, for it is not imposed as an obligation of citizenship. Although the power of taxation generally cannot properly be considered of feudal origin, yet in its application to real property it assumes a decidedly feudal character. If the power to tax real property rested solely upon the obligations of citizenship, then it could only be levied upon those proprietors of lands who were citizens. As a matter of fact, all lands situated within the jurisdiction of the government which levies the tax are taxed for their proportionate share. The levying of a tax upon land and the enforcement of the levy, are usually proceedings *in rem* against the land, and not *in personam* against the proprietor.[2]

The right of eminent domain surely can rest only upon

[1] Tiedeman on Real Property, § 19.
[2] See *post*, § 129.

§ 115

the claim that the State is the absolute proprietor of all lands within its jurisdiction, which consequently makes all private owners merely tenants of the State.[1]

Our conclusion therefore is that there is no "private property in land" in the sense in which Mr. Spencer and Mr. George employ the term, and the provisions of the law in respect to the tenancy of lands are in strict conformity with the principles they advocate. It may be, as Mr. George asserts, that certain cunning men in days gone by cheated society out of its dues, and obtained from it fee simple tenancies without rendering an adequate equivalent; and it may be true (we shall not question the proposition in this place), that the present returns to the State for the private enjoyment of these tenancies are grossly inadequate to the benefits thus received: Mr. George may possibly be just in his claim that taxation of lands ought to be increased far beyond its present rate; but the economic problem would be very much simplified, if it is clearly understood that the scheme proposed for the nationalization of land involves no legal, as it does an economic, revolution.

§ 116. **Regulation of estates — Vested rights.** — If it be true that the absolute property in land is in the State, it must follow as a logical consequence that, in the grant of lands to private individuals, the State may impose whatever conditions and terms, under which the land is to be acquired, that may be deemed wise or necessary. For example, the United States government may institute whatever regulations it pleases for the sale of the public lands of the West. The right to acquire a private property in land is a privilege and not a right. The State may refuse altogether to sell, or exact whatever returns in the way of rents or public duties it pleases. But when the right to the public enjoyment of lands is purchased by the individual, it becomes a vested

---

[1] See *post*, § 121.

§ 116

right, of which he cannot be divested by any arbitrary rule of law. There are several clauses of the constitutions which contain an express or implied prohibition of such interferences with vested rights ; but the principal protection to vested rights is that guaranteed by the clause which declares that " no man shall be deprived of his * * * property, except by the judgment of his peers or the law of the land." It is not necessary in this place to discuss in general what is meant by vested rights, and what are considered to be such.[1] It is sufficient for us to be able to say that when one becomes the tenant of the State, or acquires the absolute title to an estate in the land, whether that estate be in fee, for life, for years, or otherwise, his interest is a vested right, which is protected by the constitutional limitations against any arbitrary changes by legislation. But naturally, until the estate is acquired, the purchaser has no absolute right to purchase any particular estate in the land. It is fully competent for the legislature to determine what estates one may acquire in lands. For example, estates tail have been abolished in most of the American States. That is, the statutes of the different States have declared what shall be the effect of an attempt to create an estate tail. In Alabama, California, Connecticut, Florida, Georgia, Kentucky, Maryland, Michigan, Minnesota, Mississippi, North Carolina, Tennessee, Texas, Wisconsin, Virginia and West Virginia, estates tail are converted into fees simple.   In Arkansas, Illinois, Kansas, Missouri, New Jersey and Vermont, the tenant in tail takes a life estate, and the heirs of his body, the remainder in fee *per formam doni*.   In Indiana and New York, the tenant takes a fee simple, if there is no limitation in remainder after the estate tail, and a life estate, where there is such a limitation.   In Delaware, Maine, Massachusetts, Pennsylvania, and Rhode Island, es-

---

[1] For a masterly exposition of this subject, see Cooley Const. Lim. 430–511.

§ 116

tates tail are not expressly abolished, but an easy mode of barring the entail by a conveyance in fee simple is provided by statute.[1]

Another notorious example of legislative interference with creation of estates in lands is furnished by the enactment of Statutes of Uses, which provide for the union in the *cestui que use* of the legal and equitable estates.[2]   In the same way are the incidents of estates being materially modified and changed by statute.   The law of mortgages is constantly undergoing a change in every State, through the enactment of statutes and by judicial legislation.   Joint tenancies have been converted into tenancies in common ; estates at will have been changed to tenancies from year to year, and estates for years declared to be estates of inheritance, with all the incidents of freehold estates.   There are many other such instances of legislative changes of the character and incidents of estates in lands, which may be ascertained by a reference to any work on Real Property.   All such legislation, however radical it may be, will be clearly free from all constitutional objections, as long as it is not made to apply to existing estates.   To declare, that hereafter no estate tail or use shall be created, does not infringe any vested right, either of the vendor or vendee, or any third person in privity with either of them.   But the effect would be very different if these statutes were made applicable to the existing estates of the prohibited kind. Whether the estate tail was converted into a fee simple or divided into a life estate in the first taker and a contingent remainder in the heirs of his body, or if the tenant in tail has the power given him to convert the estate into a fee simple by a conveyance; in any one of these three cases of legislation, the application of it to existing estates tail would violate the constitutional prohibition of interference with

---

[1] Tiedeman on Real Prop., § 2, n. ; 1 Washb. on Real Prop. 112, note; Williams on Real Prop. 35, Rawle's note.
[2] Tiedeman on Real Prop., §§ 459–470.

§ 116

vested rights. Of course the heirs of the body have no vested rights,[1] but the reversioner or remainder-man, after the estate tail has.[2] Mr. Cooley states that "in this country estates tail have been very generally changed into estates in fee simple, by statutes the validity of which is not disputed."[3] If the reversion or remainder after an estate tail be a vested right, and without exception the recognized authorities on the law of real property are agreed that these interests are vested rights, the conclusion is irresistible, that laws, changing estates tail into fees simple, are unconstitutional if applied to estates tail already created, when the laws were passed. Mr. Cooley says: "No other person (than the tenant in tail) in these cases has any vested right, either in possession or expectancy, to be affected by such change; and the expectation of the heir presumptive must be subject to the same control as in other cases."[4] In a note to the above statement[5] he says that "the exception to this statement, if any, must be the case of a tenant in tail after possibility of issue extinct; where the estate of the tenant has ceased to be an inheritance, and a reversionary right has become vested." There cannot be any doubt whatever, that the conversion of an estate tail after possibility of issue extinct into a fee simple, would be in violation of the vested rights of the reversioner or remainder-man. For the estate tail after possibility of issue extinct is but a life estate.[6] But, in respect to the matter of being a vested right, there is no difference between the remainder or reversion after an ordinary

---

[1] See, post, § 117.

[2] Tiedeman on Real Prop., §§ 385, 398, 538; 2 Washb. on Real Prop. 737, 738; 2 Washb. on Real Prop. 546, 690.

[3] Cooley Const. Lim. 441, citing, in support of the proposition, De Mill v. Lockwood, 3 Blatchf. 56.

[4] Cooley Const. Lim. 441, 442, citing, 1 Washb. on Real Prop. 81-84.

[5] p. 442.

[6] Tiedeman on Real Prop., § 51; 1 Washb. on Real Prop. 110, 111; 2 Sharswood Blackstone, 125.

§ 116

estate tail, and one after an estate tail *after possibility of issue extinct.* There is no uncertainty as to the title in either case. The failure of issue in both simply determines when the reversion or remainder shall take effect in possession, and the uncertainty or impossibility of ever enjoying the estate in possession, never makes a remainder contingent.[1] It is true that in England the remainder after an estate tail was liable to be defeated by a common recovery, when suffered or instituted by the tenant in tail for the purpose of cutting off the entail.[2] And if common recoveries or some other mode of barring the entail had been previously recognized in this country, the remainder after the estate tail would be properly considered a contingent interest instead of a vested right, and could be further regulated by statute. Thus, for example, in Massachusetts, the tenant in tail can make a conveyance in fee simple, thus barring the contingent interest of the remainder-man or reversioner. Another statute might very well be enacted, making the existing estates tail a fee simple, while they remain in the possession of the tenant in tail. Since the interest of the reversioner or remainder-man was already liable to be defeated by the arbitrary will of the tenant in possession, it was not a vested right, and, therefore, not protected by the constitutional limitations.

For the same reason, the right of survivorship in a joint tenancy cannot be considered a vested right. Apart from the fact, that the title to the interest of the co-tenant under the doctrine of survivorship, could not until his death become

---

[1] Tiedeman on Real Prop., § 401; Fearne Cont. Rean. 216; 4 Kent Com. 202; 2 Washb. on Real Prop. 547; Croxall *v.* Shererd, 5 Wall. 288; Pearce *v.* Savage, 45 Me. 101; Brown *v.* Lawrence, 3 Cush. 390; Williamson *v.* Field, 2 Sandf. Ch. 533; Allen *v.* Mayfield, 20 Ind. 293; Marshall *v.* King, 24 Miss. 90; Manderson *v.* Lukens, 23 Pa. St. 31; Maurice *v.* Maurice, 43 N. Y. 380; Furness *v.* Fox, 1 Cush. 134; Blanchard *v.* Blanchard, 1 Allen, 223.

[2] Williams on Real Prop. 253; 1 Spence Eq. Jur. 144; 2 Prest. Est. 460; Page *v.* Hayward, 2 Salk. 570.

§ 116

vested in the survivor, the co-tenant had the power to defeat the right of survivorship by his own conveyance of his undivided interest. The conveyance of a joint tenant's share in the joint tenancy converts it into a tenancy in common, as between the assignee and the other joint tenants.[1] It is, therefore, not difficult to justify on constitutional grounds the statute of Massachusetts which converted existing joint-tenancy into tenancies in common.[2] In the same way the enactment of a statute, converting existing trusts, which could not be executed by the English Statute of Uses, into legal estates, could not be considered unconstitutional, except where the effect would be to materially change the beneficial character of the rights of the *cestui que trust*. The title of the trustee is not a vested right which would be protected by these constitutional limitations. He holds it in trust for the *cestui que trust*, and if the latter ·has not been harmed by the transfer of the land to him, the trustee can not complain. A law may be passed, abolishing the doctrine of " a use upon a use," and convert into legal estates all uses that remain unexecuted in consequence of this doctrine. It may possibly be claimed that in active trusts the trustee has a vested right to the compensation which the law allows him for the performance of his duties under the trust. But the claim is manifestly untenable. If the performance of his duties is rendered unnecessary by the transfer of the legal estate to the *cestui que trust*, he has not earned his compensation. One cannot be said to have a vested right to earn compensation by the performance of duties which have by law become unnecessary.

---

[1] Tiedeman on Real Prop., § 238; 1 Washb. on Real Property, 647, 648; Co. Lit. 273b. And the right of survivorship will *pro tanto* be defeated by a mortgage of a joint tenant's interest in a joint tenancy. York *v.* Stone, 1 Salk. 158; 1 Eq. Cas. Abr. 293; Simpson *v.* Ammons, 1 Binn. 175.

[2] Holbrook *v.* Finney, 4 Mass. 565 (3 Am. Dec. 243); Miller *v.* Miller, 16 Mass. 59; Annable *v.* Patch, 3 Pick. 360. See Bombaugh *v.* Bombaugh, 11 Serg. & R. 192.

§ 116

Under the English Statute of Uses, which has been adopted without change in most of our States, the separate use to a married woman cannot be executed into a legal estate, because she cannot hold the legal estate free from the control of the husband, as she can the use or equitable estate.[1] A statute, which converted such an existing estate into a legal estate, without providing for its remaining her separate property, would clearly be unconstitutional, as being in violation of vested rights. On the other hand, if a statute is passed, which declares that married women shall hold their legal estates as well as equitable estates free from the control or attaching rights of the husband, the use to a married woman which remained unexecuted by the statute, only on account of her disability to nold the legal estate independently of her husband, would at once become executed into a legal estate under the old Statute of Uses, without any express legislation to that effect.[2]

§ 117. **Interests in expectancy.** — Interests in expectancy, when distinguished from vested rights, are held not to be under the protection of the constitution, and may, therefore, be modified, changed, or completely abolished by subsequent legislation.[3] A purely contingent interest, to which there cannot be any present fixed title, cannot be considered a vested right. Where the vesting of a right depends under existing laws upon the future concurrence of certain circumstances or facts, the repeal of those laws will operate to defeat the expectant interest. " A person has no property, no vested interest, in any rule of the common law. * * * Rights of property, which have been created by the common law, cannot be taken away without

[1] Tiedeman on Real Prop.,§ 469.
[2] See Sutton v. Aiken, 62 Ga. 733; Bratton v. Massey, 15 S. C. 277; Bayer v. Cockerill, 2 Kan. 292.
[3] Cooley Const. Lim. 440.

§ 117

due process; but the law itself, as a rule of conduct, may be changed at the will, or even at the whim of the legislature, unless prevented by constitutional limitations." [1]

For the reason that an interest in expectancy is not to be considered a vested right, it is the universally recognized rule of constitutional law that the right of inheritance of the heir presumptive is liable to be modified or entirely defeated by a legislative change in the law of descent. The law of descent varies according to the civil polity of each State, or, as Blackstone has it, it is "the creature of civil polity and *juris positivi*." Independently of positive law, the heir acquires no rights whatever in his ancestor's property. For public reasons, and with an incidental recognition of the moral right to the inheritance of those who stand in the most intimate blood relationship with the deceased owner, the law declares that property, which the owner leaves at his death undisposed of by grant or demise, shall descend to those named by the statute and in the order given. The expectant heir's right of inheritance rests altogether upon this command of positive law. A repeal of the law before the death of the ancestor would take away all authority for his claim of inheritance. It is, therefore, a well recognized and undisputed rule of law that the statute of descent, in force when the ancestor dies, determines the right of inheritance : *nemo est hæres viventis*.[2] But when the ancestor dies, and under the then existing statute of descent, the property is cast upon a particular individual as heir, the right of property becomes a vested right, and like

---

[1] Waite, Ch. J., in Munn *v.* Illinois, 94 U. S. 113, 134.

[2] Cooley Const. Lim. 441; Story on Confl. Laws, § 484; Tiedeman on Real Prop. § 664; Potter *v.* Titcomb, 22 Me. 300; Miller *v.* Miller, 10 Met. 393; In re Lawrence, 1 Redfield Sur. Rep. 310; Smith *v.* Kelly, 23 Miss. 167; Marshall *v.* King, 24 Miss. 85; McGaughey *v.* Henry, 15 B. Mon. 383; Jones *v.* Marable, 6 Humph. 116; Price *v.* Talley, 10 Ala. 946; Eslava *v.* Farmer, 7 Ala. 543; Sturgis *v.* Ewing, 18 Ill. 176; Emmert *v.* Hays, 89 Ill. 11. Cooley Const. Lim. 441.

§ 117

all other vested rights, however acquired, it cannot be affected by subsequent legislation.

Of the same character are the rights which the husband and wife acquire in the real and other property of each other, by virtue of the marital relation existing between them. By rule of positive law, for more or less public reasons, these rights are granted. They do not depend upon contract, and do not emanate from the marriage contract. The acquisition of these rights is merely an incident of the marriage, made so by law.[1] If, therefore, the law upon which the claim to these marital rights of property rests, is repealed before the rights become vested, the expectant right would be defeated, because there would be no foundation for the claim of an existing right. The common law provided that the husband on his marriage would acquire an estate during coverture in all of the lands of the wife which she then owned, and, from the time of purchase, in all other lands which she may subsequently acquire.[2] Until she acquires a title to the lands by purchase or otherwise, the right to an estate in the lands is merely expectant. A law which provides that married women shall hold their lands and other property free from the attaching rights of the husband, would not be unconstitutional if made to apply to those already married, provided it was not allowed to affect the husband's vested rights in the property, acquired by the wife before the pas-

---

[1] "Dower is not the result of contract but a positive institution of the State, founded on reasons of public policy. To entitle to dower, it is true, there must be a marriage, which our law regards in some respects as a civil contract. So the death and seisin of lands by the husband during the coverture are also necessary to establish a right to this estate. But they are not embraced by, nor are they the subjects of the marriage contract. The estate is by law made an incident of the marriage relation and the death and seisin of one of the parties are conditions on which it comes into existence. It stands, like an estate by the curtesy, on the foundations of positive law." Moore v. City of New York, 8 N. Y. 110.

[2] Tiedeman on Real Prop., § 90; 1 Bla. Com. 442; 1 Washb. on Real Prop. 328, 329.

§ 117

sage of the remedial statute. The statute can constitutionally cut off the husband's expectant interests in the property of the wife, acquired by her subsequently.[1] The same principles will apply to tenancies by the curtesy, and to dower. Until the birth of a child, who was capable of inheriting the estate, the husband's curtesy was merely an expectant interest. Upon the birth of the child, the tenancy became initiate. The title vests in him absolutely. His right of possession as tenant by the curtesy is postponed until the wife's death, but the estate is so far a vested right upon the birth of issue, that he may convey it away, and it is subject to sale under execution for his debts.[2] Any law which provided for the abolition of tenancy by the curtesy, could not constitutionally be made to apply to those cases, in which the tenancy by the curtesy has become a vested right by the birth of issue, and a concurrence of all the other conditions, which are necessary to the existence of the tenancy. For in such cases the tenancies by the curtesy have become vested rights.[3] But the law

---

Westervelt v. Gregg, 12 N. Y. 202; Norris v. Beyea, 13 N. Y. 273; Pugh v. Ottenheimer, 6 Ore. 231 (25 Am. Rep. 513); Bishop Law of Married Women, §§ 45, 46. In Massachusetts it has been held that the husband's contingent interest as husband, in the right of property to which the wife is entitled subject to a contingency, is so far a vested right that it cannot be affected by remedial legislation. Dunn v. Sargent, 101 Mass. 336. See Plumb v. Sawyer, 21 Conn. 351; Jackson v. Lyon, 9 Cow. 664; Pritchard v. Citizen's Bank, 8 La., 130 (23 Am. Dec. 132.)

[2] Tiedeman on Real Prop., §§ 108, 109; Mattocks v. Stearns, 9 Vt. 326; Roberts v. Whiting, 16 Mass. 186; Litchfield v. Cudworth, 15 Pick. 28; Watson v. Watson, 13 Conn. 88; Burd v. Dansdale, 2 Binn. 80; Lancaster Co. Bk. v. Stauffer, 10 Pa. St. 398; Van Duzer v. Van Duzer, 6 Paige 366; Day v. Cochrane, 24 Miss. 261; Canby v. Porter, 12 Ohio, 79. Equity will not interfere in behalf of the wife or children. Van Duzer v. Van Duzer, 6 Paige, 366.

[3] Hathon v. Lyon, 2 Mich. 93; Long v. Marvin, 15 Mich. 60. In Illinois, the husband's curtesy is by statute given the character of the wife's dower. It, is therefore, in that State, subject to change by statute, until the death of the wife makes it a vested right. Henson v. Moore, 104 Ill. 403.

§ 117

could apply to all the property of those already named, who have had no children, capable of inheriting the estate. And while the birth of issue and its death before the acquisition of the property by the wife will be a sufficient performance of this condition, to enable the husband's tenancy by the curtesy to attach, as soon as the property is acquired by the wife ;[1] yet until the property is acquired, the right to the tenancy by the curtesy in such property is so far an interest in expectancy, that it may be taken away by statute.

On the other hand, the wife's dower is inchoate until the death of her husband. Neither he nor his creditors can by any act deprive her of her dower during coverture ;[2] and it is so far a mere expectant interest, that she can neither assign, release, nor extinguish it, except by joining in the deed of her husband. It cannot during coverture be considered even a *chose in action;* and it is not affected by any adverse possession, although such possession is sufficient to bar the husband's interest in the land.[3] Although the authorities are not altogether unanimous, the overwhelming weight of authority recognizes the dower during coverture as being so far inchoate and an interest in expectancy, that it may be changed, modified, or altogether abolished by statute.[4] There is no unconstitutional interference with vested

[1] Tiedeman on Real Prop., § 108; Williamson Real Prop., 228, Rawle's note; Dubs *v.* Dubs, 31 Pa. St. 154; Lancaster Co. Bk. *v.* Stauffer, 19 Pa. St. 398.

[2] Tiedeman on Real Prop., §§ 115, note, 126.

[3] Tiedeman on Real Prop., § 115; Durham *v.* Angier, 20 Me. 242; Moore *v.* Frost, 3 N. H. 127; Gunnison *v.* Twitchell, 38 N. H. 68; Learned *v.* Cutler, 18 Pick. 9; Moore *v.* New York, 8 N. Y. 110; McArthur *v.* Franklin, 16 Ohio St. 200. But see Somar *v.* Canaday, 53 N. Y. 298 (13 Am. Rep. 523); White *v.* Graves, 107 Mass. 325 (9 Am. Rep. 38); Buzick *v.* Buzick, 44 Iowa, 259 (24 Am. Rep. 740), in which the inchoate dower is considered as a vested interest, so far as to enable a wife for its protection to secure in equity a cancellation of a deed, containing her renunciation of dower, which had been procured by the fraud of the purchaser.

[4] Barbour *v.* Barbour, 46 Me. 9; Merrill *v.* Sherburne, 1 N. H. 199 (8 Am. Dec. 52). See Ratch *v.* Flanders, 29 N. H. 304; Jackson *v.* Edwards, 7 Paige, 391; *s. c.* 22 Wend. 498; Moore *v.* City of New York, 4

rights, as far as the dower right is concerned, whether it is by statute increased, diminished, or completely abolished. But where the dower estate is enlarged in the lands already possessed by the husband, there is a clear violation of his vested rights, because the incumbrance upon his estate has been increased. It would be the same, in respect to the wife's property, if the husband's tenancy by curtesy or other marital rights in her property were enlarged by statute, after the property had been acquired. It is unquestionably the prevailing rule of construction, that the widow's dower right in the lands, which her husband has conveyed away during his lifetime, is governed by the law in force at the time of alienation. But since the dower right in all cases is inchoate during the coverture, even in the lands which have been aliened by the husband, it is in this case as much subject to legislative change, as long as it is not enlarged, as if the property was still in the possession of the husband, and while the presumption of law may be against the application of a statute, regulating dower, to estates which have already been conveyed away, there is no constitutional objection in the way of its application to

Sandf. S. C. 456; *s. c.* 8 N. Y. 110; Melizet's Appeal, 17 Pa. St. 449; Phillips *v.* Disney, 16 Ohio 639; Weaver *v.* Gregg, 6 Ohio St. 547; Noel *v.* Ewing, 9 Ind. 37; Logan *v.* Walton, 12 Ind. 639; May *v.* Fletcher, 40 Ind. 575; Carr *v.* Brady, 64 Ind. 28; Pratt *v.* Tefft, 14 Mich. 191; Guerin *v.* Moore, 25 Minn. 462; Bennett *v.* Harms, 51 Wis. 25; Henson *v.* Moore, 104 Ill. 403, 408, 409; Lucas *v.* Sawyer, 17 Iowa, 517; Sturdevant *v.* Norris, 30 Iowa, 65; Cunningham *v.* Welde, 56 Iowa, 369; Ware *v.* Owens, 42 Ala. 212; Walker *v.* Deaver, 5 Mo. App. 139; Magee *v.* Young, 40 Miss. 164; Bates *v.* McDowell, 58 Miss. 815. *Contra,* Royston *v.* Royston, 21 Ga. 161; Moreau *v.* Detchmendy, 18 Mo. 522; Williams *v.* Courtney, 77 Mo. 587; Russell *v.* Rumsey, 35 Ill. 362; Steele *v.* Gellatly, 41 Ill. 39. See Dunn *v.* Sargent, 101 Mass. 336, 340. In Indiana, it has been held that dower may be increased, as well as diminished, in the lands owned by the husband at the time when the statute was enacted. Noel *v.* Ewing, 9 Ind. 37. A contrary conclusion has been reached in North Carolina. Sutton *v.* Asken, 66 N. C. 172 (8 Am. Rep. 500); Hunting *v.* Johnson, 66 N. C. 189; Jenkins *v.* Jenkins, 82 N. C. 202; O'Kelly *v.* Williams; 74 N. C. 281.

§ 117

such cases, if the intention of the legislature is clearly manifested. It is true, as Mr. Cooley states:[1] that if the dower is diminished, the purchaser will get a more valuable estate for which he had not paid an equivalent consideration. But if it is the wish of the legislature that this shall be done, no provision of the constitution has been violated, for there has been no infringement of vested rights. This proposition was carried to such a logical extreme in Indiana, that, in declaring a statute, abolishing the common-law dower, and giving the wife an estate in fee in one-third of her husband's land in lieu of dower, to apply to the lands granted by the husband to purchasers for value, it was held that her common-law dower in such lands was abolished by the statute; while she could not claim the enlarged dower in such lands, because the statute would then interfere with the vested rights of the purchaser. Thus, she was deprived of both the statutory dower, and the dower at common-law.[2] It may be doubted whether, in such a case, the legislature intended that the statute should operate in that manner; but if the intention to have the statute apply to such cases is established, judged by the principles of constitutional construction previously deduced, there can be no doubt that the statute can be made to apply to such cases, even when its application will have the effect of depriving the widow of her dower, at common law, without succeeding in vesting in her the greater estate, intended by the statute to take the place of the dower at common law. But a statute, which simply provided for the enlargement of the dower at common law into an estate in fee could not be construed, when applied to estates that

---

[1] Cooley Const. Lim. 442, n. 4.

[2] Strong v. Clem, 12 Ind. 37; Logan v. Walton, 12 Ind. 639; Bowen v. Preston, 48 Ind. 367; Taylor v. Sample, 51 Ind. 423. See Davis v. O'Farrall, 4 Greene, 168; O'Ferrall v. Simplot, 4 Iowa, 381; Moore v. Kent, 37 Iowa, 20; Craven v. Winter, 38 Iowa, 471; Kennedy v. Insurance Co., 11 Mo. 204.

§ 117

have been granted away, so as to deprive the wife of her common-law dower; for the dower at common-law would be abolished inferentially from the enlargement of the estate by the operation of the statute ; and since the statute cannot apply to such cases, because it would infringe upon the vested rights of the purchaser, the wife's dower in the lands of the husband's purchaser would remain unchanged at common law. It is probable that the Indiana court was in error in not placing this construction upon the statute in question.

But every future interest in property is not an interest in expectancy. A vested estate of future enjoyment is as much a vested right as an estate in possession.[1] Vested remainders and reversions are, therefore, vested rights, and cannot be changed or abolished by statute. We have already discussed the character of a remainder or reversion after an estate tail, and have concluded that they are vested rights not subject to legislative change or modification.[2] If the remainder or reversionary interest were contingent, the conclusion would possibly be different.

But is a contingent remainder, a contingent use or a conditional limitation,[3] so far an interest in expectancy, that it may be defeated by subsequent legislation? In those cases in which the interest is contingent, because the person who is to take the contingent estate is not yet born, it may be reasonable enough to claim that the interest is not a vested right. Until one is born, or at least conceived, he cannot be considered as the subject of rights under the law. He certainly cannot have a vested right in or to anything. A statute might very properly destroy such a contingent interest. This class of cases may

---

[1] Cooley Const. Lim. 440. See *ante*, § 116.

[2] See *ante*, § 116.

[3] The term "conditional limitation" is here employed as a general term, including shifting uses and executory devises. See Tiedeman on Real Prop., §§ 281, 398, 418, 536, 537.

§ 117

possibly include also those, in which the contingency arises from an uncertainty as to which of two or more living persons shall be entitled to take, as where the limitation is to the heirs of a living person. No man's heirs can be ascertained until his death, although one may be the presumptive or apparent heir of another. The heir presumptive or apparent cannot be said to have a vested right to such an estate, in the sense in which the term "vested right" is employed in the law of real property ; but the same may be said of any contingent interest, whether it be a remainder, a use, or a conditional limitation. The person, who is to take the estate upon the happening of the contingency, can in none of these cases claim to have a vested estate in the land ; but may not the expectant owner of the contingent interest claim to have a vested, indefeasible right to the estate, whenever the contingency happens? Even in the law of real property, where the term "vested estate" is used in an extremely technical sense, the contingent remainderman, as well as the expectant owner of a shifting use or executory devise, is deemed to be so far possessed of vested rights in the estate as to be able, at least in equity, to make a valid assignment of the interest.[1] It would seem, therefore, that the interest in such cases would be so far a vested right that it would be beyond the reach of legislative interference. Another reason may be assigned why a statute could not operate to destroy such contingent interests, viz. : that, being created by act of the owner of the property, instead of arising by operation of law, its subsequent taking effect in possession does not depend upon the continuance of the present laws. A change in the law can only operate to defeat the contingent estate, by imposing upon the owner a prohibition against doing with the estate, what he could do without the aid of law. In all the common examples of interests in expectancy, which have been changed or abol-

---

[1] Tiedeman on Real Prop., §§ 411, 530.

§ 117

ished by statute, the interest is the creature of positive law, and does not vest upon any act of disposition of the owner of the land. Its taking effect in possession must consequently depend upon the continued existence of the law, which authorizes and creates it. The repeal of the law, before it vests, does not operate retrospectively, in defeating the inchoate estate. But a law would most certainly operate retrospectively, making that unlawful or impossible which was possible and lawful when it was done, which changes or destroys the interest of a contingent remainderman, or executory devisee. Being retrospective, it will be void if it infringes any vested right, even though it does not amount to a "vested estate," as the term is understood in the law of real property.

Another interesting question is, how far powers of appointment may be changed or abolished by statute. A law would act retrospectively, if it were made to avoid the deed or grant of a power of appointment, and, if it interfered with vested rights, would be unconstitutional. A special power of appointment, to appoint the estate to certain persons under certain conditions and in accordance with directions given, would give to these beneficiaries a vested right to the exercise of their power in their favor, within the restrictions and limitations imposed by the donor, and the donee of the power can not suspend or extinguish the power by a release.[1] It would be reasonable to claim that no statute could be so framed as to change or destroy such a power, because it would interfere with vested rights. But where the power was general, the donee having the power to appoint to whom he pleases, there is certainly no vested right to the exercise of the power in the person or persons to whom he might ultimately appoint the estate. But he would have an absolute right to the exercise of the power, either for himself or in trust for others; and this vested right would be violated by a statute,

[1] Tiedeman on Real Prop. § 561.

§ 117

which either took away the power, or imposed upon its exercise limitations that did not exist at the time when the power was created, and which have the effect of materially reducing the value of the power. Such a statute would consequently be unconstitutional and void.

§ 118.   **Limitation of the right of acquisition.** — One of the incidental rights of private property in lands is the right to acquire land.   Land being the free gift of nature, the regulation of it by the government must be directed in the interest of all, and as every one is guaranteed by the constitution the equal protection of the law, and inequality or partiality in the bestowal of privileges is prohibited, every one may be said to have an indefeasible right to acquire land, by complying with the general laws, which have been enacted for regulating its disposition.   As long as there is a public domain, every one has a right to buy of the government, if he pays the price asked for the land. But where all the public lands have been taken up, the only way left open for the subsequent acquisition of land is by purchase from other private owners.   If no one is willing to sell, one's right to acquire lands has in no way been violated.   But if a seller can be found, any law which would interfere with the purchase, that is, prohibit a particular person or class of persons from acquiring any property in land whatever, would be an unconstitutional violation of a right which belongs to every citizen.   Thus an ordinance was held to be unconstitutional by the Supreme Court of Texas, which absolutely prohibited any prostitute or lewd woman from residing in, or inhabiting any room, house, or place in the city, and forbade the leasing of any such premises to such a person.[1]   Even a chronic breaker of the laws has a right to possess a lodging-house.   He has no right to purchase or lease a house for the purpose of

[1] Milliken v. City Council, 54 Texas 388 (38 Am. Rep. 629).

prosecuting his criminal or nefarious trade, and even though it is a moral certainty that the criminal will use the house or room he occupies for immoral or criminal purposes, he can not be deprived of the use of said room or house as a lodging-house. The citizen has a constitutional right to acquire a local habitation, and no law can impose an absolute prohibition.

It is true that if the Christian principle of the universal brotherhood of man were recognized as a principle of constitutional and international law, and nations merely considered as convenient and subordinate subdivisions of this world-wide brotherhood, we would accord to the alien, as well as to the citizen, the equal right to acquire a homestead within our borders. But this principle of Christianity has never been adopted into our law or into the law of any nation, civilized or uncivilized. On the contrary, international law is constructed on the idea of nationality as a cornerstone. The nations of the world are recognized by international law as distinct and independent political entities, having exclusive control over the country and people within their borders, and owing nothing to the people living outside of their jurisdictions. Although an alien born is entitled to the equal protection of the laws, instituted for the benefit of the citizen, while he is sojourning in the country, he has no absolute right to come into our country or to remain there. Unlike the citizen, he can at any moment be compelled to leave,[1] with or without cause, unless he has acquired a right of ingress under a treaty with his own government. The alien, therefore, cannot be considered as having any absolute right to purchase or acquire lands.

It has long been the policy of England and of the States of this country to deny to the alien the right to hold lands within their borders. In many of the Western States,

[1] See *ante,* § 60.

§ 118

statutes have been passed granting to the alien the unlimited right to purchase and hold lands, and many millions of acres are now the property of foreign capitalists, who have never lived in this country and never expect to.

But while an absolute prohibition against the acquisition of lands by a particular person or class of persons would be unconstitutional, it would not be impossible to impose limitations upon the quantity of land which any one person may own. The agrarian evil, known under the name of "landlordism," resulting from the concentration of lands into the hands of a relative few, and the formation of large farms, is one that will threaten every community at some stage of its political existence. It may be considered by some, with some show of reason, to be questionable, whether the situation would be improved by a statute, which prohibited any one person from holding more than a given quantity of land ; but no serious constitutional objection can be raised to such legislation. It would certainly be a constitutional exercise of police power, as long as it was not made to operate against vested rights, by making void the purchase of lands that have already been completed.[1]   In New-York there is a constitutional prohibition of agricultural leases for a longer period than twelve years.[2] Applied to future purchasers, even providing for the confiscation without compensation of the lands acquired in excess of the quantity allowed by law, the law would most unquestionably be constitutional.

When it is said that the citizen has a natural right to acquire a certain quantity of land for lawful purposes, domestic corporations are not included under that term. It is probably true that corporations already created with the power to purchase lands, whose charters are not subject to repeal by the legislature, have as indefeasible a right to

---

[1] As to the right of expropriation, see *post*, § 121b.
[2] Clark *v.* Barnes, 70 N. Y. 301 (32 Am. Rep. 306).

purchase lands as the natural person; but statutes of mortmain may, subject to this exception, be passed prohibiting absolutely the acquisition of lands by corporations. The rights and powers of a corporation depend altogether upon the will of the legislature.

§ 119. **Regulation of the right of alienation.** — It can hardly be questioned that the government, in making sale of public lands, may provide that the interest which is thus granted shall not be assigned. For land being the absolute property of the State, any condition may be imposed in the original grant of it, that the welfare of the community may seem to require. If effective measures for the prevention of the concentration of lands in the hands of a few are considered essential to the prosperity of the State, the government may lawfully impose an absolute prohibition against alienation, for the purpose of attaining that end.

But in no State is there any law depriving the owner of lands of the right of alienation (except that in some of the States, statutes have been enacted which declare estates for years of short duration, and tenancies from year to year, to be inalienable without the consent of the landlord); nor did the common-law at any time prohibit alienation altogether. Under the feudal system, absolute alienation, of a kind which would shift to the shoulders of the alienee the burden of performing the duties which the feudal tenure imposed upon the tenant, was prohibited, but it was always possible to sublet the land to another, while the original tenant remained liable to the lord for the rendition of the services due to him.[1] On the contrary, the history of the law of real property reveals a constant struggle on the part of the common classes, to remove all restrictions upon the alienation of lands. The statute *quia emptores*,[2] declared

[1] Tiedeman on Real Prop., §§ 21, 23.
[2] 18 Edw. I.

§ 119

void all conditions which absolutely prohibited the alienation of estates in fee, permitting grantors to impose limitations upon the power of alienation in the grant of
any estate less than a fee. So, also, when the courts, by
judicial legislation, developed the law of uses and executory
devises, the rule against perpetuity was adopted, which
prohibited the suspension of alienation by the creation of
contingent estates, beyond a life or lives in being, and
twenty-one years thereafter.[1] The same limitation rests
in effect upon the creation of contingent remainders.[2] A
constant change of ownership has always been considered
salutary to the public welfare.

Inasmuch, therefore, as the private property in land,
already acquired, has been procured subject to no condition
against alienation, the right of alienation is as much a vested
right as the right of possession or the right of enjoyment;
and a law, which materially diminishes this right of alienation, without having for its object the prevention of
injuries to others, or which takes away the right altogether,
is an unconstitutional interference with vested rights.
That the right of free alienation is a vested right, which
cannot be modified or taken away by subsequent legislation,
while the land remains in the possession of the present
landholders, cannot be questioned; and it is equally certain that the government may, in its future grant of the
public lands to private individuals, absolutely prohibit
the alienation of these lands without the consent of the
State : but it is exceedingly doubtful, whether it is constitutional or unconstitutional to apply the statutory prohibition to lands, already the property of private persons, after
they have been sold to others, subject to the statutory restriction upon alienation. There is certainly no interference with any vested right of the subsequent purchaser,

---

[1] Tiedeman on Real Prop., § 544; 2 Washb. on Real Prop. 580.
[2] Tiedeman on Real Prop., § 417; 2 Washb. on Real Prop. 701, 702.

§ 119

but there may be some ground for the claim that the operation of the statute would diminish materially the chances of sale, and consequently would infringe upon the vested right of alienation of the present owners, in a manner not permitted under constitutional limitations.   But this position does not seem to be tenable.   While the vested right of alienation cannot by subsequent legislation be taken away altogether, an indirect restriction upon the right, resulting from the denial of the right of alienation to subsequent purchasers and the consequent diminution of sales, would not be properly considered a deprivation of a vested right.   It is no more so than the effect of a statute, which prohibited the purchase by one person of more than a specified quantity of land.   In both cases, the exercise of police power is reasonable, and the indirect burden imposed upon present owners is but what may be expected from the exercise of the ordinary police power of the State.

While the vested right of alienation cannot be taken away altogether, its exercise may be subjected to reasonable regulations, which are designed to prevent the practice of fraud, and to facilitate the investigation of titles.   The statutory regulation of conveyancing is in some of the States very extensive, providing for almost every contingency, while in others the legislation has been limited.   But in all the States it will be found to be necessary, in order to effect a valid transfer, to comply with certain statutory requisitions.   It is not necessary to speak of them in detail.   They all have the same general object in view, and their constitutionality has never been and cannot be questioned.   These requirements do not deprive the land owner of his right of alienation.   They only regulate his exercise of the right, with reasonable objects in view.   But is hardly necessary to state that such statutory regulations can only have a lawful application to future conveyances.   Laws for

§ 119

the conveyance of estates are unconstitutional as far as they affect conveyances already made.[1]

But the vested right of alienation which the land owner acquires as a natural incident of his property rests upon the natural power, in the absence of lawful restrictions, to give away or sell what belongs to him. The natural right can only exist as long as his natural dominion over the property lasts, viz. : during his life. His natural dominion over his property terminates with his death. He may sell or give away, as he pleases, as long as he does not violate the rights of creditors, up to the last moment of his life, and his right of alienation *inter vivos* cannot be taken away by statute; but after death he ceases to exercise a natural dominion over his property, and if he has any power of disposition after death, it must rest upon positive law, and must change or disappear with the modification or repeal of the law. It is therefore held that no one has a vested right to dispose of lands by will, in accordance with the laws in force when he acquired them. His right to devise depends upon the laws in existence at his death. The new statute may be made to apply to future purchasers of lands, and not to present owners, but it will apply to the latter, if they are not expressly excluded from the operation of the statute.[2]

§ 120. **Involuntary alienation.**—Except the power which the court of chancery possesses in certain cases, and which

---

[1] Greenough *v.* Greenough, 11 Pa. St. 489; Reiser *v.* Tell Association, 39 Pa. St. 137; James *v.* Rowland, 42 Md. 462.

[2] " A party who acquires property does not acquire with it the right to devise such property according to the law as it exists at the time he acquires it. Wills and testaments, rights of inheritance and succession are all of them creatures of the civil or municipal law, and the law relating to or regulating any of them may be changed at the will of the legislature. But no change in the law made after the death of the testator or intestate will affect rights which became vested in the devisee, heir or representative by such death." Sturgis *v.* Ewing, 18 Ill. 176. See Emmert *v.* Hays, 89 Ill. 11.

§ 120

of course is subject to repeal or regulation by the legislature, the power to effect an involuntary alienation rests upon legislative enactment. As a general proposition, the legislature cannot divest one of his vested rights against his will. It can enact laws for the control of property and of its disposition, but it cannot take the private property of one man and give it to another.[1] But there are certain well-known exceptions to this general rule, where the interference of the legislature is necessary to save and protect the substantial interests of individuals on account of their own inability to do so, or to promote the public good. In some of the State constitutions there is a provision against the enactment of special laws, operating upon particular individuals or upon their property. In those States, therefore, involuntary alienation can only be effected by a general law, applicable to all persons under like circumstances. But in the absence of such a constitutional provision, the transfer of lands may be made by special acts of the legislature, as well as under a general law.[2] But wherever such a transfer by special act of the legislature would involve the assumption of judicial power, it would be generally held void, under the common constitutional provision which denies to the legislature the exercise of such powers.[3]

One of the most important, and the most easily justified, cases of involuntary alienation, is one affecting the property of persons under legal disability. Where persons are under a legal disability which prevents them from making a

---

[1] Wilkinson v. Leland, 2 Pet. 658; Adams v. Palmer, 51 Me. 494; Commonwealth v. Alger, 7 Cush. 53; Varick v. Smith, 5 Paige, 159; Matter of Albany Street, 11 Wend. 149; John and Cherry Street, 19 Wend. 676; Taylor v. Porter, 4 Hill, 147; Heyward v. Mayor, 7 N. Y. 324; Bowman v. Middleton, 1 Bay, 252; Russell v. Rumsey, 35 Ill. 374; Good v. Zercher, 12 Ohio, 368; Deutzel v. Waldie, 30 Cal. 144.

[2] Sohier v. Mass. Gen. Hospital, 3 Cush. 483; Kibby v. Chitwood, 4 B. Mon. 95; Edwards v. Pope, 4 Ill. 473.

[3] Rice v. Parkman, 16 Mass. 326; Jones v. Perry, 10 Yerg. 59; Lane v. Dorman, 4 Ill. 238; Edwards v. Pope, 4 Ill. 473.

§ 120

valid sale of their property, and such sale and reinvestment
of the proceeds of sale are necessary for the conservation
of their interests, the State, in the capacity of *parens
patriæ*, has the power to authorize a sale by the guardians
of such persons. This may be done by special act or by
a general law.[1] The law which imposes the disability may
very properly provide against the injurious consequences of
such disability. But the property of persons who are not
under a disability cannot be sold by authority of the courts,
on the ground that such a sale would be beneficial.[2] In
most of the States there are general laws authorizing the
courts to empower the guardians of minors, lunatics and
other persons under disability, to make sale of the real
property of such persons.

The law also provides for sales of real property by
the administrators and executors of the deceased owner.
Where one dies without having made proper provision,
for such contingencies, it is often necessary that some
one should be authorized to make a sale of the lands
for the purpose of making an effective administration,
and to protect and satisfy the claims of those who are interested in the property. If the deceased leaves a will he
very often, perhaps generally, empowers the executor to
make sale of the land, when necessary. Where the executor has the testamentary power, his sales are presumed to
be under this power, and there is no need of a resort to the
statutory power.[3] But these express testamentary powers
are supplemented by statutes, which authorize courts of pro-

---

[1] Sohier *v.* Mass. Gen. Hospital, 16 Mass. 326; *s. c.* 3 Cush. 483; Davidson *v.* Johonot, 7 Metc. 395; Cochran *v.* Van Surlay, 20 Wend. 365;
Estep *v.* Hutchman, 14 Serg. & R. 435; Doe *v.* Douglass, 8 Blackf. 10;
Kirby *v.* Chitwood, 4 B. Mon. 95; Shehan *v.* Barnett, 6 B. Mon. 594; Jones
v. Perry, 10 Yerg. 59.

[2] Wilkinson *v.* Leland, 2 Pet. 658; Adams *v.* Palmer, 51 Me. 494; Sohier
v. Mass. Gen. Hospital, 3 Cush. 483; Heyward *v.* Mayor, 7 N. Y. 324;
Ervine's Appeal, 16 Pa. St. 256; Palairet's Appeal, 67 Pa. St. 479.

[3] Payne *v.* Payne, 18 Cal. 291; White *v.* Moses, 21 Cal. 44.

§ 120

bate to order a sale of the decedent's lands by the administrator or executor, whenever this is necessary to the full
performance of his duties.   Thus, if the personal property
is not sufficient to satisfy all the debts, the administrator or
executor may, under order of the court, make a valid sale of
the lands, and the proceeds of sale will constitute in his
hands a trust fund out of which the claims of the creditors
must be satisfied.[1]

By the early common law, lands were inalienable for any
purpose, and consequently they could not be sold to pay
the debts of the owner.   But as trade and commerce increased, it became necessary that the creditors should be
provided with means for satisfying their claims by compulsory process against the debtor's property.   In compliance
with the popular demand, the statutes merchant and statutes
staple were passed, which created in favor of the creditors
an estate in the debtor's land, whereby he was enabled to
enter into possession and satisfy himself out of the rents
and profits.[2]   These statutes have been abolished in England,
where they are superseded by the *writ of elegit*, which bears
a close resemblance to the American statutes of execution.
In all the American States there are statutes which provide
that, when a creditor obtains judgment against his debtor,
he may cause a writ of execution to be issued against the
property of the debtor, under which the sheriff is authorized to make sale of the real property, and to execute the
proper deeds of conveyance.   In order to further protect
the creditor, it is provided by most of the State statutes
that the judgment, when properly docketed, creates a lien
upon all the debtor's real property, which attaches to, and
binds, the land into whosesoever hands it may come.   The
judgment lien enables the creditor to sell the land under execution, although it has been conveyed away by the debtor

---

[1] See Tiedeman on Real Prop., § 756; 3 Washb. on Real Prop. 209.
[2] 2 Bla. Com. 161, 162.

§ 120

to a purchaser for value.　It is not necessary to attempt to justify these cases of involuntary alienation.　When a judgment for debt is rendered, it determines that one man owes another so much property, expressed and estimated in money, and it is a very natural police regulation to give the property to whom it is due.

The cases are numerous in which the court of chancery has the power to decree a sale and conveyance, and it will be impossible to enumerate them.　The more common cases are the decree of sale in the foreclosure of a .mortgage, in the enforcement of an equitable lien, in an action for specific performance of a contract for the sale of lands, in the confirmation of defective titles, and the sale of equitable estates to satisfy the claims of creditors.　In all these cases, originally, the court in its decree ordered the holder of the legal title, or the owner of the land, to make the proper deeds of conveyance, upon pain of being punished for contempt of court.　If the individual was obstinate or beyond the jurisdiction of the court, the court was powerless to effect a conveyance.[1]　But now courts of equity generally possess the power to authorize some officer of the court, usually the master, to execute the necessary deeds of conveyance, and such deeds will be as effectual in passing an indefeasible title as the sheriff's deed under execution.[2]

Generally when a title is defective through some informality in the execution of the conveyance, upon a proper case being made out, the court of equity will afford an ample remedy by decreeing a reformation of the instrument.[3] But cases do arise where, through the absence or death of

---

[1] Ryder v. Innerarity, 4 Stew. & P. 14; Mummy v. Johnston, 3 A. K. Marsh. 220; Sheppard v. Commissioners of Ross Co., 7 Ohio, 271.

[2] 3 Washb. on Real Prop. 219; Tiedeman on Real Prop., § 758.

[3] Adams v. Stevens, 49 Me. 362; Brown v. Lamphear, 35 Vt. 260; Andrews v. Spurr, 8 Allen, 416; Metcalf v. Putnam, 9 Allen, 97; Conedy v. Marcy, 13 Gray, 373; Prescott v. Hawkins, 16 N. H. 122; Caldwell v. Fulton, 31 Pa. St. 484; Keene's Appeal, 64 Pa. St. 274; Mills v. Lockwood, 42 Ill. 111; Gray v. Hornbeck, 31 Mo. 400.

§ 120

the parties, or through a want of knowledge as to who they are, it is impossible to obtain a reformation in chancery; and even in cases where the equitable remedy is only troublesome and inconvenient, and the defect is only an informality, which does not go to the essence of the conveyance, and which does not create any doubt as to the intention to make a valid conveyance; the power of the legislature to interfere and cure the defect by special act has been generally sustained by the courts of those States, where special acts are not inhibited by the constitution.[1]

The compulsory partition of a joint estate, by allotment or by sale of the premises and distribution of the proceeds of sale, is another recognized class of involuntary alienations. The co-tenants of a joint estate may make a voluntary partition by mutual conveyance to each other of their share in different parts of the estate; that is, by dividing up the estate into several parcels, and making conveyance of one parcel to each, all joining in the deed or deeds, a partition can be made.[2] This was effected merely by the joint exercise of the right of alienation. The consent of all had to be obtained, for all had to join in the deed of partition. Involuntary partition is quite different. This gives one co-tenant the right to take away the property of another against his will, and compel him to accept in the place of it a different interest in the land, or his share in the proceeds of sale. At common law, no suit for partition of a joint estate could have been sustained against the will of any one of the co-tenants, except in the case of an estate in coparcenary; and it was not until the reign of Henry VIII. that any legal action was provided for compulsory partition. The distinction, made by the common law

---

[1] See Wilkinson *v.* Leland, 2 Pet. 627; *s. c.* 10 Pet. 294; Watson *v.* Mercer, 8 Pet. 88; Kearney *v.* Taylor, 15 How. 494; Adams *v.* Palmer, 51 Me. 494; Sohier *v.* Mass. Gen. Hospital, 3 Cush. 483; Chestnut *v.* Shane's Lessee, 16 Ohio, 599; Tiedeman on Real Prop., § 755.

[2] Tiedeman on Real Prop., § 260; 1 Washb. on Real Prop. 676.

§ 120

in this connection between estates in coparcenary and other joint estates, rests upon the fact that the estate in coparcenary arises by operation of law, by descent to the heirs, without the consent of the co-tenant. It was but reasonable that the common law should provide a means of converting the estate in coparcenary into estates in severalty. The other joint estates, are created by and with the consent of the co-tenants, for they are always created by purchase, and they may be presumed to have intended that the estate should ever remain a joint estate, at least as long as all the co-tenants do not agree to a partition. But, yielding to the pressure of public opinion, which has always in England and in this country demanded the removal of all restrictions against the free alienation of land, and the regulation of estates in land in such a manner that a change of ownership may take place in the easiest possible manner, statutes were passed in the reign of Henry VIII., and likewise in the different States of the Union, creating a legal action for the compulsory partition in all joint estates except estates in entirety.[1] The right of compulsory partition of all joint estates, as an invariable incident of these estates, except in the case of tenancies in entirety, has come down to us as an inheritance from the mother country, and all joint estates in the United States have been created in actual or implied contemplation of the possibility of a compulsory partition. Consequently no question can arise as to the constitutionality of laws providing for compulsory partition. It would be different if the right of compulsory partition were granted now for the first time, and the statute was made to apply to existing joint estates. So far as it applied to existing joint estates, the law would be unconstitutional, because of its interference with vested rights. But all subsequently created joint estates would take effect

---

[1] Tiedeman on Real Prop., §§ 261, 262, 290; 1 Washb. on Real Prop. 651, 676; Williams on Real Prop. 103.

§ 120

subject to this provision for compulsory partition, and no one's rights are violated. No partition could be made of a tenancy in entirety, principally because a man and his wife could not sue each other. The right of compulsory partition was therefore not an incident of tenancies in entirety.[1] It has been much mooted, whether tenancies in entirety were not by implication converted into tenancies in common by statutes, which in general terms give to married women, in respect to their property, the rights and powers of single women. Although there are a few cases, in which the courts have held that tenancies in entirety were inferentially abolished,[2] the majority of the cases deny that these statutes have had any effect upon the law of estates in entirety, and that a conveyance of lands to a man and wife makes them tenants in entirety, with the common-law rights and incidents of such tenancies, now, as before the statute.[3] The right to the continued existence of the tenancy in entirety, except when it is destroyed by a voluntary partition, is a vested right which cannot be taken away by subsequent legislation. A statute, which gave to tenants in entirety the right of compulsory partition would be unconstitutional, so far as it was made to apply to existing tenancies in entirety.

A statute of Kentucky[4] authorized the sale of real estate in fee, upon the petition of the life tenant, with or without the consent of the tenant in remainder or reversion. The object of the statute was the same which prompted the

----

[1] Tiedeman on Real Prop., § 242; 1 Washb. on Real Prop. 673.

[2] Clark v. Clark, 56 N. H. 105; Cooper v. Cooper, 76 Ill. 57; Hoffman v. Steigers, 28 Iowa, 302.

[3] Marburg v. Cole, 49 Md. 402 (33 Am. Rep. 266, Hulett v. Inlow, 57 Ind. 412 (26 Am. Rep. 64); Hemingway v. Scales, 42 Miss. 1 (2 Am. Rep. 586); McCurdy v. Canning, 64 Pa. St. 39; Diver v. Diver, 56 Pa. St. 106; Bennett v. Child, 19 Wis. 365; Fisher v. Provin, 25 Mich. 347; Grover v. Jones, 52 Mo. 68; Robinson v. Eagle, 29 Ark. 202; Goelett v. Gori, 31 Barb. 314; Meeker v. Wright, 75 N. Y. 262.

[4] Civil Code, § 491.

§ 120

grant of the right of compulsory partition, viz. : to facilitate the change of ownership in lands. The statute was declared to be unconstitutional, except in its application to cases in which the reversioner or remainder-man is laboring under some disability, such as infancy, insanity, or the like. It was claimed that in no other case could a citizen be deprived of the right to manage his property without state interference.[1] There cannot be any doubt of the unconstitutionality of the law when it is applied to existing life estates, remainders and reversions, although such laws have been sustained in Massachusetts and Connecticut.[2] The application of the statute to such cases would operate to deprive persons of their vested rights, and consequently would be unconsti-

---

[1] Glossom v. McFerran, 79 Ky. 236.

[2] Statute authorized sale of lands on petition of life tenant:—

"It is said by the petitioners that this resolution deprives them of their interest in the property against their will and is therefore void, not only as opposed to natural justice, but as in conflict with the provisions of the constitution of the state. It was held by this court in the case of Richardson v. Monson, 23 Conn. 94, that the statute which authorizes the sale of lands held in joint tenancy, tenancy in common, or coparcenary, whenever partition cannot conveniently be made in any other way, is constitutional. That case was ably discussed by counsel, who offered some arguments against the constitutionality of the statute, which have been urged upon our consideration against the validity of this resolution. It is difficult to see any distinction in principle between the two cases. When a sale is made of real estate held in joint tenancy, the tenant opposed to the sale is as much deprived of his estate by the change which is made, as these petitioners are of their property, by the change authorized by this resolution. In either case the parties are not subjected to a loss of their property. It is simply changed from one kind to another." Linsley v. Hubbard, 44 Conn. 109 (26 Am. Rep. 431).

"The Legislature authorizes the sale, taking care that the proceeds shall go to the trustees for the use and benefit of those having the life estate, and of those having the remainder, as they are entitled under the will. This is depriving no one of his property, but is merely changing real estate into personal estate, for the benefit of all parties in interest. This part of the resolve, therefore, is within the scope of the powers exercised from the earliest times, and repeatedly adjudged to be rightfully exercised by the legislature." Sohier v. Mass. Gen. Hospital, 3 Cush. 496; Rice v. Parkman, 16 Mass. 326.

§ 120

tutional.   But in its application to future cases, the statute
violates no provisions of the constitution, for like the statutory right of compulsory partition, it would attach as an
ordinary incident to all subsequently created estates for life,
and in remainder or reversion: no vested right would be invaded, for the vested rights of those, who would be affected
by the compulsory sale, would be acquired subject to the
exercise of this power.

Another case of involuntary alienation occurs under the
operation of the so-called *betterment laws.*   Under the common law maxim, *quidquid plantatur solo, solo cedit,* whatever is annexed to the soil, whether by the owner or by a
stranger, without the consent of the owner, becomes a part
of the soil, in legal contemplation, and consequently the
property of the owner of the soil.   If a stranger makes an
erection upon the land, with the consent of the owner, the
property in the house or other erection remains in the
licensee, and he can remove it whenever the license is revoked.   If he does not then remove it, he loses his right to
it, and it becomes the property of the owner of the soil.[1]

If the building is erected by a stranger without the
consent of the owner of the soil, it at once becomes
the property of the latter, although the stranger has
made the improvements, believing in good faith that
he had a good title to the land.[2]   So far as the principle

[1] Tapley v. Smith, 18 Me. 12; Russell v. Richards, 10 Me. 429; Keyser
v. School District, 35 N. H. 480; Coleman v. Lewis, 27 Pa. St. 291; Reid
v. Kirk, 12 Rich. 54; Yates v. Mullen, 24 Ind. 278; Mott v. Palmer, 1
Const. 571; Hinckley v. Baxter, 13 Allen, 139; Antoni v. Belknap, 102 Mass.
200; Kutter v. Smith, 2 Wall 491; O'Brien v. Kustener, 27 Mich. 292;
Ham v. Kendall, 111 Mass. 298; Goodman v. Hannibal & St. Joseph R. R.
Co., 45 Mo. 33.

[2] Osgood v. Howard, 6 Greenl. 452; Aldrich v. Parsons, 6 N. Y. 55c;
Dame v. Dame, 38 N. H. 429; Ogden v. Stock, 34 Ill. 522; Rogers v.
Woodbury, 15 Pick. 156; Mott. v. Palmer, 1 Const. 571; West v. Stewart,
7 Pa. St. 122; Webster v. Potter, 105 Mass. 416; Powell v. M. & B. Mfg.
Co., 3 Mason, 369; 2 Kent's Com. 334-338; Tiedeman on Real Prop., §
702.

§ 120

was applied to *bona fide* holders of land under a mistaken claim of title, it gave to the owner of land property to which he could make no moral or equitable claim. His title to the improvements vested simply under the operation of the technical legal rule just stated. In order to remedy this gross injustice of the common law, statutes have been passed in many of the States known as *betterment laws,* which generally, in substance, provide that upon the recovery of land from one who has been a *bona fide* disseisor under color of title, the plaintiff shall reimburse the defendant for the improvements, which he has made under the mistaken belief that he was the owner of the land, or transfer the title to the defendant, upon the payment of the value of the land without the improvements. Although differing somewhat in detail, they all substantially conform to this description. The constitutionality of the statutes has been repeatedly questioned, but they have invariably been sustained.[1]

The constitutionality of these laws has been generally sustained in their application to improvements already made under a mistaken claim of title, as well as to those made after the enactment of the statutes. Judge Story held[2] that such a law could not constitutionally be made to apply to improvements made before its passage. Mr. Cooley states that this decision was rendered under the New Hampshire constitution, which forbade retrospective laws.[3] But, even

---

[1] See Brown *v.* Storm, 4 Vt. 37; Whitney *v.* Richardson, 31 Vt. 300; Brackett *v.* Norcross, 1 Me. 89; Withington *v.* Corey, 2 N. H. 115; Bacon *v.* Callender, 6 Mass. 303; Fowler *v.* Halhert, 4 Bibb, 54; Hunt's Lessee *v.* McMahon, 5 Ohio 132; Longworth *v.* Worthington, 6 Ohio, 9; Ross *v.* Irving, 14 Ill. 171; Childs *v.* Shower, 18 Iowa, 261; Pacquette *v.* Pickness, 19 Wis. 219; Armstrong *v.* Jackson, 1 Blackf. 374; Coney *v.* Owen, 6 Watts, 435; Steele *v.* Spruance, 22 Pa. St. 256; Lynch *v.* Brudie, 63 Pa. St. 206; Griswold *v.* Bragg, 48 Conn. 577; Dothage *v.* Stuart, 35 Mo. 570; Fenwick *v.* Gill, 38 Mo. 510; Ormond *v.* Martin, 37 Ala. 598; Pope *v.* Macon, 23 Ark. 644; Howard *v.* Zeyer, 18 La. An. 407; Love *v.* Shartzer, 31 Cal. 487.

[2] In Society, etc., *v.* Wheeler, 2 Gall. 105.

[3] Cooley Const. Lim. 479, note.

§ 120

independently of this special constitutional provision, and applied to betterment laws generally, the position of Judge Story is sound. Under the legal maxim: *quidquid planta-tur solo, solo cedit,* the improvements already made, when the statute was passed, had become the absolute property of the real owner of the land, and a statute which took away the right to these improvements would interfere with vested rights, and for that reason would be unconstitutional. But inasmuch as the right to the improvements subsequently made would depend upon the continued existence of this common-law rule, its repeal or change would prevent the right from vesting, and so far as these statutes gave to the *bona fide* disseisor of the land the right to the improvements made by him after the enactment of the statute, it would not violate any constitutional provision. If the statute did not go farther in the adjustment of the antagonistic rights of the two claimants, the statute would create in them a species of joint estate. But the statute proceeds to give to the real owner of the land his election to pay the *bona fide* disseissor the value of the improvements, or to transfer to him the title to the land, upon receiving payment of the value of the land without the improvements. This latter provision of the statute without doubt works an interference with vested rights, for a man's right of property has been either charged with a burden, in the shape of liability for improvements which he has not directed to be made, or given to another on account of no fault of his own. But circumstances and facts, which cannot be changed in order to place the parties in *statu quo,* have created between them a *quasi*-joint estate of such a nature that the property cannot be mutually profitable without a partition. Compulsory partition of a peculiar kind is ordered, viz: the owner of the land is obliged to pay for the improvements, or to sell the land to the other claimant. When applied to the improvements, which are made after the enactment of the statute, the statute is as constitutional as the laws which

§ 120

provide for the compulsory partition of ordinary joint estates. "Betterment laws, then, recognize the existence of an equitable right, and give a remedy for its enforcement where none has existed before. It is true that they make a man pay for improvements which he has not directed to be made; but this legislation presents no feature of officious interference by government with private property. The improvements have been made by one person in good faith, and are now to be appropriated by another. The parties cannot be placed *in statu quo*, and the statute accomplishes justice as nearly as the circumstances of the case will admit, when it compels the owner of the land, who, if he declines to sell, must necessarily appropriate the betterments made by another, to pay the value to the person at whose expense they have been made. The case is peculiar; but a statute cannot be void as an unconstitutional interference with private property, which adjusts the equities of the parties as nearly as possible according to natural justice." [1] It was held in Ohio that a statute was unconstitutional, which gave to the occupying claimant the right to buy the land or receive payment for the improvements he had made. The right of election should be given to the owner of the land. The court say : " The occupying claimant act, in securing to the occupant a compensation for his improvements as a condition precedent to the restitution of the lands to the owner goes to the utmost stretch of the legislative power touching this subject. And the statute, * * * providing for the transfer of the fee in the land to the occupying claimant, without the consent of the owner, is a palpable invasion of the right of private property, and clearly in conflict with the constitution." [2]

It would seem reasonable, also, to maintain that in order that the claim for improvements under the better-

---

[1] Cooley Const. Lim. 480.
[2] McCoy *v.* Grandy, 3 Ohio St. 463.

ment laws may be made, the improvements must be permanent annexations. Where the improvements consist of clearing or draining lands, the benefit has become absolutely inseparable from the land; but where the improvements consist of houses and other buildings, they could be removed in most cases, at least when they were frame buildings. Where the buildings are constructed upon firm and permanent foundation imbedded in the soil, particularly when the buildings are made of brick or stone, the cost of removal would in most cases almost amount to the value of the improvement, and to compel a removal would be almost as unjust as to give the improvements to the owner of the land. But when the buildings are frames, resting temporarily upon blocks, or upon the ground, by analogy, the distinction beeween permanent and temporary annexations, which obtain in the law of fixtures, may be recognized in this connection, and in the last case the occupying claimant may be permitted to remove his temporary structure, but cannot claim any compensation for it under the betterment laws.[1]

SECTION 121. Eminent domain.
      121a. Exercise of power regulated by legislature.
      121b. Public purpose, what is a.
      121c. What property may be taken?
      121d. What constitutes a taking?
      121e. Compensation, how ascertained.

§ 121. **Eminent domain.** — It has been already explained[2] that all lands were originally the common property of the human race; necessarily so, since land is the free gift of nature, and not the product of man's labor. It was also shown that, under the present law of real property, the private owner of lands acquires only a tenancy of more or less limited

[1] For a discussion of the law of eminent domain, see next section, § 121; for the limitations upon the power of taxation, see *post*, § 129.
[2] See § 115.

§ 121

duration under the absolute and ultimate proprietorship of
the State, as the representative of organized society, subject
to certain conditions, one of which is that the State may at
any time, on payment of its value, reclaim the tenancy so
granted to private individuals, whenever the public exigencies require such confiscation. This right of confiscation of
private lands for public purposes is called the right of eminent domain. Mr. Cooley speaks of eminent domain as
referring, not only to those superior rights of the State in
the private lands of the individual, but also to any lands
which the State may own absolutely, such as public buildings, forts, navigable rivers, etc.[1] It seems to me that this
more comprehensive use of the term unnecessarily con-
founds it with "*public* domain," and deprives it of its
technical and special signification. Mr. Cooley also defines
the term to mean "that superior right of property pertaining to the sovereignty by which the private property
acquired by its citizens under its protection may be taken or
its use controlled for the public benefit without regard to
the wishes of its owners,"[2] including personal, as well as
real property, except money and rights of action.[3] There
is some foundation for this use of the term in the writings
of political economists and publicists, and in the *dicta* of
judges.[4] It is also true that personal property may be for-

---

[1] Cooley on Const. Lim. 647, 648.

[2] Cooley on Const. Lim. 649.

[3] Cooley on Const. Lim. 652, 653. "Generally it may be said, legal
and equitable rights of every description are liable to be thus appropriated. From this statement, however, must be excepted money, or that
which in ordinary use passes as such, and which the government may
reach by taxation, and also rights in action, which can only be available
when made to produce money; neither of which can it be needful to take
under this power."

[4] "The right which belongs to the society or to the sovereign of disposing, in case of necessity, and for the public safety of all the wealth
contained in the State, is called the eminent domain." McKinley, J., in
Pollard's Lessee *v.* Hagan, 3 How. 212, 223. In this case, as in all other
actual cases of the exercise of the right of eminent domain, the thing appropriated was land.

§ 121

cibly taken from private owners for public uses, whenever
extreme necessity requires it, as in the case of war or of a
a general famine.[1] But, inasmuch as the grounds for the
justification of this involuntary appropriation of private
property to public purposes are different, according as the
property is real or personal, the former resting upon the
claim of a superior property in lands, the other upon the
illogical plea of urgent and overruling necessity, it is wise
to confine the term "eminent domain" to the cases of land
appropriation, and employ some other term to signify the
official appropriation of personal property. Eminent
domain, therefore, is the superior right of the State to
appropriate for public purposes the private lands within
its borders, upon payment of a proper compensation for the
property so taken.

§ 121*a*. **Exercise of power regulated by legislature.** —
The exercise of this right is in the first instance reposed in
the legislature. Until the legislature by enactment determines the occasions when the conditions under which, and
the agencies by which, the power of appropriation may be
exercised, there can be no lawful appropriation of lands to
public purposes. The exercise of the right is a legislative
act, and requires no judicial confiscation of the land, in
order to divest the private owner of his title.[2] Except
so far as the exercise of the power may be limited
and controlled by provisions of the constitution, the necessity for its exercise is left to the legislative discretion.
The courts cannot question the necessity for the taking,

---

[1] See *post*, § 137.

[2] " It requires no judicial condemnation to subject private property to
public uses. Like the power to tax, it resides with the legislative department to whom the delegation is made. It may be exercised directly
or indirectly by that body; and it can only be restrained by the judiciary
when its limits have been exceeded or its authority has been abused or
perverted." Kramer *v.* Cleveland & Pittsburg R. R. Co., 5 Ohio St. 140,
146.

§ 121*a*

provided the land is taken for a public purpose.   The legislative determination of the necessity is final, and is not
subject to review by the courts.

The following quotation, from an opinion of Judge Denio,
of the New York Court of Appeals,[1] will be sufficient to
explain the reasons by which the exclusion of this question
from judicial investigation, and the consequent denial to the
property owner of the right to be heard in his behalf, may
be justified.   The learned judge says : " The question then
is, whether the State, in the exercise of the power to appropriate the property of individuals to a public use, where the
duty of judging of the expediency of making the appropriation, in a class of cases, is committed to public officers, is
obliged to afford to the owners of the property an opportunity to be heard before those officers when they sit for the
purpose of making the determination.   I do not speak now
of the process for arriving at the amount of compensation
to be paid to the owners, but of the determination whether,
under the circumstances of a particular case, the property
required for the purpose shall be taken or not; and I am of
the opinion that the State is not under any obligation to
make provision for a judicial contest upon that question.
The only part of the constitution which refers to the subject is that which forbids private property to be taken for
public use without compensation, and that which prescribes
the manner in which the compensation shall be ascertained.

" It is not pretended that the statute under consideration
violates either of these provisions.   There is, therefore, no
constitutional injunction on the point under consideration.
The necessity for appropriating private property for the use
of the public or of the government is not a judicial question.   The power resides in the legislature.   It may be
exercised by means of a statute which shall at once designate the property to be appropriated and the purpose of the

---

[1] People v. Smith, 21 N. Y. 595.

§ 121a

appropriation; or it may be delegated to public officers, or, as it has been repeatedly held, to private corporations established to carry on enterprises in which the public are interested. There is no restraint upon the power, except that requiring compensation to be made. And where the power is committed to public officers, it is a subject of legislative discretion to determine what prudential regulations shall be established to secure a discreet and judicious exercise of the authority. The constitutional provision securing a trial by jury in certain cases, and that which declares that no citizen shall be deprived of his property without due process of law, have no application to the case. The jury trial can only be claimed as a constitutional right where the subject is judicial in its character. The exercise of the right of eminent domain stands on the same ground with the power of taxation. Both are emanations of the law-making power. They are the attributes of political sovereignty, for the exercise of which the legislature is under no necessity to address itself to the courts. In imposing a tax, or in appropriating the property of a citizen, or a class of citizens, for a public purpose, with a proper provision for compensation, the legislative act is itself due process of law; though it would not be if it should undertake to appropriate the property of one citizen for the use of another, or to confiscate the property of one person or a class of persons, or a particular description of property upon some view of public policy, where it could not be said to be taken for a public use. It follows from these views that it is not necessary for the legislature, in the exercise of the right of eminent domain, either directly, or indirectly through public officers or agents, to invest the proceedings with the forms or substance of judicial process. It may allow the owner to intervene and participate in the discussion before the officer or board to whom the power is given of determining whether the appropriation shall be made in a particular case, or it may provide that the officers shall

§ 121a

act upon their own views of propriety and duty, without the aid of a forensic contest. The appropriation of the property is an act of public administration, and the form and manner of its performance is such as the legislature in its discretion may prescribe." [1]

While the exercise of the right of eminent domain belongs primarily to the legislature, it is not necessary for it directly to make the appropriation to public uses. Since the exercise of the power is only permissible in the advancement of the public interests, if that requirement is complied with, it is also within the legislative discretion to determine whether the confiscation shall be made by it, or by some other corporate body or individual to whom the power is delegated. If the public interests are subserved best, when the right is exercised by a municipal corporation or a railroad company, there can be no constitutional objection to the delegation of the power, for the burden upon private property is not thereby increased. The grant of the power to a town, city, county or school district, needs no special defense, because the delegate of the power is in each instance only a local branch of the general State government. It is the government in every case which makes the confiscation. But when the power is granted to a corporation, composed of private persons, who procure a grant of the power for the purpose of making a profit out of it; although the use to which the land is put may serve to satisfy a public want, there is more

---

[1] See also United States v. Harris, 1 Sumn. 21; Spring v. Russell, 3 Watts, 294; Varick v. Smith, 5 Paige Ch. 137 (28 Am. Dec. 417); People v. Smith, 21 N. Y. 595; Cooper v. Williams, 7 Me. 273; Perry v. Wilson, 7 Mass. 395; Aldridge v. Railroad Company, 2 Stew. & Port. 199 (23 Am. Dec. 307); O'Hara v. Lexington, etc., R. R. Co., 1 Dana, 232; Henry v. Underwood, 1 Dana, 247; Waterworks Co. v. Burkhardt, 41 Ind. 364; Ford v. Chicago, etc., R. R. Co., 14 Wis. 609. But the question, whether the appropriation shall be made, may be submitted by the legislature to a vote of the people, or to some court or jury. Iron R. R. Co. v. Ironton, 19 Ohio St. 299. And in Michigan, the submission of the question of necessity to a jury, is made by the constitution an indispensable requirement. Mansfield, etc., R. R. Co. v. Clark, 23 Mich. 519; Arnold v. Decatur, 29 Mich. 11.

§ 121a

or less disposition to question the constitutional propriety
of the delegation of the power. But the constitutional
objection is deemed to be untenable. In granting to a
private corporation the right of eminent domain, the State
does not consider the benefit to the stockholders of the corporation, but rather the public benefit derived from the construction and maintenance of a turnpike, a railroad, etc.
It is true that government may undertake these public
improvements, but it is the prevailing opinion that the best
interests of the public are subserved by granting the right to
a private corporation which assumes, in return for the right
of eminent domain and the private gain to be got out of the
business, to satisfy the public want; and the legislature has
uniformly been held to hold within its discretion the power
of exercising this right or of delegating it, according as the
one course or the other seems best to promote the public
welfare.[1]   Not only is this permissible, but it is also held to
be constitutionally unobjectionable to delegate to the corporation or individual, along with the exercise of the right
of eminent domain, the power to determine finally upon the
necessity for the taking, without any judicial investigation.[2]

[1] Wilson v. Blackbird Creek Marsh Co., 2 Pet. 245; Stevens v. Middle-
sex Canal, 12 Mass. 466; Boston Mill Dam v. Newman, 12 Pick. 467;
Lebanon v. Olcott, 1 N. H. 339; Petition of Mt. Washington Road
Co., 35 N. H. 134; Eaton v. Boston C. & M. R. R. Co., 51 N·
H. 504; Armington v. Barnet, 15 Vt. 745; White River Turnpike v. Centra-
R. R. Co., 21 Vt. 590; Bradley v. N. Y. & N. H. R. R. Co., 21 Conn. 294;
Olmstead v. Camp, 33 Conn. 532; Beekman v. Saratoga & Schenectady R.
R. Co., 3 Paige, 73 (22 Am. Dec. 679); Bloodgood v. Mohawk & Hudson
R. R. Co., 18 Wend. 9; Whiteman's Ex'rs v. Wilmington, etc., R. R. Co.,
2 Harr. 514; Raleigh, etc., R. R. Co. v. Davis, 2 Dev. & Bat. 451; Swan v.
Williams, 2 Mich. 427; Pratt v. Brown, 3 Wis. 603; Gilmer v. Lime Point,
18 Cal. 229.
[2] People v. Smith, 21 N. Y. 595; Lyon v. Jerome, 26 Wend. 484; Matter of Fowler, 53 N. Y. 60; N. Y. Central, etc., R. R. Co v. Met. Gas Co.,
63 N. Y. 326; Hays v. Risher, 32 Pa. St. 169; Chicago, etc., R. R. Co. v.
Lake, 71 Ill. 333; North Missouri R. R. Co. v. Lackland, 25 Mo. 515;
North Mo. R. R. Co. v. Gott, 25 Mo. 540; Bankhead v. Browny, 25 Iowa,
540; Warren v. St. Paul, etc., R. R. Co., 18 Minn. 384.

§ 121a

But while the power of the legislature to determine the mode and occasion of the exercise of the right of eminent domain is not restricted by constitutional limitations, when the legislature has prescribed the conditions and established regulations for the exercise of the right, the performance of the conditions and the observance of the regulations become an indispensable condition precedent to the exercise of the right, and any failure to comply with the requirements of the statute, will invalidate the confiscation of property. There must be a most scrupulous observance of all those provisions which were designed to serve as a protection to the interests of the land owner.[1]

---

[1] " The statute says that, after a certain other shall have been passed, the company may then proceed to take private property for the use of its road; that is equivalent to saying that the right shall not be exercised without such subsequent act. The right to take private property for public use is one of the highest prerogatives of the sovereign power; and here the legislature has, in language not to be mistaken, expressed its intention to reserve that power until it could judge for itself whether the proposed road would be of sufficient public utility to justify the use of this high prerogative. It did not intend to cast this power away, to be gathered up and used by any who might choose to exercise it." Gillinwater v. Miss., etc., R. R. Co., 13 Ill. 1, 4. See Baltimore, etc., R. R. Co. v. Nesbit, 10 How. 395; Stacy v. Vt. Cent. R. R. Co., 27 Vt. 39; Burt v. Brigham, 117 Mass. 307; Wamesit Power Co. v. Allen, 120 Mass. 352; Lund v. New Bedford, 121 Mass. 286; Nichols v. Bridgeport, 23 Conn. 189; Judson v. Bridgeport, 25 Conn. 426; Bloodgood v. Mohawk, etc., R. R. Co., 18 Wend. 9; Reitenbaugh v. Chester Valley, R. R. Co., 21 Pa. St. 100; State v. Seymour, 35 N. J. L. 47; W. Va. Transportation Co. v. Volcanic Oil & Coal Co., 5 W. Va. 382; Supervisors of Doddridge v. Stout, 9 W. Va. 703; Decatur Co. v. Humphreys, 47 Ga. 565; Cameron v. Supervisors, etc., 47 Miss. 264; St. Louis, etc., R. R. Co. v. Teters, 68 Ill. 144; Mitchell v. Illinois, etc., Coal Co., 68 Ill. 286; Chicago, etc., R. R. Co. v. Smith, 78 Ill. 96; People v. Brighton, 20 Mich. 57; Power's Appeal, 29 Mich. 504; Kroop v. Forman, 31 Mich. 144; Moore v. Railway Co., 34 Wis. 173; Bohlman v. Green Bay, etc., R. R. Co., 40 Wis. 157; Delphi v. Evans, 36 Ind. 90; Ellis v. Pac. R. R. Co., 51 Mo. 200; United States v. Reed, 56 Mo. 565; Commissioners v. Beckwith, 10 Kan. 603; St. Joseph, etc., R. R. Co. v. Callender, 13 Kan. 496; Stanford v. Worn, 27 Cal. 171; Brady v. Bronson, 45 Cal. 640; Stockton v. Whitmore, 50 Cal. 554; Paris v. Mason, 37 Texas, 447.

§ 121*a*

It is also recognized as an invariable corollary to this rule, that the grants of the right of eminent domain are to be strictly construed, and the powers delegated are not to be extended by construction beyond the express limitation of the statute. "There is no rule more familiar or better settled than this; that grants of corporate power, being in derogation of common right, are to be strictly construed; and this is especially the case where the power claimed is a delegation of the right of eminent domain, one of the highest powers of sovereignty pertaining to the state itself, and interfering most seriously and often vexatiously with the ordinary rights of property." [1]

But there are two constitutional limitations, imposed very generally upon the exercise of the right of eminent domain, and it is also a judicial question whether the legislature, in the exercise of the right, has fully complied with their requirements. One has reference to the ascertainment and payment of the compensation to the land owner for the loss of his land, which will be discussed subsequently,[2] and the second provides that the private land of the individual shall not be taken in the exercise of the right of eminent domain except for public purposes. It is a legislative question whether the public exigencies require the appropriation, but it is clearly a judicial question, whether a particular confiscation of land has been made for a public purpose.[3]

---

[1] Currier v. Marietta, etc., R. R. Co., 11 Ohio St. 228, 231. See W. Va. Transportation Co. v. Volcanic Oil & Coal Co., 5 W. Va. 382; Bruning v. N. N. Canal & Banking Co., 12 La. Ann. 541; Gilmer v. Lime Point, 19 Cal. 47.

[2] See *post*, § 121d.

[3] Tyler v. Beacher, 44 Vt. 648; Olmstead v. Camp, 33 Conn. 551; Beckman v. Railroad Company, 3 Paige, 45 (22 Am. Dec. 679); Matter of Deansville Cemetery Association, 66 N. Y. 569 (23 Am. Rep. 86); Scudder v. Trenton, etc., Co., 1 N. J. Eq. 694 (23 Am. Dec. 756); Loughbridge v. Harris, 42 Ga. 500; Harding v. Goodlett, 3 Yerg. 40 (24 Am. Dec. 546); Chicago, etc., R. R. Co. v. Lake, 71 Ill. 333; Water Works Co. v. Burkhardt, 41 Ind. 364; Ryerson v. Brown, 35 Mich. 333 (24 Am. Rep. 564); Bankhead v. Brown, 25 Iowa, 540.

§ 121a

§ 121*b*. **Public purpose, what is a.** — The authorities are unanimous in the recognition of the abstract proposition, that the legislature cannot in the exercise of the right of eminent domain, even when the compensation is made on the most liberal terms, take the land from a private owner and appropriate it to any but a public use.[1] But a careful reading of the authorities fail to develop any definite meaning for the term " public use." As long as the government exercises the right directly and for the State's immediate benefit, no difficulty is experienced in determining what is a public use. There can be no doubt that land is devoted to a public use, when it is taken for the purpose of laying out parks, and

---

[1] " The right of eminent domain does not imply a right in the sovereign power to take the property of one citizen and transfer it to another, even for a full compensation, where the public interest will be in no way promoted by such transfer." Beekman *v.* Saratoga, etc., R. R. Co., 3 Paige, 73 (22 Am. Dec. 679). " It is true there is neither in our constitution, nor in the constitution of the other States, any express provision forbidding, that private property should be taken for the private use of another or any constitutional provision forbidding the legislature to pass laws, whereby the private property of one citizen may be taken and transferred to another for his private use without the consent of the owner. It was doubtless regarded as unnecessary to insert such a provision in the constitution or bill of rights, as the exercise of such arbitrary power of transferring by legislation the property of one person to another, without his consent, was contrary to the fundamental principles of every republican government; and in a republican government neither the legislative, executive nor judicial department can possess unlimited power. Such a power as that of taking the private property of one and transferring it to another for his own use, is not in its nature legislative, and it is only legislative power, which by the constitution is conferred on the legislature. Such an act, if passed by the legislature, would not in its nature be law, but would really be an act of robbery, the exercise of an arbitrary power, not conferred on the legislature." Varner *v.* Martin, 21 W. Va. 548. See, also, to the same effect, Bloodgood *v.* Mohawk, etc., R. R. Co., 18 Wend. 955; Matter of Albany St., 11 Wend. 149 (25 Am. Dec. 618); Embury *v.* Conner, 3 N. Y. 511; N. Y., etc., R. R. Co. *v.* Kip, 46 N. Y. 546 (7 Am. Rep. 383); Teneyck *v.* Canal Co., 18 N. J. 200 (37 Am. Dec. 233); Edgewood R. R. Co.'s appeal, 79 Pa. St. 277; Concord R. R. Co. *v.* Greely, 17 N. H. 47; Buckingham *v.* Smith, 10 Ohio, 288; Cooper *v.* Williams, 5 Ohio, 391 (24 Am. Dec. 299); Pratt *v.* Brown, 3 Wis. 603; Sadler *v.* Langham, 34 Ala. 311.

§ 121*b*

public gardens,[1] for the construction of public buildings of
all kinds,[2] aqueducts, drains and sewers,[3] and the building of
levees on the banks of the Mississippi.[4] It is likewise
freely admitted that the State may appropriate lands without limitation for the purpose of laying out streets and
highways. In all these cases of the exercise of the right
of eminent domain, the land is taken for the general use of
the public, and therefore is devoted to a public use. If in
any one of these cases the land was to be used by a few private individuals, and not by the public generally, it would
not be a taking for a public use, and consequently it would
be unlawful.

There has been considerable doubt felt and expressed
concerning the constitutionality of State statutes, providing for the opening and maintenance of so-called private
roads, at the expense of the person or persons who may be
benefited thereby. These statutes usually provide that
some local offices or officers, usually the county court, shall
in all cases, where the public necessity will not justify the
opening of a public road, to be constructed and maintained
at the expense of the county, authorize, under certain limitations, those persons who will be benefited by the opening of such a road, to construct and maintain it at their own
expense, and to appropriate whatever land is needful.

[1] Owners of Ground v. Mayor, etc., of Albany, 15 Wend. 374; Matter
of Central Park Extension, 16 Abb. Pr. 56; Brooklyn Park Commissioners
v. Armstrong, 45 N. Y. 234 (6 Am. Rep. 70); County Court v. Griswold,
58 Mo. 175.

[2] Hooper v. Bridgewater, 102 Mass. 512; Williams v. School District,
33 Vt. 271; Long v. Fuller, 68 Pa. St. 170.

[3] Ham v. Salem, 100 Mass. 350; French p. White, 24 Conn. 174; Gardner v. Newburg, 2 Johns. Ch. 162 (7 Am. Dec. 526); Reddall v. Bryan,
14 Md. 444; Kane v. Baltimore, 15 Md. 240; Burden v. Stein, 27 Ala.
104; Matter of Drainage of Lands, 34 N. J. L. 497; People v. Nearing,
27 N. Y. 306; Reeves v. Treasurer of Wood Co., 8 Ohio St. 333; Anderson
v. Kerns Draining Co., 14 Ind. 199; Hildreth v. Lowell, 11 Gray, 345.

[4] Mithoff v. Carrollton, 12 La. Ann. 185; Cash v. Whitworth, 13 La.
401· Inge v. Police Jury, 14 La. Ann. 117.

§ 121b

The constitutionality of these statutes has been attacked, on the ground that the roads, thus established, were private and not for the benefit of the general public.[1] The difficulty in the way of a clear understanding of the matter is increased by a failure to appreciate the difference between a public and a private road. If one or more individuals have the power to appropriate land for the opening of a road for their exclusive benefit, from which they may shut out the general public, and which they may maintain or discontinue at their pleasure, without any supervisory control on the part of the State or municipal authorities, the road is most certainly a private one, and the forcible appropriation of land for it is a taking of private property without due process of law. But if the road is open to the general public, and the persons, for whose special benefit the road was established, have not the power of closing it up at will, but upon them the expense of constructing it and maintaining it is imposed ; even though they may at will discontinue the repairs, the road is a public one, notwithstanding it is called by the statute authorizing it a private road, and it is opened for the special benefit of those, who assume the expense of its construction and maintenance. It being open to the public, the fact that there is no pressing public need for the road is not open to judicial investigation. The legisla-

---

[1] Taylor v. Porter, 4 Hill, 140; Buffalo & N. Y. R. R. Co. v. Brainard, 9 N. Y. 100; Tyler v. Beacher, 44 Vt. 648 (8 Am. Rep. 398); Bradley v. N. Y., etc., R. R. Co., 21 Conn. 294; Pittsburg v. Scott, 1 Pa. St. 809; Varner v. Martin, 21 W. Va. 534; Young v. McKenzie, 3 Ga. 31; Hickman's Case, 4 Harr. 580; Sadler v. Laugham, 34 Ala. 311; Reeves v. Treasurer of Wood Co., 8 Ohio St. 333; Wild v. Deig, 43 Ind. 45 (13 Am. Rep. 399); Stewart v. Hartman, 46 Ind. 331; Blackman v. Halves, 72 Ind. 515; Osborn v. Hart, 24 Wis. 89 (1 Am. Rep. 161); Nesbit v. Trumbo, 39 Ill. 110; Dickey v. Tennison, 27 Mo. 373; Bankhead v. Brown, 25 Iowa, 540; Witham v. Osburn, 4 Ore. 318 (18 Am. Rep. 287). But see Whittingham v. Bowen, 22 Vt. 317; Bell v. Prouty, 43 Vt. 279; Proctor v. Andover, 42 N. H. 348; Pocopson Road, 16 Pa St. 15; Harvey v. Thomas, 10 Watts, 63; Ferris v. Bramble, 5 Ohio St. 109; Robinson v. Swope, 12 Bush, 21; Sherman v. Brick, 32 Cal. 241, in which such the constitutionality of appropriations is more or less sustained.

§ 121b

ture is the sole judge of the necessity for the appropriation of private lands to a public use. The following quotation from an opinion of the Supreme Court of Iowa will amply illustrate the limitations upon the power of establishing " private " roads over private lands: " The State may properly provide for the establishment of a public road or highway to enable every citizen to discharge his duties. The State is not bound to allow its citizens to be walled in, insulated, imprisoned, but may provide them a way of deliverance. The State may provide a public highway to a man's house, or a public highway to coal or other mines. If the road now in question had been established as a public road under the general road law, as we confess we do not see why it might not have been, there would be in our minds no doubt of its validity, although it does not exceed a half mile in length, and traverses the lands of but a single person. For the right to take land for a public road, that is, a road demanded by public convenience, as an outlet to a neighborhood, or it may be as I think for a single farmer, without other means of communication, cannot depend upon the length of the road, or the number of persons through whose property it may pass.

" With respect to the act of 1866, we are of opinion that the roads thereunder established are essentially private, that is, the private property of the applicant therefor, because : *First*, the statute denominates them private roads. If these roads are not private and different from ordinary and public roads, there was no necessity for these provisions. *Secondly*, such a road may be established upon the petition of the applicant alone; and he must pay the costs and damages occasioned thereby, and perform such other conditions as to fences, etc., as the board may require. *Thirdly*, the public are not bound to keep such roads in repair, and this is a satisfactory test as to whether a road is public or private.[1]

---

[1] The second and third reasons for holding the road to be a private one

§ 121*b*

Fourthly, we see no reason when such a road is established, why the person at whose instance it was done might not lock the gates opening into it or fence it up, or otherwise debar the public of any right thereto. Could not the plaintiffs, in this case, having procured the road in question, abandon it at their pleasure? Could they not relinquish it to the defendants without consulting the board of supervisors? If this is so, does it not incontestably establish the fact, that it is essentially *private?* For it must be private if it is of such a nature, that the plaintiffs can at their pleasure use or forbid its use, abandon or refuse to abandon it, relinquish or refuse to relinquish it? If the act of 1866 is valid, might not the plaintiffs, having procured the road, use it for laying down a horse or tramway, and forbid everybody from using the road, and even exclude all persons therefrom? Who could prevent it? These conditions make the great difference between such a road and a public highway, and demonstrate the essentially private character of the road."[1]

here stated, rather establish a rebuttable than a conclusive presumption in favor of its private character. The establishment of the road upon the petition of the applicant, and its construction and maintenance at his expense, are not necessarily inconsistent with its being a public road, if the public have the use of it, and cannot be excluded from it.

[1] Dillon, Ch. J., in Bankhead *v.* Brown, 25 Iowa, 545. "The use, convenience and advantage of the public, contemplated by the law, are benefits arising out of the aggregate of such improvements, to which a particular road so established contributes to a greater or less degree. But no limitation upon the power of the court, in regard to any proposed road, is to be found in the degree of accommodation, which it may extend to the public at large. That is a matter which addresses itself not to the authority, but the discretion of the court. It cannot be predicated of any road that it will be of direct utility to all the citizens of the county. It may accommodate in travel and transportation but a small neighborhood, or only a few individuals. Still, when established, it may be used at pleasure by all the citizens of the county or country; and the public is interested in the accommodation of all the members of the community." Lewis *v.* Washington, 5 Gratt. 265. See Varner *v.* Martin, 21 W. Va. 534, for a most exhaustive review of the law and authorities on this subject.

§ 1215

The difficulty of determining what is a public use becomes greater and more perplexing, when the attention is turned to those cases in which the right of eminent domain is exercised, not by the State or municipality, by some private stock corporation, which undertakes the performance of the public work, in consideration of the tolls and other returns they are permitted to require of the public for the outlay of the capital they have made.   We have already seen[1] that the right of eminent domain may be delegated to private individuals and corporations, provided it is exercised in the promotion of some public good.   It is plain enough that the establishment of railroads, turnpikes, canals and other means of transportation and locomotion is as much a public use as the construction of public streets or highways.   The facts, that they are established and owned by private individuals or corporations, and that the general public must pay a certain fee or toll for the privilege of using them, do not affect their legal character.   For, as Mr. Cooley says, " the common highway is kept in repair by assessments of labor and money ; the tolls paid upon turnpikes, or the fares on railways, are the equivalents to these assessments ; and when these improved ways are required by law to be kept open for use by the public impartially, they also may properly be called highways, and the use to which land for their construction is put be denominated a public use." [2]

We again reach contested ground, when we inquire into the power of the government to authorize the exercise of the right of eminent domain in the condemnation of lands for manufacturing and industrial purposes.   The question has usually arisen in the request for the condemnation of lands on the banks of a river, for the establishment of some sort of mill run by water power.   Before the days of steam, water was the only motive power, and sometimes a whole commu-

[1] See § 121.
[2] Cooley on Const. Lim. 660, 661.

§ 121b

nity would depend for milling facilities upon the caprice or avarice of one or more men. It is true that at present a mill site on the river bank is not so essential to industrial activity, but it is still important on the ground of economy, water power being cheaper than steam. In most ot the States, in which the question has arisen, such appropriations of land have been sustained as being for the public good, if not for a public use.[1] But in New York and other States the power of exercising the right of eminent domain in favor of manufacturing and milling industries is denied.[2]

In pronouncing the opinion of the Supreme Court of Massachusetts in favor of such an exercise of the right of eminent domain, Shaw, Ch. J., said: "It is then contended that if this act was intended to authorize the defendant company to take the mill power and mill of the plaintiff, it was void because it was not taken for public use, and it was not within the power of the government in the exercise of the right of eminent domain. This is the main question. In determining it we must look to the declared purposes of the act; and if a public use is declared, it will be so held, unless it manifestly appears by the provisions of the act that they can have no tendency to advance and promote such public use. The declared purposes are to improve the navigation of the Merrimac River

---

[1] Fisher v. Manufacturing Co., 12 Pick. 67; Boston & Roxbury Mill Co. v. Newman, 12 Pick. 467; Olmstead v. Camp, 33 Conn. 532; Great Falls Manuf. Co. v. Fernald, 47 N. H. 444; Ash v. Cummings, 50 N. H. 591; Jordan v. Woodward, 40 Me. 317; Crenshaw v. State River Co., 6 Rand. 245; Burgess v. Clark, 13 Ired. 109; Smith v. Connelly, 1 T. B. Mon. 58; Shackleford v. Coffey, J. J. Marsh. 40; Newcome v. Smith, 1 Chand. 71; Thien v. Voegtlander, 3 Wis. 461; Pratt v. Brown, 8 Wis. 603; (but see Fisher v. Horricon Co., 10 Wis. 351; Curtis v. Whipple, 24 Wis 350;) Miller v. Troosh, 14 Minn. 365; Venard v. Cross, 8 Kan. 248; Harding v. Funk, 8 Kan. 315.

[2] Hay v. Cohoes Company, 3 Barb. 47; Ryerson v. Brown, 35 Mich. 333 (24 Am. Rep. 564); Loughbridge v. Harris, 42 Ga. 500; Tyler v. Beacher, 44 Vt. 648 (8 Am. Rep. 398); Saddler v. Laugham, 34 Ala. 311. In the last two cases, the right to condemn lands for mill sites was recognized, provided the mill owners were required to serve the public impartially.

and to create a large mill power for mechanical and manufacturing purposes.   *   *   *   That the improvement of
the navigation of a river is done for the public use, has been
too frequently decided and acted upon to require authorities,
and so to create a wholly artificial navigation by canals.
The establishment of a great mill power for manufacturing
purposes, as an object of great interest, especially since
manufacturing has come to be one of the great public indus-
trials pursuits of the commonwealth, seems to have been regarded by the legislature and sanctioned by the jurisprudence
of the commonwealth, and in our judgment rightly so, in
determining what is a public use, justifying the exercise of
eminent domain.   *   *   *   That the erection of this dam
would have a strong and direct tendency to advance both
these public objects, there is no doubt.'' [1]   On the same
general grounds, in the exercise of the right of eminent
domain, lands have been appropriated for use as a cemetery. [2]
A careful reading of the authorities forces one to the conclusion that the term *public use* is either misused or is given
a peculiar meaning in the law of eminent domain, very
different from what it generally bears in other branches of
the law, and this thought is most strongly forced upon us
in learning from the cases that the establishment of a private mill is such a public use as will justify the exercise of
the right of eminent domain in its favor. [3]

[1] Hazen *v.* Essex Company, 12 Cush. 475.

[2] Edgecombe *v.* Burlington, 46 Vt. 118; Balch *v.* Commissioners, 103
Mass. 106; Evergreen Cemetery *v.* New Haven, 43 Conn. 234; Matter of
Deansville Cemetery, 66 N. Y. 569. But in the last the power to condemn
lands for cemetery purposes was denied to a strictly private corporation.

[3] '' Reasoning by analogy from one of the sovereign powers of government to another is exceedingly liable to deceive and mislead. An object
may be public in one sense and for one purpose, when in a general sense
and for other purposes it would be idle or misleading to apply the same
term. All governmental powers exist for public purposes, but they are not
necessarily to be exercised under the same conditions of public interest.
The sovereign police power which the State exercises is to be exercised only
for the general public welfare, but it reaches to every person, to every

§ 121*b*

Indeed, it would appear more correct to say, that while the term *public use* was originally employed in the law of eminent domain as meaning a use by some governmental agency, the ever increasing complications of modern civivilization have compelled an application of the right of eminent domain to other than public or governmental uses, and the meaning of the term *public use* was broadened from

kind of business, to every species of property within the commonwealth. The conduct of every individual, and the use of all property and of all rights is regulated by it, to any extent found necessary for the preservation of the public order, and also for the protection of the private rights of one individual against encroachments by others. The sovereign power of taxation is employed in a great many cases where the power of eminent domain might be made more immediately efficient and available, if constitutional principles could suffer it to be resorted to; but each of these has its own peculiar and appropriate sphere, and the object which is *public* for the demands of the one is not necessarily of a character to permit the exercise of the other. (That Eminent Domain and Taxation are but special phases of police power, and not distinct and separate powers of government, see *ante*, § 1.)

"If we examine the subject critically we shall find that the most important consideration in the case of eminent domain is the necessity of accomplishing some public good which is otherwise impracticable; and we shall also find that the law does not so much regard the means as the need. The power is much nearer akin to that of the public police than to that of taxation; it goes but a step further, and that is in the same direction. Every man has an abstract right to the exclusive use of his own property for his own enjoyment in such manner as he shall choose; but if he should choose to create a nuisance upon it, or to do anything which would preclude a reasonable enjoyment of adjacent property, the law would interfere to impose restraints. He is said to own his private lot to the center of the earth, but he would not be allowed to excavate it indefinitely, lest his neighbor's lot should disappear in the excavation. The abstract right to make use of his own property in his own way is compelled to yield to the general comfort and protection of the community, and to a proper regard to relative rights in others. The situation of his property may even be such that he is compelled to dispose of it because the law will not suffer his regular business to be carried on upon it. A needful and lawful species of manufacture may so injuriously affect the health and comfort of the vicinity that it cannot be tolerated in a densely settled neighborhood, and therefore the owner of a lot in that neighborhood will not be allowed to engage in that manufacture upon it, even though it be his regular and legitimate business. * * *

§ 121*b*

time to time in order to cover these new applications of the right, until now the term is synonymous with *public good*, and justifies the following language of Chancellor Walworth. In defining what is a public use,[1] he said: " If the public interest can be in any way promoted by the taking of private property, it must rest in the wisdom of the legislature to determine, whether the benefit to the public will be of sufficient importance to render it expedient for them to exercise the right of eminent domain, and to authorize an interference with the private rights of individuals for that purpose. It is upon this principle that the legislatures of several of the States have authorized the condemnation of lands for mill sites, where from the nature of the country such mill sites could not be obtained for the accommodation of the inhabitants, without overflowing the lands thus condemned. Upon the same principle of public benefit, not only the agents of the government, but also individuals and corporate bodies, have been authorized to take private

Eminent domain only recognizes and enforces the superior right of the community against the selfishness of individuals in a similar way. Every branch of needful industry has a right to exist, and the community has a right to demand that it be permitted to exist, and if for that purpose a peculiar locality already in possession of an individual is essential, the owner's right to undisturbed occupancy must yield to the superior interest of the public. A railroad cannot go around the farm of every unwilling person, and the business of transporting persons and property for long distances by rail, which has been found so essential to the general enjoyment and welfare, could never have existed if it were in the power of any unwilling person to stop the road at his boundary, or to demand unreasonable terms as a condition of passing him. ▼The law interferes in these cases, and regulates the relative rights of the owner and of the community with as strict regard to justice and equity as the circumstances will permit. It does not deprive the owner of his property, but it compels him to dispose of so much of it as is essential on equitable terms. While, therefore, eminent domain establishes no industry, it so regulates the relative rights of all that no individual shall have it in his power to preclude its establishment." People *v.* Township Board of Salem, 20 Mich. 452.

[1] Beekman *v.* Schenectady and Saratoga R. R. Co., 3 Paige, 45, 73 (22 Am Dec. 679).

§ 121*b*

property for the purpose of making public highways, turnpike roads and canals; of erecting and constructing wharves and basins; of establishing ferries; of draining swamps and marshes, and of bringing water to cities and villages. In all such cases the object of the legislative grant of power is the public benefit derived from the contemplated improvement which is to be effected directly by the agents of the government, or through the medium of corporate bodies, or of individual enterprise." In commenting upon this language of Chancellor Walworth, Judge Cooley says:[1] "It would not be entirely safe, however, to apply with much liberality the language above quoted, that, ' where the public interest can be in any way promoted by the taking of private property,' the taking can be considered for a public use. It is certain that there are very many cases in which the property of some individual owners would be likely to be better employed or occupied to the advancement of the public interest in other hands than in their own; but it does not follow from this circumstance alone, that they may rightfully be dispossessed. It may be for the public benefit that all the wild lands of the State be improved and cultivated, all the low lands drained, all the unsightly places beautified, all dilapidated buildings replaced by new; because all these things tend to give an aspect of beauty, thrift, and comfort to the country and thereby to invite settlement, increase the value of lands, and gratify the public taste; but the common law has never sanctioned an appropriation of property based upon these considerations alone; and some further element must therefore be involved before the appropriation can be regarded as sanctioned by our constitutions." It is true that the common law has never sanctioned the condemnation of private property for all the purposes enumerated by Judge Cooley; and it is likewise true, that in condemning lands for

[1] Cooley Const. Lim. 660.

§ 121*b*

such purposes, it could not, with any proper use of the term, be called a taking for a public use; but there is nothing in our constitutions which require a taking for a public use. We have, as the sole authority for the requirement, the judicial opinion that it is unrepublican to take private property for any but a public use; but we claim that the courts, at least in later years, meant that private property cannot be taken, except to promote some public good, when they required it to be a taking for a public use. There is, therefore, no constitutional limitation upon the power of the government, to declare an appropriation of lands in the possession of private persons for the construction of mills, the improvement of wild lands, the drainage of low lands, and for the promotion of any public benefit, where the avarice or selfishness of the private owner necessitates a condemnation of such lands. It is unquestionably unconstitutional and inconsistent with republican principles, for a government arbitrarily to take the property of one man and give it to another, or to do so in any case where the public interest will not thereby be promoted. There is certainly some danger of an arbitrary or unreasonable exercise of the power, since the legislature is the supreme judge of the necessity of the condemnation; and it may be wise to impose such limitations upon the power of the legislature as will serve as safeguards against arbitrary interferences with private property: but it cannot be said to be unrepublican to require the owners of lands to so use them as will best promote the public welfare. It is highly republican in principle to place the public good (*res publica*) above the selfish interest of the individual; and inasmuch as the ultimate property in lands is vested in the State for the common benefit, it is not unreasonable to claim that all private property in lands is acquired and held, subject to the condition, among others, that it may be reclaimed by the State whenever the public interests demand it. There is nothing fundamentally

§ 121*b*

unjust in such a principle, although it may easily be made
the cover for some arbitrary and iniquitous transactions.
During the present year, (1886) a bill was proposed by the
English cabinet to make a forced purchase of the lands of
Irish landlords, and to divide up the land into small holdings, and sell the same to the Irish tenantry on easy terms.
The object of the bill was to remedy the agrarian evil,
which at some time in its history troubles every thickly
settled community; and while it was vigorously and successfully opposed, the objections to its passage were
economical and not constitutional. In a less justifiable
case, the Prussian landtag, at the instance of Prince Bis-
marck, has expropriated the lands of the hostile Polish
population of Posen, in order to provide for a German settlement. Any taking of land from one man and giving it
to another in this country, would at the present day be unjustifiable, because land is not yet scarce enough ; or, more
correctly stated, the population is not yet large enough to
make expropriation of lands a public necessity. But if a
similar state of affairs were to arise in one of the American
States as exists in Ireland to-day, and the public order and
peace was daily and hourly threatened by the lack of small
land holdings, and the exactions of absentee landlords ; if
the quiet and order of prosperous times could be restored
by an expropriation of the land of large land owners, it
would be eminently republican for the State to do so,
taking care that the expropriation does not extend beyond
the public necessity. If the land owner is rendering his
equivalent to society for his ownership of the lands, there
will be no agrarian evil ; and he is not entitled, as against the
superior demands of society, to the unearned increment,
where he does not add to it by the expenditure of capital or
labor.

§ 121c. **What property may be taken.** — Every species of real property may be taken in the exercise of the
§ 121c

right of eminent domain. Not only the land itself may be taken, but also anything which may actually, or in legal contemplation, be considered a part of the land : All buildings and other structures that may be in the way of the public use of the condemned lands ; [1] the streams of water,[2] the stone, gravel and wood that may be needed for the promotion of the public improvement,[3] apart from the land itself. An easement may be acquired over the land, while the land remained private property, and so also may franchises be condemned.[4] But in all cases no more of the property can be taken than is necessary to serve the public purpose for which it is condemned. No other considerations will justify the taking of the whole of a man's property, when only a part is needed, and the excessive appropriation must under all circumstances be held to be unconstitutional. This limitation is best explained by a reference to the facts of a case, which arose in the State of New

---

[1] Wells *v.* Somerset, etc., R. R. Co., 47 Me. 345.

[2] Gardner *v.* Newburg, 2 Johns. Ch. 162 (7 Am. Dec. 526); Johnson *v.* Atlantic, etc., R. R. Co., 35 N. H. 569; Baltimore, etc., R. R. Co. *v.* Magruder, 35 Md. 79 (6 Am. Rep. 310).

[3] Jerome *v.* Ross, 7 Johns. Ch. 315 (11 Am. Dec. 484); Wheelock *v.* Young, 4 Wend. 647; Lyon *v.* Jerome, 15 Wend. 569; Bliss *v.* Hosmer, 15 Ohio, 44; Watkins *v.* Walker Co., 18 Texas, 585.

[4] West River Bridge *v.* Dix, 6 How. 507; Richmond R. R. Co. *v.* Louisa R. R. Co., 13 How. 71; State *v.* Noyes, 47 Me. 189; Armington *v.* Barnet, 15 Vt. 745; White River Turnpike Co. *v.* Vt. Cent. R. R. Co., 21 Vt. 590; Pistaque Bridge Co. *v.* New Hampshire Bridge, 7 N. H. 35; Boston Water Power Co. *v.* Boston, etc., R. R. Co., 23 Pick. 360; Central Bridge Co. *v.* Lowell, 4 Gray 474; *In re* Rochester Water Commissioners, 66 N. Y. 413; Commonwealth *v.* Pa. Canal Co., 66 Pa. St 41 (5 Am. Rep. 329); *In re* Towanda Bridge, 91 Pa. St. 216; Tuckahoe Canal Co. *v.* R. R. Co., 11 Leigh 42 (36 Am. Dec. 374); Chesapeake, etc., Canal Co. *v.* Baltimore, etc., R. R. Co., 4 Gill & J. 5; No. Ca., etc., R. R. Co. *v.* Carolina Cent., etc., R. R. Co., 83 N. C. 489; New Orleans, etc., R. R. Co. *v.* Southern, etc., Tel. Co., 53 Ala. 211; Little Miamia, ect., R. R. Co. *v.* Darton, 23 Ohio St. 510; New Castle, etc., R. R. Co. *v.* Peru, etc., R. R. Co., 3 Ind. 464; Lake Shore, etc., R. R. Co. *v.* Chicago, etc., R. R. Co , 97 Ill. 506; Central City Horse Railway Co. *v.* Fort Clark, ect., R'y Co., 87 Ill. 523.

§ 121c

York.[1] By a statute, municipal corporations were authorized, in condemning a part of a city lot for the purpose of
extending or widening the streets, to appropriate the whole,
if it was deemed advisable, and to sell or otherwis e dispose
of the part not needed for the improvement of the street.
The statute was pronounced unconstitutional. In delivering the opinion of the court, the Chief Justice, Savage,
said: " If this provision was intended merely to give to
the corporation capacity to take property under such circumstances with consent of the owner, and then to dispose
of the same, there can be no objection to it ; but if it is to
be taken literally, that the commissioners may, against the
consent of the owner, take the whole lot, when only a part
is required for public use, and the residue to be applied to
private use, it assumes a power which, with all respect, the
legislature did not possess. The constitution, by authorizing the appropriation of private property to public use,
impliedly declares that for any other use private property
shall not be taken from one and applied to the private use
of another. It is in violation of natural right ; and if it is
not in violation of the letter of the constitution, it is of its
spirit, and cannot be supported. This power has been supposed to be convenient when the greater part of a lot is
taken, and only a small part left, not required for public
use, and that small part of but little value in the hands of
the owner. In such case the corporation has been supposed best qualified to take and dispose of such parcels, or
gores, as they have sometimes been called; and probably
this assumption of power has been acquiesced in by the
proprietors. I know of no case where the power has been
questioned, and where it has received the deliberate sanction of this court. Suppose a case where only a few feet, or
even inches, are wanted, from one end of a lot to widen a
street, and a valuable building stands upon the other end

---

[1] Matter of Albany St., 11 Wend. 151 (25 Am. Dec. 618).

§ 121c

of such lot; would the power be conceded to exist to take the whole lot, whether the owner consented or not? The quantity of the residue of any lot cannot vary the principle. The owner may be very unwilling to part with only a few feet; and I hold it equally incompetent for the legislature thus to dispose of private property, whether feet or acres are the subject of this assumed power."[1] It has also been held, that in establishing a public improvement, it is the duty of those who are exercising the right of eminent domain to avoid as much as possible the diversion of streams, and to construct whatever culverts and bridges may be necessary to keep the streams in their regular channels.[2]

Another application of the same principle would lead to the conclusion, that where the fee simple estate in the land was not needed, only a less estate or an easement should be taken; and that the taking of the fee under such circumstances would be an unlawful appropriation. In the absence of statutory regulations to the contrary, it is certainly a conclusive presumption, that where less than a fee is needed for the public use, and a joint occupation of the land by the public and by the private individual was possible as in the case of a highway, the fee is not taken for the public use, and if there should be at any time a discontinuance of the public use, the land would be relieved of the public easement, and become again the absolute property of the original owner.[3] But in some of the States, it is

[1] See to the same effect, Dunn v. City Council, Harp. 129; Baltimore, etc., R. R. Co. v. Pittsburg, etc., R. R. Co., 17 W. Va. 812; Paul v. Detroit, 32 Mich. 108. In Embury v. Conner, 3 N. Y. 511, it was held that this excessive appropriation of land beyond what is needed for the public use was permissible, provided it was not done against the consent of the owner.

[2] See Proprietors, etc. v. Nashua R. R. Co., 10 Cush. 388; March v. Portsmouth, etc., R. R. Co., 19 N. H. 372; Rowe v. Addison, 34 N. H. 306; Haynes v. Burlington, 38 Vt. 350; Boughton v. Carter, 18 Johns. 405; Stein v. Burden, 24 Ala. 130; Pettigrew v. Evansville, 25 Wis. 223; Arimond v. Green Bay Co., 31 Wis. 316.

[3] Rust v. Lowe, 6 Mass. 90; Barclay v. Howell's Lessee, 6 Pet. 498;

§ 121c

now provided by the statute that in appropriation of lands for highways, the fee shall be held to be condemned, and not simply a public easement acquired.[1] And it would seem plausible that in the case of an ordinary highway the fee might be needed for use as a highway, since the demands of modern civilization require the soil of the streets of a city to contain imbedded in it the gas, water and sewer pipes, the telephone, telegraph, and electric light wires, etc., as well as to be used as a highway, thus rendering a joint occupation of the land by the public and the private owner impossible. It is by no means unreasonable, therefore, to provide for the condemnation of the fee in the beginning, instead of allowing successive condemnations of the soil, as the public demands each particular use to which it can be put. But it is hard to see the reason why in the condemnations of land, for other purposes, for railroad purposes, for example, the fee should be taken; and unless the necessity of taking the fee is proven, the taking would be an unlawful condemnation of private property.[2] But if the fee is necessary, the taking of the fee for any purpose is lawful; and it seems to be the prevailing opinion that the question,

---

Weston v. Foster, 7 Met. 297; Dean v. Sullivan R. R. Co., 22 N. H. 316; Blake v. Rich, 34 N. H. 282; Jackson v. Rutland, etc., R. R. Co., 25 Vt. 150; Giesy v. Cincinnati, etc., R. R. Co., 4 Ohio St. 308; Jackson v. Hathaway, 15 Johns. 447; Henry v. Dubuque & Pacific R. R. Co., 2 Iowa, 288; Elliott v. Fair Haven etc., R. R. Co., 32 Conn. 579, 586; Imlay v. Union Branch R. R. Co., 26 Conn. 249; State v. Laverack, 34 N. J. 201; Railroad Co. v. Shurmeir, 7 Wall. 272.

[1] People v. Kerr, 37 Barb. 357; s. c. 27 N. Y. 188; Brooklyn Central, etc., R. R. Co. v. Brooklyn City R. R. Co., 33 Barb. 420; Brooklyn & Newton R. R. Co. v. Coney Island R. R. Co., 35 Barb. 364; Protzman v. Indianapolis, etc., R. R. Co., 9 Ind. 467; New Albany & Salem R. R. Co. v. O'Dailey, 13 Ind. 353; Street Railway v. Cummingsville, 14 Ohio St. 523; State v. Cincinnati Gas Co., 18 Ohio St. 262; Millburn v. Cedar Rapids, etc., R. R. Co., 12 Iowa, 246; Franz v. Railroad Co., 55 Iowa, 107; Moses v. Pittsburg, etc., R. R., 21 Ill. 516.

[2] New Orleans, etc., R. R. Co. v. Gay, 32 La. Ann. 471. In Illinois the condemnation of the fee for railroad purposes is expressly forbidden. Const. Ill. 1870, art. 2, § 13.

§ 121c

whether it is necessay is a legislative, and not a judicial one. The declaration of the legislature, that the fee is necessary, is, therefore, final and conclusive.[1]

But while the appropriation of land, in the exercise of the right of eminent domain, must be confined to the necessity; on the other hand, that amount may be appropriated, not only what is directly necessary for the public use, but also whatever is incidentally needed, such as the workshops and depots of railroads.[2] But the appropriation of lands for such incidental purposes must fall within a fair construction of the grant of power by the legislature, in order to be allowable; for the power to make such an appropriation cannot be justified by a consideration of its convenience or appropriateness, if it is not expressly conferred. Thus it was held that where a railroad company was granted the power " to enter

[1] In Hayward v. Mayor, etc., of New York, 7 N. Y. 314, 325, it is said that the power of deciding upon the need of the fee, " must of necessity rest in the legislature, in order to secure the useful exercise and enjoyment of the right in question. A case might arise where a temporary use would be all that the public interest required. Another case might require the permanent, and apparently the perpetual, occupation and enjoyment of the property by the public, and the right to take it must be co-extensive with the necessity of the case, and the measure of compensation should, of course, be graduated by the nature and the duration of the estate or interest of which the owner is deprived." In this case the the land was appropriated for the purpose of extending the almshouse. See, also, Brooklyn Park Commissioners v. Armstrong, 45 N. Y. 234 (6 Am. Rep. 70); Dingley v. Boston, 100 Mass. 544; Baker v. Johnson, 2 Hill, 343; Munger v. Tonawanda R. R. Co., 4 N. Y. 349; Rexford v. Knight, 11 N. Y. 308; Coster v. N. J. R. R. Co., 22 N. J. 227; Plitt v. Cox, 43 Pa. St. 486; Water Works Co. v. Burkhart, 41 Ind. 364.

[2] N. Y. & Harlem R. R. Co. v. Kip, 46 N. Y. 546 (7 Am. Rep. 385); Chicago, etc., R. R. Co. v. Wilson, 17 Ill. 123; Low v. Galena, etc., R. R. Co., 18 Ill. 324; Giesy v. Cincinnati, etc., R. R. Co., 4 Ohio St. 308. In Eldridge v. Smith, 34 Vt. 484, it was held that the erection of buildings for the manufacture of cars, or for leasing to the employes of the road, was not so necessary to the conduct and management of a railroad, as to justify the condemnation of lands for such purposes. But it was held competent for the railroad company to appropriate lands for piling wood and lumber used in the construction and conduct of the road.

§ 121c

upon any land to survey, lay down and construct its road,"
" to locate and construct branch roads," etc. ,to take land
" for necessary side tracks," and " a right of way over
adjacent lands sufficient to enable such company to construct and repair the road," it was not authorized, after it
had located the road, and was constructing its main road
along the north side of a town, to appropriate a temporary
right of way for a term of years along the south side, which
was to be used while the main road was being built.[1]

§ 121d. **What constitutes a taking.** — In order to lay the
foundation of a claim for compensation for the taking of property in the exercise of the right of eminent domain, it is not
necessary that there should be an actual or physical taking of
the land. Whenever the use of the land is restricted in any
way, or some incorporeal hereditament is taken away, which
was appurtenant thereto, it constituted as much a taking as if
the land itself had been appropriated.[2] The flowing of
lands,[3] the diversion of streams,[4] the appropriation of
water fronts, on streams where the tide does not ebb and
flow,[5] and, likewise, in navigable streams, the condemnation
of an exclusive wharfage,[6] are only a few instances of the

[1] Currier v. Marietta, etc., R. R. Co., 10 Ohio St. 121.

[2] Pampelly v. Green Bay, etc., Co., 13 Wall. 166; Hooker v. New
Haven, etc., R. R. Co., 14 Conn. 146; Eaton v. Boston, C. & M. R. R. Co.,
51 N. H. 504; Glover v. Powell, 10 N. J. Eq. 211; Ashley v. Port Huron,
35 Mich. 296; Arimond v. Green Bay, etc., Co., 31 Wis. 316.

[3] Grand Rapids Booming Co. v. Jarvis, 30 Mich. 308; Eaton v. Boston,
etc., R. R. Co., 51 N. H. 504; Brown v. Cayuga, etc., R. R. Co., 12 N. Y.
486; Norris v. Vt. Cent. R. R. Co., 28 Vt. 99.

[4] Harding v. Stanford Water Co., 41 Conn. 87; Proprietors, etc., v.
Nashua & Lowell R. R. Co., 10 Cush. 388; March v. Portsmonth, etc., R.
R. Co., 19 N. H. 372; Rome v. Addison, 34 N. H. 306; Johnson v. Atlantic,
etc., R. R. Co., 35 N. H. 569; Haynes v. Burlington, 38 Vt. 350; Bough-
ton v. Carter, 18 Johns. 405; Baltimore, etc., R. R. Co. v. Magender, 34
Md. 79 (6 Am. Rep. 310); Stein v. Burden, 24 Ala. 130; Pettigrew v.
Evansville, 25 Wis. 223.

[5] Varick v. Smith, 9 Paige, 547.

[6] Murray v. Sharp, 1 Bosw. 539.

§ 121d

exercise of the right of eminent domain, in which the property taken is incorporeal. In respect to the appropriation
of water fronts, according to the older authorities, if the
stream was a navigable one, that is, one in which the tide
ebbed and flowed, and the title to the bed of which was in
the State, the appropriation to public uses of the water front
was held not to involve any taking of property for which
compensation had to be made ;[1] and this has also been held
to be the rule in reference to those fresh water streams, which
are practically navigable, and the title to whose beds is in
the state.[2] But these cases have not been followed by later
adjudications, so far as they assert the right to take away
from the riparian proprietor all access to the navigable
stream by and over his land. This right of access to the
stream is declared to be an incorporeal hereditament, appurtenant to the abutting land, which cannot be taken away
without proper compensation.[3]

The diversion of navigable streams is also a taking of
property, for which compensation must be made to the
riparian owner. Although the riparian owner has no property in the water, or in the bed of the stream, he has a
right to make a reasonable use of it, and since a diversion
of the stream will interfere with the reasonable use, perhaps deprive him altogether of its use, compensation must
be made to him for this loss, as being a taking of property.[4]

It frequently happens in the experience of municipal life

[1] Gould v. Hudson River R. R. Co., 6 N. Y. 522; Pennsylvania R. R. Co.
v. N. Y., etc., R. R. Co., 23 N. J. Eq. 157; Stevens v. Paterson, etc., R.
R. Co., 34 N. J. 532.

[2] Tomlin v. Dubuque, etc., R. R. Co., 32 Iowa, 106 (7 Am. Rep. 176).

[3] Railway v. Renwick, 102 U. S. 180; Yates v. Milwaukee, 10 Wall. 497;
Chicago, etc., R. R. Co. v. Stein, 75 Ill. 41. As to rights of property in
highways, see post.

[4] People v Canal Appraisers, 13 Wend. 355; Gardner v. Newburg, 2
Johns. Ch. 162; Bellinger v. N. Y. Central R. R. Co., 23 N. Y. 42; Morgan
v. King, 35 N. Y. 454; Hatch v. Vermont Cent. R. R. Co., 25 Vt. 49; Thunder Bay, etc., Co. v. Speechly, 31 Mich. 332; Emporia v. Soden, 25 Kan. 588
(37 Am. Rep. 265).

§ 121d

that in order to prevent an accidental fire from becoming a general conflagration, one or more houses which stand in the path of the fire will be destroyed by means of explosions or otherwise, in order to check it. It is never done, except in cases where the destroyed houses would have inevitably been consumed by the fire. The owners of these houses, therefore, have not suffered any loss by their destruction; and on this ground, and on the plea of overruling necessity, such destruction of buildings have been held not to be an appropriation under the right of eminent domain, and no claim for compensation can be made by the owners. And where a municipal officer orders the destruction, the municipal corporation is not liable for damages, in the absence of a statute to that effect.[1]

But the consequential or incidental injury to property, resulting from the lawful exercise of an independent right, is never held to be a taking of property in the constitutional sense, where the enjoyment of the right or privilege does not involve an actual interference or disturbance of property rights. " In the absence of all statutory provisions to that effect, no case, and certainly no principle, seems to justify the subjecting a person, natural or artificial, in the prudent pursuit of his own lawful business, to the payment of consequential damage to others in their property or business. This always happens more or less in all rival pursuits, and often where there is nothing of that kind. One mill or one store or school injures another. One's dwelling is undermined, or its lights darkened, or its prospect obscured, and thus materially lessened in value by the erection of other buildings upon lands of other proprietors.

---

[1] Taylor v. Plymouth, 8 Met. 462· Ruggles v. Nantucket, 11 Cush. 433; Stone v. Mayor, etc., of N. Y., 25 Wend. 157; Russell v. Mayor, etc., of N. Y., 2 Denio, 461; American Printworks v. Lawrence, 21 N. J. 248; American Print Works v. Lawrence, 23 N. J. 590; White v. Charleston, 1 Hill (s. c.) 571; Keller v. Corpus Christi, 50 Texas 614 (32 Am. Rep. 513); Conwell v. Emrie, 2 Ind. 35; Field v. Des Moines, 39 Iowa, 575; McDonald v. Redwing, 13 Minn. 38; Sirocco v. Geary, 3 Cal. 69.

§ 121d

One is beset with noise or dust or other inconvenience by the alteration of a street, or more especially by the introduction of a railway, but there is no redress in any of these cases. The thing is lawful in the railroad as much as in the other cases supposed. These public works came too near some and too remote from others. They benefit many and injure some. It is not possible to equalize the advantages and disadvantages. It is so with everything, and always will be. Those most skilled in these matters, even empirics of the most sanguine pretensions, soon find their philosophy at fault in all attempts at equalizing the ills of life. The advantages and disadvantages of a single railway could not be satisfactorily balanced by all of the courts in forty years ; hence they would be left, as all other consequential damage and gain are left, to balance and counterbalance themselves as they best can."[1] Thus there is no taking of property, if the owner of a fishery finds it reduced in value in consequence of improvement in the navigation of the river,[2] or a spring is destroyed, or other damage done to riparian land by the same or similar causes,[3] or when the value of adjoining property is

[1] Hatch v. Vt. Central R. R. Co., 25 Vt. 49; Richardson v. Vermont Cent. R. R. Co., 25 Vt. 465; Railroad Company v. Richmond, 96 U. S. 521; Davidson v. Boston & Maine R. R. Co., 3 Cush. 91; Kennett's Petition, 24 N. H. 135; Hooker v. New Haven, etc., R. R. Co., 14 Conn. 146; Gould v. Hudson River R. R. Co., 6 N. Y. 522; People v. Kerr, 27 N. Y 188; Zimmerman v. Union Canal Co., 1 Watts & S. 846; Monongahela Navigation Co. v. Coons, 6 Watts & S. 101; Shrunk v. Schuylkill Navigation. Co., 14 Serg. & R. 71; Harvey v. Lackawanna, etc., R. R. Co., 47 Pa. St. 428; Tinicum Fishing Co. v. Carter, 61 Pa. St. 21; Fuller v. Edings, 11 Rich. L. 239; Edings v. Seabrook, 12 Rich. L. 504; Alexander v. Milwaukee, 16 Wis. 247; Murray v. Menefee, 20 Ark. 561.

[2] Shrunk v. Schuylkill Navigation Co., 14 Serg. & R. 71. See Parker v. Milldam Co., 20 Me. 353 (37 Am. Dec. 56); Commonwealth v. Chapin, 5 Pick. 199 (16 Am. Dec. 386); Commonwealth v. Look, 108 Mass. 452; Carson v. Blazer, 2 Binn. 475 (4 Am. Dec. 463).

[3] Commonwealth v. Richter, 1 Pa. St. 467, Green v. Swift, 47 Cal. 536; Brown v. Cayuga, etc., R. R. Co., 12 N. Y. 486; Davidson v. Boston &

§ 121d

affected by a change in the grade of the street.[1]
In reference to this matter, Mr. Justice Miller has said[2]
that the decisions, which have denied the right of compensation " for the consequential injury to the property of an
individual from the prosecution of improvement of roads,
streets, rivers, and other highways," " have gone to the
extreme and limit of sound judicial construction in favor
of this principle, and in some cases beyond it ; and it remains true that where real estate is actually invaded by
superinduced additions of water, earth, sand, or other material, or by having any artificial structure placed on it, so
as effectually to destroy or impair its usefulness, it is a
taking within the meaning of the constitution." The
greatest difficulty has been experienced in applying these
principles to the police regulations of the highways or public streets, in consequence of the variety of uses to which

Maine R. R. Co., 3 Cush. 91; Sprague v. Worcester, 13 Gray, 193; Transportation Co. v. Chicago, 99 U. S. 635.

[1] Gozzler v. Georgetown, 6 Wheat. 593; Smith v. Washington, 20 How.
(U. S.) 135; Callendar v. Marsh, 1 Pick. 418; Bender v. Nashua, 17 N. H.
477; Skinner v. Hartford Bridge Co., 29 Conn. 523; Green v. Reading, 9
Watts, 382; O'Connor v. Pittsburg, 18 Pa. St. 187; In re Ridge Street, 29
Pa. St. 391; Matter of Furman Street, 17 Wend. 649; Wilson v. Mayor, etc.,
of New York, 1 Denio, 595; Graves v. Otis, 2 Hill, 466; Radcliffe's Ex'rs
v. Mayor, etc., Brooklyn, 4 N. Y. 195; Pontiac v. Carter, 32 Mich. 164; Lafayette v. Bush, 19 Ind. 326; Macy v. Indianapolis, 17 Ind. 267; Vincennes
v. Richards, 23 Ind. 381; Roberts v. Chicago, 26 Ill. 249; Murphy v. Chicago, 29 Ill. 279; Creal v. Keokuk, 4 Greene (Iowa) 47. But see, *contra,*
Atlanta v. Green, 67 Ga. 386; Johnson v. City of Parkersburg, 16 W. Va.
402 (37 Am. Rep. 779) ; McComb v. Akron, 15 Ohio, 474 (18 Ohio, 229) ;
Crawford v. Delaware, 7 Ohio St. 459. In the last two cases it is held
that when the grade of streets is first established, the consequential injury
to adjoining property does not constitute a taking of property; but when
the grade has once been established, and the adjoining property improved
with reference to the existing grade, a change in grade, causing damage,
would give rise to a claim for compensation. In O'Brien v. St. Paul, 25
Minn. 331, it is held that if the change in the grade of a street deprives
the abutting land of its lateral support, it is a taking of property in the
exercise of the right of eminent domain.

[2] Pumpelly v. Green Bay, etc., Co., 13 Wall. 166, 180.

26   § 121*d*

the demands of modern life require them to be put.   It has
already been explained that, in most of the cities and village communities of this country, the public have only an
easement of a right of way over the land used as a road,
while the title to the soil remained in the owners, subject
to the public easement.   But in some of the States (notably
New York and Indiana), it is provided by statute that the
fee of land appropriated for highway purposes shall always
be vested in the State.[1]   It is clear that any appropriation
of the highway to other purposes, which would be inconsistent with, or different from, its use as a street, would be
a taking of the private property of the abutting owner,
where the soil remained his property subject to the public
easement.[2]   But it is not so clear whether such an appropriation of the highway would require the payment of compensation to the abutting owners, in cases where the fee of
the road is in the State.   If any right of property has been
invaded in making the appropriation, compensation must
be made, otherwise not.   It has been very generally held
that the proprietors of adjoining property have, as an easement over the land used as a highway, the right to the free
and unobstructed use of the street, and any interference with
such use was a taking of property, for which compensation
had to be made.[3]   In New York, where the fee of the

---

[1] See *ante*, § 121c.

[2] All the cases cited *post*, in connection with the discussion of the
right of the State to authorize the construction of horse and steam
railways on the highways, support this general proposition.   They only
differ as to whether the running of these railways is inconsistent with
the use of the land as a highway.

[3] Haynes v. Thomas, 7 Ind. 38; Protzman v. Indianapolis, etc., R. R.
Co., 9 Ind. 467; New Albany & Salem R. R. Co. v. O'Daily, 13 Ind. 453;
Indianapolis R. R. Co. v. Smith, 52 Ind. 428; Crawford v. Delaware, 7
Ohio St. 459; Street Railway v. Cummingsville, 14 Ohio St. 523; State v.
Cincinnati Gas, etc., Co., 18 Ohio St. 262; Grand Rapids, etc., R. R. Co. v.
Heisel, 38 Mich. 62 (31 Am. Rep. 306); Pekin v. Winkel, 77 Ill. 56; Lack-
land v. North Missouri R. R. Co., 31 Mo. 180; Green v. Portland, 32 Me.
431; Brown v. Duplessis, 14 La. Ann. 842.   But see, *contra*, Millburn v.

§ 121d

streets is in the State, the earlier cases seemed to deny to the abutting land owner any right of property in the street, as a highway, which would be invaded by a different appropriation of the land.[1] But in a late case,[2] it has been held, not only that the abutting land owner has, as appurtenant to his land, an incorporeal right of property in the free and unrestricted use of the street or highway, but also a right to the free passage of light and air over the land used as a street, and any interference with either right would constitute a taking of property, for which compensation must be made. Judge Danforth said, in delivering the opinion of the court, that the land in question was " conceded to be a public street. But besides the right of passage, which the grantee as one of the public, acquired, he gained certain other rights as purchaser of the lot, and became entitled to all the advantages which attached to it. The official survey — its filing in a public office — the conveyance by deed referring to that survey and containing a covenant for the construction of the street and its maintenance, make as to him and the lot purchased a dedication of it to the use for which it was constructed. The value of the lot was enhanced thereby and it is to be presumed that the grantee paid, and the grantor received an enlarged price by reason of this added value. There was thus secured to the plaintiff the right and privilege of having the street forever kept open as such. For that purpose, no special or express grant was necessary; the dedication, the sale in reference to it, the conveyance of the abutting lot with its appurtenances, and the consideration paid were of themselves suf-

---

Cedar Rapids, etc., R. R. Co., 12 Iowa, 246; Franz v. Railroad Co., 55 Iowa, 107.

1 People v. Kerr, 37 Barb. 357; s. c. 27 N. Y. 188; Ferring v. Irwin, 55 N. Y. 486; Kellinger v. Forty Second St., etc., R. R. Co., 50 N. Y. 206; Brooklyn Park Commissioners v. Armstrong, 45 N. Y. 234 (6 Am. Rep. 70); Coster v. Mayor, etc. 43 N. Y. 399.

2 Story v. New York Elevated R. R. Co., 90 N. Y. 122, 145, 146.

§ 121*d*

ficient.[1] The right thus secured was an incorporeal hereditament; it became at once appurtenant to the lot, and formed ' an integral part of the estate ' in it. It follows the estate and constitutes a perpetual incumbrance upon the land burdened with it. From the moment it attached, the lot became the dominant, and the open way or street the servient tenement.[2] Nor does it matter that the acts constituting such dedication are those of a municipality. The State even, under similar circumstances, would be bound, and so it was held in the City of Oswego v. Oswego Canal Co. : [3] ' In laying out the village plot,' says the court, ' and in selling the building lots, the State acted as the owner and proprietor of the land ; and the effect of the survey and sale, in reference to the streets laid down on the map, was the same as if the survey and sale had been made by a single individual.' [4] Lesser corporations can claim no other immunity, and all are bound upon the principle that to retract the promise implied by such conduct, and upon which the purchaser acted, would disappoint his just expectation.

" But what is the extent of this easement? what rights or privileges are secured thereby? Generally it may be said, it is to have the street kept open, so that from it access may be had to the lot, and light and air furnished across the

---

[1] Citing Wyman v. Mayor of N. Y., 11 Wend. 487; Trustees of Watertown v. Cowen, 4 Paige, 510.

[2] Citing Child v. Chappell, 9 N. Y. 246; Hills v. Miller, 3 Paige, 256; Trustees of Watertown v. Cowen, 4 Paige, 514.

[3] 6 N. Y. 257.

[4] It is a fact, at least in the more modern of our cities, that the public streets were originally indirect dedications by the owner to the public, by laying out a plat, and selling lots, bounded by certain streets, set forth in the plat. The sale of the lots imposed upon the land, over which the street was laid out, at least as against the owner of the land, an easement that the land shall be forever kept open as a street for the use of the lot owners. And the subsequent acceptance by the public of the street so dedicated can certainly make no change, in this regard, in the rights of the lot owners.

§ 121*d*

open way.   The street occupies the surface, and to its uses the rights of the adjacent lots are subordinate, but above the surface there can be no lawful obstruction to the access of light and air, to the detriment of the abutting owner. To hold otherwise would enable the city to derogate from its own grant, and violate the arrangement on the faith of which the lot was purchased.   This, in effect, was an agreement, that if the grantee would buy the lot abutting on the street, he might have the use of light and air over the open space designated as a street.   In this case, it is found by the trial court, in substance, that the structure proposed by the defendant,[1] and intended for the street opposite to the plaintiff's premises, would cause an actual diminution of light, depreciate the value of the plaintiff's warehouse and thus work to his injury.   In doing this thing, the defendant will take his property as much as if it took the tenement itself.   Without air and light, it would be of little value. Its profitable management is secured by adjusting it in reference to the right obtained by his grantor over the adjoining property.   The elements of light and air are both to be derived from the space over the land, on the surface of which the street is constructed, and which is made servient for that purpose.   He therefore has an interest in that land, and when it is sought to close it, or any part of it, above the surface of the street, so that light is in any measure to his injury prevented, that interest is to be taken, and one whose lot, acquired as this was, is directly dependent upon it for a supply, becomes a party interested and entitled, not only to be heard, but to compensation.''[2]

---

[1] A railroad elevated fifteen feet above the surface.

[2] In a strong dissenting opinion, Judge Earl said: " If the plaintiff has an unqualified private easement in Front Street for light and air and for access to his lot, then such easement cannot be taken or destroyed without compensation to him.   Arnold v. Hudson River R. R. Co., 55 N. Y. 661).   But whatever right an abutter, as such, has in the street is subject to the paramount authority of the State to regulate and control the street, for all the purposes of a street, and to make it more

§ 121d

It is reasonable for us, therefore, to conclude that, whether the public owns the fee in the road-bed or only an easement to be used as a public way, in either case there is an interest in the road-bed left in the abutting owner, which might be affected by an appropriation of the street or road to other purposes, but the character of the private interest changes with the nature of the public interest. Where the fee is in the public, the abutting proprietor has an incorporeal right to the use of the highway as such, and, if the New York

suitable for the wants and convenience of the public. The grade of a street may, under authority of law, be changed and thus great damage may be done to an abutter. The street may be cut down in front of his lot so that he is deprived of all feasible access to it, and so that the walls of his house may fall into the street, and yet he will be entitled to no compensation (Radcliff's Ex'rs v. The Mayor, etc., 7 N. Y. 195; O'Connor v. Pittsburg, 18 Pa. St. 187; Callendar v. Marsh, 1 Pick. 418); and so the street may be raised in front of his house so that travelers can look into his windows and he can have access to his house only through the roof or upper stories, and all light and air will be shut away, and yet he would be without any remedy. The legislature may prescribe how streets shall be used, as such, by limiting the use of some streets to pedestrians or omnibuses, or carriages or drays, or by allowing them to be occupied under proper regulations for the sale of hay, wood or other produce. It may authorize shade trees to be planted in them, which will to some extent shut out the light and air from the adjoining houses. Streets cannot be confined to the same use to which they were devoted when first opened. They were opened for streets in a city and may be used in any way the increasing needs of a growing city may require. They may be paved; sidewalks may be built; sewer, water and gas pipes may be laid; lamp-posts may be erected, and omnibuses with their noisy rattle over stone pavements, and other new and strange vehicles may be authorized to use them. All these things may be done, and they are still streets, and used as such. Streets are for the passage and transportation of passengers and property. Suppose the legislature should conclude that to relieve Broadway in the city of New York from its burden of travel and traffic it was necessary to have an under ground street below the same; can its authority to authorize its construction be doubted? And for the same purpose could it not authorize a way to be made fifteen feet above Broadway for the use of pedestrians? Where the streets become so crowded with vehicles that it is inconvenient and dangerous for pedestrians to cross from one side to another, can it be doubted that the legislature could authorize them to be bridged, so that pedestrians could pass over them, and that it could do this with-

§ 121d

case [1] will be fully indorsed by subsequent adjudication, to the free passage of light and air over the street. If the fee is in the abutting land owner, the bed of the road is his property, subject only to the public easement, that it shall be left open for use as a highway. The abutting land owner may do anything with the land that is not inconsistent with the full enjoyment of the right of way by the public. Thus, the private owner has a right to plant trees in the street, to construct cellars extending to the middle of the street, and to depasture his cattle in the street in front of his own land, where the right has not been taken away by police regulations in the interest of the public. And a law, which granted to another the right of pasturage in such a street or road, would operate as an exercise of the right of eminent domain, and constitute a taking of property. [2] The Supreme Court of the United States has held that " on the general question as to the rights of the public in a city street, we cannot see any material difference in principle

out compensation to the abutting owners, whose light and air and access might to some extent be interfered with? These improvements would not be a destruction of or a departure from the use to which the land was dedicated when the street was opened; but they would render the street more useful for the very purpose for which it was made, to wit: travel and transportation. If by these improvements the abutting owners were injured, they would have no constitutional right to compensation, for the reason that no property would be merely consequential. And if the public authorities could make these improvements, then the legislature could undoubtedly authorize them to be made by *quasi*-public corporations, organized for the purpose, as it can authorize plank-road and turnpike companies to take possession of highways and take toll from those who use them." (pp. 186–188.)

[1] Story *v.* N. Y. Elevated R. R. Co., *supra*.

[2] Tonawanda R. R. Co. *v.* Munger, 5 Denio, 255; Woodruff *v.* Neal, 28 Conn. 165. In Ohio, by an ancient custom, the right of pasturage in the public highways was held to be in the public. Kerwhacker *v.* Cleveland, etc., R. R. Co., 3 Ohio St. 172. In Adams *v.* Rivers, 11 Barb. 390, it was held that trespass would lie in favor of the abutting proprietor and against one who stood in the public highway and abused the proprietor, on the ground that he was there without license, and using the land for other purposes than as a highway.

§ 121*d*

with regard to the extent of those rights, whether the fee is in the public or in the adjacent land owner, or in some third person. In either case, the street is legally open and free for the public passage, and for such other public uses as are necessary in a city, and do not prevent its use as a thoroughfare, such as the laying of water-pipes, gas-pipes and the like.''[1] It may be reasonable to hold, at the present day, that the use of the road-bed for the laying of water, gas, and sewer pipes, was contemplated in the original condemnation of the land for use as a highway, and was considered in the estimation of damages ; but it is altogether inconsistent with reason and the nature of things to assert as a general proposition, that the rights of the public in the streets are the same, whether the fee is in the public or is private property.[2]

It is more difficult at times to answer satisfactorily the question of fact, whether a particular use of a street is inconsistent with its use as a highway, and the question has oftenest been applied to the construction of turnpikes, horse and steam railways along the highway.

The only essential difference between an ordinary highway and a turnpike is that the former is kept in repair by the public by means of taxation, general or special, and

---

[1] Barney v. Keokuk, 94 U. S. 324, 440.

[2] Judge Cooley says: ''The practical difference in the cases is, that when the fee is taken, the possession of the original owner is excluded; and in the case of city streets where there is occasion to devote them to many other purposes besides those of passage, but nevertheless not inconsistent, such as for the laying of water and gas-pipes, and the construction of sewers, this exclusion of any private right of occupation is important, and will sometimes save controversies and litigation. But to say that when a man has declared a dedication for a particular use, under a statute which makes a dedication the gift of a fee, he thereby makes it liable to be appropriated to other purposes, when the same could not be done if a perpetual easement had been dedicated, seems to be basing important distinctions upon a difference which after all is more technical than real, and which in my view does not affect the distinction made.'' Cooley, Const. Lim. 687n. See Bloomfield, etc., Co. v. Calkins, 62 N. Y. 386.

§ 121d

the public generally may use it without charge ; while the
turnpike is owned and conducted by a private corporation,
and a toll is required of all who use it. Since in both cases
the public have an indefeasible right to use the road, the
establishment of a turnpike over the common highway is not
an appropriation of the street to a different purpose. The
payment of toll is only an equivalent of the taxation and
the highway labor, which in the case of an ordinary highway might be required of the abutting land owner for keeping the road in repair.[1]

The question, whether the construction of a railroad along
a highway is such an appropriation of the land to different
uses as will support the claim of compensation of the abutting land owners, is very hard to answer satisfactorily. The
decisions on the subject are at variance, and the grounds upon
which the decisions are placed are not always the same, and
sometimes confusing. In some of the cases, great stress is
laid upon the fact, that the fee is or is not in the public.[2]
But the authorities and facts will only justify this distinc-

[1] "When a common highway is made a turnpike or a plank-road, upon
which tolls are collected, there is much reason for holding that the owner
of the soil is not entitled to any further compensation. The turnpike or
the plank-road is still an avenue for public travel, subject to be used in
the same manner as the ordinary highway was before, and, if properly
constructed, is generally expected to increase rather than diminish the
value of property along its line; and though the adjoining proprietors
are required to pay toll, they are supposed to be, and generally are fully
compensated for this burden by the increased excellence of the road, and
by their exemption from highway labor upon it." Cooley Const. Lim. 677,
678. See Commonwealth v. Wilkinson, 16 Pick. 175 (24 Am. Dec. 624);
Murray v. County Commissioners, 12 Met. 455; Benedict v. Goit, 3 Barb.
459; Wright v. Cartey, 27 N. J. 76; State v. Laverack, 34 N. J. 201;
Douglass v. Turnpike Co., 22 Md. 219 ; Chagrin Falls, etc., Plank-road Co.
v. Cane, 2 Ohio St. 419; Bagg v. Detroit, 5 Mich. 336. But see Williams
v. Natural Bridge Plank-road Co., 21 Mo. 580.

[2] See Moses v. Pittsburg, etc., R. R. Co., 21 Ill. 516, 522; People v.
Kerr, 37 Barb. 357; s. c. 27 N. Y. 188; Millburn v Cedar Rapids, etc., R.
R. Co., 12 Iowa, 246; Franz v. Railroad Co., 55 Iowa, 107, and the other
cases cited in this connection.

§ 121d

tion: If the new use of the highway is inconsistent with its character as a highway, where the fee is in the abutting land owner, it is a taking of property for which compensation must be made, whatever incidental benefits or injuries the land owner may sustain from the new use ; and even if he has sustained no injury whatever, for incidental injuries never constitute a taking of property in the law of eminent domain.   But if the fee is in the public, any use of the highway will not operate as a taking of the property of the abutting land owner, which does not interfere with his ordinary use of the street.[1]   Probably this distinction might assist in explaining away many of the differences of opinion, which now make the cases on this subject confusing and perplexing.   Where the fee is not in the public, it seems to be the opinion of an overwhelming majority of the cases, that the construction of an ordinary steam railway along a public street was a taking of the property of the owners of the fee for a different use, for which compensation had to be made.   " It is true that the actual use of the street by the railroad may not be so absolute and constant as to exclude the public also from its use.   With its single track, and particularly if the cars used upon it were propelled by horse-power, the interruption of the public easement in the street might be very trifling and of no practical consequence to the public at large.   But this question cannot affect the question of right of property, or of the increase of the burden upon the soil.   It would present simply a question of degree in respect to the enlargement of the easement, and would not affect the principle, that the use of a street for the purposes of a railroad imposed upon it a new burden." [2]

---

[1] See Protzman v. Indianapolis, etc., R. R. Co., 9 Ind. 467; New Albany, etc., R. R. Co. v. O'Daily, 13 Ind. 353; Crawford v. Delaware, 7 Ohio St. 459; Street Railway v. Cumminsville, 14 Ohio St. 541.

[2] Wager v. Troy Union R. R. Co., 25 N. Y. 526, 532. See Inhabitants of Springfield v. Conn. River R. R. Co., 4 Cush. 71; Imlay v. Union Branch

§ 121d

In deciding that the construction of an ordinary railroad as a public street or highway was a new taking of the property of the owner of the fee, the Supreme Court of Connecticut presented a very strong argument in favor of the proposition, which is as follows: "When land is condemned for a special purpose on the score of public utility, the sequestration is limited to that particular use. Land taken for a highway is not convertible into a common. As the property is not taken, but the use only, the right of the public is limited to the use, the specific use, for which the proprietor has been divested of a complete dominion over his own estate. These are propositions which are no longer open to discussion. But it is contended that land once taken and still held for highway purposes may be used for a railway without exceeding the limits of the easement already acquired by the public. If this is true, if the new use of the land is within the scope of the original sequestration or dedication, it would follow that the railway privileges are not an encroachment on the estate

R. R. Co., 26 Conn. 249; Presbyterian Society, etc., *v.* Auburn etc., R. R. Co., 3 Hill, 567; Williams *v.* N. Y. Central R. R. Co., 16 N. Y. 97; Carpenter *v.* Oswego, etc., R. R. Co., 24 N. Y. 655; Mahon *v.* N. Y. Central R. R. Co., 24 N. Y. 658; Starr *v.* Camden & Atlantic R. R. Co., 24 N. J. 592; Central R. R. Co. *v.* Hetfield, 29 N. J. 206; So. Ca. R. R. Co. *v.* Steiner, 44 Ga. 546; Donnaher's Case, 16 Miss. 649; Cox v. Louisville, etc., R. R. Co., 48 Ind. ⅋178; Schurmeier *v.* St. Paul, etc., R. R. Co., 10 Minn. 82; Gray *v.* First Division, etc., 13 Minn. 315; Ford *v.* Chicago, etc., R. R. Co., 14 Wis. 609, 616; Pomeroy *v.* Chicago, etc., R. R. Co., 16 Wis. 640; Cox *v.* Louisville, etc., R. R. Co., 48 Ind. 178; Cosby *v.* Railroad Co., 10 Bush (Ky.), 288; Railroad Co. *v.* Combs, 10 Bush, 382 (19 Am. Rep. 67); 2 Dillon Municipal Corp., § 725. See *contra*, Mifflin *v.* Railroad Co., 16 Pa. St. 182; Cases of Phila. & Trenton R. R. Co., 6 Whart. 25 (36 Am. Dec. 202); Struthers *v.* Railroad Co., 87 Pa. St. 282; Lexington, etc., R. R. Co. *v.* Applegate, 8 Dana, 289 (33 Am. Dec. 497). See, also, West Jersey R. R. Co. *v.* Cape May, etc., Co., 34 N. J. Eq. 164; Com. *v.* Erie, etc. R. R. Co., 27 Pa. St. 339; Snyder *v.* Pennsylvania R. R. Co., 55 Pa. St. 340; Peddicord *v.* Baltimore, etc., R. R. Co., 34 Md. 463; Wolfe *v.* Covington, etc., R. R. Co., 15 B. Mon. 404; Houston, etc., R. R. Co. *v.* Odum, 53 Tex. 343.

§ 121*d*

remaining in the owner of the soil, and that the new mode
of enjoying the public easement will not enable him rightfully to assert a claim to damages therefor.   On the contrary, if the true intent and efficacy of the original condemnation was not to subject the land to such a burden as
will be imposed upon it when it is confiscated to the uses
and control of a corporation, it cannot be denied that in the
latter case the estate of the owner of the soil is injuriously
affected by the supervening servitude ; that his rights are
abridged, and that in a legal sense his land is again taken
for public uses.   Thus it appears that the court have simply to decide whether there is such an identity between a
highway and a railway, that statutes conferring a right to
establish the former include an authority to construct the
latter.

" The term ' public highway,' as employed in such of our
statutes as convey the right of eminent domain, has certainly
a limited import.   Although, as suggested at the bar, a navigable river or a canal is, in some sense, a public highway,
yet an easement assumed under the name of a highway
would not enable the public to convert a street into a canal.
The highway, in the true meaning of the word, would be
destroyed.   But as no such destruction of the highway is
necessarily involved in the location of a railway track upon
it, we are pressed to establish the legal proposition that a
highway, such as is referred to in these statutes, means, or
or at least comprehends a railroad.   Such a construction is
possible only when it is made to appear that there is a substantial practical or technical identity between the uses of
land for highway and for railway purposes.   No one can
fail to see that the terms ' railway ' and ' highway ' are
not convertible, or that the two uses, practically considered, although analogous, are not identical.   Land, as
ordinarily appropriated by a railroad company, is inccn-
venient and even impassible to those who would use it
as a common highway.   Such a corporation does not hold

§ 121d

itself bound to make or keep its embankments and bridges in a condition which will facilitate the *transitus* of such vehicles as ply over an ordinary road.

"A practical dissimilarity obviously exists between a railway and a common highway, and is recognized as the basis of a legal distinction between them. It is so recognized on a large scale when railway privileges are sought from legislative bodies, and granted by them. If the terms 'highway' and 'railway' are synonymous, or if one of them includes the other by legal implication, no act would be more superfluous than to require or to grant authority to construct railways over localities already occupied as highways. If a legal identity does not subsist between a highway and a railway, it is illogical to argue that, because a railway may be so constructed as not to interfere with the ordinary uses of a highway, and so as to be consistent with the highway right already existing, therefore such a new use is included within the old use. It might as well be urged that if a common or a canal, laid out over the route of a public road, could be so arranged as to leave an ample roadway for vehicles and passengers on foot, the land should be held to be originally condemned for a canal or a common, as properly incident to the highway use.

"There is an important practical reason why courts should be slow to recognize a legal identity between the two uses referred to. They are by no means the same thing to the proprietor whose land is taken; on the contrary, they suggest widely different standards of compensation. One can readily conceive of cases, where the value of real estate would be directly enhanced by the opening of a highway through it; while its confiscation for a railway at the same or a subsequent time would be a gross injury to the estate, and a total subversion of the mode of enjoyment expected by the owner, when he yielded his private rights to the public exigency. But essential distinctions also exist between highway and railway powers, as conferred by stat-

§ 121*d*

ute — distinctions which are founded in the very nature of the powers themselves. In the case of the highway, the statute provides that, after the observance of certain legal forms, the locality in question shall be forever subservient to the right of every individual in the community to pass over the thoroughfare so created at all times. This right involves the important implication that he shall so use the privilege as to leave the privilege of all others as unobstructed as his own, and that he is therefore to use the road in the manner in which such roads are ordinarily used, with such vehicles as will not obstruct or require the destruction of the ordinary modes of travel thereon. He is not authorized to lay down a railway track, and run his own locomotive and car upon it.

"No one ever thought of regarding highway acts as conferring railway privileges, involving a right in every individual, not only to break up ordinary travel, but also to exact tolls from the public for the privilege of using the peculiar conveyances adapted to a railroad. If a right of this description is not conferred when a highway is authorized by law, it is idle to pretend that any proprietor is divested of such a right. It would seem that, under such circumstances, the true construction of highway laws could hardly be debatable, and that the absence of legal identity between the two uses of which we speak was patent and entire.

"Again, no argument or illustration can strengthen the self-evident proposition that, when a railway is authorized over a public highway, a right is created against the proprietor of the fee, in favor of a person, or artificial person, to whom he bore no legal relation whatever. It is understood that when such an easement is sought or bestowed, a new and independent right will accrue to the railroad corporation as against the owner of the soil, and that, without any reference to the existence of the highway, his land will forever stand charged with the accruing servitude. Ac-

§ 121d

cordingly, if such a highway were to be discontinued, according to the legal forms prescribed for that purpose, the railroad corporation would still insist upon the express and independent grant of an easement to itself, enabling it to maintain its own road on the site of the abandoned highway. We are of opinion, therefore, as was distinctly intimated by this court, in a former case[1] that, to subject the owner of the soil of a highway to a further appropriation of his land to railway uses is the imposition of a new servitude upon his estate, and is an act demanding the compensation which the law awards when land is taken for public purposes.'" The dissimilarity of highways and railways cannot be more strikingly presented than by a consideration of the numerous safeguards that are thought necessary to be thrown around the public, when a railroad crosses a highway. The bells must be rung, the whistle must be blown, the speed must be slackened, and very often bars are laid across the highway, so that vehicles and foot passengers cannot attempt to cross the track while the train is passing. How much greater would be the inconvenience to the public if a railroad track was laid along the highway, instead of across it.

But where the fee of the highway is in the public, the cases pretty generally hold that the establishment of a railroad along a highway is not such a taking of property of the adjoining land owner as will require the payment of compensation.[2] It cannot be doubted that in no case

---

[1] See opinion of Hinman, J., in Nicholson *v.* N. Y., etc., R. R. Co., 22 Conn. 74, 85.

[2] Milburn *v.* Cedar Rapids, etc., R. R. Co., 12 Iowa, 246; Clinton *v.* Cedar Rapids, etc., R. R. Co., 24 Iowa, 455; Franz *v.* Railroad Co., 55 Iowa, 107; Grand Rapids, etc., R. R. Co. *v.* Heisel, 38 Mich. 62 (31 Am. Rep. 306); Grand Rapids, etc., R. R. Co. *v.* Heisel, 47 Mich. 393; Harrison v. New Orleans, etc., R. R. Co., 34 La. Ann. 462 (44 Am. Rep. 438); Protzman *v.* Indianapolis, etc., R. R. Co., 9 Ind. 467; New Albany, etc., R. R. Co. *v.* O'Daily, 13 Ind. 353; Chicago, etc., R. R. Co. *v.* Joliet, 79 Ill. 25; Moses *v.* Pittsburg, etc., R. R. Co., 21 Ill. 516, 522. In this last case,

§ 121*d*

does the consequential depreciation in value of adjoining property, as a result of the construction of a steam railway along the street, constitute a taking of property which requires a payment of compensation, any more than the ordinary and reasonable exercise of any right gives rise to liability for incidental injuries to others. The appropriation of a highway to other purposes must interfere with some positive right of property, in order that it may be considered a taking of property. Where the public does not own the fee, any other and different use of the highway

Caton, C. J., said: "By the city charter, the common council is vested with the exclusive control and regulation of the streets of the city, the fee simple title to which we have already decided is vested in the municipal corporation. The city charter also empowers the common council to direct and control the location of railroad tracks within the city. In granting this permission to locate the track in Beach Street, the common council acted under an express power granted by the legislature. So that the defendant has all the right which both the legislature and the common council could give it, to occupy the street with its track. But the complainant assumes higher ground, and claims that any use of the street, even under the authority of the legislature and the common council, which tends to deteriorate the value of his property on the street, is a violation of that fundamental law which forbids private property to be taken for public use without just compensation. This is manifestly an erroneous view of the constitutional guaranty thus invoked. It must necessarily happen that streets will be used for various legitimate purposes, which will, to a greater or less extent, discommode persons residing or doing business upon them, and just to that extent damage their property; and yet such damage is incident to all city property, and for it a party can claim no remedy. The common council may appoint certain localities, where hacks and drays shall stand waiting for employment, or where wagons loaded with hay or wood, or other commodities, shall stand waiting for purchasers. This may drive customers away from shops or stores in the vicinity, and yet there is no remedy for the damage. A street is made for the passage of persons and property; and the law cannot define what exclusive means of transportation and passage shall be used. Universal experience shows that this can best be left to the determination of the municipal authorities, who are supposed to be the best acquainted with the wants and necessities of the citizens generally. To say that a new mode of passage shall be banished from the streets, no matter how much the general good may require it, simply because streets were not so used in the days of Blackstone, would hardly comport with

§ 121d

would be a taking, whatever effect it may have upon the adjoining property, as has been already fully explained, for there would be a fresh appropriation of the property of the owners of the fee.   But when the fee is in the State, the adjoining land owner has only an easement in the street, which entitles him to a reasonable enjoyment of it as a street, and an appropriation of it to other purposes, for example, for the construction of a steam railway, will constitute a taking of the property of the abutting proprietor, only when

the advancement and enlightenment of the present age. Steam has but lately taken the place, to any extent, of animal power for land transportation, and for that reason alone shall it be expelled the streets? For the same reason camels must be kept out, although they might be profitably employed. Some fancy horse or timid lady might be frightened by such uncouth objects. Or is the objection not in the motive-power used, but because the cars are larger than were formerly used, and run upon iron, and confined to a given track in the street? Then street railroads must not be admitted; they have large carriages which run on iron rails, and are confined to a given track. Their momentum is great, and may do damage to ordinary vehicles or foot passengers. Indeed we may suppose or assume that streets occupied by them are not so pleasant for other carriages or so desirable for residences or business stands, as if not thus occupied. But for this reason the property owners along the street cannot expect to stop such improvements. The convenience of those who live at a greater distance from the center of a city requires the use of such improvements, and for their benefit the owners of property upon the street must submit to the burden, when the common council determine that the public good requires it. Cars upon street railroads are now generally, if not universally, propelled by horses; but who can say how long it will be before it will be found safe and profitable to propel them with steam, or some other power besides horses? Should we say that this road should be enjoined, we could advance no reason for it which would not apply with equal force to street railroads; so that consistency would require that we should stop all. Nor would the evil which would result from the rule we must lay down stop here. We must prohibit every use of a street which discommodes those who reside or do business upon it, because their property will else be damaged. This question has been presented in other States, and in some instances, where the public have only an easement of the street, and the owner of the adjoining property still holds the fee in the street, it has been sustained; but the weight of authority, and certainly, in our apprehension, all sound reasoning is the other way."

§ 121*d*

his reasonable enjoyment of the street as such is denied to him. The noise, smoke, etc., do not involve any taking of property, however much it may depreciate the value and the desirability of the adjoining property. This would seem to be the better doctrine, and such is the opinion of the Indiana courts.[1]

But the courts are almost unanimously of the opinion that the appropriation of the street to the use of an ordinary horse railway, designed to convey passengers and property from one part of a city to another, is not a new taking of property, for which compensation must be made, whether the fee is in the State or in the abutting land owner. The use of the highway by a horse car company is held to be consistent with its use as a highway, and to constitute no interference with the reasonable enjoyment of the adjoining property-owner.[2] But the abutting land owner is only entitled to a reasonable use of the street as such, and the infliction on him of a mere inconvenience in the use of the street, by the construction of a street railway, will not

---

[1] Protzman *v.* Indianapolis, etc., R. R. Co., 9 Ind. 467; New Albany, etc., R. R. Co. *v.* O'Daily, 12 Ind. 551; *s. c.* 13 Ind. 353. See, also, Street Railway *v.* Cumminsville, 14 Ohio St. 523; Grand Rapids, etc., R. R. Co., 38 Mich. 62 (31 Am. Rep. 306); *s c.* 47 Mich. 393.

[2] For cases, in which the fee was in the adjoining proprietor, see Attorney-General *v.* Metropolitan R. R. Co., 125 Mass. 515 (28 Am. Rep. 264); Commonwealth *v.* Temple, 14 Gray, 75; Elliott *v.* Fairhaven, etc., R. R. Co., 32 Conn. 579; Hinchman *v.* Railroad Co., 17 N. J. Eq. 75; *s. c.* 20 N. J. Eq. 360; City Railroad Co. *v.* City Railroad Co., 20 N. J. Eq. 61; Street Railway *v.* Cumminsville, 14 Ohio St. 523; Hobart *v.* Milwaukee City R. R. Co., 27 Wis. 194 (9 Am. Rep. 461). In Craig *v.* Railroad Co., 39 Barb. 449; *s. c.* 39 N. Y. 404; Wager *v.* Railroad Co., 25 N. Y. 526, it was held that there was no difference between the horse and steam railways. In both cases, there must be a payment of compensation for a new taking of property from the owners of the fee. For cases, in which the fee was in the public, see People *v.* Kerr, 27 N. Y. 188; Kellinger *v.* Street Railroad Co., 50 N. Y. 206; Metropolitan R. R. Co. *v.* Quincy R. R. Co., 12 Allen, 262; Street Railway *v.* Cumminsville, 14 Ohio St. 523; Chicago *v.* Evans, 24 Ill. 52; Hess *v.* Baltimore, etc., Railway Co., 52 Md. 242 (36 Am. Rep. 371.

§ 121*d*

constitute a taking. Thus, it was held in New York, that the construction of a street railway, so near to the sidewalk as not to leave space enough for the standing of vehicles between the track and the sidewalk, was a taking of property in the constitutional sense.[1] And the same opinion was expressed in Wisconsin concerning a street railway whose tracks prevented the owner of a store from having his drays stand transversely to the sidewalk, while unloading goods.[2] While the running of a street railway does not ordinarily interfere with the reasonable enjoyment of the street by the adjoining land owners, still it might, under peculiar circumstances, interfere very seriously with the ordinary use of the street, as where the street is very narrow, and at the same time a great business thoroughfare ; and whenever that happens, the construction of the railway would constitute a taking of property, for which compensation can be demanded.   Mr. Cooley seems to think that under such circumstances, the property owner would, in the light of the authorities, be without a remedy.[3]   But while the proprietor of the adjoining property may be incommoded to some extent by the construction and maintenance of a street railway, without entitling him to compensation, his complete exclusion from the ordinary use of the street, or an extraordinary and unreasonable interference with such use, would support a claim for compensation, as being a taking of property in the exercise of the right of eminent domain. Such, at least, appears to us to be a reasonable deduction from the authorities, which hold that any interruption of the reasonable use of the streets by the abutting land owner will constitute a taking of property.

It has sometimes happened that land, which had been appropriated for the opening of a street, is afterwards used

---

[1] Kellinger *v.* Street R. R. Co., 50 N. Y. 206; People *v.* Kerr, 27 N. Y. 188.

[2] Hobart *v.* Milwaukee City R. R. Co., 27 Wis. 194 (9 Am. Rep. 461).

[3] Cooley Const. Lim. 683.

§ 121*d*

for the erection of a market, or public scale, etc. This
cannot be done in any case without payment of compensation, because the use of the land as a market is inconsistent
and interferes with its use as a street.[1]

§ 121e. Compensation, how ascertained. — It does not
fall properly within the scientific scope of a work on Police
Power to enter into a detailed account of the rule and proceedings for the ascertainment and measurement of the
compensation, that is to be paid to one whose land is taken
away from him in the exercise of eminent domain. That
subject belongs more properly to a work on practice or on
damages. But there are certain constitutional principles
involved in the subject, which will require a cursory consideration.

While the condemnation of land for public purposes is
in no sense a judicial act, the determination of the amount
of compensation is a judicial act, which requires, for a final
adjudication, a trial of the facts before a court, with a due
observance of all those constitutional safeguards that are
thrown around private rights, for their protection against
arbitrary or tyrannical infringements. The legislature cannot fix the limits of compensation, nor can it be done in
any *ex parte* proceeding. But a jury is not necessary, unless
the constitution expressly provides for a jury trial.[2]

---

[1] State *v.* Laverack, 34 N. J. 201; State *v.* Mayor, etc., of Mobile, 5
Port. 279 (30 Am. Dec. 564); Angell on Highways, § 243, *et seq. ;* Barney
v. Keokuk, 94 U. S. 324.

[2] Charles River Bridge *v.* Warren Bridge, 7 Pick. 344; *s. c.* 11 Pet. 420,
571; People *v.* Kniskern, 54 N. Y. 52; Petition of Mt. Washington Co., 35
N. H. 134; Ligat *v.* Commonwealth, 19 Pa. St. 456, 460; People *v.* Tall-
man, 36 Barb. 222; Clark *v.* Miller, 54 N. Y. 528; Baltimore, etc., R. R.
Co. *v.* Pittsburg, etc., R. R. Co., 17 W.Va. 812; Power's Appeal, 29 Mich.
504; Lamb *v.* Lane, 4 Ohio St. 167; Hood *v.* Finch, 8 Wis. 381; Boon-
ville *v.* Ormrod, 26 Mo. 193; Dickey *v.* Tennison, 27 Mo. 373; Rich *v.*
Chicago, 59 Ill. 286; Cook *v.* South Park Com., 61 Ill. 115; Ames *v.* Lake
Superior, etc., R. R. Co., 21 Minn. 241. See Putnam *v.* Douglass Co., 6

§ 121e

Another question relates to the time when the compensation should be made. According to the constitutions of many of the States, the payment of compensation must always precede or accompany the condemnation of the land. But where such constitutional provisions do prevail, it is held to be no violation of them for public officers, or the officers and agents of the corporation, in whose favor the right of eminent domain is to be exercised, to enter upon the land, before the payment of compensation, for the purpose of surveying and selecting the land for condemnation.[1] In the absence, however, of such a constitutional requirement, at least in the case of the appropriation of land by the State or municipal authorities, it is not necessary to provide for the payment of compensation before the appropriation. It is sufficient, if an easy remedy is provided for the recovery of the compensation by the land owner at his own instance.[2]

Ore. 378 (25 Am. Rep. 527); Conn. River R. R. Co. *v.* County Commissioners, 127 Mass. 50 (34 Am. Rep. 338).

[1] Cushman *v.* Smith, 34 Me. 247; Nichols *v.* Somerset, etc., R. R. Co., 43 Me. 356; Bloodgood *v.* Mohawk, etc., R. R. Co., 14 Wend. 51; *s. c.* 18 Wend. 9; State *v.* Seymour, 35 N. J. 47; Walther *v.* Warner, 25 Mo. 277; Fox *v.* W. P. R. R. Co., 31 Cal. 538.

[2] Charlestown Branch R. R. Co. *v.* Middlesex, 7 Met. 78; Haverhill Bridge Proprietors *v.* County Commissioners, 103 Mass. 120 (4 Am. Rep. 518); Conn. River R. R. Co. *v.* Com., 127 Mass. 50 (34 Am. Rep. 338); Talbot *v.* Hudson, 16 Gray, 417; Ash *v.* Cummings, 50 N. H. 591; Orr *v.* Quinby, 54 N. H. 590; Calkins *v.* Baldwin, 4 Wend. 667 (21 Am. Dec. 168); Bloodgood *v.* Mohawk, etc., R. R. Co., 18 Wend. 9; Gardner *v.* Newburg, 2 Johns. Ch. 162 (7 Am. Dec. 526); Rexford *v.* Knight, 11 N. Y. 308; Chapman *v.* Gates, 54 N. Y. 132; Hamersly *v.* New York, 56 N. Y. 533; Loweree *v.* Newark, 38 N. J. 151; Long *v.* Fuller, 68 Pa. St. 170; Callison *v.* Hedrick, 15 Gratt. 244; Southwestern R. R. Co. *v* Telegraph Co., 46 Ga. 43; Buffalo, etc., R. R. Co. *v.* Ferris, 26 Tex. 588; White *v* Nashville, etc., R. R. Co., 7 Heisk. 518; Simms *v.* Railroad Co., 12 Heisk. 621; Taylor *v.* Marcy, 25 Ill. 518; People *v.* Green, 3 Mich. 496; Brock *v.* Hishen, 40 Wis. 674; State *v.* Messenger, 27 Minn. 119; Harper *v.* Richardson, 22 Cal. 251. But the land owner must be able to institute the suit for the recovery of the compensation of his own motion, and without the interposition of some State officer. Shepherdson *v.* Milwaukee, etc., R. R. Co., 6 Wis. 605; Powers *v.* Bears, 12 Wis. 213; In the absence of a statutory

§ 121e

But this can hardly be taken as an emphatic determination that such is a constitutional requirement in the absence of an express provision to that effect. It is rather a consideration of what provisions the legislature ought to make for the protection of the land owner, so that he should not be. left to the mercy of a possibly dishonest or bankrupt corporation, and run the risk of losing both his land and his money.[1] And most of the State statutes do make such provisions.

SECTION 122. Regulation of the use of lands — What is a nuisance?
    122a. What is a nuisance, a judicial question.
    122b. Unwholesome trades in tenement houses may be prohibited.
    122c. Confinement of objectionable trades to certain localities.
    122d. Regulation of burial grounds.
    122e. Laws regulating the construction of wooden buildings.
    122f. Regulation of the right to hunt game.
    122g. Abatement of nuisances — Destruction of buildings.

§ 122. **Regulation of the use of lands — What is a**

provision for compensation, the land owner may resort to his common-law remedy. Hooker v. Haven, etc., Co., 16 Conn. 146 (36 Am. Dec. 477). It is not unconstitutional, after providing a proper remedy for the recovery of the compensation, to limit the time in which the remedy may be pursued. Charleston Branch R. R. Co. v. Middlesex, 7 Met. 78; Rexford v. Knight, 11 N. Y. 308; Callison v. Hedrick, 15 Gratt. 244; Cupp v. Commissioners of Seneca, 19 Ohio St. 173; People v. Green, 3 Mich. 496; Taylor v. Marcy, 25 Ill. 518; Gilmer v. Lime Point, 18 Cal. 229. But where the property is taken by a private corporation, instead of by the State, an inclination is manifested by some of the authorities to hold it necessary on general principles that payment of compensation precede or accompany the condemnation. "The settled and fundamental doctrine is, that government has no right to take private property for public purposes, without giving just compensation; and it seems to be necessarily implied that the indemnity should, in cases which will admit of it, be previously and equitably ascertained, and be ready for reception, concurrently in point of time with the actual exercise of the right of eminent domain." Kent, Chancellor, in 2 Kent, 329, note. See, also, to the same effect, Loweree v. Newark, 38 N. J. 151; State v. Graves, 19 Md. 351; Dronberger v. Reed, 11 Ind. 420; Shepherdson v. Milwaukee, etc., R. R. Co, 6 Wis. 605; Powers v. Bears, 12 Wis. 213.

[1] See Ash v. Cummings, 50. N. H. 591; Memphis & Charleston R. R. Co.

§ 122

nuisance? — The reasonable enjoyment of one's real estate is certainly a vested right, which cannot be interfered with or limited arbitrarily. The constitutional guaranty of protection for all private property extends equally to the enjoyment and the possession of lands. An arbitrary interference by the government, or by its authority, with the reasonable enjoyment of private lands is a taking of private property without due process of law, which is inhibited by the constitutions. But it is not every use which comes within this constitutional protection. One has a vested right to only a reasonable use of one's lands. It is not difficult to find the rule which determines the limitations upon the lawful ways or manner of using lands. It is the rule, which furnishes the solution of every problem in the law of police power, and which is comprehended in the legal maxim, *sic utere tuo, ut alienum non lœdas.* One can lawfully make use of his property only in such a manner as that he will not injure another. Any use of one's lands to the hurt or annoyance of another is a nuisance, and may be prohibited. At common law that is a nuisance, which causes personal discomfort or injury to health to an unusual degree. As it has been expressed in a preceding section,[1] the right of personal security against acts, which will cause injury to health or great bodily discomfort, cannot be made absolute in organized society. It must yield to the reasonable demands of trade, commerce and other great interests of society. While the State cannot arbitrarily violate the right of personal security to health by the unlimited authorization of acts which do harm to health, or render one's residence less comfortable, there is involved in this matter the consideration of what constitutes a reasonable use of

v. Payne, 37 Miss. 700; Walther *v.* Warner, 25 Mo. 277; Carr *v.* Georgia R. R. Co., 1 Ga. 524; Southwestern R. R. Co., *v.* Telegraph Co., 46 Ga. 43; Henry *v.* Dubuque, etc., R. R. Co., 10 Iowa, 540; Curran *v.* Shattuck, 24 Cal. 427.

[1] § 18.

§ 122

one's property. At common law this is strictly a judicial
question of fact, the answer to which varies according to
the circumstances of each case.   One is expected to endure
a reasonable amount of discomfort and annoyance for the
public good, which is furthered by the permission of trades
and manufactures, the prosecution of which necessarily
involves a certain amount of annoyance or injury to the inhabitants of the neighborhood.   In all such cases, it is a
question of equity, on whom is it reasonable to impose the
burden of the inevitable loss, resulting from this clashing
of interests; and independently of statute it is strictly a
judicial question, and all the circumstances of the case
must be taken into consideration.[1]   But the legislature frequently interferes to modify the common law of nuisances;
sometimes legalizing what were nuisances before the enactment, and sometimes prohibiting, as being nuisances, what
were not considered to be such at common law.   No legislative act can justify a nuisance, which is willfully committed and which serves no useful purpose.   But when the
objectionable act serves a useful purpose, and supplies a
public want, the private right of personal security against
nuisances must yield to the public necessity, whenever a
legislative act calls for the sacrifice.   It is a constitutional
exercise of police power to legalize a nuisance, if the public
exigencies should require it.   It is of course a matter of
legislative discretion, whether the legalization of the nuisance is required by the public necessities.   Thus it has
been held to be lawful for the legislature to authorize the
ringing of bells and the blowing of whistles by the loco-
motives of railroads at the times when, and in the places
where, it would otherwise be a nuisance.   The public safety
required the imposition of this burden upon the comfort
and quiet of those who may thereby be disturbed.[2]   In the

[1] See *ante*, § 18.
[2] Sawyer *v.* Davis, 136 Mass. 239 (49 Am. Rep. 27); Pittsburg, Cin. &
St. L. R. R. Co. *v.* Crown, 57 Ind. 45 (33 Am. Rep. 73).

§ 122

same manner the legislature may authorize the prosecution of certain trades and occupations in localities, which would, under like circumstances, be considered a nuisance at common law. But in all these cases of legalization of nuisances, the legislative interference must promote some public good. If the benefit, derived from the authorization of the nuisance, is altogether of a private character ; if it can in no legitimate sense be considered as a public benefit, the legislative interference is unwarranted, and it is the duty of the courts to declare the statute to be unconstitutional. It is a question for the legislature whether the public needs require the legalization of the nuisance ; but it is a judicial question whether such a legislative act serves a public want.

On the other hand, through the interference of the legislature, the doing of acts may be prohibited on the ground of being nuisances, which otherwise have been held to be permissible, because of the public benefit resulting from these acts. The courts may determine, independently of statute, that the public benefit from a certain unwholsome or annoying trade far outweighs the personal discomfort or injury to health, which attends the prosecution of the trade, and for that reason may refuse to prohibit ; but the legislature is not precluded from reaching a different conclusion. Granting that the act or trade produces discomfort or injury to health, it is ultimately a legislative question whether the public welfare requires the imposition of this burden. No one has a natural right to do that which injures another. If the law permits him to do this it is a privilege, which may be revoked at any time by the proper authority. The police power of the government is reposed in the legislature. It is quite a common experience for the legislature, either to prohibit altogether, or to regulate the

§ 122

doing of that which works an annoyance or injury to others.[1]

§ 122a. **What is a nuisance, a judicial question.**— It is clearly within the legislative discretion to determine whether the private interest or the public good shall yield in a case where the two are antagonistic, and to prohibit or permit the doing of what promotes the public welfare and at the same time causes personal discomfort or injury ; and its judgment cannot be subjected to a review by the courts. The courts cannot reverse the legislative decree in such a case ; it is not in any sense a judicial question. But the police power of the legislature, in reference to the prohibition of nuisances, is limited to the prohibition or regulation of those acts which injure or otherwise interfere with the rights of others. The legislature cannot prohibit a use of lands, which works no hurt or annoyance to the neighbors or adjoining property. The injurious effect of the use of the land furnishes the justification for the interference of the legislature. The legislative prohibition or regulation of the use and enjoyment of one's private property in land is in violation of constitutional principles, which is not confined to the prevention of a nuisance. A certain use of lands, harmless in itself, does not become a nuisance, because the legislature has declared it to be so. The legislature can determine whether it will permit or prohibit the doing of a thing which is harmful to others, in the proper considera- tion of the public welfare ; but it cannot prohibit as a nui- sance an act which inflicts no injury upon the health or

---

[1] " Unwholesome trades, slaughter houses, operations offensive to the senses, the deposit of gunpowder, the application of steam power to propel cars, the building with combustible materials, and the burial of the dead, may all be interdicted by law, in the midst of the dense masses of population, on the general and rational principle, that every person ought so to use his property as not to injure his neighbors; and that private interests must be made subservient to the general interests of the community." 2 Kent Com. 340.

§ 122a

property of others. If the harmful or innocent character
of the prohibited use of lands furnishes the test for determining the constitutionality of the legislative prohibition,
it is clearly a judicial question, and is certainly not within
the legislative discretion, whether the prohibited act or acts
work an injury to others. If they do not cause injury
or annoyance to others, the attempted legislative interference is unwarranted by the constitution, and it is the duty
of the courts to declare it to be unconstitutional. The following language from an opinion of the Supreme Court of
New Jersey will serve to fortify the position here taken on
the limitation of the legislative power to declare what is a
nuisance : " Assuming the power in this board [of health]
derived from the legislature, to adjudge the fact of the
existence of a nuisance, and also assuming such jurisdiction
to have been regularly exercised, and upon notice to the
parties interested, still, I think, it is obvious that, in a case
such as that before this court, the finding of the sanitary
board cannot operate, in any respect, as a judgment at law
would, upon the rights involved. It will require but little
reflection to satisfy my mind, accustomed to judge by legal
standards, of the truth of this remark. To fully estimate
the character and extent of the power claimed, will conduct
us to its instant rejection. The authority to decide when
a nuisance exists, is an authority to find facts, to estimate
their force, and to apply rules of law to the case thus made.
This is a judicial function, and it is a function applicable to
a numerous class of important interests. The use of land
and buildings, the enjoyment of water rights, the practice
of many trades and occupations, and the business of manufacturing in particular localities, all fall, on some occasions,
in important respects, within its sphere. To say to a man
that he shall not use his property as he pleases, under certain conditions, is to deprive him *pro tanto*, of the enjoyment
of such property. To find conclusively against him, that
a state of facts exists with respect to the use of his property,

§ 122a

or the pursuit of his business, which subjects him to the condemnation of the law, is to affect his rights in a vital point. The next thing to depriving a man of his property, is to circumscribe him in its use, and the right to use property is as much under the protection of the law as the property itself, in any other respects, is, and the one interest can no more than the other be taken out of the hands of the ordinary tribunals. If a man s property cannot be taken away from him except upon trial by jury, or by the exercise of the right of eminent domain upon compensation made, neither can he, in any other mode, be limited in the use of it. The right to abate public nuisances, whether we regard it as existing in the municipalities, or in the community, or in the hands of the individual, is a common-law right, and is derived in every instance of its exercise, from the same source — that of necessity. It is akin to the right of destroying property for the public safety in case of the prevalence of a devastating fire or other controlling exigency. But the necessity must be present to justify the exercise of the right, and whether present or not, must be submitted to a jury under the guidance of a court. The finding of a sanitary committee, or of a municipal council, or of any other body of a similar kind, can have no effect whatever, for any purpose, upon the ultimate disposition of a matter of this kind."[1] To the same effect is the following quotation

---

[1] Hutton v. City of Camden, 39 N. J. 122 (23 Am. Rep. 209). See Manhattan Fertilizing Co. v. Van Keuren, 8 C. E. Green, 251; Weil v. Ricord, 9 C. E. Green, 169. "The common council, in the exercise of the power to declare nuisances, may not declare anything such which cannot be detrimental to the health of the city, or dangerous to its citizens, or a public inconvenience, and even then not when the thing complained of is expressly authorized by the supreme legislative power in the State. Its legislation must be subordinate to that of the State, the power to which it owes its existence. When its acts of legislation are brought before this court, whose high duty it is to see that inferior tribunals, vested with a limited jurisdiction, whether legislative or judicial, do not exceed their power, we must determine whether these are valid or not. I cannot think an ordinance declaring the running of any loco-

§ 122a

from the opinion of the Supreme Court of the United States in a case in which the constitutionality of a city ordinance was questioned, which declared certain wharf structures to be nuisances and provided for their removal : " The mere declaration by the City Council of Milwaukee that a certain structure was an encroachment or an obstruction did not make it so, nor could such a declaration make it a nuisance unless it in fact had that character.   It is a doctrine not to be tolerated in this country, that a municipal corporation, without any general laws either of the city or of the State, within which a given structure can be shown to be a nuisance, can, by a mere declaration that it is one, subject it to removal by any person supposed to be aggrieved, or even by the city itself.   This would place every house, every

motive or train of cars upon any track in the city, at a greater rate than one mile in six minutes a removable nuisance, or declaring the stopping of a train of cars for one moment upon the track of a railroad authorized by law, where the track does not cross a street or a public square, a removable nuisance, is a fair or legal exercise of the power to declare nuisances and provide for their removal. * * * The doing of such acts cannot interfere with the public health or expose the inhabitants of the city to danger or inconvenience.   I do not see why any railroad depot, or track, or freight house, any train of cars in motion or stationary at any point in the city, cannot under the same power, with equal propriety, be declared nuisances, if the common council should so determine." State v. New Jersey, etc., R. R., 29 N. J. L. 170.   " There is a difference between abating a nuisance and declaring what shall be a nuisance. For the definition of a nuisance, and consequent ascertainment of the subjects to which their power of abating or removing may be extended, the council must refer to the general law, just as they must, in requiring the performance of patrol duty, learn what that duty is.   In derogation of the ordinary rights of property, they may abate or remove anything which by law is a nuisance, and in an action against them proof, that a thing was a nuisance, and was therefore removed or destroyed, would constitute their justification.   But they have no power to declare that to be a nuisance which is not, or to dispense with other proof of the noxious character of a thing, by showing that by an ordinance they had declared that all such things should be nuisances." Dissenting opinion of Wardlaw, J., in Crossby v. Warren, 1 Rich L. 388; Lakeview v. Setz, 44 Ill. 81. See Baldwin v. Smith, 82 Ill. 163.

§ 122a

business, and all the property of the city, at the uncontrolled will of the temporary local authorities." [1]

§ 122*b*. **Unwholesome trades in tenement houses may be prohibited.** — Perhaps the judicial character of the power to determine what is a nuisance, is best displayed in the consideration of a late case from the New York Court of Appeals,[2] in which an act of the legislature was declared to be unconstitutional, which made it a misdemeanor to manufacture cigars, in cities of more than five hundred thousand inhabitants, in any tenement house occupied by more than three families, except on the first floor of the house, on which there may be a store for the sale of cigars and tobacco.   In delivering the opinion of the court, Judge Earle said: "It is plain that this law interferes with the profitable and free use of his property by the owner or lessee of a tenement house who is a cigar maker, and trammels him in the application of his industry and the disposition of his labor, and thus, in a strictly legitimate sense, it arbitrarily deprives him of his property and of some portion of his personal liberty.   The constitutional guaranty that no person shall be deprived of his property without due process of law may be thus violated without the physical taking of property for public or private use.   This guarantee would be of little worth if the legislature could, without compensation, destroy property or its value, deprive the owner of its use, deny him the right to live in his own house or to work at any lawful trade therein.   If the legislature has the power under the constitution to prohibit the prosecution of one lawful trade in a tenement house, then it may   prevent   the   prosecution   of   all   trades therein."   *   *   *   "All laws which impair or trammel these rights, which limit one in his choice of a trade or a profession, or confine him to work or live in a specified

---

[1] Yates *v.* Milwaukee, 10 Wall. 505.
[2] In the matter of Jacobs, 98 N. Y. 98 (50 Am. Rep. 636).

§ 122*b*

locality, or exclude him from his own house, or restrain his
otherwise lawful movements (except in police regulations)
are infringements upon his fundamental rights of liberty,
which are under constitutional protection." * * * In
speaking of the limitations upon the police power of the
government, he continues : "Under it the conduct of an
individual, and the use of property may be regulated so as
to interfere to some extent with the freedom of the one and
the enjoyment of the other, and in cases of great emergency, engendering overruling necessity, property may be
taken and destroyed without compensation, and without
what is commonly called due process of law. The limit
of the power cannot be accurately defined, and the
courts have not been able or willing definitely to circumscribe it. But the power, however broad and extensive,
is not above the constitution. It furnishes the supreme
law, and so far as it imposes restraints the police power
must be exercised in subordination thereto." * * *
" Generally, it is for the legislature to determine what laws
and regulations are needed to protect the public health and
secure the public comfort and safety, and while its measures
are calculated, intended, convenient and appropriate to accomplish these ends, the exercise of its discretion is subject
to the review of the courts. If it passes an act ostensibly
for the public health, and thereby destroys or takes away
the property of a citizen or interferes with his personal
liberty, then it is for the courts to scrutinize the act and see
whether it really relates to and is convenient and appropriate to promote the public health." Whether the court was
correct in holding this statute to be unconstitutional, because
the regulation did not tend to promote the public health,
need not be discussed here. The principle is clearly settled, that the court did not exceed its power, in pronouncing the law to be unconstitutional on that ground. But the
court would have trespassed upon the powers of the legislature, if it had undertaken to pass upon the necessity of the

regulation. It falls within the legislative discretion to decide upon the necessity for the exercise of its police power.

It can not be questioned that the State has the power to prohibit the prosecution of all unwholesome or injurious trades and employments in these large tenement houses in our metropolitan cities, in which the people are often huddled together like cattle. The manufacture of cigars is considered by some to so taint the atmosphere as to endanger the health of the occupants of the house. If this be true, then the legislature has undoubtedly the power to prohibit the prosecution of this trade in a tenement house occupied by three or more families. The injurious effect upon the health of the cigarmaker's family may not furnish the proper justification for legislative interference, except in behalf of minor children. For since the wife and grown children, in the theory of law, if not in fact, voluntarily subject themselves to the unwholesome odors of the tobacco, they do not need and cannot demand the protection of the law. But where a house is occupied by more than one family, the other families have a right to enjoy the possession of their parts of the house, free from the unwholesome or disagreeable odors of a trade that is being plied by another in the same house.

A very common evil is the washing of soiled clothes in tenement houses. There can be very little doubt that infectious and contagious diseases may be communicated and spread over a large area through the medium of soiled clothes, and if the legislature were to see fit to prohibit washerwomen from plying their trade in tenement houses, I cannot see what constitutional objection could be raised to such and similar regulations, even though their enforcement may impose very great hardships upon those who can least bear them. Granting that the prohibited trade is unwholesome to the occupants of the house, the

§ 122*b*

advisability of the prohibition must be referred to the legislative discretion.

§ 122c. Confinement of objectionable trades to certain localities.[1] — As long as a trade does not injure the public health, and is the source of no annoyance whatever to the inhabitants of the locality in which it is conducted, it cannot lawfully be prohibited. Every man has a constitutional right to follow on his premises any calling, provided it does not in any way interfere with another's reasonable enjoyment of his premises. But if the prosecution of a certain trade affects another injuriously, the State may so regulate the trade that the injury may be avoided or reduced to a minimum. If the trade is in itself, and necessarily, harmful to one's neighbors, or to the public health, it may be prohibited altogether. But if it can be prosecuted under certain limitations, so as to avoid injury to others, the police regulation must be confined to the imposition of these needed restrictions, and the trade cannot be absolutely prohibited.[2]

The police regulation cannot extend beyond the evil to be remedied. Where, therefore, certain trades and employments, which serve some useful purpose and add something to the world's wealth, are harmful to the inhabitants of the locality, in which they may be conducted ; and the harm may be avoided altogether, or considerably reduced, by confining them to localities, in which the pop-

[1] See *ante*, § 104 on the police control of employments in respect to locality.

[2] "Conceding that the power 'to abate and remove' should be construed as including the power to prevent, yet this preventive power could only be exercised in reference to those things that are nuisances in themselves and necessarily so. There are some things which in their nature are nuisances, and which the law recognizes as such; there are others which may or may not be so, their character in this respect depending on circumstances." Lake View *v.* Setz, 44 Ill. 81.

ulation is sparse and the residences are few ; it is altogether
permissible to prohibit the prosecution of these trades in
other localities.   The instances of this kind of regulation
are very numerous.   Slaughter-houses have been confined
to certain localities,[1] the sale of fresh meat and vegetables
has been prohibited except in the public markets, where the
articles exposed for sale may be conveniently inspected.[2]
In the same way may the manufacture of pressed hay [3] and
the storage of cotton and other combustible material,
such as oil and gunpowder, be prohibited in the densely
settled parts of the city, and the prosecution of such trades
be confined to certain less dangerous localities.   In the
same way may the sale of intoxicating liquors be prohibited
in certain localities, for example, within a certain distance
of the State insane asylum, university or State capitol,[4]
provided it be conceded that the sale of intoxicating liquors
in those localities, in a legal sense, threatens an injury to
the public.[5]   But in all these cases the prohibition must be
confined to the removal of the evil to be guarded against
There cannot be an absolute prohibition of a trade in a locality in which it may be prosecuted without annoyance or
inconvenience to the neighboring residents.   Thus it has

[1] Cronin v. People, 82 N. Y. 318; Metropolitan Board of Health v.
Heister, 37 N. Y. 661; Slaughter-house Cases, 16 Wall. 36; Milwaukee v.
Gross, 21 Wis. 241;

[2] Buffalo v. Webster, 10 Wend. 99; Bush v. Seaburg, 8 Johns. 418;
Winnsboro v. Smart, 11 Rich. L. 551; Bowling Green v. Carson, 10 Bush,
64; New Orleans v. Stafford, 27 La. Ann. 417 (21 Am. Rep. 563); Wartman v. Philadelphia, 33 Pa. St. 202; St. Louis v. Weber, 14 Mo. 547; Ash
v. People, 11 Mich. 347; Leclaire v. Davenport, 13 Iowa, 210.   Contra,
Bethune v. Hayes, 28 Ga. 560; Caldwell v. Alton, 33 Ill. 416; Blooming.
ton v. Wahl, 46 Ill. 489.

[3] Mayor City of Hudson v. Thorn, 7 Paige, 261.

[4] State v. Joyner, 81 N. C. 534; Ex parte McClain, 61 Cal. 436 (44 Am.
Rep. 554); Dorman v. State, 34 Ala. 216; Boyd v. Bryant, 35 Ark. 69 (37
Am. Rep. 6); Trammell v. Bradley, 37 Ark. 356; Bronsin v. Oberlin, 41
Ohio St. 476 (52 Am. Rep. 90).

[5] See ante, § 103.

§ 122c.

been held to be unreasonable to prohibit the establishment of a steam engine within the limits of the city.[1]

In Kentucky, a statute was enacted, forbidding any person from carrying on the stabling business within a specified distance of the grounds of a named agricultural society during the maintenance of its fairs, and imposing a penalty for the breach of the law. In a suit, brought under the statute, it could not be established that the prosecution of the business of stabling in that locality was likely to produce any public harm, and the court therefore declared the regulation to be an unconstitutional interference with the right of enjoyment of private property.[2]

Another curious and questionable exercise of police power, in prohibiting objectionable trades in certain localities, is to be found reported in the case of Commonwealth v. Bearse.[3] A statute was passed, prohibiting the establishment of any store, tent, or booth, for the purpose of vending provisions and refreshments, or for the exhibition of any kind of show or play, within one mile of the camp-meeting grounds during the time of holding any camp or field meeting for religious purposes, except with the consent of those having the camp-meeting in charge, provided that no one will be required to suspend any regular, usual, and established business, which is being conducted within such limits.[4] The object of the statute was to prevent the disturbance of the religious meeting by the presence of hucksters and peddlers, who are drawn thither purely by the desire to barter with those who are in attendance upon the meeting. Inasmuch as no one's regular business is interfered with, the owner of contiguous land is only prohibited from so using his land as to make a profit out of the camp-meeting, to the annoyance of those who have assembled there for worship. This

[1] Baltimore v. Redecke, 49 Md. 217 (33 Am. Rep. 239.)
[2] Commonwealth v. Bacon, 13 Ky. 210 (26 Am. Rep. 189).
[3] 132 Mass. 542 (42 Am. Rep. 450).
[4] Mass. Statute of 1867, ch. 59.

§ 122c

limitation upon the right of enjoyment of one's lands was declared to be a constitutional exercise of police power. The court say: " It is contended that the defendant's use of his own land is subjected to the will of another; that he cannot under this law use it for an otherwise lawful purpose, except with the consent of another. But no general control has been assumed over his land; no lawful and established business that he has is interfered with. If it be that of selling provisions and refreshments, he may continue it, although the camp-meeting has assembled. If he purposes to make a use of his land that he would not have made but for the assembling of the camp-meeting, that is not an improper police regulation which requires him to obtain the consent of its authorities. * * * If a business were in its character such as was, or was liable to become, a nuisance, the legislature might entirely forbid it. It would equally provide that it should not be maintained except with the consent of those in whose vicinity it was to be carried on, on account of the inconveniences attending it. This does not compel one to submit to others the inquiry whether he shall use his own land in a lawful way, but it is a legislative decision that such use is not lawful or permissible, unless consent is obtained from those who are already using their property in such a way that they may be annoyed." Confined within these narrow limits, it is probable that the constitutionality of the regulation may be sustained, on the ground that the business of catering to the wants of those in attendance on the camp-meeting may become a nuisance, unless it is regulated in this manner. But a law could not be sustained, which compelled a man to suspend his regularly established business during the time of holding the meeting, because in the regular prosecution of his business he might supply the wants of the camp-meeting company. Such a law would be an unconstitutional interference with the natural right of enjoyment of one's property.

§ 122c

§ 122*d*. **Regulation of burial-grounds.** — The burial of the dead within the limits of towns and cities has always been and still is, a common evil. In the past little attention was paid to sanitary regulations of any kind, and the injurious effect of the burial of the dead in thickly settled communities was seldom considered. But in some communities public opinion has been aroused on the subject, and laws have been passed, which prohibited interments within certain limits. In all the cases in which the constitutionality of this law was brought into question, it has been conceded that the legislature may regulate the burial of the dead, and prohibit it in those localities in which it will prove injurious to the public health;[1] but it is doubtful how far such a police regulation may be prevented directly or indirectly, by agreements, that a cemetery shall be established in a given locality. In New York it was held that a grant of land by the municipal corporation, for the purpose of a cemetery, with covenants of quiet enjoyment, did not prevent the passage of an ordinance prohibiting interments in that part of the city. It was no impairment of a contract, as municipal corporations have no power to make a contract, controlling or taking away their police power.[2] But it has been held in Illinois that the legislature has no right to prohibit the burial of the dead in the grounds of a cemetery company, which it has been authorized to lay out for that purpose. The court say : "A cemetery is not a nuisance *per se* and the subject of legislative prohibition. The legislature has the constitutional right to pass laws regulating the interment of the dead, so as to prevent injury to the health of the community, and this in respect to a private

---

[1] Brick Presb. Church *v.* Mayor, etc., 5 Cow. 538; Coates *v.* Mayor, etc., 7 Cow. 585; Kincaid's Appeal, 66 Pa. St. 423 (5 Am. Rep. 377); City Council *v.* Wentworth St. Baptist Church, 4 Strobh. 310; Lake View *v.* Rose Hill Cemetery Co., 70 Ill. 192.

[2] Brick Presbyterian Church *v.* Mayor, etc., 5 Cow. 538; Coates *v.* Mayor, etc., 7 Cow. 585.

§ 122*d*

corporation acting under its charter, as well as with individuals. But the legislature cannot prohibit the burial of the dead in lands purchased and laid out at great expense by a corporation chartered for the purpose. Such a statute is unconstitutional, as impairing the obligation of the contract contained in the charter."[1] The regulations of the burial of the dead have so far been confined to the prohibition of burial in the compact parts of a city, or within the city boundary. It is also held by some[2] that a cemetery is not a nuisance *per se*, and consequently the interment of the dead cannot be prohibited altogether. Of late, the advocates of cremation of dead bodies have been urging the unwholesomeness of burial as a reason why cremation should be adopted in its stead, as a means of disposing of corpses. If the burial of the dead does not cause or threaten injury to the public health, burial could not lawfully be prohibited; but if it is proven to be a fact that the interment of dead bodies does injure the public health, and is a fruitful source of the transmission of disease, as it is claimed to be by many scientists, it cannot be doubted that the State may prohibit burial and compel the remains of the dead to be cremated, or disposed of in some other harmless way.

In addition to the regulation of the locality in which burial is permitted, there are usually some regulations concerning the manner of interment, the object of which is to prevent any deterioration of the public health, as, for example, that the grave must be of a certain depth, and that the interment shall not be made without special license from the health officer.

§ 122e. **Laws regulating the construction of wooden buildings in cities.** — Another great danger, which threat-

---

[1] Lake View *v.* Rose Hill Cemetery Co., 70 Ill. 192 (22 Am. Rep. 71). See *post* for the general discussion of the restriction upon the exercise of police power contained in the charters of private corporations.

[2] See Lake View *v.* Rose Hill Cemetery Co., 70 Ill. 192 (22 Am. Rep. 71).

§ 122e

ens all thickly settled communities, is that of more or less extensive conflagrations, resulting from accidental fires. Every house, everywhere, is subject in a greater or less degree to the danger of destruction by fire; but it is only when the buildings are closely built, that the danger of fire being communicated from an adjoining building becomes great enough to call for special regulations for preventing the spread of such accidental fires. The danger of destruction by fire is least when the buildings are constructed of more or less non-combustible material. It would probably be considered unreasonable to require all buildings to be absolutely fire proof, but it is a common regulation in the large cities to prohibit the erection of wooden buildings, or of buildings with wooden, or shingle roofs. This regulation has often been subjected to judicial criticism, and the constitutionality of it has invariably been sustained.[1] The increase in the danger of a general conflagration, resulting from the construction of wooden buildings in the heart of a large city, furnishes ample justification for the regulation. But the proprietor has the right to erect on his lands whatever kind of buildings or other structures he may please, provided he does not, in doing so, threaten, or do, harm to others; and, as long as he does not put others in danger, he may even set fire to his own house, without committing any punishable wrong.[2] While, therefore, it is lawful for the State to prohibit the erection of wooden

---

[1] See Wadleigh v. Gilman, 12 Me. 403; Welch v. Hotchkiss, 39 Conn. 144; Vanderbelt v. Adams, 7 Cow. 349; Corp. of Knoxville v. Bird, 12 Lea, 121 (47 Am. Rep. 326). In the case of Knoxville v. Bird, a city ordinance, prohibiting the erection of wooden buildings, was sustained in its application to cases, in which a contract for the construction of the building was made before the passage of the ordinance, and remained unexecuted; the passage of the law against the erection of such buildings made illegal all contracts for their construction, and released all parties to the contract from the obligations thereby assumed. Cordes v. Miller, 39 Mich. 581 (33 Am. Rep. 330).

[2] Bloss v. Tobey, 2 Pick. 320; Hennesey v. People, 21 How. Pr. 239.

§ 122e

buildings in thickly settled communities, because of the
danger of fire, it would certainly not be lawful to apply the
same regulation to suburban and country property, on which
the buildings are far apart ; for the danger of a general conflagration is reduced to so low a minimum, that, if the
danger existed at all, it could not be appreciably increased
by the erection of wooden buildings.

§ 122*f*. **Regulation of the right to hunt game.** — It is
a very common police regulation, to be found in every
State, to prohibit the hunting and killing of birds and other
wild animals in certain seasons of the year, the object of the
regulation being the preservation of these animals from
complete extermination by providing for them a period of
rest and safety, in which they may procreate and rear their
young. The animals are those which are adapted to consumption as food, and their preservation is a matter of
public interest. The constitutionality of such legislation
cannot be questioned.

§ 122*g*. **Abatement of nuisances — Destruction of**
buildings. — Nuisances may always be abated. The fact
of being a nuisance having been established, the thing may
be destroyed, removed, or so regulated that it will cease to
be a nuisance. In certain cases of extreme necessity, the
private individual may, without the aid of government, abate
or remove the nuisance ; in other cases the government must
through its proper department interfere. But in all these
cases the interference with the enjoyment of private property, whether by the State or by the individual, must be
justified by the proof of two facts, viz. : first, that the
property, either *per se* or in the manner of using it, is a
nuisance, and secondly, that the interference does not extend beyond what is necessary to correct the evil. To extend the exercise of the power of abatement, beyond the point
of necessity, would make the interference unlawful. But

§ 122*g*

for the purpose of removing a nuisance, the State may go to any length, even so far as to destroy houses and other buildings, where they are in fact nuisances. If a house is falling into decay, and endangering the public safety, or it is irretrievably unhealthy, and consequently threatening evil to the public health,[1] or is *per se*, for any other reason, a nuisance, it may certainly be destroyed, and it is not unusual to find municipal regulations of this character. But where the nuisance consists, not in the building itself, but in the use to which it is put, the building cannot be destroyed. The interference by the State must be confined to the prohibition of the wrongful use. A good illustrative case is to be found in the Michigan reports. The city of Detroit passed an ordinance, providing for the demolition of all buildings used for the purpose of prostitution. It was no doubt thought that, apart from being a severe punishment to the owners of the houses for letting them for this unlawful purpose, it would be a most effective effort to suppress the social vice, by destroying the buildings best adapted for carrying on the immoral trade. Whatever good motive may have induced the enactment of the ordinance, it was clearly unconstitutional, as being an interference with private property beyond what was necessary to abate or remove the nuisance, and such was the opinion of the Supreme Court of Michigan. In delivering its opinion, the court said: " It is said that the house was a nuisance. This may be very true ; but it was a nuisance in consequence of its being the resort of persons of ill-fame. That which constitutes or causes the nuisance may be removed ; thus if a house is used for the purpose of a trade or business, by which the health of the public is endangered, the nuisance may be abated, by removing whatsoever may be necessary to prevent the exercise of such trade or business ; so a house in which gaming is carried on, to the injury of the

---

[1] Theilan *v.* Porter, 14 Lea, 622 (52 Am. Rep. 173).

§ 122*g*

public morals; the individual by whom it is occupied may be punished by indictment and the implements of gaming removed; and a house in which indecent and obscene pictures are exhibited is a nuisance, which may be abated by the removal of the pictures. Thousands of young men are lured to [some of] our public theaters, in consequence of their being a resort, nightly, of the profligate and abandoned; this is a nuisance. Yet in this, and in the other cases stated, it will not be contended that a person would be justified in demolishing the house, for the obvious reason that to suppress the nuisance such an act was unnecessary. So in the case before us the nuisance was not caused by the erection itself, but by the persons who resorted there for the purpose of prostitution. The authority given to the town to suppress bawdy houses does not support and authorize an ordinance directing the demolition of buildings, in which such nuisance is committed."[1]

§ 123. **How far use of land may be controlled by requirement of license?** — Inasmuch as certain uses, to which lands may be put, require police regulation and supervision, in order to prevent the threatened public injury, by bringing those cases within the strict control of the police, it is quite reasonable for the State to require the issue of licenses, before it is lawful to do those things upon the land, which are likely to endanger the public welfare in any way. For example, in order to enforce the law against the erection or enlargement of wooden buildings, it would be reasonable to require a permit or license, before one can lawfully make any improvement or repairs to his buildings.[2] In the same manner may the city require a license or permit to construct any kind of building, so that it may take the proper precautions against the danger to the public,

[1] Welch v. Stowell, 2 Dougl. (Mich.) 332.
[2] Welch v. Hotchkiss, 39 Conn. 140 (12 Am. Rep. 383).

§ 123

resulting from house-building.   This is a very common police regulation.   The requirement of a license and of a small
license fee, large enough to cover the cost of issuing the license, and of maintaining the necessary police supervision,
cannot be questioned in any case where the act or thing,
for which the license is required, contains some element of
danger to the public.   All such uses of lands are subject to
police regulation, and the legislature is the supreme judge
of the kind of regulation that the public welfare requires,
subject only to the power of the court to confine all police
regulations to the prevention of the threatened public
injury.   But one does not need any license from the State,
nor can he be required to procure one, to make a harmless
use of his lands.   His right to use them is a natural right,
which he possesses independently of positive or statutory
law.[1]   As has been already fully explained,[2] a license,
strictly so-called, is an authority to do that, which on account of its possible danger to the public is subjected to
police regulation, and which for that reason is rightly declared to be unlawful without the license.   It is not required
of the individual for the purpose of increasing the revenues
of the city or State, although the public treasury may be
benefited incidentally by the exaction of a license fee.   It
is a police regulation, which is only justifiable when it is instituted to avert or regulate some threatened public injury.
While it is probably true that a license tax, as a tax, in
the absence of special constitutional restrictions, may be
imposed upon a particular use of lands, as upon certain
trades and occupations, which are in no way likely to prove
harmful to the public ; the license tax must be tested by the
consideration of the constitutional restrictions upon the

[1] See Ah He v. Crippen, 19 Cal. 491; Ah Lew v. Choate, 24 Cal. 562, in
which it was held that a man's right to mine on his own land cannot be
controlled by the imposition of a license.

[2] See ante, § 101, in which the whole subject of licenses, as distinguished
from taxation, is exhaustively treated.

§ 123

power of taxation ; and where a municipal corporation has
not the power under its charter to impose a license tax
as a tax, it cannot impose it as a police regulation upon
those who do not make use of their lands in any dangerous
manner.[1]

§ 124. **Improvement of property at the expense and
against the will of the owner.** — It has long been an
established rule of law, and it is still so in the absence of a
modifying statute, that the owner of lands is not responsible for any annoyance or discomfort, proceeding from some
natural cause, and not from the act of some individual ; and
he cannot be made to respond in damages for his failure to
remove the cause of annoyance, even though the public
health of the neighborhood is seriously affected.   Thus the
owner of swamp lands cannot be held responsible for the
injury to the health of the neighbors, caused by the deadly
exhalations of his swamp.   The owner of land is responsible for the injury or annoyance flowing from the construction of artificial swamps, and the keeping of stagnant water ;
but he is, independently of statute, under no obligation to
drain a natural swamp, in order to improve the public
health of the community.[2]   It cannot be questioned that
the owner of swamps or other unhealthy lands may be
compelled to allow them to be drained, and to be otherwise
cleared of things which affect the public.   For while the
owner of lands is not responsible for the continuance of a
natural nuisance, he has no indefeasible right to its continuance ; and the State may remove such a nuisance, with
or without the owner's consent, provided the expense of

[1] State *v.* Hoboken, 33 N. J. 280.   In this case the ordinance directed
that owners of land should be assessed a certain amount for the privilege
of building vaults in front of their dwellings.   It was held to be no
license in the sense of being a police regulation, and, as a license tax, it
could not be referred to the charter power to " regulate " t he construction
of such vaults.   But see *ante*, § 101.

[2] Reeves *v.* Treasurer, 8 Ohio St. 333.

§ 124

removing it is borne by the State and not imposed upon the owner. In many of the States, statutory provisions have been made for the compulsory drainage of swamp lands, and the only cause for disputing the constitutionality of such legislation is the provision that the entire cost of drainage shall be imposed upon the owner. The constitutionality of such legislation has, as a reasonable exercise of the police power of the State, been generally sustained,[1] on the general ground that the State may impose upon the owner the duty of draining his low lands, in consideration of the consequent increase in the value of his lands. The Supreme Court of Wisconsin justifies such legislation in the following language : " It would seem to be most reasonable that the owners of the lands drained and reclaimed should be assessed to the full extent, at least of his special benefits, for he has received an exact equivalent and a full pecuniary consideration therefor, and that which is in excess of such benefits should be paid on the ground that it was his duty to remove such an obvious cause of malarial disease and prevent a public nuisance. The duty of one owner of such lands is the duty of all, and in order to effectually enter upon and carry out any feasible system of drainage through the infected district, all such owners may be properly grouped together to bear the general assessment for the entire cost proportionably. Assessment in this and similar cases is not taxation." [2] The cases generally sustain the position of the Wisconsin court, and justify the imposition upon the owner of the entire cost of drainage, whether it

---

[1] Donnelly v. Decker, 58 Wis. 461 (46 Am. Rep. 637) ; Norfleet v. Cromwell, 70 N. C. 634 (16 Am. Rep. 787); Anderson v. Kerns, 14 Ind. 199; O'Reilly v. Kankakee Val. Draining Co., 32 Ind. 169; Draining Co. Case, 11 La. Ann. 338; Woodruff v. Fisher, 17 Barb. 224; French v. Kirkland, 1 Paige, 111; Williams v. Mayor of Detroit, 2 Mich. 560; Phillips v. Wickham, 1 Paige, 590; Sessions v. Crunkleton, 20 Ohio St. 349; Bancroft v. Cambridge, 126 Mass. 438; Dingley v. Boston, 100 Mass. 544; Davidson v. New Orleans, 96 U. S. 97; Hadgar v. Supervisors, 47 Cal. 222.

[2] Donnelly v. Decker, 58 Wis. 461 (46 Am. Rep. 637).

§ 124

exceeds or falls within the special benefits he receives from the drainage ; but in New Jersey it has been definitely settled that the assessment upon land owners for the drainage of the low lands must be limited to the amount of special benefits so imparted to them, and any additional assessment is unconstitutional.[1] All the cases agree that the compulsory drainage is never justifiable except when the public health requires it. It can never be ordered purely for private gain.[2]

---

[1] Pequest Case, 41 N. J. L. 175; Tidewater Co. *v.* Coster, 3 C. E. Green, 518; State *v.* Driggs Drainage Co., 45 N. J. L. 91. "The owners of these lands could not be convicted of maintaining a public nuisance because they did not drain them; even though they were not the owners of the lands upon which the obstructions are situated. It does not appear by the act or the complaint that the sickness to be prevented prevails among inhabitants of the wet lands, nor whether these lands will be benefited or injured by draining; and certainly, unless they will be benefited, it would seem to be partial legislation to tax a certain tract of land, for the expense of doing to it what did not improve it, merely because, in a state of nature, it may be productive of sickness." Woodruff *v.* Fisher, 17 Barb. 224.

[2] State *v.* Driggs Drainage Co., 45 N. J. L. 91. In Woodruff *v.* Fisher, 17 Barb. 224, the court say: "If the object to be accomplished by this statute may be considered a public improvement, the power of taxation seems to have been sustained upon analogous principles. Citing People *v.* Mayor, etc., of New York, 4 N. Y. 419; Thomas *v.* Leland, 24 Wend. 65; Livingston *v.* Mayor, etc., New York, 8 Wend. 85 (22 Am. Dec. 622). But if the object was merely to improve the property of individuals, I think the statute would be void, although it provided for compensation. The water privileges on Indian River cannot be taken or affected in any way solely for the private advantage of others, however numerous the beneficiaries. Several statutes have been passed for draining swamps, but it seems to me that the principle above advanced rests upon natural and constitutional law. The professed object of this statute is to promote public health. And one question that arises is, whether the owners of large tracts of land in a state of nature can be taxed to pay the expense of draining them, by destroying the dams, etc., of other persons away from the drowned lands, and for the purposes of public health. This law proposes to destroy the water power of certain persons against their will, to drain the lands of others, also, for all that appears against their will; and all at the expense of the latter, for this public good. If this taxation is illegal, no mode of compensation is provided, and all is illegal."

§ 124

If it be conceded that the owners of low lands are under a legal obligation to remove from their lands all natural as well as artificial caus es of injury to the public health, it cannot be denied that the State may, by appropriate legislation, co mpel the performance of this duty ; and if the land owner refuses to drain his land, to drain it for him and compel him to reimburse the State for the entire cost of drainage, whatever relation it bears to the increase in the value of the land. The burdensome character of the duty does not affect the obligation to perform it, and it would not be u nconstitutional to impose upon the land owner the payment of the cost of drainage, in excess of the special benefits he has received from the improvement. On the other hand, if it be true that there is no natural obligation upon the land owner to remove from his land all nuisances produced by natural causes, the entire cost of compulsory drainage cannot be imposed by statute upon those who own such lands at the time when the statute was enacted. The State may in the grant of its public lands impose upon the purchaser whatever conditions and duties the public welfare may seem to demand ; and so, likewise, may the State provide that all future purcaasers of swamps and other low lands shall drain them of the stagnant water, for in both cases there is no interference with vested rights, which our constitutions prohibit. But it is an unconstitutional interference with vested rights, to impose this statutory obligation upon those who possess such lands when the statute was adopted. Providing for the limitation of the assessment on the land owner to the amount of special benefit received by him from the drainage, is an attempt to make an equitable adjustment of what would otherwise be a clear violation of the rights of property; but it is altogether illogical and untenable. It is as much a violation of the rights of property to compel the owner to pay for improvements to his lands, which he did not order and does not want, as to impose on him the entire cost of removing a

§ 124

natural nuisance, which it was not his duty to abate. The State has the right, either to impose on the land owner the payment of the entire cost of drainage, or to exact nothing. As taxation, this special assessment would seem to offend the constitutional provisions, which require that all taxation shall be equally distributed.[1]

SECTION 125. Regulation of non-navigable streams — Fisheries.
   125a. Conversion of non-navigable into navigable streams.

§ 125. **Regulation of non-navigable streams — Fisheries.** — Where two tracts of land are divided by a navigable stream, the general rule is that the boundary line is the low water mark on the adjoining shore, and the soil or bed of the stream is the property of the State.[2] But if the stream is not navigable, the boundary line is the center of the current of the stream, commonly called the *filum aquæ*, and the owners of the shore have a right of property in the bed of the stream up to this *filum aquæ*. In neither case does any one acquire any exclusive right of property in the stream of water. The riparian owner, in the case of a non-navigable stream, may make a reasonable use of the water, even appropriating absolutely a portion of it, in the form of water or of ice, but no one has a right to assume absolute control of the stream, unless from beginning to end it lies wholly within his lands. Where a non-navigable stream passes over the lands of two or more adjacent owners, the adjacent riparian owners have mutual easements upon the soil of each for the free and unrestricted flow of the water. The riparian owners have the right to use the water to a reasonable extent, but can not so use it as to di-

---

[1] See *post*, § 129.

[2] As to what is, and is not, a navigable stream, see Tiedeman on Real Property, § 835; 1 Washb. on Real Prop. 413; and cases cited in these treatises.

§ 125

minish the flow or corrupt the water.[1]   It may be said with
truth that almost any use of a stream of water is likely to
corrupt it, and, in the absence of statutory regulation, what
is and is not a lawful use of the stream, is a judicial question, to be determined by the consideration of the circumstances of the case, including the economic necessities and
industries of the community through which the stream
passes.

The maintenance of a tannery or saw mill may not be a
nuisance in one locality, while it may be considered one
in some other locality.   And, independently of statute, if
the riparian proprietors make a certain use of a stream
for some time, the fact that it renders the stream unfit
for another use, which some other riparian owner wishes
to make of it, does not make the customary use of the
stream a nuisance.   But the legislature may, in consideration of the public interest, prohibit any use of a non-
navigable stream, which interferes with another use of it,
when the public welfare demands that the stream should
be adapted to the latter use.   Thus, an act of the legislature was declared to be constitutional, which prohibited the
use of all streams entering into a reservoir, in any way that
would pollute or corrupt the water.[2]   But it can hardly
be doubted that, if such a stream had been previously
used in connection with a tannery, or other business, which
would render the water of the stream unfit for drinking
purposes, the subsequent establishment of a reservoir, draw-
ing its water from this stream, and the prohibition of the
tannery or other like business, could not be sustained, so
far as the prohibition or destruction of the objectionable
business is concerned, unless provision was made for payment of compensation to the owner of the tannery or other

---

[1] Washburn v. Gilman, 64 Me. 163 (18 Am. Rep. 246); Richmond
Manuf. Co. v. Atlantic Delaine Co., 10 R. I. 106 (14 Am. Rep. 658); Jacobs
v. Allard, 42 Vt. 303 (1 Am. Rep. 331).
[2] State v. Wheeler, 44 N. J. L. 88.

§ 125

like business for the loss he has thus sustained. Such a
prohibition would be a taking of private property for a public
use, within the meaning of the constitutional provision,
which requires the payment of compensation for the property so taken.

The riparian owner is prohibited from erecting or maintaining a dam across the stream, and causing an overflow
of the land above or diminishing the volume of the stream
below.[1] But whenever the public welfare requires it, or it
serves in any way to promote the public good, the legislature may authorize the construction and maintenance of such
dams, provided compensation is made to all riparian
proprietors, who may have been injured thereby.[2] While
the maintenance of a dam, without legislative sanction and
without the consent of the riparian owners, is a trespass,
if made and maintained for the statutory period of limitation under a claim of right to do so, an absolute right
to its maintenance may thus be acquired; and it has
been held that one, who has maintained a dam across
a non-navigable stream for twenty-one years, cannot be
required by statute to construct and maintain a passage-way
over the same for fish.[3] The owner of the dam cannot be
compelled at his own expense to maintain this passage-way,
but the State can undoubtedly authorize those, who may be
thereby benefited, to construct the passage-way at their
expense, taking care to compensate the owner of the dam
for whatever damage he has suffered.[4]

It is not permissible at common law to divert a stream
from its regular channel, if by so doing injury results to the

[1] Sampson v. Hoddinot, 1 C. B. (N. S.) 590; Colburn v. Richards, 13
Mass. 420, Anthony v. Lapham, 5 Pick. 175.

[2] Lee v. Pembroke Iron Co., 57 Me. 481 (2 Am. Rep. 59); Gray; v. Harris, 107 Mass. 492 (9 Am. Rep. 61); Proctor v. Jennings, 6 Nev. 83 (3 Am.
Rep. 240).

[3] Woolever v. Stewart, 36 Ohio St. 146 (38 Am. Rep. 566).

[4] Commonwealth v. Pa. Canal Co., 66 Pa. St. 41 (5 Am. Rep. 329).

§ 125

owners above or below.[1] Water may be diverted from the channel for any reasonable use, but it can only be detained as long as it is necessary and reasonable, and it must be returned to the channel before it passes to the land of the riparian proprietor below.[2] But what would otherwise be an unlawful or unreasonable diversion or detention of the stream may be legalized by legislative authorization, upon payment of compensation for all damage suffered by the other riparian owners.

Another, sometimes valuable, right of property in non-navigable streams, which may be subjected to police regulation, is the right to catch the fish of the stream. The riparian owners have the right to fish on their own banks, and in any part of the stream which lies within their boundary line. Unless the catching of fish is conducted with reason, either the fish may be altogether exterminated, or the enjoyment of the right by one may interfere with the equal enjoyment of the right by others. For the protection of the fish, and for the maintenance of equality in respect to the right to fish, the State can rightly regulate fisheries, providing that the regulations are reasonable, and do not extend beyond the prevention of the threatened injuries.[3]

§ 125a. **Conversion of non-navigable into navigable streams.** — Whether a stream is a navigable or a non-navi-

---

[1] Elliott v. Fitchburg P. R. Co., 10 Cush. 191; Macomber v. Godfrey, 108 Mass. 219 (11 Am. Rep. 349); Tuthill v. Scott, 44 Vt. 525 (5 Am. Rep. 301).

[2] Clinton v. Myers, 46 N. Y. 511 (7 Am. Rep. 373); Arnol v. Foot, 12 Wend. 330; Miller v. Miller, 9 Pa. St. 74; Pool v. Lewis, 46 Ga. 162 (5 Am. Rep. 526).

[3] See Holyoke Co. v. Lyman, 15 Wall. 500; Commonwealth v. Chapin, 5 Pick. 199; Commonwealth v. Essex Co., 13 Gray, 247; Weller v. Snover, 42 N. J. L. (13 Vroom), 341; Doughty v. Conover, 42 N. J. L. (13 Vroom), 192. In the last case, the statute under consideration prohibited the use of fishing nets at certain times of the year in particular counties. See, also, Commrs. of Inland Fishing v. Holyoke Water Power Co., 104 Mass. 446 (6 Am. Rep. 247).

§ 125a

gable stream must, be determined by a consideration of its condition in a state of nature. A stream that is unnavigable in fact cannot, by dredging and the removal of obstructions, be converted into a navigable stream so as to affect the rights of the riparian owners in the stream or in its bed, except in the exercise by the State of the right of eminent domain. The conversion of a non-navigable into a navigable stream would be a taking of private property for a public use, which is only possible on payment of full compensation to the riparian owners.[1] It is sometimes supposed that in the case of Carondelet Canal & Navigation Co. v. Parker,[2] the State undertook to convert a non-navigable into a navigable stream without payment of compensation to the riparian owners, and in the syllabus of the case as reported in the American Reports, it is stated that the State may authorize a private corporation to convert an unnavigable stream into a navigable stream, and charge tolls for the improvements. But a careful study of the case will reveal the fact that the bayou St. John was really in legal contemplation a navigable stream, although practically unnavigable for most if not all commercial purposes. But, on payment of compensation, the right of property in a non-navigable stream may be forfeited by its conversion into a navigable stream, in the same manner as all other rights of property in lands must fall under the exercise of the right of eminent domain.

§ 126. **Statutory liability of lessors for the acts of lessees.** — Independently of statute, the lessor is not in any manner responsible for the wrongful acts of his lessee. The

---

[1] See Hathorn v. Stinson, 12 Me. 183; Bradley v. Rice, 13 Me. 200; Waterman v. Johnson, 13 Pick. 261; Wood v. Kelley, 30 Me. 47; Paine v. Woods, 108 Mass. 170, in which it has been settled that if a natural pond or lake is raised by artificial means, the boundary line will continue to be at low water mark of the pond in its natural state.

[2] 29 La. Ann. 430 (29 Am. Rep. 339).

§ 126

owner of an estate for years in lands is, during the continuance of the tenancy, as independent an owner, so far as
the liability to the State or to the individual is concerned,
as the tenant in fee.   Certain uses of lands may be prohibited, because of their injurious effect upon the person or
property of others, and the doing of such acts at once becomes unlawful.   The State may punish the wrong-doer by
the imposition of penalties or otherwise, and the individual
who has suffered damage in consequence of the wrongful
act, may recover damages of him in the proper action.

It is often a difficult matter to secure the enforcement of
a public regulation, particularly if it concerns the manner
of using premises, which does not involve a direct trespass
upon the rights of others.   Inasmuch as the proprietor
of lands is only a tenant of the State, the terms and conditions of whose tenancy may be so regulated as that the
public good may not suffer, the State may impose upon the
landlord the duty of securing the enforcement of the law
in respect to the prohibited use of the premises, by imposing on him a penalty for leasing his lands with the intent or
knowledge that the premises will be used for unlawful purposes ; and the State may also provide it to be his duty, as well
as right, to enter upon the land for the purpose of forfeiting
the lease, whenever it comes to his knowledge that the
lessee is making an unlawful use of the premises.   The
performance of this police duty may become very burdensome, but the constitutionality of the law which imposes
it can not be questioned.   Thus it has been held to be
reasonable to impose a penalty on the owner of a house for
permitting his house to be used for prostitution.[1]   But
while the State may impose this police duty upon the lessor
to prevent the lessee from making an unlawful use of the
premises, he can only be required to exercise reasonable care

---

[1] McAlister v. Clark, 33 Conn. 91; People v. Erwin, 4 Den. (N. Y.) 129;
Territory v. Dakota, 2 Dak. 155.

§ 126

in the performance of the duty ; and his responsibility under•such statutes is confined to those cases in which he has actual knowledge of the wrongful use of the property.   It is furthermore true, that the State cannot, in imposing this police duty, as was done in one case by the New York legislature, declare the lessor to be responsible to third persons who may have been damaged by the unlawful use of the premises.   The New York statute, just referred to, created a cause of action for damages in favor of the person or property which was damaged by the act of an intoxicated person against the owner of real property, whose only connection with the injury is that he leased the premises where the liquor causing the intoxication was sold or given away, with the knowledge that intoxicating liquors were to be sold thereon.   The act was declared by the New York Court of Appeals to be constitutional,[1] but we hope to show that it was an amazing, and altogether unconstitutional, interference with civil liberty and private property. The language of the court indicates that they appreciated the practical scope and effect of the statute, and it will be profitable for the reader to quote from the opinion of the court, in describing the character of this piece of legislation. The court say :   " To realize the full force of this inquiry it is to be observed that the leasing of premises to be used as a place for the sale of liquors is a lawful act, not prohibited by this or any other statute.   The liability of the landlord is not made to depend upon the nature of the act of the tenant, but exists irrespective of the fact whether the sale or giving away of the liquor was lawful or unlawful, that is, whether it was authorized by the license law of the State, or was made in violation of that law. Nor does the liability depend upon any question of negligence of the landlord in the selection of the tenant, or of the tenant in selling the liquor.   Although the person to

[1] Bertholf *v.* O'Reilly, 74 N. Y. 509 (30 Am. Rep. 323).

§ 126

whom the liquor is sold is at the time apparently a man
of sober habits, and, so far as the vendor knows, one whose
appetite for strong drink is habitually controlled by his reason and judgment, yet if it turns out that the liquor sold
causes or contributes to the intoxication of the person to
whom the sale or gift is made, under the influence of which
he commits an injury to person or property, the seller and
his landlord are by the act made jointly and severally responsible.   The element of care or diligence on the part of
the seller or landlord does not enter into the question of
liability.   The statute imposes upon the dealer and the
landlord the risk of any injury which may be caused by the
traffic.   It cannot be denied that the liability sought to be
imposed by the act is of a very sweeping character, and
may in many cases entail severe pecuniary liability ; and its
language may include cases not within the real purpose of
the enactment.   The owner of a building who lets it to be
occupied for the sale of general merchandise, including
wines and liquors, may under the act be made liable for
the acts of an intoxicated person, where his only fault is
that he leased the premises for a general business, including the sale of intoxicating liquors, in the same way as
other merchandise.   The liability is not restricted to the
results of intoxication from liquors sold or given away to
be drunk on the premises of the seller.   There is no way
by which the owner of real property can escape possible
liability for the results of intoxication, where he leases or
permits the occupation of his premises, with the knowledge that the business of the sale of liquors is to be carried
on upon the premises, whether alone or in connection with
other merchandise, or whether they are to be sold to be
drunk on the premises or to be carried away and used elsewhere.''   In declaring the act to be constitutional, the
court continue: "There are two general grounds upon
which the act in question is claimed to be unconstitutional ;
first, that it operates to restrain the lawful use of real

§ 126

property by the owner, inasmuch as it attaches to the particular use a liability, which substantially amounts to
prohibition of such use, and, as to the seller, imposes a
pecuniary responsibility, which interferes with the traffic in
intoxicating liquors, although the business is authorized by
law; and, secondly, that it creates a right of action unknown
to the common law and subjects the property of one person
to be taken in satisfaction of injuries sustained by another,
remotely resulting from an act of the person charged, which
act may be neither negligent nor wrongful, but may be
in all respects in conformity with the law. * * * The
right of the State to regulate the traffic in intoxicating
liquors, within its limits, has been exercised from the foundation of the government, and is not open to question.
The State may prescribe the persons by whom and the conditions under which the traffic may be carried on. It may
impose upon those who act under its license such liabilities
and penalties as in its judgment are proper to secure society against the dangers of the traffic and individuals against
injuries committed by intoxicated persons under the influence of or resulting from their intoxication. * * * It
is quite evident that the act of 1873 may seriously interfere
with the profitable use of real property by the owner.
This is especially true with respect to a building erected
to be occupied as an inn or hotel, and especially adapted to
that use, where the rental value may largely depend upon the
right of the tenant to sell intoxicating liquors. The owner
of such a building may well hesitate to lease his property
when by so doing he subjects himself to the onerous liability imposed by the act. The act in this way indirectly
operates to restrain the absolute freedom of the owner in
the use of his property, and may justly be said to impair
its value. But this is not a taking of his property within
the constitution. He is not deprived either of the title or
the possession. The use of his property for any other lawful purpose is unrestricted, and he may let or use it as a

§ 126

place for the sale of liquors, subject to the liability which the act imposes. The objection we are now considering would apply with greater force to a statute prohibiting, under any circumstances, the traffic in intoxicating liquors, and as such a statute must be conceded to be within the legislative power, and would not interfere with any vested rights of the owner of real property, although absolutely preventing the particular use, *a fortiori* the act in question does not operate as an unlawful restraint upon the use of property. * * * The act of 1873 is not invalid because it creates a right of action and imposes a liability not known to the common law. There is no such limit to legislative power. The legislature may alter or repeal the common law. It may create new offenses, enlarge the scope of civil remedies, and fasten responsibility for injuries upon persons against whom the common law gives no remedy. We do not mean that the legislature may impose on one man the liability for an injury suffered by another, with which he has no connection. But it may change the rule of the common law which looks only to the proximate cause of the mischief, in attaching legal responsibility, and allow a recovery to be had against those whose acts contributed, although remotely, to produce it. This is what the legislature has done in the act of 1873. That there is or may be a relation in the nature of cause and effect, between the act of selling or giving away intoxicating liquors, and the injuries for which a remedy is given, is apparent, and upon this relation the legislature has proceeded in enacting the law in question. It is an extension by the legislature of the principle, expressed in the maxim *sic utere tuo ut alienum non lœdas* to cases to which it has not before been applied, and the propriety of such an application is a legislative and not a judicial question."[1]

Conceding that the sale of intoxicating liquors may be

---

[1] Bertholf *v.* O'Reilly, 74 N. Y. 524 (30 Am. Rep. 323).

§ 126

prohibited altogether, or subjected to whatever other police regulations the legislature may see fit to impose, and this we do not admit to be true, without most material qualifications,[1] the claim is still made that this kind of legislation is unconstitutional. The State may impose upon the lessor the police duty of preventing, as far as it lies in his power, the lessee from making an unlawful use of the premises, and may impose upon him penalties for his failure to eject the lessee. This is a legitimate police regulation. It is simply compelling the owner of property to perform a duty to the public which no one can do so well as he; and he cannot complain if the profits of his property have been diminished by the regulation. Neither he nor his lessee has an indefeasible right to make use of his property in a way to injure another in person or property. And he as well as the lessee can be made to respond in damages to any one who has suffered injury by and through his unlawful act. But in order that any one may recover damages of another, he must show that the damages were caused by the wrongful act. It is only on such a showing that any one can maintain a suit for damages. It is not a subject for police regulation to determine what is the cause of the damage. It is a judicial question of fact, to be determined in a judicial inquiry, free from any control on the part of the legislature. The legislature cannot determine when the legal relation of cause and effect exists between two facts. It will probably be granted that in one sense the relation of cause and effect exists between any two facts that may be selected. In organized society the lives of men are so intimately bound up with each other, there is so much influence and counter influence, that it is difficult to say whether anything now known would have happened, if some antecedent fact had not occurred, it matters not how remote. To apply the

---

[1] For a discussion of limitation upon the power of the government to prohibit the sale of intoxicating liquors, see, *ante*, § 103.

§ 126

reasoning to the facts of the case in question, for the purpose of easier illustration, if the lessor had done his duty to the public in preventing an unlawful use of the premises, the injury to the third person would not have occurred through this intoxication, but likewise the injury would not have happened, if the lessee had not broken the law in making the prohibited use of the land.   Nay, further, the joint wrongful acts of the lessor and lessee would not have caused the injury, if the purchaser had not been guilty of the vice, and, under the peculiar circumstances of the present case, the crime, of intoxication.   Here are three unlawful acts, following each other in the order of sequence, followed by an injury to a third person.   The common-law rule, which made the proximate cause responsible for the damage, to the exclusion of the remote cause, would have declared the intoxicated person to be alone responsible. Indeed, when one considers the fact that the same damage could have been caused as easily by an intoxication produced by liquor bought from some other dealer, within or without the State in which the sale of it is prohibited or regulated, and as easily, whether the lessor did or did not know of the sale of the liquor by his lessee ; when it is still further considered that in the New York case there would have been no violation of law, had no injury been inflicted on another by the intoxicated person, the conclusion become irresistible that the damage was not caused by the wrongful act of the lessor or the lessee.   The New York court holds that the legislature " may change the rule of the common law, which looks only to the proximate cause of the mischief, in attaching legal responsibility and allow a recovery to be had against those whose acts contribute, although remotely, to produce it. ''   If this rule of the common law was itself a police regulation, it would of course be subject to legislative change ; but it has been established by the accumulated experience of ages as the best rule for the ascertainment of the cause of a damage, and is no more

§ 126

subject to legislative change than is the law of gravitation.[1]
This subject, and the facts of this particular case,[2] has
been given this extended consideration, because it was
an extraordinary exercise of police power, and furnished a
most striking example of the great uncertainty that now
prevails in the legal minds of this country, concerning the
constitutional limitations upon the police power of the government.

§ 127. **Search Warrants — Sanitary Inspection.**—The
security of the privacy of one's dwelling, not only against
private individuals, but also as against the officers of the
law, or the frequent and unrestrained interference with this
privacy by the common police officers, more than anything
else distinguishes a free country, one governed by officials
under constitutional limitations, from a country, in which
political absolutism is checked only by the limitations of
nature.   The dwelling of the continental European, particularly the Frenchman, must open at the command of the
police officer, whenever a crime has been committed, and
suspicion rests upon him.   His closets and other private
apartments are broken open, his private papers ruthlessly
scattered about or taken away, to be subjected to the
inspection of some other official without any specific description of the persons or things which are to be apprehended ;
and without any proof beyond a mere suspicion, that the
house contains the person or thing sought for.   But under a
constitutional government, of which the liberty of the citizen
is the corner stone, the privacy of one's dwelling is rarely
ever invaded, and then only in extreme cases of public
necessity, and under such limitations as will serve to protect
the citizen from any unusual disturbance of his home life.
The common law maxim, " Every man's house is his castle"

---

[1] See, *ante*, § 68, for a further and more general discussion of this
question of remote and proximate cause.

[2] Bertholf *v.* O'Reilly, *supra.*

§ 127

is guaranteed in this country by an express constitutional provision, which declares that "the right of the people to be secure in their persons, houses, papers, and effects, against unreasonable searches and seizures, shall not be violated; and no warrants shall issue but upon probable cause, supported by oath or affirmation, and particularly describing the place to be searched, and the persons or things to be seized." [1] Except in accordance with, and under the restrictions of this, constitutional provision, one may close his doors against all intruders, and resist their entrance by the use of all the force that may be necessary for the protection of the property, even to the extent of taking the life of the trespasser.[2] The constitutional guaranties of the security of one's dwelling enable the Englishman and American to feel that there is a reality in these beautiful words of Lord Chatham, which have been so often quoted: "The poorest man may, in his cottage, bid defiance to all the forces of the crown. It may be frail; its roof may shake; the wind may play through it; the storm may enter; the rain may enter; but the King of England may not enter; all his force dares not cross the threshhold of the ruined tenement."

But the necessities of organized society do require that at times the doors of the private dwellings shall be opened for the admission of the officers of the law, and principally as an aid to the prosecution of crimes. But, before that is permissible, a search warrant must be obtained from a court of competent jurisdiction, which is authorized by law to grant it; it must be issued to an officer of the law, and never to the complainant; it can only be granted upon a showing of probable cause for believing that a proper case has arisen for the exercise of this police power; and lastly,

[1] U. S. Const. Amend., § art. 4. Similar provisions are to be found in each of the State constitutions.

[2] Bohannan v. Commonwealth, 8 Bush, 481 (8 Am. Rep. 474); Pond v. People, 8 Mich. 150.

§ 127

the warrant must contain a particular description of the premises to be searched, and the person or things to be taken into custody.[1] A failure to comply with any one of these requirements will render the warrant defective, and the entrance into the dwelling under it an unlawful invasion. In other countries search warrants are issued upon the barest suspicion that the house contains a criminal or things that are for some reason subject to seizure, and often, too, for the sole purpose of procuring evidence wherewith to convict the criminal. The only fact that is required to be established by *prima facie* evidence is that a crime has been committed by some one, known or unknown, it matters not which, and it is in the judgment of the police officer advisable that a particular house shall be searched in the interest of justice.

Under no circumstances can a search warrant be issued in this country for the sole purpose of securing the necessary evidence for the State. Whenever the police officer shows probable cause for believing that stolen goods are secreted in the house of the supposed thief or some other person, and in all other cases where the house contains the goods, the possession and use of which constituted the crime, that house may be searched, and so far, and in these cases, the State may, with the aid of a search warrant, procure evidence of the guilt of the accused. But ordinarily this is not permitted. A man's letters and papers and other effects cannot be searched in the aid of a criminal prosecution against him. Not only is this prohibited by the spirit of the constitutional provision in reference to the issue of search warrants, but likewise by another provision[2] which provides that no one " shall be compelled in any criminal

---

[1] Bishop Crim. Procedure, §§ 240–246, 716–719; 2 Hale P. C. 142, 150; Archbold Cr. Law, 145, 147.

[2] U. S. Const. Amend. art 5. The same provision is to be found in most, if not all, of the State constitutions.

§ 127

case to be a witness against himself."[1] But, as already stated, where the crime or misdemeanor consists of the possession or use of things, which are prohibited by the law, either because of their injurious effect upon the public, or because the goods belong to another, or when there is an unlawful detention of persons, search warrants may be issued for their recovery, when satisfactory evidence of their being stored in a particular dwelling is presented to the judicial officer who issues the warrant. Thus search warrants have been granted to search for stolen goods, for counterfeit money, forged bills and notes, for goods held in violation of the revenue laws of the United States [2] in violation of the laws against lotteries and gambling in general [3] for obscene publications and intoxicating liquors kept in violaticn of the liquor laws [4] and for the recovery of public books and records which have been taken from the proper custody.   Search warrants have also been issued for the purpose of securing the release of females supposed to be forcibly concealed in houses of ill-fame ; for the recovery of minor children, who have been enticed or forcibly taken away from their parents or guardian, and probably in any case of probably unlawful detention of a human being.[5]   Search warrants may also be granted in aid

[1] "To enter a man's house by virtue of a warrant, in order to procure evidence, is worse than the Spanish Inquisition, — a law under which no Englishman would wish to live an hour." Lord Camden in Entinck v. Carrington, 19 State Trials, 1029; s. c. 2 Wils. 275; Hackle v. Money, 2 Wils. 205; Leach v. Money, 19 State Trials, 1001 ; s. c. 3 Burr. 1692; s. c. 1 W. Bl. 555; Wilkes v. Wood, 19 State Trials, 1153; Archbold Cr. Law, 141; Cooley Const. Lim. 371, 372.

[2] Sandford v. Michals, 13 Mass. 286 (7 Am. Dec. 151) ; Sallee v. Smith, 11 Johns. 500.   See Locke v. United States, 7 Cranch, 339; The Luminary, 8 Wheat. 401; Henderson's Distilled Spirits, 14 Wall. 44.

[3] Commonwealth v. Dana, 2 Met. 329; Day v. State, 7 Gill, 321; Lowery v. Rainwater, 70 Mo. 152 (35 Am. Rep. 420).

[4] State v. Brennan's Liquors, 25 Conn. 278; Hibbard v. People, 4 Mich. 125; Fisher v. McGirr, 1 Gray, 1; Gray v. Kimball, 42 Me. 299; Allen v. Colby, 47 N. H.445.

[5] Cooley Const. Lim. 372.

§ 127

of those sanitary and other police regulations, which are designed to prevent the storage of gunpowder or other explosive or inflammable materials in such large quantities that it will endanger the public safety, or to check or regulate the accumulation of offal or garbage to the injury of the public health. It would also be a reasonable regulation to compel the search of the house or premises for the discovery of persons suffering from some dangerously infective disease, and whom the law required to be cared for in the public lazaretto ; or to see that after the recovery of such a person from an infectious disease the house is properly disinfected. In consideration of the reasonableness of these sanitary regulations, it is supposed that in the enforcement of them, one's house may be searched in opposition to his wishes and by force, without a search warrant.[1] But it is probable that in a clear case of the resistance of the entrance of the health officer, a search warrant would be required. These regulations are however so reasonable that it is rarely, if ever, necessary for the officer to do more than to show his general authority.

The search warrant cannot be issued in aid of civil process, but one may be ejected from his dwelling in pursuance of a decree of ejectment without a formal search warrant.[2] As a general proposition an officer may go to serve a process wherever the subject-matter of the process may be. But, except for the purpose of making

[1] Cooley's Principles of Const. Law p. 211.

[2] " Search warrants were never recognized by the common law as processes which might be availed of by individuals in the course of civil proceedings, or for the maintenance of any mere private right; but their use was confined to the case of public prosecutions instituted and pursued for the suppression of crime, and the detection and punishment of criminals. Even in those cases, if we may rely on the authority of Lord Coke, their legality was formerly doubted; and Lord Camden said they crept into the law by imperceptible practice. But their legality has long been considered to be established on the ground of public necessity; because without them felons and other malefactors would escape detection." Merrick, J., in Robinson v. Richardson, 13 Gray, 456.

§ 127

an arrest or seizure in criminal cases and in the few cases
in which search warrants are issued in the enforcement of
sanitary and other police regulations, the service of process is subject to this limitation, that the officer cannot
break open the outer door.   But if the outer door is found
open, the officer may break open any inner door, if that be
necessary for the service of the process.[1]

Another important requisite, is that the warrant must
specify and describe particularly the place to be searched,
and the person or thing sought after.   The description of
the house must be sufficiently particular, in order that it
may be distinguished from others.   A description that is
equally applicable to two or more buildings is defective, and
an erroneous or defective description will vitiate the warrant, and make the entrance under it an unlawful trespass.[2]   If a warrant is issued to search a dwelling-house,
the adjoining barn cannot under this warrant be forcibly
entered.[3]   The same regulations apply to the persons or
things to be taken into custody.   They must be particularly
described, in order that the warrant may be free from objection.   The warrant for the arrest of a person under a
fictitious name, without any further description, whereby
he may be identified, would be defective,[4] and so likewise
if the things to be seized are described generally as " goods,

---

[1] Semayne's Case, 5 Co. 91; Smith Lead. Cas. 213; Ilsley v. Nichols,
12 Pick. 270; Swain v. Mizner, 8 Gray, 182; Oystead v. Shed, 13 Mass.
520; People v. Hubbard, 24 Wend. 369; Snydecker v. Brosse, 51 Ill. 357;
Bailey v. Wright, 38 Mich. 96.

[2] Sandford v. Nichols, 13 Mass. 286 (7 Am. Dec. 151); Allen v.
Staples, 6 Gray, 491; McGlinchy v. Barrows, 41 Me. 74; Humes v.
Tabor, 1 R. I. 464; Ashley v. Peterson, 25 Wis. 621; Bell v. Rice, 2 J. J.
Marsh. 44 (9 Am. Dec. 122).

[3] Jones v. Fletcher, 41 Me. 254; Downing v. Porter, 8 Gray, 539;
Bishop Cr. Procedure, §§ 716, 719. And when a building is to be
searched, it is usually necessary to give the name of the owner or occupant. Stone v. Dana, 5 Met. 98.

[4] Commonwealth v. Crotty, 10 Allen, 403.

§ 127

wares and merchandise.'' [1] It is considered highly objectionable, on principle, for the warrant to be used in the night time ; and while there is no constitutional provision which prohibits a search under a warrant in the night, statutes invariably provide that the search shall be made in the day, except in a few urgent cases of felony.[2]

It is also necessary for the warrant to direct that the person or things seized shall, if found, be taken to the magistrate, who issued the warrant, in order that there may be a judicial examination of the facts, and a disposition of the persons or things according to law.   A search warrant is fatally defective, which does not provide for this subsequent judicial examination, but leaves the disposition of the person or things to the judgment of the ministerial officer.[3]

When the warrant complies with all the requirements of the law, the officer is protected from liability in damages for whatever force he may find it necessary to use in the execution of the warrant, even though the persons or things sought after should not be found.[4] But he must keep strictly within the limits of his warrant, and should he enter dwellings, arrest persons, or seize things, not falling within the description contained in the warrant, he is liable in damages for the unwarranted trespass.[5]

§ 128. Quartering soldiers in private dwellings. — It

[1] Sandford v. Nichols, 13 Mass. 286 (7 Am. Dec. 151).

[2] 2 Hale P. C. 150; Cooley Const. Lim. 370.

[3] 2 Hale P. C. 150; Fisher v. McGirr, 1 Gray, 1; Greene v. Briggs, 1 Curt. 311; State v. Snow, 3 R. I. 64; Bell v. Clapp, 10 Johns. 263 (6 Am. Dec. 339); Hibbard v. People, 4 Mich. 126; Matter of Morton, 10 Mich. 208; Sullivan v. Oneida, 61 Ill. 242; Lowry v. Rainwater, 70 Mo. 152 (35 Am. Rep. 420); Hey Sing Jeck v. Anderson, 57 Cal. 251.

[4] 2 Hale P. C. 151; Barnard v. Bartlett, 10 Cush. 501; Cooley Const. Lim. 374.

[5] Crozier v. Cudney, 6 B. & C. 232; 9 D. & R. 224; State v. Brennan's Liquors, 25 Conn. 278.

§ 128

is provided by the United States constitution,[1] and by almost every State constitution, that " no soldier shall in time of peace be quartered in any house without the consent of the owner, nor in time of war, but in a manner to be prescribed by law." At the present time, and in this country, the necessity for this constitutional provision does not seem to be very urgent, and it is not. But at the time when the provision was incorporated into the constitution, the practice was so common in some countries, and the danger of its being generally adopted in our own country [it had in colonial days been occasionally resorted to] appeared to be sufficiently imminent in order to justify its enactment. It is well that there should be an unequivocal declaration on so important a matter ; for no more efficient means of oppression of a people can be devised than the power, at all times and without any limitation, to throw upon an objectional person the burden of housing and supporting a company of soldiers. The constitutional provision just cited, protects the house of the citizen against all such intrusions in time of peace, and in war the matter is required to be specially regulated by law. It is safe to say, however, that, with the present temper of public opinion, the exercise of this power would not be tolerated now, even in time of war, unless provision is made for the full compensation of those on whom this burden should be made to fall.[2]

SECTION. 129. Taxation — Kinds of taxes.
    129a. Limitations upon legislative authority.

§ 129. **Taxation—Kinds of taxes.** — The functions of a government can only be exercised and kept in operation with the aid of material means furnished by the people ;

---

[1] U. S. Const. Amend., art. 3.
[2] See *post*, § 137, in reference to forcible appropriation of private property in time of war.

§ 129

and no government could be properly called stable, which had to depend upon voluntary contributions. The exaction of these means, therefore, is a power which a government inherently and necessarily possesses without any express grant. A tax, is, in its most comprehensive sense, any charge or assessment levied by the government for public purposes upon the persons, property, and privileges of the people within the taxing district or State. It is a forced contribution of means towards the support of the government.

Taxes may assume very many forms, varying according to the thing, privilege, or right which is taxed. They may take the form of duties, imposts and excises, and the taxes imposed by the general government are confined to these. The power to impose these indirect taxes is expressly granted to the United States government. The constitution provides [1] that "the congress shall have power to levy and collect taxes, duties, imposts, and excises to pay the debts, and provide for the common defense and general welfare of the United States; but all duties, imposts and excises shall be uniform throughout the United States." Duties and imposts are the taxes levied upon importations into this country, and under this express power it is claimed that the general government may establish a protective tariff, which has already been shown to be in violation of constitutional liberty.[2] Excises are the taxes laid upon the manufacture and sale of articles of merchandise, upon licenses to follow certain occupations, and upon the enjoyment of franchises or privileges. The internal revenue tax upon the manufacture and sale of intoxicating liquors and tobacco are at present the only excises levied by the general government.[3] But there is no limitation upon the power of the

[1] Const. U. S., art. I, § 8, ch. 1.

[2] See *ante*, § 91.

[3] Since the above was written at the last session of Congress, 1885–1886, a law was passed imposing a tax upon the sale and manufacture of oleomargarine.

§ 129

government in selecting the subjects of taxation ; and during the late civil war, and immediately thereafter, there were taxes, in the form of stamp duties on matches, bank checks, legal papers and the like. The United States government is also authorized by the constitution to impose direct taxes, which has been held to include any capitation and land taxes,[1] subject to the limitation that they must be apportioned among the several States according to the representative population.[2]

A very common form of State and municipal taxation is the exaction of license fees for the privilege of pursuing any occupation or profession, a tax, therefore, upon occupations. The constitutional character of the license tax, and its points of distinction from the license fee exacted in connection with the police regulation of an occupation, the pursuit of which is likely to prove dangerous or injurious to society, have already been fully explained in another place,[3] and need not be discussed in this connection. The States have also at times imposed a poll-tax upon the citizen, and made the payment of it a condition precedent to the exercise of the right of suffrage. But this mode of taxation incurs great popular disfavor, and is very rarely, if at all, employed now. The most common form of State and municipal taxation is the taxation of property, both real and personal, and there is a fundamental difference between the character of taxation generally, including the taxation of personal property, and the character of taxation of real property. Taxation, generally, is imposed upon citizens and resident aliens, resting upon the permanent or temporary allegiance they owe to the government ; and they are supposed to re-

---

[1] Hylton v. United States, 3 Dall. 171; Pacific Ins. Co. v. Soule, 7 Wall. 433; Veazie Bank v. Fenno, 8 Wall. 533; Springer v. United States, 192 U. S. 586.

[2] Const. U. S. art. I, § 2; art. I, § 9.

[3] See ante, § 101.

§ 129

ceive a fair equivalent for these involuntary contributions in the domestic peace and order, and the protection to their rights of person and property, which a stable government ensures. The obligation to pay taxes in such cases rests upon the fact of domicile and citizenship. But the taxation of real property rests upon other grounds. In its application to real property, taxation assumes a decidedly feudal character. If the power to tax real property rested solely upon the obligations of citizenship or domicile, as most of the legal authorities seem to hold,[1] then it could only be levied upon those proprietors of lands who were citizens. At the time when the earlier cases, which have been cited, were decided, no one but a citizen could become the proprietor of lands in the United States, and this coincidence no doubt caused the learned judges to make the statements, upon which the claim of a connection between citizenship and taxation of real property rests. But since then the restriction upon the proprietorship of lands by aliens has been removed in most of the States, and now all land situated within the jurisdiction of the government which levies the tax are taxed for their proportionate share, whether the land is owned by citizens or aliens, residents or non-residents. The levying of a tax upon land, and the enforcement of the levy, are proceedings *in rem* against the land, and not *in personam* against the proprietors.[2] Taxation of real property is nothing more than the *reditus* which the tenant of a feud paid to the lord of the manor for the enjoyment of the land; in this country, in the case

---

[1] Providence Bank *v.* Billings, 4 Pet. 561; McCulloch *v.* Maryland, 4 Wheat. 428; Opinions of Judges, 48 Me. 591; People *v.* Mayor, etc., 4 N. Y. 422; Clark *v.* Rochester, 24 Barb. 482; Phila. Assn., etc., *v.* Wood, 39 Pa. St. 73; Moale *v.* Baltimore, 5 Md. 314; Doe *v.* Deavors, 11 Ga. 79; Chicago *v.* Larned, 34 Ill. 279; Davison *v.* Ramsay Co., 18 Minn. 481.

[2] Cooley on Tax. 360. In some of the States, however, a distinction it made by statute between the resident and non-resident lands as they are called, imposing a personal liability upon the owners of the residens lands. Cooley on Tax. 278, 279.

§ 129

tenancies in fee, the State taking the place of the intermediate landord, as in England, the king did in the case of tenancies *in capite*.   Indeed the obligation of citizenship is a modern outgrowth of the allegiance of the feudal system, which the vassal or tenant of land owed through his lord to the king, as the lord paramount or ultimate proprietor of the lands of the kingdom.   The obligation of citizenship, apart from the obligations of a tenant of lands, was unknown to the feudal age.[1]   But whatever may be the proper theory in respect to the character and the authority of taxation, the power of the government to levy the proportionate share of taxes upon the lands owned by aliens has never been questioned, and an exemption of such lands from the operation of the levy would most surely meet with popular demonstrations of disapproval.

§ 129*a*. **Limitations upon legislative authority.** — The power of a government to impose taxes is almost without limitation and necessarily so, because of the varied character of governmental functions and needs.   Chief Justice Marshall has almost denied the existence of any limitations upon the power of taxation.   He said, in one case, "the power of taxing the people and their property is essential to the very existence of government, and may be legitimately exercised on the objects to which it is applicable or the utmost extent to which the government may choose to carry it.   The only security against the abuse of this power is found in the structure of the government itself.   In imposing a tax, the legislature acts upon its constituents. This is, in general, a sufficient security against erroneous and offensive taxation.   The people of a State, therefore, give to their government a right of taxing themselves and their property ; and as the exigencies of the government

---

[1] Tiedeman on Real Prop. § 20; 1 Washb. on Real Prop. 46, citing 3 Guiz. Hist. Civ. 108.

§ 129*a*

cannot be limited, they prescribe no limits to the exercise of this right, resting confidently on the interest of the legislator, and on the influence of the constituents over their representative, to guard them against its abuse." It is " unfit for the judicial department to inquire what degree of taxation is the legitimate use, and what degree may amount to the abuse, of the power."[1]

It is undoubtedly true that the power of the legislature to determine the rate of taxation is limited only by its wise discretion, and may be extended so as to involve a complete confiscation of all the taxable property within the State, if the payment of such a tax could be enforced. There would be no redress in the courts for such an abuse of the power. It is also true that the selection of the objects of taxation is without limitation, except those imposed by the United States constitution, and arising out of the inter-relation of the Federal and State governments.[2]

The State may freely determine upon what occupations and manufactures to impose a license or excise tax, and may exempt others from the burden of taxation with or without laudable reasons ; it may determine what is taxable property, and exempt from the levy any kind of property in the exercise of its discretion. The arbitrary character of the exemptions in any of these cases furnishes no ground for an appeal to the courts.[3] But, usually, as a matter of

[1] McCulloch v. Maryland, 4 Wheat. 316, 428, 430. See, also, Providence Bk. v. Billings, 4 Pet. 514; Kirtland v. Hotchkiss, 100 U. S. 491; Portland Bk. v. Apthrop, 12 Mass. 252; Herrick v. Randolph, 13 Vt. 525; Armington v. Barnet, 15 Vt. 745; Thomas v. Leland, 24 Wend. 65; People v. Mayor, etc., of Brooklyn, 4 N. Y., 491; Kirby v. Shaw, 19 Pa. St. 258; Sharpless v. Mayor, etc., 21 Pa. St. 145; Weister v. Hade, 52 Pa. St. 474; Wingate v. Sluder, 6 Jones (N. C.), 552; West. Un. Tel. Co. v. Mayor, 28 Ohio St. 521; Board of Education v. Mclandsborough, 36 Ohio St. 227.

[2] As to which, see *post*, § 210.

[3] Brewer Brick Co. v. Brewer, 62 Me. 62 (16 Am. Rep. 395; Durach's Appeal, 62 Pa. St. 491; Stratton v. Collins, 43 N. J. 563; New Orleans

§ 129a

course, there is a public reason, upon which the exemption may be justified. For the promotion of the public welfare, educational and religious institutions and their property are often exempted from taxation, and the right to make the exemption has been rarely questioned.[1] For the purpose of lightening the burden of the poorer classes, and relieving the State of the danger of consequent pauperism, the State may very properly exempt from taxation the tools and other means of support of the wage-earner. But it has been held to be unconstitutional to make exemptions from taxation on account of sex or age, as for example, widows, maids and female minors. Such an act was declared to be void.[2] Classes or kinds of property may be exempted, as well as classes of persons.[3] But the legislature of the State must determine for itself what shall be objects of taxation. The county or municipal authorities cannot be permitted or authorized by the legislatures to make the exemptions.[4] Statutory exemptions are always very strictly construed against the individual and in favor of the public;[5] and ordinarily a general exemption by the State from taxation does not extend to assessments by the municipal authorities for a local improvement.

v. Fourchy, 30 La. Ann. pt. 1, 910; New Orleans *v.* People's Bank, 32 La. Ann. 82; State *v.* North, 27 Mo. 464; People *v.* Colman, 3 Cal 46.

[1] It is no violation of the constitutional principle of religious liberty to exempt the property of religious institutions from taxation. Trustees of Griswold College *v.* State, 46 Iowa, 275 (26 Am. Rep. 138).

[2] State *v.* Indianapolis, 69 Ind. 375 (35 Am. Rep. 223).

[3] Butler's Appeal, 73 Pa. St. 48; Sioux City *v.* School District, 55 Iowa, 150.`

[4] Farnsworth Co. *v.* Lisbon, 62 Me. 451; Wilson *v.* Mayor, etc., of New York, 4 E .D. Smith, 675; State *v.* Parker, 33 N. J. 213; State *v.* Hudson, etc., Commissioners, 37 N. J. 11; Hill *v.* Higdon, 5 Ohio St. 243; State *v.* County Court, 19 Ark. 360; Weeks *v.* Milwaukee, 10 Wis. 242; Wilson *v.* Supervisors of Sutter, 47 Cal. 91.

[5] Railway Co. *v.* Philadelphia, 101 U. S. 528; State *v.* Mills, 34 N. J. 177; Trustees of M. E. Church *v.* Ellis, 38 Ind. 3; Nashville, etc., R. R. Co. *v.* Hodges, 7 Lea, 663.

[6] Seamen's Friend Society *v.* Boston, 116 Mass. 181; Universalist

§ 129*a*

In reference to these matters, as just explained, the power of taxation is practically without limitation, at any rate subject to very few limitations. But it would not do to say that every legislative act, which assumes the exercise of the power of taxation, will be constitutional. Levies can be made upon the property of the individual which will transcend the object of taxation, as well as violate its spirit. The levy of a tax is only permissible, except under a tyrannical government, when it is made for a public purpose, and it is proportioned uniformly among the objects or subjects of taxation. When a tax is imposed for some private or individual benefit, or is not uniformly imposed upon those who ought to bear it, it is perfectly proper, nay, it is the duty of the courts to interfere and prohibit what may be justly called an extortion.[1] But the term "public purpose" must not be used in this connection in any narrow sense. Taxes are levied for a public purpose, not only when they

---

Society v. Providence, 6 R. I. 235; Brewster v. Hough, 10 N. H. 138; Seymour v. Hartford, 21 Conn. 581; Matter of Mayor, etc., 11 Johns. 77; Patterson v. Society, etc., 24 N. J. 385; Pray v. Northern Liberties, 31 Pa. St. 69; Baltimore v. Cemetery Co., 7 Md. 517; Orange, etc., R. R. Co. v. Alexandria, 17 Gratt. 185; Lafayette v. Orphan Asylum, 4 La. Ann. 1; Broadway Baptist Church v. McAtee, 8 Bush, 508 (8 Am. Rep. 480); Cincinnati College v. State, 19 Ohio, 110; Palmer v. Stumph, 29 Ind. 329; Peoria v. Kidder, 26 Ill. 351; Lockwood v. St. Louis, 24 Mo. 20; Le Fever v. Detroit, 2 Mich. 586; Hale v. Kenosha, 29 Wis. 599.

[1] "It is the clear right of every citizen to insist that no unlawful or unauthorized exaction shall be made upon him under the guise of taxation. If any such illegal encroachment is attempted, he can always invoke the aid of the judicial tribunals for his protection, and prevent his money or other property from being taken and appropriated for a purpose and in a manner not authorized by the constitution and laws." Bigelow, Ch. J., in Freeland v. Hastings, 10 Allen, 570, 575. See, also, to the same effect, Hooper v. Emery, 14 Me. 375; Allen v. Jay, 60 Me. 124 (11 Am. Rep. 185); Talbot v. Hudson, 16 Gray, 417; Weismer v. Douglass, 64 N. Y. 91 (21 Am. Rep. 588); Tyson v. School Directors, 51 Pa. St. 9; Washington Avenue, 69 Pa. St. 352 (8 Am. Rep. 255); People v. Township Board of Salem, 20 Mich. 452; People v. Supervisors of Saginaw, 26 Mich. 22; Ferguson v. Landram, 5 Bush, 230; Morford v. Unger, 8 Iowa, 82; Hansen v. Vernon, 27 Iowa, 28.

§ 129a

are designed to pay the salaries of government officials, to erect and keep in repair government buildings ; to maintain the public roads, harbors and rivers in a fit condition, and to provide for the defenses of the country. Taxes may not only be levied for such purposes, but also for all purposes of public charity. It is a public purpose to erect with State funds, obtained from taxes, penitentiaries, orphan and lunatic asylums, hospitals and lazarettos, public schools and colleges.[1] It is a public purpose to provide pensions for the soldier and other employees of the government, when they have become disabled in service or superannuated.[2] And wherever there is a reasonable doubt as to the character of the purpose for which the tax was levied, the doubt should be solved in favor of the power of the legislature to lay the tax.[3] But if the purpose be truly private ; if the tax in effect takes the property of one man and gives it to another, it is illegal and it is the duty of the courts to enjoin its collection.[4] For example, it has been held unlawful to

[1] But it is only for the support of public charities that the government may tax the people. A levy of a tax for donation to some private benevolent or charitable institution is void. St. Mary's Industrial School *v.* Brown, 45 Md. 310.

[2] Booth *v.* Woodbury, 32 Conn. 118; Speer *v.* School Directors of Blairville, 50 Pa. St. 150.

[3] " To justify the court in arresting the proceedings and declaring the tax void, the absence of all public interest in the purposes for which the funds are raised must be clear and palpable; so clear and palpable as to be perceptible by every mind at the first blush." Per Dixon, Ch. J., in Brodhead *v.* City of Milwaukee, 19 Wis. 624, 652. See Spring *v.* Russell, 7 Me. 273; Mills *v.* Charleton, 29 Wis. 411 (9 Am. Rep. 578.)

[4] " The legislature has no constitutional right to * * * lay a tax, or to authorize any municipal corporation to do it, in order to raise funds for a mere private purpose. No such authority passed to the assembly by the general grant of the legislative power. This would not be legislation. Taxation is a mode of raising revenue for public purposes. When it is prostituted to objects in no way connected with the public interest or welfare, it ceases to be taxation and becomes plunder. Transferring money from the owners of it into the possession of those who have no title to it, though it be done under the name and form of a tax, is unconstitutional for all the reasons which forbid the legisla-

§ 129*a*

levy taxes in aid of manufacturing and other private industrial enterprises,[1] for the relief of farmers, whose crops
have been destroyed, to supply them with seeds and provisions,[2] or for making loans to persons whose homes have
been destroyed by fire.[3] It has also been held illegal to
pay a subscription to a private corporation that is to be
devoted to a private purpose.[4] On the other hand,
it has been repeatedly held that the legislature may
authorize counties and municipal corporations to subscribe for capital stock in railroad companies in aid
of their construction and may levy a tax in order to
pay the subscription.[5] Since the legislature is pro-

<hr>

ture to usurp any other power not granted to them." Black, Ch. J., in
Sharpless v. Mayor, etc., 21 Pa. St. 147, 168.

[1] Loan Association v. Topeka, 20 Wall. 655; Opinions of Judges, 58
Me. 590; Allen v. Jay, 60 Me. 124 (11 Am. Rep. 185); Commercial Bank
v. Iola, 2 Dill. 353.

[2] State v. Osawkee, 14 Kan. 418. But the United States, as well as
the State governments, have frequently come with the public funds to the
rescue of the people of sections which have been inundated by floods, or
devastated by disease or fire; and it would seem that the State aid under
such circumstances differed little if at all from the ordinary bestowal
of alms upon the poor, and is equally justifiable, as being a public
charity.

[3] Lowell v. Boston, 111 Mass. 454 (15 Am. Rep. 39).

[4] Weismer v. Douglass, 64 N. Y. 91 (21 Am. Rep. 586).

[5] Zabriskkie v. Cleveland, C. &. R. R. Co., 23 How. 381; Bissell v.
City of Jeffersonville, 54 How. 287; Amey v. Allegheny City, 24 How.
364; Curtis v. Butler Co., 24 How. 435; Mercer Co. v. Hacket, 1 Wall. 83;
Gelpcke v. City of Dubuque, 1 Wall. 175; Seybert v. City of Pittsburg, 1
Wall. 272; Van Hortrup v. Madison City, 1 Wall. 291; Meyer v. City of
Muscatine, 1 Wall. 384; Havemeyer v. Iowa Co., 3 Wall. 294; Thomson v.
Lee Co., 3 Wall. 327; Rogers v. Burlington, 3 Wall. 654; Mitchell v. Bur-
lington, 4 Wall. 270; Campbell v. City of Kenosha, 5 Wall. 194; Riggs v.
Johnson, 6 Wall. 166; Lee Co. v. Rogers, 7 Wall. 181; City of Kenosha, 9
Wall. 477; Chicago, B. & Q. R. R. Co. v. County of Otoe, 16 Wall. 667;
Gilman v Sheboygan, 2 Black, 510; Tipton Co. v. Rogers L. & M. Works,
103 U. S. 523. The cases from the State courts are too numerous to cite
in detail. But see, to the same effect, Supervisors of Portage Co. v.
Wis. Cent. R. R. Co., 121 Mass. 460; Augusta Bank v. Augusta, 49 Me.
507; Williams v. Duanesburg, 66 N. Y. 129; Brown v. County Comrs., 21

§ 129a

hibited from making levies for private purposes, it cannot authorize municipal corporations to do so.[1]

But great difficulty is experienced in enforcing an observance of this limitation, if any desire is manifested to violate it, since the legislature usually makes one levy of tax in a gross sum to cover all the probable expenditures of the government during the fiscal year, and there is rarely, if ever, a special levy for each item of expenditure. It would certainly hamper very seriously the operations of government, if each taxpayer were allowed to question the legality of the levy, because one of the proposed items of expenditure is not for a public purpose. In such a case the interest of the individual must yield to the public good, and apart from a change of representatives at the next election, there is probably no remedy, unless the treasurer or other disbursing officer should refuse to apply the public funds to the unlawful purpose. But if a special stamp or license tax should be levied for a private purpose, the taxpayer can resist the payment, and demand from the ordinary courts protection against the actions of the tax collector.

A tax levy may also be open to objection because it does not comply with the constitutional requirement of uniform apportionment. The language of the State constitutions in in this connection is not invariably the same, and in some of them the language is sufficiently variant to account for the contradiction of authorities; but as a general proposition, they are considered to make about the same requirement. Taxation must be equal and uniform, but the constitutions do not require that the same rule of uniformity should be employed in the apportionment of all taxes. No one rule of uniformity can be devised, which will be applicable to all kinds of taxation, and consequently for each mode of taxation there must be a special rule of apportion-

Pa. St. 37; St. Louis *v.* Alexander, 23 Mo. 483; Smith *v.* Clark Co., 54 Mo. 58.

[1] Attorney-General *v.* Eau Claire, 37 Wis. 400.

§ 129*a*

ment. Thus, for example, the taxation of property is apportioned according to the value, it being considered that such an apportionment will bring about a more perfect equalization of the tax than any other rule. But in laying a tax upon professions and occupations, a different rule of uniformity must be followed.[1] And the usual rule is to establish a scale of taxation upon the occupations, graded in proportion to their relative profits. The meaning, therefore, of this constitutional limitation is that whatever the rule of apportionment is, it must be uniformly and impartially applied to all objects of the special taxation.[2] There cannot be any partial discrimination between persons or property living in the same taxing district, and falling within the established rule of apportionment. The State has the right to determine the limits of the taxing district,[3]

---

[1] As to the uniformity of the tax on occupations, see *ante*, § 101.

[2] See State Railroad Tax Cases, 92 U. S. 575; Cummings *v.* National Bank, 101 U. S. 153; Oliver *v.* Washington Mills, 11 Allen, 268; Tidewater Co. *v.* Costar, 18 N. J. Eq. 518; Kittanning Coal Co. *v.* Commonwealth, 78 Pa. St. 100; Galtin *v.* Tarborough, 78 N. C. 119; Youngblood *v.* Sexton, 32 Mich. 406; Bureau Co. *v.* Railroad Co., 44 Ill. 229; Marsh *v.* Supervisors, 42 Wis. 502; Philles *v.* Hiles, 42 Wis. 527; Ex parte Robinson, 12 Nev. 263; Sanborn *v.* Rice, 9 Minn. 273; New Orleans *v.* Dubarry, 33 La. Ann. 481 (39 Am. Rep. 273); State *v.* Rolle, 30 La. Ann. 991; Walters *v.* Duke, 31 La. Ann. 668; State *v.* Cassidy, 22 Minn. 312 (21 Am. Rep. 765). But see, *contra*, Sims *v.* Jackson, 22 La. Ann. 440; State *v.* Endom, 23 La. An. 663; State *v.* So. Ca. R. R. Co., 4 S. C. 376.

[3] But the tax district must be of uniform character, so that the tax shall fall upon those who are almost equally benefited by the expenditure. It has thus been held unlawful for a legislature to extend the limits of a city so as to include farming lands, and thus increase the revenue of the city. City of Covington *v.* Southgate, 15 B. Mon. 491; Arbegust *v.* Louisville, 2 Bush, 271; Swift *v.* Newport, 7 Bush, 37; Morford *v.* Unger, 8 Iowa, 82; Langworthy *v.* Dubuque, 13 Iowa, 86; Fulton *v.* Davenport, 17 Iowa, 404; Buell *v.* Ball, 20 Iowa, 282; Bradshaw *v.* Omaha, 1 Neb. 16; Durant *v.* Kauffman, 34 Iowa, 194. But see, *contra*, Stilts *v.* Indianapolis, 55 Ind. 515; Giboney *v.* Cape Girardeau, 58 Mo. 141; Martin *v.* Dix, 52 Miss. 53 (24 Am. Rep. 661); New Orleans *v.* Cazelear, 27 La. Ann. 156. See, also, Kelly *v.* Pittsburg, 85 Pa. St. 170; Hewitt's Appeal, 88 Pa. St. 55; Weeks *v.* Milwaukee, 10 Wis. 242.

§ 129*a*

but when the taxing district is established, and the rule of apportionment determined upon, the tax must be uniformly apportioned throughout the taxing district.   There cannot be different rules of apportionment for different persons or different sections of the district.[1]

The charge of illegality, because of the violation of the constitutional requirement of equality and uniformity in the apportionment, is most commonly brought against local assessments co-called.   It is very common at the present day for municipal corporations, instead of providing for the improvement of the streets, the construction of sewers and drains, and other local arrangements for the promotion of health and comfort, by the imposition of a general tax, collectible from all the taxpayers of the city according to the value of their taxable property, to apportion the cost of the improvement among those contiguous proprietors who are more directly benefited by the improvement.   There are two modes of apportionment of the cost of these local improvements, both of which have been sustained as being a substantial compliance with the constitutional requirement of uniformity.   One method is a more or less arbitrary apportionment of the cost according to the legislative judgment of the benefit received by each proprietor from the improvement,[2] while it has in other cases been held to

---

[1] Pine Grove v. Talcott, 19 Wall. 666, 675; Knowlton v. Supervisors of Rock Co., 9 Wis. 510; Exchange Bank v. Hines, 3 Ohio St. 1, 15; Kent v. Kentland, 62 Ind. 291 (30 Am. Rep. 182); State v. New Orleans, 15 La. Ann. 354; Chicago, etc., R. R. Co. v. Boone Co., 44 Ill. 240; Fletcher v. Oliver, 25 Ark. 289; Commissioners of Ottawa Co. v. Nelson, 19 Kans. 234 (27 Am. Rep. 101); East Portland v. Multnomah Co., 6 Ore. 62.   But see, contra, Gillette v. Hartford, 31 Conn. 351; Serrill v. Philadelphia, 38 Pa. St. 355; Benoist v. St. Louis, 19 Mo. 179.

[2] People v. Mayor, etc., of Brooklyn, 4 N. Y. 419; Livingston v. New York, 8 Wend. 85 (22 Am. Dec. 622); Wright v. Boston, 9 Cush. 233; Jones v. Boston, 104 Mass. 461; Nichols v. Bridgeport, 23 Conn. 189; Cone v. Hartford, 28 Conn. 363; State v. Fuller, 34 N. J. 227; McMasters v. Commonwealth, 3 Watts, 292; Weber v. Reinhard, 73 Pa. St. 370 (13 Am. Rep. 747); Alexander v. Baltimore, 5 Gill, 383; Howard v. The

§ 129a

be equally lawful to make a taxing district of one street of
a city, and apportion the cost of improvements among
abutting proprietors in proportion to the frontage of their
lots.[1] The reasoning of the courts is invariably that in
local assessments, as in the case of a general tax, there is
a more or less successful attempt at uniformity, although
the rules of apportionment may be different. "A property
tax for the general purposes of the government, either of
the State at large, or of a county, city, or other district, is
regarded as a just and equitable tax. The reason is obvious. It apportions the burden according to the benefit,
more nearly than any other inflexible rule of general taxation. A rich man derives more benefit from taxation in
the protection and improvement of his property than a
poor man, and ought therefore to pay more. But the
amount of each man's benefit in general taxation cannot be
ascertained and estimated with any degree of certainty;
and for that reason a property tax is adopted, instead of an
estimate of benefits. In local taxation, however, for special purposes, the local benefits may in many cases be seen,
traced, and estimated to a reasonable certainty.[2] At least

Church, 18 Md. 451; Scoville v. Cleveland, 1 Ohio St. 126; Sessions v.
Crunkleton, 20 Ohio St. 349; Maloy v. Marietta, 11 Ohio St. 636; Bradley
v. McAtee, 7 Bush, 667 (3 Am. Rep. 309); Hoyt v. East Saginaw, 19 Mich.
39; Sheley v. Detroit, 45 Mich. 431; Cook v. Slocum, 27 Minn. 500; Lafayette v. Fowler, 34 Ind. 140; Peoria v. Kidder, 26 Ill. 351; Garrett v.
St. Louis, 25 Mo. 505; Uhrig v. St. Louis, 44 Mo. 458; Burnett v. Sacramento, 12 Cal. 76. See, contra, State v. Charleston, 12 Rich. 702.

[1] Williams v. Detroit, 2 Mich. 560; Northern R. R. Co. v. Connelly,
10 Ohio St. 159; Lamsden v. Cross, 10 Wis. 282. Contra, McBean v.
Chandler, 9 Heisk. 349; Perry v. Little Rock, 32 Ark. 31.

[2] People v. Mayor, etc., of Brooklyn, 4 N. Y. 419, 427. In Ohio, the
legislature has expressly authorized the municipal governments to
apportion local assessments, either according to the frontage of lots or
their assessed value. In declaring this law to be constitutional, Peck, J.
says: " It is said that assessments as distinguished from general taxation, rest solely upon the idea of equivalents; a compensation proportioned to the special benefits derived from the improvement, and that in

§ 129a

this has been supposed and assumed to be true by the legislature, whose duty it is to prescribe the rules on which
taxation is to be apportioned, and whose determination of
this matter being within the scope of its lawful power, is
conclusive."

the case at bar, the railroad company is not, and in the nature of things
cannot be in any degree benefited by the improvement. It is quite true
that the right to impose such special taxes is based upon a presumed
equivalent, but it by no means follows that there must be in fact such
full equivalent in every instance, or that its absence will render the
assessment invalid. The rule of apportionment, whether by the front
foot or a percentage upon the assessed valuation must be *uniform*, affecting all the owners and all the property abutting on the street alike. One
rule cannot be applied to one owner, and a different rule to another owner.
One could not be assessed ten per cent, another five, another three, and
another left altogether unassessed, because he was not in fact benefited.
It is manifest that the actual benefits resulting from the improvement
may be as various almost as the number of the owners and the uses to
which the property may be applied. No general rule, therefore, could be
laid down which would do equal and exact justice to all. The legislature have not attempted so vain a thing, but have prescribed two
different modes in which the assessment may be made, and left the city
authorities free to adopt either. The mode adopted by the council
becomes the statutory equivalent for the benefits conferred, although in
fact the burden imposed may greatly preponderate. Northern Indiana R.
R. Co. *v.* Connelly, 10 Ohio St. 159. See, generally, Willard *v.* Presbury,
14 Wall. 676; Allen *v.* Drew, 44 Vt. 174; Washington Avenue, 69 Pa. St.
352 (8 Am. Rep. 255); Craig *v.* Philadelphia, 89 Pa. St. 265; Philadelphia
v. Rule, 93 Pa. St. 15; Hill *v.* Higdon, 5 Ohio St. 243; Ernst *v.* Kunkle,
5 Ohio St. 520; White *v.* People, 94 Ill. 604; Palmer *v.* Stumph, 29 Ind.
329; St. Joseph *v.* O'Donaghue, 31 Mo. 345; Hines *v.* Leavenworth, 3
Kan. 186; Burnett *v.* Sacramento, 12 Cal. 76; Chambers *v.* Satterlee, 40
Cal. 497. See for an exhaustive treatment of this subject, Cooley Const.
Lim. 616, 634; 2 Dill. Mun. Corp., §§ 752, 761.

NOTE.—The subject of taxation is so extensive that it is itself sufficient
to constitute the subject of a separate volume, and an exhaustive treatment of it in the present connection would have swelled the volume
beyond reasonable proportions. Moreover, the power of taxation is not
commonly considered a branch of the police power. While I am convinced
that it is scientifically correct to consider taxation as the imposition of a
burden in the exercise of the police power of the government, the fact

§ 129a

that the subject has been fully and thoroughly treated by distinguished writers (see Cooley Const. Lim. 592, 646; 2 Dillon Mun. Corp., §§ 735, 822; Sedgwick on Statutory and Constitutional Law, ch. 10), has led me in explaining the power of taxation as a branch of police power, to content myself with stating the constitutional objections that might be made to different forms of taxation, supporting the statements by a liberal citation of authorities.

§ 129*a*

CHAPTER XI.

POLICE REGULATION OF PERSONAL PROPERTY.

SECTION 135. Laws regulating the creation and acquisition of interests in personal property — Real and personal property herein distinguished.

135a. Statute of uses and rule against perpetuity, as regulations of personal property.

136. Regulation and prohibition of the sale of personal property.

136a. Laws regulating disposition of personal property by will.

137. Involuntary alienation.

138. Control of property by guardian.

139. Destruction of personal property on account of illegal use.

140. Laws regulating use of personal property.

140a. Prohibition of possession of certain property.

140b. Regulation and prohibition of the manufacture of certain property.

140c. Carrying of concealed weapons prohibited.

140d. Miscellaneous regulations of the use of personal property.

141. Laws regulating the use and keeping of domestic animals.

141a. Keeping of dogs.

141b. Laws for the prevention of cruelty to animals.

142. Regulation of contracts and other rights of action.

143. Regulation of ships and shipping.

§ 135. **Laws regulating the creation and acquisition of interests in personal property — Real and personal property herein distinguished.** — It has been shown in a previous section,[1] that the private property in lands is acquired from the State, and is held in subordination to the absolute property in lands, which is vested in, and can never be aliened by the State, as the representative of the public in organized society. It was also asserted and explained,[2] that in consequence of the public origin of all

---

[1] See, *ante,* § 115.
[2] See, *ante,* § 116.

private property in land, there was but one constitutional limitation upon the power of the legislature to regulate the acquisition and transfer of estates in land, viz.: that such regulations must not interfere or conflict with vested rights. Not only in the primary acquisition of land from the State, but also in the acquisition of it from former private owners, the State has the unrestricted power to determine the conditions and form of transfer, and the character of the estates so created, as long as there is no interference with vested right by a material obstruction or practical denial of the right of alienation of a vested estate. The regulations may be arbitrary in the extreme, but they cannot be subjected to any serious constitutional objection.

It is different, however, with personal property. All personal property is the product of some man's labor, and whether the owner has acquired it by his own labor, by inheritance or by exchange, his interest is a vested right of the most unlimited character. He does not hold it by any favor of the State, and in consequence of his possession of it he has assumed no peculiar obligation to the State. He has the right, therefore, to acquire it in any manner that he pleases, provided in so doing he does not interfere with or threaten the rights of others. Laws for the regulation of the conveyance of real property may be altogether arbitrary, provided the burden so imposed upon alienation does not amount to a practical prohibition of alienation. But in order that a similar regulation of the transfer of personal property may be lawful, it must serve some public good, and whether it does promote the public welfare is a judicial and not a legislative question. In neither case is there any likelihood that an arbitrary and wholly unreasonable regulation of the conveyance of property will be attempted. In both cases the legislature would usually be prompted to regulate conveyancing only by some public consideration, and hence the distinction here made, between real and personal property, in its application to the regulation of con-

§ .135

veyancing, does not possess much practical importance.
But a case may arise, in which the attempted regulation
could, under this distinction, be declared unconstitutional,
and hence it is highly proper that the distinction should be
presented in this connection.   The ordinary legislation, in
the regulation of the conveyance of both real and personal
property, has for its object either the prevention of fraud,
the removal of doubt concerning the validity of one's title,
or the facilitation of investigations of titles.   For some one
or more of these reasons, the sale of personal property is
declared to pass a good title, as against a subsequent purchaser, or incumbrancer, only when the possession has been
delivered, or the bill of sale is recorded ; the chattel mortgage
is required to be recorded ; and all transfers of property
are avoided in favor of existing creditors, which are not made
upon some valuable and substantial considerations.   All of
these are reasonable regulations, for the restraint upon the
rights of alienation and acquisition is but slight and serves
a worthy and public purpose ; for every one is interested in
the prevention of fraud as he is of all other trespasses on
the rights of others.

But there is a greater likelihood of an arbitrary or unnecessary regulation of the interests or estates which one may
acquire in personal property.   As has been already explained, the State has the unrestricted power to determine
the kinds and characteristics of the estates which may be
created in lands ; but the estate or interest in personal property may be as varied and unique as human ingenuity may
devise, subject to the one limitation imposed by the nature
of the article of personal property.   Thus, for example, it
is common to find it stated in law books that a future estate
may be created in personal property, where the present
enjoyment does not involve necessarily a consumption of
the thing itself.[1]   Of course, the creation of an estate in

---

[1] Tiedeman on Real Prop., § 546.

§ 135

personalty of such a character, that it will prove a public injury or a private wrong, may be prohibited, and all regulations of the creation of estates and interests in personal property may be instituted, which have in view the prevention of such wrongs.   But, except in a few rare cases, it is difficult to see how any interest in personal property can be created which will have an injurious effect on the public or third persons.   One exceptional case is that of an interest so limited as to deprive creditors of the right to subject the property to their lawful demands.   A law, declaring void all conditions against sale for debts, is undoubtedly constitutional, for the public is directly interested in enforcing the payment of a debt.   The contraction of a debt is a voluntary subjection of property to liability for it, and the possession of property, free from this liability for debt, would tend to induce and increase that wild and irresponsible speculation which does so much to produce fluctuations in values and financial disasters.   It is, therefore, proper to prohibit such a limitation of both real and personal property.

§ 135a. **Statute of uses and rule against perpetuity as regulations of personal property.** — It was proper and constitutional for the legislature or parliament to enact the statute of uses, which has for its object the abolition of all uses, or other equitable interests, held separately from the legal title and estate, so far as it was held to apply to real property.   For, although the creation of such equitable interests was charged to be conducive to the perpetration of fraud,[1] and that was the reason assigned for the enactment, the real purpose was the conservation and protection of those legal rights in land, such as the king's right of forfeiture on account of attainder, alienage and treason, and the manorial lord's wards, marriages, reliefs, heriots,

---

[1] Tiedeman on Real Prop., § 459; 1 Sudg. on Powers (ed. 1856), 78.

§ 135a

escheats, aids, etc., which were special privileges imposed upon the tenants as burdens of tenure, and the evasion of which constituted the alleged perpetration of fraud. Inasmuch as the State can impose whatever conditions and limitations upon tenancies of land it pleases, uses and trusts issuing out of land may be abolished altogether. And although the limitation of the operation of the statute to uses issuing out of freehold estates in lands was the result of a technical construction of the statute, induced by the opposition of bench and bar to the statute itself, and not by any consideration of constitutional limitations upon the power of Parliament or of the American legislature to enact the statute; if the question were to be raised anew, the application of a statute, abolishing uses and trusts, to personal property may be resisted on the ground that it is unconstitutional to prohibit the creation of trusts in personal property.[1] The owner, as well as the purchaser of personal property, has a right to have the property in question conveyed to trustees to be held in trust; and the liberty and right of property of both are invaded in an unconstitutional manner, when a legislature undertakes to prohibit the creation of trusts in personal property.

In New York all passive trusts have been abolished, and only certain active trusts, enumerated in the statute, are now permitted. All other express trusts are converted by the statute into legal estates by the transfer of the seisin and estate to the *cestui que trust*.[2] So far as the statute limits the creation of active trusts in personal property, the constitutionality of the law must depend upon the evil effect upon others of the creation of such a trust. No active trust in personal property can be prohibited which does not have some immoral or illegal purpose. It may be

---

[1] The term "personal property," it must be observed, is used in this connection in the sense of chattels personal, including movable property of all kinds, but excluding chattel interests in lands.

[2] Tiedeman on Real Prop., § 470; N. Y. Rev. Stat., p. 727.

§ 135a

different with passive trusts.   Since such legislation, as the
New York statute just mentioned, is, whenever copied,
usually accompanied with the statutory removal of all disabilities in respect to separate property from married
women, there can be no sound or substantial reason for the
existence of passive trusts.   The creation of them may not
produce any direct or positive harm, but they certainly
tend to complicate the administration of the law, and for
that reason the prohibition of them may possibly be
justified.

Another case of regulation of the creation of interests
in personal property, which may be subjected to serious
criticism, is the application of the rule against perpetuity
to personal property.   In limiting the creation of future
interests by will, the application of the rule can be easily
justified, for the power to dispose of any property by will,
in any manner whatever, depends upon the legislative discretion.[1]   But in its application to future interests in personal property, created by conveyances *inter vivos*, it is
hard, if at all possible, to find any constitutional justification for such legislation.   Personal property is the product
of man's labor, and he has the right during his life to make
whatever use of it, or to dispose of it to any one, in any
way, and under any terms that he pleases, provided that in
so doing he does not inflict or threaten the infliction of any
wrong or damage on others.   It may be said that the prosperity of a country is advanced when the national wealth is
not accumulated in the hands of a few, and the rule against
perpetuity operates as a check upon such dangerous accu-
mulations.   But if such a reason served as a justification
of this exercise of police power, it would justify the more
severe, but, in principle, similar legislation, which would
compel a man to confine his earnings to a certain amount,
a regulation which has been urged by some labor reformers

---

[1] See *ante*, § 119, and *post*, § 136

§ 135*a*

as a solution of the present industrial problems.   There is
no trespass, direct or indirect, upon the rights of others,
in limiting a future interest in personal property, beyond a
life or lives in being.   And since the power to make such
perpetual limitations of personal property does not depend,
as does the like power in respect to real property, in any
sense upon the sanction or grant of the State, it cannot be
curtailed or taken away.

The application of the ordinary constitutional limitations to the exercise of police power in cases like these, may
excite surprise, and is certainly novel.   The general impression, both professional and popular, has been that there is
no limitation upon the power of the legislature to regulate such matters.   The long acquiescence in the legiti-
macy of such legislation tends to confirm the accepted
doctrine, in opposition to the view here advocated.   But if
it be true that no regulation by the government of the
natural rights of the individual is constitutional, which does
not promote the public welfare by the prevention of a trespass upon the rights of others, it must be conceded that in
cases like these, the limitations upon the power of the government have their full force and effect, and that it is the
duty of the courts to see that the legislature in the exercise of its police power keeps within these constitutional
limitations.

§ 136. **Regulation and prohibition of the sale of personal property.** — It is one of the absolute rights of the
individual to be free from unreasonable restraints upon the
sale or transfer of his personal property.   The right to
sell or transfer one's property is as much an inalienable
right as that of enjoyment of the property free from unnecessary restrictions.   Of course, the right to sell may be
subjected to whatever regulations may be needed to prevent any threatened injury to the public or to third persons.   In the discussion of the police regulation of trades

§ 136

and employments, the regulation and prohibition of the sale of personal property, as a trade or occupation, have been discussed at length ;[1] and, inasmuch as all such regulations are designed to control the sale of merchandise, as a trade, they are considered and criticised in the character of restraints upon the liberty of exercising a lawful calling, rather than as an invasion of the rights of property. In the main, the same objections apply to a police regulation, whether it is considered to be an infringement of personal liberty or of the rights of property. It will, therefore, not be necessary to discuss all such regulations in detail in this place, as it would be hardly more than a repetition of what has already been written.[2] But in the application of the principles there set forth, as limiting the police regulation of employments and of the sale of personal property, a distinction should be drawn between the selling of personal property as a trade, and as a solitary or occasional exercise of a right of ownership. The sale of certain personal property, as a trade, may be liable to become harmful to the public, and for that reason may properly be subjected to police regulation ; whereas the mere act of selling the article of merchandise, independently of being the ordinary occupation of the seller, would contain no element of danger to the public, and therefore cannot be subjected to any police regulation whatever : and wherever the two acts can be separated, the regulation must be confined to those cases in which the selling, on account of its frequency, or of its connection with the sale of other similar articles of merchandise, assumes the character of a trade or occupation. Regulations for the prevention of fraud are, probably in every case, applicable to the unusual, as well as the ordinary, sale of personal property ; so that, for example, in order to make a valid sale, as against a second purchaser,

---

[1] See *ante*, chapter IX, and particularly §§ 89, 93, 95, 96, 101, 102, 103.

[2] See, especially, §§ 89, 102, 103.

§ 136

the possession must be delivered, independently of the frequency or infrequency of the act. But there are other cases of police regulation, which are designed to correct evils, which only arise in connection with the prosecution of a trade or occupation. Thus, for example, the sale of unwholesome food by a grocer may be prohibited altogether, in the course of his regular business, for his business is the sale of food for human consumption ; and the sale by him of unwholesome food to his regular customers will almost necessarily inflict injury on the public health. And so would the sale of such food be likely to prove harmful to the public, if it should be sold by any casual owner for the purpose of being used as an article of food. But if it were sold, independently of one's business as a vendor of human food, for some other lawful purpose, its sale could not be prohibited, for it contains no element of danger to the public health.

Conceding the position maintained in a previous section,[1] that the sale of liquor in saloons, to be drunk on the premises, is the only case of the sale of intoxicating liquors which may be prohibited ; and that the ground for the justification of prohibition in that case is the fact, that liquor saloons are the resort of all the more or less lawless elements of society, and consequently the public peace is endangered by their presence in the community ; it is easy to understand how the prohibition of liquor saloons may be justified, and yet the application of the prohibitory law to an unusual or single case of the sale of liquor, to be drunk on the premises, by one who is not a saloon keeper, may be resisted on constitutional grounds. The latter case could not threaten a disturbance of the public peace, any more than the intemperate use of liquor, in whatever way it may be procured, is likely to do so. The cases, in which this distinction would

[1] See *ante*, § 103.

§ 136

be likely to find application, are rare, and the subject need not be given any further attention.

§ 136*a*. **Laws regulating disposition of personal property by will.** — The right of disposing of one's property as one pleases, by transfer or conveyance *inter vivos*, is an indefeasible incident of the right of property in personalty. The transfer of real property may, under certain limitations, be restrained or prohibited according to the discretion of the legislature, since lands are acquired by grant from the State,[1] subject to the right of the State to determine the conditions and terms upon which they are to be held. But that cannot be done with personal property. Personal property is the product of man's labor, instead of being the free gift of nature, and one's right of property is derived from the exercise of dominion over the thing.

It is a part of that lawful dominion over the thing, that the owner has the right to sell or give it away. But the natural right of property, and consequently the natural right of disposition of it, lasts only as long as the natural dominion. When that control which one may claim in consequence of the actual or constructive possession of the thing ceases, the natural right of disposition ceases ; and if one has under the law any further control of the thing, it must rest upon positive law. It is, therefore, a legislative privilege, and can therefore be taken away by the same power which gave it. It will, therefore, be conceded that the right to dispose of personal property by will rests upon positive or statutory law, and is therefore subject to legislative regulation and prohibition without limitation. It is not disputed that such is the rule in respect to the disposition of lands by will,[2] for we know that the present right to devise lands depends upon the authority of the English

---

[1] See *ante*, § 119.
[2] See *ante*, § 119.

§ 136*a*

statute of wills, enacted in the reign of Henry VIII., or
of some American statute, designed to take the place of the
English statute; whereas the right to dispose of personalty
by testament comes down to us as a common-law right.[1]
But there can be no doubt that the right to bequeath personal property is as much the creature of positive law, as
the right to devise lands.   This was the position taken by
the Supreme Court of Ohio in a case, in which an act of the
legislature was sustained, which provided that a bequest,
by a testator leaving issue living, to any religious or charitable purpose shall be void, if made within twelve months
of the testator's death.   The enactment operated as a restraint upon the right to dispose of his personal property
by will.   In delivering its opinion, the court said : " We
hold that the right to acquire property implies the right to
dispose of it.   But the inalienable rights here declared, as
well as those implied, are possessed by living, not dead
men.   A disposition by will does not take effect during the
testator's life, but operates only after his death.   While
the right of testamentary disposition may be, as Mr. Redfield in his work on wills says, instinctive, it nevertheless
depends solely on municipal law, and has never been regarded as a natural or inalienable right.   It has always
been subject to the control of legislative power, and such
power is not limited in this State by a constitutional provision." [2]

§ 137.   **Involuntary alienation.** — It is true with personal,
as with real property, that as a general rule the property of
one man cannot by legislative enactment be taken away and
given to another.   Not only is this true in respect to known
and recognized owners of personal property, but it is also
true, where the property is not claimed by any visible or

---

[1] See 2 Bla. Com. 491, 492.
[2] Patton v. Patton, 39 Ohio St. 590.

known owner. Thus it was held in North Carolina to be unconstitutional for the State by statute to appropriate the unclaimed dividends of private corporations to public uses.[1] For the same reasons the legislative diversion of a bequest to a different use, than what was provided by the donor, was held to be unconstitutional, although in both cases the State was the beneficiary. The diversion was an interference with the reversionary interest of the donor's heirs.[2] But, notwithstanding this general rule, there are a few exceptional cases in which the State may lawfully dispose of one's personal property against his will. They are principally the same as have already been explained and justified in reference to the involuntary alienation of real property ;[3] and, the reasons for this exercise of police power being the same in both cases, there is no need for a repetition in this place. It seems to be very doubtful whether there is any room for the application of the principles of eminent domain to personal property. Mr. Cooley says that the State may, in the exercise of its eminent domain, appropriate to a public use private property of every description.[4] This is confounding the meaning of terms. Eminent domain means that superior and absolute right of property which the State, as the legal representative of organized society, has in the lands within its borders, and subordinate to which all private property therein is held. In cases of extreme public necessity, it is quite probable that the State may appropriate the personal property of the citizen on payment of its full value. At least this is the case in time of war. The governments of all civilized nations exercise this power of appropriation of personal property, in order to supply them-

---

[1] University of North Carolina v. N. C. R. R., 76 N. C. 103 (22 Am. Rep. 671).

[2] Trustees Brooks Academy v. George, 14 W. Va. 411 (35 Am. Rep. 760).

[3] See *ante*, § 120.

[4] Cooley Const. Lim. 649, 652, 653.

§ 137

selves with whatever is needful in the prosecution of the
war ; and the forcible and irregular seizure of property by
military commanders have been justified, when the necessity was urgent and such as will admit of no delay, and
where the civil authority would be too late in providing the
means required for the occasion.[1]   Not only does the State,
in time of war, appropriate whatever personal property they
may need for the prosecution of the war, as food or ammu-
nition or weapons of warfare, but it more frequently makes
forced loans of capital from its people by compelling them
to accept its treasury notes as legal tender in payment of
debts both public and private.[2]   And it is quite likely that
the State may, in any other case of extreme necessity, appropriate whatever of private property may be needful to
satisfy some urgent general want.   Suppose, for example,
in the case of a general failure of the crops, a famine should
occur, and those who did possess stocks of provisions refused to sell at any reasonable price, or refused to sell
at all, while people were brought to the extremity of star-
vation.   Could not the State compel those who had a
" corner " on the provision market to deliver up their property for the public good, on payment of a reasonable price?
Every one has a right to put whatever price on his goods his
judgment, his cupidity, or other feeling, may prompt, and the
State cannot ordinarily regulate the price of commodities.[3]
But when the public want of food becomes so great, that
the failure to satisfy it will be sure to give rise to serious
disturbances of the public peace and the violent appropriation of the food that is denied them, it is idle to speak of the
sacredness of private property.   It cannot be doubted that
an official appropriation of articles of food, under circumstances of such urgent necessity, would be judicially justi-

---

[1] Farmer *v.* Lewis, 1 Bush (Ky.), 66. See Harmony *v.* Mitchell, 1
Blatchf. 549; Mitchell *v.* Harmony, 13 How. 115.

[2] See *ante,* § 90.

[3] See *ante,* § 95.

§ 137

fied on the plea of necessity, however illogical it may seem. But all other means of satisfying the public hunger must first have been exhausted, before the selfish proprietor of the scarce articles of food may be forcibly subjected to instruction in the graces of Christian charity.[1]

§ 138. **Control of property by guardian.** — The control of the ward's property is so common an authority of the guardian, that it is altogether unnecessary to refer to cases in support of the constitutionality of a law which invests the guardian with this control over the property of the infant ward. The helplessness of the minor, and his inability to manage his property in a careful manner, resulting from his immaturity, constitute sufficient reasons for taking from him the control of his property. The powers of the guardian are dependent upon the provisions of the law, and are constantly subject to legislative regulation and change. The common law gave to the guardian of a minor the power to manage his real estate, lease it and collect the rents, make repairs, etc., but he had not the power to make a sale of it in fee, without an order from a court of equity. And this is the general rule, in this country, at the present day.[2] But the guardian has, in the absence of statutes to the contrary, the ordinary power of selling and disposing of the personal property of the minor, whenever he should deem it advisable to do so.[3] And it seems that, after a guardian has been appointed and has taken charge of the ward's estate, he acquires such a vested interest in the property during the guardianship, that a law would be unconstitutional, because it deprived him of a vested right, which provided for the sale of the minor's property by another, even though the other person be the mother of the ward.[4]

[1] As to the sale of estrays, see *post*, § 141.
[2] See Schouler Dom. Rel. 480–487.
[3] See Schouler Dom. Rel. 461–479.
[4] Lincoln *v.* Alexander, 52 Cal. 482 (28 Am. Rep. 639).

§ 138

Not only is it a legitimate exercise of police power to place the control of a minor's property in the hands of a guardian; but it is equally competent to place under guardianship the person and property of all other persons, who from any cause may become unable to take care of themselves. There can be no doubt of the power to treat the insane in this manner. And it has been held to be competent, in the exercise of the police power, to place habitual drunkards under guardianship. The assumption by the guardian of the control of the property of the drunkard would not be an unlawful deprivation of property. The derangement of mind, resulting from habitual drinking, would place him in the same category with the ordinary insane.[1] The claim has also been made that the property of spendthrifts may be taken from them and placed under the control of a guardian or curator.[2] But it would appear to be a very difficult matter to determine just what degree of extravagance will make the possessor of property a spendthrift. And before that difficulty could be overcome, it would be necessary to determine what makes one a spendthrift. Webster defines a spendthrift to be "one who spends money profusely or improvidently." If that be taken as a correct definition, it would be difficult to discover in it the element which would justify this exercise of police power. If it be established that his improvident expenditures are the acts of a deranged mind, then he could lawfully be placed under guardianship, on the ground that he is suffering from a form of dementia. But if a perfectly sane man chooses to spend a fortune in high living; prefers the pleasures of a riotous life, with poverty in advanced years, to an equable and moderate expenditure of his income, with the enjoyment of ease and comfort through life, and a proper provision for his heirs; who can lawfully hinder him

[1] Wadsworth v. Sharpsteen, 8 N. Y. 388· Imhoff v. Whitmer, 21 Pa. St. 243; Devin v. Scott, 34 Ind. 67.
[2] See Schouler Dom. Rel. 404.

§ 138

from making the choice? A man can do what he please
with his own property, provided he does not interfere with
or transgress some vested right of another. He may, like
Raphael Aben Ezra, give away his entire fortune, and become a beggar and a wanderer upon the face of the earth ;
and no one in a free State dare deny him that privilege.
And what he could give away, without receiving any equiv-
lent therefor, he may dispose of in riotous living.

§ 139. **Destruction of personal property on account
of illegal use.**[1] — In a variety of cases, it has been provided, as a penalty for the infraction of the law, that the
implements used in the prosecution of an unlawful trade, or
in the doing of an illegal act, shall be seized and destroyed.
It is a most common provision in the laws for the regulation and prohibition of the sale of intoxicating liquors.[2]
The same provision has been made to apply to nets
and other implements employed in illegal fishing ;[3] so also
in respect to the stock in trade of a gambler.[4] But in all
of these cases the seizure and destruction must rest upon a
judgment of forfeiture, procured at the close of an ordinary trial, in which the owner of the property has had a full
opportunity to be heard in defense of his property.[5] Conceding in every case the illegality of the use to which the
property has been put, the constitutionality of the statute
cannot be questioned, when the proper hearing is provided
for before condemnation.

[1] In respect to the destruction of domestic animals for being nuisances, see *post*, § 141.

[2] State *v.* Miller, 48 Me. 576; State *v.* Snow, 3 R. I. 54; Greene *v.*
James, 2 Curt. 187.

[3] Jeck *v.* Anderson, 57 Cal. 251 (40 Am. Rep. 115); Weller *v.* Snover,
42 N. J. L. (13 Vroom) 341.

[4] Lowry *v.* Rainwater, 70 Mo. 152 (35 Am. Rep. 420).

[5] Greene *v.* James, 2 Curt. 187; Jeck *v.* Anderson, 57 Cal. 251 (40 Am.
Rep. 115); Lowry *v.* Rainwater, 70 Mo. 152 (35 Am. Rep. 420).

§ 139

SECTION.   140. Laws regulating the use of personal property.
140a. Prohibition of possession of certain property.
140b. Regulation and prohibition of the manufacture of certain property.
140c. Carrying of concealed weapons prohibited.
140d. Miscellaneous regulations of the use of personal property.

§ 140. **Laws regulating the use of personal property.**— While personal property is protected by constitutional limitations against all unnecessary interference and regulation, it is a standard rule of police power that one must not make such a use of his property as to injure another ; and consequently the use and enjoyment of personal property may be subjected to such police regulations as may be necessary to prevent any threatened injury to the public. The proof of the existence of a threatened injury, and of the appropriateness of the proposed regulation as a remedy, will always justify the interference. Its efficacy is not a matter for judicial consideration. Laws for the regulation of the use of personal property may be as varied as the uses to which such property can be put; and it is only possible to a refer to few exemplary cases, which have come up before the courts for construction.

§ 140a. **Prohibition of possession of certain property.**— In the first place, the very possession of personal property, coupled with an intent proven or presumed, may be such a public evil as to justify the prohibition of such a possession. Thus, a Rhode Island statute forbade the possession, with intent to sell or exchange, of adulterated milk, and it was declared to be constitutional.[1] But the unlawful intent would, in such a case, have to be proven. Without this intent, the possession of the adulterated milk neither produces nor threatens any harm to the public; and since adulterated milk may be put to some other use, which is not, and cannot,

[1] State v. Smyth, 14 R. I. 100 (51 Am. Rep. 344).

§ 140a

be prohibited, the unlawful intent to sell cannot be presumed
from the mere possession.   But it is different when the
thing cannot be put to any unobjectionable use.   In such a
case the thing cannot be presumed to be of any value to its
owner except on the hypothesis ; that he intends to make
this injurious use of it, and hence the wrongful intent may
be presumed from the act of the possession.   Thus the
constitutionality of a statute was sustained which imposed
a penalty upon any one who should have in his possession
any dead game in certain seasons of the year.[1]

§ 140b. Regulation and prohibition of manufacture of
certain property. — As a general proposition, it can hardly
be doubted that one has a constitutional right to change
the form and condition of his personal property to whatever extent he may see fit ; and he may make a business of
manufacturing a given article, provided he does not
threaten the public with any injury.   And it may be safely
stated that the manufacture of no useful article may be
prohibited altogether.   If the article can be put to a lawful
and rightful use, it matters not how likely it will be used
in a way harmful to the public, the right to manufacture
it cannot be prohibited altogether.   As has been already
explained, in setting forth the various regulations that may
be applied to trades and occupations,[2] the manufacture
of the article may be subjected to whatever regulations
may be necessary to guard the public against injury in the
process of manufacture, or afterwards in a wrongful use of it.
Those who engage in its manufacture may be required to
submit to a certain examination, in order to ascertain their
fitness for the business, and to take out a license, if the manufacture requires such regulations.   And if the danger to the
public of a wrongful and illegitimate use of the manufac-

[1] Phelps v. Racey, 60 N. Y. 10 (19 Am. Rep. 140).
[2] See ante §§ 89, 101–105.

§ 140b

tured article be so imminent as to call for such legislation, as seems very likely to happen with reference to the manufacture of dynamite, nitro-glycerine, and other like explosive compounds, the manufacture of it for the purpose of sale, that is, as a business, may be prohibited to all but a few licensed manufacturers or the agents of the State. But if, in the actual manufacture of the thing, without police supervision, as in the case of dynamite, there is no danger to the public, the fact that it can be put to a wrongful use will not justify legislation which prohibits the owner of the raw material to manufacture the article which he does not intend to sell, but to make use of in a legitimate way. The manufacture of dynamite may be prohibited, as a business, to all but licensed manufacturers, because his intention to sell makes it very likely or at least possible that the identical stuff will be employed in some unlawful way. But when one manufactures it for his own lawful use, he has done nothing to disturb the public safety.

The regulations concerning the manufacture of metallic money are of this character of police regulations. It is true, that the sole power of coining money is given by the United States constitution to the national government.[1] But, except as a restriction upon the power of the States, the constitutional provision was not necessary. It certainly was not needed to authorize the prohibition of the manufacture of metallic money by the individual. For whatever scientific objections may be made to such regulations by sociological writers, it cannot be denied that the free and indiscriminate coinage would lead to the perpetration of many frauds of those who are least able to discover them. For this reason the government reserves to itself the right to coin money, and punishes severely any counterfeiting of the coins of this and any other country.[2] Not

[1] U. S. Const.
[2] See U. S. Rev. Statutes, §§ 5457, 5458. See *post*, § 206.

§ 140*b*

only this, but it is also prohibited to any one to manufacture for distribution, as an advertisement, or for any otherwise lawful purpose, any metallic pieces with shape and impressions so resembling the shape and impressions of money coins, that there is danger that they may be made the means of practicing frauds upon the unwary.[1]

But in all these cases it is a judicial question whether the manufactured article is calculated to prove an instrument of trespass on the rights of other, and the prohibition of its manufacture can only be justified by an affirmative answer to this inquiry. The absolute prohibition of the manufacture of intoxicating liquors can only be justified by proof of the fact that intoxicating liquors cannot be put to some beneficial use. This is conceded to be false by all, whatever may be their other views on legislation in aid of temperance, and most of the present legislation permit its manufacture and sale for medicinal and mechanical purposes. If the position of temperance reformers, that the use of intoxicating liquors as a beverage is a wrong or trespass on society, cannot be successfully assailed, then the constitutionality of a law, which prohibited the manufacture of it except by certain licensed manufacturers, or by the State officers, could not be questioned. Although it would be unreasonable to confine its manufacture to licensed agents of the State, merely for the purpose of preventing the sale to habitual drunkards, lunatics and minors — great as that evil is, the number of such purchasers does not bear comparison with the immense number of those who buy and use it in moderation; — still the constitutionality of the regulation could not be attacked, for the necessity of the legislation is a legislative and not a judicial question.[2]

§ 140c. **Carrying of concealed weapons prohibited.** —

---

[1] See U. S. Rev. Stat. § 5462.
[2] See *ante*, § 103, for a general discussion of the prohibition of the liquor trade.

§ 140c

For the purpose of preventing or reducing the number of street affrays, which, it is claimed, the habit of carrying concealed weapons increases to a most alarming frequency, in most of the States there are now statutes in force, prohibiting the carrying of concealed weapons. Apart from a provision of the constitutions of the United States, and of the several States, which guarantees to every citizen the right to bear arms, there cannot be any serious constitutional objection raised to this regulation. It cannot be questioned that the habit of carrying concealed weapons tends to engender strife, for the very act indicates the expectation of a possible use for the weapons. The prohibition of carrying concealed weapons is, therefore, an appropriate remedy for the suppression of street affrays. The American constitutions guarantee to every citizen the right to possess and bear arms, in time of peace as well as in war; and no binding law can be passed by Congress or by a State legislature, prohibiting altogether the carrying of weapons of warfare. But the law against the carrying of concealed weapons is not a total prohibition. It is only a reasonable regulation, established to prevent a serious injury to the public in the enjoyment of this constitutional right. It only prohibits the carrying of *concealed* weapons, and does not interfere with any other mode of carrying them. It is the concealment which is calculated to produce harm to the public. Any one, carrying a weapon for a laudable purpose, will not desire to conceal it. The law against the carrying of concealed weapons has in many cases been declared to be constitutional.[1]

---

[1] Munn *v.* State, 1 Ga. 243; Aymette *v.* State, 2 Humph. 154; State *v.* Buzzard, 4 Ark. 18; State *v.* Reid, 1 Ala. 612; State *v.* Mitchell, 3 Blackf. 229; State *v* Jumel, 13 La. Ann. 399; State *v.* Smith, 11 La. Ann. 633; English *v.* State, 35 Tex. 472 (14 Am. Rep. 374); State *v.* Wilforth, 74 Mo. 528 (41 Am. Rep. 330). In Haile *v.* State, 38 Ark. 564 (42 Am. Rep. 3), a statute was held to be constitutional which prohibited the carrying of army pistols, unless uncovered and in the hand.

§ 121c

§ 140*d*. **Miscellaneous regulations of the use of personal property.** — In Missouri, a municipal ordinance conferred upon one person the right to remove and appropriate all carcasses of animals found in the city and not slain for food, to the exclusion of the owner. The statute was subjected to judicial construction, and it was held to be unconstitutional, so far as it applied to carcasses, which have not become a nuisance, although not slain for use as food.[1] As long as the carcasses of animals are not a nuisance to the public, because of their effect upon the public health, they are as much protected by constitutional guaranties, as the live animals.

The agricultural communities of the South suffer greatly from the depredations of thieves on the unharvested crop, and particularly from the stealing of cotton. As a means of checking this pillage, a statute was enacted in Alabama, which made it unlawful " for any person to transport or move after sunset and before sunrise of the succeeding day," within certain counties. " any cotton in the seed," but permitted the owner or producer to remove it from the field to the place of storage. This was held to be a reasonable police regulation, and not an unconstitutional interference with the rights of private property.[2] It is a rather peculiar regulation, and may possibly be open to scientific objection, but it is no doubt constitutional. It is made in the interest of the farmer ; and since the statute reserves to the owner or producer the right to remove the cotton after nightfall from the field to a place of storage, the regulation may be considered as being confined to the prohibition of all trading or dealing in cotton after sunset and before sunrise, and does not interfere with any other harmless use of it by the owner.

---

[1] River Rendering Company *v.* Behr, 77 Mo. 91 (46 Am. Rep. 6).
[2] Davis *v.* State, 68 Ala. 58 (44 Am. Rep. 128).

§ 140*d*

SECTION 141. — Laws regulating use and keeping of domestic animals.
141a. — Keeping of dogs.
141b. — Laws for the prevention of cruelty to animals.

§ 141. **Laws regulating use and keeping of domestic animals.** — The common law has always recognized a right of property in domestic and domesticated animals, the keeping of which serves some useful purpose, such as cows, sheep, fowls, horses, oxen, etc. ; and now a certain right of property is recognized in every species of animal, which may be subjected to the control of man, whether they retain their wild nature, or whether it is completely subdued. The only difference between the right of property in a cow or other completely domesticated animal and in some wild or half-tamed beast, is the degree of care required in the keeping of them, in order to prevent injury to the public. For the common law required the owner of every kind of animal to so guard and keep him, as that no injury should result to another ; and gave to the one injured a right of action for damages against the owner of the animal, if he had not exercised that degree of care which in ordinary cases may be required to avert an injury to others.[1] Thoroughly domesticated animals, such as cattle, sheep, swine, and the like, which may reasonably be presumed to exhibit no vicious propensity, are at common law permitted to go at large, and the owner is only responsible for damages when he permits the animal to go at large, when he knows of his vicious propensity. For without such knowledge, he could not have anticipated any injury to others, and he was therefore guilty of no negligence.[2] But all animals, whether tame or wild, are liable in quest of food to trespass upon the lands adjoining the highway ; and the owner of an animal incurred at common law a liability for all trespasses made by animals which he

[1] Cooley on Torts, 348–350.
[2] Cooley on Torts, p. 341–348, and cases there cited.

§ 141

allowed to go upon the highway unattended.[1] But if one is driving cattle through the highway, as one has a right to do, independently of statute, and one of the animals should get away from the herd, and trespass upon the adjoining land ; if he has exercised all the care that may be expected, under the circumstances, from a reasonably prudent man, the owner of the land cannot recover of him for the damage. It is a case of *damnum absque injuria.*[2]

Respect for public decency would require the owners of stallions and bulls to keep them carefully housed, and the law may very properly prohibit the keeping and exhibition of them in public places.[3]

This is a summary statement of the common-law rights of property in animals and their attendant duties. But of course these may be subjected to further statutory regulation, and they have been. In every State the keeping of live stock is under police regulation. In some communities the common-law rule still prevails, that the owners of stock are liable for all trespasses of their stock upon the lands of others, although there is no enclosure about the land, where they allow their stock to roam at large. In other communities the owners of lands are required to maintain enclosures that will be an effective barrier to all trespasses of stock, and a right of action is given for only those trespasses which occur in spite of the enclosure. The clash of interest between stock-raising and farming calls for the interference of the State by the institution of police regulations; and whether the regulations shall subordinate the stock-raising interest to that of farming or *vice versa,* in the case of an irreconcilable difference, as is the case with respect to the going-at-large of cattle, is a matter for the legislative discretion, and is not a judicial question. In the exercise of this general power of control over the keeping of live

---

[1] Cooley on Torts, and cases there cited.
[2] Cooley on Torts, 341.
[3] Nolin *v.* Franklin, 4 Yerg. 163.

§ 141

stock, the State or municipal corporation may prohibit altogether the running at large of such animals, and compel the owners to keep them within their own enclosures; and provide as a remedy for enforcing the law that the animals found astray shall be sold, after proper notice to the owner, and time allowed for redemption, paying over to the owner the proceeds of sale, after deducting what is due to the State in the shape of penalty.[1]

§ 141a. **Keeping of dogs.** — Laws for the regulation of the keeping of dogs are very much more common than the regulation of property in any other kind of domestic animals, and deserve special consideration. The right of property in a dog, although supposed at common law to be less valuable, and consequently less deserving of legal protection, has always been recognized. But in consequence of the tendency to be vicious, the dog's life has always been somewhat precarious. No one at common law has a right to kill a dog that is doing no harm, and has exhibited no vicious propensities, even though he may be trespassing upon another's land.[2] But not only may one kill any animal *damage feasant*, if it be necessary for the protection of life and property;[3] but also where a ferocious dog, addicted to biting mankind, is suffered to run at large unmuzzled, it is a common nuisance, and any person may kill it, independently of statute; and independently of the question whether it was doing or threatening mischief at the time of the killing, or whether the owner had notice of its disposition.[4] But no one has, independently of statute, a

[1] Campen v. Langley, 39 Mich. 451 (33 Am. Rep. 414); Wilcox v. Hemming, 58 Wis. 144 (46 Am. Rep. 625); Rockwell v. Nearing, 35 N. Y. 302; Campbell v. Evans, 45 N. Y. 356; Cook v. Gregg, 46 N. Y. 439; Varden v. Mount, 78 Ky. 86 (39 Am. Rep. 208); Roberts v. Ogle, 38 Ill. 459.

[2] Brent v. Kimball, 60 Ill. 21 (14 Am. Rep. 35); Matthew v. Fiestel, 3 E. D. Smith, 90; Dodson v. Moch, 4 Dev. & B. L. 146.

[3] Aldrich v. Wright, 53 N. H. 398.

[4] Putnam v. Payne, 13 Johns. 312; Maxwell v. Palmerton, 21 Wend.

§ 141a

right to kill a fierce or dangerous dog, if it is kept on the
owner's premises and not allowed to go at large.[1]

But the duties of the owners of dogs may be and are
frequently changed by statute. The following lengthy
quotation from an opinion of the Supreme Court of Massachusetts, gives an interesting account of the "dog" legislation in that State, and will serve as an index of similar
legislation in other States. It is given in full, because
neighborly disputes over dogs are a frequent source of bad
feeling and expensive litigation :—

"There is no kind of property over which the exercise of
this power (of police regulation) is more frequent or necessary than that which is the subject of the present action.
In regard to the ownership of live animals, the law has long
made a distinction between dogs and cats and other domestic
quadrupeds, growing out of the nature of the creatures
and the purpose for which they are kept. Beasts which
have been thoroughly tamed, and are used for burden or
husbandry, or for food, such as horses, cattle and sheep, are
as truly property of intrinsic value and entitled to the same
protection as any kind of goods. But dogs and cats, even
in a state of domestication, never wholly lose their wild
nature and destructive instincts, and are kept either for
uses which depend on retaining and calling into action those
very natures and instincts, or else for the mere whim or
pleasure of the owner; and, therefore, although a man
might have such a right of property in a dog as to maintain
trespass or trover for unlawfully taking or destroying it,
yet he was held, in the phrase of the books, to have
'no absolute and valuable property' therein which could
be the subject of a prosecution for larceny at common

407; Dunlap v. Synder, 17 Barb. 561; People v. Board of Police, 15 Abb.
Pr. 167; Brown v. Carpenter, 26 Vt. 638; Woolf v. Chalker, 31 Conn.
121.

[1] Perry v. Phipps, 10 Ired. L. 259.

§ 141a

law, or even, according to some authorities, of an action of detinue or replevin, or a distress for rent, or which could make him responsible for the trespasses of his dog on the lands of other persons, as he would be for the trespasses of his cattle.[1] And dogs have always been held by the American courts to be entitled to less legal regard and protection than more harmless and useful domestic animals.[2]

" The damages sought to be prevented by the dog laws of the commonwealth, as declared in the preambles to the earlier ones, are sudden assaults upon persons, worrying, wounding and killing of neat cattle, sheep and lambs, ' distressing evils from canine madness' and other injuries occasioned by dogs. These statutes, which have been the subject of repeated consideration and revision by the legislature, with a view of securing these objects, and of affording means for ascertaining the owners and making them liable for the mischievous acts of their dogs, have accordingly not only provided that any person might kill a dog assaulting him, or attacking cattle or sheep, out of its owner's enclosure ; and that the owner should be responsible, in either single, double, or treble damages, for mischief committed by his dog ; but have also declared that it should be lawful to kill any dog, as to which the requirements of law had not been complied with under circumstances which have varied in successive statutes. At first it was only any dog ' found strolling out of the inclosure or immediate care of its owner,' after due notice to him that it was suspected of being dangerous or mischievous ; then ' not having a collar and certified ' to the assessor; and, by later statutes, ' any dog found going at large, not wearing a

---

[1] Vin. Abr. Trespass Z; Replevin A; 2 Bla. Com. 193; 3 Bla. Com. 7; 4 Bla. Com. 234, 235; Milton v. Faudrye, Pop. 116; s. c. nom. Millen v. Fawer, Bendl. 171; Mason v. Keeling, 1 Ld. Raym. 608; s. c. 12 Mod. 336; Read v. Edwards, 17 C. B. (N. S.) 245; Regina v. Robinson, 8 Cox Crim. Cas. 115.

[2] Putnam v. Payne, 13 Johns. 312; Brown v. Carpenter, 26 Vt. 638; Woolf v. Chalker, 31 Conn. 121.

§ 141a

collar; ' ' found and being without a collar ;' ' being without a collar ; ' ' going at large, and not registered in the town clerk's office, or the tax on which had not been paid ; ' ' going at large and not licensed and collared ;' or, finally, all dogs, not licensed and collared, as required by statute, ' whenever and wherever found.' For the last ten years the statutes have also declared it to be the duty of certain public officers to cause such dogs to be destroyed under the circumstances pointed out ; and have given a remedy against the town or country for any injury done by dogs to other domestic animals.

" These statutes have been administered by the courts according to the fair construction of their terms, and without a doubt of their constitutionality. Under the statute of 1812, chapter 146, which required the owner or keeper of any dog to put a collar about its neck, to be constantly worn, with the name and residence of the owner marked thereon, and declared it to be lawful to kill any dog ' found and being without a collar as aforesaid ' (omitting the qualifications of other statutes, of ' going at large ' or ' out of the immediate care of its owner '), it was held that no action could be maintained for killing a dog without such a collar, out of his owner's inclosure, although under his immediate care ; Chief Justice Shaw saying: ' We think it was the intention of the legislature not to give the owner of a dog a right to maintain an action for destroying him, unless he had, in fact, given that security to the public which the act required.' [1] And a person who, instead of killing a dog being without a collar, converted him to his own use, was held liable to the owner in trover, because in the words of Chief Justice Shaw: ' The object of the statute is, not to confer a benefit on an individual, but to rid society of a nuisance by killing the dog.' [2] Similiar statutes have been

---

[1] Tower v. Tower, 18 Pick. 262.

[2] Cummings v. Perham, 1 Met. 555.

§ 121a

held in other States to be reasonable and constitutional regulations of police.[1] The statute under which this defendant justifies provides that the mayor of cities and chairmen of selectmen of towns, shall within ten days from the first day of July, annually, ' issue a warrant to one or more police officers or constables, directing them to proceed forthwith either to kill or cause to be killed all dogs within their respective cities or towns, not licensed and collared according to the provisions of this act, and to enter complaint against the owners or keepers thereof; and any person may, and every police officer and constable shall, kill or cause ' to be killed all such dogs, whenever and wherever found.' [2] The warrant here provided for, being general in its form, not founded on oath, nor containing any special designation of object, is not indeed a legal warrant of search and seizure; it is rather an appointment of the officer who is to be specially charged with the duty of executing the authority conferred by the statute. The statute makes it the duty of every police officer and constable to kill or caused to be killed, all dogs not licensed and collared according to its provisions, ' whenever and wherever found.' There are no express restrictions of time or place, and no limitation, as in earlier statutes, to dogs going at large, or out of the owner's enclosure or his immediate care. Any restrictions upon the authority of the officer arise by implication, from regard to the sanctity of the dwelling house or the danger of a breach of the peace. But it is unnecessary in the present cases very closely to consider the extent of such restrictions, if any, which are to be implied upon the power and duty of the officer to abate what the law has declared to be in substance and effect a public nuisance. The regulations imposed by the statute upon the ownership and keeping of dogs are reason-

[1] Morey v. Brown, 42 N. H. 373; Carter v. Dow, 16 Wis. 298.
[2] Statutes 1867, ch. 130, § 7.

§ 141a

able and easy to be complied with. If any dog is an object of value or of affection to its owner, he has only to procure and record a license and put on a collar, in order to bring it under the protection of the law.

" It is agreed that neither of these plaintiffs had complied with the statute in these respects, and there is nothing in the facts agreed in either of the cases from which it can be inferred that the defendant committed any trespass upon the plaintiff's premises, or any act tending to a breach of the peace. Under the defendant's authority and duty to kill or cause to be killed all dogs not licensed and collared, ' whenever and wherever found,' he had clearly a right peaceably to enter for that purpose, without permission, upon the close of the owner or keeper of such a dog, and there kill it." [1]

Regulations of this general character are to be found in very many, if not most, of the States. In Georgia and New Hampshire, the constitutionality of laws has been sustained, which authorized the killing of all dogs without a collar.[2] And it has frequently been held lawful for the State, as an encouragement for the rearing of sheep, to discourage the keeping of dogs by the requirement of a license fee for each dog.[3] And, conceding the right of the State to require a license fee for the keeping of a dog, which is intended to operate as a check upon the keeping of dogs, the amount of the license is not open to judicial revision. It cannot be confined by judicial intervention to the mere expense of issuing the license. In order to operate as a restraint upon the keeping of dogs, the amount of the license must be large enough to make it burdensome to keep

---

[1] Blair v. Forehand, 100 Mass. 136 (1 Am. Rep. 94).

[2] Morey v. Brown, 42 N. H. 373; Cranston v. Mayor of Augusta, 61 Ga. 572.

[3] Mitchell v. Williams, 27 Ind. 62; Carter v. Dow, 16 Wis. 298; Tenney v. Lenz, 16 Wis. 566; State v. Cornwall, 27 Ind. 62;Holts v. Roe, S. C. Ohio, 5 Ohio Law J. 605.

§ 141a

·dogs, and, as has been fully explained in connection with the discussion of licenses in general,[1] the imposition of such licenses, as a restraint upon the doing of some thing which inflicts or threatens to inflict injury on the public, is free from all constitutional objections.[2]

In many of the States compensation is given by statute to the owners of the sheep killed by dogs, and a summary proceeding is usually provided for recovering damages from the owner of the dog. But in order to be constitutional, the act must provide for a judicial examination of the wrong done and the damage suffered, with a full opportunity for the owner of the dog to be heard. In New Hampshire a statute of this kind was declared to be unconstitutional so far as it undertook to bind the owner of the dog by the amount of damages, which had been fixed by the selectmen of the town without giving him an opportunity to be heard on the question of damages.[3]

§ 141*b*. **Laws for the prevention of cruelty to animals.** — From a scientific standpoint, perhaps the most curious phase of the exercise of police power is embodied in the laws for the prevention of cruelty to animals. These laws now prevail very generally throughout the United

---

[1] See *ante*, § 101.

[2] " We cannot assent to the position taken by appellant, that if the sum required for a license exceeds the expense of issuing, the act transcends the licensing power and imposes a tax. By such a theory the police power would be shorn of all its efficiency. The exercise of that power is based upon the idea that the business licensed or kind of property regulated, is liable to work mischief, and therefore needs restraints, which shall operate as a protection to the public. For this purpose the license money is required to be paid. But if it could not exceed the mere expense of issuing the license, its object would fail altogether. * * * We have no doubt, therefore, that the legislature may, in regulating any matter that is a proper subject of police power, impose such sums for licenses as will operate as partial restrictions upon the business, or upon the keeping of particular kinds of property." Tenney *v.* Lenz, 16 Wis. 567.

[3] East Kingston *v.* Towle, 48 N. H. 57 (2 Am. Rep. 170).

§ 141*b*

States, and public sentiment is in most communities unusually active in its support, and is not restrained by any difficulty in finding a scientific justification for the law.   The enactment and enforcement of the law are prompted by a tender sympathy for the dumb brutes, who while serving human ends are being subjected to cruelty.   These statutes are designed, as the language of the statutes expressly indicates, for the prevention of cruelty to animals.   Whose rights are protected by the enactment?   Those of the animals?   Are animals, other than human beings, recognized as the subjects of rights?   Cruelty to animals might be claimed as an offense against public morality and the public sense of mercy. But that is in the nature of an afterthought, suggested as an escape from the logical dilemma, with which one is otherwise confronted in the consideration of these laws.   Whatever may be said to the contrary, in the enactment of these laws, there is an unconscious, if not admitted, recognition of legal rights in the dumb animals, who are subjected to man's dominion.   They are by such legislation placed in the same legal relation to the freeman as the slave was in the days of slavery.   Both are the property of the freeman; the master's power of control was limited only by just such laws, as the one now under consideration, which were designed to prevent cruelty in their treatment.   It is the torture to the animal that is prohibited, wherever it was done.[1]   If the law was considered and justified merely as the prohibition of an offense against the public sense of mercy,   and involved no recognition of rights in the dumb animals, the operation of the law would have to be confined to public acts of cruelty, such as unmerciful beating on the streets and other thoroughfares.   But it is plain that the ordinary law for the prevention of cruelty to animals is broken as much by cruel treatment in the stable as in the public highway; whether done in the presence of a large assembly,

[1] See State v. Pugh, 15 Mo. 509.

§ 141b

as in the cock-pit, or with no others present than the person whose anger or pure maliciousness induces the act of cruelty. The animals so protected must be recognized as subjects of legal rights. And why should they not be so recognized? Is it not self-conceit for man to claim that he alone, of all God's creatures, is the possessor of inalienable rights?

§ 142. **Regulation of contracts and rights of action.** The validity of an ordinary contract cannot be impaired by State legislation, for it is protected from such an attack by an express provision of the Federal constitution.[1] Any law, therefore, which changes the character of the obligation, either by diminishing or increasing its burden, is void because it impairs the obligation.[2] The obligation of the contract, which is thus protected from impairment, is civil and not moral; that is, the law must be legal, according to the provisions of the law in force when the contract was made, in order that it may claim this protection. An illegal contract creates or supports no rights, in short, has no legal existence.[3] It will not be necessary to explain in this place

---

[1] "No State shall pass any law impairing the obligation of a contract." U. S. Const., art. I, § 10.

[2] Douglass v. Pike Co., 101 U. S. 677; McCracken v. Hayward, 2 How. 608, 612; Ogden v. Saunders, 12 Wheat. 213; People v. Ingersoll, 58 N. Y.; Goggans v. Turnipseed, 1 S. C. 40 (7 Am. Rep. 23); Stein v. Mobile, 49 Ala. 362 (20 Am. Rep. 283); Van Baumback v. Bade, 9 Wis. 559. And the constitutional prohibition applies to changes in the State constitutions as well as to amendments of the statutes. White v. Hart, 13 Wall. 646; Osborn v. Nicholson, 13 Ark. 654; Oliver v. Memphis, etc., R. R. Co., 30 Ark. 128; Jacoway v. Denton, 25 Ark. 641.

[3] "It is the civil obligation which [the constitution] is designed to reach; that is, the obligation which is recognized by, and results from, the law of the State in which it is made. If, therefore, a contract when made is by the law of the place declared to be illegal, or deemed to be a nullity, or a *nude pact*, it has no civil obligation; because the law in such cases forbids its having any binding efficacy or force. It confers no legal right on the one party, and no corresponding legal duty on the other. There is no means allowed or recognized to enforce it; for the maxim is *ex nudo pacto non oritur actio*. But when it does not fall within the pre-

§ 142

how far laws may be enacted for the regulation of subsequent contracts, for this matter has been fully discussed in another connection.[1] Nor is it necessary or appropriate to explain here in detail what is included under the term " contract," in the sense in which the word is used in the constitutional provision referred to.[2] The term contract is here employed in the sense of " executory contract," an agreement between two or more, for a valuable consideration, to do or give something.

The constitutional provision against impairing the obligation of contracts is held to be binding only upon the States. But there can be no doubt that similar action by Congress would likewise be unconstitutional, because it would deprive one of his property without due process of law.[3]

All rights of every description may be violated, and inasmuch as the law prohibits the individual from redressing his own wrong, he is entitled to an appropriate action in the law courts of the country. A denial of this right of action would be as much an interference with the right that has been violated, as the original trespass was. If the violated right is a broken contract, an absolute refusal of all remedy would impair the obligation of a contract in a constitutional sense, and the law taking away all remedies would be void.[4] For a like reason, a law, which would take away all remedies for the violations of other rights, whether of persons or of property, would ap-

dicament of being either illegal or void, its obligatory force is co-extensive with its stipulations." Story on Constitution, § 1380.

[1] See ante, §§ 90, 93–100.

[2] For a discussion of this subject see Cooley Const. Lim., pp. 331–346· Whether the character of corporations fall properly within the meaning and scope of this provision, see post, § 188.

[3] See ante § 93.

[4] Osborne v. Nicholson, 13 Wall. 662; Call v. Hagger, 8 Mass. 430; Penrose v. Erie Canal Co., 56 Pa. St. 46; Thompson v. Commonwealth, 81 Pa. St. 314; West v. Sansom, 44 Ga. 295; Rison v. Farr, 24 Ark. 161; Griffin v. Wilcox, 21 Ind. 370; McFarland v. Butler, 8 Minn. 116; Jackson v. Butler, 8 Minn. 117.

§ 142

pear to violate the legal sanctity of the substantive right. If it be a right of property that has been transgressed, the deprivation of the right of action would be an interference with vested rights ; and so also would it be an infringement of one's personal security, if a right of action was denied for a trespass upon one's person or liberty. But it has been held by the United States Supreme Court that a constitutional convention of a State may take away existing rights of action, provided the obligation of a contract is not impaired, or a punishment inflicted.[1] There is certainly no express provision of the constitution which protects these rights of action from interference by legislation; but it would seem to us that the constitution protects from undue interference the right to resort to the courts for redress of one's wrongs, as much as it does the right to pursue a harmless occupation. They are equally essential to the pursuit of happiness. It would be an act of tyranny for a government to deny the right to redress one's own wrongs, and at the same time to refuse an appropriate remedy. It is probable that the Supreme Court would have decided differently, if the constitutional provision under consider ation had had reference to other rights of action than those growing out of the conflict of war.

But as long as a substantial remedy is provided, the character of it may be changed at the pleasure of the legislature; and when it applies to the enforcement of a contract, such a change, however material, will not be considered to impair the obligation of a contract, even though the change is to a less desirable or convenient remedy.[2] The most radical

---

[1] Drehman *v.* Stifel, 41 Mo. 184; *s. c.* 8 Wall. 595. See Hess *v.* Johnson, 3 W. Va. 645. In the first case, the constitutional provision took away all rights of action for anything done by the State or Federal military anthorities during the civil war.

[2] Ogden *v.* Saunders, 12 Wheat. 213; Beers *v.* Haughton, 9 Pet. 329; Tennessee *v.* Sneed, 96 U. S. 69; Simpson *v.* Savings Bank, 56 N. H. 466; Danks *v.* Quackenbush, 1 N. Y. 129; Morse *v.* Goold, 11 N. Y. 281; Baldwin *v.* Newark, 38 N. J. 158; Moore *v.* State, 43 N. J. 203; Evans *v.* Mont-

§ 142

changes are permissible, as long as a substantial remedy remains. Thus a law may take away from existing contracts the right to confine the debtor, and yet not impair the obligation of the contract. "Confinement of the debtor may be a punishment for not performing his contract, or may be allowed as a means of inducing him to perform it. But the State may refuse to inflict this punishment, or may withhold this means, and leave the contract in full force. Imprisonment is no part of the contract, and simply to release the prisoner does not impair the obligation." [1]

The rules of evidence may also be changed without affecting the substantive rights involved. No one can be said to

---

gomery, 4 Watts & S. 218; Penrose v. Erie Canal Co., 56 Pa. St. 46; Baumgardner v. Circuit Court, 4 Mo. 50; Porter v. Mariner, 50 Mo. 364; Smith v. Van Gilder, 26 Ark. 521; Coosa River St. B. Co. v. Barclay, 30 Ala. 120; Halloway v. Sherman, 12 Iowa, 282; Smith v. Packard, 12 Wis. 371; Bronson v. Newberry, 2 Dougl. (Mich.) 38; Rockwell v. Hubbell's Admrs. 2 Dougl. (Mich.) 197.

[1] Marshall, C. J., in Sturges v. Crowninshield, 4 Wheat. 122. See Mason v. Haile, 12 Wheat. 370; Penniman's Case, 103 U. S. 714; Matter of Nichols, 8 R. I. 50; Sommers v. Johnson, 4 Vt. 278 (24 Am. Dec. 604); Ware v. Miller, 9 S. C. 13; Maxey v. Loyal, 38 Ga. 531; Bronson v. Newberry, 2 Dougl. (Mich) 38. A judgment lien may be taken away by the repeal of the statute authorizing it. Watson v. N. Y. Cent. R. R. Co., 47 N. Y. 157; Woodbury v. Grimes, 1 Col. 100. But see, *contra*, Gunn v. Barry, 15 Wall. 610. The time of the lien may also be extended before it has expired (Ellis v. Jones, 51 Mo. 180), or the mode of securing it changed before it has attached. Whitehead v. Latham, 83 N. C. 232. See, also, Williams v. Haines, 27 Iowa, 251, in which a statute, which allowed the want of consideration to be set up in defense of an action on a sealed instrument, was held to be constitutional, because it did not impair the obligation of the contract. On the other hand, where by statute the stockholders are made personally liable for the contracts of the corporation, a statute taking away this liability cannot be made to apply to existing contracts. Hawthorn v. Calef, 2 Wall. 10; Corning v. McCullough, 1 N. Y. 47; Story v. Firman, 25 N. Y. 214; Morris v. Wrenshall, 34 Md. 494; Brown v. Hitchcock, 36 Ohio St. 667; Providence Savings Institute v. Skating Rink, 52 Mo. 452. So, also, may the distress for rent be taken away from existing leases. Van Rensselaer v. Snyder, 9 Barb. 302; *s. c.* 13 N. Y. 299; Guild v. Rogers, 8 Barb. 502. And the distress for rent may be abolished, even in cases in which the parties have expressly stipulated for it. Conkey v. Hart, 14 N. Y. 22.

§ 142

possess " a right to have one's controversies determined by
existing rules of evidence."[1] These rules are always subject
to change and modification by the legislature, and a new rule
can be made to apply to existing rights of action, without interfering with vested rights or impairing the obligation of a
contract. Thus, a law could apply to existing rights of action,
which permitted parties in interest to testify.[2] In the same
way may a statute apply to existing rights of action, which
changed the burden of proof from the plaintiff to defendant,
as, for example, where a tax title is made by statute *prima
facie* evidence of a compliance with the regulations for the
sale of land.[3] But a statute cannot preclude the right to a
judicial examination into the facts of a case, by making a
certain set of circumstances conclusive evidence of the existence of the right of the plaintiff to recover or to be non-
suited. Except in the case of estoppel, where a man is
denied the right to question the truth of his representations
which he has made falsely to another's hurt, there can be
no prejudgment of one's rights by the creation of conclusive presumptions.[4]

---

[1] Cooley Const. Lim. 452.

[2] Rich *v.* Flanders, 39 N. H. 304; Southwick *v.* Southwick, 49 N. Y. 510.
So, also, a statute which admits parol evidence to contradict a written
instrument. Gibbs *v.* Gale, 7 Md. 76. See, generally, Ogden *v.* Saun-
ders, 12 Wheat. 213; Webb *v.* Den, 17 How. 576; Fales *v.* Wadsworth, 23
Me. 553; Pratt *v.* Jones, 25 Vt. 303; Neass *v.* Mercer, 15 Barb. 318;
Howard *v.* Moot, 64 N. Y. 262; Commonwealth *v.* Williams, 6 Gray, 1;
Karney *v.* Paisley, 13 Iowa, 89.

[3] Hand *v.* Ballou, 12 N. Y. 541; Forbes *v.* Halsey, 26 N. Y. 53; Lacey
v. Davis, 4 Mich. 140; Wright *v.* Dunham, 13 Mich. 414; Delaplaine *v.*
Cook, 7 Wis. 44; Lumsden *v.* Cross, 10 Wis. 282; Adams *v.* Beale, 19
Iowa, 61; Abbott *v.* Lindenbower, 42 Mo. 162; *s. c.* 46 Mo. 291.

[4] Tift *v.* Griffin, 5 Ga. 185; Little Rock, etc., R. R. Co. *v.* Payne, 33
Ark. 816 (34 Am. Rep. 55); Abbott *v.* Lindenbower, 42 Mo. 162; *s. c.* 46
Mo. 291; Young *v.* Beardsley, 11 Paige, 93; East Kingston *v.* Towle, 48
N. H. 57 (2 Am. Rep. 174); Allen *v.* Armstrong, 16 Iowa, 508; Conway *v.*
Cable, 37 Ill. 82; White *v.* Flynn, 23 Ind. 46; Groesbeck *v.* Seeley, 13
Mich. 329; Lenz *v.* Charlton, 23 Wis. 478; Taylor *v.* Miles, 5 Kan. 498 (7
Am. Rep. 558); Wright *v.* Cradlebaugh, 3 Nev. 341. In the case last cited

§ 142

It has also been very generally held to be no impairment of the substantive rights of action, if a law should be enacted exempting certain property of the debtor from execution, to an extent not permitted when the contract was executed or the judgment was obtained. "Regulations of this description have always been considered, in every civilized community, as properly belonging to the remedy to be exercised or not, by every sovereignty, according to its own views of policy or humanity. It must reside in every State to enable it to secure its citizens from unjust and harassing litigation, and to protect them in those pursuits which are necessary to the existence and well being of every community."[1] But an act, which exempted all the property of the debtor from execution, would, like the law which deprived the creditor of all remedies, be void because it im-

the court say: "We apprehend that it is beyond the power of the legislature to restrain a defendant in any suit from setting up a good defense to an action against him. The legislature could not directly take the property of A. to pay the taxes of B. Neither can it indirectly do so by depriving A. of the right of setting up in his answer that his separate property has been jointly assessed with that of B., and asserting his right to pay his own taxes without being incumbered with those of B. * * * Due process of law not only requires that a party shall be properly brought into court, but that he shall have the opportunity when in court to establish any fact which, according to the usages of the common law, or the provisions of the constitution, would be a protection to him or his property."

[1] Taney, C. J., in Bronson *v.* Kinzie, 1 How. 311, 315; Quackenbush *v.* Danks, 1 Denis, 128; *s. c.* 3 Denio, 594; *s. c.* 1 N. Y. 129; Morse *v.* Goold, 11 N. Y. 281; Hill *v.* Kessler, 63 N. C. 437; Martin *v.* Hughes, 67 N. C. 293; In re Kennedy, 2 S. C. 216; Hardeman *v.* Downer, 39 Ga. 425; Maull *v.* Vaughn, 45 Ala. 134; Sneider *v.* Heidelberger, 45 Ala. 126; Farley *v.* Dowe, 45 Ala. 324; Breitung *v.* Lindauer, 37 Mich. 217; Sprecker *v.* Wakeley, 11 Wis. 432; Coleman *v.* Ballandi, 22 Minn. 144; Cusic *v.* Douglass 3 Kan. 123. But, of late, there has been a change in the current of judicial authority, and the tendency now is to deny the constitutionality of the changes in the exemption laws in their application to existing contracts. See, to that effect, Duncan *v.* Burnett, 11 S. C. 333 (32 Am. Rep. 476); Wilson *v.* Brown, 58 Ala. 62 (29 Am. Rep. 727); Johnson *v.* Fletcher, 54 Miss. 628 (28 Am. Rep. 388).

§ 142

paired the obligation of a contract.[1] It has been held, on
the other hand, that homestead laws cannot be made to
restrict the right of execution on existing contracts, where
there had previously been no homestead law.[2] But a homestead can be claimed against judgments procured on existing rights of action arising out of torts, since these claims
do not become debts until they are reduced to judgment.[3]

Another interesting phase of the regulation of rights of
action is involved in the enactment of bankruptcy and insolvency laws. The power of the United States, by the enactment of bankrupt laws, to provide for the release of the debtor
from his contractual obligations on the surrender of his assets
to his creditors, cannot be questioned, because the power is
expressly given by the Federal constitution.[4] And it has
been settled by the decisions of the United States Supreme
Court that the several States may provide similar legislation, subject to the paramount control of Congress. When
there is a federal bankrupt law, it supersedes the State
law of insolvency ; but the latter come into operation again
upon the repeal of the national bankrupt law.[5] But the
State insolvent law, not being authorized by an express constitutional provision, cannot be made to apply to existing

---

[1] State v. Bank of South Carolina, 1 S. C. 63.

[2] Gunn v. Barry, 15 Wall. 610; Edwards v. Kearzey, 96 U. S. 595;
Homestead Cases, 22 Gratt. 266 (12 Am. Rep. 507) ; Garrett v. Cheshira,
69 N. C. 396 (12 Am. Rep. 647) ; Lessley v. Phipps, 49 Miss. 790.

[3] Parker v. Savage, 6 Lea, 406.

[4] U. S. Const., art. I., § 8.

[5] See Sturgis v. Crowninshield, 4 Wheat. 122; Farmers' and Mechanics'
Bk. v. Smith, 6 Wheat. 131; Ogden v. Saunders, 12 Wheat. 213; Baldwin v.
Hale, 1 Wall. 223. But the State insolvent laws can have no application
to contracts made without the State, or to those made between citizens of
different States, unless all the parties to the contract come into court and
voluntarily submit to the operation of the State laws. McMillan v.
McNeil, 4 Wheat. 209; Ogden v. Saunders, 12 Wheat. 213; Clay v. Smith,
3 Pet. 411; Boyle v. Zacharie, 6 Pet. 348; Suydam v. Broadnax, 14 Pet.
67; Cook v. Moffat, 5 How. 295; Baldwin v. Hale, 1 Wall. 223; Baldwin
v. Bank of Newbury, 1 Wall. 234; Gilman v Lockwood, 4 Wall. 409.

§ 142

contracts, since they cannot be considered as having been made in contemplation of such a law. State insolvent laws can only apply to future contracts.[1]

While a law would be invalid which denied to one all remedy for the redress of his wrongs; and while resort to the courts for a vindication of one's rights may be considered as an absolute right, which cannot be arbitrarily taken away ; it is nevertheless true that it is not the duty of the State to keep its courts open indefinitely for the institution of private suits. It has performed fully its duty to the citizen, when it has opened its courts to him for a reasonable time after the right of action has accrued. It is also injurious to the public welfare to permit suits upon stale claims ; for the permission of them gives an opportunity for the perpetration of fraud and the infliction of injustice, in consequence of the intermediate loss of evidence and death of witnesses, which prevent the defendant from meeting and disproving the claim of the plaintiff. For these reasons it has for time immemorial, and in all systems of jurisprudence, been considered wise and proper, by the enactment of statutes of limitation, to compel all rights of action to be prosecuted within a reasonable length of time after the action has accrued. And it is also the settled rule of American constitutional law that the amendments to the statutes of limitation can be made to apply to existing contracts without impairing their obligation in a constitutional sense, provided after the enactment a reasonable time is given for the institution of the suit.[2]

[1] Ogden v. Saunders, 12 Wheat. 213.

[2] See Terry v. Anderson, 95 U. S. 628; Proprietors, etc., v. Laboree, 2 Me. 294; Call v. Hagger, 8 Mass. 423; Smith v. Morrison, 22 Pick, 430; Davidson v. Lawrence, 49 Ga. 335; Kimbro v. Bk. of Fulton, 49 Ga. 419; Hart v. Bostwick, 14 Fla. 162; Barry v. Ransdell, 4 Met. (Ky.) 292; O'Bannon v. Louisville, 8 Bush, 348; Blackford v. Pettier, 1 Blackf. 36; DeMoss v. Newton, 31 Ind. 219; Price v. Hopkin, 13 Mich. 318; Osborne v. Jaines, 17 Wis. 573; State v. Messenger, 27 Minn. 119; Adamson v. Davis, 47 Mo.

§ 142

§ 143. Regulation of ships and shipping. — In consequence of the exposure to the dangers of the sea, there would be more or less danger of accident and damage to others, in the use of ships, if there were not some legal regulation of their construction and management. All police regulations are therefore lawful, which are designed, and tend, to diminish the dangers of sea voyaging. They are not subject to any constitutional objections.

In the first place, it is lawful to prohibit the use of unseaworthy vessels, and to provide for the inspection of all vessels and the condemnation of those that are defective.[1] The United States government under the Federal statutes have appointed officers, whose duty it is to perform this service to the traveling public. It is also common to limit by law the number of passengers and the amount of freight which a vessel may be permitted to carry ;[2] and it is not unreasonable to require the master or purser of a vessel to furnish to some public officer a statement of the amount of freight or the number of passengers he may have on board.[3] The overloading of a boat with freight or passengers may be considered an actual trespass upon the right of personal security of all those who may be on board of the vessel.

The skill or ignorance of the master or captain, and other officers in charge of the vessel, is of the utmost importance to those who entrust their person or property to their care ; and it is consequently permissible to require all those who are applicants for such positions to submit to examinations into their qualifications, and receive a certificate of qualification, without which they cannot assume the

268; Keith v. Keith, 26 Kan. 27. See a fuller discussion of the subject in Cooley Const. Lim. 448–451.

[1] Thus, it was held to be a reasonable regulation, which provided for the inspection of boilers of vessels. Bradley v. Northern, etc., Co., 15 Ohio St. 553.

[2] St. Louis v. McCoy, 18 Mo. 238; St. Louis v. Boffinger, 19 Mo. 13.

[3] Canal Commissioners v. Willamette Transp. Co., 6 Ore. 219.

duties of such a post.   This is so common and reasonable a regulation that it has never been questioned.[1]

The navigation of a vessel also requires some regulation by law to remove doubt and uncertainty, and to insure uniformity in the rules.   The principal legal rules of navigation are those relating to the use of colored lights at night, the regulation of fog signals, and the rules for steering when two or more vessels come into close neighborhood. These regulations are designed to prevent collision, and a detailed discussion of them may be found in any work on shipping and admiralty.   It is not necessary to mention them here.   We are only concerned with a consideration of the constitutionality of such laws in general.   This regulation by law of the rules of navigation consists chiefly in adopting as legal and binding rules those which had met with the approval of the best part of the marine world, and the object of the interference of the government is to secure fixity and uniformity.   The constitutionality of these police regulations has never been questioned.

The navigation of a vessel in mid-ocean involves no special difficulty to any one who is at all skilled in navigation.   But the entrance into a harbor does require a peculiar knowledge of the coast and of the currents in and out of the bay or river.   It would, therefore, be reasonable to require all vessels, on entering a harbor, to be placed in charge of a licensed pilot, and, inasmuch as the law makes it obligatory upon the pilot to beat up and down the coast in search of vessels, which are bound for the port, it is held to be reasonable to compel the master or captain to accept the services of the first pilot who offers.[2]

---

[1] See *ante*, § 87, in respect to the police regulation of skilled trades and learned professions.

[2] Thompson *v.* Spraigue, 69 Ga. 409 (47 Am. Rep. 760).   See Sherlock *v.* Alling, 93 U. S. 99.   As to whether the United States or the States have the power to regulate the matter of pilotage, see *post*, 204.

§ 143

CHAPTER XII.

POLICE REGULATION OF THE RELATION OF HUSBAND AND WIFE.

SECTION 149. Marriage. a natural *status*, subject to police regulation.

150. Constitutional limitations upon the police control of marriages.

151. Distinction between natural capacity and legal capacity.

152. Insanity as a legal incapacity.

153. The disability of infancy in respect to marriage.

154. Consanguinity and affinity.

155. Constitutional diseases.

156. Financial condition — Poverty.

157. Differences in race — Miscegenation.

158. Polygamy prohibited — Marriage confined to monogamy.

159. Marriage indissoluble — Divorce.

160. Regulation of the marriage ceremony.

161. Wife in legal subjection to the husband — Its justification.

162. Husband's control of wife's property.

163. Legal disabilities of married women.

§ 149. **Marriage, a natural status, subject to police regulation.** — Whatever may be one's views concerning the philosophical origin of the institution of marriage; it matters not whether it is viewed as a divine institution and a sacrament, or as the natural result of the social and physiological forces; all are agreed that it has its foundations in nature, and is not a human contrivance. Mankind cannot be conceived as existing without this *status*, for the marital relation is co-existent with, and must have accompanied, the beginning of the creation. The natural element of marriage is discoverable in like relationships among most, if not all, of the lower animals. It is, therefore, but a natural *status*, one that is brought into existence by natural forces, and cannot be successfully prevented or abolished. The natural *status* of marriage works for the good or woe of mankind, according as it is founded in purity and rests upon sound spiritual and physical foundations, or assumes a contrary character. The welfare of society is inseparably wrapped up with the success of the marital relations of its members : and ill-assorted marriages, marriages between persons who are either mentally or physically unfit to enter into the relation, will surely bring harm to society ; while appropriate marriages constitute the very foundation of society, and its welfare depends upon the fostering and encouragement of them. Indeed nations have often provided inducements to enter into the relation, at times when the general extravagance of the people deterred them from assuming the responsibilities of husband and wife. If, therefore, a happy marriage between competent parties redounds to the lasting benefit of society, and a marriage between persons, who through mental or physical deficiencies are incapable of contracting a happy marriage, produces harm to the State, surely the State is interested in promoting and encouraging the former, and discouraging and preventing the latter. The State may, therefore, institute regulations having that purpose in view, in the exercise of the ordinary police power. The right of the State to regulate marriages, determining the capacities of parties, and the conditions of marriage, has never been questioned. Indeed, it would be absurd to assert that the State could not prohibit polygamy, and deny the right of marriage to persons whose marriage, on account of their deficiencies, or on account of their near relationship to each other, is likely to be harmful to society in one or more ways. Mr. Bishop says :[1] " The idea, that any government could, consistently with the general well being, permit marriage to become merely a thing of bargain between men and women, and not regulate it by its own power, is too absurd to require refutation." The tendency of modern thought is to recognize no limit to the power of the government to regulate marriage.

[1] 1 Mar. & Div., § 1

§ 149

Chief Justice Cockburn, in one case, said that the Parliament could deny the right of marriage altogether. It is not likely that others would go so far in recognition of the police power of the State, for it is generally conceded that marriage is "a thing of natural right,"[1] and cannot be denied except for some good legal reason. But it does not seem to be settled what are good reasons, and who shall determine what they are. Mr. Bishop says: "Surely it (the government), will retain the right to regulate whatever pertains to marriage in its own way, and to modify the incidents of the relation from time to time as itself pleases."[2] And while he recognizes the natural right to marry, the only benefit derived from this recognition, is to throw all presumption in favor of the legality of the marriage, and requiring the courts to sustain the validity of a marriage, "unless the legal rule which is set up to prevent this conclusion is distinct and absolute, or some impediment of nature intervenes."[3] Judge Cooley admits that the State's control of marriage is not unlimited, but finds it difficult to determine the limitations. He says: "If the regulations apply universally and impartially, a question of constitutional law can scarcely arise upon them, for every independent State must be at liberty to regulate the domestic institutions of its people as shall seem most for the general welfare. A regulation, however, that should apply to one class exclusively, and which should not be based upon any distinction between that class and others which could be important to the relation, must be wholly unwarranted and illegal. This principle is conceded, but it is not easy to determine what regulation would come within it."[4]

[1] 1 Bishop Mar. & Div., § 13; Cooley's Principles of Const. Law, p. 228.

[2] 1 Bishop Mar. & Div., § 12. See, also, Pennoyer v. Neff, 95 U. S. 714.

[3] 1 Bishop Mar. & Div., § 13.

[4] Cooley's Principle of Const. Laws 228.

§ 149

§ 150. **Constitutional limitations upon the police control of marriages.** — It has been often asserted and explained in the preceding pages that the police power can only extend to the imposition of such restraints and burdens upon natural right as are calculated to promote the general welfare by preventing injury to others, individually or as a community. If this be the true limitation of police power generally, and the governmental regulation of marriage be conceded to be an exercise of police power, the constitutionality of a police regulation of marriage may be tested by determining whether the regulation is designed to, and does, prevent a threatening injury to society or to others. If there is no threatening injury and, so far as the judicial eye can discern, the regulation is arbitrary and unnecessary, the court would pronounce against the constitutionality of the regulation. Marriage being a natural right, one is deprived of his liberty and the pursuit of happiness if such a regulation is permitted to prevent his marriage. If it is only doubtful that the marriage would prove injurious to others or to society, it would, of course, be proper, in conformity with a general rule of constitutional construction, to solve the doubt in favor of the validity of the regulation. But in a clear case of arbitrary regulation, — *i.e.*, where there is no threatening evil outcome of the marriage which the regulation is designed to prevent, it is clearly the duty of the court to declare the regulating law unconstitutional.

For the purpose of testing their constitutionality, regulations of marriage may be divided into those which are designed to prevent injury to society and to third persons, and those which are intended to afford protection to the parties to the contract of marriage. In order that a regulation may be constitutional, it must fall into one of these classes.

They may also be divided into the following classes: (1) Those which relate to the capacity of parties to enter

§ 150

into a perfect marriage state; (2) those which require certain forms of ceremony; and (3) those which are intended to provide for proper harmony and conduct of the parties to each other in the marriage state, in respect to their actions generally and also in respect to the control of their property. The constitutionality of police regulations of marriage will be discussed in this order.

§ 151. **Distinction between natural capacity and legal capacity.** — While marriage, when consummated, constitutes a *status*, as a result of the execution of the contract to marry, a valid contract must precede a valid marriage; and the validity of the contract of marriage is determined by the same principles which govern ordinary contracts. Among those elementary principles are, the requirement of two persons competent to contract, the agreement, and a consideration, which in the case of the contract of marriage constitutes each other's promise respectively. The law cannot compel an individual to marry against his will, for it is not a duty to the State to marry. His consent or agreement is necessary to the validity of the contract. When, therefore, the consent is not present, whether it arises from mental inability to give the consent, or from duress or fraud, the contract of marriage, and hence the marriage itself, must be declared void. Hence the marriages of the insane, except during a lucid interval, or of a child of such tender age and immature mind that he cannot be supposed to understand the nature of the contract and therefore cannot be held to have given his consent, are void or voidable, from the very nature of the case. The rules of law which provide for the avoidance of such marriages only lend the aid of the courts to the more effective enforcement of the laws of nature, and do not involve the exercise of police power, since there are no restrictions imposed upon the right of marriage but those

which nature herself commands. Police power is exerted
only when an artificial incapacity is created.

§ 152. **Insanity as a legal incapacity.** — If the parties
to the contract of marriage are of sane mind when the
contract of marriage is made and performed, the subsequent or previous insanity does not affect the validity of the
marriage *status*. Having entered into the *status* through a
valid contract, the capacity to contract ceases to be of
value, since the contract is merged by its performance into
a *status*. But if the blood of either of the parties is
tainted with insanity, there is imminent danger of its
transmission to the offspring, and through the procreation
of imbecile children the welfare of the State is more or
less threatened. It may not be the policy of the State to
impose restrictions upon the marriage of those who suffer
from mental unsoundness of a constitutional character, or
the danger to the State may not be sufficiently threatening;
but if the proper legislative authority should determine
upon the establishment of such restrictions, even though
they amounted to absolute prohibition, there can be no
question as to their constitutionality. The danger to the
State arising from the imbecility of the offspring has
always been considered an all-sufficient justification of the
State interference and regulation of marriage.

§ 153. **The disability of infancy in respect to marriage.** — In the general law of contracts, all minors are
declared incapable of making a valid contract, and the law
determines the age when they attain their majority and are
freed from this disability. In most of the States the age
of twenty-one is selected for both sexes, while in some
of the States females become of age at eighteen. It matters not what may be the age determined upon, the imposition of the disability is an exercise of police power, and is
justified on the ground that on account of his immaturity the
§ 153

minor is not on equal terms with the adult, and for his own
protection he is rendered unable to subject himself to possible extortion or imposition.   If it were the policy of the law
to impose the same liability upon the right of marriage, the
further, and perhaps more important, reason may be urged
that persons of such youthful age are unable to provide
properly for the wants of a family, and as a protection to
the State against pauperism the youth may be prohibited
from marriage altogether until he arrives at the age of
twenty-one, and his marriage declared absolutely void.
But for various cogent reasons, especially the danger of
increasing immorality and the delicacy of the situation of
both parties, arising from the avoidance of the marriage
of persons under age, infancy is no disqualification [1] to the
entrance into a completely valid marriage.   If the minor
is of the requisite physical capacity, the marriage will be
valid, notwithstanding infancy ; while the contract to marry,
like all other executory contracts, is voidable by the infant,
although binding upon the adult with whom he may have
contracted.[2]   But, arising out of the parental control,
authorized by the law, a minor may be prevented by his
parents from marrying, if he does not elude them.   The
law requires the consent of the parents to the marriage
only as a preliminary justification of the marriage, but the
want of the consent does not invalidate the marriage if it
is actually consummated   The present policy of the law is
opposed to such stringency, but it would be a lawful exercise of police power to make the consent of the parents
necessary to the validity of the marriage.

While infancy in itself does not furnish any ground for
invalidating a marriage, the physical incapacity arising from

[1] 1 Bishop Mar. & Div., § 144; Gavin *v.* Burton, 8 Ind. 69.

[2] 1 Bishop Mar. & Div., § 143; Hunt *v.* Peake, 5 Cow. 475; Williard *v.*
Stone, 17 Cow. 22; Hamilton *v.* Lomax, 26 Barb. 615; Cannon *v.* Alsbury,
1 A. K. Mar. 76; Kester *v.* Stark, 19 Ill. 328; Warwick *v.* Cooper, 5 Sneed,
659; Schouler Dom. Rel. 32.

§ 153

a tender age constitutes a natural incapacity, like general impotence, to perform one of the obligations of the marital relation, and more or less affects the validity of the marriage. The physical incapacity of a child renders the marriage inchoate, and it is completely valid only when there is cohabitation after his arrival at the age of puberty. The incapacity is natural; but in order to avoid the necessity of an actual investigation, in each particular case, into the physical capacity of the infant bride or bridegroom, the law provides that males under fourteen and females under twelve shall be held to be physically incapable of performing the marital functions. This regulation was derived from the civil Roman law, and in the warm southern climate the law no doubt represented correctly the physiological fact that at these ages the average child attained the full powers of a man or woman. But in the more northern latitudes the growth is slower, and children are usually immature at these ages, and changes have constantly been made in the law, in order that it may more readily conform to the actual age of puberty. Such a change has been made in North Carolina and Iowa, and perhaps in other States.[1] But the appointment of an age when the physical capacity will be presumed, is a police regulation, and is plainly justifiable on the ground that it promotes the general welfare to avoid the delicate examinations that would otherwise be necessary to establish the fact of capacity, and the law cannot be called into question if it should vary from the physiological facts.

The common law also provides that the marriage of persons, either of whom is under the age of seven, is a mere nullity.[2] Probably the prohibition rests in this case upon the ground of absolute mental and physical incapacity.

In all of these cases of police regulation of marriage

---

[1] 1 Bishop Mar. & Div., § 142.
[2] 1 Bishop Mar. & Div., § 147.

§ 153

between or by minors, the immaturity of mind or body constitutes the justification for the interference with the natural right, and their constitutionality admits of no question.

§ 154. **Consanguinity and affinity.** — In all systems of jurisprudence, beginning with the laws of Moses, marriages between persons of the nearer degrees of relationship by consanguinity have been prohibited; and in some of these cases, notably that of parent and child, the act of marriage has been declared a crime and punishable as such. The legal justification of this prohibition lies in the birth of imbecile and frail offspring, which is the constant if not invariable fruit of such marriages. The injury to be avoided by the prohibition consists not only of that which threatens the State in the increase of pauperism through the birth of persons likely to become paupers, but also the injury to the offspring. One might, if allowed a certain latitude of speech, be said to have a natural right to come into this world with normal faculties of mind and body, and the prevention of the birth of issue is justifiable when the parties cannot transmit, at least to a reasonable degree, a *mens sana in corpore sano*. It can never be questioned that the marriage of very near relations has this disastrous effect, although it may be a proper subject for debate at what degree of relationship marriage would be safe. Still, granting the danger of such marriages, the determination of the degrees of relationship, within which marriage is to be prohibited, must be left to the legislative discretion; and although it is strictly a judicial question whether consanguinity is likely to make a particular marriage disastrous or dangerous, it must be a flagrant case of arbitrary exercise of legislative power, in order to justify judicial interference. It is a general rule of constitutional construction

§ 154

that all doubts as to the constitutionality of a legislative act must be solved in favor of the legislature.[1]

In England, the relationship by affinity, *i.e.*, by marriage, has been held to be a ground for prohibiting marriage with the relations of the deceased wife or husband, within the same degrees in which consanguinity constitutes a bar to a valid marriage.[2] The reason for this prohibition is set forth in the leading case of Butler *v.* Gastrill,[3] in this language: " It was necessary in order to perfect the union of marriage, that the husband should take the wife's relations in the same degree, to be the same as his own, without distinction and *vice versa;* for if they are to be the same person, as was intended by the law of God, they can have no difference in relations, and by consequence the prohibition touching affinity must be carried as far as the prohibition touching consanguinity ; for what was found convenient to extinguish jealousies amongst near relations, and to govern families and educate children amongst people of the same consanguinity, would likewise have the same operation amongst those of the same affinity. And when we consider who are prohibited to marry by the Levitical law, we must not only consider the mere words of the law itself, but what, by a just and fair interpretation, may be deduced from it." If the tests, heretofore given for determining the constitutionality of laws for the regulation of marriage be reliable, no such reasoning as this would justify the prohibition in this country. It would have to be demonstrated that marriages between persons nearly related by affinity produce imbecile or weak offspring, or will otherwise antagonize the public interests, in order that their prohibition may be constitutionally unobjectionable. But there will be very little occasion for testing the constitutionality of this law in this country. Affinity was, and probably still

---

[1] Cooley Const. Lim. 218.
[2] 1 Bishop Mar. & Div., §§ 314, 315, 316.
[3] Gilb. ch. 156, 158.

§ 154

is, in Virginia, a ground for invalidating marriages, to the same extent as consanguinity,[1] but marriages with the deceased wife's sister, as Mr. Bishop expresses it, " in most of the States, are not only not forbidden, but deemed commendable. It would be difficult to find a person who would object to such a union, or pretend that the laws permitting it had wrought injury." [2]

§ 155. **Constitutional Diseases.**— If the possibility or probability of the procreation of imbecile offspring be a justification of the laws which prohibit the marriage of near relations and of those afflicted with constitutional insanity, so likewise the danger of transmission to the offspring will justify the enforcement of laws which prohibit the marriage of those who are suffering from constitutional diseases, which may be transmitted to the fruit of the marriage, or which so deplete the constitutions of the parents that the birth of healthy, vigorous children becomes impossible. Such would be leprosy, syphilis, and possibly, tuberculosis. The same reasoning, which has been presented to support the impediments of insanity and consanguinity, applies to the proposed impediment of constitutional diseases, and a repetition of it is unnecessary. This power has not been exercised in this country to the writer's knowledge.

§ 156. **Financial condition — Poverty.** — Not only is the welfare of society threatened by the transmission of a shattered mental or physical constitution to the children, but also by bringing them into the world, when the parents are not possessed of the means sufficient to provide for them. The only difficulty in the enforcement of such a law, as in the cases of constitutional insanity and disease, lies in determining in what cases the danger is threatening enough to

---

[1] Com. *v.* Perryman, 2 Leigh, 717; Hutchins *v.* Com., 2 Va. Cas. 331; Com. *v.* Leftwich, 5 Rand. 657; Kelly *v.* Scott, 5 Gratt. 479.

[2] 1 Bishop Mar. & Div., § 319.

justify the interference of the law ; and in the case of poverty, there is the further difficulty of proving the condition of pauperism, which would operate as a bar to marriage. It would probably be impossible to enforce the rule against any but public paupers, those who are dependent upon the public alms, and can, therefore, be easily identified. Such a regulation at one time prevailed in Maine, and it was held, when the constitutionality of the law was called into question, that the State may by statute prohibit the marriage of paupers.[1]

§ 157. **Differences in race — Miscegenation.** — When the negro race in this country was for the most part held in slavery, the degradation of a state of servitude operated to create a most powerful prejudice against the black man, although he was a free man. As an outcome of this prejudice, and a popular sense of superiority, the legislatures of very many of the States of this country, particularly in the South, passed laws for the prohibition of marriages between whites and blacks. These laws for the most part still remain upon the statute book, notwithstanding the full and complete recognition of the rights of citizenship of the black man. In some of the States, marriages between the Indian and white race are also prohibited. Although there is occasionally an attempt made to show some physiological reason for the prohibition, it cannot be denied that the real cause is an uncontrollable prejudice against the black man, and a desire to maintain the inequality of his present social condition. Whatever other reason may be proclaimed, this is the controlling reason. If this be true, if the law has no better foundation than racial prejudice, is the State justified, under the general constitutional limitations, in prohibiting the marriage of a white man and a black woman, or *vice versa*, when the prejudice is not felt

---

[1] Brunswick *v.* Litchfield, 2 Me. 28.

§ 157

by them? Is it not an unwarrantable act of tyranny to prohibit such a marriage, simply because the community is prejudiced against it? Some attempt has been made to show that the mixture of blood will cause a general decay of the national strength, either through enfeebled constitutions or sterility; but it does not appear that the truth of the proposition has ever been established. At any rate, in no other country, except where slavery has lately prevailed, has such a law ever been enacted. Unless it can be established beyond a reasonable doubt that the intermarriage of white and black may be expected to produce frail and sterile offspring, or threatens the general welfare in some other well defined way, the duty of the courts is to pronounce these laws unconstitutional, because they deprive the parties, so disposed to marry, of their right of liberty without due process of law. But the prejudice of race has been too strong even in the judicial minds of the country to secure for these laws a scientific consideration, and hence they have been repeatedly held to be constitutional.[1]

[1] See Bailey v. Fiske, 34 Me. 77; Medway v. Natick, 7 Mass. 88; Medway v. Needham, 16 Mass. 157. In Massachusetts the statute was repealed in 1843. State v. Hooper, 5 Ire. 201; State v. Ross, 76 N. C. 242; State v. Kennedy, 67 N. C. 25. " It is stated as a well authenticated fact that the issue of a black man and a white woman, and that of a white man and black woman intermarrying, they cannot possibly have any progeny, and such a fact sufficiently justifies those laws which forbid the intermarriage of blacks and whites laying out of view other sufficient grounds for such enactments." State v. Jackson, 80 Mo. 175. It has been held that the fourteenth amendment of the constitution of the United States does not apply to such laws, since the prohibition is upon white and black alike. State v. Hairston, 63 N. C. 451; State v. Reinhardt, 63 N. C. 547; State v. Kenney, 76 N. C. 251 (22 Am. Rep. 683); State v. Gibson, 36 Ind. 389 (10 Am. Rep. 42); Lonas v. State, 3 Heisk. (Tenn.) 287; Ex rel. Hobbs, 1 Woods, 537; Green v. State, 58 Ala. 190 (29 Am. Rep. 739); Hoover v. The State, 59 Ala. 59; Frasher v. State, 3 Tex. App. 263 (30 Am. Rep. 131); Kinney's Case, 30 Gratt. 858. Judge Cooley says: "Many States prohibit the intermarriage of white persons and negroes; and since the fourteenth amendment this regulation has been contested as the offspring of race prejudice, as establishing an unreasonable discrimination, and as depriving one class of the equal protection of the laws.

§ 157

§ 158. **Polygamy prohibited — Marriage confined to monogamy.** — While voicing the universal moral sentiment of a higher civilization, the laws against polygamy likewise furnish to society a protection against the evils arising from the degradation of its females and the procreation of more children than one man is able to support. In monogamy, it is often difficult for the husband and father to provide the proper means of support for the offspring of his only wife ; and in polygamy the difficulty would be greatly increased if the system did not make plodding slaves of the women. There can be no question that the system of polygamy brings about a moral degradation of the women, treating them as mere animals, designed simply to gratify the animal passions of the man who owns them. The wife of a many-wived husband cannot feel for him the noble and ennobling sentiment of love in its higher phase, for the relation she bears to him is anything but ennobling. Then, again, it is estimated, with a reasonable show of accuracy, that the population of the world is nearly equally divided between the two sexes, the adult female predominating to a small extent. If polygamy were legalized, the logical consequence would be that a proportion of men, the number increasing in proportion to the average number of wives to each married man, would be prevented from entering into the marriage state ; because through competition a wife had become a luxury, if one could be procured at all, and such men would seek the gratification of their sexual

Strictly, however, the regulation discriminates no more against one race than against the other; it merely forbids marriages between the two. Nor can it be said to so narrow the privilege of marriage as practically to impede or prevent it. Race prejudice no doubt has had something to do with establishing it, but it cannot be said to be so entirely without reason in its support as to be purely arbitrary. The general current of judicial decision is, that it deprives a citizen of nothing that he can claim as a legal right, privilege or exemption." Cooley Principles of Const. Law, 228, 229.

§ 158

desires in illicit concubinage. Polyandry is and must be the invariable complement of polygyny.

But, at this late day, it is not necessary to point out the evils of polygamy, for the accumulated experience of the oriental world confirms the injurious character of the system, which the moral consciousness of the occidental world had discovered, as if by inspiration. So generally and naturally is the evil character of polygamy recognized that the leading American authority on the law of marriage, without any qualification or preliminary explanation, defines marriage to be " the civil *status* of *one man* and *one woman* united in law for life, for the discharge, to each other and the community, of the duties legally incumbent on those whose association is founded on the distinction of sex."[1] There can be no doubt as to the constitutionality of laws against polygamy, under the general constitutional provisions; but of late the right of government to prohibit and punish polygamy in cases, where its practice is commanded, or at least sanctioned by one's religion, is questioned on the ground that it is a violation of religious liberty, and hence contravenes the constitutional provision, relating to religious liberty. The question has been raised under the United States statutes, which relate to the practice of polygamy among the Mormons of Utah. It has been held by the Supreme Court of the United States that the constitutional guarantee of religious liberty does not extend its protection to the crimes committed under the sanction of religion.[2]

§ 159. **Marriage indissoluble — Divorce.** — Free from legal limitations, in other words, in the absence of police regulations, the status of marriage would not be of any fixed or definite duration. On the contrary, its continued existence would depend upon the mutual good will of the

[1] 1 Bishop Mar. & Div., § 3.
[2] See Reynolds *v*. United States, 98 U. S. 145.

§ 159

parties ; and it could be dissolved at any time that either of them declines to continue the relation, or its duration could be determined by the agreement of the parties : it would require no great degree of imagination, under such a state of affairs, to classify marriages, in reference to their duration, into those for life, for an uncertain period which may last during life, for years, from year to year, or at will. And this was practically the condition of the law of marriage at one time in the Roman empire.[1]

But the best interests of society, as well as those of the offspring, require that the relation should be permanent ; and the teachings of morality and religion made this economic necessity a divine command and procured legislative interference, sweeping away all doubts as to the right of the State to interfere.   Indeed, morals, religion, political economy and law were so intimately blended together at the time when marriages were first regulated by the State (the beginning antedates the historic age), that probably the reader of the present volume will be astonished to find reasons presented and urged as a justification of this State interference.   But it is clear that but for the evil to society or to the offspring, society could not exact of a married couple the duty to maintain the relation any longer than they chose to do so.   The moral or religious element cannot in itself furnish a foundation for legislation, although I am sure that the religious teachings on the subject were themselves prompted by a consideration of the evils flowing from marriages loosely contracted and easily dissolved.   So many, and such great evils were supposed to flow from them, that in past time we find churchmen, moralists, and jurists, alike demanding that marriages be declared absolutely indissoluble, except for causes arising before marriage, which invalidated the marriage itself.   But since it was not in the power

---

[1] See Sandar's Justinian, p. 102, to the effect that marriage under Roman law was dissoluble by mutual consent, otherwise at the instance of one party only for certain violations of the marriage vow.

§ 159

of the State to compel ill-suited couples to live in harmony, or bring them together, if they had separated, they sanctioned the separation and legalized it; while the bond of marriage still held them together, and prevented their remarriage to others. Such was the English and American common law. The State of South Carolina makes it a subject of loud boasts that she clings to these views of social and moral necessity, even in these degenerate days of easy divorces. "The policy of this State has ever been against divorces. It is one of her boasts that no divorce has ever been granted in South Carolina." [1] But this State stands alone in its adherence to the old law of divorces, while all of her sister States permit divorces for one or more causes, arising subsequent to the marriage, which, under the common law, justified only a divorce *a mensa et thoro;* a separation which deprived the parties of all their marital rights, but kept them bound together, unable to contract a new marriage. The weakness of human nature being considered, but one moral result might be expected from a denial of the right of divorce, in cases where the parties are unable to live together in peace, viz. : illicit connections increase in number to an alarming extent. In speaking of the position taken by South Carolina, Mr. Bishop says : [2] "So it has become necessary to regulate, by statute, how large a proportion a married man may give of his property to his concubine, [3] — superfluous legislation, which would never have been thought of, had not concubinage been common. Statutes like this are unknown, because not required in States where divorces are freely granted." [4]   On the other hand,

[1] Ch. Dargan in Hair *v.* Hair, 10 Rich. Eq. 163, 174.

[2] 1 Bishop Mar. & Div., § 38.

[3] See Denton *v.* English, 3 Brev. 147; Canady *v.* George, 6 Rich. Eq. 103; Cusack *v.* White, 2 Mill, 279.

[4] "In this county," says Judge Nott, "where divorces are not allowed for any cause whatever, we sometimes see men of excellent characters unfortunate in their marriages, and virtuous women abandoned or driven away houseless by their husbands, who would be doomed to celibacy and

it might well be said that the facility with which divorces can be obtained is calculated to make the parties more uneasy under the friction that is present in different quantities in almost all marriages, and less disposed to sacrifice self-will on the altar of their common good ; while the remarriage of divorced parents to others must certainly have a demoralizing influence over the offspring. It has also been asserted that loose divorce laws tend to diminish the growth of population by making it more difficult to provide for the rearing of the children of the divorced and remarried parents. Perhaps laws which grant divorces to a limited extent, for breaches of the marital duties, and yet keep distinctly in view the stability of the marital relation, are best calculated to avoid both the Scylla and Charibdis of this vexed and much discussed problem of society. " It is the policy of the law, and necessary to the purity and usefulness of the institution of marriage, that those who enter into it should regard it as a relation permanent as their own lives; its duration not depending upon the whim or caprice of either, and only to be dissolved when the improper conduct of one of the parties (the other discharging the duties with fidelity as far as practicable under the circumstances) shall render the connection wholly intolerable, or inconsistent with the happiness or safety of the other." [1] Whatever view may be entertained as to the wisdom of denying or granting divorces, and there are all shades of opinion on this subject, the right of the State to regulate the matter has never been seriously questioned. Whether divorces shall be granted or not, is a matter that addresses itself to the discretion of the legislature.

solitude if they did not form connections which the law does not allow, and who make excellent husbands and virtuous wives still. Yet they are considered as living in adultery, because a rigorous and unyielding law, from motives of policy alone, has ordained it so." Cusack v. White, 2 Mill, 279, 292.

[1] Simpson, J., in Griffin v. Griffin, 8 B. Mon. 120.

§ 159

§ 160. **Regulation of the marriage ceremony.** — It requires no painstaking elucidation of the grounds upon which to justify State regulation of the ceremony, by which is established an institution, in which the welfare of the State is so vitally concerned, as marriage. It is certainly not unreasonable for the State to provide a fixed, certain mode of entering into marriage, provided the ceremony, thus selected, is of such a character, that no one would be prevented from entering into the *status*, on account of religious scruples, or an inability to comply, which did not arise from his legal incapacity for marriage. According to the old English law, the marriage was held to be invalid, unless the ceremony was performed by a clergyman of the Church of England.[1] So, also, in the Papal States, before their annexation to the kingdom of Italy in 1870, no marriage was valid unless it was solemnized by one in holy orders in the Catholic Church. A religious ceremony has been required in other countries. It is manifest that, while the State may prescribe that a religious ceremony, possessing certain features, shall constitute a valid solemnization of the marriage, it would be a violation of the religious liberty, guaranteed to all by the American constitutions, if the State compelled one, against his will, to submit to a religious ceremony of marriage, or else be denied the privilege of entering into the marriage state. The ceremony prescribed by the State, and made obligatory upon all, must be of such a character that all can conscientiously comply. A regulation, like the German law of marriage, which makes a ceremony before a civil magistrate necessary to the validity of a marriage, would not violate any constitutional right, not even of those who view marriage in the light of a religious sacrament, for the religious ceremony is not forbidden.

The policy of our country, in the main, has been to leave

---

[1] See Reg. *v.* Millis, 10 Cl. & F. 534. The decision in this case was by a divided court, and the conclusion has been warmly opposed, although acquiesced in, in England. See 1 Bishop Mar. & Div., §§ 270-282.

§ 160

the law of marriage, in respect to the formality of its solemnization, as it was in all Christendom before the Council of Trent, which declared it to be a sacrament and enjoined a religious ceremony, viz. : that no particular ceremony is required, simply a valid contract in *verba de præsenti*, by which the parties assume to each other the relation and duties of husband and wife. And where statutes provide for the issue of a marriage license, they do not make the license necessary to the validity of the marriage, the only effect of the statute being that the minister or magistrate who performs the ceremony is subject to a fine, if he officiates in a case in which no license has been granted.[1] But the present state of the law furnishes no argument against the constitutionality of a statute which required some formal ceremony, subject to the exceptions and limitations already mentioned.

§ 161. **Wife in legal subjection to the husband — Its justification.** — As a matter of abstract or natural justice, the husband and wife must stand on a plane of equality ; neither has the right of control, and both can claim the enjoyment of the same general rights. There are many conscientious people who think differently ; but apart from the influence or teachings of the Bible on this subject, with every such person the thought is but the resultant of his desires and prejudices. Considering the married couple in a state of isolation, eliminating every influence they may exert upon other individuals, their offspring for example, or upon the general welfare of the State, the conclusion is irresistible, that any subjection by law of the wife to the commands of the husband would be a deprivation of the wife's liberty without due process of law, and, therefore,

---

[1] See State *v.* Madden, 81 Mo. 421, in which the constitutionality of a law was contested and sustained, which made it a misdemeanor for any one to solemnize a marriage where the parties have not previously obtained a license.

§ 161

void under our constitutional limitations. And such would likewise be the conclusion, considering the couple in their relation to society and to their offspring, if the ideal marriage became the rule, and absolute harmony and compatibility of temper prevailed in every household. This is, however, at least for the present, an unattainable ideal. There are many individual couples, who have attained this ideal of the domestic relation, where each is "solicitous of the rights of the other," and where "committing a trespass" is "the thing feared, and not being trespassed against," and self-sacrifice, not encroachment, the ruling principle.[1] With such couples there is no subjection of the wife to her husband, and there is never any inequality of position, where the true, genuine sentiment of love inspires every act; for the subjection of one to the other is incompatible with the reign of love. But this is not always the case. Indeed, such a relation between husband and wife constitutes the exception, rather than the rule. In the words of Herbert Spencer,[2] "to the same extent that the triumph of might over right is seen in a nation's political institutions, it is seen in its domestic ones. Despotism in the State is necessarily associated with despotism in the family." The remnant of the savage within us still nurses the desire to rule, and the instinct of selfishness, when unchastened by the principles of altruism, is displayed in the dealings of husband with wife, as of man with man. Might is right, between whatever parties the question may arise. Left, therefore, in a state of nature, it will be a rare exception that the parties to a marriage will sustain an equality of rights; as a general rule, one of them will be the ruler while the other will be the subject, sometimes submissive, but usually more or less rebellious. In most cases, in which this state of affairs exists at all, the

---

[1] Spencer's Social Statics, p. 188.
[2] Social Statics, p. 179.

§ 161

contention and discord continue during life, unless before
death a beneficent divorce law enables the parties to take
leave of each other and go their way alone.   Discord in the
family destroys all the benefits that might be expected to
accrue to the community, even if it does not amount to a
positive breach of the peace.   It demoralizes the offspring
as well as the parties themselves ; and if by a regulation of
their conduct towards each other the State could secure a
reasonable degree of harmony, the result would justify the
interference as tending to promote the general welfare.
How shall this intercourse be regulated?   Shall the State
require the maintenance of substantial equality between
two people whom nature has endowed unequally, both mentally and physically?   I do not mean in this connection to
assert and defend the position, often taken, that women are
essentially and radically inferior to men.   I merely desire
to make the statement, that as a general proposition the
man rules, it may be by greater intellectual strength, or it
may be by brute force, probably in most cases by the latter.
It sometimes happens, but it is the exception, that the
woman is the strongest, and she then rules, whatever the
law might have to say upon the subject.   The maintenance
of a fictitious equality, one that is not the legitimate product of the social forces, by the mandate of the law, even
if that were possible, and it is not, would not tend to
increase harmony in the domestic relations.   Left to
themselves the stronger will rule, and the stronger will
rule notwithstanding the law proclaims an equality.
Harmony can only be approximated by legalizing the rule
of the stronger, at the same time placing around it such
safeguards as will secure for the weaker protection against
the tyranny and cruelty of the stronger.   The wife is not
subjected by the law to the control of the husband, because
the husband has a right to rule, but because he is generally
the stronger, and will have the mastery even though the
law might give the control to the weaker.   If women were

§ 161.

usually the stronger sex, the husbands would be in subjection to them, as they are now, when the husband finds more than his match in his wife. In the management of the things and interests which they hold in common, the husband rules by nature as by law.

Legalizing his natural control, the ancient law in many countries held him responsible to others for all the acts of trespass which the wife may commit. Even to this day, in most of the States, a husband is responsible to third persons for all wrongs against them committed by his wife; while he is to a certain extent responsible to the State for all the crimes committed by his wife in his presence. Whichever of these facts, the husband's control or his responsibility for his wife's acts, be considered the primal fact, the other must be the legitimate and necessary consequence. In proportion that his power of control is diminished, must his responsibility for her acts be lessened, until the happy era is reached, when there will be neither control nor responsibility. But what degree of control and responsibility is to be permitted is left to the legislative discretion.

§ 162. **Husband's control of wife's property.** — Starting out with the proposition, that in the eye of the law husband and wife are looked upon as one person, a duality of which the husband is the head and legal representative, the legal personality being merged in that of her husband, the necessary logical consequence is that he acquires, either absolutely or during coverture, all the rights of property which she possessed, for rights can only be predicated of a legal personality. For this reason, therefore, in the days when the study of law was an exercise in the rigid rules of logic, instead of an earnest effort to discover the means by which substantial justice may be meted out, the wife's property passed upon marriage, with herself, under the control of the husband. There were other reasons, which might have

§ 162

appeared important in the primeval days of tne common law, and justified in the minds of the framers of the law this legal absorption by the husband of the wife's property, as well as herself. Under the early law as now, the husband was obliged to support the wife, and it was thought but fair that he should have the management and control of all the property that she might have, in consideration of this obligation to support. But probably the best reason for tnis rule may be found in the fact, that when the feudal system prevailed, there were no obligations of citizenship, except such as arose out of the relation of lord and vassal in respect to the land which the latter may hold under the lord, and for which the vassal had to render services of various kinds, usually of such a nature that only a man could perform them.[1] When, therefore, lands were acquired by a woman, by descent or otherwise, who subsequently married, her husband had to perform the services due to the lord, and it was but just that he should have the credit of it. The same reasons did not apply to personal property, but in this rude age personal property was inconsiderable; and consisted chiefly of such that a married couple would use in common, household goods and domestic animals, which after a long use in common with like property of the husband, would well nigh pass beyond the possibility of identification, and because of this difficulty the law gave to the legal representative of the duality all such property that was not capable of easy identification as constituting part of the wife's paraphernalia. These reasons are not presented as the justification of such a law at the present day. So grossly unjust has it been felt to be for years and centuries, that with the aid of equity's corrective influence over the common law, whereby the hard logic of the common law may be respected and yet substantial justice be within the reach of all, it has been

---

[1] See Tiedeman on Real Property § 20; 1 Washb. on Real Prop. 46, citing 3 Guizot Nat. Hist. Civ. 108.

§ 162

possible for any one about to convey property, whether real or personal, to a woman, or for the young woman herself, before marriage, to so settle her property, that it shall remain her separate property, free from the control of her husband, notwithstanding the rules of the common law. And it is probably on account of the means furnished by equity jurisprudence of escape from the hardships of the common law in this respect, that the statutory changes, now so common, were not made ages ago. Indeed, it is the firm conviction of many jurists that statutes, which give to married women the same absolute and exclusive control over their property, which they had when single, do not confer upon woman an unmixed good. For while she is thus given the unlimited power of control over her property, she may ruin herself financially by giving heed to the persuasions of her husband, against which she cannot usually hold out, more readily than she could when, under the rules of equity, her separate property is settled upon her, with limitations upon her power of control, imposed for her own protection. But there can be no doubt that the common law in respect to the property rights of married women, in the present age, cannot be justified by any rule or reason known to constitutional law, however just it may have been under the feudal system. But it is to be supposed that, in consequence of the proverbial conservatism of the law, and the remarkable longevity of common-law principles, the wrong can only be remedied by statutory changes.[1]

§ 163. **Legal disabilities of married women.**— It is also a consequence of the legal theory, that the personality of the wife is lost in that of the husband, that married women

---

[1] "Marriage is not simply a contract; but a public institution, not reserved by any constitutional provision from legislative control; and all rights in property, growing out of the marital relation, are alike subject to regulation by the legislative power." Noel v. Ewing, 9 Ind. 37.

are placed under various legal disabilities, the most important of which is that they cannot make a valid contract. If they could not hold property in their individual capacity, it would hardly be consistent to give them the power to make contracts in their own names. As agents of their husbands they could make any contracts that came within the scope of their expressed or implied authority, but they were not allowed to make contracts, the performance of which they could not guarantee, since their property was not subject to their control. When equity provided a way, in which a married woman could hold separate property, she was permitted in equity to make contracts in respect to such property, and the creditors could enforce such claims against the separate estate by instituting the proper action in a court of equity. This was but just, for the disability to contract was but a consequence of the common-law rule, which gave to the husband the complete control of her property. When, therefore, by statutory changes, her property rights are secured to the married woman, free from the control of her husband, there can be no reason or justice in retaining the common-law disability to make a contract, except as a protection to herself against the evil designs of her husband. It is no doubt permissible for the law to provide this protection by making void all her contracts and gifts of property to her husband, but the disability must be kept within these limits, in order to be consonant with common justice.

§ 136

CHAPTER XIII.

POLICE REGULATION OF THE RELATION OF PARENT AND CHILD, AND OF GUARDIAN AND WARD.

SECTION 165. Original character of the relation of parent and child — Its political aspect.
  166. No limitation to State interference.
  166a. People v. Turner.
  167. Compulsory education.
  168. Parents' duty of maintenance.
  169. Child's duty to support indigent parents.
  170. Relation of guardian and ward altogether subject to State regulation.
  171. Testamentary guardians.

§ 165. Original character of the relation of parent and child — Its political aspect. — The early history of all the Aryan races, from whom the modern European races have sprung, reveals the family, with the husband and father as autocrat, as the primal social and political organization, upon which subsequently the broader organizations of tribe and nation were established. The tribe was a union of families, of Gentes, and the nation a union of tribes. But the family organization remained intact, and the tribal government was represented by the father or head of the family. The other members of the family did not have a voice in the administration of the tribal affairs, nor did the government of the tribe have any control of the concerns of the family. The father and head of the family ruled its members without constraint, could command the services of the child, make a valid sale of the adult children as well as the minor, and punish them for offenses, inflicting any penalty which his wisdom or caprice may suggest, even to the taking of life. Nor did this police control extend only to the offenses committed against the members of the same family. The members of one family bore no legal relation to those of another, except the two heads. If the member of one family was guilty of a trespass upon the rights of a member of another family, the head of the latter family demanded redress from the head of the former, and he would inflict the proper punishment upon his offending kinsman, or else prepare to bear the responsibility of the act in an appeal to the tribal authorities.

It is not necessary to enter into the details of the family relation, in its political character. It is sufficient for the present purposes to say that it is in the political character of the family as an institution of government, that the father is given this absolute control over the children and others forming the family of which he is the head and ruler. It is not in his natural capacity of a sire that the justification of this control is to be found. When, therefore, the family ceases to be a subdivision of the body politic, and becomes a domestic relation instead of a political institution, we expect to find, and we do find as a fact, that this absolute control of the children is taken away. The children, like the father, become members of the body politic, and acquire political and civil rights, independently of the father. Then this supreme control is transferred to the State, the father retaining only such power of control over his children during minority, as the promptings of nature and a due consideration of the welfare of the child would suggest. By the abolition of the family relation as a political institution, the child, whatever may be his age, acquires the same claim to liberty of action as the adult, viz.: the right to the largest liberty that is consistent with the enjoyment of a like liberty on the part of others; and he is only subject to restraint, so far as such restraint is necessary for the promotion of the general welfare or beneficial as a means of protection to himself. The parent has no natural vested right to the control of his child. Except in the day when the family was a political institution of which the father was the king or

§ 165

ruler, his power over the child during minority is in the nature of a trust, reposed in him by the State (or it may, historically, be more correct to say, which the State reserved to the father, when the political character of the family was abolished), which may be extended or contracted, according as the public welfare may require. To recognize in the father any absolute right to the control of his child, would be to deny that " all men are born free and equal.'' For if the child is subject to the commands of the father, as a matter of abstract right, there can be no limitation upon the parental control, except what may be necessary to promote the general welfare, for the prevention of cruelty to the children, and for the protection of the rights of members of other families ; the political powers of the father of the patriarchal age could not be taken away from him and vested in some other State organization. The father has as much a right to control the actions of his child when he is over twenty-one years of age as when he is below that age. Liberty, therefore, as we understand it, was not created for him ; the heads of families alone are freemen. But it is said that men are free to do as they please, when they become of age. By what authority are they denied their full liberty until they reach the age of twenty-one? Is a youth of twenty, by nature, less free than the youth of twenty-one? Is it because the father has a natural right to control the actions, and command the obedience, of the youth of twenty, and had not the same power of control over the youth of twenty-one? We have seen that in his political character the father exercised the same absolute control over the members of his family, whatever may be the age of the child or other member of the family. With the abolition of the family, as a political institution, the parental control was limited to the period of minority of the child, and the adult was free to do as he pleased, being only amenable to the State or society for infractions of its laws. If all men are born free and equal, are entitled to the

§ 165

equal protection of the law, they can claim the enjoyment of equal liberty, whether they be children or parents, infants or adults, under or over twenty-one years of age. It is only, therefore, as a police regulation, that the subjection of minor children to the control of parents may be justified under constitutional limitations. The authority to control the child is not the natural right of the parents; it emanates from the State, and is an exercise of police power.

§ 166. **No limitation to State interference.** — If it be true that the control of children, by whomsoever the control is exerted, is an exercise of police power, and can be justified only as such, on constitutional principles, then the parental control is a privilege or duty, and not a natural right; and this view meets with a tacit acquiescence, as long as the limitations upon the parental control are confined to the ordinary ones, with which long usage has made us familiar. Thus we readily acknowledge the right of the State to punish the parent for inflicting cruel and excessive punishment; and in a clear case of cruel treatment, we would not be shocked if the authorities were to take the child away from the parent. But we are startled if the rule is carried to its extreme limit in laying down the proposition, that, being a privilege, the State may take away the parental control altogether, and assume the care and education of the child, whenever in the judgment of the legislature such action may be necessary for the public good, or the welfare of the child. And such has been, with few exceptions, the opinion of the courts of this country. Thus, at common law, and everywhere in America, in the absence of statutory regulation to the contrary, the father has the absolute control of his minor children, to the exclusion of a similar right in the mother. Is this discrimination against the mother in recognition of the father's natural right to the custody of the child? If this were true, the legislature of New Jersey exceeded its powers when it provided by stat-

§ 166

ute that the mother, in cases of separation, shall have the custody of children of tender age. But the Supreme Court of that State held that the act was constitutional. In rendering the decision the court said : —

" The argument (that the act is unconstitutional) proceeds upon the assumption that the parent has the same right of property in the child that he has in his horse, or that the master has in his slave, and that the transfer of the custody of the child from the father to the mother is an invasion of the father's right of property. The father has no such right. He has no property whatever in his children. The law imposes upon him, for the good of society and for the welfare of the child, certain specified duties. By the laws of nature and of society he owes the child protection, maintenance, and education. In return for the discharge of those duties, and to aid in their performance, the law confers on the father a qualified right to the services of the child. But of what value, as a matter of property, are the services of a child under seven years of age? But whatever may be their value, the domestic relations and the relative rights of parent and child are all under the control and regulation of municipal laws. They may and must declare how far the rights and control of the parent shall extend over the child, how they shall be exercised, and where they shall terminate. They have determined at what age the right of the parent to the services of the child shall cease and what shall be an emancipation from his control." [1]

It has also been held that Congress has power to enlist minors in the navy or army, without the consent, and against the wishes of the parents.[2]

In New York, also, it has been held that the commissioners of public charity have the power, under the statutes of

[1] Bennett v. Bennett, 13 N. J. Eq. 114.
[2] See United States v. Bainbridge, 1 Mason, 71.

§ 166

that State, to bind out to apprenticeship a child left to their care by the father, without providing the means of support, against the father's will or without his consent.[1]

§ 166*a*. **People v. Turner.** — But in a late decision of the Supreme Court of Illinois the natural right of the parent to the custody of his minor child has been recognized and affirmed, and an act of the legislature declared unconstitutional, which empowered certain officers to commit to the reformatory school all minors under a certain age, when he is found to be without the proper parental care.[2]   The Court say :

" The contingencies enumerated, upon the happening of either of which the power may be exercised, are vagrancy, destitution of proper parental care, mendicancy, ignorance, idleness, or vice.   Upon proof of any one the child is deprived of home, and parents, and friends, and confined for more than half of an ordinary life. . It is claimed that the law is administered for the moral welfare and intellectual improvement of the minor, and the good of society.   From the record before us we know nothing of the management. We are only informed that a father desires the custody of his child, and that he is restrained of his liberty.   Therefore we can only look at the language of the law and the power granted.

" What is proper parental care?   The best and kindest parents would differ in the attempt to solve this question. No two scarcely agree; and when we consider the watchful supervision which is so unremitting over the domestic affairs of others, the conclusion is forced upon us that there is not a child in the land who could not be proved, by two or more witnesses, to be in this sad condition.   Ignorance, idleness, vice, are relative terms.   Ignorance is always pre-

---

1 People *v.* Weisenbach, 60 N. Y. 385.
2 People *v.* Turner, 55 Ill. 280 (8 Am. Rep. 645).

§ 166*a*

ferable to error, but at most is only venial. It may be general, or it may be limited. Though it is sometimes said that ' idleness is the parent of vice,' yet the former may exist without the latter. It is strictly an abstinence from labor or employment. If the child performs all its duties to parents and to society, the State has no right to compel it to labor. Vice is a very comprehensive term. Acts, wholly innocent in the estimation of many good men would, according to the code of ethics of others, show fearful depravity. What is the standard to be? What extent of enlightenment, what amount of industry, what degree of virtue, will save from the threatened imprisonment? In our solicitude to form youth for the duties of civil life, we should not forget the rights, which inhere both in parents and children. The principle of the absorption of the child in, and its complete subjection to the despotism of, the State is wholly inadmissible in the modern civilized world."

" The parent has the right to the care, custody and assistance of his child. The duty to maintain and protect it is a principle of natural law. He may even justify an assault and battery in the defense of his children, and uphold them in their lawsuits. Thus the law recognizes the power of parental duty, strongly inculcated by writers on natural law, in the education of children. To aid in the performance of these duties and enforce obedience parents have authority over them. The municipal law should not disturb this relation except for the strongest reasons. The ease with which it may be disrupted under the laws in question; the slight evidence required, and the informal mode of procedure, make them conflict with the natural right of the parent. Before any abridgement of the right, gross misconduct, or almost total unfitness on the part of the parent should be clearly proved. This power is an emanation from God, and every attempt to infringe upon it, except from dire necessity, should be resisted in all well governed States. In this country the hope of the child in

§ 166a

respect to its education and future advancement is mainly dependent upon the father; for this he struggles and toils through life; the desire of its accomplishment operating as one of the most powerful incentives to industry and thrift. The violent absorption of this relation would not only tend to wither these motives to action, but necessarily in time alienate the father's natural affections.

" But even the power of the parent must be exercised with moderation. He may use correction and restraint, but in a reasonable manner. He has the right to enforce only such discipline as may be necessary to the discharge of his sacred trust; only moderate correction and temporary confinement. We are not governed by the twelve tables, which formed the Roman law. The fourth table gave fathers the power of life and death and of sale over their children. In this age and country such provisions would be atrocious. If a father confined or imprisoned his child for one year, the majesty of the law would frown upon the unnatural act, and every tender mother and kind father would rise up in arms against such monstrous inhumanity. Can the State, as *parens patriæ*, exceed the power of the natural parent, except in punishing crime?

" These laws provide for the ' safe keeping,' of the child, they direct his ' commitment ' and only a ' ticket of leave,' or the uncontrolled discretion of a board of guardians, will permit the imprisoned boy to breathe the pure air of heaven outside his prison walls, and to feel the instincts of manhood by contact with the busy world. The *mittimus* terms him ' a proper subject for commitment;' directs the superintendent to ' take his body ' and the sheriff indorses upon it, ' executed by delivering the body of the within named prisoner.' The confinement may be from one to fifteen years, according to the age of the child. Executive clemency cannot open the prison doors, for no offense has been committed. The writ *habeas corpus*, the writ for the security of liberty, can afford no relief, for the sovereign power of

§ 166*a*

the State, as *parens patriœ*, has determined the imprisonment beyond recall. Such a restraint upon natural liberty is tyranny and oppression. If, without crime, without the conviction of any offense, the children of the State are to thus confined for the 'good of society,' then society had better be reduced to its original elements, and free government acknowledged a failure." [1]

In a later case, arising under a subsequent statute, act of May 29, 1879, which provides for the committal to the industrial school of dependent infant girls, who are beggars, wanderers, homeless or without proper parental care, it was held that the act was constitutional, and was distinguished from the act under consideration in People *v.* Turner; by better provisions for a judicial hearing before commitment under the act.[2] Laws committing homeless children to industrial schools have in other States been generally maintained.[3]

The opposite views of this most interesting phase of police

[1] This case was also published in the American Law Register, vol. 10 (N. s.), p. 372, with an able annotation by Judge Redfield. The following is a quotation from the annotation: —

"We have read this decision with great admiration. There can be no question, it is a very creditable advance in favor of liberty among the children of white parents, as well as those of more sombre hue. All classes of men, and women too, under this decision, may keep their own children at home and educate them in their own way. This is a very wonderful advance in the way of liberty. It must certainly be a great comfort to a devout Roman Catholic, father or mother, to reflect that now his child cannot be driven into a Protestant school and made to read the Protestant version of the Holy Scriptures. And what is more, his or her child cannot be torn from home and immured in a Protestant prison, for ten or more years, and trained in what he regards a heretical and deadly faith, to the destruction of his own soul. This is right and we hope the court will be able to maintain this noble stand upon first principles."

[2] Ex parte Ferrier, 103 Ill. 367 (42 Am. Rep. 10).

[3] Prescott *v.* State, 19 Ohio St. 184 (2 Am. Rep. 388) ; Roth *v.* House of Refuge, 31 Md. 329; Milwaukee Industrial School *v.* Supervisors of Milwaukee Co., 40 Wis. 328 (22 Am. Rep. 702) ; House of Refuge *v.* Ryan, 37 Ohio St. 197.

§ 166*a*

power are thus presented to the reader with great particularity, and the solution of the problem depends upon the nature of the parent's claim to the custody of the child. If it is the parent's natural right, then the State cannot arbitrarily take the child away from the care of the parents; and any interference with the parental control must be justified as a police regulation on the grounds that the assumption of the control of the child by the State is necessary for the public good, because of the evil character of the parents; and like all other similar cases of restraint upon natural right, the commitment of the child to the care of the State authorities must rest upon a judicial decree, after a fair trial, in which the parents have the right to appear and defend themselves against the charge of being unfit to retain the custody of the child. Whereas, if the parental control be only a privilege or duty, granted or imposed by the State, it rests with the discretion of the legislature to determine under what circumstances, if at all, a parent may be entrusted with the rearing of his child, and it is not a judicial question whether the legislative judgment was well founded.[1]

[1] "The duties and authority pertaining to the relation of parent and child have their foundations in nature it is true. Nevertheless all civilized governments have regarded this relation as falling within the legitimate scope of legislative control. Except in countries which live in barbarism, the authority of the parent over the child is nowhere left absolutely without municipal definition and regulation. The period of minority is fixed by positive law, when parental control shall cease. Within this, the age when the child may marry at its own will is in like manner defined. The matter of education is deemed a legitimate function of the State and with us is imposed upon the legislature as a duty by imperative provisions of the constitution. The right of custody, even, is sometimes made to depend upon considerations of moral fitness in the parent to be entrusted with the formation of the character of his own offspring. In some countries, and even in some of our American States, education has for more than a century been made compulsory upon the parent, by the infliction of direct penalties for its neglect. The right of the parent to ruin his child either morally or physically has no existence in nature. The subject has always been regarded as within the purview of legislative authority. How far this interference should extend is a

§ 166a

But while we may reach the conclusion, that there is no constitutional limitation to the power of the State to interfere with the parental control of minors, it does not necessarily follow that an arbitrary denial of the parental authority will in every case be enforcible or beneficial. The natural affection of parents for their offspring is ordinarily the strongest guaranty that the best interests of the child as well as of society will be subserved, by leaving the child to the ordinary care of the parents, and providing for State interference in the exceptional cases, when the parents are of such vile character, that the very atmosphere of the home reeks with vice and crime ; and when it is impossible for the child, under its home influences, to develop into a fairly honest man. The natural bond, between parent and child, can never be ignored by the State, without detriment to the public welfare ; and a law, which interferes without a good cause with the parental authority, will surely prove a dead letter. "Constitutions fail when they ignore our nature. Plato's republic, abolishing the family, making infants but the children of the State, exists only in the imagination."[1] These are, however, considerations by which to determine the wisdom of a law ; they cannot bring the constitutionality of the law into question, enabling the courts to refuse to carry the law into execution in any case that might arise under it.

§ 167. **Compulsory education.** — One of the popular phases of police power at the present day is the education of the children at the expense of the State. For many years it has been the policy of every State in the Union to

question, not of constitutional power for the courts, but of expediency and propriety, which it is the sole province of the legislature to determine. The judiciary has no authority to interfere with this exercise of the legislative judgment; and to do so would be to invade the province which by the constitution is assigned exclusively to the law-making power." State *v.* Clottu, 33 Ind. 409.

[1] Bliss on Sovereignty, p. 17.

bring the common school education within the reach of the poorest child in the land, by establishing free schools ; and in the estimation of many the best test of the civilization of a people or a State is the condition of its public schools; the more public schools, properly organized, the more civ- ilized.   Whatever may be the view one may hold of the question of compulsory education, none but the most radi- cal disciple of the *laissez-faire* doctrine will deny to the State the right to establish and maintain free schools at the public expense, provided the attendance upon such schools be left to the discretion of the child or its parents.   When, however, the State is not satisfied with simply providing schools, the attendance to which is free to all ; but desires to force every child to partake of the State bounty, against its will and the wishes of its parents, perhaps against the honest convictions of the parent that attend- ance upon the public schools will be injurious to the child : when this exercise of police power is attempted, it will meet with a determined opposition from a large part of the population.   For reasons already explained,[1] the child who is altogether bereft of parental care, cannot in- terpose any legal objection ; for he is presumed to be mentally incapable of judging what will best promote his welfare.   But it becomes a more serious question when the child has parents, and they oppose his attendance upon the public school.   If the children do not go to any school, it does not appear so hard to compel the children to attend the State schools ; but it is an apparent wrong for the State to deny to the parent his right to determine which school the child shall attend.   And yet the constitutionality of the law, in its application to the two cases, must be governed by the same law.   If the control of children is a parental right, instead of a privilege or duty, then in neither case is the State authorized to interfere with the parental authority,

---

[1] See *ante*, § 50.

§ 167

unless the parent is morally depraved or insane: while the interference in both cases would be constitutional, if the parental control is held to be a privilege or duty, according to the point of view. It is probable that, under the influence of the social forces now at work the latter view will prevail, and compulsory education become very general, at least to the extent of requiring every child to attend some school within the specified ages.

§ 168. **Parent's duty of maintenance.**—The law of every civilized nation imposes upon the parent the duty to maintain and support the child during his period of infancy, when he is unable to support himself. Having brought the child into the world, he owes this duty, not only to the child, but to society as well, and the legal enforcement of this duty is a justifiable exercise of police power. Probably no one will dispute this, as long as the duty is confined to the support of the child during the time when it is physically or mentally incapable of providing for its own maintenance; and the duty may be made to last as long as the incapacity exists, notwithstanding it is permanent and will continue through life to old age. But when there is no actual incapacity, and the child is really able to provide for him or herself, may the State impose upon the parent the duty to support the child during the time that the State requires the child to be in attendance upon the schools? This might very properly be considered a doubtful exercise of police power. Still, if the education is necessary to make the child a valuable citizen, and can be made compulsory; as long as this requirement is kept within the limits of necessity, it would seem that the maintenance of the child during its attendance upon the school would be as much the duty of the parent, as to provide for the child's physical wants during its early infancy. If the question is ever raised, and this is quite likely in any effort to make com-

§ 168

pulsory education a realized fact, it will probably be settled in favor of the power of the State to impose this duty.

§ 169. **Child's duty to support indigent parents.** — Blackstone says: " The duties of children to their parents arise from a principle of natural justice and retribution. For to those who gave us existence, we naturally owe sub. jection and obedience during our minority, and honor and reverence ever after ; they who protected us in the weakness of infancy are entitled to our protection in the infirmity of their age ; they who by sustenance and education have enabled their offspring to prosper, ought in return to be supported by that offspring in case they stand in need of assistance." [1]   In the support of the claim of a moral duty the reasons assigned by Blackstone are all sufficient, but they cannot constitute the basis of a legal duty.   Independently of statute in England and in this country, the child is under no legal duty to support its aged parents.[2] But statutes have been passed in England and in most of of the United States, providing for the legal enforcement of this obligation, at least to the extent of relieving the public from the support of the paupers.[3]   The same legal duty has been imposed upon children by the laws of other countries, for example, the Athenians.[4]   On what ground can the imposition of these statutory duties be justified? Gratitude is the reason assigned by Blackstone for the exaction of the moral duty. Will the law undertake to compel children to manifest to their parents gratitude for past care and maintenance? That is clearly not the object of the statutes. Their object is to relieve the community of

[1] 1 Bl. Com. 453.
[2] Rex v. Munder, 1 Stra. 190; Lebanon v. Grifflin, 45 N. H. 558; Stone v. Stone, 32 Conn. 142; Edwards v. Davis, 16 Johns. 281; Reeve Dom. Rel. 284.
[3] Schouler Dom. Rel. 365; 2 Kent, 208.
[4] 1 Bl. Com. 453; 2 Kent's Com. 207.

§ 169

the necessity to support the aged and indigent.   As a protection against an increased public burden, the law compels the child to support his parents.   The State has a clear right to compel the parent to maintain his infant child, because the father or mother is responsible for its birth.   They brought the child into the world, primarily and, in ordinary cases, chiefly to gratify their own desires ; and it is but just that the State should compel the parents to relieve the community of the necessity of supporting their offspring.   But the child has done nothing, which in any legal sense would make him responsible to the public to provide his aged parents with the means of support.   The law can never be invoked for the purpose of enforcing pure moral obligations ; nor can a law be justified by the fact that its enforcement compels incidentally the performance of a moral or religious duty.   Clearly, there is no reason arising out of the relation of parent and child, upon which can be rested a legal duty of the child to support the parent.   If it can be justified on constitutional grounds at all, as an exercise of police power, it can only be as a special tax upon the child, and is constitutional or not, according as special taxes are permitted or prohibited by the limitations of the constitution.

§ 170. **Relation of guardian and ward altogether subject to State regulation.** — Inasmuch as the guardian is ordinarily appointed by a court of the State in which the minor resides, there can be no doubt that the rights, obligations and duties of guardian and ward to each other are subject to the almost unlimited control of the State.   The guardianship is instituted for the benefit of the minor, and it is for the legislature to determine what will advance his interests.   But there is some doubt involved in determining the limitations of police power in the control and regulation of the powers and duties of

§ 170

§ 171. **Testamentary guardians.** — They are those who are appointed by testament by the parent of the minor child. It is permitted by the law of England and of the United States for the father to appoint by testament a guardian by will, and it might very well be urged that if the parent has a natural right to the care and control of his minor child, he would have a right to determine who shall succeed him in the enjoyment of this right. The one position is no more unreasonable than the other. But the argument in favor of the right to appoint testamentary guardians is historically weakened by the fact that it did not exist at common law, the privilege being granted for the first time by statute (12 Charles, II). " It is clear by the common law a man could not, by any testamentary disposition, affect either his land or the guardianship of his children." [1] It is our own opinion that all guardianships are trusts or privileges, and do not confer upon the guardians any absolute rights ; and such has been the conclusion of the courts, in the few cases in which the question has been raised. [2]

---

[1] Lord Alvanley in Ex parte Chester, 7 Ves. 370. But see Coke Lit. 87*b*, in which there are statements calculated to throw doubt upon the correctness of this position, at least so far as the guardianship of the ward's person is concerned.

[2] Beaufort *v.* Berty, 1 P. Wms. 703; Gilbert *v.* Schwenck, 14 M. & W. 488.

§ 171

CHAPTER XIV.

POLICE REGULATION OF THE RELATION OF MASTER AND SERVANT.

SECTION 175. Terms " master and servant " defined.
176. Relation purely voluntary.
177. Apprentices.
178. State regulation of private employments.
179. State regulation of public employments.

§ 175. Terms "master and servant" defined. — Although these terms were originally referable only to the case of menial or domestic servant, making one of the domestic relations, strictly so-called,[1] they have been so extended in their application as now to be synonymous with employer and employee.   A servant in the legal sense includes now, not only the menial servants of the household, but every class of persons, who for a compensation obligate themselves to render certain services to another. It may be true that in another age and under an earlier civilization, " the relation of master and servant presupposes two parties who stand on an unequal footing in their mutual dealings ;"[2] but that cannot be said of the relation at the present day, and under the American law.   Certain employments denote and compel the recognition of social inferiority.   But in the sight of the law the servant stands on a plane of equality with his master, and the constitution guarantees a like protection to the rights of both.

§ 176. Relation purely voluntary.— The relation of master and servant is purely voluntary, resting upon the contract of the parties, and as a general proposition it must

---

[1] See Schouler Dom. Rel. 599.
[2] Schouler Dom. Rel. 599.

ever remain voluntary. The relation ordinarily cannot rest upon compulsion. Every man has a natural right to hire his services to any one he pleases, or refrain from such hiring; and so, likewise, it is the right of every one to determine whose services he will hire. " It is a part of every man's civil rights," says Mr. Cooley,[1] " that he be left at liberty to refuse business relations with any person whomsoever, whether the refusal rests upon reason, or is the result of whim, caprice, prejudice, or malice. With his reasons neither the public nor third persons have any legal concern. It is also his right to have business relations with any one with whom he can make contracts; and if he is wrongfully deprived of this right by others, he is entitled to redress." This natural right is not limited simply to the formation of the relation of master and servant. Each party has the right to stipulate the terms and conditions upon which he will enter into the relation and refuse to form it, if the other party declines to yield to his demands. Government, therefore, cannot exert any restraint upon the actions of the parties, nor interfere, except at the call of one of the parties, to enforce his rights under the contract which constitutes the basis of the relation. The law may establish certain presumptions of the intentions of the parties, where they have not expressly agreed otherwise; but the right to agree upon whatever terms they please cannot be in any way abridged, as long as there is no trespass upon the rights of third parties or of the public.

§ 177. **Apprentices.** — But apprenticeships constitute an exception to this general rule; the ground for the exception being the minority of the apprentice when he enters into service. His right to make a valid contract for apprenticeship constitutes a legal exception to his general disability, and is, therefore, subject to whatever regulations

---

[1] Cooley on Torts, p. 278.

the State may see fit to impose.   The immaturity of the apprentice places him on an equal footing with his master, and he deserves and requires the protection of the law.

§ 178. **Regulation of private employment.** — But between adults, employer and employed, since all men are free and equal, and are entitled to the equal protection of the law, neither party can be compelled to enter into business relations with the other, except upon his own terms, voluntarily and free from any coercion whatsoever. . The State has no right to interfere in a private employment and stipulate the terms upon which the services are to be rendered.

Ordinarily, this proposition will be readily conceded, particularly if one considers the question in its bearings upon his own affairs.   A feeling of indignation arises within us at the contemplation of State interference to determine the wages we shall pay to our domestic servants.   But in so far as the question is removed from its relation to our own affairs, so that it becomes less and less influenced by our prejudice and self-interest, the contemplation of the social inequalities of life, and the truly heartless, if not iniquitous, oppression which is afforded by reason of these inequalities; when we see, more and more clearly each day, that the tendency of the present process of civilization is to concentrate social power into the hands of a few, who, unless restrained in some way, are able to dictate terms of employment to the masses, who must either accept them or remain idle; when at best they are barely enabled to provide for the more pressing wants of themselves and families, while their employers are, at least apparently, accumulating wealth to an enormous extent: when all this injustice exists, or seems to exist, the impulse of a generous nature is to call loudly for the intervention of the law to protect the poor wage-earner from the grasping cupidity of the employer.   That there is much suffering among the working

§ 178

classes there can be no doubt. And although there may be room for conjecture, whether the suffering is not largely due to their own improvidence and a desire to imitate the luxurious habits of the rich, rather than the oppression of the capitalists, it is certainly true that the employers occupy a vantage ground, by which they are enabled to appropriate to themselves a larger share of the profits of the enterprise. But he has acquired this superior position, this independence, through the exertions of his powers ; he is above, and can to some extent dictate terms to, his employees, because his natural powers are greater, either intellectually or morally ; and the profits which naturally flow from this superiority, are but just rewards of his own endeavors. At any rate, no law can successfully cope with these natural forces.

But there is undoubtedly a certain amount of unrighteous oppression of the working classes. In making the contract of hiring, the employer and workman deal with each other at arm's length. Generally speaking, so far at least as the settlement of the terms of hiring is concerned, their rights and interests are antagonistic. It is to the interest of the employer to get a given amount of work done for the lowest wages possible, and it is the interest of the wage-earner to get the highest wages obtainable for the given amount of work. If the parties cannot agree upon the terms which will be mutually profitable, can the law determine this dispute for the contesting parties ? By statute 30 and 31 Vict., ch. 105,[1] " equitable councils of conciliation," composed of delegates selected by the masters and workingmen, were empowered to adjust all such disputes, and determine the rate of wages to be paid to the workmen. As long as the submission of such disputes to such a council be left voluntary, the statute could meet with no constitutional objection, if it should be enacted in any of

[1] 1867.

§ 178

the American States. But its constitutionality would be very doubtful, if the submission was made compulsory. There is an irreconcilable inconsistency in seeking the protection of the law and yet proclaiming one's equality before the law. As soon as the law places one for any just reason under a disability, or gives to another a privilege not enjoyed in common by all,[1] protection from oppression becomes a duty of the State, so far as the disability or its cause, or the grant of the privilege, produces or renders the oppression possible. The law can only guarantee to men, on a legal plane of equality, protection against trespasses upon their rights. To place the working classes under special protection against the aggression of capital, beyond the careful and strict enforcement of their rights; to compel the employer to pay the rate of wages, determined by the State to be equitable, is to change the government from a government of freemen to a paternal government, or a despotism, which is the same thing.

But even if this reasoning should not be sufficient to prove the unconstitutionality of State interference in the relation of master and servant, the very futility of such interference would at least cast a doubt upon its constitutionality. Law can never create social forces. On the contrary, law is the resultant of the social forces. If the social forces at work at any given time produce an inequality in the material conditions of classes of society, and give rise to the oppression of one class by another; if the inferior class is not naturally strong enough to resist the oppression, when free from legal restraints, no law can afford it protection. For how can the workingman secure the enforcement of a law made for his protection, when the protection of the State is required, because his needs and the necessities of his family compel him to submit to the unrighteous exactions of the capitalist. Will not the

1 See *ante*, § 93.

§ 178

same needs and necessities force him to place by his vote men in the various State offices whose antipathy to his interests will make the law a dead letter, if not secure its repeal? In England, where suffrage is limited, such a law is somewhat reasonable, because those for whose benefit it was enacted are under legal disability. But in this country where suffrage is universal, and the wage-earners constitute a vast majority of the voters, if they are unable to assert their claims without the aid of law, they cannot do so with its aid. And thus their inefficacy confirms the unconstitutionality of laws, which are designed to protect the workman against the oppression of the employer. Laws, therefore, which are designed to regulate the terms of hiring in strictly private employments, are unconstitutional, because they operate as an interference with one's natural liberty, in a case in which there is no trespass upon private right, and no threatening injury to the public. And this conclusion not only applies to laws regulating the rate of wages of private workmen, but also any other law, whose object is to regulate any of the terms of hiring, such as the number of hours of labor per day, which the employer may demand. There can be no constitutional interference by the State in the private relation of master and servant except for the purpose of preventing frauds and trespasses.

§ 179. **Public employments.** — But when the employment is connected with a public interest, and particularly when it is connected with the enjoyment of a franchise or privilege, not enjoyed by private individuals, — a privilege which is granted because it will promote the public welfare, such as the railroad, the telegraph, the telephone, and the like, — the public is interested in the proper conduct of the business ; and any disturbance of, or interference with, its regular and orderly prosecution will materially affect the public interest. Where the privilege is a monopoly, as is practically the case with the telegraph in the United

States, a general disagreement of the employer with his operatives may often stop the wheels of industry and produce
a general paralysis of all commercial energies ; and although
the operatives of the railroad or of the telegraph are no more
entitled to the aid of the law in enforcing their demand, or
in securing better terms from their employers, than the
strictly private workman, any disagreement between the
railroad and telegraph companies and their employees affects
the public interest by interfering with their means of communication and transportation ; and to promote the general
welfare, not to aid the operatives, it is a legitimate exercise
of the police power of the State to compel both parties to
submit their claims to a competent tribunal, thus adjusting
their differences, and preventing an injury to the public.
There may be a practical inability to enforce even such a
a law, because of the powerful political influence of the
capitalists ; but it is nevertheless justifiable, on constitutional
grounds, because the legal equality is disturbed in these
cases by the grant to the corporation of a franchise, a privilege not obtainable by the workman.

§ 179

CHAPTER XV.

POLICE REGULATION OF CORPORATIONS.

SECTION 188. The inviolability of the charters of private corporations.
189. Police control of corporations.
190. Freedom from police control, as a franchise.
191. Police regulation of corporations in general.
192. Laws regulating rates and changes of corporations.
193. Police regulation of foreign corporations.
194. Police regulation of railroads.

§ 188. **The inviolability of the charters of private corporations.** — At a very early day, it was decided by the Supreme Court of the United States that the charter of a private corporation constituted a contract between the State and the stockholders or members of the corporation, by which the State, in consideration of the public benefit, and of the investment of capital in the corporate business, grants to these capitalists the power to act together as one legal personality, with corporate powers and liabilities, separate and apart from the individual responsibilities of the members. The opinion of Chief Justice Marshall, in the leading case on this subject,[1] has been so often affirmed by the Federal courts, as well as by the State Courts,[2] that it may now

---

[1] Dartmouth College v. Woodward, 4 Wheat. 518.

[2] See Planters' Bank v. Sharp, 6 How. (U. S.) 301; Trustees, etc., v. Indiana, 14 How. (U. S.) 268; Piqua Bank v. Knoop, 16 How. (U. S.) 369; Hawthorne v. Calef, 2 Wall. 10; Binghamton Bridge Case, 3 Wall. 51; State v. Moyes, 47 Me. 189; Wales v. Stetson, 2 Mass. 143; Central Bridge v. Lowell, 15 Gray, 106; Grammar School v. Burt, 11 Vt. 632; Backus v. Lebanon, 11 N. H. 19; People v. Manchester, 9 Wend. 351; Commonwealth v. Cullen, 13 Pa. St. 133; Cleveland, etc., R. R. Co. v. Speer, 56 Pa. St. 325; Zabriskie v. Hackensack, etc., R. R. Co., 17 N. J. Eq. 178; State v. Mayor of Newark, 35 N. J. L. 157; Bank of Old Dominion v. McVeigh, 20 Gratt. 457; Bank of State v. Bank of Cape Fear, 13 Ired. 75; Mills v. Williams, 11 Ired. 558; Young v. Harrison, 6 Ga. 130; State v. Accommodation Bank,

§ 188· (574)

be laid down as a settled principle of constitutional law, that an act of incorporation is such a contract between the State and the incorporators as is protected by the clause of the Federal constitution, which denies to the States the power to pass any law impairing the obligation of a contract.[1] Any law, therefore, of a State which impairs the corporate rights, or which repeals, annuls or amends the corporate charter, against the wishes of the members of the corporation, impairs the obligation of a contract, and is consequently void; unless the power, so to amend, annul or repeal the charter, is reserved to the State in the charter or by the general laws of the State, in force at the time that the charter was granted. It is now a very common statutory or constitutional provision that all charters of private corporations are held subject to the power of the State to repeal or amend. But, even in the case of such a reservation, the charter cannot be so amended or repealed as to interfere with the vested rights of property, which the stockholders may have acquired by and through the corporation.[2]

26 La. Ann. 288; State v. Tombeckbee Bank, 2 Stew. 30; Commercial Bank v. State, 14 Miss. 599; Mobile, etc., R. R. Co. v. Moseley, 52 Miss. 127; Sala v. New Orleans, 2 Woods (U. S. C. C.), 188; State v. Southern, etc., R. R. Co., 24 Tex. 80; Hamilton v. Keith, 5 Bush, 458; Marysville Turnpike Co v. How, 14 B. Mon. 429; Mechanics' Bank v. DeBolt, 1 Ohio St. 591; Edwards v. Jagers, 19 Ind. 407; Flint v. Woodhull, 25 Mich. 99; Bruffett v. G. W. Ry. Co., 25 Ill. 353; St. Louis v. Manufacturers' Sav. Bank, 49 Mo. 574; Farrington v. Tennessee, 95 U. S. 679.

[1] See an ingenious argument against the correctness of the decision of the court in the Dartmouth College Case, in 8 Am. Law Rev. 190. The writer of the article, inter alia, makes the point that, inasmuch as the author of this clause of the constitution, Judge Wilson, of Pennsylvania, afterwards of the Supreme court of the United States, was a Scotch lawyer, and therefore learned in the Roman or Civil law, we must look to that system for the real meaning of the phrase " obligation of a contract." In the Roman law, obligatio ex contractu, invariably meant a pecuniary liability.

[2] Holyoke Co. v. Lyman, 15 Wall. 500; Inland Fishery Commissioners v. Holyoke Water Power Co., 104 Mass. 446; Worcester v. N. and W. R. R. Co., 109 Mass. 103; Thornton v. Marginal Freight Railway, 123 Mass 32.

§ 188

§ 189. **Police control of corporations.** — It has been supposed that, because it is the settled law of this country that the legislature of a State cannot repeal or amend the charter of a private corporation, unless the power is expressly reserved, these perpetual corporations are placed beyond the reach of the ordinary police power of the State ; that, while all the rights of the natural person are subject to the exercise of the police power in the interest of the public, these corporations are free from this burden, because the slightest police regulation operates as a restriction of the enjoyment of the corporate franchise, and hence impairs the obligation of a contract. Such a construction of the operation of this constitutional provision is not only scientifically absurb, but it is in violation of the ordinary rules of constitutional construction, which provide for a strict construction of all grants by the State to the individual. Apart from the question whether the State can barter away its police power,[1] the intention of a legislature to place a private corporation beyond the reach of the police power of the State ; to grant to a corporation the right to do what it pleases in the exercise of its corporate powers, it matters not how much injury is inflicted upon the public, and yet be subject to no control or restraint, which is not provided by the laws in force when the charter was granted ; is so manifestly unreasonable, that we cannot suppose that the legislature so intended, unless this extraordinary privilege is expressly granted. It cannot be implied from the grant of the charter. The subjection of existing corporations to new police regulations does not involve a repeal or amendment of the charters, for an act of incorporation simply guarantees to the incorporators the right to act and do business as a corporate body, subject, of course, to the laws of the land, and the legitimate control of government. The legal *status* of the corporation, as an artificial person, does not

---

[1] As to which, see *post*, § 190.

§ 189

differ from the natural person, except so far as the charter may reserve or grant special privileges or impose peculiar burdens. As a general proposition, corporations are included under the name of " persons " in coming within the operation of the law. In order that the law may apply to corporations, it is not necessary that they be expressly named.[1] Thus general laws, relating to the validity or enforcement of contracts, are applicable to corporations, although persons are only mentioned.[2] So, also, are corporations included in the operation of laws relating to real estate, in which there is reference only to " inhabitants " and " occupiers." [3] Corporations are taxpayers, like natural persons, although the tax laws should speak only of " persons," " individuals," or " inhabitants ;" [4] and a law, relating to practice or procedure, which refers to " persons " or " residents," would also include corporations within its operation.[5] But where the law, on account of the peculiar

[1] Beaston v. Farmers' Bk., 12 Pet. 102; U. S. v. Amedy, 11 Wheat. 392; People v. Utica Ins. Co., 15 Johns. 382; Planters' & Mechanics' Bk. v. Andrews, 8 Porter, 404. Compare School Directors v. Carlisle Bk., 8 Watts, 291; Blair v. Worley, 1 Scam. 178. And see, Com. v. Phœnix Bk., 11 Metc. 129; Androscoggin Water Power Co. v. Bethel Steam Mill Co., 64 Me. 441.

[2] Mott v. Hicks, 1 Cow. 513; State of Indiana v. Woram, 6 Hill, 33; State v. Nashville University, 4 Humph. 157; Commercial Bk. v. Nolan, 8 Miss. 508.

[3] Curtis v. Kent Water Works, 7 B. & C. 314; State v. Nashville University, 4 Humph. 157; King v. Gardner, Cowper, 79; Lehigh Bridge Co. v. Lehigh Coal & Nav. Co., 4 Rawle, 8.

[4] Otis v. Weare, 8 Gray, 509; People v. Utica Ins. Co., 15 Johns. 358; International L. Ass. Co. v. Comrs., 28 Barb. 318; Ontario Bk. v. Bunnell, 10 Wend. 186; Baldwin v. Trustees, 37 Me. 369; Curtis v. Kent Water Works, 7 B. & C. 314.

[5] Knox v. Protection Ins. Co., 9 Conn. 430; Mayor of Mobile v. Rowland, 26 Ala. (N. S.) 498; Planters' Bk. v. Andrews, 8 Porter, 404; Trenton Bk. v. Haverstick, 6 Halst. 171; Mineral Point R. R. v. Keep, 22 Ill. 9; City of St. Louis v. Rogers, 7 Mo. 19; Bushel v. Commonwealth Ins. Co., 15 Serg. & R. 176; Eslava v. Ames Plow Co., 47 Ala. 384; Brauser v. New England Fire Ins. Co., 21 Wis. 506; Bristol & Chicago & Aurora R. R. 15 Ill. 436; Bk. of No. America v. Dunville, etc., R. R., 82 Ill. 493; Western

§ 189

character of the corporation as a legal entity, relates to matters which are connected with and can only concern natural persons, the law cannot apply to corporations. For example, a corporation cannot be a rebel within the operation of the confiscation acts of the United States.[1]

The act of incorporation, therefore is a governmental act of creation. It creates a legal, artificial personality which becomes the subject of rights, and like any other legal personality holds these rights subject to the ordinary laws of the State. Unless there is an express reservation of a freedom from the restraint of police regulations, it would be an exceedingly liberal, and hence wrongful, construction of the constitutional protection against the impairment of the obligation of contracts, to place corporations above and beyond the ordinary police power of the State. As a general proposition, the principle here advocated has been recognized and adopted by the courts generally. It is only in the application of the principle to a particular case that any doubt as to its correctness is felt or expressed.

The leading case on the subject is that of Thorpe *v.* Rutland, etc., R. R. Co.,[2] in which Judge Redfield has discussed fully and at length the police control of corporations. In referring to the general police power of the State by which persons and property are subjected to all kinds of restraints and burdens, in order to secure the general comfort, health, and prosperity of the State, of the perfect " right in the legislature to do which no question ever was, or upon acknowlededgd general principles, ever can be made, so far as natural persons are concerned," he says : —

" It is certainly calculated to excite surprise and alarm, that the right to do the same in regard to railways should be made a serious question. This objection is made gener-

Transportation Co. *v.* Scheu, 19 N. Y. 408.   See Olcott *v.* Tioga R. R., 20 N. Y. 210; Commercial M. F. Ins. Co. *v.* Duerson, 28 Gratt. 631.

[1] Risley *v.* Phœnix Bank, 83 N. Y. 318.
[2] 27 Vt. 150.

§ 189

ally upon two grounds : 1. That it subjects corporations to a virtual destruction by the legislature; and 2. That it is an attempt to control the obligation of one person to another, in matters of merely private concern. * * *

" All the cases agree that the indispensable franchises of corporations can not be destroyed or essentially modified. This is the very point upon which the leading case of Dartmouth College v. Woodward, was decided, and which every well considered case in this country maintains. But when it is attempted upon this basis to deny the power of regulating the internal policy of railroads, and their mode of transacting their general business, so far as it tends unreasonably to infringe the rights or interests of others, it is putting the whole subject of railway control quite above the legislation of the country. * * * This is a control by legislative action, coming within the operation of the maxim, *sic utere tuo ut alienum non lœdas*, and which has always been exercised in this manner in all free States, in regard to those whose business is dangerous and destructive to other persons, property, or business. Slaughterhouses, powder mills, or houses for keeping powder, unhealthy manufactories, keeping of wild animals, and even domestic animals, dangerous to persons or property, have always been regarded as under the control of the legislature. It seems incredible how any doubt should have arisen upon the point now before the court. And it would seem it could not, except from some undefined apprehension, which seems to have prevailed to a considerable extent, that a corporation did possess some more exclusive powers and privileges upon the subject of its business, than a natural person in the same business, with the equal power to pursue and accomplish it, which I trust has been sufficiently denied." [1] * * *

[1] See, also, to the same effect, Gowen v. Penobscott R. R. Co., 44 Me. 140; Cummings v. Maxwell, 45 Me. 190; Commonwealth v. Intoxicating Liquors, 115 Mass. 153; Lord v. Litchfield, 36 Conn. 116 (4 Am Rep. 41); Frankford, etc., Ry. Co. v. Philadelphia, 58 Pa. St. 119; Taggert v.

§ 189

§ 190. **Freedom from police control, as a franchise.** —
The claim has often been made that, if it is stipulated in
the charter of a corporation that it shall not be subjected to
a specific police regulation, such a contract is binding upon
all the subsequent legislatures, and they are powerless to
prevent an injury to the public by instituting this regulation.   In other words, it is claimed, that the State may, by
contract irrevocably preclude itself from the exercise of its
ordinary police power, it matters not what evil consequences
to the public may thereby be prevented.   The recognition
of this doctrine would, if often acted upon, certainly hamper the government in its effort to protect its citizens from
threatening dangers.   The dangerous character of the doctrine is particularly noticeable in its application to the police
control of corporations.   The franchise of the corporation,
even if it consists only in the privilege of acting and doing
business in a corporate capacity, enables it, as against the
private individual, to occupy a vantage ground; its power
for harming and controlling the rights and interests of individuals is thereby greatly increased, and the necessity for
police control, in order that the rights of individuals may
not be exposed to the danger of trespass, is proportionately
increased.   To recognize in a legislature the power by a
contract to tie the hands of all future legislatures, and deprive them of the power to interpose regulations that may
become needful as a protection to the public against the
aggressions or other unlawful acts of the corporation, would
be a specimen of political suicide.   It has, therefore, been
often decided, in the American courts, Federal and State,
that the State cannot barter away, or in any way curtail its

Western, etc., R. R. Co., 24 Md. 563; Haynes v. Carter, 9 La. Ann. 265;
Louisville, etc., R. R. Co. v. Ballard, 2 Met. (Ky.) 165; Blair v. Milwau-
kee, etc., R. R. Co., 20 Wis. 254; Reapers' Bank v. Willard, 24 Ill. 433;
Bank of Republic v. Hamilton, 21 Ill. 53; Dingman v. People, 51 Ill. 277;
State v. Herod, 29 Iowa, 123; Gorman v. Pac. R. R. Co., 26 Mo. 441; Ex
parte N. E. & S. W. R. R. Co., 37 Ala. 679.

exercise of any of those powers, which are essential attributes of sovereignty, and particularly the police power, by which the actions of individuals are so regulated as not to injure others; and any contract, by which the State undertakes to do this, is void, and does not come within the constitutional protection.[1] In a late case, it has been definitely settled that the power to regulate the actions of individuals and corporations, for the promotion of the public health and the public morals, can never be restricted or suppressed by any contract or agreement of the State. In delivering the opinion of the court, ———, J. says : " The appellant insists that, so far as the act of 1869 partakes of the nature of an irrepealable contract, the legislature exceeded its authority, and it had no power to tie the hands of the legislature in the future from legislating on that subject without being bound by the terms of the statute then enacted. This proposition presents the real point in the case. Let us see clearly what it is. It does not deny the power of that legislature to create a corporation, with power to do the business of landing live stock and providing a place for slaughtering them in the city. It does not deny the power to locate the place where this shall be done exclusively. It does not deny even the power to give an exclusive right, for the time being, to particular persons or to a corporation to provide this stock landing, and to establish this slaughterhouse. But it does deny the power of that legislature to continue this right so that no future legislature, not even the same body, can repeal or modify it, or grant similar privileges to others. It concedes that such a law, so long

<hr>

[1] See Beer Company *v.* Massachusetts, 97 U. S. 25; Fertilizing Company *v.* Hyde Park, 97 U. S. 659; Stone *v.* Mississippi, 101 U. S. 814; Thorpe *v.* Rutland, etc., R. R. Co., 27 Vt. 140, 149; People *v.* Commissioners, 59 N. Y. 92; Hammett *v.* Philadelphia, 65 Pa. St. 146 (3 Am. Rep. 615); Hirn *v.* State, 1 Ohio St. 15; Bradley *v.* McAtee, 7 Bush, 667 (3 Am. Rep. 309); Indianapolis, etc., R. R. Co. *v.* Kercheval, 16 Ind. 84; Toledo, etc., R. R. Co. *v.* Jacksonville, 67 Ill. 37; Chicago Packing Co. *v.* Chicago, 88 Ill. 221.

§ 190

as it remains on the statute book as the latest expression of the legislative will, is a valid law, and must be obeyed, which is all that was decided by this court in the Slaughter-house Cases. But it asserts the right of the legislature to repeal such a statute, or to make a new one inconsistent with it, whenever, in the wisdom of such legislature, it is for the good of the public it should be done. Nor does this proposition contravene the established principle that the legislature of a State may make contracts on many subjects which will bind it, and will bind succeeding legislatures for the time the contract has to run, so that its provisions can neither be repealed, nor its obligations impaired. The examples are numerous where this has been done, and the contract upheld. The denial of this power, in the present instance, rests upon the ground that the power of the legislature intended to be suspended is one so indispensable to the public welfare that it cannot be bargained away by contract. It is that well known but undefined power, called the police power. * * * While we are not prepared to say that the legislature can make valid contracts on no subject embraced in the largest definition of police power, we think that, in regard to two subjects so embraced, it cannot by any contract, limit the exercise of those powers to the prejudice of the general welfare. These are the public health and the public morals. The preservation of those is so necessary to the best interests of the social organization, that a wise policy forbids the legislative body to divest itself of the power to enact laws for the preservation of health and the repression of crime." [1]

On the principle, that the State cannot barter away its police power, it has been held lawful for the State to prohibit all lotteries, and to apply the law to existing lottery companies.[2] So, also, is it possible for the State to pro-

---

[1] Butchers' Union Slaughter-house, etc., Co. v. Crescent. City Live Stock, etc., Co., 111 U. S. 746.

[2] Stone v. Mississippi, 101 U. S. 814; State v. Morris, 77 N. C. 512;

§ 127

hibit the sale and manufacture of liquor, although it has previously issued licenses, authorizing the prosecution of these trades,[1] and such prohibitory laws may be enforced against existing corporations, whose charters empower them to carry on the prohibited trade.[2] In like manner, may laws incorporated in the charter for the government of a corporation, in its relation to the public, be repealed or amended.[3] But it has been held in Illinois that, while the State may regulate the interment of the dead, and in the first instance prescribe the localities in which burial will be permitted, yet it is not possible for the legislature to prohibit burial upon lands purchased and laid out as a cemetery at great expense, by a corporation, which has been chartered for that purpose.[4]

Bass v. Nashville, Meigs, 421 (33 Am. Dec. 154); Mississippi Soc. of Arts v. Musgrove, 44 Miss. 820; Moore v. State, 48 Miss. 147 (12 Am. Rep. 367); State v. Woodward, 89 Ind. 110 (46 Am. Rep. 160). See, contra, Broadbent v. Tuscaloosa, etc., Association, 45 Ala. 170; Kellum v. State, 66 Ind. 588.

[1] Calder v. Kurby, 5 Gray, 597; Commonwealth v. Brennan, 103 Mass. 70; La Croix v. County Comrs., 50 Conn. 321 (47 Am. Rep. 648); Met. Board of Excise v. Barsie, 34 N. Y. 657; Baltimore v. Clunity, 23 Md. 449; Fell v. State, 42 Md. 71 (20 Am. Rep. 83); McKinney v. Salem, 77 Ind. 213. Contra, Adams v. Hatchett, 27 N. H. 289; State v. Phalen, 3 Harr. 441; Boyd v. State, 36 Ala. 329. A license for the prosecution of any trade, which tends to be injurious to the public, may be revoked by a subsequent prohibitory law. State v. Burgoyne, 7 Lea, 173. See, generally, State v. Cook, 24 Minn. 247; Pleuler v. State, 11 Neb. 547. See ante, §§ 101–103.

[2] Beer Company v. Massachusetts, 91 U. S. 25; Commonwealth v. Intoxicating Liquors, 115 Mass. 153.

[3] Bank of Columbia v. Okely, 4 Wheat. 235; Baltimore, etc., R. R. Co. v. Nesbit, 10 How. 395; Railroad v. Hecht, 95 U. S. 170; s. c. 29 Ark. 661; Gowen v. Penobscot R. R. Co., 45 Me. 140; Ex parte N. E. & S. W. R. R. Co., 37 Ala (N. S.) 679; Howard v. Kentucky, etc., Ins. Co., 13 B. Mon. 282.

[4] Lakeview v. Rose Hill Cemetery Co., 70 Ill. 192. But see, contra, Brick Presbyterian Church v. Mayor, etc., 5 Cowen, 538; Coates v. Mayor, etc., 7 Cow. 585; Kincaid's Appeal, 66 Pa. St. 423; City Council v. Wentworth Street Baptist Church, 4 Strobh. 310. See, also, ante, § 122d.

§ 190

§ 191. **Police regulation of corporations in general.** — But the corporation is no more subject to arbitrary regulations than is the individual. In order that the regulation of a corporation may be within the constitutional limitations of police power, it must have reference to the welfare of society by the prevention or control of those actions which are calculated to inflict injury upon the public or the individual. As in all other cases of the exercise of the police power, the police regulations of corporations must be confined to the enforcement of the maxim, *sic utere tuo, ut alienum non lædas,* subject to the observance of which every corporate charter must be supposed to have been granted. Any attempt, under the guise of police regulations, to repeal or amend the charter, or to abridge any of the corporate rights and privileges, would of course be unconstitutional and void.[1] The property of the corporation cannot be confiscated, under pretense of being a police regulation, without payment of compensation. Thus, it was held unconstitutional for a law to require an existing turnpike company to set back its first gate two miles from the corporate limits of a town, which had grown up at the original gate, under penalty of forfeiting all right to tolls.[2] The two miles of road, included within the existing turnpike, might have been confiscated in the exercise of the power of eminent domain, but compensation for the loss would have been required. So, also, would it be unlawful to compel a railroad or turnpike to permit certain persons to make use of the road without paying the cus-

---

[1] State *v.* Noyes, 47 Me. 189; Washington Bridge Co. *v.* State, 18 Conn. 53; Benson *v.* Mayor, etc., of N. Y. 10 Barb. 223; Hegeman *v.* Western R. R. Co., 13 N. Y. 9; Commonwealth *v.* Pennsylvania Canal Co., 66 Pa. St. 41; Bailey *v.* Philadelphia, etc., R. R. Co., 4 Harr. 389; People *v.* Jackson, etc., Plank Road Co., 9 Mich. 285; Attorney-General *v.* Chicago, etc., R. R. Co., 35 Wis. 425; Sloan *v.* Pacific R. R. Co., 61 Mo. 24.

[2] White's Creek Turnpike Co. *v.* Davidson Co., 3 Tenn. Ch. 396. See Detroit *v.* Plankroad Co., 13 Mich. 140.

tomary toll.[1] And while it is permissible to prohibit a corporation from doing the thing, or engaging in the business, for which it was created, no law can make the corporation responsible for the damages suffered by the public, as a consequence of what the corporation was authorized to do. Thus, for example, where the legislature authorized the construction of a bridge over a navigable stream, of such dimensions that it would necessarily become an obstruction to the navigation of the river, the bridge company could not be made responsible to those whose navigation of the stream was impeded, for that would in effect be a deprivation of the corporate rights.[2] So, also, would it be unlawful for the legislature to provide by a subsequent law for the complete forfeiture of the charter as a penalty for a prohibited act which under the existing law was a cause for only a partial forfeiture, because the enforcement of the new penalty against a corporation for acts already done would operate to impair the obligation of contracts.[3] But there is no constitutional objection to the application to existing corporations of new remedies for the attainment of justice, and to secure a performance of the corporate duties to the public.[4] For example, it is lawful for a legislature to extend the individual liability of the stockholders of a bank for any debt thereafter incurred.[5] A law is valid, also, which provides that existing corporations shall maintain their corporate organizations for a limited period after their dissolution, and continue their capacity for being sued, for the purpose of winding up its affairs.[5]

---

[1] Pingry v. Washburn, 1 Aiken, 264.

[2] Bailey v. Philadelphia, etc., R. R. Co., 4 Harr. 389.

[3] People v. Jackson, etc., Plankroad Co., 9 Mich. 285.

[4] Crawford v Branch Bank, 7 How. 279; Gowen v. Penobscot R. R. Co., 44 Me. 140; Commonwealth v. Cochituate Bank, 3 Allen, 42.

[5] Stanley v. Stanley, 26 Me. 196; Coffin v. Rich, 45 Me. 507; Hathorne v. Calef, 53 Me. 471; Child v. Coffin, 17 Mass. 64; Gray v. Coffin, 9 Cush. 200.

[6] Lincoln, etc., Bank v. Richardson, 1 Greenl. 79· Franklin Bank v.

Corporations may also be required to submit to an inspection of their affairs by a public official, in order to ascertain any breaches of duty to the public.[1] And the
legislature may lawfully provide the extreme remedy of
dissolving the bank or other corporation, whenever, upon
examination by the public inspector, it should be found in
an insolvent condition.[2] In the case last cited,[3] it was held
that a law was constitutional, which provided for the
judicial dissolution of an insurance company, chartered under the laws of the State, whenever the auditor upon examination of its affairs, should be of the opinion that its
financial condition is such as to render its further continuance hazardous to those who are insured in the company.
In pronouncing the law to be constitutional the court says:

" With certain constitutional limitations, the rights of
all persons, whether natural or artificial, are subject to such
legislative control as the legislature may deem necessary
for the general welfare, and it is a fundamental error to
suppose there is any difference in this respect between the
rights of natural and artificial persons. They both stand
precisely upon the same footing. While personal liberty
is guaranteed by the constitution to every citizen, yet, by
disregarding the rights of others, one may forfeit not only
his liberty, but even life itself. So a corporation, by refusing to conform its business affairs as to defeat the ob-

Cooper, 36 Me. 179; Foster v. Essex Bank, 10 Mass. 245; Nevitt v.
Bank of Port Gibson, 6 Smedes & M. 513. And a State law of this kind
may be made to apply to foreign corporations, in the endeavor to secure
a just distribution of their assets lying within the jurisdiction of the
State, which enacted the law. McGoon v. Scales, 9 Wall. 31; Stetson v.
City Bank, 2 Ohio St. 114; Lewis v. Bank of Kentucky, 12 Ohio St.
132.

[1] Hunter v. Burnsville Pike Co., 56 Ind. 213; Commonwealth v. Farmers' and Mechanics' Bank, 21 Pick. 542. See Planters' Bank v. Sharp,
5 How. 340.

[2] Commonwealth v. Farmers' & Mechanics' Bank, 21 Pick. 542; Nevitt
v. Bank of Port Gibson, 6 Smedes & M. 513; Ward v. Farwell, 97 Ill. 693.

[3] Ward v. Farwell, *supra.*

§ 191

jects and purposes of its promoters, and the design of the legislature in creating it, may forfeit the right to further carry on its business, and also its existence as an artificial being. The fact that the stockholders may be personally injured by declaring a forfeiture of the company's franchises, and causing its affairs to be wound up in a case of this kind, is not a sufficient reason why it should not be done, if the further continuance of its business would be dangerous to the community. In the proper exercise of the police power, laws are often enacted by the legislature for the common good which materially affect the value of certain kinds of property, by which a particular class of persons are injured; yet such consequences do not at all affect the validity of the legislation, and to such losses the maxim *damnum absque injuria* applies. It is generally said one may do as he pleases with his own property, but this is subject to the important qualification — he must please to do with it as the law requires. * * * The maxim *sic utere tuo, ut alienum non lœdas*, applies to all such cases. * * *

"These general principles would seem to warrant the conclusion that the legislature is authorized, in the proper exercise of the police power, to adopt such necessary legislation and regulations as will effectually protect the community from losses incident to a public business, conducted by a corporation under a charter from the State, where such business has become hazardous, and will probably result in financial distress and disappointed hopes to those who, ignorant of its condition, do business with it.'"[1]

§ 192. **Laws regulating rates and charges of corporations.** — The right of the legislature to regulate the rates and charges of a corporation has frequently been the subject of litigation in the courts of this country. The estab-

---

[1] Ward *v.* Farwell, 97 Ill. 608, 609

lishment of extensive and rich corporations, which are
often enabled by their combined capital and by the possession of special franchises to make a practical monopoly
of the business in which they are engaged, and consequently to demand of those, who are compelled by circumstances to have business dealings with the corporations,
extortionate and unequal charges. For these reasons,
there is a general popular demand for legislative regulation
of the rates and charges of the corporations.

The general power of the government to regulate prices
has already been fully explained,[1] and the constitutional
limitations discussed. It will not be necessary to repeat
here what has been stated there. It was ascertained by a
study of the cases that where the government by the grant
of a more or less exclusive franchise increases the economic
powers of a person or persons, so as to create a monopoly
against those to whom the franchise is denied, it had the
power to regulate the charges of such person or persons, so
that the public may obtain that reasonable enjoyment of the
benefits arising out of the monopoly, which indeed was
the consideration or inducement of the grant of the
franchise.[2] The Supreme Court of the United States
has even gone further in the recognition of the legislative power to regulate prices, and asserted that, when
circumstances make of a particular business "a virtual
monopoly," the legislature may prevent extortion by
the regulation of prices.[3] But in order to justify the
legislative regulation of the charges of corporations, it will
not be necessary to go to the length of this decision. In
the first place, if the power to repeal or amend the charter
is reserved to the State, no question can arise; for in the
exercise of the power to amend, the legislature may require,

---

[1] See *ante*, § 93.

[2] See *ante*, § 93.

[3] Waite, Ch. J., in Munn *v.* Illinois, 94 U. S. 113. See the criticism of
this decision in § 93.

§ 192

as a condition of the continuance of the corporate existence, the observance of whatever police regulation it may see fit to establish, in the same manner, and to the same extent, that it may impose conditions of every sort and kind, in the original grant of the charter.   When the power to amend or repeal is not reserved, the question becomes important, whether the corporation may be subjected to this regulation.   In regard to police regulations generally, we have seen[1] that the corporation occupies no vantage ground above the individual ; that both corporations and natural persons may be subjected to the same regulations under like circumstances ; and that the institution of new and more burdensome regulations, after the creation of the corporation, does not constitute any infringement of the corporate rights, provided no attempt is made, under the guise of police regulation, to destroy or impair any of the substantial rights of the corporation.   It is, therefore, not difficult, under the principles explained and set forth in a previous section,[2] to justify the regulation of the rates and charges of railroads, turnpikes, telegraph and telephone companies, and other corporations, to which the government has granted some special franchise — to each of the corporations named is given the right to appropriate land in the exercise of the right of eminent domain, without which it would be almost impossible to construct their lines or road — for the grant of the franchise made these corporations legal monopolies, as against the public, and consequently they became subject to police regulation, in order to protect the public from extortion.   It has been generally held, with only one or two exceptions, that the legislature may regulate the charges of corporations of this kind.[3]

[1] See *ante*, § 189.
[2] § 93.
[3] Railroads — Chicago, etc., R. R. *v.* Iowa, 94 U. S. 115; Peck *v.* Chicago, etc.,R.R., 94 U. S. 164, 176; Union Pac. Ry. *v.* U. S., 99 U. S. 700; Cin., H. & D. R. R. Co. *v.* Cole, 29 Ohio, 125; Iron R. R. Co. *v.* Lawrence

§ 192

Whether corporations, which receive no franchise or privilege from the government, may be subjected to State regulation of their charges in the conduct of their business, for example, a corporation engaged in the flour milling or cotton manufacturing business, depends upon other grounds. Under the principle established in Munn *v.* Illinois,[1] such a regulation may be easily justified, where the business under peculiar circumstances has become a virtual monopoly. So, also, may a corporation of this kind be subjected to such a regulation, because the very creation of the corporation, which constitutes an authority for the compact combination of the capital of many persons in one business, may be considered a special franchise, increasing the power of those who compose the corporation, over the property and the necessities of others. There has been no need for the regulations of the charges of such corporations, and consequently we have no adjudications upon the subject, except the case of Munn *v.* Illinois.

It has been stated, as the generally accepted doctrine, that the State cannot make a valid contract in limitation of the exercise of its police power.[2] But a disposition is displayed by the authorities to make of the power to regulate the charges of corporations an exception to this general rule, by denying to the legislature the power to regulate such charges by subsequent laws, where the power to do so

---

Furnace Co., 29 Ohio St. 208; Chicago & Alton R. R. Co. *v.* People, ex rel Koerner, 67 Ill. 11 (16 Am. Rep. 599); Ruggles *v.* People, 91 Ill. 256; Illinois Cent. R. R. Co. *v.* People, 95 Ill. 313; Blake *v.* Winona etc., R. R. Co., 19 Minn. 418 (18 Am. Rep. 345); *s. c.* 94 U. S. 180; Mobile & M. R. R. Co. *v.* Steiner, 61 Ala. 559. *Contra*, Atty-Gen. *v.* Chicago, etc., R. R. Co., 35 Wis 425; Philadelphia, etc., R. R. Co. *v.* Bowers, 4 Houst. 506. Gas and water companies — Spring Valley Waterworks *v.* Schottler, 110 U. S. 347; State *v.* Columbus Gaslight, etc., Co., 34 Ohio St. 216 (32 Am. Rep. 390). Ferry companies — Parker *v.* Metropolitan R. R. Co., 109 Mass. 507. Telephone Companies — Hockett *v.* State, Sup. Ct. Ind. Cent. L. J., July 9, 1886.

[1] 94 U. S. 113.

[2] See *ante*, § 197

§ 192

is denied by the charter, or where the lawful charges are stipulated in the charter. Chief Justice Waite, of the Supreme Court of the United States, expressed the opinion of the court on this point, in the following language:—

"This company, in the transaction of its business, has the same rights and is subject to the same control as private individuals under the same circumstances. It must carry when called upon to do so, and can charge only a reasonable sum for the carriage. In the absence of any legislative regulation upon the subject, the courts must decide for it, as they do for private persons when controversies arise, what is reasonable. But when the legislature steps in and prescribes a maximum of charge, it operates upon this corporation the same as it does upon individuals engaged in a similar business. It was within the power of the company to call upon the legislature to fix permanently this limit and make it a part of the charter, and, if it was refused, to abstain from building the road and establishing the contemplated business. If that had been done the charter might have presented a contract against future legislative interference. But it was not ; and the company invested its capital, relying upon the good faith of the people and the wisdom and impartiality of the legislators for protection against wrong under the form of legislation regulation." [1]

§ 193. **Police regulation of foreign corporations.** — It is provided by the United States constitution [2] that " the citizens of each State shall be entitled to all the privileges and immunities of citizens of the several States ; " and under this clause of the constitution the citizen of one State is

---

[1] Ch. J. Waite in Chicago, etc., R. R. Co. v. Iowa, 94 U. S. 155. See, also, Spring Valley Water Works v. Schottler, 110 U. S. 347; Hamilton v. Keith, 5 Bush, 458; Illinois Cent. R. R. Co. v. People, 95 Ill. 113; Sloan v. Pacific R. R. Co., 61 Mo. 24 (21 Am. Rep. 397;) Farmers' Loan, etc. v. Stone, et. al., U. S. C. C. Miss., 18 Cent. L. J. 472.

[2] U. S. Const., art. IV., § 2, cl. 1.

§ 193

protected against any discrimination in another State between himself and the citizens of the latter State. He is
entitled to the equal enjoyment of the privileges of the citizen, and any arbitrary discrimination between him and the
citizen of the latter State in the matter of police regulations, would be in violation of this constitutional provision.
But corporations are not considered to be citizens within
the operation of this guaranty. The legal existence of a
corporation is confined to the territory of the State which
brings the corporation into existence. The corporations of
one State are not entitled to the privileges or immunities of
the citizens of the several States, and consequently they
cannot claim the right to transact business in any other
State but the one in which they were created. If they are
permitted to exercise their corporate powers in any other
State, it is a privilege and not a guaranteed right. A State
may, without violating any provision of the constitution of
the United States, prohibit altogether the doing of business
by foreign corporations within its territory; and if the
privilege is granted, it may be coupled with all sorts of
conditions, the performance of which constitutes a condition precedent to the enjoyment of the privilege; and these
requirements will not be open to constitutional objection,
because they are not made applicable to domestic corporations.[1] It is even permissible for the State legislature to

[1] Liverpool Ins. Co. v. Mass., 1 Wall. 506; Bank of Augusta v. Earle,
13 Pet. 519; Purdy v. N. Y. & N. H. R. R. Co., 61 N. Y. 353; Tatem v.
Wright et al., 23 N. J. L. 429; Slaughter v. Commonwealth, 13 Gratt.
767; Osborn v. Mobile, 44 Ala. 493; Commonwealth v. Milton, 12 B. Mon.
212; People v. Thurber, 13 Ill. 554; Wood Mowing Machine Co. v. Caldwell, 54 Ind. 270 (23 Am. Rep. 641); Am. Union Tel. Co. v. W. U. Tel.
Co., 67 Ala. 26 (42 Am. Rep. 90). It is very common to subject foreign
insurance companies to special and strict police regulations. Exempt
Firemen's Fund v. Roome, 93 N. Y. 313 (45 Am. Rep. 217); Thorne v.
Travelers' Ins. Co., 80 Pa. St. 15 (21 Am. Rep. 89); Cincinnati M. H.
Assurance Co. v. Rosenthal, 55 Ill. 85 (8 Am. Rep. 626); Pierce v. People,
106 Ill. 11 (46 Am. Rep. 683); Fire Department of Milwaukee v. Helfenstein, 16 Wis. 136. See Doyle v. Ins. Co., 94 U. S. 535.

§ 193

provide for the exaction of a penalty from any agent of a foreign corporation (in this case it was an insurance company), who shall act without authority from the State, although the contract is made out of the State, and provides that he shall be deemed the agent of the other party to the contract.[1] But a foreign corporation cannot be taxed for the purchase of raw material, which is shipped from the taxing State to its native State for manufacture, for that cannot be considered a " doing of business within the commonwealth." [2] In the absence of special regulations, whenever a corporation does business in another State, it is so far considered a corporation of that State as to be amenable to its ordinary police regulations.[3]

§ 194. **Police regulation of railroads.** — The police regulation of the management of railroads is extremely common and varied, and consequently the exercise of police power over them has more frequently been the subject of litigation. But there is no more need for a judicial determination of the limitations upon police power in this phase of its exercise than in any other. The same principles govern its exercise in every case. Every one, whether a corporation or a natural person, must so enjoy and make use of his rights as not to injure another; and the State may institute whatever reasonable regulations may be necessary to prevent injury to the public or private persons. Here, as elsewhere, however, the exercise of police power must be confined to those regulations which may be needed, and which do actually tend, to prevent the infliction of injury upon others. And it is a judicial question whether a particular regulation is a reasonable exercise of police power. The public necessity of the exercise of the police power in

[1] Pierce v. People, 106 Ill. 11 (46 Am. Rep. 683).
[2] Commonwealth v. Standard Oil Co., 101 Pa. St. 119.
[3] Peik v. Chicago, etc., R. R. Co., 94 U. S. 164; Milnor v. N. Y., etc., R. R. Co., 53 N. Y. 164; McGregor v. Erie Railway, 35 N. J. L. 115.

any case is a matter addressed to the discretion of the legislature; but whether a given regulation is a reasonable restriction upon personal rights is a judicial question.[1]

A disposition is manifested in some of the cases to claim for the railroad company the application of the same rule of reasonableness, as would be applicable to regulations of the private property of individuals; that is, prohibiting all regulations of railroads and of their property, which would not be applicable generally to the private property of individuals. But the reasonableness or unreasonableness of a police regulation is subject to variation with a change of circumstances, and in the character of the subject of the regulation. A regulation may be reasonable when directed

---

[1] "What are reasonable regulations, and what are the subjects of police powers must necessarily be judicial questions. The law-making power is the sole judge when the necessity exists, and when, if at all, it will exercise the right to enact such laws.

"Like other powers of government, there are constitutional limitations to the exercise of the police power. The legislature cannot, under the pretense of exercising this power, enact laws not necessary to the preservation of the health and safety of the community that will be oppressive and burdensome upon the citizen. If it should prohibit that which is harmless in itself, or command that to be done which does not tend to promote the health, safety or welfare of society, it would be an unauthorized exercise of power, and it would be the duty of the court to declare such legislation void."

"An ordinance of the city which required a railroad to keep flagman by day and red lantern by night at a certain street crossing, when the company had only a single track, over which only its usual trains passed, and where it did not appear that the crossing was unusually dangerous, or more so than ordinary crossings, was held not to be a reasonable requirement, and therefore within the constitutional limitation on the exercise of the police power.

"A regulation that would require a railroad to place a flagman at such places where danger to public safety, in judgment of prudent persons, might be apprehended at any time, would be a reasonable one." Toledo, etc., R. R. v. Jacksonville, 67 Ill. 37. See, also, Chicago & Alton R. R. Co. v. People, 67 Ill. 11; State v. East Orange, 12 Vroom, 127; City of Erie v. Erie Canal Co., 59 Pa. St. 174; Phila. W. B. R. R. Co. v. Bowers, 4 Houst. 506; Ladd v. Southern C. P. & M. Co., 53 Tex. 172; Sloan v. Pac. R. R. Co., 61 Mo. 24.

§ 194

against the use of certain kinds of property, while it would be unreasonable, if applied to other and different kinds of property, the enjoyment or use of which does not threaten the injury, against which the regulation was directed.   But there can be no doubt that a corporation cannot be subjected to a regulation, which would not be applicable to a natural person under like circumstances.   The police regulations resemble greatly the regulation of the use of the common highways, and a comparison of them, as set forth in the following language of a distinguished judge, will assist in reaching a clear understanding of the scope of police power in the regulation of railroads.   In Chicago, B. & Q. R. R. Co. *v.* Attorney-General of Iowa,[1] Dillon, J., says : —

" In all civilized countries the duty of providing and preserving safe and convenient highways to facilitate trade and communication between different parts of the State or community is considered a governmental duty.   This may be done by the government directly, or through the agency of corporations created for that purpose.   The right of public supervision and control over highways results from the power and duty of providing and preserving them.   As to ordinary highways these propositions are unquestioned. But it is denied that they apply to railways built by private capital, and owned by private corporations created for the purpose of building them.   Whoever studies the nature and purposes of railways constructed under the authority of the State by means of private capital will see that such railroads possess a twofold character.   Such a railway is in part public and in part private.   Because of its public character, relations, and uses, the judicial tribunals of this country, State and national, have at length settled the law to be that the State, to secure their construction, may exert in favor of the corporation authorized by it to build the road both its power of eminent domain and of taxation.

1 9 West. Jur. 347.

§ 194

This the State cannot do in respect of occupations or purposes private in their nature. * * * In its public character a railroad is an improved highway, or means of more rapid and commodious communication, and its public character is not divested by the fact that its ownership is private. * * * In its relations to its stockholders, a railroad, or the property in the road and its income is private property, and, subject to the lawful or reserved rights of the public, is invested with the sanctity of other private property. The distinction here indicated marks with general accuracy the extent of legislative control, except where this has been surrendered or abridged by a valid legislative contract. Over the railway as a highway, and in all its public relations, the State, by virtue of its general legislative power, has supervision and control; but over the rights of the shareholders, so far as these are private property, the State has the same power and no greater than over other private property." [1]

---

[1] "We apprehend there can be no manner of doubt that the legislature may, if they deem the public good requires it, of which they are to judge, and in all doubtful cases their judgment is final, require several railroads in the State to establish and maintain the same kind of police which is now observed upon some of the more important roads in the country for their own security or even such a police as is found upon the English railways and those upon the continent of Europe. No one ever questioned the right of the Connecticut legislature to require trains upon all their roads to come to a stand before passing draws in bridges; or of the Massachusetts legislature to require the same thing before passing another railroad. And by parity of reason may all railways be required so to conduct themselves, as to other persons, natural or corporate, as "not unreasonably to injure them or their property. And since the business of railways is specially dangerous, they may be required to! bear the expense of erecting such safeguards, as will render it ordinarily safe to others, as is often required of natural persons under such circumstances.

"There would be no end of illustrations upon this subject, which in detail are more familiar to others than to us. It may be extended to the supervision of the track, tending switches, running upon the time of other trains, running roads with a single track, using improper rails, not using proper precautions by way of safety beams in case of the breaking of axle trees, number of brakemen upon train with reference to number

§ 194

As has already been intimated, the number of police regulations of railroads is very great, and the character of them is as varied. For the purpose of illustrating the scope of these regulations, it will only be necessary to refer to the more important ones, which have been passed upon by the courts.

For example, in the exercise of the ordinary police power of the State, it has been held to be reasonable to require all railroads to fence their tracks, not alone for the protection of the live stock of the abutting owners. Indeed, the chief object of the statute is probably to protect the traveling public against accidents occurring through collision of trains with cattle.[1] One exercise of the power to require railroads to fence their tracks does not preclude a second regulation of the same kind, providing for other and different fences.[2] And the railroad company can not relieve

---

of cars, employing intemperate or incompetent engineers and servants, running beyond a given rate of speed and a thousand similar things, most of which have been made the subject of legislation or judicial determination, and all of which may be." Thorpe v. Rutland, etc., R. R. 27 Wis. 140. See, also, Richmond, F. & P. R. R. Co. v. City of Richmond, 26 Gratt. 83; s. c. 96 U. S. 521; People v. Boston, etc., R. R. Co., 70 N. Y. 569; State v. East Orange, 12 Vroom, 127; Phila., W. & B. R. R. Co. v. Bowers, 5 Houst. 506; Cin. H. & D. R. R. Co. v. Sullivan, 32 Ohio St. 152; Pittsburg, C. & St. L. R. R. Co. v. Brown, 67 Ind. 45 (33 Am. Rep. 73); Toledo, W., etc., R. R. Co. v. Jacksonville, 67 Ill. 37; Galveston, etc., R. R. Co. v. Gierse, 51 Tex. 189.

[1] Sawyer v. Vt., etc., R. R. Co., 105 Mass. 196; Wilder v. Maine Cent. R. R. Co., 65 Me. 332; Smith v. Eastern R. R. Co., 35 N. H. 356; Bulkley v. N. Y., etc., R. R. Co., 27 Conn. 497; Bradley v. Buffalo, etc., R. R. Co., 34 N. Y. 429; Penn. R. R. Co. v. Riblet, 66 Pa. St. 164 (5 Am. Rep. 360); Thorpe v. Rutland, etc., R. R. Co., 27 Vt. 140; Indianapolis, etc., R. R. Co. v. Marshall, 27 Ind. 300; New Albany, etc., R. R. Co. v. Tilton, 12 Ind. 10; Indianapolis, etc., R. R. Co. v. Kercheval, 16 Ind. 84; Toledo, etc., R. R. Co. v. Fowler, 22 Ind. 316; Indianapolis, etc., R. R. Co. v. Parker, 29 Ind. 471; Ohio & Miss. R. R. Co. v. McClelland, 25 Ill. 140; Gorman v. Pac. R. R. Co., 26 Mo. 441; Jones v. Galena, etc., R. R. Co., 16 Iowa, 6; Winona, etc., R. R. Co. v. Waldron, 11 Minn. 575; Blewett v Wyandotte, etc., R. R. Co., 72 Mo. 583; Kan. Pac. Ry. Co. v. Mower, 16 Kan. 573; Louisville & Nashville, R. R. Co. v. Burke, 6 Caldw. 45.

[2] Gillam v. Sioux City, etc., R. R. Co., 26 Minn. 268.

§ 194

itself from the obligation to erect and maintain the fence by any contracts with the abutting owners.[1] The railroad company is, of course, liable for whatever injury is done to persons or property in consequence of any neglect in maintaining the fence.[2] In the absence of special legislation, the judgment will be confined to the recovery o f the actual damages suffered in consequence of the neglect. But the statute may constitutionally make the company liable for double the value of the stock killed by reason of the neglect to properly maintain the fences. This requirement is justified on the same grounds as the authority to recover exemplary or punitory damages.[3] And it may also be provided by statute that the railroad company may be held liable for all losses of property, occurring in consequence of the neglect of the railroad in the maintenance of the fences, although the owner may be guilty of contributory negligence.[4] But there must be some violation of the law,

---

[1] New Albany, etc., R. R. Co. v. Tilton, 12 Ind. 3; New Albany, etc., R. R. Co. v. Maiden, 12 Ind. 10. See Poler v. N. Y. Cent. R. R. Co., 16 N. Y. 476; Shepherd v. Buff., N. Y. & Erie R. R. Co., 35 N. Y. 641.

[2] As to what degree of care is required of railroads in this connection, see Chicago, etc., R. R. Co. v. Barsie, 55 Ill. 226; Antisdel v. Chicago, etc., R. R. Co., 26 Wis. 145; Lemmon v. Chicago, etc., R. R. Co., 32 Iowa, 151.

[3] Cairo, etc., R. R. Co. v. People, 92 Ill. 97 (34 Am. Rep. 112); Barnett v. Atlantic, etc., R. R. Co., 68 Mo. 56 (30 Am. Rep. 773); Spealman v. Railroad Co., 71 Mo. 434; Humes v. Mo. Pac. R. R. Co., 82 Mo. 22 (52 Am Rep. 369); Tredway v. Railroad Co., 43 Iowa, 527; Welsh v. Chicago, B. & Q. R. R. Co., 53 Iowa, 632; Little Rock & Ft. Scott R. R. Co. v. Payne, 33 Ark. 816 (34 Am. Rep. 55). Contra, Madison, etc., R. R. Co. v. Whiteneck, 8 Ind. 217; Indiana Cent. R. W. Co. v. Gapen, 10 Ind. 292; Atchison & Neb. R. R. Co. v. Baty, 6 Neb. 37 (29 Am. Rep. 356). It is also competent to include attorney's fees as part of the damages that may be recovered. Peoria, etc., R. R. Co. v. Duggan, 109 Ill. 537 (50 Am. Rep. 619.

[4] Corwin v. N. Y. & Erie R. R. Co., 13 N. Y. 42; Horn v. Atlantic, etc., R. R. Co., 35 N. H. 169; O'Bannon v. Louisville, etc., R. R. Co., 8 Bush, 348; Jeffersonville, etc., R. R. Co. v. Nichols, 30 Ind. 321; Jeffersonville, etc., R. Co. v. Parkhurst, 34 Ind. 501; Illinois Cent. R. R. Co. v. Arnold, 47 Ill. 173; Hinman v. Chicago, etc., R. R. Co., 28 Iowa, 491.

§ 194

or some act of negligence, on the part of the railroad company, in order that the company may be held liable for damages suffered from the running of trains. A statute which makes a railroad responsible " for all expenses of the coroner and his inquest, and of the burial of all persons who may die on the cars, or who may be killed by collision or other accident occurring to such cars, or otherwise," is, therefore, properly declared to be unconstitutional, so far as it is applied to cases of loss, in which the company has not been guilty of negligence or of a violation of some legal duty.[1] The State may in like manner regulate the grades of railways, generally, and particularly at the points where they cross highways or other railways, and provide for an apportionment of the expense of making the crossings ;[2] and prescribe the rate of speed at which highways and other railways may be crossed,[3] and while running within the corporate limits of a city or town.[4] The State may institute other regulations, having the protection of life in view, such as requiring all railroad companies to ring their bell or blow the whistle of the engine on approaching a crossing or highway ;[5] or to place and keep flagmen at such places, and at such

---

[1] Ohio & Mississippi R. R. Co. v. Lackey, 78 Ill. 55 (20 Am. Rep. 259). But see Pennsylvania R. R. Co. v. Riblet, 66 Pa. St. 164 (5 Am. Rep. 360), in which it was held to be competent for the legislature to compel an existing railroad to repair all fences along its route that may be destroyed by fire from its engines. See, to the same effect, Lyman v. Boston, etc., R. R. Co., 4 Cush. 288; Gorman v. Pac. R. R. Co., 26 Mo. 441; Rodemacher v. Milwaukee, etc., R. R. Co., 41 Iowa, 297 (20 Am. Rep. 592).

[2] Fitchburg, R. R. Co. v. Grand Junction R. R. Co., 1 Allen, 552; s. c., 4 Allen, 198; Pittsburg, etc., R. R. Co. v. S. W. Penn. R. R. Co., 77 Pa. St. 173.

[3] Mobile, etc., R. R. Co. v. State, 51 Miss. 137.

[4] Rockford, etc., R. R. Co. v. Hillmer, 72 Ill. 235; Chicago, Rock Island, etc., R. R. Co. v. Reidy, 66 Ill. 43; Mobile & Ohio R. R. Co. v. State, 51 Miss. 137; Horn v. Chicago, etc., R. R. Co., 38 Wis. 463; Haas v. Chicago & N. W. R. R. Co., 41 Wis. 44.

[5] Veazie v. Mayo, 45 Me. 560; s. c. 49 Me. 156; Commonwealth v. Eastern R. R. Co., 103 Mass. 254 (4 Am. Rep. 555); Bulkley v. N. Y. & N. H. R. R. Co.. 27 Conn. 486; Stuyvesant v. Mayor, etc., of New York,

§ 194

times of the day, when the traffic and the passage of numbers of people make such a regulation reasonable and necessary.[1] It is also a lawful exercise of police power to require a railroad to construct a bridge in passing over a public highway, instead of crossing it at the same grade;[2] or to prohibit a railroad from constructing its tracks or running cars on any street so near the depot of another railroad, as to interfere with a safe and convenient access to the latter road.[3]

The State may also make all kinds of reasonable regulations for insuring a fair and impartial carriage of all persons and property. The right to regulate the charges of corporations in general has already been fully explained,[4] and the railroad companies may be subjected to such regulations, as well as any other corporation. In consequence of the racial prejudice, there is a disposition in some parts of the country to make invidious distinctions in the accommodations provided for the white and black passengers. While it is in violation of the common-law rights of the negro, as well as of the constitutional and statutory provisions, which guarantee to the negro equal privileges in the use and enjoyment of the public conveyances, hotels,

---

7 Cow. 588; Pittsburg, Cin. & St. L. R. R. Co. v. Brown, 67 Ind. 45 (33 Am. Rep. 73); Galena v. Chicago U. R. R. Co. v. Dill, 22 Ill. 264; Ohio & M. R. R. Co. v. McClelland, 25 Ill. 140; Chicago, etc., R. R. Co. v. Triplett, 38 Ill. 482; Clark's Administrator v. Hannibal & St. Jo. R. R. Co., 36 Mo. 202.

[1] Toledo, etc., R. R. Co. v. Jacksonville, 67 Ill. 37; Lake Shore & M. S. Ry. Co. v. Cincinnati, S. & C. Ry. Co., 30 Ohio St. 604.

[2] People v. Boston & Albany R. R. Co., 70 N. Y. 569. But it would be unconstitutional to require railroad companies to build crossings at the intersection of their road with a highway, which had been constructed after the railroad has been built. City of Erie v. Erie Canal Co., 59 Pa. St. 174; Ill. Cent. R. R. Co. v. Bloomington, 76 Ill. 447.

[3] Portland, S. & P. R. R. Co. v. Boston and Maine R. R. Co., 65 Me. 122.

[4] See, ante, § 192. The State may require all railroad companies to post up in its stations schedules of the rates of fare and freight, without violating any constitutional provision. Railroad v. Fuller, 17 Wall. 560.

§ 194

and places of amusement,[1] if the railroad company should deny to him the use of the first-class and sleeping cars;[2] yet it is lawful for them to provide separate cars for the two races, provided their appointments and conveniences are equally good.[3] It is also held to be a lawful exercise of police power to require railroads to draw the cars of other corporations as well as their own, at reasonable times and for a reasonable compensation, to be agreed upon by the parties or fixed by the railroad commissioners.[4]

In order that the inhabitants of the country, through which a railroad passes, may be assured a reasonable use of the regular trains, the legislature may determine at what stations and for what length of time, all trains shall be required to stop,[5] and all agreements of railroad companies, which limit the location of stations, are void because against public policy.[6]

It has also been held to be competent for a State to prohibit the running of freight trains on Sundays.[7]

Indeed, it would be impossible to mention in detail all the police regulations to which railroad corporations are now subjected in the interests of the public. The test of their constitutionality is, in every case, whether they are

[1] As to the constitutionality of these laws in general, see, *ante*, § 92.

[2] Alexander & Washington R. R. Co. *v.* Brown, 17 Wall. 445; Chicago & N. W. Ry. Co. *v.* Williams, 55 Ill. 185; Coger *v.* N. W. Union Packet Co., 37 Iowa, 145.

[3] West Chester & P. R. R. Co. *v.* Miles, 55 Pa. St. 209; Central R. R. Co. *v.* Green, 86 Pa. St. 421; Chicago & N. W. Ry. Co. *v.* Williams, 55 Ill. 185.

[4] Rae *v.* Grand Trunk Ry. Co., 14 Fed. Rep. 401.

[5] Railroad Commissioners *v.* Portland, etc., R. R. Co., 63 Me. 269 (18 Am. Rep. 208); State *v.* New Haven, etc., R. R. Co., 43 Conn. 351; Davidson *v.* State, 4 Tex. Ct. App. 545 (30 Am. Rep. 166); Chicago & Alton R. R. Co *v.* People, 105 Ill. 657.

[6] St. Joseph & Denver City R. R. Co. *v.* Ryan, 11 Kan. 602 (15 Am. Rep. 357); Marsh *v.* Fairburg, etc., R. R. Co., 64 Ill. 414 (16 Am. Rep. 564); St. Louis, etc., R. R. Co. *v.* Mathers, 71 Ill. 592 (22 Am. Rep. 122).

[7] State *v.* Balt. & Ohio R. R. Co., 24 W. Va. 783 (49 Am. Rep. 290).

§ 194

designed, and do tend, to protect some public or private right from the injurious act of the railroad company. And the most complete legislation of this kind is that which provides for the general supervision of the railroads by commissioners, appointed by the State, and given full power to make inspection of the working and management of the roads. The constitutionality of this State supervision cannot well be doubted. "Our whole system of legislative supervision through the railroad commissioners acting as a State police over railroads, is founded upon the theory that the public duties devolved upon railroad corporations by their charter are ministerial, and, therefore, liable to be thus enforced." [1]

[1] Railroad Commissioners v. Portland, etc., R. R. Co., 63 Me. 269 (18 Am. Rep. 208).

§ 194

CHAPTER XVI.

THE LOCATION OF POLICE POWER IN THE FEDERAL SYSTEM OF
GOVERNMENT.

SECTION 200. *The United States government one of enumerated powers.*
201. Police power generally resides in the States.
202. Regulations affecting interstate commerce.
203. Police control of navigable streams.
204. Police regulation of harbors Pilotage laws.
205. Regulation of weights and measures.
206. Counterfeiting of coins and currencies.
207. Regulation of the sale of patented articles.
208. War and rebellion.
209. Regulation of the militia.
210. Taxation.
211. Regulation of offenses against the laws of nations.
212. The exercise of police power by municipal corporations.

§ 200. **The United States government one of enumerated powers.** — Very frequently, during the first century of our national existence, the government of the United States has assumed powers, which were highly essential to the promotion of the general welfare, but which were not expressly delegated to the Federal government. The exercise of such powers has always met with the vehement objection of the party in opposition (although each of the great national parties has in turn exercised such questionable powers, whenever public necessities or party interest seemed to require it); the objection being that the constitution did not authorize the exercise of the power, since there was no delegation of it by the constitution. Popular opinion, concerning the fundamental character of the Federal government, was formulated in the adoption of the tenth amendment to the constitution, which provides that "the powers, not delegated to the United States by the constitution, nor prohibited by it to the States, are reserved to the States

(603)   § 200

respectively or to the people." Relying upon this amendment as the authority for it, it has become the universally recognized rule of constitutional construction that, adopting the language of an eminent writer on constitutional law, "the government of the United States is one of enumerated powers, the national constitution being the instrument which specifies, and in which the authority should be found for the exercise of, any power which the national government assumes to possess. In this respect it differs from the constitutions of the several States, which are not grants of powers to the States, but which apportion and impose restrictions upon the powers which the States inherently possess."[1]

The so-called "strict constructionists" have maintained that the United States can exercise no power but what is *expressly* granted by the constitution. But this rule was at times applied so rigidly by the party in opposition, whenever it was desirable to prevent the enactment of an obnoxious law, that the right was denied to the United States to exercise even those powers which, although not expressly delegated, were so necessary to the effectuation of the express powers, that it cannot be supposed that the framers of the constitution did not intend to grant them. In numerous instances, the question of constitutional construction has been brought for settlement before the Supreme Court of the United States; and it is now firmly settled, that the Federal government can exercise, not only the powers which are expressly granted, but also those powers, the grant of which can be fairly implied from the necessity of assuming them, in order to give effect to the express

---

[1] Cooley Const. Lim. 10, 11. See also, to the same effect, Marshall, Ch. J., in Gibbons *v.* Ogden, 9 Wheat. 1; Story, J., in Martin *v.* Hunter's Lessee, 1 Wheat. 304, 326; Waite, Ch. J., in United States *v.* Cruikshanks, 92 U. S. 542; Calder *v.* Bull, 3 Dall. 386; Trade-mark Cases, 100 U. S. 82; Briscoe *v.* Bank of Kentucky, 11 Pet. 257; Gilman *v.* Philadelphia, 3 Wall. 713; and numerous judicial utterances of the same import in the State reports.

§ 200

grant of powers. "The government of the United States can claim no powers which are not granted to it by the constitution; and the powers actually granted must be such as are expressly given, or given by necessary implication." [1]

This doctrine of implied powers gave to the Federal constitution that elasticity of application, without which the permanency of the Federal government would have been seriously endangered. [2] But at the same time it produced the very evil, in a greater or less degree, the fear of which urged the strict constructionists to oppose its adoption, viz.: that it would open the way to the most strained construction of express grants of power, in order to justify the exercise of powers that could not be fairly implied from the express grants. Indeed, the country has often been presented with the spectacle of United States judges and legislators, engaged in justifying questionable but necessary assumptions of power by the general government, by laboriously twisting, turning and straining the plain literal meaning of the constitutional provisions, seeking to bring the powers in question within the operation of some express grant of power. For illustration I will refer only to two extreme cases, the Louisiana purchase, and the issue of treasury notes with the character of legal tender.

In the case of the Louisiana purchase, the exercise of the questionable power was so plainly beneficial to the whole country, that it was generally acquesced in. But the claim

---

[1] Story, J., in Martin v. Hunter's Lessee, 1 Wheat. 304, 326; Ch. J. Marshall in Gibbon v. Ogden, 9 Wheat. 1, 187, and other cases cited *supra*.

[2] "While the principles of the constitution should be preserved with a most guarded caution, it is at once the dictate of wisdom and enlightened patriotism to avoid that narrowness of interpretation, which would dry up all its vital powers, or compel the government [as was done under the confederation], to break down all constitutional barriers, and trust for its vindication to the people, upon the dangerous political maxim, that the safety of the people is the supreme law (*salus populi suprema lex*); a maxim which might be used to justify the appointment of a dictator, or any other usurpation." Story on Constitution, § 1292.

§ 200

of an express or implied power to make the purchase was so palpably untenable, that the transaction has been tacitly admitted to have been an actual but necessary violation of the constitution.   Even Mr. Jefferson, to whom the credit of effecting the purchase of Louisiana was justly and chiefly due, was of the opinion that there was no warrant in the constitution for the exercise of such a power, and recommended the adoption of an amendment to the constitution, authorizing its purchase.   In speaking of the objections, that were urged against the project, Judge Story says: " The friends of the measure were driven to the adoption of the doctrine that the right to acquire territory was incident to national sovereignty; that it was a resulting power, growing necessarily out of the aggregate power confided by the Federal constitution, that the appropriation might justly be vindicated upon this ground, and also upon the ground that it was for the defense and general welfare." [1]

An equally remarkable case of a strained construction of constitutional provisions is the exercise by Congress of the power to make the United States treasury notes legal tender in payment of all debts, public and private.   The exercise of this power is not so plainly beneficial; on the contrary it has been considered by many able publicists to be both an injurious and a wrongful interference with the private rights of the individual.[2]   For this reason, the assumption of the power by the national government has not met with a general acquiescence; and the constitutionality of the acts of Congress, which declared the treasury notes to be legal tender, has been questioned in numerous cases, most of which have found their way by appeal to the Supreme Court of the United States.   In Hepburn v. Griswold,[3] the

[1] Story on Constitution, § 1286.

[2] See ante, § 90, for a full discussion of power of the United States Government to make its treasury notes legal tender in paymenta of debts.

[3] 8 Wall. 603.

§ 200

acts of Congress of 1862 and 1863 were declared to be unconstitutional, so far as they make the treasury notes of the United States legal tender in the payment of pre-existing debts. In the Legal Tender Cases,[1] the opinion of the court in Hepburn v. Griswold was overruled, and the acts of 1862 and 1863 were declared to be unconstitutional in making treasury notes legal tender, whether they applied to existing debts, or those which were created after the enactment of these statutes, the burden of the opinion being that Congress has the right, as a war measure, to give to these notes the character of legal tender. In 1878, Congress passed an act, providing for the reissue of the treasury notes, and declared them to be legal tender in payment of all debts. In a case, arising under the act of 1878, the Supreme Court has finally affirmed the opinion announced in 12 Wallace, and held further that, the power of the government to make the treasury notes legal tender, when the public exigencies required it, being admitted, it becomes a question of legislative discretion, when the public welfare demands the exercise of the power.[2] A perusal of these cases will disclose the fact that the members of the court and the attorneys in the causes, have not referred to the same constitutional provisions for the authority to make the treasury notes legal tender. Some have claimed it to be a power, implied from the power to levy and carry on war; some refer it to the power to borrow money, while others claim it may be implied from the grant of power to coin money and regulate the value of it. It will not be necessary for the present purpose to demonstrate that this power is not a fair implication from the express powers mentioned. A careful reading of all the opinions in the cases referred to will at least throw the matter into hopeless doubt and uncertainty, if it does not convince the reader that in

[1] 12 Wall. 457.
[2] Juillard v. Greenman, 110 U. S. 421.

§ 200

assuming this position, violence has been done by the court to the plain literal meaning of the words. There are only too many cases, in which forced construction has been resorted to, in order to justify the exercise of powers which are deemed necessary by public opinion. No change in the rules of construction will prevent altogether the tendency to strain and force the literal meaning of the written constitution, in order to bring it into conformity with that unwritten constitution, which is the real constitution, and which is slowly but steadily changing under the pressure of popular opinion and public necessities, checked only by the popular reverence for the written word of the constitution. But all justification for this violent construction can be removed by correcting a most surprising error in constitutional construction, an error which has produced an anomaly in constitutional law.

A stable and enduring government can not be so constructed, that no branch of it can exercise a given power, unless it is granted by the constitution, expressly or by necessary implication. A government, as a totality, may properly be compared to a general agent, who does not require any specific delegation of power, in order to do an act, provided it falls within the scope of the agent's general authority. A government, like a general agent, may have express restrictions or limitations imposed upon the general powers. But in the absence of a prohibition, the right to exercise a given power, which falls within the legitimate scope of governmental authority, must be vested in some branch of the government.

Referring to the Federal system, it is claimed, in the assertion of this principle, that either the general government or the several State governments may exercise such a power, unless its exercise is prohibited to both by the Federal constitution. I do not mean to say that constitutional conventions never attempt to lay down a different rule. On the contrary, if the great men, who have contributed to the

§ 200

building up of American constitutional law, have been free from error in their construction of the tenth amendment to the Federal constitution, the adoption of that amendment was an attempt to do this impossible thing ; and the attempt has resulted in repeated violations of the constitution, as construed by them, by the assumption by Congress of powers, which were not expressly delegated nor fairly implied. The Louisiana purchase and the Legal Tender Cases, already referred to, furnish sufficient illustration of the truth of the statement. Cases of the same character will surely arise from time to time, and each repetition will diminish the popular reverence for the written constitution ; an evil which every earnest jurist would like to prevent. The difficulty lies in the interpretation and construction of the tenth amendment.

According to the prevailing interpretation of that amendment, in order that the United States may by treaty make a purchase of foreign territory, or declare by act of Congress that the treasury notes shall be legal tender in payment of all public and private debts, the power must be granted by the constitution. It is clear that the State governments cannot exercise these powers, for the exercise of them is expressly prohibited to the States. But if it can be shown that this interpretation of the tenth amendment is erroneous, — unless the common law maxim, *communis error facit jus* is recognized as binding in this case,— it must be conceded that the United States may exercise these and other like powers, although they are not expressly or impliedly granted.[1] There is no reason why the real meaning of that amendment should not be given effect, in construing the constitutionality of such acts. For no rule

---

[1] It must not be understood from what is said that the writer recognizes in the national government the power to make its treasury notes legal tender. On the contrary, the power is denied to both State and Federal government on the ground that the Federal constitution expressly prohibits to both the exercise of the power. See *ante*, § 90.

§ 200

of construction is binding upon the courts and other departments of the government, which does not rest for its authority upon some provision of the written constitution.[1] The tenth amendment reads as follows: " The powers, *not delegated to the United States by the constitution, nor prohibited by it to the States,* are reserved to the states respectively, or to the people." It is clear that, if a given power is not prohibited to the States, the general government cannot exercise it, unless there is an express delegation of the power. The amendment declares that such powers are reserved to the States or to the people. But if a given power is prohibited to the States, but not delegated to the United States (the right to make purchase of foreign territory, for example), can it be said that under this amendment the exercise of this power is reserved to the States? The very prohibition to the States in the Federal constitution forbids such a construction. It may be claimed that in such a case the power would be reserved " to the people." But that claim cannot be sustained. The reservation of the powers (referred to in this amendment), in the alternative, " to the States respectively or to the people," evidently involves a consideration of the possibility that the State constitutions may prohibit to the States the exercise of the power that is reserved, and in that case the power would be reserved to the people. What powers " are reserved to the States respectively, or to the people?" The answer is, those powers which are " *not* (*neither*) delegated by the constitution to the United States, *nor* prohibited by it to the States." These

---

[1] " As men whose intentions require no concealment generally employ the words which most directly and aptly express the idea they intend to convey, the enlightened patriots who framed our constitution, and the people who adopted it, must be understood to have employed words in their natural sense, and to have intended what they have said. * * * We know of no rule for construing the extent of such powers, other than is given by the language of the instrument which confers them, taken in connection with the purposes for which they were conferred." Chief Justice Marshall in Gibbons *v.* Ogden, 9 Wheat. 1.

§ 200

two clauses, which contain the exceptions to the operation of the amendment, are not in the alternative. In order that it may be claimed under this amendment that a power is " reserved to the States respectively or to the people," it must avoid both exceptions, *i. e.*, it must be a power which is *neither* delegated to the United States, *nor* prohibited to the States. It cannot be successfully claimed that a power is reserved under this provision, which is prohibited by the Federal constitution to the States, for the reason that it is not delegated to the United States. The conclusion, therefore, is that the United States government is one of enumerated powers, so far that it cannot exercise any power which is not prohibited by the constitution to the States, unless it is expressely or impliedly delegated to the United States. But those powers, which are prohibited to the States, and which fall legitimately within the scope of governmental authority, may be exercised by the United States, unless they are also prohibited to the United States. There need not be any express or implied grant of such powers to the national government.

It is not pretended or claimed that the construction of the tenth amendment here advocated conforms more nearly to the intentions of the framers of the constitution than that which has generally been accepted by writers upon the constitutional law of the country. Indeed, the early history of the United States reveals forces of disintegration in the politics of that day, equal or almost equal to the forces of consolidation, which would incline one to suppose that the intentions of the law-makers in the formation of the constitution were embodied in that construction of constitutional provisions which would most effectually hamper and curtail the powers of the national government. The great struggle of the wise men of those days was to secure for the Federal government the delegation of sufficient power to establish an independent government, and it may be said with truth that the Federal constitution was wrested from an unwilling

§ 200

people. It would, therefore, be impossible to show that the construction of the tenth amendment here advocated was in conformity with the intentions and expectations of those whose votes enacted the amendment. It is freely admitted that the prevailing construction is without doubt what the framers of the amendment intended. But the intentions of our ancestors can not be permitted to control the present activity of the government, where they have not been embodied in the written word of the constitution. Where the written word is equally susceptible of two constructions, one of which reflects more accurately the intention of the writer, the preference is given to that construction. But when this construction is discovered by the practical experience of a century to be pernicious to the stability of the government and in violation of the soundest principles of constitutional law; when the alternative construction is grammatically the only possible one, and relieves the constitutional law of the country of a serious embarrassment, it is but reasonable that the latter construction should be adopted, and its adoption would not violate any known rule of constitutional construction.

§ 201. **Police power generally resides in the States.** — But this discussion concerning the true construction of the tenth amendment of the United States constitution only affects the location of those phases of police power, which are denied by the constitution to the States, and which are neither granted nor prohibited to the United States, as in the case of making anything else besides gold and silver legal tender in the payment of private and public debts, or in the purchase of foreign territory, and the like; and the question in such cases is not, whether the power to do these things resides in the Federal or State government, but whether the power can be exercised at all. In all ordinary cases of police powers, the meaning and legal effect of the tenth amendment is clear, viz. : that unless the exercise of

§ 201

a particular police power is granted by the United States government, expressly or by necessary implication, the power resides in the State government, and may be exercised by it, unless the State constitution prohibits its exercise. It may, therefore, be stated, as a general proposition that with the few exceptions, which are mentioned in the succeeding sections, the police power in the United States is located in the States. The State is intrusted with the duty of enacting and maintaining all those internal regulations which are necessary for the preservation and the prevention of injury to the rights of others. The United States government cannot exercise this power, except in those cases in which the power of regulation is granted to the general government, expressly or by necessary implication. For example, it was held unconstitutional for Congress to declare it to be a misdemeanor for any one to mix naptha and illuminating oils, and offer the adulterated article for sale, or to prohibit the sale of petroleum that is inflammable at a less than the given temperature. This was a police regulation that could only be established by the States.[1] So, also, it has been held to be unconstitutional for Congress to undertake to regulate the equal rights of citizens to make use of the public conveyances, hotels and places of amusement. In order to give full effect to the fourteenth amendment, which prohibited the States from passing or enforcing any law, which denied to any person within its jurisdiction the equal protection of the laws, Congress passed an act which declared that all persons within the jurisdiction of the United States shall be entitled to the full and equal enjoyment of the accommodations, advantages, facilities and privileges of inns, public conveyances on land and water, theaters and other places of public amusement, subject only to the conditions and limitations established by law, and applica-

[1] United States *v.* De Witt, 9 Wall. 41; Patterson *v.* Commonwealth, 11 Bush, 311; *s. c.* 97 U. S. 501.

§ 201

ble alike to the citizens of every race and color, regardless of any previous condition of servitude.[1] The ordinary police regulation of employments and professions is most certainly within the powers of the State governments. Independently of the fourteenth amendment to the national constitution, it would not be within the power of Congress to enact a law, which provided for the compulsory formation of business relations, for such regulations fall within the ordinary police power of the State. The fourteenth amendment merely prohibits a State from passing or enforcing any law, which denied to any person equality before the law. If a State should not deem it proper to provide that the hotels of the State shall be open for the reception and entertainment of all persons who may apply, Congress cannot supply the deficiency by any enactment of its own, for in such a case there has been no violation of the fourteenth amendment. The amendment is violated only when the States attempt by legislation to establish an inequality in respect to the enjoyment of any rights or privileges. It has, therefore, been held by the United States Supreme Court that the civil rights bill, the act of 1875 just mentioned, is unconstitutional because it invades the police jurisdiction of the States.[2]

§ 202. **Regulations affecting interstate commerce.** — In article I., section 8, clause 3 of the United States constitution, it is provided that Congress shall have power "to regulate commerce with foreign nations, and among the several States, and with the Indian tribes." In conformity with this constitutional provision it has been held that whenever Congress exercises this form of regulation over foreign and interstate commerce, State regulations must invariably give way, and the regulations by Congress of commerce

---

[1] Laws of 1875, ch. 114.

[2] Civil Right's Cases, 109 U. S. 3. See Ex parte Yarborough, 110 U. S. 651.

§ 202

may descend to the minutest details, providing regulations of the most local character in the exercise of this power. But in the absence of congressional regulations, the State may institute the ordinary reasonable police regulations in aid of commerce. Thus it is lawful for a State to provide for the inspection of tobacco, which is intended to be shipped to some point outside of the State, it being an ordinary police regulation, not designed to interfere with commerce but to facilitate the detection of fraud in the sale of this article.[1] So, also, in the exercise of its police power, may the State exact a license fee from all non-resident salesmen or merchants, who are engaged in interstate commerce.[2] But under the guise of a police regulation, the exports and imports cannot be subjected to a State tax.[3] Any attempt, therefore, of a State to lay such a tax, will be void.[4] If the business in question contains an element of danger to the public, it may be subjected to regulations designed to protect the public against injury; it may be made subject to inspection, and a license fee may be exacted in aid of its inspection laws. That is an ordinary police regulation. But where a license is exacted of importers or exporters as a source of revenue, the license is a tax, and consequently is laid in violation of the constitution of the United States.[5] But exports and imports are free from

---

[1] Turner v. Maryland, 107 U. S. 38.

[2] Ward v. State, 31 Md. 279; s. c. 12 Wall. 418; Speer v. Commonwealth, 23 Gratt. 935 (14 Am. Rep. 164); Ex parte Robinson, 12 Nev. 263 (28 Am. Rep. 794). But where there is a discrimination made by the license law between resident and non-resident salesmen or merchants, the requirement of a license is unconstitutional. Walling v. Michigan, 116 U. S. 446; Van Buren v. Downing, 41 Wis. 122; Marshalltown v. Blum, 58 Iowa, 184 (43 Am. Rep. 116); State v. McGinniss, 37 Ark. 362; In re Watson, 15 Fed. Rep. 511.

[3] The imposition of a State tax on exports and imports is prohibited by art. I., § 10 of United States Constitution.

[4] Nathan v. State, 8 How. 73; Commonwealth v. Erie Ry Co., 62 Pa. St. 286 (1 Am. Rep. 399), reversed in 15 Wall. 232.

[5] State v. North, 27 Mo. 464; Brown v. Maryland, 12 Wheat. 419.

§ 202

taxation by the State only so long as they are found in that character. Before the article has become an export, or after the original package of the import has been broken and the article is offered for trade within the State, it may be subjected to taxation by the State, in common with other property from which it cannot then be distinguished.[1] But the police regulation of foreign and interstate commerce by the State, in the absence of like regulations on the part of the general government, must be confined to those local regulations which, while they interfere with commerce more or less materially, may be enforced without giving to the State authorities an extra-territorial power of control over the commerce of the country. For this reason and perhaps for others, the State laws which undertake to regulate the rates of fare and freight of railroads, are held to be unconstitutional, so far as they are made to apply to the interstate traffic of the railroad. To regulate the rates of fare and freight of railroads, charged by a railroad for transportation from one State into another is an unconstitutional interference with the national power of control over commerce.[2] So, also, is it impossible for a State, in regulating the time and manner of making transfers of subjects of commerce, transported by railway carriage from one point to another within the State to extend the application of the regulation to freight that is being transported to some point

---

[1] "No State can tax an export as such, except under the limitations of the constitution. But before the article becomes an export, or after it ceases to be an import, by being mingled with other property in the States it is a subject of taxation by the State. A cotton broker may be required to pay a tax on his business, or by way of license, although he may buy and sell cotton for foreign exportation." Nathan v. State, 8 How. 73. See, also, Brown v. Houston, 33 La. Ann. 843 (39 Am. Rep. 284; State v. North, 27 Mo. 464.

[2] Kaiser v. Ill. Cent. R. R. Co., 18 Fed. Rep. 151; s. c. 5 McCrary C. C. 496; Louisville, etc., R. R. Co. v. Tenn. R. R. Comrs. 19 Fed. Rep. 679; Ill. Cent. R. R. Co. v. Stone, 20 Fed. Rep. 468; Pac. Coast S. S. Co. v. Cal. R. R. Comrs., 18 Fed. Rep. 10; Carton v. Ill. Cent. R. R. Co., 59 Iowa, 148 (44 Am. Rep. 672); s. c. 22 Am. Law Reg. (N. S.) 373, note.

§ 202

beyond the State.[1] On the other hand, it has been held in Illinois to be constitutional for the State to prohibit unjust discrimination in freight and passenger charges, and to extend the prohibition to interstate commerce.[2]

§ 203. **Police control of navigable streams.** — A navigable stream is one of which the public generally may make use in the interests of commerce and social intercourse. It is a highway, like the street or public road, to which every one has the right of access, and which every one may use in any manner consistent with the equal enjoyment of the stream by others. Any exclusive appropriation of the stream,[3] or other interference with the ordinary use of the stream, is a nuisance, which any one may abate, by the removal of the obstructions to navigation, who may feel incommoded thereby.[4]

The determination of what makes a stream navigable, and consequently public, is a question for the court. The legislature cannot, by legislation, declare a stream navigable, which in fact is not so, for that would in effect be a taking of private property for a public use, which is only possible in the exercise of the right of eminent domain, and upon payment of compensation.[5] According to the English com-

---

[1] Council Bluffs v. Kansas City, etc., R. R. Co., 45 Iowa, 338 (24 Am. Rep. 773).

[2] People v. Wabash, St. L. & Pac. Ry, 104 Ill. 476; Wabash, St. L. & Pac. Ry. v. People, 105 Ill. 231.

[3] Commonwealth v. Charlestown, 1 Pick. 180; Kean v. Stetson, 5 Pick. 492; Arnold v. Mundy, 6 N. J. 1; Bird v. Smith, 8 Watts, 434.

[4] Inhabitants of Arundel v. McCulloch, 10 Mass. 70; Selman v. Wolfe, 27 Tex. 78; State v. Moffett, 1 Greene (Iowa), 247. In Maine it has been held to be a public right, when the streams are frozen over, to pass over them on foot or in vehicles, which cannot be interfered with, by cutting and removing the ice, without special authority of the State. French v. Camp, 18 Me. 433.

[5] Treat v. Lord, 42 Me. 552; Morgan v. King, 18 Barb. 284; s. c. 35 N. Y. 454; Glover v. Powell, 10 N. J. Eq. 211; Baker v. Lewis, 33 Pa. St. 301; Weise v. Smith, 3 Ore. 445 (8 Am. Rep. 621); American River Water Co. v. Amsden, 6 Cal. 443.

§ 203

mon law, all streams were navigable in which the tide ebbed and flowed.[1] In England this is not the arbitrary rule, which it would be, if applied without qualification to the streams of this country. With the exception of the Thames, above tide-water, there are no streams in England which are practically and actually navigable, except those in which the tide ebbs and flows ; and there are no tide-water streams of any importance, which are not actually navigable. But in the United States the situation is altogether different. Here, there are fresh-water streams which are navigable, and tidal streams which are not navigable. The application of the common-law rule, in its literal exactness, to the streams of this country would, therefore, result only in absurd conclusions. The courts of this country have been discussing the problem for many years, and have come to different conclusions on the various branches or sub-divisions of the question. So far as the question concerns the location of the title to the bed of the stream, it need not be considered in this connection.[2] Here, the question relates to the right of the public to make use of the stream, as a highway. In respect to this phase of the question, the courts very uniformly repudiate the common-law rule, in its literalness, and, seizing hold of the essence of the rule, declare that every stream, which is sufficiently deep and wide to float boats and rafts, used in the interests of commerce and agriculture, is navigable, and the public have a right to use it.[3]

[1] Commonwealth v. Chapin, 5 Pick. 199; People v. Tibbetts, 19 N. Y. 523; Lorman v. Benson, 8 Mich. 18.

[2] As to this branch of the question, see Tiedeman on Real Prop., § 835.

[3] The Daniel Ball, 10 Wall. 557; The Montello, 20 Wall. 439; Spring v. Russell, 7 Me. 273; Brown v. Chadbourne, 31 Me. 9; Ingraham v. Wilkinson, 4 Pick. 268; Commonwealth v. Alger, 7 Cush. 53; Claremont v. Carlton, 2 N. H. 369; Canal Comrs. v. People, 5 Wend. 423; People v. Platt, 17 Johns. 195; Morgan v. King, 25 N. Y. 454; Palmer v. Mulligan, 3 Caines, 315; Shrunk v. Schuylkill Co., 14 Serg. & R. 71; Cates v. Wadling-

§ 203

As a general proposition, the power to regulate the use of navigable rivers resides in the States, through which the rivers flow. And the only constitutional limitation upon the State's power of control, as against the United States government, is that which arises by implication from the express grant to Congress of the power to regulate foreign and interstate commerce. Inasmuch as a large part of this commerce is carried on by the use of the navigable streams of the country, it has been uniformly held by the courts, both Federal and State, that the Federal power to regulate commerce includes the power to institute regulations for the use and control of those streams which are used in the prosecution of foreign and interstate commerce. But inasmuch as all streams may be used in the carrying on of the domestic commerce, and serve other local interests, the congressional power of control does not exclude State regulation altogether. The power of the State to regulate the streams, which may be used in interstate commerce, is unaffected, as long as Congress does not exercise its power; and in any case the State regulations are void only as far as they conflict with the regulations of Congress.[1]

ton, 1 McCord, 580; Commissioners, etc., v. Withers, 29 Miss. 21; Rhodes v. Otis, 33 Ala. 578; Elder v. Barnes, 6 Humph. 358; Gavit v. Chambers, 3 Ohio, 495; Blanchard v. Porter, 11 Ohio, 138; Depew v. Board of Comrs., etc., 5 Ind. 8; Board of Comrs. v. Pidge, 5 Ind. 13; Moore v. Sanborn, 2 Mich. 519; Dorman v. Benson, 8 Mich. 18; Middleton v. Pritchard, 4 Ill. 560; McManus v. Carmichael, 3 Iowa, 1; Weise v. Smith, 3 Ore. 445 (8 Am. Rep. 621).

[1] Cooley Const. Lim. 730; Wilson v. Black Bird Creek Marsh Co., 2 Pet. 245; Wheeling Bridge Case, 13 How. 518; s. c. 18 How. 421; Gilman v. Philadelphia, 3 Wall. 713; Withers v. Buckley, 20 How. 84; Gibbons v. Ogden, 9 Wheat. 1; Escanaba Company v. Chicago, 107 U. S. 678. Under the power to regulate commerce, Congress may regulate sale, mortgage, etc., of United States vessels engaged in interstate trade. Shaw v. McCandless, 36 Miss. 296. As to how far State legislature may authorize condemnation of ships as unseaworthy by tribunals constituted by State authority, in absence of any general regulation made by Congress, see Janney v. Columbus Ins. Co., 10 Wheat. 418.

§ 203

In the absence, therefore, of congressional legislation, the State may regulate the conduct and management of ships, their speed, etc., while making use of these watery highways; and the only other limitation upon the power of the State, which may be suggested by a study of police power in general, is that the regulation must be reasonable as tending to prevent an injurious use of the stream.[1] Thus, in order to prevent damage to vessels from a loose and careless floating of logs down the stream, the State may provide by law that the logs shall be bound together into rafts or enclosed in boats, and be placed under the control and supervision of men, who are required to be reasonably skilled in the management of rafts, and to be actually in charge of them.[2] In like manner are the fisheries in a navigable stream subject to the police regulation of the State. Thus, it was held to be constitutional for a State to forbid non-residents to catch fish for the manufacture of manure and oil, in the navigable waters of the State.[3]

Where the United States government has issued coasting licenses to vessels to engage in interstate commerce on certain navigable streams, no State law can interfere with the enjoyment of the license, by granting to one or more persons the exclusive privilege of navigating the streams in question.[4] But except so far as the stream may be used, or is susceptible of use, in interstate or foreign commerce, it is within the police power of the State to grant exclusive rights to its use.[5] This right of granting exclusive privil-

---

[1] See People v. Jenkins, 1 Hill, 469; People v. Roe, 1 Hill, 470.

[2] Craig v. Kline, 65 Pa. St. 399 (3 Am. Rep. 636). See Harrigan v. Conn. River Lumber Co., 129 Mass. 580 (37 Am. Rep. 387).

[3] Brothers v. Church, 14 R. I. 398 (51 Am. Rep. 410). See, generally, People v. Reed, 47 Barb. 235; Phipps v. State, 22 Md. 380; Gentile v. State, 29 Ind. 409.

Gibbons v. Ogden, 9 Wheat. 1; Ogden v. Gibbons, 4 Johns. Ch. 150; s. c. 17 Johns. 488; Steamboat Company v. Livingston, 3 Cow. 713. See Gilman v. Philadelphia, 3 Wall. 713; The Daniel Ball, 10 Wall. 557.

[5] Veazie v. Moor, 14 How. 568. In this case, the stream over which

§ 203

eges in the use of a navigable stream is very commonly exercised in the creation of ferries, and the grant of exclusive ferry privileges. The establishment of a ferry across a navigable stream does not materially interfere with the ordinary navigation of the stream; and consequently the power of the State to create and regulate ferries in no case conflicts with the police control of Congress over navigable streams, unless Congress should by actual legislation, in the exercise of its power, supersede the subordinate State control.[1] Not only may the State grant an exclusive privilege to the navigation of a stream, but it may grant an exclusive privilege to fish in the stream,[2] or to cut ice when the river is frozen over. It is also a common exercise of proprietary power, in South Carolina, for the State to grant to corporations and individuals the exclusive right to dig phosphate rock in the beds of the navigable streams of the State.

The State has also the power to improve the navigable streams of the State, or to authorize private corporations and individuals to make the improvements, and charge toll of those who make use of the stream, as compensation for the improvements. This is but a reasonable exercise of police power, and the coasting licenses of the United States government create no exemption from liability to the regulation. All vessels may alike be required to pay toll.[3]

the exclusive privilege extended was that part of the Penobscot River, which was intercepted from communication by boats with the sea by a fall and several dams, and consequently was not susceptible of use in interstate commerce. See, also, People v. Tibbetts, 19 N. Y. 523; Livingston v. Van Ingen, 9 Johns. 50; McReynolds v. Smallhouse, 8 Bush, 447.

[1] Conway v. Taylor's Ex'r, 1 Black. 603; Fanning v. Gregorie, 16 How. 524; Wiggins Ferry Co. v. East St. Louis, 107 U. S. 365; Parker v. Metropolitan, etc., R. R. Co., 109 Mass. 506; People v. Mayor, etc., of New York, 32 Barb. 102; Chilvers v. People, 11 Mich. 43; Marshall v. Grimes, 41 Miss. 27.

[2] See Tinicum Fishing Co. v. Carter, 90 Pa. St. 85 (35 Am. Rep. 632.)

[3] Thames Bank v. Lovell, 18 Conn. 500; Kellogg v. Union Co., 12

§ 203

The State has also the power to authorize the construction of bridges across the navigable streams within its border; and if the stream is not one, that is or can be used in foreign and inter-state commerce, the power of the State to authorize its construction can in no case be questioned, because the bridge will materially interfere with the ordinary navigation of the stream.

The legislative determination of the public needs cannot in such a case be controlled by the judicial discretion.[1] The State may also license the construction of piers, extending into the current of the navigable stream; and it has been held that one is not entitled to damages for injury to his fishery, resulting from the construction of the pier.[2] But in respect to the streams, which are subject to the control of Congress, because they are used in the conduct of interstate commerce, the authority to construct a bridge may be granted by Congress or the State legislature. If Congress grants the authority, the interference of the bridge with interstate commerce will constitute no objection to the legality of the structure, the determination of Congress that it causes only a reasonable interference with the navigation of the stream being conclusive, in the same manner as a like determination of the State legislatures is, in respect to bridges over streams not adapted for use in interstate commerce. But if the State legislature authorize the construction of a bridge over a stream used in interstate

Conn. 6; Zimmerman v. Union Canal Co., 1 Watts & S. 346; Benjamin v. Manistee, etc., Co., 42 Mich. 628; Nelson v. Sheboygan Nav. Co., 4 Mich. 7 (38 Am. Dec. 222); Wisconsin River Improvement Co. v. Manson, 43 Wis. 255 (28 Am. Rep. 542); McReynolds v. Smallhouse, 8 Bush, 447; Carondelet Canal, etc., Co. v. Parker, 29 La. Ann. 430 (29 Am. Rep. 339).

[1] Commonwealth v. Breed, 4 Pick. 460; Dover v. Portsmouth Bridge, 17 N. H. 200; Depew v. Trustees of W. & E. Canal, 5 Ind. 8; Illinois, etc., Co. v. Peoria Bridge, 28 Ill. 467; Chicago v. McGinn, 51 Ill. 266 (2 Am. Rep. 295).

[2] Tinicum Fishing Co. v. Carter, 90 Pa. St. 85 (35 Am. Rep. 632).

§ 203

commerce, — inasmuch as the interference with interstate
commerce by the State is only permissive, and secondary
to the primary control of Congress, — the judgment of the
legislature, that the bridge causes only a reasonable interference with navigation, which is justifiable by the increased
facilities for rapid transportation which the bridge affords,
is not conclusive, and the ultimate decision, in the absence
of congressional action, rests with the Federal courts, who
are deemed to have the power to pass upon the reasonableness of the interference with navigation, and to cause the
bridge to be removed, if it is found to interfere materially
with the use of the stream in foreign or interstate commerce.[1]

But, even after a bridge has been condemned by the court
because of its unreasonable interference with interstate
commerce, Congress may interpose in the exercise of its
power to regulate commerce, and declare the bridge to be
a lawful structure.[2]

These interferences with the general navigation of a
stream by the public do not constitute the limitation of the
State control of streams, which cannot be used for foreign
and interstate commerce. Congress has no control over
these streams, and it seems to be the universally recognized
rule that there is no limit to the power of the State to regulate their use. It is even held to be lawful to obstruct such
a stream by the erection of dams, even to the extent of prohibiting navigation altogether. If the person who con-
structs the dam keeps within the authority given him he is
in no way responsible to those who may be damaged by the
obstruction.[3]

[1] Wheeling Bridge Case, 13 How. 518; Columbus Ins. Co. v. Peoria
Bridge Co., 6 McLean, 70; Columbus Ins. Co. v. Peoria Bridge Co., 6
McLean, 209; Jolly v. Terre Haute Drawbridge Co., 6 McLean, 237;
United States v. New Bedford Bridge, 1 W. & M. 401 · Commissioners of
St. Joseph Co. v. Pidge, 5 Ind. 13.

[2] Wheeling Bridge Case, 18 How. 421.

[3] Wilson v. Black Bird Creek Marsh Co., 2 Pet. 245; Parker v. Cutler

§ 203

§ 204. Police regulation of harbors — Pilotage laws. —
Under the constitutional grant to the United States of the
power to regulate foreign and interstate commerce is included, also, the power to regulate the harbors, and the
conduct and management of ships within the harbors. But
as long as Congress does not exercise this implied power, it
rests with the States to provide all those local regulations
of the use of harbors, which are aids to commerce rather
than restrictions or interferences, and which go far towards
eliminating the chances of injurious accidents which are
more or less present in the absence of police regulations.
Thus it is lawful for the State or municipal corporation to
prescribe when a vessel may lie in the harbor, how long she
may remain there, what light she must show at night, and
other similar regulations, without coming into conflict with
any law of Congress.[1] So, also, may the State prescribe
quarantine laws for the detention of vessels on entering a
harbor, whenever for any reason the landing of the passengers, or the discharge of the cargo, is likely to endanger the
health of the city.[2]

Mill Dam Co., 21 Me. 353; People *v.* Vanderbilt, 28 N. Y. 396; Hinchman
v. Patterson, etc., R. R. Co., 17 N. J. Eq. 75; Roush *v.* Walter, 10 Watts,
86; Zimmerman *v.* Union Canal Co., 1 Watts & S. 346; Brown *v.* Commonwealth, 3 Serg. & R. 273; Bailey *v.* Phila., etc., R. R. Co., 4 Harr.
389; Hogg *v.* Zanesville Co., 5 Ohio, 257; Depew *v.* Trustees of W. & E.
Canal Co., 5 Ind. 8; Neaderhouser *v.* State, 28 Ind. 257; Stoughton *v.*
State, 5 Wis. 291; Commissioners *v.* Withers, 29 Miss. 21; Eldridge *v.*
Cowell, 4 Cal. 80.

[1] The James Gray *v.* The John Fraser, 21 How. 421. See Mobile *v.*
Kimball, 102 U. S. 691; Escanaba Company *v.* Chicago, 107 U. S. 678.
In Vanderbilt *v.* Adams, 7 Cow. 349, an act of the legislature of New York
was sustained as constitutional which authorized the harbormasters of
the city of New York to regulate the moorings and movements of all
ships and vessels in the current of East and North Rivers, and to remove
from the wharves such vessels as were not employed in discharging or
receiving freight, in order to make room for vessels waiting for an opportunity to come up to the wharf.

[2] License Cases, 5 How. 504, 632; Railroad Co. *v.* Husen, 95 U. S. 465.
In St. Louis *v.* McCoy, 18 Mo. 238, an ordinance of the city of St. Louis

It is also lawful for a city, so far as the Federal authority is concerned, to require the payment of a tax or license fee from all boats coming into the harbor, or mooring at the city landings. The imposition of such a tax does not constitute an interference with interstate commerce in the constitutional sense.[1] But all charges laid by the local authorities for the enjoyment of the facilities furnished to vessels, must be so computed as not to constitute a tonnage duty. By the United States constitution,[2] the States are prohibited from laying any tonnage of duty without the consent of Congress. For example, the State board of harbor commissioners for the port of Charleston, South Carolina, under the authority given by the State to levy fees and port charges to defray the expenses of the police regulation of the harbor, imposed a scale of charges on vessels entering the port according to the " length over all " in feet. It was held by the Supreme Court of the State that the charges were unlawful because they were a tonnage duty.[3] But on the other hand, it has been held by the Supreme Court of the United States that the charge for the use of the wharf is not unlawful, as being a tonnage duty, because the amount of the fees is regulated according to the tonnage of freight.[4] But the harbor charges must be reasonable, and be imposed in consideration of any service rendered, or benefit received. If the law provides for the exaction of certain fees from all vessels entering the harbor,

was sustained which prescribed that boats coming from below Memphis, and having had on board, at any time during the voyage, more than a specified number of passengers, should remain in quarantine for a specified period. See, also, St. Louis v. Boffinger, 18 Mo. 13.

[1] Wiggins Ferry Co. v. East St. Louis, 107 U. S. 365; Wheeler, etc., Transportation Co. v. City of Wheeling, 9 W. Va. 170 (27 Am. Rep. 552); City of New Orleans v. Eclipse Towboat Co., 33 La. Ann. 647 (39 Am. Rep. 279).

[2] Art. I., § 10, ch. 3.

[3] Harbor Commissioners v. Pashley, 19 S. C. 315. See Inman Steamship Co. v. Tinker, 94 U. S. 238.

[4] Packet Company v. Keokuk, 95 U. S. 80.

§ 204

whether any service is rendered to it or not, the law is unconstitutional as being a restriction upon commerce.[1]

Another very important police regulation of commerce consists in the pilotage laws. Every ordinary sailing master is able to convey his vessel with safety in the open sea to any part of the world. His general knowledge of the science of navigation is a sufficient guaranty of safety to all on board. But a special knowledge of the shoals and currents of a harbor is necessary, in order that it may be entered with safety, and for this reason, it is the universal custom of all civilized nations to require that all vessels, in entering a harbor, shall be in charge of a pilot, specially licensed by the State, or at least to provide such pilots for the use of those who may desire their services under the power to regulate commerce. Congress clearly possesses the right to establish pilot regulations. But as long as Congress does not assume this power, it is but reasonable to conclude that the States may exercise the power, as they had done before the formation of the present union.

In order to remove all doubt as to the power of the States to establish pilot regulations, the first Congress passed this act: —

" All pilots in the bays, inlets, rivers, harbors, and ports of the United States shall continue to be regulated in conformity with the existing laws of the States respectively, wherein such pilots may be, or with such laws as the States may respectively hereafter enact for the purpose, until further legislative provision shall be made by Congress." [2]

Notwithstanding this statutory declaration, the State pilotage laws have frequently been attacked, for being an invasion of the power of Congress, but they have been uniformly sustained in the absence of regulations by Congress.[3] It is

---

[1] Webb v. Dunn, 18 Fla. 721.
[2] U. S. Rev. Stat. 4235.
[3] Cooley v. Wardens, 12 How. 299; Ex parte McNiell, 13 Wall. 236; the

§ 204

lawful for the States to exact the payment of pilotage fees, in whole or in part, by those owners or masters of vessels, who decline the service of a pilot, for it is within the power of the State to compel every vessel on entering a harbor of the State, to accept the service of a licensed pilot.[1] Nor is it any violation of the provisions of the constitution for a State to discriminate in the amount of pilotage between vessels in foreign commerce and those engaged in the coasting trade.[2] It has also been held lawful for a State to require the masters of vessels bound to ports in that State to accept the services of the first licensed pilot, who offers himself.[3] The only regulation of pilots established by Congress, is that contained in an act of Congress, passed in 1837, which is as follows: —

" That it shall be lawful for the master or commander of any vessel coming in or going out of any port situated upon waters, which are the boundary between two States, to employ any pilot duly licensed or authorized by the laws of either of the States bounded on the said waters, to pilot said vessel to or from said port; any law, usage or custom to the contrary notwithstanding."[4]

§ 205. **Regulation of weights and measures.** — Congress is given the power " to fix the standard of weights and measures."[5] The grant of power excludes the like power of the States, whenever Congress exercises the power; but until Congress does, there can be no constitu-

Panama, Deady 27; Ex parte Siebold, 100 U. S. 385; Wilson v. McNamee, 102 U. S. 572; State v. Penny, 19 S. C. 218.

[1] Cooley v. Wardens, 12 How. 299.

[2] Collins v. Relief Society, 73 Pa. St. 94.   See Cooley v. Wardens, 12 How. 299.

[3] Thompson v. Spraigue, 69 Ga. 409 (47 Am. Rep. 760).

[4] U. S. Rev. Stat. 4236.   See Henderson v. Spofford, 59 N. Y. 131.

[5] U. S. Const., art. I., § 8, cl. 5.

§ 205

tional objection to the regulation of these subjects by the States.[1]

§ 206. **Counterfeiting of coins and currency.** — It is also declared by the national constitution that Congress may " provide for the punishment of counterfeiting the securities and current coin of the United States." [2]   There is no need of an express grant of this power, for it would be necessarily implied from the grant of power to regulate the coinage and currency of the United States.[3]   But the offense of counterfeiting is not only a crime against the United States government, but is also a trespass upon the rights of those who are induced to receive the counterfeit coin.   The punishment of the offense against the government clearly comes within the jurisdiction of the United States.   But, in the absence of an express prohibition, it would be competent for a State to punish counterfeiting, as an offense against the individual.[4]   Congress has lately passed an act providing for the punishment of counterfeiting the coins and currency of foreign nations, and a prosecution has been instituted in the United States court at St. Louis, in a case in which a band of counterfeiters were convicted of the crime of counterfeiting the currency of Brazil.   The constitutionality of the statute was attacked on the ground that the power to punish the counterfeiting of foreign coin was not granted by the constitution, nor could it be implied from any express power ; but the validity of the statute was sustained on the ground that the power to enact it was included in the grant of the power to define and punish " offenses against the law of nations." [5]   There can be no doubt of the correctness of this decision.   When the

---

[1] Weaver v. Fegely, 29 Pa. St. 27.

[2] U. S. Const., art. I., § 8, cl. 6.

[3] Story on Constitution, § 1123.

[4] Fox v. Ohio, 5 How. 410.   See United States v. Marigold, 9 How. 560; Moore v. Illinois, 14 How. 13.

[5] U. S. Const., art. I., § 8, cl. 10.

§ 206

wrong done to the individual by receiving a counterfeit bill
or coin is alone considered, it is clearly a subject for the
State police regulation, and cannot be considered a subject
for congressional legislation, whether the coin that is counterfeited is foreign or domestic. But when the wrong to
the government, whose coin or currency is counterfeited, is
considered, the character of the offense is changed. Instead of being a subject of internal police regulation,
exclusively, it constitutes a subject of international law.
It is an offense against the law of nations. And although
it might not be declared to be so by the existing code of
international law, Congress is given the power to *define*, as
well as punish, offenses against the law of nations, and it can
undoubtedly, in the exercise of this power, provide for
punishing the counterfeiting of foreign coin. The exercise
by Congress of this implied power will not exclude the
States from the exercise of their ordinary police power
over the offense against the individual wronged by the deception.

§ 207. **Regulation of the sale of patented articles.** —
The constitution of the United States contains also a provision,[1] authorizing Congress to promote inventions by
providing for the issue of exclusive patent rights to invent-
ors. The power has been exercised, and the number of
patented articles offered for sale in the United States is
legion. In the exercise of the police power over trades and
professions, the States very frequently establish regulations,
which directly or indirectly interfere with or restrict the
sale of patented articles, and the constitutionality of such
regulations has often been questioned on that account. But
they have been generally sustained, if they were in other
respects free from constitutional objection. Thus, it was
held to be lawful to restrain the sale of adulterated provis-

---

[1] U. S. Const., art. I., § 8, cl. 8.

§ 207

ions without a stamp, although the article sold was patented. Congress cannot grant under the patent law the right to practice deception in the sale of adulterated articles ;[1] and if the adulterated article is injurious when used in the manner for which it was intended, the sale of it may be prohibited altogether.[2] But, unless there is fraud or deception in the manufacture of the patented article, it is very probable that the State could not nullify the patent by a prohibition of the sale of the patented article, on the ground that its sale involves elements of danger to the public.

Within this limitation, however, the sale of the patented article is subject to reasonable regulation by the State. For example, for the purpose of preventing fraudulent practices in the sale of patent rights, it was provided by statute in Indiana that vendors of patent rights shall file with the county clerk an authenticated copy of the letters patent, with an affidavit that they are genuine and have not been revoked or annulled, and that the vendors have authority to sell. The statute was sustained as not being in violation of the rights of the patentee, nor an invasion of the jurisdiction of Congress.[3] But a State law was declared in Nebraska to be unconstitutional, which provided that no one shall sell any patent right within the State until he has first submitted his letters patent to a county judge and obtained his approval.[4] It is also held to be constitutional for a State to impose a license tax upon the sale of patented articles by an ordinary trader, as for example, peddlers of

---

[1] Palmer v. State, 39 Ohio St. 236 (48 Am. Rep. 429). As to the general right of the State to regulate the sale of patented articles, see Jordan v. Overseers, 4 Ohio, 295; In re Brosnahan, 4 McCrary C. C. 1 (18 Fed. Rep. 62); Patterson v. Kentucky, 97 U. S. 501; Webber v. Virginia, 103 U. S. 344.

[2] Patterson v. Kentucky, 97 U. S. 501.

[3] Brechbill v. Randall, 102 Ind. 528 (52 Am. Rep. 695).

[4] Welch v. Phelps, 14 Neb. 134.

§ 207

sewing machines.[1] But it seems to be considered unconstitutional for a State to impose a license tax upon the sale by the patentee of his patented article.[2]

§ 208. **War and rebellion.** — It is provided by the constitution that Congress shall have the power " to declare war, to grant letters of marque and reprisal, and make rules concerning captures on land and water." [3] We are not concerned in this connection with the general war powers of the government, except so far as the exercise of them bears upon the citizens of the United States. Under the authority " to grant letters of marque and reprisal, and make rules concerning captures on land and water," it is held to be a legitimate means of prosecuting war to seize and confiscate the property of the enemy, and this right is also claimed for the United States against its citizens who have engaged in rebellion.[4] On the same grounds, it has been held to be lawful as a war measure, to emancipate by proclamation the slaves of those who are engaged in rebellion.[5] Congress may also in the suppression of a rebellion establish military tribunals for the trial of military offenses in those sections of the country which constitute the seat of war, and where in consequence civil law is superseded by military law. But where the courts of the country are open for the hearing of criminal offenses, and hostilities are not in such close proximity as to prevent the courts from enforcing their decrees, the jurisdiction of the civil courts cannot be invaded by a military court.[6]

In further support of the war power of the United States,

---

[1] Howe Machine Co. v. Gage, 100 U. S. 676.

[2] State v. Butler, 3 Lea (Tenn.), 222.

[3] U. S. Const., art. I., § 8, cl. 11.

[4] Miller v. United States, 11 Wall. 268; Tyler v. Defrees, 11 Wall. 331; The Grape Shot, 9 Wall. 129; The Prize Cases, 2 Black, 635.

[5] Slayback v. Cushman, 12 Fla. 427; Weaver v. Lapsley, 42 Ala. 601; Hall v. Keese, 31 Tex. 504; Dorris v. Grace, 24 Ark. 326.

Ex parte Mulligan, 4 Wall. 2.

§ 121

Congress is empowered to "raise and support armies." [1] The manner of "raising" an army, the mode of enlistment, must be determined by acts of Congress. As long as the enlistments are voluntary, no constitutional question can arise. Although it has been questioned whether the government could make forced enlistments, it cannot be seriously doubted that Congress possesses this power, and under the government of the Confederate States, whose constitution made a similar grant of power to the Confederate Congress, it was held that the general government possessed this power to compel citizens of the country to perform military service in its armies, in time of war. [2]

§ 209. **Regulation of the militia.** — Congress is authorized to "provide for organizing, arming and disciplining the militia, and for governing such part of them as may be employed in the service of the United States, reserving to the States respectively the appointment of the officers, and the authority of training the militia according to the discipline prescribed by Congress." [3] The actual control of the militia is, therefore, reserved to the States, until the President of the United States has exercised the power, which may be given him by Congress [4] to call the State militia into the service of the Uinted States, when the militia becomes for the time being a part of the United States army ; and although the States may regulate the appointment of the officers of the militia, not only are these officers subject to the orders of the President, but are also subordinate to those officers who may be placed by the President over them in

---

[1] U. S. Const., art. I., § 8, cl. 12.

[2] Barber *v.* Irwin, 34 Ga. 27; Ex parte Tate, 39 Ala. 254; Ex parte Coupland, 26 Tex. 386.

[3] Const., art. I., § 8, cl. 16.

[4] Congress is authorized to "provide for calling forth the militia, to execute the laws of the Union, suppress insurrections, and repel invasions." U. S. Const., art. I., § 8, cl. 13.

§ 209

general command of the army or of divisions of the army.[1] And when the President, in pursuance of the authority of Congress calls out the militia of the State, he may make his requisition upon the Governor of the State, or directly upon the militia officers. Any one refusing to obey this call, subjects himself to punishment under the military laws.[2]

As already stated, the power to regulate and control the militia of the country is expressly reserved to the States; and hence it cannot be doubted that the power of maintaining a militia was not intended to be included in the prohibition by the constitution of the keeping of troops in time of peace by the States.[3] Not only is that true, but it is competent for a State to make it unlawful for any body of men, other than the regularly organized volunteer militia of the State, and the troops of the United States, with an exception in favor of students in educational institutions in which military instruction is given, to associate themselves together as a military company, or to drill or parade with arms in any city or town of the State, without the license of the Governor. Such a statute is not inconsistent with any constitutional provision, and is a reasonable regulation in the interest of public order.[4]

§ 210. **Taxation.** — The power of taxation may of course be exercised by both the Federal and State governments. Neither could exercise the other powers vested in it, without the authority to provide by taxation the means of securing the execution of the laws. The constitution of the United States expressly declares that "the Congress shall have power to levy and collect taxes, duties, imposts and excises to pay the debts and provide for the common defense and general welfare of the United States; but all duties, im-

---

[1] See Kneedler v. Lane, 45 Pa. St. 238.
[2] Houston v. Moore, 5 Wheat. 1; Martin v. Mott, 12 Wheat. 19.
[3] U. S. Const., art. I, § 10, cl. 3; Luther v. Borden, 7 How. 1.
[4] Dunne v. People, 94 Ill. 120 (34 Am. Rep. 213).

§ 210

posts and excises shall be uniform throughout the United States." [1]   There are only two express limitations upon the power of Congress to levy a tax.   One is to the effect that " no tax or duty shall be laid on articles exported from any State." [2]   But it has been held that this provision of the constitution is not violated by the regulation which required, as a precaution against fraud, that certain articles intended for export shall be stamped.   This is not a tax.   It is an ordinary police regulation.[3]

It is also provided that " no capitation or direct tax shall be laid, unless in proportion to the census or enumeration hereinbefore directed to be taken." [4]   But the term *direct taxes* is used in the constitution in a peculiar sense and includes only capitation and land taxes.[5]

Congress is expressly authorized to impose a license tax upon all trades, manufactures and other occupations.   But it is not in the exercise of the ordinary police power.   The ordinary police regulation of trades and professions falls within the power of the States, and the United States cannot determine what trades are injurious, and may therefore be restrained by the imposition of a license.   The license fee, which the United States government may exact as a condition precedent to the pursuit of any employment or the manufacture and sale of any product, is a tax, and does not operate directly as an ordinary police regulation.   As a measure for enforcing the payment of the license tax, no doubt Congress may prohibit the prosecution of the trade, if the tax is not paid ; and in order that illicit trade may be detected, Congress may provide the most stringent regula-

[1] U. S. Const., art. I, § 8, cl. 1.
[2] U. S. Const., art. I, § 9, cl. 5.
[3] Pace v. Burgess, 92 U. S. 372.
[4] U. S. Const., art. I, § 2; § 9, cl. 4.
[5] Hylton v. United States, 3 Dall. 171; Pac. Ins. Co. v. Soule, 7 Wall. 433; Veazie Bank v. Fenno, 8 Wall. 533; Springer v. United States, 102 U. S. 586.

§ 210

tions for the inspection of the premises of those who are engaged in the trade in question, and require the goods to be stamped, and the like. But these regulations are only lawful as means devised for the collection of the tax, and not as a police measure, designed to restrain the prosecution of the trade. If Congress declares that its purpose, in exacting a license fee, was to lay a tax, or if there is no declared purpose, and the act of Congress falls fairly within the power of Congress to impose a license tax, the constitutionality of the act cannot be questioned on the ground that it is a police regulation, designed to restrict or suppress the objectionable trade or manufacture. The general rule of constitutional construction applies, which provides that when the language of a statute admits of two constructions, one of which keeps the statute within the constitutional limitations, and the other causes it to violate them, the former construction is invariably adopted. Nor is it possible to give the latter construction, in order to secure an avoidance of the statute on the ground of unconstitutionality, even though it is known beyond a reasonable doubt from facts outside of the statute, that this construction will conform more nearly with the real purpose of the legislators. An interesting case of this kind has lately occurred. At the last meeting of Congress (1886), an act was passed, laying a tax upon the sale and manufacture of oleomargarine, and providing a rigid system of inspection and stamping of the goods. The law in form is a legitimate exercise of the congressional power of taxation, and it may be true that some of the members of Congress supported the measure for the purpose of raising revenue. But it can hardly be doubted that the promoters and original advocates of the bill intended it to operate as a restriction upon the sale of oleomargarine in the dairy interests, and the raising of revenue was to them a matter of secondary, if any, importance. But these occult intentions of the advocates of the bill, even if they could be judicially established, could not

§ 210

affect the constitutionality of the law, as far as it does not contain regulations not suitable as a means for securing a proper collection of the tax.[1] Congress is not only unable to prohibit or restrict the prosecution of a trade by the requirement of a license, but it is also denied the power, by granting a license, to authorize the prosecution of a trade, which is prohibited by the laws of the State.[2]

In the federal state, the independence of the Federal and State governments of each other must be guaranteed by the express or implied limitations of the constitution, in order that the success of the system may be assured. And to such an extent is this limitation upon the power of both considered necessary, that it has been held by the courts that neither the United States nor the State can tax the agencies of the government of the other. The State cannot lay a tax upon the securities of the national government.[3] Nor

[1] See Veazie Bank v. Fenno, 8 Wall. 533; National Bank v. United States, 101 U. S. 1.

[2] License Tax Cases, 5 Wall. 462; Pervear v. Commonwealth, 5 Wall. 475; McGuire v. Commonwealth, 3 Wall. 387; Commonwealth v. Thornley, 6 Allen, —; Commonwealth v. O'Donnell, 8 Allen, 548, Commonwealth v. Holbrook, 10 Allen, 200; Block v. Jacksonville, 36 Ill. 301; State v. Carney, 20 Iowa, 82; State v. Stulz, 20 Iowa, 488; State v. Baughman, 20 Iowa, 497.

[3] " That the power to tax involves the power to destroy; that the power to destroy may defeat and render useless the power to create; that there is a plain repugnance in conferring on one government a power to control the constitutional measures of another, which other, with respect to those measures, is declared to be supreme over that which exerts the control, are propositions not to be denied." Marshall, Ch. J., in McCulloch v. Maryland, 4 Wheat. 316, 413; Weston v. Charleston, 2 Pet. 449; Bank of Commerce v. New York City, 2 Black, 620; Bank Tax Case, 2 Wall. 200; Society for Savings v. Coite, 6 Wall. 594; Van Allen v. Assessors, 3 Wall. 573; People v. Commissioners, 4 Wall. 244; Bradley v. People, 4 Wall. 459; Banks v. The Mayor, 7 Wall. 16; Bank v. Supervisors, 7 Wall. 26. Revenue stamps are not taxable. Palfrey v. Boston, 101 Mass. 329. United States treasury notes are not taxable. Montgomery Co. v. Elston, 32 Ind. 27. See People v. United States, 93 Ill. 30 (34 Am. Rep. 155), in which the power of the State to tax the property of the United States held by private individuals for any purpose, was denied. See State v. Jackson, 33 N. J 450.

§ 210

can the United States lay a tax upon the securities and other agencies of the State government.[1] "In respect to the reserved powers, the State is as sovereign and independent as the general government. And if the means and instrumentalities employed by the government to carry into operation the powers granted to it are necessarily, and for the sake of self-preservation, exempt from taxation by the States, why are not those of the States depending upon their reserved powers, for like reasons, equally exempt from Federal taxation? Their unimpaired existence in the one case is as essential as in the other. It is admitted that there is no express provision in the constitution that prohibits the general government from taxing the means and instrumentalities of the States, nor is there any prohibiting the States from taxing the means and instrumentalities of that government. In both cases the exemption rests upon necessary implication, and is upheld by the great law of self-preservation; as any government, whose means employed in conducting its operations are subject to the control of another and distinct government, can only exist at the mercy of that government, of what avail are these means if another power may tax them at discretion?" [2] For these reasons it has been held that the State cannot tax the property of a bank, or the bank itself, which has been established by the United States government, as a governmental agency, as was the old Bank of the United States, or the present national banks.[3] So, also, has it been held incompetent for a State to tax the salary of a United States official, or for the United States to tax the salary of a State official.[4] On the same ground, it has been held that the act of Congress, de-

---

[1] Collector v. Day, 11 Wall. 113; Ward v. Maryland, 12 Wall. 418; Railroad Company v. Peniston, 18 Wall. 5; Fifield v. Close, 15 Mich. 505.

[2] Nelson, J., in Collector v. Day, 11 Wall. 113, 124.

[3] McCulloch v. Maryiaed, 4 Wheas. 316; Osborn v. United States Bank, 9 Wheat. 738. See National Rank v. Commonwealth, 9 Wall. 353.

[4] Dobbins v. Commissioners of Erie Co., 16 Pet. 435; Collector v. Day, 11 Wall. 113; Freedman v. Sigel, 10 Blatchf. 327.

§ 210

claring that papers used in judicial process, either as pleadings or as evidence, shall be invalid unless stamped, was unconstitutional in its application to the State courts.[1] And it has likewise been held incompetent for the United States to declare an ordinary contract or deed, which is valid according to the State law, invalid because it has not been stamped.[2]

§ 211. **Regulation of offenses against the law of nations.** — Congress is also given the power " to define and punish piracies and felonies committed on the high seas, and offenses against the law of nations." Piracy is usually defined to be the equivalent of robbery in law, being a forcible deprivation of property upon the high seas.[3] But a robbery at sea committed in a vessel sailing under the flag of another nation and by one not a citizen of the United States is not such a piracy, as may be punished in the courts of the United States.[4]

§ 212. **The exercise of police power by municipal corporations.** — A large part of the police power of the State is exercised by the local governments of municipal corpora-

[1] Carpenter v. Snelling, 97 Mass. 452; Green v. Holway, 101 Mass. 243 (3 Am. Rep. 339); Atkins v. Plimpton 44 Vt. 21; Griffin v. Ranney, 35 Conn. 239; People v. Gates, 43 N. Y. 40; Moore v. Moore 47 N. Y. 467 (7 Am. Rep. 466); Hale v. Wilkinson 21 Gratt. 75; Haight v. Grist, 64 N. C. 739; Smith v. Short, 40 Ala. 385; Davis v. Richardson, 45 Miss. 499 (7 Am. Rep. 732); Bumpass v. Taggart, 26 Ark. 398 (7 Am. Rep. 623); Union Bank v. Hill, 3 Cold. 325; Hunter v. Cobb, 1 Bush, 239; Warren v. Paul, 22 Ind. 276; Craig v. Dimmock, 47 Ill. 308; Jones v. Estates of Keep, 19 Wis. 369; Sammons v. Holloway, 21 Mich. 162 (4 Am. Rep. 465); Burson v. Huntington, 21 Mich. 415 (4 Am. Rep. 497); Duffy v. Hobson, 40 Cal. 240.

[2] Moore v. Quirk, 105 Mass. 49 (7 Am. Rep. 499); Sayles v. Davis, 22 Wis. 225.

[3] 4 Bl. Com. 71-73; 1 Kent, 183. See United States v. Smith, 5 Wheat. 153; United States v. Brig Malek Adhel, 2 How. 210.

[4] United States v. Palmer, 3 Wheat. 610; United States v. Kessler, Baldw. 15.

§ 212

tions, and the extent of their police power depends upon the limitations of their charters.   They are creatures of the State, and the superior control of the State is almost without limit.   The police power of a municipal corporation must depend upon the will of the legislature, and in order that a city, town or county may exercise a particular police power, it must be fairly included in the grant of powers by the charter.   The construction of the common phraseology of municipal charters, in order to determine what police powers fell within their provisions, would consume too much space to justify an exhaustive discussion in this connection.   The subject has already received a full and able treatment by a distinguished American jurist,[1] and does not fall properly within the scope of a treatise on the constitutional limitation upon the American police power.   For these reasons, no attempt has been made to present rules for the construction of the charter grants of police power to municipal corporations.   The police regulations of a municipal corporation only concern us in this connection, when they contravene some constitutional limitation, and from this standpoint all the ordinary police regulations have been criticised in these pages.

[1] See Dillon on Municipal Corporations.

§ 212

INDEX.

[*The references in index are to pages.*]

ABATEMENT,
   of nuisances — destruction of buildings, 440–442.

ABORTION,
   criminal element of, 30, 31.

ABSTRACT,
   justice, principles of, effect of, on police power, 5–9.

ACCUSED,
   entitled to counsel, 89–91.

ACQUISITION,
   of real estate, limitations of, 351–354.
   of interest in personal property regulated, 483–486.

ADMINISTRATION,
   and execution, sale of lands by, 359, 360.

ADULTERATION,
   prohibiting sale of, 292.

ADVICE,
   of counsel, how far defense in malicious prosecution, 63–65.

AFFINITY,
   as an objection to marriage, 533–535.

ALIENATION,
   of lands, regulation of, right of, 354–357.
   involuntary, 357–370.
   of personal property, 493–496.

AMUSEMENTS,
   right to attend, 231, 232.

APPRENTICES, 568–572.

ARRESTS,
   lawful, 81–85.
   without warrant, 83–85.

ASSESSMENTS,
> local, as a mode of taxation, 479–482.

BAIL, 80, 81.

BANKRUPTCY AND INSOLVENCY LAWS, 521, 522

BAR-ROOMS,
> prohibition of, 307, 309, 311.

BATTERY,
> in self-defense, 25–30.

BEGGING,
> prohibited, 122, 123.

BEQUESTS,
> regulation of, 492, 493.

BETTERMENT LAWS, 366–370.

BIBLE,
> in public schools, 161–163.

BILLS OF ATTAINDER, 72–74.

BLASPHEMY,
> distinguished from religious criticism, 166–171.

BODY AND LIMB,
> security to, 22–29,

BOYCOTTING, 252–255.

BREAD,
> regulation of weight of, 208.

BRIDGES,
> erection of, over navigable streams, 622–623.

BUILDINGS,
> construction of wooden, regulated, 438–440.
> destruction of to abate nuisance, 440–442.

BURIAL GROUNDS,
> regulation of, 437, 438.

BUSINESS RELATIONS,
> compulsory formation of, 226–232.

CAPITAL PUNISHMENT, 19–22.

CHANCERY,
> transfer of lands by courts of, 360.

CHAPLAINS,
appointed for Congress, Legislatures, army and navy, 160, 161.

CHARGES AND RATES,
of corporations regulated by law, 587–591.

CHARTERS,
of private corporations inviolable, 574, 575.

CHRISTIANITY,
how far recognized by law, 160–163, 166–170.

CHURCH,
legal relation of, to State, 156–166.
State control of, 163–166.

CITIZENSHIP,
distinguished from domicile, 137, 138.

CITIZENS,
public duties of, 146, 147.

CLERICAL PROFESSION,
regulation of, 204, 206–207.

COINS AND COINAGE,
regulation of, 210, 211, 220–222.
counterfeiting, 628, 629.

COMBINATIONS,
in restraint of trade, prevention of, 245–251.

COMMERCE,
interstate and foreign, regulations affecting, 614–617.

COMMON CARRIER,
compulsory carriage by, 228–231.

COMPETENCY,
of witnesses, determined by religious faith, 174, 175.

COMPULSORY,
carriage by common carriers, 228–231.
education, 561–563.
emigration, 141–144.

CONCEALED WEAPONS,
prohibition of carrying of, 502, 503.

CONFINEMENT,
for infectious and contagious diseases, 102, 103.
of criminals, 97–101.
of the insane, 103–110.
to answer for a crime, 79–81.
of habitual drunkards, 114–116.

CONSANGUINITY,
and affinity, as objections to marriage, 533–535.

CONSCRIPTION,
to armies and navies in time of war, 632.

CONSTITUTIONAL LIMITATIONS,
construction of, 10–13, 68.
upon police power, 13–15.
upon police regulation of religion, 159–166.

CONTAGIOUS AND INFECTIOUS DISEASES,
confinements for, 102, 103.

CONTRACTS,
regulation of, and rights of action, 515–522.
bankruptcy and insolvency laws, 521–522.
option, when illegal, 262, 271.

CONVEYANCES,
of land, regulation of, 354–357.

CONVICT,
control and punishment of in prison, 97, 98.
lease system, 98–101.

COPYRIGHT,
as a monopoly, 317.

CORNERING THE MARKET,
prohibited, 248–251.

CORPORAL PUNISHMENT, 23–25.

CORPORATIONS,
police regulations of, 574–602.
inviolability of charters of private, 574, 575.
police control of, 576–579.
freedom from police control, as a franchise, 580–583.
police regulation of, in general, 584–587.
laws regulating rates and charges of, 587–591.
police regulation of foreign, 591–593.
police regulation of railroads, 593–602.

COVERTURE,
estate during, 343–348.

CRIME,
effect of, on right, 70.
confinement to answer for, 79–81.
and vice distinguished, 148–153.
punishment of insane for, 110–114.
not permitted under guise of religious worship, 171–174.

CRIME — *Continued.*
drunkenness a, 302
suicide as a, 18–19.

CRIMINALS,
police supervision of habitual, 124–131.
confinement of, 97–101.

CRITICISM,
of officers and candidates for office, 45–52.

COUNSEL,
accused's right of, 89–91.
advice of, how far defense in malicious prosecution, 63–65.

CRUELTY TO ANIMALS,
laws for the prevention of, 513–515.

COUNTERFEITING,
of coins and currencies, 628, 629.

CURRENCY,
regulation of the, 210–224.

CURTESY,
when interest in expectancy, 344, 345.

DANGEROUS CLASSES,
police control of, 102–136.

DEFECTIVE TITLES,
perfected by legislative enactment, 361, 362.

DESTRUCTION OF PROPERTY,
on account of illegal use, 498.

DISABILITY,
of married women, 549, 550.
sale of lands belonging to persons under legal, 358, 359.

DISEASES,
as a legal objection to marriage, 535.
confinement for infectious and contagious, 102, 103.

DISORDERLY,
religious meetings on public streets, 172–174.

DIVORCES, 539–542.

DOGS,
keeping of, 507–513.

DOMESTIC ANIMALS,
laws regulating use of, 505–515.

DOMICILE,
citizenship distinguished from, 137, 138

DOWER,
when an interest in expectancy, 345–348.

DRAINAGE,
of lands, at expense of owner, and against his consent, 444–448,

DRESS,
how far subject to police regulations, 155, 156.

DRUNKARDS,
confinement of habitual, 114–116.
when drunkenness a criminal offense, 302.

DUE PROCESS OF LAW,
in criminal trials, 70–72.

DYNAMITE,
prohibition of sale of, 298.

EDUCATION,
compulsory, 561–563.

EMIGRATION,
prohibition of, 141.
compulsory 141–144.

EMINENT DOMAIN, 370–422.
exercise of power regulated by legislature, 372–378.
public purpose, what is a, 379–391.
expropriation, 391.
what property may be taken, 391–397.
what constitutes a taking, 397–420.
compensation, how ascertained, 420–422.

EMPLOYMENTS,
State regulations of private and public, 569–573.

EMPLOYER AND EMPLOYEE,
State regulation of relation of, 567–573.
(see master and servant.)

ENGROSSING, FORESTALLING,
and regrating, 242–245.

EQUITABLE ESTATES,
converted into legal estates by statute of uses, 337, 340, 341.

ESTATE,
during coverture, when interest in expectancy, 343.
tail, abolished or modified by statute, 336–339.

ESTATE— *Continued.*
in land, police regulation of, 335–341.
equitable, converted into legal by statute of uses, 337, 340, 341.

EXECUTION,
sale of lands under, 360, 361.

EXECUTORS AND ADMINISTRATORS,
sale of lands by, 350–360.

EXEMPTION AND HOMESTEAD,
laws, 520, 521.

EXPATRIATION, 138–140.

EXPECTANCY,
interests in, 341–357.

EX POSTE FACTO LAWS, 74–79

EXPOSURE,
of one's person, 155–156.

EXPROPRIATION,
of lands for settlement of small holdings, 391.

FEDERAL GOVERNMENT,
location of police power in, 603–639.
(see police power in the Federal system of government, location of.)

FISHERIES,
regulation of non-navigable streams, 448–451.

FOREIGN CORPORATION,
police regulation of, 591–593.

FORESTALLING, REGRATING AND ENGROSSING, 242–245.

FRANCHISE,
may be exclusive, 315–326.
license to prosecute a prohibited trade is a, 318–327.

FRAUD,
regulations for the prevention of, in sale of goods, 207–209.

FREEDOM OF SPEECH,
and of the press, 189–193.

FUTURES,
dealing in, when legal, 262–271.

GAMBLING HOUSES,
prohibition of, 291.

GAME,
  regulation of right to hunt, 440.

GAS PIPES,
  laying of may be exclusive franchise, 316–317.

GUARDIAN AND WARD,
  relation of, 565, 566.
  control of property by guardian, 496–498.
  testamentary guardian, 566.

HABITUAL CRIMINALS,
  police supervision of, 124–131.

HABITUAL DRUNKARDS,
  confinement of, 114–116.

HARBORS,
  police regulation of, 624–627.

HARD LABOR,
  required of convicts, 98.

HAY,
  manufacture of pressed a monopoly, 324.

HEALTH,
  security to legalized nuisances, 32–34.

HEIR'S INTEREST,
  is an interest in expectancy, 342.

HIGHWAY,
  extraordinary use of, is a franchise, 316, 317.
  land appropriated for.
  (see eminent domain.)
  appropriated for use of railroads, 409–420.

HOMESTEAD AND EXEMPTION LAWS, 520, 521.

HOMICIDE,
  justifiable in defense of one's rights, 25–30.

HUSBAND AND WIFE,
  regulation of relation of, 525–550.
  marriage a natural status, subject to police regulation, 525–527.
  constitutional limitations upon police control of marriage, 528, 529.
  distinction between natural and legal capacity, 529, 530.
  insanity as a legal incapacity, 530.
  disability of infancy in respect to marriage, 430–533.
  consanguinity and affinity, 533–535.
  constitutional diseases, 535.
  financial condition, 535, 536.

HUSBAND AND WIFE — *Continued.*
    differences in race, miscegenation, 536, 537.
    polygamy prohibited, 538, 539.
    marriage indissoluble — divorce, 539–542.
    regulation of marriage ceremony, 543, 544.
    wife in legal subjection to the husband, its justification, 544-547.
    husband's control of wife's property, 547–549.
    legal disabilities of married women, 549, 550.
    estate during coverture, interest in expectancy, 343.
    curtesy, when interest in expectancy, 344, 345.

ILL-FAME,
    prohibition of houses of, 291.

IMMIGRATION,
    prohibition of, 144, 145.

IMPORTATIONS,
    legislative restraint of, 224–226.

IMPRISONMENT,
    for crime, 79–81, 97–101.

IMPROVEMENT,
    of property, at expense of owner and against his consent, 444–448.

INDIANS,
    regulation of the, 143, 144.

INDICTMENT,
    by grand jury, 91, 92.

INFECTIOUS AND CONTAGIOUS DISEASES,
    confinements for, 102, 103.

INFORMATION,
    prosecution by, 91, 92.

INHERITANCE,
    and interest in expectancy, 342.

INJURIOUS ARTICLES OF CONSUMPTION,
    prohibiting sale of, 294, 295.

INNKEEPERS,
    compulsory entertainment by, 228, 231.

INSANE,
    confinement of the, 103–110.
    control of, in asylum, 110.
    punishment of, for crime, 110–114.

INSANITY,
    as a legal incapacity to marriage, 530.

INSOLVENCY AND BANKRUPTCY LAWS, 521, 522.

INSPECTION OF GOODS, 207, 208.

INSURANCE COMPANIES,
 license may be required of, 281.

INTEREST IN EXPECTANCY, 341–351.

INTEREST AND USURY LAWS, 238–241.

INTERSTATE COMMERCE,
 regulations affecting, 614–617.

INTOXICATING LIQUORS,
 prohibiting sale of, 298–311.
 licensing sale of, 274–276.

INVENTIONS,
 patent to, a monopoly, 317.

INVOLUNTARY ALIENATION,
 of lands, 357–370.
 scope of legislative authority, 358.
 by persons under legal disability, 358–359.
 sales by executors and administrators, 359–360.
 under execution, 360.
 by decree of chancery, 361.
 confirming defective titles, 361–362.
 partition, 363–366.
 betterments, 366–370.
 eminent domain, 370–422.
 of personal property, 493–496.

JOINT ESTATES.
 regulated by statute, 337, 339, 340.
 partition of, 362–364.
 tenancies, converted into tenancies in common, 337, 339, 340.

LABOR,
 required of convicts, 98.

LAND TENURE, 328–335.

LAND,
 what is private property in, 328–335.
 How far use of may be controlled by requirement of license, 442–444.
 (see use of land.)

LAW,
 regulation of the practice of, 204, 205.

LAWS OF NATIONS,
offenses against the, 638.

LEARNED PROFESSIONS,
regulations of, 200, 204.
regulations of practice in the, 204–207.

LEASE OF CONVICTS, 98–101.

LEGAL PROFESSION,
regulation of, 200–203.

LEGAL TENDER,
regulation of, 210–224.

LESSORS,
statutory liability of, for acts of lessees, 452–460.

LIBERTY,
personal, defined and how guaranteed, 66–69.

LICENSE.
as police regulation distinguished from tax, 278–289.
how far use of land may be controlled by requirement of, 442–444.
of trades and occupations, 271–289.
revoked by prohibition of trade, 287, 288.

LIFE
security to, 17.

LIMITATIONS,
upon police power of United States, 1–16.
upon religious worship permissible, 171–174.

LIQUOR,
prohibition of sale of, 298–311.
regulations of the trade, 274–311.

LOCALITY,
police control of employments in respect to, 311–315.

LOTTERIES,
prohibition of, 291.

LUMBER,
public surveying of, 208.

LUNATICS,
confinement of, 103–110.
prohibiting sale of liquors to, 302–304.

MALICIOUS PROSECUTION, 59–65.
advice of counsel, how far defense in, 63–65.

MANUFACTURE,
> of personal property regulated, 502–504.
> (see licenses, trades and occupation; personal property.)

MARKETS,
> keeping of, made a monopoly, 324.
> "cornering" prohibited, 248–256.
> prohibition of private and establishment of public, 312–314.

MARRIAGE,
> regulation of, 525–550.
> (see husband and wife.)

MARRIED WOMEN,
> legal disabilities of, 549, 550.

MASTER AND SERVANT,
> regulation of relation, 567–573.
> terms "master and servant" defined, 567.
> relation purely voluntary, 567, 568.
> apprentices, 568–572.
> State regulation of private employment, 569–572.
> State regulation of public employments, 572–573.

MEDICINE,
> regulation of practice of, 202, 203, 205, 206.
> compulsory submission to medical and surgical treatment, 31, 32.

MENDICANCY,
> prohibited, 122, 123.

MERCANTILE REPORTS,
> how far privileges, 37, 55.

MERCHANDISE,
> regulation of sale of certain articles of, 207–210.

MILITIA,
> regulation of, 632, 633.

MINISTERS,
> regulation of the duties of, 206, 207.
> no restriction as to who may be, 204.

MINORS,
> State control of, 131–136.

MISCEGENATION,
> prohibited, 536, 537.

MONOPOLIES,
> of certain trades created by law, 315, 327.

MORALITY AND RELIGION,
police control of, 148–188.

MUNICIPAL CORPORATION,
exercise of police power by, 638, 639.

NATURALIZATION, 140.

NAVIGABLE STREAMS,
police control of, 617–623.

NEGLIGENCE,
contracts against liability for, prohibited, 255–259.

NITRO-GLYCERINE,
prohibition of sale of, 298.

NON-NAVIGABLE STREAMS,
conversion of, 451, 452.

NUISANCES,
legalized, 32–34.
what are, 422–426.
judicial question, 426–430.
unwholesome trades in tenement houses prohibited, 430–433.
confinement of objectionable trades to certain localities, 433–436.
regulation of burial grounds, 437, 438.
laws regulating construction of wooden buildings, 438–440.
abatement of, 440.
destruction of buildings, 440–442.

OCCUPATIONS AND TRADES,
police regulation of, 194–327.
(see police regulation of trades and professions.)
Prohibition of, in general, 289–298.

OILS,
regulation of sale of, 207.

OLEOMARGARINE,
prohibition of sale of, 295–297.

OPTION CONTRACTS,
when illegal, 262–271.

PATENT,
to invention a monopoly, 317.

PATENTED ARTICLES,
regulation of sale of, 629–631.

PARENT AND CHILD,
    regulation of relation of, 551–566.
    original character of relation of its political aspect, 551–554.
    no limitation to State interference, 554–561.
    compulsory education, 561–563.
    parent's duty of maintenance, 563, 564.
    child's duty to support indigent parents, 564, 565.
    relation of guardian and ward, subject to State regulation, 565.
    testamentary guardian, 566.

PARTITION,
    of joint estates, 362–364.

PERPETUITY,
    rule against, in relation to personal property, 488, 489.

PERSONAL LIBERTY,
    defined and how guaranteed, 66–69.

PERSONAL PROPERTY,
    regulation of sale of certain articles of, 207–210.
    police regulation of, 483–524.
    acquisition of interest in, 483, 486.
    real and personal property therein distinguished, 484–486.
    statute of uses and rule against perpetuity as regulations of personal property, 486–489.
    regulation and prohibition of sale of personal property, 489–492.
    disposition of, by will, 492, 493.
    involuntary alienation, 493–496.
    control of property by guardian, 496–498.
    destruction of personal property on account of illegal use, 498.
    laws regulating use of, 499–515.
    prohibition of possession of certain, 499, 500.
    regulation and prohibition of manufacture of certain, 500–502.
    carrying of concealed weapons prohibited, 502, 503.
    manufacture of regulated, 504.
    miscellaneous regulation of use of, 504.
    laws regulating use of domestic animals in general, 505–507.
    keeping of dogs, 507–513.
    laws for the prevention of cruelty to animals, 513–515.
    regulation of contracts and rights of action, 515–522.
    regulation of ships and shipping, 523–524.

PILOTAGE LAWS, 624–627.
    defendants, in criminal prosecution, 92–95.

PEINE FORTE ET DURE, 92.

POISON,
    regulation of sale of, 209, 210.

POLICE POWER,
    defined and explained, 1–4.
    constitutional limitations upon, 13–15.
    abstract justice no limitation upon, 5–9.
    control of criminal classes, 70–101.
    control of dangerous classes, 102–136.
    control of insane, 103–114.
    control of habitual drunkards, 114–116.
    control of vagrants, 116–122.
    control of morality and religion, 148–188.
    control of minors, 131–136.
    regulation of citizenship and domicile, 137–147.
    regulation of religion, constitutional restrictions, 159–166.
    supervision of habitual criminals, 124–131.
    supervision of prostitutes, 131.
    regulation of personal property, 483–524.
    (see personal property.)
    in its relation to corporations, 574–602.
    (see corporations.)
    regulation of real property, 328–482.
    (see real property.)
    regulation of trades and professions, 194–327.
    (see trades and professions.)
    in the Federal system of government, location of, 603–639.
    United States government one of enumerated powers, 603–612.
    generally, resides in the States, 612–614.
    regulations affecting interstate commerce, 614, 617.
    police control of navigable streams, 617–623.
    police regulation of harbors, pilotage laws, 624–627.
    regulation of weights and measures, 627, 628.
    counterfeiting of coins and currencies, 628, 629.
    regulation of sale of patented articles, 629–631.
    war and rebellion, 631, 632.
    regulation of militia, 632, 633.
    taxation, 633–638.
    regulation of offenses against the laws of nations, 638.
    exercise of, by municipal corporations, 638–639.

POLYGAMY,
    prohibited, 538, 539.

POST-OFFICE AND POST ROADS,
    government monopolies, 326, 327.

POVERTY,
    as a legal objection to marriage, 535, 536.

POWER OF APPOINTMENT,
    when interests in expectancy, 350, 351.

PRACTICE OF LAW,
    regulation of the, 204, 205.

PRELIMINARY CONFINEMENT,
    to answer for a crime, 79–81.

PRESS,
    police regulation of the, 180–193.

PRICES AND CHARGES,
    regulation of, 233–238.

PRIVATE RIGHTS,
    table of, 16.

PRIVATE PROPERTY,
    in land, what is, 328–335.

PRIVILEGE,
    of legislators, 37–40.
    in judicial proceedings, 40–45.
    by government may be made exclusive, 315–326.

PRIVILEGED COMMUNICATIONS, 35–39.

PROCESS FAIR ON ITS FACE, 81–83.

PROFESSIONS,
    regulation of, 1 4–327.

PROHIBITION,
    of emigration, 141.
    of sale of railroad tickets by scalpers, 292, 293.
    of sale of personal property, 294, 295, 298, 311, 489–492.
    of unwholesome trade in tenement house, 430–433.
    of private market, 312, 314.
    of possession of certain personal property, 499, 500.
    of manufacture of certain articles, 500, 502.
    of carrying concealed weapons, 502, 503.

PROSTITUTION,
    police supervision of, 131.
    houses of, prohibited, 291.

PROTECTIVE TARIFF, 224–226.

PUBLIC POLICY,
    general prohibition of contracts on ground of, 271.

PUBLICATIONS,
    through the press, how far privileged, 52–59.

PUNISHMENT,
    capital, 19–22.

PUNISHMENT — *Continued.*
  when cruel and unusual, 21, 22, 24.
  of criminal insane, 110–114.

PURCHASE OF REAL ESTATE,
  limitation of the, 351–354.

QUARTERING SOLDIERS,
  in private dwellings, 466, 467.

RAILROADS,
  appropriation of highways for use of, 409–420.
  as a government monopoly, 326, 327.
  police regulation of, 593–602.
  regulation of rates and charges of, 587–591.

RATES AND CHARGES,
  of corporations, regulated by law, 587–591.

REAL PRORERTY,
  police regulations of, 328–482.
  what is meant by " private property in land?" 328–335.
  regulation of estates — vested rights, 335–341.
  interests of expectancy, 341–351.
  limitation of the right of acquisition, 351–354.
  regulation of the right of alienation, 354–357.
  involuntary alienation, 357–370.
  eminent domain, 370–422.
  exercise of power regulated by legislature, 372–378.
  public purpose, what is a, 379–391.
  what property may be taken, 391–397.
  what constitutes a taking, 397–420.
  compensation, how ascertained, 420–422.
  regulation of the use of lands — what is a nuisance? 422–426.
  what is a nuisance, a judicial question, 426–430.
  unwholesome trades in tenement houses may be prohibited, 430–433.
  confinement of objectionable trades to certain localities, 433–436.
  regulation of burial grounds, 437, 438.
  laws regulating the construction of wooden buildings, 438–440.
  regulation of right to hunt game, 440.
  abatement of nuisances — destruction of buildings, 440–442.
  how far the use of land may be controlled by the requirement of
    license, 442–444.
  improvement of property at the expense, and against the will of the
    owner, 444–448.
  regulation on non-navigable streams — Fisheries, 448–451.
  conversion of non-navigable into navigable streams, 451, 452.

REAL PROPERTY — *Continued.*
    statutory liability of lessors for the acts of lessees, 452–460.
    search warrants, 460–466.
    quartering soldiers in private dwellings, 466, 467.
    taxation, 467–482.

REGRATING, FORESTALLING AND ENGROSSING, 242–245.

RELIGION,
    police regulation of, constitutional restrictions upon, 159–166.
    crime not permitted under guise of, 171–174.
    criticism and blasphemy distinguished, 166–171.
    limitation upon worship permissible, 171–174.
    discrimination in respect to admissibility of testimony, 174, 175.
    exercises in Congress and Legislatures of States, 160, 161.
    in public schools, 161–163.
    meetings in public thoroughfares, 172–174.

REMAINDERS,
    when interests in expectancy, 348–350.

REMOTE CAUSE,
    not subject of police regulation, 151–152.

REPUTATION,
    security to, 35–65.

RESTRAINT OF TRADE,
    combinations in, prevention of, 245–251.

REVERSIONS,
    not interest in expectancy, 348.

RIGHT OF ACTION,
    regulation of contracts and, 515–522.

RIGHTS,
    how affected by crime, 70.

RULE AGAINST PERPETUITY,
    in relation to personal property, 488, 489.

SALE,
    of certain articles of merchandise, regulation of, 207–210.

SALOONS,
    prohibition of, 307, 309–311.

SCALES,
    regulation of weighing by public, 208, 209.

SCALPERS,
    ticket, prohibited from carrying on the business, 292, 293.

SEARCH WARRANTS, 460–466.

SECURITY,
to health — legalized nuisance, 32–34.
to limb and body, 22–29.
to life, 17, 18.
to reputation, 35–65.
privileged communications, 35–59.
malicious prosecution, 59–65.

SHIPS AND SHIPPING,
regulation of, 523, 524.

SKILLED TRADES,
regulation of, 200.

SLAUGHTER-HOUSES,
confined to certain localities, 312, 319–327.
establishment of public, 315.
made a monopoly, 319–327.

SLAVERY,
abolished, 66.

SOLDIERS,
in private dwellings, quartering, 466, 467.

SPECULATION,
prevention of, 241–245.

SPEECH,
freedom of, 189–193.

STATUTE OF USES,
application to personal property, 486–488.

STATUTE
of limitations, applicable to existing causes of action, 522.

STREAMS,
fisheries, 448–451.
regulation of non-navigable, 448–451.
conversion of non-navigable into navigable, 451, 452.
police control of navigable, 617–623.

STREETS,
extraordinary use of, may be exclusive franchise, 316, 317.

SUICIDE,
as a crime, 18, 19.

SUMPTUARY LAWS, 153–156.

SUNDAY LAWS,
constitutionality of, 175–188.

SURGICAL AND MEDICAL TREATMENT,
compulsory submission to, 31, 32.

SELF-PRESERVATION,
no excuse for homicide of innocent person, 26–28.

TABLE,
of private rights, 16.

TARIFFS,
for protection, 224–226.

TAXATION, 467–482; 633–638.
as licensing trades and occupations 271-289.
Kinds of, 467-471.
Limitations upon legislative authority, 471–482.
Local assessments as mode of, 479-482.
Relation of State and Federal governments in regard to, 633–638.

TELEGRAPH,
as a government monopoly, 326–327.

TENANCY,
in common, joint tenancy converted into, 337, 339, 340.

TENDER,
regulation of legal 210–224.

TENEMENT HOUSES,
prohibition of unwholesome trades in, 430–433.

TENURE,
in land, 328–335.

THEATER,
right to visit, 231–232.

TICKET SCALPERS,
prohibited from plying their vocation, 292–293.

TRADES AND PROFESSIONS,
regulation of, 194–327.
General proposition, 194–198.
prohibition as to certain classes, 198–200.
skilled, regulation of, 198–200.
learned professions, 200–204.
regulation of practice in the learned professions, 204–207.
regulation of sale of certain articles of merchandise 207–210.
Legal tender and the regulation of the currency 210–224.
Legislative restraint of importations — protective tariffs, 224–226.
Compulsory formation of business relations, 226–232.
Regulation of prices and charges, 233–238.

TRADES AND PROFESSIONS — *Continued.*
Prevention of speculation, 241–245.
Prevention of combinations in restraint of, 245–251.
boycotting, 252–255.
contracts against liability for negligence prohibits, 255–259.
wagering contracts prohibited, 259–271.
general prohibition of contracts on the grounds of public policy, 271.
licenses, 271–289.
prohibition of occupations in general, 289–298.
prohibition of the liquor trade, 298–311.
police control of employments in respect to locality, 311–315.
monopolies, 315–327.
license to prosecute a prohibited, is a franchise, 318–327.
unwholesome, prohibited, 430–433.
objectionable, confined to certain localities, 433–436.

TREASURY NOTES OF U. S.,
legal tender, 210–224.

TRIAL OF THE ACCUSED,
constitutional requirements, 85–89.
must be speedy, 86–87.
must be public, 87–89.
accused entitled to counsel, 89–91.
indictment by grand jury, 91–92.
plea of defendant, 92–95.
trial by jury, 95.
legal jeopardy, 95–97.

UNITED STATES,
is government of enumerated powers, 603–612.
police powers between States and, 603–639.
(see police power in the Federal system of government.)

U. S. TREASURY NOTES,
legal tender, 210–224.

UNWHOLESOME,
food, prohibition of sale of, 293–298.
trades in tenement houses prohibited, 430–433.
trades, confined to certain localities, 433–436.

USE OF LAND,
regulation of, what is a nuisance, 422–426.
what is a nuisance, a judicial question, 426–430.
unwholesome trades in tenement houses prohibited, 430–433.
confinement of objectionable trades to certain localities, 433–436.
regulation of burial grounds, 437, 438.

USE OF LAND — *Continued.*
laws regulating construction of wooden buildings, 438–440.
regulation of right to hunt game, 440.
abatement of nuisances, destruction of buildings, 440–442.
of personal property, laws regulating, 499–515.
(see personal property.)

USES, STATUTE OF,
in relation to personal property, 486–488.

USURY AND INTEREST LAWS, 238–241.

VAGRANCY,
prohibited, 116–122.

VESTED RIGHTS,
in real property, 335–341.

VICE,
and crime distinguished, 148–153.
not subject of police regulations, 148–151.

WAGERING CONTRACTS,
prohibited, 259–271.

WAR AND REBELION, 631–632.

WAREHOUSES,
right to make use of, 230.

WATER WORKS,
construction of, may be an exclusive franchise, 317

WIFE,
in legal subjection to husband, its justification, 544–547.
dower, when an interest in expectancy, 345–348.
legâl disabilities, 549, 550.
property, under control of husband, 547–549.
(see husband and wife.)

WILL,
laws regulating disposition of personal property by, 492–473.

WITNESSES,
religious test of competency of, 174, 175.

WOODEN BUILDINGS,
laws regulating construction of, 438–440.